M.L. Jhingan is an alumnus of the University of Delhi who after his M.A., worked as Research Assistant on a project of Dr.V.K.R.V. Rao, the then Director, Delhi School of Economics. Dr. Jhingan taught economics to postgraduate classes for over three decades and had been contributing to academic journals.

He is the author and co-author of a number of widely acclaimed textbooks on Economics and Management that sell in India and abroad. His books combine theoretical rigour and lucid exposition of the various concepts and theories of economics.

His most popular and the best selling text, The Economics of Development and Planning, was published 50 years ago in 1966 . Dr.Jhingan also guided Ph.Ds in India and abroad. Prof. Jhingan was Head of Economics Department and Principal, Government Post Graduate Evening College, Bhiwani and retired as Deputy Director, Higher Education, Haryana.

HISTORY OF ECONOMIC THOUGHT

3rd Edition

Dr. M.L. Jhingan.
Retired Deputy Director.
Higher Education, Haryana
Dr. M. Girija.
Dr. L. Sasikala.
Deptt. of Economics
Sri Sarada College for Women.
Salem-636016.
Tamilnadu.

Simply the text!
VRINDA PUBLICATIONS (P) LTD.

VRINDA PUBLICATIONS (P) LTD.

B-5, Ashish Complex (opp. Ahlcon Public School),
Mayur Vihar, Phase-I, Delhi-110 091
Tel. : 22755315, 22755316
E-mail—vrinda@ndf.vsnl.in
http://www.vrindaindia.com

First Edition : 2003
Reprinted : Two Times
Second Edition: 2006/Reprinted Four Times
Third Edition: 2011/Reprinted : Six Times
Reprint: 2025

e Textbook Available

ISBN 978-81-8281-389-2
(HISTORY OF ECONOMIC THOUGHT-3RD EDITION)

Typeset by : Kumud Printographics, Delhi-53
Printed at : Nisha Enterprises,

PREFACE TO THE THIRD EDITION

The authors feel great pleasure in putting forth the third edition of the book which has been revised and recast. Besides revising and updating the chapters 4, 5, 6, 11, 16, 22, 25 and 26 following new chapters have been added:

- Jeremy Bentham
- Welfare Economics
- Development of Economic Theories

The authors believe that the readers will find this edition of the book even more useful than the previous one. The authors are grateful to students and teachers who have favoured them with their useful suggestions.

Suggestions for the improvement of the book shall be most welcome

Authors

Preface to the First Edition

Writing a book on "History of Economic Thought" is a tough task, as it is a very vast subject covering the entire spectrum of economic thinkers of all nations. However, a modest attempt has been made by the authors to cover the syllabi of all the Indian Universities. The book is based mainly on U.G.C. model curriculum. It is written for both Graduate and Post-Graduate students. At the end of each chapter, review questions have been given. The authors hope that the book will be of immense use to the students of various Indian Universities. The authors are much grateful to Mr. Dinesh Kant Managing Director, Vrinda Publications (P) Ltd. Delhi for publishling the book in a commendable manner.

The authors will be pleased to receive constructive criticisms and suggestions towards the improvement of the book.

Authors

Preface to the Second Edition

This is a thoroughly revised and enlarged edition of the book in which new matter has been added in a number of chapters. Some of the important additions are :

- Smith's Theory of Distribution of Growth and of Economic Development.
- Ricardo's Theory of Economic Growth.
- Comparison of Malthus and Ricardo.
- Marx's Theory of Capitalist Development and Crisis.
- Jawaharlal Nehru's Economic Thought.

The author's hope that the present edition will be more useful to both students and teachers. Suggestions for further improvement of the book will be welcomed.

Authors

CONTENTS

Chapter 1

Nature and Significance of History of Economic Thought

INTRODUCTION

History of Economic Thought as the title implies deals with the origin and development of economic ideas and their interrelations. It is a historical account of economic doctrines. Prof. Haney has defined it as "a critical account of the development of economic ideas, searching into their origin, interrelations and manifestations". According to Prof. Bell, "It is the study of the heritage left by the writers on economic subjects".

Prof. Schumpeter holds that "economic thought is the sum total of all the opinions and desires concerning economic subjects especially concerning with public policies of different times and places". Schumpeter further says that the history of economic thought traces the historical change of attitudes. It also speaks about the economic problems and the approaches to those problems.

History of Economic Thought is different from Economic History and History of Economics. While History of Economic Thought deals with the development of economic ideas, Economic History is a study of the economic development of a country. On the other hand, History of Economics deals with the science of economics.

Even though Economic History and History of Economic Thought constitute seperate branches of study, they are closely related. Economic ideas are directly and indirectly motivated by the economic conditions and environment of the country. Ideas and environment are equally important and hence close relationship between History of Economic Thought and Economic History.

History of the development of economic ideas can be studied under three periods, namely : 1. Ancient, 2. Medieval 3. Modern.

Further the history of Economic Thought may be broadly divided into two parts. The first part deals with the origin and the development of economic ideas before the development of economics as a science. The second part deals with the economic ideas after the development of economics as a science.

History of economic thought can be studied and analysed by adopting different approaches.

1. Chronological approach
2. Conceptual approach
3. Philosophical approach
4. Deductive (or) Classical approach
5. Inductive approach
6. Neo-classical approach
7. Welfare approaoch
8. Institutional approach
9. Keynesian approach

1. Chronological Approach. In this approach, economic ideas are discussed in order of time. The economic ideas of different economists can be presented yearwise and can be studied. In this approach we can find a continuity in the economic ideas of different economists.

2. Conceptual Approach. It speaks about the evolution of different economic concepts (ideas) and the interdependence of these concepts. Conceptual approach can also be called as ideological approach.

3. Philosophical Approach. This was first adopted by the Greek philosopher, Plato. In the past, economics was considered as a hand maid of ethics. Naturally philosophical approach was adopted by the early writers to discuss the economic ideas.

4. Deductive Approach. The classical economists adopted deductive method. They believed in the universal application of economic laws.

5. Inductive Approach. The Historical School emphasised the inductive method. These economists believed that the laws of economics are not universal in nature.

6. Neo-classical Approach. This approach aims at improving the classical ideas by modifying them. Neo-classical approach was first adopted by Marshall. The Neo-classical approach believed that "Induction and Deduction are necessary for the science of economics just as the right and left feet are necessary for walking".

7. Welfare Approach. It aims at providing the basis for adopting policies which are likely to maximise social welfare.

8. Institutional Approach. The institutionalists questioned the validity of classical ideas and gave importance to psychological factors.

9. Keynesian Approach. A major development in modern economics is associated with the name of J.M. Keynes. His approach is new and different from the classical school. It takes into consideration the operation of business cycles that affect the entire economic policies. Keynesian approach deals with the problem of the economy as a whole.

Significance Of History Of Economic Thought

There are two views with regard to the importance of study of Histroy of Economic Thought. One group of economists believed that there is no need to study the history of Economic Thought because it is a history of errors. Whereas another group believed that one cannot possess knowledge of any economic doctrine until one knows something of its history. So a study of History of Economic Thought is important for the following reasons:

1. The study of History of Economic Thought clearly shows that there is a certain unity in economic thought and this unity connects us with ancient times.
2. The study of Economic Thought will help us to understand the origin of economics.
3. Economic ideas have been instrumental in shaping the economic and political policies of different countries.
4. Economic ideas are conditioned by time, place and circumstances.
5. A study of Economic Thought provides a broad basis for comparison of different ideas. It will enable a person to have a well-balanced and reasonable judgement.
6. Through the study of Economic Thought the student will realise that economics is different from economists.
7. The study of the subject helps us to avoid the mistakes committed by earlier economic thinkers.
8. The study of History of Economic Thought will enable us to know the person responsible for the formulation of certain important principles.

In short, the significance of the study of History of Economic Thought can hardly be overemphasized. It is an important tool of knowledge.

Difficulties In The Study Of History Of Economic Thought

However, it must be remembered that History of Economic Thought is selective and interpretative in nature. In other words the authors select those topics in which they are interested. They also explain the facts in their own manner. If authors leave out certain important facts and emphasize others, their judgements are biased. For example, the famous book, "A History of Economic Doctrines"—written by Gide and Rist leaves out discussions on ancient economic ideas, medieval economic thought and the contributions made by Mercantilists.

Further, complete history should deal with modern economic thought also. That means it should include the contributions made by Marshall, A.C. Pigou, J.M. Keynes etc. In this respect it can also be said that Alexander Gray's "The Development of Economic Doctrines" is incomplete.

Inspite of the above defects, the study of History of Economic Thought enables one to understand the subject clearly.

QUESTIONS

1. What do you mean by 'History of Economic Thought'?
2. State the differences between the 'History of Economic Thought' and 'Economic History'.
3. Explain how the 'History of Economic Thought' and 'Economic History' of a country are closely related
4. Analyse the significance of the study of the History of Economic Thought.
5. Discuss the nature and scope of History of Economic Thought.

Chapter 2

ANCIENT ECONOMIC THOUGHT

INTRODUCTION

The study of ancient economic thought may not appear to be very fascinating to modern students, but there can be little doubt that for a clear understanding of economic theories and institutions in a proper sequence, such a study has more than a mere historical value. It gives us an insight into the life, habits and customs of ancient communities and also provides a wider spectrum of the growth of modern economics. It sheds light on the origin of economic thought and the factors responsible for its development. Ideas do not grow in isolation and are passed on from one generation to another with the necessary modifications and adaptations. Hence they have to be judged in their historical perspective. The study of ancient economic thought not only provides the necessary bridge between ancient and modern but also between accidental and oriental economic thought. Its importance lies not only in providing a continuity of ideas but also in an understanding of the interaction of these ideas in their proper relationship. In short, this is at once a link between old and new, between East and West and between ethics and economics.

ECONOMIC THOUGHT OF HEBREWS

The beginnings of the science of economics and economic institutions are often traced back to the Hebrew and Jewish times. The society discussed in the Old Testament mentioned some of the characteristics of modern capitalism and private property. The Hebrews belong to the ancient civilizations of the world. Their period dates back to 2500 B.C. It is believed by some scholars that Western Civilization has its origin in Hebrew civilization. Division of labour, market, exchange, money etc., were the institutions of those times. The philosophers of those times were real founders of all social theories even though their writings were in a scattered form.

The economic philosophy of the Hebrews was simple. The society in which they lived was also a simple one. Economic problems were never studied separately. Economics, Politics, Ethics and Philosophy were interconnected. But religion and ethics were given greater importance. Economic life was controlled by priests. They gave importance to agriculture. The Hebrews had definite ideas on subjects such as interest, agriculture, property, taxation etc.

Economic Ideas

Interest

The Mosaic Law prohibited interest taking or usury (high rate of interest). However, the Hebrew prophets did not use the term interest. The law applied only to the Hebrews. Lending of money at interest to strangers was allowed. The Hebrews were asked not to collect interest from poor people because the poor borrowed money mainly for consumption purposes. This rule was modified in the times of Solomon when charging of interest at low rate was justified. Security for loans was in the nature of a "pledge" with well-defined rules for it. Thus the ideas of Hebrews on interest were more or less similar to those expressed by ancient Hindu thinkers.

Just Price

Both Hebrews and Hindus exercised great care in formulating laws against false weights and measures and adulteration of articles of consumption. These were strictly prohibited by the Hebrews. Monopoly and speculation were even more strictly prohibited. Raising market prices for speculative means was disapproved. There were also ceiling on the profits of retail shopkeepers which could not exceed the limit of 16 2/3 percent. The export of food grains was also prohibited and in times of scarcity and famine, hoarding of food grains was not permitted. Thus the concept of just price included correct weight, competitive price and reasonable rate of profit.

Labour and Wages

The Hebrews realised the dignity of labour but the pride of place was given to agricultural labour. There was no labour problem as we have these days. Wage workers were common. The Hebrews did not lay down rules for regulating the relation between the employer and employee. The chief regulations were concerning mercy and justice to them. Payments were made in kind.

Agriculture

Hebrews gave preference to agriculture. A Hebrew maxim runs as follows, "Although trading gives greater profit, there may be loss in a moment. Therefore never hesitate to buy land". This shows that how agriculture had become the supreme occupation. At that time the purpose of lawgivers was to fix the people in agricultural life which was a settled one. There was a tendency on the other hand to disregard trade and the mercantile community. Perhaps it is for this reason that Hebrews did not enter into commerce and manufacture to any great extent.

Seventh and Jublee Year

There was a very peculiar institution of Seventh and Jubilee year among the Hebrews. The Hebrews left their land fallow in the seventh year after cultivating it for six years. This was done with the object of preserving the fertility of the soil. The slaves serving for six years were freed in the seventh year. In this year all debts should be cancelled.

The Jubilee year was another peculiar institution of the Hebrews. The Jubilee year was the fiftieth year. According to this provision the land sold to someone was to be returned to its owners in the 50th year. In those days land was the main form of wealth. They tried to prevent concentration of wealth and also the acquisition of land of small holders by owners of large estates. By the institution of Seventh and Jubilee year the Hebrews desired to prevent inequality in wealth.

Money

The Hebrews seemed to have understood the functions of money. Money was used mainly in the form of bullion. There was no question of stamped money.

Sabbath

The sabbath was the corner stone of Hebrew Economic thought. It was their weekly day of rest, relaxation and good living. It was enjoyed by the masters of the house and his family as well as the slaves and the servants. According to Spiegel, "the institution of the weekend was a social invention that has no parallel in the civilization of Greek, Rome or other ancient culture".

Property

In those days land was the main form of property. Wealth was measured in lands, slaves, talents, silver, and other precious metals. The owner of a plot of land was the owner of all resources above and below the surface of land. According to the Law of Inheritance the first claim on property went to the eldest son. If there was no son it went to the daughter and in the absence of a daughter it might go to the close relatives like brothers, uncles etc.

Trade

In those days only surplus corn was sold in the market. The Hebrew wives were Craft - Women who used to spin wool and flax. Commerce flourished in the reign of King Solomon. He made successful voyages to distant lands, including India.

Taxes

Taxes did not exist in the Hebrew economy. Labour service was utilised for the construction of bridges, roads and other public utility services. Customs and toll tax were also collected. The toll tax was known as a tribute realised from every male for the maintenance of temples. Hebrew laws helped the dependants, fatherless and widows. The corner portion of the fields and vineyards were available for the poor.

Conclusion

On the whole the economic life of Hebrews was very simple. Their life was dominated by the priestly class. Religion, law, ethics, philosophy and economic ideas were bound together. Their educational system was very much influenced by religion and ethics. Though their economic ideas were simple and scattered they had a greater power to influence the minds of people. According to Eric Roll, "the views of the Hebrews may appear extremely primitive to modern economics, their power to influence men's minds is not necessarily inferior to that of many a refined and scientific theories."

Greek Economic Thought

The Greeks were the first to develop an economic theory, but it appeared in the form of 'incidental observations, thrown off in the pursuit of a more worthy end'. "It is in the Greek writers that theorizing on economic matters first explicitly emerges" said Alexander Gray. Though the Greeks being the pioneers in many branches of knowledge, they did not contribute much to the growth of economic ideas. There was no demarcation between politics, economics and ethics. The ancient world was founded on a system of caste distinctions. The masters did not give due respect to odd jobs done by slaves. In the absence of freedom of choosing one's occupation there was hardly any incentive for economic activities. However, Haney says that "the part played by the Greek ideas in the development of modern economic thought demands no small attention".

Credit goes to Plato for giving some attention to the economic aspects of social organisation. The Greek philosopher who really laid the foundation of economics as a science was Aristotle. According to Eric Roll, "Plato was the first of a long line of reformers and his student Aristotle was the first analytical economist".

Plato (427-347 BC)

Plato was a Greek philosopher. He was born in Athens in an aristocratic family. He was a pupil of Socrates. He taught mathematics and philosophy in the first great school of philosophers - the Academy, founded by him. His famous writings, 'The Republic' and 'The Laws' are the most important sources of his economic thought. Credit goes to Plato for giving some attention to the economic aspects of social organistaions. Eric Roll says that "he attempted to offer a systematic exposition of the principles of society and of the origin of the city state, as well as a plan for the ideal social structure". He regarded economics a branch of ethics and politics.

Origin of The State

Plato traced the origin of the state to economic considerations. Plato said "a state arises out of the needs of mankind. No one is self-sufficient. All of us have many wants". The state in order to supply the necessary commodities to satisfy human wants gathered together. The partners and helpers of this gathering is called as the state. In Plato's ideal state there were two classes, the rulers and the ruled. The rulers were the king and warriors and the ruled were artisans and unskilled workers. The members of the ruling class must be set apart from early childhood and they should be educated in philosophy and the arts of war because they will have to protect the state against foreign attack. At the age of thirty they will have to pass an examination. This examination selects the future philosopher king and those who cannot pass are concerned with general administrative duties.

Plato distinguished five types of government.

1) Aristocracy – rule by the best.
2) Timocracy – rule by the soldiers.
3) Oligarchy – rule by a few.
4) The rule of the wealthy and
5) Democracy.

Division of Labour

Plato's main contribution was in his account of division of labour. By division of labour he simply meant the division of employment as an aid to social organisation. He based the origin of the state on division of labour. According to Plato the essential needs of mankind are food, clothing and shelter. Therefore a city state must include a builder, a weaver, a farmer and a shoe maker or a representative of some other similar occupation. Every individual should do the work that is suitable for him. As a consequence all commodities are produced more plentifully, easily and of a better quality. The division of labour into various trades was thus recognised as a necessary condition to economic welfare even though division of each trade into various tasks was not conceived by him. Moreover he did not consider the necessity of a wider market for the application of the priciples. Thus Plato's idea of division of labour is different from that of Adam Smith. Smith's division of labour is determined by the market, but Plato's division of labour determines the market. Secondly to Adam Smith the advantages of division of labour go to only the employers, but to Plato it is beneficial to the entire society. Thirdly the cost of division of labour according to Plato is the difference in skill and talent. But according to Adam Smith division of labour leads to differences in skill and talent.

Size of Population

The problem of population was also analysed by Plato. The size of population in his state was assumed on the basis of the best results of division of labour. He provided a careful regulation of population to maintain stability in the economy. The right number of population suggested by Plato for a state was 5040. Only such a number provided opportunity for everyone to be familiar with all the other persons and help the economy to achieve self-sufficiency. It also helps to reap maximum productive efficiency. If the number showed a decreasing tendency, the state should offer prizes to encourage the growth of population. But if the number exceeds 5040 new colonies must be established.

Money

Plato recognised the value of money as medium of exchange. He did not favour the idea of allowing gold and silver to be used by the common men. Instead he suggested the use of domestic coins for payment of wages and other transactions. He wanted the state to have a common hellenic currency for the use of ambassadors, travellers, visitors etc.

Interest

Plato prohibited interest taking for loans. but later on he permitted interest taking as a penalty for delayed payment.

Value

Plato considered value as an inherent quality of the commodity. A man should not attempt to raise the price, but simply ask the value of the commodity.

Agriculture

Like the Hebrews, the Greeks too considered agriculture as the most desirable occupation.

Riches (Wealth) And Poverty

Plato criticized riches and poverty. He was of the view that riches made a man careless while poverty led to inefficiency. To him great riches and happiness cannot exist together because the rich people spend a part of their wealth without any justice. Plato had suggested an ideal property arangement. Only farmers and artisans were allowed to get property while the rulers and the administrators were not allowed to enjoy the property rights. He realised that, the city was divided into two parts namely, city of the poor and the rich, These two parts were always at war with each other.

Slavery

Plato regarded slavery as a permanent factor in the civilization of mankind. In his book 'The Laws' he stated that the treatment of the slaves should be liberal. Foreigners who were defeated in war and were taken as prisoners should be made slaves. In his city state, the slaves formed about 1/3 of the population and they performed most of the economic functions.

Communism

Plato's ideas regarding communism are extremely remarkable. Plato's communism is the most talked about and misunderstood part of his philosophy. In his ideal state the property should be collectively owned. Plato advocated communism to eliminate the evils of caste system. Plato's ideal state was not a communist state in the strict sense of the term. Though the aim was to abolish class conflict, it was not to be achieved on the basis of equality of opportunities. There were two classes, the ruler comprising of guardians and auxiliaries and the ruled called artisans. The members of the ruling class were to be well educated in the arts of war and philosophy. According to Prof. Haney, "Plato's communism did not stand for an absolute mechanical equality, but recognised authority and class distinctions".

Education

Plato stated that both boys and girls should receive the same kind of education. His idea on education is more important in the modern days.

Conclusion

Plato's contributions made definite progress in economic thinking of his time. His economic ideas show that he was essentially a child of his time. He recognised division of labour and it was adopted as a means of easier and better production. However, he did not recognise acquired skill, elimination of waste etc., as later economists were to admit its merits. Plato was a man of peace. He was the first thirteen who made economics a handmaid of ethics. At best we could consider Plato not as an economist but only as a social reformer.

ARISTOTLE

Introduction

Aristotle was the first analytical economist who laid the foundation of the science of Economics. He was the student of Plato and tutor to Alexander, the great. He did not produce any economic treatise. Anyhow it was from him the writers of Middle Ages got their main ideas. Though there is no continual analysis his scattered ideas especially private property, usury, and the just price had a greater influence on subsequent economic thought. Even though Aristotle was the student of Plato he differed from him on important issues like the origin of the state, private property, communism etc. Plato was a deductive thinker, Aristotle followed the inductive method and therfore a more practical one. While Plato was a radical thinker, Aristotle was conservative one. The reasoning of Aristotle is less imaginative and more logical and scientific than that of Plato. The main ideas of Aristotle was found in 'Politics' and 'Ethics'.

Contributions of Aristotle to Economic Thought

Idea of State

According to Aristotle the state originates out of the needs of mankind. He explains the origin of the state in terms of household. The household is an association formed to satisfy the wants of the family members. The village grows out of a number of households and finally the state comes into existence. Man is by nature a social animal, so the state is possible because all men live together in a society. The aim of the state is promotion of good life. Thus Aristotle attributes the origin of the state to economic and political causes.

In Aristotle's Ideal state, there would be two classes—the ruler and the ruled. The former was classified as military class, statesmen, magistrates and the priest. The ruled were farmers, craftsmen, and labourers. The members of the ruling class would perform their duties according to their respective age. For example, they were soldiers when they were young and strong, statesmen in the middle age and priests in the old age.

Private Property

While Plato advocated public property Aristotle supported the institution of private property.

Aristotle argued that public property would not be looked after as carefully as private property. To him private property was superior to public property on five grounds—progress, peace, practice, pleasure and philanthropy. Private property is more productive than public property. The principle "what is everybody's business is nobody's business" can be applied here. Hence, Aristotle said that property should be private. When there is private property they will make much progress because everyone will be attending to his own business.

Communism is not conducive to social peace. Quarrels are bound to develop when the principle of equal wages for equal work is not followed. Under public property there is the possibility of someone doing more work but getting small reward. The practical experience shows that private property is good than public property. Private property enables people to be sympathetic. The institution of private property will promote good conduct among the citizens. If a man has property he can have a part of it for himself and share the rest with his friends. Further, Aristotle was against the imposition of ceiling on private property. Rather he pleaded for checking the growth of population. If population is not checked, it will result in poverty which is the root cause of revolution and crime. Aristotle wanted the owners of private property to accept public responsibility. The property owners must act as trustees of the society. A similar idea was given by Gandhiji.

Scope of Economics

The word economics is of Greek origin and it means management of the household. Aristotle developed the theory of economics while discussing the elements of household management. There were two elements, namely, economics and chrematistics, the former concerned with the art of consumption of wealth in the satisfaction of wants and the later with the art of acquiring wealth either by making money or by exchange. Aristotle speaks two types of exchange—natural and unnatural. Natural form of exchange satisfies the human wants. The un- natural form of exchange aims at momentary gains. Aristotle speaks about two kinds of uses. One is the proper use which is similar to economy proper or value-in use. The other is similar to science of supply. For example, a shoe can be used for wearing and for exchange. Both are uses of the shoe. The first type of use is economy proper and the second one is value-in-exchange or chrematistics. By saying this Aristotle laid the foundation for value in-use and value-in-exchange, which were later popularised by Adam Smith. Barter is also natural branch of chrematistics. Thus, natural chrematistics concern the satisfaction of natural wants by natural uses of a commodity while exchange is an unnatural process of money making because man goes on undertaking this activity even after he has reached the point of satiety.

Money

Aristotle's theory of money explains "what money is and what money does". Aristotle explained the necessity of money while Plato explained about only one important function of money namely'medium of exchange,' Aristotle explained the other functions of money, namely, store of value and measure of value.

Aristotle advocated a non-communist society. In such a society there would be barter, then the difficulties of barter would result in the introduction of money. He believed that money came into existence through legislations.

Aristotle's treatment of money is said to be the best part of his economic thought. He said that money came to be introduced to facilitate commercial dealings. In the opinion of Schumpeter, Aristotle's theory should be called the Metalist theory of money in contrast with Cartel theory of money propounded by Plato.

Interest

According to Aristotle interest taking was the most unnatural of all the methods of getting wealth, said Schumpeter. Money served only as a medium of exchange, it cannot be regarded as productive. As one piece of money could not produce another, interest was unjust. Money had no business to increase from hand to hand. In those days money was borrowed by the poor persons for consumption purposes and therefore interest taking was considered unjust.

Slavery

Aristotle's views regarding division of labour, inheritance, population and slavery were more or less similar to that of Plato. He supported the institution of slavery. He divided slaves into natural slaves and legal slaves. The natural slaves were inferior to others, both in body and mind. Those conquered in war were treated as legal slaves.

Aristotle's Criticism of Plato's Communism

Aristotle did not fall in line with Plato in so far as the community of property was concerned. Under common ownership of property, people will not look after it carefully as it will be under private ownership. To him ownership of property was a natural instinct of man. Aristotle had a new idea that property should be private, but the use of it should be common. Thus Aristotle modified Plato's theory of Communism. He did not accept the extreme individualism of the Greeks. He wanted more and more goods under common use without affecting individual proprietary rights.

Monopoly

Aristotle defined monopoly as a position in a market of a single seller. He condemned it as unjust.

Conclusion

Aristotle laid the foundation of the science of Economics. He may be rightly called 'the first analytical economist'. He adopted inductive method to explain the origin and growth of the city state. His ideas on private property are valid even today. In the field of exchange also he laid the foundation for the distinction between value-in-use and value-in-exchange. Moreover his treatment of money is the best part of his economic thought. On the whole, Aristotle's contribution to the development of economic thought was more important and his ideas developed in his "Ethics" exerted greater influence on the writers of the Middle Ages.

ROMAN ECONOMIC THOUGHT

The contribution of Romans to the development of economic thought is very little. Their main field of interest was jurisprudence and their writings were very much influenced by Greek thought. The Greeks were thinkers, keen and analytic, whereas Romans were men of action, warriors and statesmen. The Greeks left a philosophy which deeply affected the ethics and economics of later thinkers but the Romans built institutions which affected law and politics.

Roman economic ideas can be gathered from three sources, namely, the jurists, the philosophers and agricultural writers. The Roman jurists were the original thinkers and the laws express the best Roman economic thought. The chief writers were Cicero, Seneca and Pliny. These philosophers praised agriculture and condemned usury. The agricultural writers like Cato, Columella and Varro dealt with many economic aspects. While praising agriculture they regarded it as the salvation of Rome.

Views on Agriculture

The Romans were mainly interested in the improvement of agriculture. Agriculture was their chief occupation. They favoured small scale farming. Cato had written more on the technical aspects of agriculture. Cato regarded an agricultural estate of 150 acres of 0live groves and 62 acres of vineyards as the ideal one. Varro advised crop growing and stock breeding. Agriculture was viewed not as an industry run for profit, but as a problem of domestic economy.

Money and Interest

Formerly, the barter system was prevalent, but later bimetalism, that is, coins of bronze and silver was adopted. At the same time Pliny favoured barter because to him, gold was the cause of the ruin of mankind. Roman jurists recognised the importance of money as medium of exchange. They treated money just like a commodity whose value was more or less changeable and essential to its function. The Romans strongly condemned usury and money lending. But there was no legislation to prevent this. In the city of Rome the usual rate of interest was 4 to 8 percent.

Division of Labour

Cicero laid emphasis on division of labour, as it had several advantages. Writers like Hutcheson and David Hume referred to Roman writers in their discussion of division of labour. They recognised geographical division of labour.

Commercial Regulations

The Roman state interfered with economic matters and commercial regulations. Fines were imposed on merchants who had stored up food grains in the expectation of high prices. Goods were inspected by the authorities, and the entire quantity was confiscated if fraud was detected. The exportation of precious metals was banned.

Labour

The Romans condemned slave labour on grounds of inefficiency. They attached more value to hired labourers than to slaves and advocated that hired labourers should be used, in place of slaves to do the work in unhealthy regions and they should be assigned more important jobs on projects employing slave labour.

Value

The Romans regarded utility should be the criterion for determining exchange value. Some commodities have greater value than their price. According to them price was determined by the forces of demand and supply. However, they did not develop more about value.

Natural Order

The Roman jurists were the original thinkers of laws. They made a distinction between human law and natural law, which had much influence on medieval and later thought. Their 'jus civile' was a national law applicable to Roman citizens, while 'jus gentium', the body of law common to different nations, gives the idea of natural law, that is to say, the idea of a body of law, which being common to all people is 'natural' to them. This idea laid the foundation stone for Smith and Physiocrats.

Private Property

The Roman ideas on property also influenced the development of economic thought. The Romans discarded the communal ownership of property. The jurists defined individual rights on property and he was free to dispose of his property. Aristotle had limited the right of property; while the Roman law of private property showed unrestricted individualism which later provided the basis for the institution of capitalism.

Conclusion

It can be concluded that the Romans added little to the stream of economic thought. The reason was that Rome produced very few social thinkers. They approached social questions from the political point of view rather than the economic. Prof. Haney has rightly observed that, 'though the Romans did not directly develop economic theory, a knowledge of their writings is essential to an understanding of the continuity of the history of economic thought. For instance, the natural law conception, which the Romans evolved from the 'jus gentium' was to exert a considerable influence on the evolution of economic thought."

QUESTIONS

1. Give an account of social divisions of the society during the ancient Greek period.
2. Analyse the economic ideas of Plato.
3. State the concepts of 'Money', 'Value' and 'Exchange' and 'Finance' as enunciated by Aristotle.
4. Elaborate some of the economic ideas of Roman Writers.
5. Write short notes on:
    (a) Plato's 'Republic'
    (b) Plato's 'Communism'
    (c) Roman Law

Chapter 3

MEDIEVAL ECONOMIC THOUGHT

INTRODUCTION

Middle Ages "is the most ill defined period in the world history," says Prof. Haney. Many writers agree that the fall of the Roman Empire in 476 A.D. seems to be the beginning of the Middle Ages. According to Dr. Ingram and others the period came to an end in 1300 A.D. But with the contributions of Gabriel Biel who seems to be the last person of this school, the period came to an end in 1500 A.D. The thousand years of Middle Ages can be divided into two periods:

(1) From 476 A.D. to 11th century in which there was not much progess, hence dubbed as dark ages.

(2) From the 12th to the 15th century, the period witnessed economic progress.

FEATURES OF MEDIEVAL SOCIETY

In the early Middle ages, economic ideas were influenced by the customs and traditions of the German Society. They did not give importance to private property. There was complete freedom of opinion. Barter was the prevailing form of exchange and profit earning was prohibited. Profit and interest were not encouraged and agriculture was given the foremost place. The later medieval society was dominated by lords and serfs. This division was influenced by the social structure of the medieval period. The feudal lords owned large estates and the landless and poor came under their patronage. The serfs had to pay taxes to the feudal lords mostly in kind for tilling their land. In turn the feudal lords gave them the right of tillage. With the development of towns and cities commercial activities made much progress. Greek cities became strong trading centres.

The medieval economic ideas are found in the writings of St. Thomas Aquinas and Nicholas Oresme.

St. Thomas Aquinas (1225-1274 A.D.)

St. Thomas Aquinas was the best representative of medieval economic thought. He has been called as scholastic philosopher. Born in Italy, he got his early education at the Benedictive monastery and University of Naples.After the completion of his academic apprenticeship, he taught Theology at various places in Rome, Paris, London and Naples. He was an extensive writer and wrote as many as 60 books of which the most important was Summa Theologica; which presents the systematic summary of economic ideas of that time.

Economic Ideas

Just Price

The most important contribution of Thomas Aquinas was Just price ("Justum Pretium"). This doctrine was based upon the concept of value. He recognised time and place utility. Just price was associated with utility or usefulness of the commodity. It was, however, believed that the exact determination of price was not possible. However, just price was subject to variations due to market fluctuations. One could charge a high price either because he had improved the commodity in some way or because of the risk he took in transporting it from one place to another. Hence charging of a higher price was justified if the seller was likely to incur a loss. The Medieval School believed that value should be equal to costs including the expenditure on labour. Selling of a defective thing was considered as fraud. In short, value was absolute and based on cost. The value thus fixed was not market price and was independent of the estimate of buyer or seller. 'Just price' was similar to that of the present 'fair value'. Thus Aquinas distinguished between 'Just price' and 'market price'. Just price was determined by law.

Usury

Lending money for earning more wealth was considered as the worst form of earning money. Like the Hebrews the Medieval church of fathers also prohibited the taking of interest. A high rate of interest was treated as the exploitation of the poor as there was absence of opportunities for the profitable investment of capital. But the lender was entitled for a compensation if the principal amount was not returned within the stipulated time. Several factors were responsible for their belief against usury. Mainly Aristotle's argument influenced Aquinas to condemn usury. Usury had been condemned by Aristotle because he regarded money as barren. Aquinas made use of the doctrine of Roman law. According to this goods were of two kinds : Consumptibles and non-consumptible, i.e., goods which were not consumed in use. He put money in the first category and stated that "to demand interest in addition to the return of loan was to seek an unnatural and unjust gain". The early condemnation of usury rested on the authority of the Bible and Aristotelian doctrine. In the hands of Aquinas the objection to usury became much more deep.

Property

St. Aquinas followed Aristotle regarding private property. There are two views, firstly, the power of acquiring and secondly, the way of spending it. The power of acquiring the property gives the rights on individual. Private property leads to an increase in the production of wealth. The method of using the property was much more important than the right of ownership. According to Aquinas the estate – private property which was legitimately acquired should be distributed among the largest possible number of people and for the support of the poor also.

Trade

Trade was considered to be unnatural and to him it meant a fall from the state of grace. But still he recognised it as a necessary evil and considered it legitimate. Acquinas argued that God himself admitted that there should be trade in the world as he had distributed resources differently among different countries. However, trade should be carried on only for the benefit of the public. Trade guilds had framed rules to check fraudulent commercial practices. The merchants should not turn a means to an end by selling the things he purchases for an abnormal profit. Speculators and middle men were also condemned.

Division of labour

Division of labour was accepted to be necessary condition in the efficient performance of economic activity. This school regarded every profession as necessary and noble provided it led to public service.

Economic functions of the state

The state was regarded as a great private economy to which the independent domestic economy idea was applied. The main source of the income of the state were the estate which included buried treasure, reversion of property to the king in the absence of the its owner, etc. Taxes in the modern sense did not exist in those days. The state was to perform the following functions : "the maintenance of population, and provision for the poor, the establishment of safe and free roads" – (Haney). A system of weights and measures and a special coinage was also emphasized. Aquinas believed that by money the king could purchase food for his subjects, in times of war. The king possessed the entire monetary control and many laws were passed to prevent counterfeiting and clipping. The circulation of foreign coins were forbidden.

Conclusion

On the whole, St. Thomas Aquinas made a great impression in economic thought. He codified the ideas and made definite improvement upon them. His ideas about private property, trade, wages, division of labour, usury etc, were greatly improved from that of his predecessors and his theory of 'just price' was a definite contribution he made to economic thought.

NICOLE ORESME

Oresme was an important medieval thinker and his treatise "On the First Invention of Money", contained various elements of contemporary economic thought. He was concentrating more upon the monetary aspects of the economy and it was due to the dominance of money in the exchange transactions of medieval society. A great change of the substitution of barter with a monetary exchange took place in the middle ages. In his book, he has given a detailed description of the origin of money and enumerated the qualities of good money. He was in favour of bimetalism and hence advocated the use of both silver and gold as money material. He emphasized that the value of money is to be derived from the value of money material or commodity. He recognised that the right of coinage should rest with the king, acting on behalf of the community and he has no right to tamper with the wealth of his subjects by altering the proportion, the weight of money (material). The gain derived from debasement is worst than usury. Debasement is thus a concealed tax which leads to dislocation of trade and impoverishment. Thus Oresme anticipated Gresham's Law about bad money when he stated that "despite all precautions they (gold and silver) are carried out to places where they are rated higher".

Conclusion

The historians dubbed the medieval period as "Dark Ages". However, this period is of great significance in the evolution of economic thought. According to Haney, it was "a period of adjustment and fusing" and " a period of transitions". It was in this period that individualism and materialism of Romans, the idealism of the Christians, the democratic individualism of Germans, restricted individualism of Aristotle—all were combined and fused by this school of men into " a consistent body of logical rules concerning the rights and duties of the classes of men, and the forms and functions of government". It was " a period of transition" because in this period domestic economy was replaced by natural economy, agriculture by manufacturers, and commerce and slavery by serfdom and free labour. The whole economic philosophy of the Middle ages might be summed in the doctrine of just price, which aimed to protect buyers from exploitation.

QUESTIONS

1. Analyse in detail the characterstic features of Medieval European Society.
2. Elaborate the economic ideas of St. Thomas Aquinas.
3. Write short notes on :
   (a) The doctrine of Just Price.
   (b) Economic functions of the State.
   (c) Significance of Medieval thought.

Chapter 4

MERCANTILISM

INTRODUCTION

The dominant system of economic thought that prevailed in Europe from 16th to 18th Century was Mercantilism. It was known by different names in different countries. In England it was called as commercial system or Mercantile system because it emphasised the importance of commerce and free trade. It was also known as "Restrictive system" because its practical policies consisted of numerous restrictions and regulations on commerce.

In France it was known as "Colbertism" after the name of Colbert, the Finance Minister of Louie the XIV. In Germany and Austria it was called "Cameralism". It was also known as "Bullionism" because of the importance given to gold and silver.

Mercantilist thinkers did not form a group, advocating a fixed line of thought and policy. They were businessmen, merchants, administrators, in different countries. They left a number of pamphlets and papers regarding economic problems. Only the later economists have analysed their writings and found certain uniformity in their ideas and policies and have grouped them together as mercantilists.

Mercantilism prevailed not only in England, France, Germany and Italy, but also in countries like Russia, Spain and Scotland. It adopted itself to the changing circumstances. Alexander Grey observed that "It had three hundred years run and so it coloured the thought and still more the actions of every country in Europe". Haney says, "Mercantilism comprises the economic views that prevailed among the European statesmen from 16th to 18th century".

FACTORS SHAPING MERCANTILISM

Some economic, political, religious and cultural factors were responsible for the emergence of mercantilism.

Economic Factors

Towards the end of the 15th century changes were taking place in the economic life of the people. Domestic economy was giving way to an exchange economy. Agriculture was giving place to industry. Trade became very important and it changed the foundation of socio-economic set-up of the middle ages. Trade necessitated the use of money which was available in the form of gold and silver. Along with the expansion of commerce there were improvements in transport, agriculture, population, etc., so the Mercantilist thought was the outcome of these developments.

Political Factors

Towards the end of the middle ages nationalism became the strong force. Europe changed greatly due to Renaissance. As a result, there was a fundamental political change. It resulted in the emergence of strong nations like England, France, Spain, etc., Feudalism came to an end and the King became more powerful. Each nation wanted to preserve its independence and considered other nations as enemies. In order to create a strong and powerful state the Mercantilists tried to regulate the political and economic activities of the people.

Religious Factors

The Reformation Movement was revolt against Roman Catholic Church. It challenged the authority of Pope. Initially the Roman Catholic Church controlled the political and economic activities of the nation. But after the Reformation the authority of the Pope was challenged.

Cultural Factors

Culturally also Europe was undergoing a sharp change. Renaissance gave a new light of learning to the people. People were made to realise that this worldly life was more important than the heavenly life. As a result, money came to occupy an important place in human activities.

Scientific Factors

In the field of science and technology great improvements and inventions were made. The discoveries of compass and printing press were of great importance, With the help of compass navigation became easier and it led to the discovery of new countries. Thus new countries opened the gates to a variety of raw materials and markets. The invention of printing press helped the spread of new ideas and knowledge.

Thus all the above factors provided an atmosphere for the development of Mercantilist thought.

1. The fundamental aim of Mercantilism was to make a country strong. The strength of a country was tested with the help of the wealth of the country, above all, in that portion of wealth which consisted of precious metals like gold and silver. So the Mercantilists attached

greater importance to bullion (gold) because it was the most durable, useful and generally acceptable form of wealth.

2. If a country has gold mines and silver mines, it can get gold and silver but if a country has no mines, it can get gold and silver through trade. The country should have a favrourable balance of trade. In other words, there should be an excess of exports over imports.
3. In the Mercantilist system of thought trade was the most important occupation. Industry and commerce were ranked second in importance. Agriculture was the least important of all. The state had an important role to play in the Mercantilist system. It should come forward to exploit the natural resources of the country to increase its exports. There was regulation of economic life by the government.

Main Ideas or Characteristics of Mercantilism

Wealth

The fundamental aim of the mercantilists was to make the country strong. The strength of the country was found in the wealth of the country, especially that portion of wealth which consisted of precious metals like gold and silver.

Mercantilism firmly believed that gold was the basis of wealth and power. Hence the mercantilist slogan was 'more gold, more wealth and more power'. All the economic activities in the country were centred around wealth. According to Gray, "Everybody thought that his country was engaged in a race with other countries and in that race it must not be the looser".

In this respect it seems that the mercantilists should have drawn inspiration from their predecessors because in ancient Greek and Roman and throughout the middle ages power was considered to be synonymous with accumulation of treasure or precious metals. Commerce was also encouraged on the same ground. To quote Columbus "Gold is a wonderful thing; whoever possesses it, is a master of everything he desires; with gold one can get souls into paradise".

This greatest importance given to precious metals may be attributed to the following reasons:

i) In the 16th century, the only form of wealth, most useful and generally acceptable was gold and silver. Naturally the mercantilist attached more importance to gold and silver.
ii) With the rise of absolute monarchy, taxation could be possible only if money was used as measure of value. Thus on the political side also money came to occupy greater importance.
iii) For conducting wars money was essential. Three things were required for war—money, more money and still more money.
iv) Mercantilists believed that trade depended on plentiful of money.
v) Money was also needed for development of exchange economy.
vi) Money in those days was identified with capital.

Thus the Mercantilists had a high regard for money. If we consider the circumstances of the day, Mercantilists were justified in attaching greater importance to gold. According to Keynes, "the Mercantilists understood the important role of money in the economic system. They studied the effects of an increase in the quantity of money on the price level and employment."

Foreign Trade

The Mercantilist theory of foreign trade is known as the balance of trade theory. The aim of this theory was to get large amount of precious metals. Foreign trade was considered to be the only source for getting gold and silver. They believed that all those nations which did not possess their own gold and silver mines could become rich after getting gold and silver from foreign countries through trade. Sir Thomas Mun the greatest representative of Mercantilist declared that, "foreign trade ought to be encouraged, for, upon it hinges the great revenue of the King, the honour of the kingdom, the noble profession of the merchant, the supply of our poor, the improvement of our lands and means of our treasure".

The mercantilists insisted that the value of export should always be greater than imports. In short, they advocated a favourable balance of trade. Hence they encouraged exports and discouraged imports. "Export more, import less and collect the balance in the form of gold and silver", was the essence of this theory. Accordingly every exporter was considered to be a close friend of the state and every importer as an enemy.

However, the mercantilists theory of foreign trade has no validity in modern times. If every nation exports more, there would be an end to international trade. Further, the mercantilists did not distinguish between particular balance of trade and general balance of trade. By general balance of trade we mean balance of the country's trade with other countries and particular country. Further, the mercantilists were ignorant of the fact that favourable balance of trade cannot be maintained for ever because if gold comes into a country more and more, there would be inflation. Thus the mercantilist theory of foreign trade is not a correct one.

Commerce and Industry

The mercantilists considered commerce and industry as the most important branches of the national economy. They wanted to increase the national productive efficiency by means of regulation of industry and commerce. They believed, that commerce and trade were the most productive occupation and agriculture was the least productive. Further, as they believed that manufacturing industries were more closely connected with commerce, they must receive all attention from the government. However, it should not be misunderstood that the mercantilists regarded agriculture as insignificant. They thought that agriculture did not contribute directly to the strength of the country.

Population

Mercantilists encouraged large population for making the nation militarily strong and for increasing its productive capacity. They believed that cheap and abundent supply of labour would keep the cost of production low. This would enable a country to sell its commodity at a lower price in the internaitional market. According to Devenant, "People were the real strength of a counrty". The mercantilists even encouraged immigration becasue they would bring wealth and enrich the country.

Natural Resources

The mercantilists wanted to utilize all the natural resources to the maximum extent so as to produce more, export more and import less. They also attached importance to agriculture in order to solve the food problem. Colonies were developed to supply the required raw materials. Further, the colonies were not allowed to export directly to foreign countries. All the commodities should be exported to the mother country only.

Wages and Rent

The mercantilists discussed the problems of production only. So they did not give much importance to the problems of distribution, especially to wages and rent.

Interest

No unanimity existed among the mercantilist writers on the subject of interest. Sir Thomas Mun, a famous mercantilist writer favoured interest taking for the loans on the ground that lending helped the poor and young merchants. It also led to the employment of the savings of the widows. Thomas Mun and his followers told that the rate of interest would be high or low depending upon the industrial conditions of the country.

Taxation

The views of the mercantilists on taxation were interesting because they were more scientific and ahead of their time. Broadly speaking the mercantilists favoured a multiple tax system based on the principle of "each should pay according to the benefits received from the state".

Theory of Value

Regarding value, both subjective and objective approaches existed. Prior to the mercantilists , value was regarded as an intrinsic quality possessed by a commodity, it depended upon the utility of the commodity. Value was thus considered to be different from price.

By the end of the mercantilist period, market value was recognised. Scarcity also determined the value of a commodity. According to the mercantilists the normal value of a commodity depended on the cost of production.

Factors of Production

Mercantilists recognised three important factors of production, namely, land, labour and capital. Here we can quote Sir William Petty's saying "Labour is the father and active principle of wealth as land is the mother". The Mercantilists emphasised the cultivation of agricultural waste lands so that food production might increase and the country might become self-sufficient and imports might be reduced.

Commercial Regulation

Mercantilists believed that commercial regulations were essential for maximising social welfare. Commercial laws were passed to restrict the import of food materials. But no regulation was applied to the import of raw materials because they were required for the industrial development of the country. The state supported the export industries and shipping which would secure a favourable balance of trade.

Role of State

The mercantilists regarded the state as the supreme power for controlling the activities of the people. State was the master and its citizens, the servants. The mercantilists believed that state intervention was necessary to solve the problems of the society. They believed that for securing success in wars a strong nation was required.

Nearly, all the mercantilist writers believed that since the total economic resources of the world were limited, the economic policy must be framed in such a manner as to increase the power of the state. As a result they suggested the policy of protection. The state policies were shaped according to this idea. Special acts were passed to encourage exports and the development of industries. Protection was given to the industries because their main objective was to maintain a favourable balance of trade.

Land Banking Schemes

Mercantilists ideas regarding money gave rise to the establishment of Land Banking Schemes. Land Bank Schemes were introduced by Chamberlin and Barbon.

Occupation

Mercantilists believed that merchants were the most profitable members of the society. To them occupation was productive only if it increased wealth of a country.

Critical Estimate of Mercantilism

Mercantilist theories and practices have been criticised by many writers. The opposition actually started towards the end of the 17th century. The storm of criticism against mercantilism was particularly strong in France. The criticism against mercantilism reached its climax towards the end of the 18th century when Adam Smith published his book "The Wealth of Nations", one fourth of which was devoted to this.

Broadly speaking, the following criticisms have been levelled against mercantilists and their policies:

1) They gave too much importance to gold and silver and neglected the importance of other commodities.
2) They exaggerated the importance of commerce and undermined the usefulness of agriculture and other branches of human history.
3) They were wrong in believing that a favourable balance of trade was the only source of prosperity.
4) Their belief that the gain of one nation was necessarily the loss of another was wrong.
5) Their ideas regarding 'utility' and 'value' were vague and abstract.
6) Their ideas about capital and interest were imperfect.
7) They lacked broad-mindedness.

But at the same time, we should not completely criticise the mercantilist doctrines and theories. While studying their ideas, one should not overlook the circumstances and problems of their times. Mercantilism was essentially a product of its age. It is no doubt true that they erred at places. But as Haney has remarked "they are far from a mass of absurdities".

Thus the mercantilist system had its own weaknesses. As an economic policy it lacked universal application. As a body of doctrines, it could not provide right guidance to statesmen of the time. They confused the means and the ends by overemphasizing the importance of bullion. Further, in their zeal to increase the total productivity of the nation, they regarded wealth and labour as the ultimate goal of human existence.

Mercantilists were not only practical administrators and traders, they also put forward such ideas which led to the development of various economic theories in modern times. Dr. Smith has rightly pointed out, "It is the mercantilists and not Smith, who are the spiritual predecessors of modern economics". Mercantilism implied a general view of society which is often overlooked. They developed a sort of macro economic approach to the problems of the society. The mercantilists emphasised the need for maximising exports not only with the idea of accumulating gold and silver, but with the hope that a prosperous export sector would provide more employment. Even the emphasis of the mercantilists on more money can be justified on economic grounds. They were aware of the dynamic functions of money. An increase in the supply of money would result in lowering the rate of interest which would serve as an inducement to invest. Knut Wicksell developed his theory of interest with the mercantilist ideas as the basis. Keynes also admired some of the mercantilist ideas. The mercantilists were aware of the fact that money is not merely a medium of exchange but a store of value. Keynes noted that the mercantilists were concerned with the economic system as a whole and they were interested in securing optimum employment of the resources. Keynes approved two mercantilist ideas - more money for business expansion and more money for lowering the rate of interest. Mercantilism paved the way for many western nations for their transformation from 'commercial capitalism' to 'industrial capitalism'. The mercantilists ideas are powerful even today. In the words of Eric Roll, "Down to the present day they all reappear from time to time in various guises as symptoms and weapons of economic conflict".

Decline of Mercantilism

Mercantilism declined due to many reasons. Under the influence of the teachings of Smith, policy of plenty began to replace the policy of power. The development of banking reduced the importance of bullion and coins. Further, the expansion of market economy showed that real estates, factories and machinery were more important items of wealth than gold and silver. The economic growth that took place during the Industrial Revolution made the society to rely on competition. It was realised that the wealth of all nations could be increased simultaneously by efficient utilisation of natural resources and through the progress made in sceince and technology.

Neo-Mercantilism

Neo-Mercantilism was a sharp reaction against the doctrine of laissez faire. It was not a movement for return to mercantilism. While mercantilism emphasised on the development of trade under state control, the neo-mercantilist policy envisaged a state activity of another kind—assistance, support, defence rather than regulation and control.

Neo-Mercantilism was different from 17th century Mercantilism in two important aspects. Firstly, these policies were dictated by the ideal of social planning. They were looked upon as temporary devices to achieve the ideal of social welfare and are to be continued as long as they are essential for planning. The old mercantilists has no such idea of planning in view. Secondly, modern mercantilist devices are enforced by reference to accurately kept statistics of trade, industry and prices. Though many mercantilists like Petty were conscious of the importance of statistics, most of the mercantilist states did not possess the elaborate organisation, required for the collection of economic statistics, nor the technique of statistical interpretation and analysis had developed enough to enable any sensible statistical control of economic policy. Though 17th century mercantilism required a lot of government regulation of economic activity, modern objectives of economic and social control were still remote to it.

Mercantilism and Under-Developed Countries

Economic ideas of the mercantilists have relevance to the under-developed countries of today. The countries in which mercantilism flourished resemble present day under-developed countries in some respects and differ from them in others. The mercantilists according to Heckscher had, "a belief in official intervention as a corrective to evils". Even today in underdeveloped countries, the state is assigned a key role in the process of economic growth. Economic development of England, France and Germany was made possible by the activities of millions of private enterpreneurs under the policy of non-intervention by those governments. But in the shortage of private enterpreneurial skill, the state has to play a dominant role in the developing countries. Not only that, it has to regulate production and distribution with the object of promoting growth with justice.

The mercantilists considered the non-agricultural sectors-foreign trade and manufacturing sectors-as strategic in the economic growth of a nation. They thought that a favourable development of foreign trade and manufacturing by state regulation and assistance, would give rise to a favourable development in agricultural and other less strategic sectors. But most of the underdeveloped countries like India are predominantly agricultural. In India, for instance, most of our traditional exports such as tea, jute, cotton, and sugar depend either directly or indirectly on agriculture. So priority has to be given for schemes of agricultural development, for, if agriculture fails, plans will fail.

With regard to population, we must follow the teachings of Malthus rather than mercantilists. There is a definite need for population control in our country. The mercantilists have assigned a most important place to money in economic development at all times. It is true that money is essential for economic development. But whenever certain bottlenecks developed in an economy, more money would mean only increase in prices. Further, the mercantilists failed to explain the conditions under which further increase in money would push up prices rather than increase employment. Thus while mercantilists recognised the role of money in economic development, they exaggerated its role and underestimated the role of real factors. More money, especially paper money may sometimes generate inflationary pressures. India is a case in point.

Capital deficiency is one of the main problems of underdeveloped countries. External assistance is uncertain and cannot be relied upon for ever. So self-help is the best help. We can promote capital formation in a country by promotion of exports. Even today gold plays an important role in international monetary transactions. Only by promotion of exports, underdeveloped countries can earn enough gold and foreign exchange. Therefore, there is every need for seeking a favourable balance of trade by maximising exports and minimising imports. This aspect of mercantilist policy has relevance to most of the underdeveloped countries. The governments of underdeveloped countries provide financial and non-financial assistance to the export sector, and imports of non-essential commodities should be restricted so as to conserve foreign exchange. Even the developed nations may be persuaded to have liberal trade terms towards their imports from underdeveloped countries. But some of the rich countries of today follow mercantilist policies in some form or other in their trade relations with poor countries. It is one of the causes for the chronic deficit in the balance of payments positions of most of the poor countries.

INFLUENCE OF MERCANTILISTS ON ECONOMIC POLICY

Most of the mercantilists recognised the effect of an export surplus on employment through its effect on price. Inflow of gold through a favourable balance of trade causes the supply of money in circulation to increase, which enhances trade and promotes employment. Mercantilists stressed more on the trade stimulating effect rather than the price-inflationary effect of increase in money supply.

Barring a few mercantilists, who held that rate of interest is determined by natural forces, the general belief was that low rate of interest was monetary phenomenon, a price for the use of money. They also believed that low rate of interest was conducive to production and employment. Thus the supply of money in circulation must be increased to lower the interest rate.

Majority of the mercantilists favoured a low wage policy as it reduced costs and prices and encouraged its demand in the foreign markets. Hence it has a favourable effect on production and employment in the domestic market. Mercantilists advocated an increase in the supply of labour and reduction in the wages of labour for the creation of sizable export surplus and to increase employment.

Mercantilists believed that full employment can be achieved through increase in labour force and its productivity. Labour force can be increased by increasing population. The policies approved by the mercantilists to increase population consisted of measures to reduce mortality, measures to reduce age at marriage and increase the proportion of the married population and measures to reduce or prevent emigration and to encourage immigration. In order to increase the productivity of labour mercantilists advocated that efforts should be directed to make the workers more willing to work. But these writers did not analyse the effects of higher wages on productivity through their effects on health and living condition.

ANTONIO SERRA

Antonio Serra was an Italian. His pamphlet, "A Brief Treatise on the causes which can make Gold and Silver abound in Kingdoms where there are no Mines", contains his mercantilist views. There are some countries blessed with gold and silver mines. But in other countries, according to Serra, the presence of gold and silver may be attributed to: (1) the quantity of industry, (2) the quantity of the population, (3) extensive trading operation, and (4) the regulations of the sovereign.

(i) The Quantity of Industry. This is the typical Mercantilist idea of preferring industry to agriculture, because, according to him, firstly, it is safer, as the cultivator of land has to depend on weather, secondly, it is subject to increasing returns whereas agriculture is not, thirdly, it has a surer market, because fruits of industry can be kept for a long time to secure a better market and fourthly, and lastly, there is more profit in industry than in agriculture.

(ii) The Quality of Population. The more diligent, hard working and eager to build up the trade are the inhabitants of a country, the more beneficial it will be to develop foreign trade and thereby get more gold and silver.

(iii) Extensive Trading Operations. The country should possess an extensive trade and trading operations preferably in the produce of foreign countries rather than that of its own.

(iv) Regulations of the Sovereign. Here Serra is somewhat feeble because, according to him, it is not easy to know how to arrange this factor well since the same case may produce different effects in different cases just like a light whistle rouses the dogs but quiets the horses. Any way the trend is clear.

Like Thomas Mun, Serra also disapproves the prohibition of the export of money. According to him, if money is exported for any purpose whatever, it must return with profit into the kingdom from which it was sent. But this goes to the root of the Mercentilist idea.

SIR THOMAS MUN

Mun was an important representative of the English mercantilists. He was born in England in 1571. His most important book was "England's Treasure by Foreign Trade". Gray rightly remarks that "Mun is perhaps the nearest approach to the perfect mercantilist".

Mun wanted to regulate the foreign trade of the country to secure a favourable balance of trade. He stated his theory of balance of trade thus: "The ordinary means to increase our wealth and treasure is by foreign trade, wherein we must ever observe this rule : to sell more to strangers yearly than we consume of theirs in vlaue". He never wanted to place restrictions on the export of billion. But he wanted to manufacture commodities at home "for then we get not only the price of our wares as they are worth here, but also the merchants' gains, the charges of insurance and freight to carry them beyond the seas". He advocated accumulation of wealth and it could be possible by reducing imports and encouraging exports. He suggested that imports should be taxed at a high rate and exports at a moderate rate. He did not want limitless accumulation of wealth because it would lead to high prices and adverse balance of trade. He also recognised the importance of taxation for national defence.

In his book, he has suggested a programme for accumulation of treasure. The main points of this programme were :

1. Mun advocated the cultivation of waste lands for producing those commodities which were hitherto imported. This would help in reducing the import of tobacco, hemp, flax etc.
2. He suggested that people should refrain from consuming foreign goods and from unnecessary change of fashions, so that their imports might be reduced.
3. Regarding exports, the requirements of neighbouring countries should be properly assessed so that the commodities which a foreign buyer could not get from other places might be sold at a higher price. As for other goods, they might be sold at a cheaper rate.
4. Commodities should be transported only through England's own ships so that price of the commodities and shipping charges might be available to the state.
5. He advocated frugal cosumption of domestic goods by English people so that more would be left for exports. Lavish consumption of domestic goods would promote employment of poor.
6. Mun suggested that English people should develop fishing in adjacent seas instead of allowing Dutch to fish in those waters.
7. England should be developed into a distributing centre so that shipping and trade could develop and the King's income might increase.
8. Mun wanted England to have trade relations with distant countries.
9. He favoured the export of money to other countries for he thought "money begets trade and trade increases money". Mere accumulation of money in the country will not lead to a quick and ample development of trade.
10. He wanted that the commodities manufactured from the imported material should be allowed to be exported free. By this measure England would be able to provide employment and increase exports and the customs of the King.
11. "We must endeavour to make the most we can of our own". This statement of Mun is very

vague and he did not try to elucidate it.

Mun praised industry and condemned idleness and luxury. He praised the "industrious Dutch" and deplored the idleness of his countrymen who spent most of their time in idleness and pleasure smoking, feasting and drinking. Mun was also aware of the fact that money was only a means to an end and that it would not serve its purpose if enough goods and services were not there to buy. He was aware of the fact that money by itself was barren.

Sir Josiah Child

Sir Josiah Child (1630-1699) favoured a surplus balance of trade and supported an export of specie if it could result in a greater eventual inflow of it. To him international trade could not be undirectional and some imports were bound to be there. Like Mun he also insisted that a nation should direct its attention to the general rather than particular trade balance. Sir Child's main contribution, however, was in terms of the relationships between rate of interest and flourishing trade and commerce. He believed that a low rate of interest encouraged expansion of trade and therefore strongly advocated for it. He supported his argument by stressing that Holland was ahead of England in trade primarily on account of the low rate of interest there. Child developed a theory of colonial economy and linked it to argument of employment at home. Colonialism implied emigration from the home country which in itself was bad. But Child found that in some cases this emigration might also create additional demand abroad for imports from the home country in which case home workers could be employed more beneficially. Thus the usefulness or otherwise of colonies depended upon the nature of individual colonies.

Philipp Von Hornick (1638-1712)

Von Hornick was an Austrian pamphleteer. According to him, "The might and eminence of a country consists in its surplus of gold and silver". All other things necessary or convenient for its subsistence should be derived from its own resources without dependence on other countries. Like Mun, Hornick has laid down certain rules for the accumulation of gold and silver.

(i) The country's soil should be exploited to the utmost and in particular, efforts should be made to discover gold and silver;

(ii) The commodities should be worked up in the country itself;

(iii) Population should be encouraged and the people turned from idleness;

(iv) Gold and silver should not be allowed to be exported or hoarded but should remain in circulation;

(v) The people should get along with their own domestic products and foreign products should be avoided as far as possible;

(vi) When it becomes absolutely necessary to obtain foreign products, this should be done by exchange with internal goods and not by gold and silver;

(vii) As far as possible the foreign goods should be imported in unfinished form and worked up in the country;

(viii) In so far as exports are concerned these should be sold in a finished form as far as possible and only in exchange with gold and silver;

(ix) No import should be allowed of goods of which there is sufficient supply in the country even if it is of a lightly inferior quality.

His fundamental doctrine is that it is better to pay more for an article which remains in the country than one which goes out because, according to him, "What once goes out stays out". The question with him is always one of foreign comparison since, according to him, the power and wealth have become relative terms, depending not on the absolute quantities of power and wealth possessed but in their relations to those of neighbouring lands. He, therefore, wants that his country, i.e., Austria, should surpass her neighbours in power and wealth by the application of various devices. This is a quite typical Mercantilist idea.

JOHANNES NEJNRICH GOTTLEB VON' JUSTI (1717-1771)

Justi was a professor of Kameral Sciences at the University of Vienna. He was a great author. His views are contained in his book entitled "Political Economy, or a Systematic Treatise on all Economic and Kameral Sciences" which was published in 1755. In this book he has summed up the Kameralistic doctrines. There is nothing new except the analysis and classifications made by him. According to him, economic science deals with the maintenance and increase of resources of private persons while the Kameral Science deals with similar subjects in relation to governments. Kameralism is demonstrated in nature and deals with the revenue of the prince, its disbursement, organization and administration of the political business of the prince.

He says that there are three great essentials leading to the prosperity of the State; freedom, safety of property rights and flourishing industry. Good government and flourishing industry and limitless increase of population may increase the wealth of a State to any extent. Although he attaches great significance to commerce and favourable balance of trade, he does not undermine the importance of agriculture.

Justi has laid down certain rules for the imposition of taxes. In brief, these rules are:

(i) Taxes should be so levied that they will be willingly paid.

(ii) They must not obstruct the progress of industry and commerce by coming in the way of freedom of conduct, credit, etc.

(iii) They must be imposed with relative equality.

(iv) They should be certain and true, and imposed upon such articles which may lead to a sure and honest collection.

(v) They should be imposed on such commodities, that their collection will require the minimum number of officers and officials.

(vi) They should be levied in such a way that the time and amount of payment would be most convenient for the people.

JOACHIM GEORGE DARIES (1714 – 1791)

Daries was a professor at the University of Jena. In 1763 he became professor of Kameral Sciences at the University of Frankfurt where he founded the Royal Academy. He wrote a book entitled "First Principles of Kameral Sciences" which was published in 1756. In this book he has tried to remove the objections raised against Kameralism. According to him there are two sources of annual income: one fixed and the other, a matter of chance. The former consists of (a) aptness in application of human force; and (b) acquired goods which can be of annual use. This he calls capital and to him capital is a surer source of income than a skill. His definition of capital is quite interesting. To him it is "that earned property which we accept as enduring so that it proves effective annually for our uses". Daries divided Kameralism into rural and urban. The former deals with the forces of nature and includes tillage and cattle rearing. The latter includes the art which helps nature in workshops and factories. The third division is that of Police Science or Polity which treats of matters as population, education, and care of the poor, etc. Lastly, there is Royal Economy, which relates to the royal income.

The analysis of costs as given by Daries is worth noting. He says that the producers should make a thorough investigation of costs and make allowance for: (a) raw materials; (b) interest on the value of such materials till the finished product is sold out; (c) the price of tools; (d) interest on their value and their depreciation; (e) labour; (f) interest on wages; (g) interest on the value of buildings used; and (h) expenses involved in marketing, accounting, etc. In the ultimate analysis, he is of the opinion that "when these items are established as a capital and the price received for the product replaces this capital with interest, the business is carried on with profit".

He does not favour the idea of completely banning the export of gold and silver. "The export of gold and silver is only to be obstructed to the extent that it does not work to the good of the State. It is, on the contrary, an evidence of political shrewdness to give foreigners gold and silver if it is possible by this to further the well-being of the State". He was opposed to the idea of imposing restrictions on trade. According to him it is not always profitable to exchange goods for precious metals. He considers the exchange of goods for goods under certain circumstances, more advantageous.

He was an orthodox Mercantilist in so far as he supported the idea of an increasing population. According to him a dense population is the source of wealth to the State. It increases the food supply, trade and income of the prince and is important for defence.

QUESTIONS

1. Analyse the factors leading to the shaping of Mercantilistm.
2. What are the chief elements of Mercantilist Thought ?
3. Explain the concept of 'Balance of Trade' as advocated by Mercantlists.
4. Discuss how mercantilist doctrines were implemented in State Policies.
5. Give a brief account of the ideas put forward by Thomas Mun.
6. State briefly the criticisms levelled against mercantilist ideas.
7. What is meant by Neo-mercantilism?
8. Write short notes on :
   (a) Mercantilist views on 'Population'.
   (b) Concept of 'Value' according to Mercantilists.

Chapter 5

Physiocracy

INTRODUCTION

Physiocracy is the collective name of those economic principles and policies which developed in France in the middle of the 18th century. Physiocracy is also known as the 'Agricultural System'. Economic thinkers who contributed to the growth and development of physiocracy have been called as physiocrats. The Physiocrats have been regarded as the founders of economic science because they were the first to grasp the general principles under-lying the economic phenomena and to evolve a theoretical system. Physiocracy is also remarked as the first school of economic thought. The term physiocracy means "Rule of Nature'.

Physiocracy may be defined as a reaction againt Mercantilism and its concepts. The physiocrats believed that the mercantile policies instead of doing any good have done great harm to the nations. So they revolted against the mercantile policies.

According to Gide and Rist, "Physiocrats must be credited with a foundation of the earliest school of economists in the fullest sense of the term. The entrance of this small group of men into the arena of history is a most touching one".

The influential French School of thinkers of the early 18th century was led by "Quesnay and Turgot". They believed in the existence of natural law which governs the universe. Their emphasis on agriculture has earned for their system of thought, the name agricultural school.

The factors that gave rise to physiocracy

In 1750, France provided a favourable climate for the emergence of physiocratic ideas. There were many economic, political and social factors that were responsible for the rise of physiocracy. Firstly, physiocracy was essentially a revolt of the French against Mercantilism. Under Colbert the famous Finance Minister of France, Mercantilism was carried to an extreme degree. As a result, there was neglect of agriculture and lot of government regulations. So there was need for an economic theory to prove that the mercantile policies were not favourable for the progress and wealth of a nation. The Physiocrats provided the theoretical basis to attack Mercantilism.

Secondly, the tax system of France was corrupt, inefficient and unjust. The nobles and the clergymen, who owned nearly 2/3rd of the lands, were exempted from direct taxation. On the other hand, the burden of taxation on the poor was very heavy. The poor were affected by taxes like salt tax, poll tax, etc.

Thirdly, the finance of the French government was in a bad condition. The unnecessary wars and the luxurious court life of King Louis the XIV and XV made the government bankrupt. So the government started borrowing loans.

Fourthly, the French farmers were exploited by the nobles and landlords in a number of ways. The landlords took large share of the produce. The government levied heavy taxes upon the farmers. Even the markets for agricultural commodities were restricted because Mercantilism was in favour of industrial goods.

Fifthly, the genral economic conditions of France were also unfavourabale. Britain had already realised that it was a wrong policy to develop trade and industry at the expense of agriculture. Agricultural revolution was taking place in England. So in France also attention was diverted to agriculture.

Lastly, there were other forces working for the change. The political and moral philosophers emphasised the importance of individual rather than wealth. They told that man must be the centre of study.

Thus as Eric Roll says, "With the physiocrats we enter an era of schools and systems in Economic Thought". Physiocrats are important in the history of economic thought because they represented the first school of economists. The mercantailists were ordinary people who emphasised only foreign trade. But the physiocrats realised the importance of various economic activities and their relation. In the physiocratic system all social factors like production and distribution are connected. In short, the physiocrats were reformers.

MAIN IDEAS OF PHYSIOCRATS

The Physiocrats contributed on the theoretical side, three important ideas, namely : 1. The concept of natural order. 2. The concept of net product. 3. The circulation of wealth.

1. Natural Order

The physiocrats had firm faith in the philosophy of natural order. Nemours called Physiocracy as "The science of natural order". Gide and Rist said "The essence of physiocratic system lay in their contribution of natural order".

Natural order has been defined by the physiocrats as the providential order made by God for the welfare of mankind. It is universal and unchangeable. The natural laws are the expression of the will of God. To discover and to understand these laws is man's first duty and to live according to them is his second duty.

According to the physiocrats the natural order is an ideal order given by God. It is different from the positive order made by men. In other words, the society which is governed by the laws of nature is an ideal society and the society which is ruled by positive laws made by the Government is an imperfect society. The moral and religious philosophy is reflected in their concept of Natural Order.

Natural order will increase the happiness of mankind. "Divine in its origin it was universal in its scope". In short, the natural order is the best and most advantageous order for the physiocrats. The physiocratic Natural order had 3 important features:

1. Natural order aimed at securing pleasure to the people.
2. It aimed to increase the rights of the people without imposing any restrictions on their liberty.
3. It stands against mercantilism.

The physiocrats believed that natural order maintained equilibrium in nature. The concept of natural order produced certain important practical results. It implied that only under conditions of freedom, man can enjoy the maximum happiness and derive maximum advantage in economic matters. There should be minimum interference in economic affairs by Government. In other words, the physiocrats advocated laissez faire policy. The physiocrats believed that the individual interests were identical with the interest of the society.

Criticisms

Physiocratic idea about natural order was vague and not clear. It was not the result of observation of external facts. It ignored the fact that the interest of the individual is not always in harmony with those of the society and the individual is not always the best judge of his own interest.

2. Net Product

The physiocratic concept of net product was the outcome of their nature philosophy. Physiocrats held agriculture supreme among all occupations, since it was the source of wealth. It is in agriculture that nature works along with man.

In the doctrine of net product the physiocrats introduced the fundamental idea of economic surplus. In the physiocratic system, agriculture has been given a dominant place because of its important role in the economic development of a country. Agriculture is the only sector which yields net product or surplus produce. In other words it is only in agriculture the net wealth produced is greater than the wealth consumed. Net product is defined as the excess of wealth produced over and above what is required. The physiocrats introduced the idea of surplus resulting from the bounty of nature which they called "Product - Net" or "Net Product".

Commerce and industry according to the physiocrats are the branches of agriculture because agriculture supports them by furnishing the necessary materials. The size of the net product shows the welfare of the community. Because of this fact the physiocrats advocated a light tax on agriculture. Net Product is the real revenue of the nation, a source from which manufacturing and commercial classes get their living.

No other sector except agriculture is capable of yielding net product. In commerce the already produced commodities are transferred from one hand to another and nothing new is produced. In industry also the raw materials are modified and no surplus is produced. In industry and commerce the wealth produced exactly equals to the wealth consumed. Thus industry and commerce are regarded as unproductive.

Thus, Prof. Haney considers "The idea of Net Product was important for the development of economic analysis. From this developed, the idea of surplus which was to play an important part in later theories".

3. The Circulation Of Wealth: (Tableau Economique).

After having discovered the source of wealth, the physiocrats turned to the problem of how wealth produced by the agriculturists gets circulated among the different classes of the society. The physiocrats must be credited with being the first school of economists who analysed the problem of distribution. The idea was first given by a famous physiocrat Quesnay through tableau economique. How much importance the physiocrats attached to the circulation of wealth is evident from what Turgot said the "it constituted the very life of the body politic, just as the circulation of blood did of the physical".

As Hector Denis said, "the discovery of the circulation of wealth in economic society occupied in the history of science the same position as is occupied by the discovery of circulation of blood in the history of Biology."

The most important contribution of physiocracy is the tableau economique. The author of this table was Quesnay. He was a doctor and so he applied his biological knowledge to the economy and compared the circulation of wealth with circulation of blood. The economic table represents the way in which circulation of wealth takes place in the economy. In his table, Quesnay has divided the society into three classes. In other words the physiocratic system is based on the division of society into the following three classes:

1. The productive class: It consisted of farmers, who cultivate the soil and pay the rent to the landlords.
2. The proprietory class included the landlords and the king.
3. The sterile class or unproductive class. This class included all those people who are engaged in non-agricultural occupations. Merchants, artisans, domestic servants, government servants, doctors, lawyers, teachers, etc. formed part of this class. It must be remembered that the physiocrats did not consider the sterile class as useless. It was unproductive in the sense that it did not produce any net product.

Among the three classes the farmers alone are the productive class because soil is the only source of wealth. After classifying the society into three classes, Quesnay traced the circulation of wealth among the three classes of the society in the following manner.

All wealth is produced by the productive class. The value of the total produce produced by the farmers in any year is equal to five million francs. Out of this agricultural class requires two million francs for their maintenance. So the two million do not circulate in the economy. The remaining produce worth of three million francs is distributed in the following manner. Since the productive class requires industrial goods, it will buy them from the sterile class for one million franc, the remaining two million francs pass on to the hands of landlords and the government in the form of rent and taxes. The proprietary class lives on these two million francs. It spends one million francs for food and the other for the purchase of industrial goods.

According to the physiocrats the sterile class or upnroductive class produces no surplus. But still it receives two million francs. The sterile class uses the two million francs for buying the necessaries of life and raw materials for industries from the productive class. Thus the two million which have come into the hands of the unproductive class return to their starting point, namely, the farmers. Thus

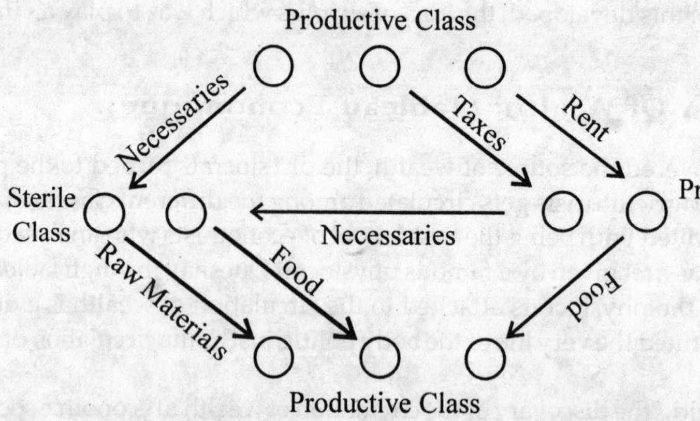

the cycle is complete. The following figure clearly shows the circulation of wealth among the three classes of people.

The tableau economique is based on the existence of a social structure, land is owned by the landlords but cultivated by the farmers who became the productive class. The net product or surplus produced by the productive class is used for the satisfaction of sterile and proprietary classes. The tableau economique assumes constant prices for the commodities. Further, it assumes that the harvest is 100 percent and the expenses of the productive and unproductive classes are equal.

In short the tableau economique explains two things.

a) How the net product circulates among the three classes ?
b) How it is re-produced each year ?

Criticism of Tableau Economique

Many complexities are involved in the circulation of wealth in a society. Today, one may be surprised to find that under the "Tableau", the class which enjoys two-fifths of the national income does nothing in return first. The reason lies in the great reverence the physiocrats had for the land owners. The adjective "Sterile" is applied not to them but to the manufacturers and artisans.

Property is the foundation of the "natural order". One might have expected that the premier position should have been given to the class which they turned productive i.e. the tillers of the soil. But the Physiocrats put proprietors above these tillers of the soil, because God, according to them, had willed that the farmers should be the first dispensers of all wealth. This idea was, undoubtedly, a great mistake on the part of the Physiocrats.

Another mistake was their failure to realise the inherent dignity of all true labour simply because it was not the creactor of wealth. In the eyes of the Physiocrats, it was the nature that produced wealth and not the worker. Hence, an industrial worker is unproductive whereas an agricultural worker is not. Since the Physiocrats lived in a feudal society, they suffered from an illusion as to the necessity for landed property similar to that which led Aristotle to defend the institution of slavery.

ITS IMPORTANCE

Growth Models

There is one more advantage from the Tableau Economique. It can help us to understand and construct models. Some fundamental truths of interdependence of various sectors is revealed by it. It also shows that a number of conditions will have to be fulfilled for an overall balance. How the expenditure behaviour of one sector determines the constraints upon other sectors is also shown by this Tableau. In the growth models, these very ideas are used. Input requirements and output supplies are worked out or assumed for different sectors. And in conjunction with other assumptions, conditions of the overall economic balance of stability are also worked out. There is no denying the fact that modern growth models are much more complex. They consider the depreciation factors, time lags, gestation periods, changing supply position of various resources, technological changes, demand changes and so on. Today's models work out conditions of stability and instability in the economy.

At that time, when the tableau economique was published it was regarded as one of the greatest achievements of human mind. Gide and Rist are of the opinion that "Physiocrats were the first to attempt a synthesis of distribution and production. They were anxious to know how wealth passed from one class to another".

Quesnay's economique table is considered as the most important contribution of physiocracy. It is regarded as a pioneering attempt at national income analysis and mathematical economics. Quesnay was interested in the statistical data and tried to estimate the value of annual output. Quesnay's net product is equal to that of Karl Marx's surplus value.

Practical Ideas of Physiocrats.

The physiocrats did not analyse the problem of value in a systematic manner. They were interested only in production. According to them, value is connected with the usefulness of the commodity. They did not differentiate between value and price. Quesnay said "What is called value is price". Value was not fixed but changed from time to time depending upon the demand.

2. Interest

As for as interest is concerned physiocrats made a difference between money and capital. In their view capital is the result of saving and so interest on capital is justified. The physiocrats allowed interest charging for the loans which were taken for agricultrual purposes because such loans were productive.

3. Population

Physiocrats encouraged large population because they believed that large population increases consumption which results in an increase in production and so wealth will increase.

4. Taxation

The physiocratic theory of taxation is connected with net product. They believed that only land produced a surplus, taxes should be paid from the surplus or net product. In short, they advocated a single tax system on agriculture. But an objection was raised against the single tax system because the government's revenue will be less. Further, this type of taxation was not justified because it ignored the other sources of wealth to the government.

5. Private Property

The physiocrats were believers in the institution of private property. The physiocrats regarded property as a tree and its branches are social institutions. In support of private property they stated that the landlords must enjoy 2/5 of the surplus because they are responsible for making land fit for cultivation. It is the landlord who provides the farmer the necessary funds for cultivation. So, if the landlords are not given their due share, they will take away the land from cultivation. At the same time, the physiocrats imposed certain duties upon the landlords. They should bring new lands under cultivation and help and protect the farmers.

6. Trade

The physiocrats thought that exchange was unproductive. Accordingly, industry and commerce were considered unproductive. So foreign trade which had assumed so much importance under mercantilism started loosing its importance. The physiocrats thought that foreign trade produced no real wealth. So some of the physiocrats even considered foreign trade as an evil. However, the physiocrats were not entirely against foreign trade. They believed that a country should exchange only those goods which it cannot produce and those which are in excess of consumption. As a result, the physiocrats advocated free trade.

7. Functions of State

In the natural order of Physiocrats, the functions of the state would be reduced to the minimum, i.e., to protect the country and the life, liberty and property of the individual. The physiocrats pointed out that the main cause for all troubles and poverty in France was due to government interference. Therefore, they advocated minimum state interference. They thought that a state must provide universal education and it should also undertake public works. Thus the functions of the physiocratic government were:

1. To preserve natural order.
2. To protect private property.
3. To spread education in natural order.
4. To undertake public works programme.
5. To eliminate international barriers.

In short, the physiocrats made the following contributions to economic theory:

a. They put economics on a scientific basis.
b. Their emphasis on the net product was notable.
c. Their analysis of capital pointed the true nature of that factor of production.
d. They made important contribution to the theory of taxation.

Thus the physiocrats by contributing many ideas occupied an important place in the history of economic thought. Inspite of their short period of life, their influence was more. Adam Simth got may ideas from the physiocrats. The physiocrats must be given a high place among those who laid the foundation for the French Revolution. They were the pioneers in the field of distribution. Again, in the field of taxation, by suggesting a single tax on land they laid the principle of shifting and incidence of taxation.

Critical Estimate of Physiocracy

Physiocracy was the revolt of the French people against Mercantilism. It is, from this angle, we have to judge the economic ideas of the physiocrats. While the mercantilists were occupied with gold, the physiocrats emphasized "Real wealth" in the form of raw produce. The Mercantilists aimed at maximising exports and minimising imports with an object of securing a favourable balance of trade. But the physiocrats in general regarded foreign trade as an evil. While the mercantilists believed in the regulation of trade and Industry, the physiocrats suggested freedom of trade and Industry.

In spite of the above merits, the physiocrats were wrong in considering agriculture alone as the productive occupation. Commerce and industry are equally important and productive. The physiocrats had a wrong idea of production. They regarded manufacture as unproductive although it creates utility. Further the physiocrats were mainly responsible for their wrong classification of labour into productive and unproductive.

The greatest defect in the physiocratic doctrine is the absence of any reference to value. The physiocrats suggested complete freedom of trade and industry. But absolute freedom of trade is not advisable.

The aim of the physiocrats was to develop agriculture. They regarded land, as the only source of wealth. So it followed that the landlords should pay the taxes. But this idea is against the interest of the agricultural class.

The weakest point in the physiocratic system is the theory of distribution. But, at the same time, we have to remember that the physiocrats made some important contributions to economic thought.

1. They put economics on a scientific basis by applying scientific methods.
2. Economic development was a major concern of the Physiocrats. They realised the importance of agriculture which give surplus for capital formation.
3. The physiocrats were the first school of economists to analyse capital and capital formation.
4. The physiocrats realised the interdependance of different classes in the economy.
5. The physiocrats insisted that the government should restrict its functions.
6. They advocated direct taxes rather than indirect taxes.
7. Lastly, the physiocrats must be given a high place among those who prepared the ground for French Revolution.

FRANCOIS QUESNAY (1694-1774)

Life and Works. Quesnay was born in 1694. He was the first in the chronological order. He belonged to a poor peasant family. After studying medicine, he established himself as a village physician and wrote several treatises and books on medical subjects and philosophical problems. He was a physician to Louis XV. He was an ardent lover of village economy and he could never reconcile himself to urban civilization. Agriculture was the vocation of his heart and he was always in mental contact with the village. He was so much impressed by the conditions of the peasantry in those days that he started writing on economic problems. At first, he started writing papers and articles anonymously or under a pseudonym in various periodicals. His first economic essays, "Firmiers" and "Grains", were published in the famous encyclopedia. Quesnay is best known for his Tableau

Economique. He laid emphasis on agriculture, demanding that it should be brought to the highest level of perfection. "Poor peasant: poor kingdom: poor king" is the maxim generally attributed to him. He was in favour of granting freedom of trade and industry so that agriculture could get enough chance to expand. The main theme of his table is the annual distribution and circulation of the output of agriculture and manufactures which have been represented by a diagram.

Quesnay's ideas, which are contained in his articles, essays, dialogue and the table can be classified as critical and positive. In the first category come those ideas which are critical of Mercantilist doctrines and policies. In this respect he was influenced by Boisguillebert. But the main difference between the two was that while the bulk of Boisguillebert's writings were directed against the financial policies of Louis XIV, Quesnay besides decrying the existing economic and social conditions desired to establish an ordere naturel, based on the laws of nature. Quesnay was a devout catholic and a rustic by sentiment, who, with his heart in the village looked upon trade and commerce with distrust. The critical aspect of his work is related to the existing conditions of France while the positive aspect is modelled after the medieval conditions.

Quesnay's social principles have permeated his teachings regarding laws of nature. Man cannot create laws just as he cannot create himself. He is only the bearer of the laws and not the legislator. Natural laws are the permanent laws, which are of two types: physical and moral. In his reasoning regarding physical laws he was influenced by Locke while in his analysis of moral laws he was influenced by St. Aquinas.

Riches. Quesnay held that the earth and its fertility were the only sources of riches and these were increased through cultivation. Riches are the consumable articles which satisfy human needs. It is the need or the utility which transforms things into riches. Agriculture gives two kinds of riches: the annual revenue to the landed proprietors and the returns to the labour and the expenses involved in cultivation. The revenue of the landed proprietors, i.e., the net product is the sum which remains after deducting the cost of tillage from total yield of the land. The net product and cultivator's returns are the measure and limit of the annual income of the nation. They are the annual fund from which all expenses, individual and national are met. The magnitude and the size of this fund depend on the price at which the produce is sold. For the creation of the net product it is necessary that the produce must be sold at just price, 'bon prix'. It is the price at which the cultivators offer their produce and is determined by taking into account their cost of production as well as the surplus value which soil contributes. In practices, 'bon prix' is ultimately determined by the demand and supply of the commodity. Freedom of trade and unrestricted competition are the essential conditions for the determination of the just price and for furthering the prosperity of agriculture.

The Productive Classes. Since land produces a surplus, Quesnay regarded proprietors and the cultivators as the productive classes. The artisans, craftsmen, professional men, merchants and traffickers were declared unproductive. The productive classes not only meet the cost of production of the commodities but also supply additional riches, which form the revenue of the nation. It is the production of these additional riches that helps us to differentiate between productive and sterile occupations.

Equality of Exchanges. Quesnay looked upon mankind as a single community, whose members exchange superfluous commodities on the basis of justice, value for value without loss or gain to any one, but to the benefit of each. The same law applies to trade between various nations. He did not uphold the exchanges which are performed through the intermediaries of merchants. According to him as long as those exchanges take place direct between producers and the consumers, they were right and in conformity with the principles of equality and justice. He was thus not against all sorts of exchanges for he thought that without the operations of the merchants the surplus produce would lose all its value. In a natural order, i.e., where trade is free, the exchanges are always equal and both countries benefit equally. This type of trade is beneficial to both the countries. But when merchants turn into traffickers, their interests and those of the nation are diametrically opposed. Undoubtedly, the traffickers bring home large gains, but these are not public gains. Quesnay, thus sums up that, "the most advantageous policy for a State is, therefore, the continual and progressive increase of its agricultural production and thus also of the product net, and utmost restriction of the gains of the traffickers, i.e., that the payments for their services should be as low as possible. The most rational means to achieve this aim is perfect freedom of trade".

On Money. Quesnay regarded money as a barren metal. It produces nothing and serves only as a measure of value and a pledge. Money, to him, was merely a statutory medium of exchange. He did not agree with those who regarded money as real wealth and claimed that money purchases all the things. His contention was that money as such is not serviceable for immediate use. It is not a consumable article. The consumable articles arise chiefly from the annual wealth of agriculture, and are distributed through the commerce by the medium of money. Money, thus, is the medium of exchange and distribution of goods, whose quantity depends upon the volume of available goods. In short, neither money nor commerce, neither merchants nor traffickers bring wealth to the nation; it is annual production of the primary goods which is the source of wealth, which gives rise to commerce and money and which provides employment to traders and merchants.

Fevourable Balance of Trade. The idea that favourable balance of trade can bring in riches to the country was intolerable for Quesnay. He said that persons who nourish such ideas forget that every sale is a purchase and that both buyers and sellers mutually exchange goods of equal value. In conditions of free trade losses and gains would be equal, but in conditions of inequality of exchanges created by custom duties or monopolies or manipulation, balance of payments cannot be equal. Quesnay was against granting privileges and tariff manipulations to boost up manufactures because it leads to the impoverishment of the farmers. The injury inflicted on agriculture is increased all the more by the manufacture of fancy goods from the imported raw materials. According to him the criterion of prosperity or poverty of a nation cannot be found in the balance of trade. A country may be poor with large exports. A country can be prosperous only when inland production and consumption are equal.

Rate of Interest. Quesnay who was vigorously advocating free competition for determining the just price, was not prepared to grant any liberty to the money-lenders and desired maximum governmental control to fix the rate of interest. According to him the rate of interest must be equal to the revenue earned from the ownership of land which a man would purchase if he does not lend out the money. The profits of commerce cannot set a standard for the rate of interest because the profits are themselves against the natural order. The revenue from agriculture, being legitimate in itself, should be the maximum standard of the rate of interest. Quesnay, like his predecessors realised that the various methods of obtaining revenue for the government were unjust and uneconomical. Since land was the source of the national income he proposed to abolish all various impositions to make the net product of agriculture the only and single source of public revenue and tithes. He wanted the proprietors of land to bear the entire burden of taxes. According to Quesnay, "the best form of government was a single authority, vested with sovereign power, but acting in conformity with the laws of nature and the positive law derived from them". Such were his ideas and he was virtually the father of political economy.

ANNE ROBER JACQUES TURGOT (1727-1781)

After Quesnay, Turgot was the most celebrated member of the Physiocratic school. He was born at Paris in 1727. He presented Physiocratic principles in a methodical way and helped in their spread. As Intendant of Limoges he introduced many reforms specially by removing restrictions from commerce. He was later on appointed as the Finance Minister when he established free trade in grain with France, abolished taxes, and suppressed the guilds. He revealed physiocracy in action.

Turgot's doctrine is to be found primarily in two small tracts, the " Eloge de Gournay" and the " "Reflexions Sur La Formationet Distribution des Richesses", besides his statements in his official and state documents. The Eloge is rather an extreme statement of laissez faire. The major portion of the book is covered by this subject. It also contains famous Physiocratic doctrine: that agriculture is the source of all revenues and that all taxes are paid by the proprietor. In Reflexions, one finds the superiority of agriculture at its full glory. The iron law of wages is one of the consequences of this superiority. The simple labourer is knocked down in his negotiations with the employer who had a wide choice because of competition among workers. Farmer is, however, in a happy position because he receives over and above his subsistence. The land is, therefore, the unique source of all wealth. The book is divided into 100 small sections and covers subjects like the division of labour, the origin and uses of money, the nature of capital and interest, and the role of agriculture. It is in a sense the restatement of physiocratic doctrines. Turgot has concluded that land revenues are the only proper source for taxes. The remainder largely deals with money and capital. He is of the view that no restrictions should be placed on the rate of interest which should be allowed to be determined solely by the course of trade.

In several important aspects Turgot differed from other writers of the physiocratic school. While agreeing that agriculture could yield a net product he has introduced some elements of a subjective theory of value. Turgot had realised that a time would come when the owner of the land would not be its cultivator and would be transformed into a wage-earner. And in this context since the labourer will be paid only a subsistence wage, the balance of the net product would become ordinary capitalised profits. Similarly, he held that those who occupied the land first became the proprietors while those who came later became the labourers. This concept seems to be in sharp contrast with that of other writers of the school. He, therefore, differed with the physiocrats on the following points. (a) productivity of agriculture and the sterility of industry. (b) landed property being no longer an institution of divine origin. It was a result of occupation and public utility, and (c) movable property holds a prominent place in his work. He recognised the worth of capital and proved the validity of interest.

Turgot was, no doubt, one of the most illustrious members of the school but he can be distinguished from other physiocrats. His book "Reflexions" appears to be a thing of great controversy. Cossa declared that the book was the first scientific treatise on social economics. Ingram liked it immensely and held that it must occupy a place among the classics of the science of economics. Turgot had a remarkable style of writing, but whatever he wrote, was taken mostly from others. He drew inspiration from Cantillon, Hume, Gournay, and Quesnay. Cantillon's Essay was more scientific while Turgot's was more voluminous. But Cantillon, Turgot and Adam Smith—all are landmarks in the development of economic science.

QUESTIONS

1. Analyse the factors responsible for the rise of physiocracy.
2. What are the theoretical concepts on which physiocrats built up their doctrines ?
3. Analyse the concept of 'Net Product'.
4. What is meant by circulation of wealth in physiocratic doctrine ?
5. What were the views of physiocrats on 'Trade'?
6. What are the criticisms levelled against physiocratic doctrine?
7. Can you altogether dismiss the physiocratic doctrine as imperfect, illusory and contradictory ?
8. What are the contributions of physiocrats to the Economic Science ?
9. Write short notes on :
   (a) Physiocracy as a School of Thought
   (b) Views of physiocrats on 'Taxation'
   (c) Sterile class in Physiocracy.

Chapter 6

PRE-CLASSICAL ECONOMISTS

WILLIAM PETTY

Petty was born in Hampshire on December 16,1623. His chief economic writings were "A Treatise of Taxes and Contributions" (1662), "A Tract Concerning Money" (1682) and "Discourses on Political Arithmetic" (1660). Petty is aptly regarded as the founder of political economy and statistical method. He is remembered for his contributions in the field of economic theory. He had a quantitative bent of mind and was the first to develop a fact-finding approach in economic enquiry. As a statistician, Petty confined himself only to the employment of quantitative data and used simple averages as the statistical technique. What distinguishes Petty in the field of economics is not his statistical method but the economic concepts which he derived from his statistical investigations. His economic ideas are the result of his brooding over the actual problems of his time and country.

Petty's most important contribution to economic theory was his theory of natural par which also included his views on rent and value. Petty's theory of natural par has three variations:

(1) Natural Par Between Land and Labour: Petty believed that land and labour were the two original factors of production capable of generating value. Petty's next step was to relate the value of land and labour by equating a piece of land producing a day's food of an average man to the day's labour of the same man. Thus, the common measure of value, that Petty singled out, was 'day's food, and it is through this measure that he was able to convert the value of land into the value of labour and thus to make a par between the two.

(2) Natural Par Between Rent and Money: Petty realised that the commonly accepted measure of value was not 'day's food' but money. The question that strained his mind was to determine the money value of the surplus product, which Petty called rent. Natural and true rent is the surplus of corn over what is used by the cultivator to meet his cultivation expenses as well as his subsistence needs. Thus, rent is simply the difference between the total production of land and the cost of producing it.

What is the money value of rent? Petty's answer is that the money value of annual rent will be equal to the surplus silver which is left after deducing the cost of production of silver (including subsistence wage of the worker working in the silver mine) from the annual production of silver. If a man produces a net surplus of silver equal to one ounce during the same period, then the price of a bushel is an ounce of silver.

Thus, Petty's theory of value is a by-product of his theory of rent and as he emphasized the importance of both land and labour in his analysis, his theory may more appreciately be called a land - labour theory of value rather than labour theory of value. In his analysis of value, Petty ignored the use-value and set aside the differences of various lands.

(3) Natural par between rent and interest: Petty also attempted to link rent with interest. Natural interest (net of risk premium) will be equal to the rent of so much land as the money lent will buy.

Petty was also the first to pen down a systematic treatise on public finance. In fact his all other economic ideas are inter - connected with his ideas of public finance. Petty singled out six heads of public expenditure: defending the country, maintaining the rulers, ensuring justice, supporting educational institutions, helping the orphanages and their dependents, and maintaining the public works like roads, streams, bridges etc.

On the revenue side, Petty regarded the tax on rent as the most suitable source of public revenue. In a new country, such a tax is the best one. In this case, land tax will be immediately capitalised because the new buyers of land will certainly take the tax into their consideration. As a result of this, land price will fall.

In old countries, the land tax will affect different classes of people differently. In case of short period lease, the land tax will compel the landlords to step up the rent and the tenants to raise the price of corn. Thus, the ultimate burden of tax will fall on the consumers. In case of a long-term lease, the landlords will not be able to pass the land tax on the tenants. On the other hand, the tenants will sell the corn at the same higher price at which the short term tenants are selling. The net effect will be that the long-term tenants will be better off after the imposition of land tax. The consumers are always the loosers. Whether the lease is for short period or for long period, the burden of land tax will fall ultimately on the consumers through higher prices.

Petty was of the view that taxes should be proportional and equitable. He justified such a tax on the ground that it will not affect the relative economic position of different tax payers and all of them will suffer the burden of tax proportionately. The revenue collected through taxes must be spent in such a way that it promotes industry and trade of the country.

Petty's other theoretical achievements were in the field of wages, money and income. Petty referred to a normative subsistence theory of wages which stated that wages should not be more than subsistence. If they are more than subsistence, the workers will prefer leisure to work. Thus, Petty hinted at the backward sloping supply curve of labour. In the field of money, he regarded velocity of money as a function of peoples' pay periods. Petty also realised the importance of national income in economic analysis. By making it clear that the national income is always equal to the national expenditure, he anticipated Keynes theory of income-expenditure equality symbolised in his famous equation: $Y = C + I$.

A review of Petty's "Treatise of Taxes and Contributions" reveals a number of analytical flaws; but inspite of these flaws, the work continues to be great because of its scientific character. Orderliness of the outer structure and consistency of the internal analysis are the two qualities which give the Treatise its status as a scientific work and rank Petty among the originators of scientific economics.

JOHN LAW

John Law (1671-1729) is better known as a man of practical affairs. But he made an important contribution to the theory of money and made a distinction between the use value and market value of a commodity. In Money and Trade Considered; with a Proposal for Supplying the Nation with Money (1705, 2nd ed., 1720), he points out that use value (which the modern terminology is 'utility' of a good) is necessary for a good to command a market value, but it does not determine the market value. The latter depends upon the relative supply and demand position. He gives the well-known examples of water and diamonds to prove his point. Water has a high use value, but on account of its abundant supply, it has a very low market value; diamonds, on the other hand, have very low use value, but command a high market value on account of their scarcity. The same idea, as extended to money, implies that money also has no imaginary value. The value of money depends upon the uses to which it is put and the service which money renders to the society is similar to the service which any other commodity provides.

John Law is remembered, more than anything else, for his suggestions for the issue of paper money so much prevalent in the modern times. However, as a typical Mercantilist he desired that the State should have stock of treasure and he wanted that the paper notes would only take the place of metallic money in transactions of the public and that bullion would then accumulate in the State's treasury. The issue of paper money resulted in severe inflation which caused much ruin. Ultimately the only property that remained was land which came to be regarded most important as envisaged in the development of French Physiocratic thought.

Also, he is generally regarded as the founder of a subjective theory of value, with special reference to the value of money. He definitely rejected the idea that money had an imaginary value. According to him, nothing had any value except for the use to which one puts it. The same was true of the money commodity even in relation to its monetary uses. The service which it rendered as money was no different from its other services or from the services of any other commodity. These views clearly make him a forerunner of Austrian School.

RICHARD CANTILLON

Richard Cantillon's "An Essay on the Nature of Commerce in General" is the most systematic statement of economic principles, before the Wealth of Nations. The Essay begins with a definition of land as the source of wealth, labour as the power which produces it, and all material goods as its constituents. It goes on to discuss the economic structure, wages, value, population and money. The second part of the book is taken up mainly with problems of money, exchange, and interest; and the third part deals with foreign trade, the mechanism of the foreign exchanges, banking and credit. It is in the last two parts that Cantillon excels in original analysis and description. For it is here that he is able to combine his insight into economic principles with his own commercial experience and to write sentences which can take their place with any modern work on those subjects. He has none of these difficulties about the mechanism of foreign payments which had troubled Locke. If a state, he says, has an export surplus for any considerable time and is drawing specie from other countries, 'the circulation will become more considerable there... money will be more plentiful there, and consequently Land and Labour will gradually become dearer there'. This will at once redress the balance of trade.

The analysis of the effects of an increase in the circulating medium is even better worked out than in Hume. Assuming an increased gold output from the mines, Cantillon is able to show how the benefits of the increased purchasing power that has become available are distributed. The owners, smelters, refiners and other workers will be the first to be able to increase their demand for food, clothes, and manufactured goods, the suppliers of these commodities will in their turn be able to increase their expenses. But the share of commodities that goes to other people in the state must of necessity be diminished, because they do not participate at first in the wealth of the mines. The path of rising prices and the ensuing changes in the distribution of wealth are then carefully traced and even international effects were not ignored. Altogether, this argument remains an excellent demonstration of an important aspect of monetary theory. Cantillon was also aware that the effects of an increase of the money commodity and those of paper money were only apparently the same. Ultimately an abundance of 'fictitious' money would vanish 'at the first gust of discredit' and would precipitate disorder.

On the question of foreign exchanges, too, Cantillon was able to express clearly the principles which underlie economic practice. He showed the relation between merchandise trade, speculation and specie movements; and he showed also their interaction with exchange rates and price-level in the mechanism of international payments. Particularly lucid was the explanation of the causes which raise or lower the exchange from parity and the way in which such movements can be foreseen and discounted.

The central questions of value, ages and price are contained in part one of Cantillon's Essay. His treatment of these is not always strikingly new. He owes more to his predecessors, and he gets less far ahead of them than he does in other matters. In particular, the analysis of value lacks some consistency; though it is perhaps for that very reason that Cantillon may be taken as one of the early representatives of the eclecticism which became a characteristic of English economic thought. His theory of value is in origin a labour theory but it is transformed into a cost-of production theory and it also contains some admixture of a supply and demand theory. The first strand of thought is derived largely from Petty, the second from Locke.

Cantillon repeats in different words Petty's theory of the origin of wealth. In chapter X of the Essay he goes on to develop a theory which is summarized in the title of that chapter. 'The Price and Intrinsic Value of a Thing in general is the measure of the Land and Labour which enter into its Production. The meaning of the subsequent analysis amounts to this: if two goods are produced by the same amount of land and labour of the same quality, they will have equal value. But the proportion in which land and labour will determine the value of particular goods will vary. In some cases – a watch-spring, for example – 'Labour makes up nearly all the value'. In Others-for example-the price of 'a Wood which it is proposed to cut down'-land is the chief determinant.

Besides making cost of production (wages of labour plus cost of material) determine value, Cantillon also distinguishes between the intrinsic value and the fluctuating price at which goods are sold in the market. A rich man who has spent much money on beautifying his estate will not necessarily get its intrinsic value when he comes to sell it. Nor will farmers get the expense of the land and labour which have entered into the production of corn if they have produced more than is necessary for consumption. The ensuing excess of supply over demand will depress the market price below the intrinsic value. Intrinsic values never alter. But because it is impossible always to apportion production among different commodities in perfect harmony with consumption, variations in market prices will occur.

The supply and demand forces are again mentioned in connection with the problem of money.

Cantillon agrees with Locke's quantity theory, but corrects it by pointing out that commodities destined for export must be excluded when the mass of commodities is compared with the volume of circulating money. He does, however, disagree with Locke's view of the value of money. Like Law, her rejects the definition which gives money an imaginary value. It is true, he said, that common consent has given gold and silver value; but so it has to everything which cannot be regarded as an absolute necessity of life. The precious metals have a value which is determined in exactly the same way as that of any other commodity, namely, by the land and labour which enter into their production.

Cantillon develops this point at some length. He gives a theory of the value of money, and of money's function as a measure of value, which is based on the labour theory of value. 'The intrinsic Value of Metals', he said, 'is like everything else proportionable to the Land and Labour that enters into their production', though their market value, like that of other goods, might vary according to supply and demand. As for acting as a measure of value, money 'must correspond in fact and reality in terms of Land and Labour to the articles exchanged for it'.

Cantillon was troubled by his dual source of value; and he procedded to inquire, in Chapter XI, whether 'some relation might be found between the value of Labour and that of the produce of the Land'. This inquiry into the Par, an expression taken from Petty, resolves itself into a discussion on ages which leads to results somewhat similar to those of Petty. The clue of the Par is to be found in the amount of subsistence required to produce a given amount of labour. From that, the amount of land which has to be allotted to this purpose can be deduced. And an equivalence between land and labour is thus established. Cantillon uses a number of examples covering slaves, serfs, craftsmen, and others; and he concludes that the intrinsic value of labour is found in the amount of land needed to support the labourer's sustenance plus an equal amount for the rearing of two children up to the age at which they can work. Cantillon speaks of two children, sine he accepts Halley's calculation that half the children that are born die before the age of seventeen.

SIR DAVID HUME (1711-1776)

Sir David Hume, though primarily a philosopher, is also known as an economist. He exerted a great influence upon Adam Smith and his followers. His special fields of interest were philosophy and literature. He had great analytical powers and great ability to harmonise divergent views. He was endowed with great powers of clarity of expression. His ideas about economic problems were quite in advance of his times and he can be classed as a liberal mercantilist. His chief work was "Political Discourses"—a collection of economic essays of which, 'Of Money', 'Of Interest', 'Of Commerce' and 'Of Balance of Trade' are the most important. He has over-emphasised the importance of money for stimulating trade. But on the whole he has followed the view held by Locke that money was only a symbol and that the amount of money possessed by a nation was of no significance. In the field of quantity theory of money he discarded the balance of trade argument and held that the movements of species would affect prices and hence the merchandise trade. He said that balance of trade of a country could not be permanently favourable or adverse and in the long run the balance of trade depends on the relative economic conditions of the countries concerned. He was thus an advocate of free trade.

The contribution of Hume to economic thought relates to the fields of money, price and interest. He regarded price to be the result of amount of money. Regarding the value of money, it was fictitious to him. Money represented commodities and its value was determined by the quantity of commodities for which it was to be exchanged. He considered the changes in the quantity of money to be of importance because they could be effective in changing the habits of the people. Changes in the quantity of money may bring about any change in the prices if the habits of the people are altered. In case prices go up as a result of an increae in money, such a rise would be beneficial because it would stimulate the industry. In this respect Hume's position is secure in economics because he analysed the problem in such a way that it was used by economists who followed him. Even Keynes may be said to have made use of his thoughts.

He held that a lower rate of interest was the surest sign of a country's flourishing state. He opposed the regulation of interest by the state. He said that the rate of interest was determined by the supply and demand of borrowers and lenders. In his opinion profits and interest were inter-dependent; the low profits of merchandise induce merchants to accept more willingly at a low interest. No man will accept low profits, where he can have high interest.

He regarded land as the source of all useful things but he had hardly any love for the landed class. In his opinion land owners who earned income without any labour were bound to be extravagant. They diminish the quantity of available capital and thus help in raising the rate of interest. On the other hand, commercial classes were all the time working in the interest of the nation by creating capital in abundance and by accepting low profits. It is thus clear that he gave ideas which were adopted by writers who followed him and it cannot be denied that he was one of the earliest forerunners of classical economics.

JAMES STEUART

Sir James Steuart (1712-1780) was the chief English Mercantilist writer of the eighteenth century. Indeed he has been called the last of the Mercantilists. Following the Stuarts into exile in 1745, he lived in France, Germany, Holland and Italy; and his book (1767) is largely a collection of observations made during this time. Its title is An Inquiry into the Principles of Political Economy, being an Essay on the Science of Domestic Policy in Free Nations, in which are particularly considered Population, Agriculture, Trade, Industry, Money, Coin, Interest, Circulation, Banks, Exchange, Public Credit and Taxes. This seems to be the first use of the term Political Economy in an English book. His idea of the science has Mercantilistic earmarks: "Economy in general is the art of providing for all the wants of a family, with prudency and frugality. What economy is in a family, political economy is in a state... The principal object of this science is to secure a certain fund of subsistence for all the inhabitants" and to render it secure. Economics is an art.

Money and banking are treated at considerable length. Steuart justifies interest, but has no clear understanding of capital. He feels that a low rate of interest would be beneficial, only governmental measures to secure it should be gradual.

The mercantilist remnant in Steuart's thought concern mainly the origin of profit, or the surplus. Steuart still spoke of a profit which arises in exchange, i.e. when a commodity is sold above its value. But he went further and admitted that such profit did not really create new wealth. He distinguished, therefore, between positive profit and relative profit. The latter represented only 'a vibration of the balance of wealth between parties'; it did not add to the existing volume of stock. Positive profit, on the other hand, did not cause any one any loss; it arose from a general increase in labour, industry, and skill and it added to the public good.

He carried a similar distinction into his explanation of value. Developing a cost-of-production theory of value, he distinguished between the real value of commodities and the profit upon alienation obtained in their sale. Real value was determined by three factors; first, the amount of it which a workman could on an average produce in a given period of time; secondly, by 'the value of the workman's subsistence and necessary expense, both for supplying his personal wants, and providing the instruments belonging to his profession' and thirdly, by the 'value of the materials, that is the first matter employed by the workman'. Given these three amounts, the real value of a good is determined. Anything above this is the profit of the manufacturer and depends on the conditions of supply and demand. The significance of this analysis is twofold. In the first place it makes the manufacturer's profit arise only in exchange and thus represents a consistent application of the mercantilist theory of the surplus. In the second place, it leads Steuart to develop a supply and demand theory of price which was very elaborate for his time.

This theory can be summarized as follows. Prices are in equilibrium when demand and work balance. (Stuart's own theory of real value shows that he thought of the harmony between market prices and intrinsic value in the same terms as Cantillon). This balance may be disturbed and the price will vary. Steuart enumerated some of the factors which would cause discrepancies between supply and demand, among which the purchasing power of the buyers and the degree of competition were the most important. H explained the mechanism of 'double competition' which would be brought into play by discrepancies between work and demand. If demand was lower than supply, sellers' competition would reduce the price, destroy profits, and even cause loses. If demand exceeded supply, buyer's competition would raise prices and profits. In the case of merchants engaged in regular trade this mechanism would work sufficiently well to make real value effective, and only variations in profits would occur. But bigger changes must not be allowed to affect equilibrium; in these, as in many other cases, Steuart was a firm believer in the desirability and efficacy of state intervention.

Steuart also tended to mercantilist views in the theory of money, and his statements on the value of money and the balance of payments are often obscure and contradictory. He was nevertheless able to correct a number of errors in the analysis of Locke and Hume. In particular, he avoided their mechanical juxta position of the mass of commodities and the quantity of money in circulation. He took up the view, which had been expressed before by Petty, that the circulation of a country could only absorb a definite quantity of money. Money, he thought, is needed within a country for two purposes: to pay the debts one owed and to buy the things one needed. The state of trade and manufacture and the habits of the people determined the demand for money: this a given quantity could satisfy. Following North, he said that any metal over and above that required for monetary purposes would be hoarded or converted into plate. Should, on the other hand, the amount of gold and silver be insufficient to sustain a country's circulation the difference would be made up by symbolic money. The result is that 'whatsoever be the quantity of money in a nation, in correspondence with the rest of the world, there never can remain, in circulation, but the quantity nearly proportional to the consumption of the rich and to the labour and industry of the poor inhabitants'.

Steuart's attitude to the economic process was old-fashioned and somewhat reactionary. His work breathes little of that air of unbridled self-interest and freedom of trade that was common at the time. But it is perhaps because of this attitude that Steuart was able to give an interesting account of the development of capitalism. He began with the origin of society (this incidentally led him to an anticipation of the Malthusian theory of population somewhat similar to that of Cantillon) and traced its structure through changes in methods of production and relations of classes. He stressed the fact that labour was the only source of an increase in the supply of the means of subsistence and developed the concept of an agricultural surplus, the division of classes and rise of industry. Finally, he brought out clearly the difference between particular forms of labour which created specific use-values, and labour as a social abstraction which created exchange-value. He called industry that form of labour which by alienation created an universal equivalent.

QUESTIONS

1. State the Economic Ideas of Petty ?
2. What are the main Economic Ideas of Locke ?
3. What are the most interesting contributions of Hume to the History of Economic Thought ?

Chapter 7

JEREMY BENTHAM

Jeremy Bentham (1748-1832) was the son of a well-to-do English lawyer and was himself trained for the bar. He did not practice law, however, but devoted his life to study and writing. He traveled considerably, and was influenced much by French thought. His works were mostly translated into French.

According to Haney, "Bentham's chief contributions to Economics lie in what he added to the philosophical, ethical and psychological basis for the science. He was essentially a social philosopher, and was more interested in government and law than in economics".

Bentham was the leader of utilitarian school. He was the author of the concept of utility. Just as Ricardo's name is associated with the theory of rent, Bentham's name is associated with the principle of utility. Bentham was the central figure of a group usually described as Philiosophical Radicals.

Bentham's important publication, so far as political economy is concerned, was "Defence of Usury" (1787). It appeared a decade after Adam Smith's "Wealth of Nations" and preceded Ricardo. His other work "An Introduction to the Principles of Morals and Legislation" (1789) had a wide influence on thought and legislative practice in England and on the continent.

Most fundamental in Bentham's thought is his hedonistic psychology. He thought that individual actions are motivated by desire for pleasure and dislike of pain, and governed by a calculated balancing of pleasures and pains. The process of motivation, as he saw it, is somewhat as follows: feelings of pleasure or pain, or both, control the emotions and "will"; the will then refers to the understanding, which calculates a balance and decides; then action follows. This is rational hedonism.

In order to maintain this position, Bentham had to believe that pleasures and pains are measurable, and he so held. But he saw the necessity of allowing for various "dimensions" of pleasure, and he admitted certain limitations or difficulties. Thus he said that pleasures differ in intensity, with degrees ranging from the faintest pleasurable feeling, which is equal to unity. Other differences lie in duration, certainty , propinquity, purity (degree of mixture with pain), fecundity (reacting to increase capacity for enjoyment), and extent (number of individuals participating). In this classficiation one sees suggestions of some of the phases of utility mentioned by Jevons and others, and of the idea of "time preference".

Bentham assumed that the feelings of different individuals are comparable, and pleasure can be measured through a "common measure" or denominator in the shape of money.

Bentham also discussed the relationship between wealth and happiness. In his "Principles of The Civil Code", he argued that the happiness of an individual is not in proportion to his wealth. From this, we may say that Bentham seemed to have some vague notions about the diminishing marginal utility of money.

A utilitarian can assume that individuals desire pleasure, and that pleasure is "good" for individuals. Bentham's utilitarianism is, a hedonistic utilitarianism, which holds that that is "good" for the individual which gives him the greatest happiness. The test of greatest happiness decides what he ought to do, determining the difference between right and wrong. The words used by Bentham to indicate this test are "benefit, advantage, pleasure, good, or happiness", and they are thus taken to be virtually synonymous.

Bentham derives from it a social ethics and a principle of government. (1) He believes not only that the principle of utility governs what individuals ought to do, but also what they shall do. (2) He believes, moreover, that society is just an aggregation of individuals, and that government should therefore be guided by the same principle. Indeed, the community, he states, is a fictitious body, and the common interest can be understood only by understanding what is the interest of the individual. In fact, the interest of community is merely "the sum of the interests of the several members who compose it," and the only way to ascertain that interest is to add individual A's pleasure-minus-pain to individual B's pleasure-minus-pain, and son on. This is the way to the greatest good of the greatest number.

On the basis of the above reasoning, Bentham reaches two conclusions which are of great importance in the development of economic thought. The first one is that "natural rights" do not exist. The other is the doctrine of laissez-faire.

Bentham believes natural rights do not exist because rights depend upon laws and laws are made by government. And governments have come into existence by force and they are perpetuated by habit.

The above line of thought provides the basis for Bentham's individualism, and his advocacy of laissez-faire and free competition. His general rule for increasing the wealth or enjoyment of the nation is that "nothing ought to be done or attempted by government". His rule of government is, "Be quiet".

Bentham argued that there was no need for government action in economic matters for the following two reasons:

1. (a) The wealth of society is nothing but the wealth of individuals who compose it; (b) each individual knows his interest better than anybody else. At another point, Bentham made the observation that "there is no true interest but individual interest".

2. Government actions is not merely inexpedient, it is injurious. Government action involves restraint upon individuals. And where there is restraint, there is pain.

Bentham advocated unlimited freedom for competition. Though competition would cause distress to some individual competitors, it would be more than offset by the benefits of others and thus promote the greatest happiness of greatest numbers. In this connection, we should note that Bentham criticized Adam Smith's concession that government should fix maximum rates of interest.

Though Bentham gave "Be quiet" as his rule of government, he allowed certain activities of government. Though he idea legislation as a "necessary evil", he said that there must be some legislation in order to establish a system of punishments and rewards that would induce individuals to pursue actions leading to the greatest happiness of the greatest number. On the agenda of the government, he allowed the state to grant patents to inventors. He recommended escheats (a kind of tax) in estates which lack near relatives, taxes on bankers and stock brokers. Above all, he said that the proper aim of legislation should be promote the hapiness at the greatest number. Thus he made place for 'general interest'. This, of course, reveals an inconsistency in his thought. For at one point he says that there is no true interest but individual interest. Now he talks in terms of 'general interest'.

While Bentham accepted the economics of Adam Smith, rejecting only Smith's proposal to regulate the interest rate, Benthamism was very different from Smithianism.

In the first place, it casts out the "nature philosophy", and substitutes rational tests for metaphysical assumptions.

In the second place, it is more purely hedonistic, and goes further in basing economic action upon rational choices as against instincts and emotions.

In the third place, it mixes ethics and moral philosophy with economics, and tends to turn the latter into a sociology.

Criticism

Firstly, there is difficulty in calculating the greatest happiness of the greatest numbers. As men are not equal, and the same pleasure may be felt by different men unequally, it would be difficult to calculate the greatest happiness of the greatest number with any assurance of success.

Secondly, Bentham equated happiness with pleasure and reduced happiness largely to terms of quantities of pleasure. 'A sum of pleasures' may be an attractive phrase. But when it comes to estimates of human happiness or misery, arithmetic in economics is not much more helpful than economics in arithmetic. For there is no proof that by pursuing the happiness of the greatest number, we shall produce the greatest happiness.

Thirdly, Bentham thought the greater the equality in "masses" of wealth possessed by individuals, the greater the chances of equality in happiness. This line of thought has serious implications. It prepares the way for the sort of mechanical quantitative treatment of social problems. Not only that, it may put some ideas into the head to a ruler. For example, the ruler may think that he can maximize human happiness by exercising control over distribution of wealth. This may lead to regimentation of life. Of course, that was not the intention of Bentham because he advocated laissez-faire policy for the state.

Fourthly, the 'principle of utility' is a subjective concept. It will make economics an inexact science. Not only that as it is an ethical concept, economics will become normative science. But the modern tendency is to make economics a positive science.

Summing up

In spite of all the criticisms, the formula of the greatest happiness of the greatest number still remains valuable in economics and politics. It supplies a 'slogan' in the popular mind and supplies a standard with which one can judge state action.

Bentham was a social reformer. He believed that education of an individual would improve his calculation of pleasure and pains. He also suggested certain legal reforms. He was a great law reformer. He suggested laws to inflict pain on individuals who acted so as to cause more pain to others, than pleasure to themselves. But this line of thought may lead to more of social action or "socialism". In a way, such ideas were leading him away from laissez-faire.

Bentham's ideas had a profound influence on a group liberal thinkers known as "philosophical radicals". J.S.Mill was one of them.

Bentham finds an important place in the history of economic thought for the following reasons:

First, he dealt a severe blow to the natural philosophy of the Physiocrats and Adam Smith.

Second, he developed rational utilitarianism as the basis for greater freedom in economic life.

Third, he was a great influence on J.S.Mill who was a champion of liberty and individualism.

Lastly, Bentham suggested the ideas of degrees of utility and their measurement to Jevons. So in a way he may be regarded as the fore-runner of marginal utility school.

Bentham will ever hold a memorable place in the history of economic thought as one who dealt a great blow to the nature philosophy, who developed rational utilitarianism as the basis for a more positive freedom in economic life, thus influencing John Stuart Mill, and who suggested the idea of degrees of utility and their measurement to Jevons.

QUESTIONS

1. Crticially examine the economic ideas of Jeremy Bentham

Chapter 8

ADAM SMITH

INTRODUCTION

After physiocracy, a body of doctrines which existed in England over a century is named as classicism in Economic Thought. These doctrines were propounded by Adam Smith and his followers during the later half of the 18th century. Adam Smith has been regarded as the father and leader of the British Classical School. The school comprised of many famous economists. Among whom the most important were besides Adam Smith, Ricardo, Malthus and J.S. Mill. In fact Smith, Ricardo and Malthus are considered as the pillars of classicism. These writers helped the development of the science of political economy by formulating new theories and expanding and elaborating the old theories.

The word 'classic' has been used in the economic literature to convey three meanings. First, it is used to refer the economic writings of the period from Adam Smith to J.S. Mill. Second, J.M. Keynes has used the term to denote the teachings of Marshall and his followers. Third, Schumpeter used the term 'classic' to mean the original work that went before. Here classical school refers to the economists who wrote between the period 1750 to 1850.

Different reasons are given for choosing the name 'classical' for this school of thought. Because of its wide popularity, it has come to be called as classic. Secondly, the doctrines of this school brought tremendous change in economic thinking and treated the subject of economics in a scientific way. Thirdly, this school is classical as it differed from other schools of thought. Finally, the doctrines of this school are followed even to-day by the modern economists. The following are the characteristic features of classical school:

1) The classical economists had faith in laissez faire. For them that Government is best which governs least.
2) Classicals advocated a market economy based on perfect competition. Production, exchange

and distribution are guided by market forces.

3) They assumed that full employment level would exist in the economy. They thought that the economy was self-adjusting and any deviation from full employment would automatically get adjusted to full employment.
4) They believed in the existence of a harmony of interests.
5) The classical economists emphasised the importance of all economic activities.
6) The classicals believed in the universality of economic laws.
7) They were the first economists who paid attention to the problems of economic growth and development.
8) They looked at the economy as a whole. Their approach was macro in nature.
9) Lastly, the classical economists believed in Say's law of market.

ADAM SMITH (1723-1790)

Adam Smith stands as an institution by himself in the history of economic thought. He is regarded as the founder of modern economics. It is no exaggeration to say that Economic science was born in 1776 with Adam Smith's 'Wealth of Nations'. He is the first economist who dealt economic problems in a systematic manner. In other words, he is the first academic economist. He has been rightly called the "Father of Political Economy". Alexander Gray has rightly said, "before Adam Smith there had been much economic discussions, with him we reach the stage of discussing economics".

LIFE AND ANTECEDENTS

Adam Smith was born in 1723 in a small town of Kirkaldy in Scotland. He studied at the Universities of Glasgow and Oxford and specialised in Mathematics, Natural Philosophy and Moral and Political sciences. At Glasgow, he worked as a Professor of Logic and later became a Professor of Moral Philosophy. In 1759, he published his "Theory of Moral Sentiments" which earned him great fame. In 1764, Smith accepted to become the Tutor of the Duke of Buccleuch. With the Duke, Adam Smith toured Europe. On his European tour, in France he met the famous Physiocrat Quesnay, Turgot and Voltaire. On his return to Scotland, he settled down to write his famous book, "An Inquiry into the Nature and Causes of the Wealth of Nations" which was published in 1776. In 1778, he was appointed as Commissioner of Customs at Edinburg which position he held till his death in 1790.

FACTORS INFLUENCING ADAM SMITH

There are three important factors that contributed to the economic thought of Adam Smith–(a) Predecessors (b) clubs and travels (c) The economic and political conditions.

a) Predecessors

Adam Smith's economic thought was influenced by the views of later mercantilists like Petty, North, Child, Tucker and Cantillon. They advocated a more liberal trade, emphasised the importance of labour and believed in the advantages of large population. From Petty, Adam Smith took his ideas on Public Finance and canons of taxation.

From Physiocrats also, Adam Smith borrowed liberally. Being a personal friend of Quesnay and Turgot, he had been deeply influenced by their ideas, particularly on freedom, self-interest, circulation of wealth and natural order. Smith borrowed liberally from his teacher at Glassgow, Francis Hutcheson the ideas regarding division of labour, changes in the value of money, taxation etc. Smith was also grateful to David Hume for many of his ideas on foreign trade, money, labour and interest. Finally the poem, "The Fable of the Bees" written by Bernard de Mandeville influenced Smiths's ideas regarding self- interest and public interest.

b) Clubs and Travels

The clubs which Adam Smith joined at Glasgow and Edinburg had also influenced his economic ideas. These clubs discussed many questions of economic importance. In addition, his travels with the Duke of Buccleuch provided him an opportunity to meet the famous physiocrats and other scholars.

c) The Economic and Political Conditions

The economic and political environment of the time also influenced the views and ideas of Adam Smith. During the later part of the 18th century, fundamental changes took place in England. Large agricultural estates were coming up. Population growth helped to increase agriculture and industrial production. Accumulation of capital facilitated the growth of commerce and transport.

In the political side, the historical event–declaration of the American Independence, emphasised the equality and freedom of all people. The slogans liberty, equality and fraternity began to be heard. Thus industrial capitalism, economic liberty, large scale farming, mobility of labour etc. enriched Adam Smith's thought.

Inspite of the fact that Smith borrowed many ideas from his predecessors, the importance of his own contributions cannot be minimised. He collected the scattered ideas, gave them a shape and enhanced their significance. His work thus created a revolution in the domain of economic thinking.

The Philosophy of Adam Smith

Adam Smith's philosophical ideas which underlie his economic thinking are found in his master piece "Wealth of Nations." Even though, there is no special mention about the system of philosophy and explicitly seen nowhere in his analysis, we can read between the lines, the philosophy that pervades the whole work.

Smith was guided by one universal principle, namely self-interest. Every individual has the desire to better his own lot. It was on this belief, that he regarded the entire economic world as a big workshop created by division of labour. He believed that human conduct was governed by self-love, sympathy, the desire to be free, a sense of propriety, a habit of labour and the propensity to satisfy his wants with the help of others. Each man is the best judge of his own interest. If complete freedom is given, he would make efforts not only to better his own lot, but also would take efforts to promote the general good. Thus "An Invisible Hand" is behind all human motives.

Based on this philosophy, Smith believed that all Government interventions in human activities were injurious. So he assigned only three functions to the Government, namely, defence, administration of justice and maintenance of public works and institutions which could not be maintained by any individual or groups.

In economic matters, Smith was a strong supporter of freedom, because he believed that the natural balance of motives proved to be effective than state interference. As a result, he supported laissez-faire doctrine.

SMITH'S NATURALISM AND OPTIMISM

In addition to the concept of the economic world as a great natural community created by division of labour, we can distinguish in Smith's works two other fundamental ideas around which his theories are framed. First is the idea of the spontaneous origin of economic institutions and secondly, their beneficient character. These two are called as "Naturalism" and "Optimism". They are closely related and frequently mixed up in his work.

Smith proved that all economic institutions created by human beings came into existence spontaneously. For this he gave many examples like division of labour, money, capital, theory of demand and supply etc. Through a process of evolution man felt the need and established various economic institutions.

Division of labour is not the effect of human wisdom. Division of labour is the result of the common instinct among men to barter and exchange. It is spontaneously developed under the influence of self-interest which acts simultaneously. This is quite clear from his statement, "It is not from the benevolence of the butcher, the brewer or the baker that we expect our dinner but from their regard to their own interest".

Similarly, money is the result of the collective instinct of people, guided by personal motives. The desire to barter and exchange gave rise to money. As people realised many difficulties in the barter system of exchange, they thought of a medium of exchange and invented money. "Money is thus, the product of the simultaneous action of a great number of people, each obeying his personal inclination". (Gide and Rist)

The same position is with capital. To Adam Smith, capital was the true source of economic life. He gave too much importance to capital and treated it as a fountain of national wealth. The accumulation of capital is mainly due to the simultaneous efforts of thousands of individuals. People, motivated by self-interest, spontaneously save something out of their income and employ these savings in productive activities.

Another example of Smith's naturalism or spontaneous origin of economic institutions is his theory of demand and supply. Producers supply commodities according to the demand. They try to secure a balance between demand and supply. Because then only, market price will be equal to normal or natural price, which is good not only for themselves but also for all.

Smith also extends his naturalism to other spheres. For example in the case of population, he maintains that variations in the wage rate regulates the supply of labour, through changes in population. If wages are more than subsistence level, prosperity of the workers leads to an increase in population. But when wages are below the subsistence level, poverty and misery cause the death of many.

For Adam Smith Naturalism and Optimism are inseperable. Economic institutions are not only natural but also beneficial. Smith believed that self interest not only creates and maintains economic institutions, but ensures that the nation progresses towards greater wealth and prosperity. Smith thus tried to prove that these spontaneous institutions were also best. Even though, this philosophy of naturalism and optimism pervades all economic theories, he never applies this concept to all. In fact optimism is intended for production and not distribution.

WEALTH OF NATIONS

Adam Smith's epoch making book "An Enquiry into the Nature and Causes of the Wealth of Nations" (shortly known as Wealth of Nations) was published in 1776. It is a masterly exposition of economic theories. Senior praised Smith for the extent and accuracy of his knowledge and the attractive style of his writing Edmund Burke considered Wealth of Nations as the most important book that has ever been written. The book deals compreshensively not only the domestic and international economy, but also discusses the problems of human welfare, material happines, jurisprudence and ethics.

Wealth of Nations consists of an introduction of three pages, followed by five books, and a short appendix. The first two books deal with the theories of production, exchange and distribution. The third book deals with the economic history of European countries, agriculture and the rise of cities and towns. The fourth book contains a critical analysis of the physiocratic and mercantilist theories. The last book deals with public finance, taxation and state interference.

Adam Smith in his book, "The Wealth of Nations" defined Economics as, "The Science of Wealth". He said that Economics is concerned with, "an enquiry into the nature and causes of wealth of Nations" Whereby "it proposes to enrich the people and the sovereign". According to Adam Smith all that economics deals with is wealth. It explains how people acquire mass wealth. It emphasises an earning and spending wealth as if wealth is everything for man. It also deals with the laws of production, distribution and consumption of wealth. This definition makes wealth as the subject matter of economics. It makes economics an independent subject and science. Its insistence on enriching the people and the soverign is still appreciated.

SMITH'S MAIN ECONOMIC IDEAS

LABOUR

The concepts "Labour" and "Division of labour" have attained significance through the excellent treatment of the subjects by Adam Smith in his "Wealth of Nations". The Physiocrats considered land alone productive. They never recognised labour as productive.

But to Adam Smith, labour is the most important factor which increases the wealth of nations. It is clearly stated in the opening sentence of the book as follows. "The annual labour of every nation is the fund which originally supplies it with all the necessaries and conveniences of life which it annually consumes and which consists always either in the immediate produce of that labour, or in what is purchased with that produce from other nations". When Smith emphasised the importance of labour, he did not underestimate the important role played by nature in production. He was aware of the fact that both physical environment and labour determined the wealth of nations.

Here Adam Smith distinguishes between productive and unproductive labour. Smith gave two definitions of productive labour: (a) that labour is productive that produces durable (vendible) commodities. It is called Durable-Vendible-commodity criterion. (b) That labour is productive that adds value to the product. This is known as value–added criterion. According to the first criterion, that labour which produces durable commodities that can be accumulated is productive labour. Whereas unproductive labour produces services which are consumed at the time of production. For example, the labour of a worker in a shoe factory is productive and that of a personal servant is unproductive.

According to the value–added criterion, productive labour not only maintains itself but also brings profits to its employers.

Adam Smith's distinction between productive and unproductive labour is faulty. Smith tried to broaden the physiocratic idea of productive labour but did not succeed. The physiocrats regarded only agricultureal labour as productive. But Smith's concept of productive labour includes all types of labour which produces tangible goods. But he did not include the services.

Division of Labour

The first chapter in Book-I of Wealth of Nations "Of the Division of Labour" emphasises the importance of division of labour. It occupies the central and dominant position in Smith's theory of production. While labour is the source of wealth, division of labour will increase the productivity of labour and thereby the wealth of a nation.

The concept of division of labour was not used by Adam Smith first. Both the name and idea existed in Mandevilla's "Fables of the Bees". The idea was also used by Harris in 1757. The only remarkable feature of Smith's division of labour is as Schumpeter points out that, "nobody, either before or after Adam Smith, ever thought of putting such a burden upon division of labour. With Adam Smith it is practically the only factor in economic progress".

According to Adam Smith division of labour "is a system of social co-operation" by which production is carried in particular activities. Adam Smith's example of pin making industry which involves 18 different operations has become a classic example. Smith has shown that an individual pin maker, working alone, could not make more than 20 pins a day. But under proper division of labour, he could produce 4800 pins a day.

Adam Smith concentrated upon the social division of labour. It emphasised the co-operation of all individuals for the satisfaction of the desires of each. Division of labour is a process by which a particular type of labour which produces goods to satisfy the individual needs are transformed into social labour which produces goods for all.

The following are the advantage of division of labour as pointed by Adam Smith :

1) It increases the productivity of labour through specialisation.
2) As work is sub-divided and done quickly, production also increases.
3) Worker's efficiency and skill increase when work is subdivided into various parts and a worker is asked to do a small part of the whole job.
4) There is saving of time and tools.
5) As production increases quickly, it forms an incentive to investors.

Adam Smith also pointed out the disadvantages of division of labour.

1) As worker is confined to one or two operations, there is no personal satisfaction of having made a full product.
2) It leads to immobility of labour because of specialisation.
3) As the same work is done repeatedly, the worker gets bored which leads to mental stagnation.

Adam Smith pointed out that division of labour was limited by the extent of the market. The wider the market for a commodity, the greater the division of labour. So in order to have a high degree of division of labour, large scale production is essential. Division of labour was limited by the availability of capital also.

CAPITAL

Smith regarded capital as a fountain of national wealth. It has a greater role to play in production. The wealth of a nation depends upon division of labour and division of labour itself is governed by capital. In his book "Wealth of Nations" capital appears in three forms : (1) as an instrument of production (2) as a fund maintaining the workers and (3) as a source of revenue.

Smith distinguished between two types of capital, namely, fixed capital and circulating capital. Smith advocated that capital could be employed in four different ways–(1) in procuring raw materials annually for the consumption of the society (2) in the manufacture of raw materials (3) in transporting the finished goods and (4) in the distribution. In other words capital is used for the cultivation of land, mines and fisheries, secondly for manufacturing, thirdly for whole sale distribution and fourthly for retail distribution.

To Smith capital formation is the result of the interaction of the self interest of individuals. Expansion of output depended on the rate of investment in a country. The rate of investment in turn, depended on savings. "Parsimony and not industry is the immediate cause of increase of capital". The ability to save was limited by income. The motive for saving and investment was profit. Profit depended on institutional environment.

Smith also recognised the role of interest in the supply of capital. He believed that a fall in the rate of interest would increase the supply of capital, because the enterpreneurs would enter the loanable fund market with a decline in the interest rate.

But Smith's ideas on capital gave rise to controversies among economists. At one place he regarded labour as the source of wealth and at another place he regarded capital as the source of wealth.

AGRICULTURE

Having been influenced by the physiocratic ideas, Adam Smith gave a high place to agriculture. Smith believed that investment in agriculture was the most productive form of capital investment because in agriculture, "nature labours along with men".

MONEY

After discussing the concept of division of labour in the first three chapters of the first book, Smith discusses about money. Regarding the origin of money, he held the view that, "Everyman.... become in some measure a merchant and therefore in effect, a currency is needed to serve as the universal instrument of commerce". Thus money is an instrument which facilitates exchange and without it large scale production and commerce would not be possible. So it is an important factor contributing to the extension of division of labour.

According to Smith, money developed spontaneously to remove the difficulties in the barter system of exchange. He stressed the two important functions of money viz., medium of exchange and measure of value.

He regarded money as the nominal price of commodities. He rejected the bullionist policies of the mercantilists which aimed at keeping surplus money at home. He demonstrated clearly that the surplus quantity of money would be exported to other countries. He suggested that the quantity of money in circulation should be determined by the level of internal economic activity.

Theory of Value

Adam Smith started his discussion of value by distinguishing between value in use and value in exchange. The first refers to the utility of the commodity and the second the power of purchasing other goods. This he explained with the "diamond–water paradox". The commodities like water possessing greatest value-in-use have little value-in-exchange. On the other hand, the commodities like diamond having little value-in-use have the greatest value-in-exchange. Even though Smith made a distinction between value in use and value in exchange, he was concerned only with the true measure of the exchangeable value.

Regarding the determination of value, Smith explained through two theories of value, namely, labour theory of value and cost of production theory of value. Smith believed that labour was the real source of value. The value of a thing depended upon the amount of labour spent for its production. According to him, the real price of everything was "the toil and trouble of acquiring it". This was the essense of his Labour Theory of Value. Thus the theory that labour is the cause of value was first formulated by the Father of Political Economy. It is the same theory which was used later on by Karl Marx to attack capitalism.

But in his cost of production theory of value, Smith gave a contradictory view. He said the value of a commodity was governed by its cost of production. This consisted of payments made to land, labour and capital. Smith could not make a clear choice between these two theories.

It must be noted that Smith not only discussed the different elements of the price of a commodity but also natural price and market price. He says that in an early primitive society where capital accumulation had not started and land was not appropriated, labour alone was the sole determinant and measure of value. Then he turns to the actual world where more than one factor of production exists, and the production of a commodity is the result of the co-operative efforts of labour, land and capital. In such a situation, the price of a commodity is the sum of the rewards paid to labour, land and capital.

Then Adam Smith proceeds to the treatment of natural and market prices. In each society, there exists an average rate of interest, wages, profit and rent, which Adam Smith calls, "the natural rates", corresponding to this is the natural price. It is the price which covers the natural rates of profits, wages and rent. Thus the concept of natural price is essentially the cost of production theory of value.

Contrary to this is the market price. The market price is the actual price prevailing in the market and is determined by the forces of demand and supply. The competitive mechanism of the market ensures the tendency towards the equilibrium or natural price in the long run. If the market price is higher than the natural price, the supply will increase and will bring the market price down to its natural price. Similarly, if the market price is less than the natural price, the supply will increase and push the market price down to the natural price. The following figures show this:

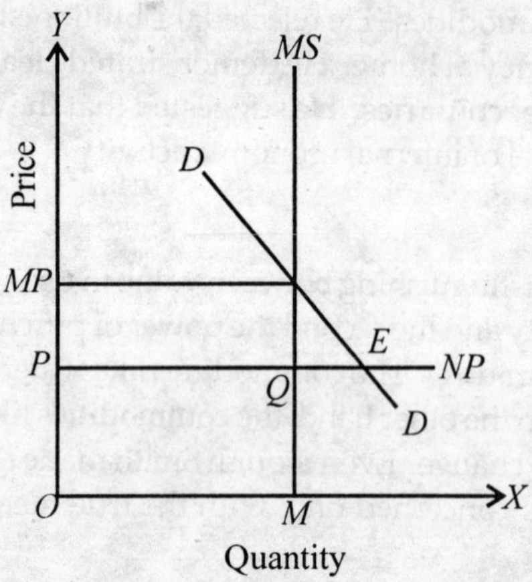

Fig 1. (A)

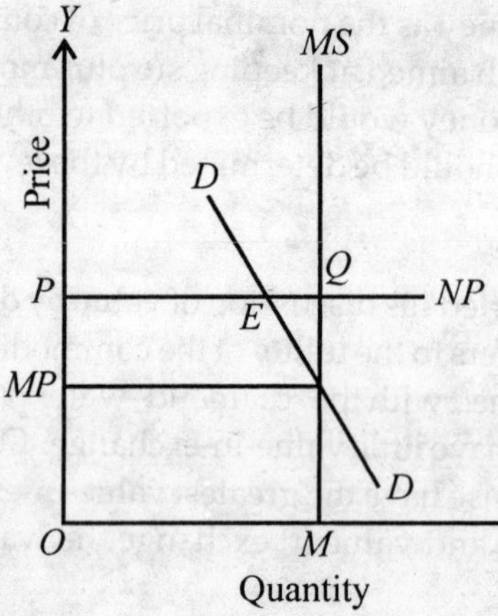

Fig 1. (B)

In figure 1. (A) demand is greater than the market supply ($PE > PQ$). So market price is above the natural price ($MP > P$). In part (B) demand is less than the market supply ($PE < PQ$) market price is less than the natural price ($MP < P$). In part (C) demand is equal to supply. So market price and natural price are equal NP = P.

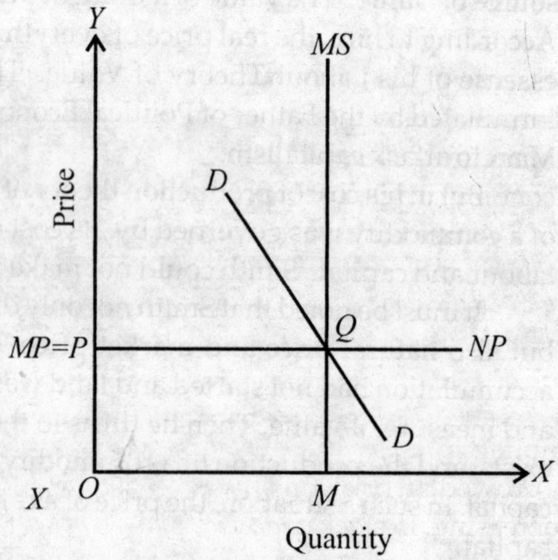

Fig 1. (C)

Critical Appraisal Of Smith's Theory Of Value

Adam Smith did not formulate a satisfactory theory of value. He himself could not choose between the two theories.

1) It is difficult to measure labour. Even though Adam Smith used time as the measuring rod, it is not a proper scale because the less skilled labour may take long time to produce a good.

2) Misdirected labour cannot have value. Even Karl Marx admits that "nothing can have value, without being an object of utility". He said, "misdirected labour does not count as labour".

3) It fails to explain the value of rare things, such as things of art and antiques.

4) The cost of production theory of value did not explain how the natural prices of the factors of production are determined. So it is empty and meaningless.

5) The cost of production theory also did not explain the change in the prices of commodities.

SMITH'S IDEAS ON DISTRIBUTION :

Rent

Smith's ideas on rent were not well formed. At some places, he is surprisingly close to the modern viewpoint on rent, at others he is hopelessly embedded in Physiocratic notions.

Rent is considered as a monopoly price paid to the landlord for the use of land. It varies with fertility and situation. Improvement in transport services tend to lower and equalise rents. *Haney* considers that except for the mistaken notion of the landlord as a monopolist and rent as a monopoly price, this viewpoint is allied to the modern concept of rent.

Gide and *Rist*, however, emphasised that Adam Smith, under the Physiocratic influence, considered rent as a gift due to the special natural powers of the soil. In manufactures, man worked without the aid of nature, hence the remuneration just covered his cost of production. In agriculture, he worked in Cooperation with nature, hence the rent of land was a special surplus available to the owner of land over and above the cost of production.

Relationship of rent and prices is not clear to Smith. His point of view shifts according to the convenience of the argument. At one place he considers rent determining price of commodities, and at another, just the opposite.

Wages

Smith's theory of wages is also confused. In fact, he had thought of practically all the theories that have been emphasised by later economists.

Generally, he talks of demand and supply of labour as the factors determining wags. The supply of labour is limited by the cost of living of workers, depending on current prices of commodities. The demand for labour is determined by the quantity of stock available, the level of national capital. In an expanding economy, higher wages will prevail due to greater demand for labour. In a stationary economy, wages will sink below the subsistence level.

Adam Smith also indicates the outlines of the Wages Fund Theory, by speaking of a "fund predestined for payment of wages". However, he does not elaborate the idea further.

Profit and Interest

Adam Smith did not clearly distinguish between profit and interest. Profit was the return on the capital. Interest was a part of profit which was to be paid to the owner for the use of the capital borrowed. In brisk business conditions, competition kept the rate of profit low, because wages were increasing. In slack conditions, the opposite happened. Wages decreased and profit went up.

Criticism

Generally, Smith's theory of distribution is confusing. He was primarily a thinker on production, on which his thought was mature enough in his earlier years. His earlier Glasgow Lectures (1763) do not deal with distribution at all. It was under the influence of the Physiocrats that he gave any thought to problems of distribution and included them in "The Wealth of Nations." Naturally enough, his theory of distribution is shoddy, inconsistent and tainted with Physiocratic errors and is in mark contrast with the remarkable lucidity of his views on production. *Gide* and *Rist* consider his treatment of distribution as the "least original" of all his work.

However, we must credit the origin of many ideas on distribution to Smith. The Wags Fund Theory was to be worked up by later classical economists. The Demand and Supply Theory of wages indicated the interdependence of resources and population, which was elaborated by Malthus.

Smith also foresaw the clash of interest involved in the problems of distribution. He talked of opposing interests of labour and capital, the tendency of wages and profits to move in opposite directions. His sympathies were with the workers and he advocated the necessity of keeping the share of labour in the national produce high. Early Socialist thinkers, who came after, had drawn abundant inspiration from his views on distribution.

The dominant note in Smith's theory of production is his optimism. He considers all productive institutions beneficent in character, but in his treatment of distribution, he was a pessimist. He was aware of the parasitism of landlords and capitalists "who love to reap where they have not sown." Gide and Rist, therefore, feel that Smith might well be considered as the fore-runner of Socialism, as socialist thought is primarily concerned with clash of interests in the distribution of wealth that smith clearly visualised.

From the classical standpoint, however, the problems of distribution were thoroughly dealt with by *Ricardo*, his immediate follower, Smith having given only a sketchy outline of the same.

Adam Smith's Theory of Economic Growth

Adam Smith's Theory of Economic Growth has not received as much attention as his Theory of Value and Distribution. He does provide an internally consistent dynamic Model. Irma Adelman rightly asserts, " The main strands of his Theory—the investigation of capital accumulation, population Growth, and labour productivity still underlie all current treatment of the problem and many of his policy recommendations are as controversial now as when they were first made".

(1) Production function

Since he recognised the existence of three factors of production, namely labour, capital and land, his production function may be expressed as

$$Y = f(K,L,N)$$

where, K = capital stock, L = Labour force, N = Land.

The production function is subject to increasing returns to scale because he did not assume diminishing marginal productivity. In his opinion, with the passage of time, the size of market will expand and in turn result in internal and external economies which will reduce the capital production. The greater degree of division of labour was expected to realise the economies of scale in production. According to him, division of labour did not depend merely on technological feasibility but on the extent of the market as well; whereas the size of the market depends on the availability of capital stock. Thus accumulation of capital is a precondition to increasing division of labour. The regulatory measures against trade have a tendency to restrict the size of the market and limit the division of labour. He recognised the importance of technological development for improvement in productivity. To understand Smith's theory of growth we should also examine the growth of labour force, capital accumulation, increase in the supply of land and the change in the institutional set up.

(2) Supply of Land and the change in Institutions

In his theory, two factors, namely supply of land and the change in institutions are comparatively less important. The rent of land therefore considered as the price paid for the use of land, is naturally a monopoly price. He nowhere explicitly stated the supply of land. Regarding institutions the change in them is determined exogenously. Institutional variable is quite important. He asserts that free trade and laissezfaire provides a highly congenial environment for economic growth. He was thus a strong believer in 'natural reason' guiding human affairs. He regarded state interference not only superfluous but harmful to economic progress. Guided by self-interest, each individual was capable of promoting his own well-being and welfare of the whole society in the process. It is wise, therefore, according to Smith to be led by the 'Invisible Land' that is motivation of the competitive market forces. As a matter of policy, therefore, Adam Smith advocated the removal of all restrictions on trade, choice of occupation and the use of property.

(3) The Growth of labour force

The rate at which the population grows in a country largely determines the growth of the labour force. According to Adam Smith rate of population growth in the long run, depends on the fund available for human sustenance. The size of the population is determined by pevailing wage rate. If actual wages exceed the subsistence wage, population will show a tendency to increase and vice-versa. The supply of labour is normally expected to be in equilibrium with the demand for labour. If the demand for labour records a continuous rise pushing wage rates upward, it induces working population to multiply faster, as a result of which supply also continually increases and vice-versa. Smith has explained the demand for labour in he framework of wage fund doctrine.

Since the supply of labour has a tendency to respond to the demand for it. Smith's argument implies that in a growing economy population will be increasing, that in declining economy it will be falling, and that in a stagnant economy characterised by the constancy of National Wealth it will be stable. In his opinion, high wage rates are consistent only with the growth of the economy.

(4) Capital accumulation

In Smith's theory Capital Accumulation has been assigned a strategic role in the growth process. To him, growth is functionally Related to rate of Investment with a fixed capital stock a country is bound to suffer stagnation. According to him, any increase in capital stock in a country generally leads to more than proportionate increase in the output on account of continuously growing division of labour. Adverse institutional developments nullify the gains of capital accumulation from the point of view of growth.

According to Smith, the Rate of Investment as a crucial factor in economic growth, is determined by the Rate of Savings. He did not visualise any possibility of leakages occurring (–) saving and investment although the two activities are not performed by the same set of people. Savings and Investment are determined by private profit. However, ability to save and investment is limited by income. Due to competition among the capitalists, Overtime when a country develops and its capital stock expands, the profit rate shows a tendency to fall. In the first place, the growing stock of capital, results in larger demand for labour which pushes up the wage rate leaving a smaller surplus to the entrepreneurs, secondly a larger capital, stock required abundant opportunities for investment which may not always exist in an economy. Therefore, when capital stock expands in a sustained manner, entrepreneurs will be able to employ it only at a lower marginal profit Ratio, that is why he postulated a downward sloping marginal efficiency of capital curve. He postulated a negatively sloped supply curve of capital implying an indirect relation between Supply of Capital and Rate of Investment. Capital accumulation stops only when Rate of Investment falls to a rate of profit which is sufficient only to compensate for the Risk premium.

(5) Agents of Growth

According to Smith, farmers, producers and businessmen are the agents of progress and economic growth. It was free trade, enterprise and competition that led farmers, producers, and businessman to expand the market which in turn made economic development possible. The functions of these three are inter-related. To Smith, development of agriculture leads to increase in construction works and commerce. When agricultural surplus arise as a result of economic development the demand for commercial services and manufactured articles rises. This leads to commercial progress and the establishment of manufactured industries. On the other hand, these developments lead to increase in agricultural production when farmers use advanced production techniques. Thus, capital accumulation decreases, economic development takes place due to the emergence of the farmer, the producer and the businessman.

(6) The Growth process

According to smith, the process of growth is cumulative. When there is prosperity as a result of progress in agriculture, manufacture of Industries and commerce, it leads to capital accumulation, Technical progress, increase in population expansion of markets, division of labour, and Rise in profits continuously. But this process is not endless. It is the scarcity of natural resources that finally stops growth.

According to Smith, in a development process of an economy both income level and capital stock rise. In addition, the rate of capital accumulation also shows a tendency to increase. Obviously this factor enhances the capital stock of an economy in succeeding periods by increased doses of investment. Another factor of vital importance which contributes to the progress of an Economy is a successive decline in the incremental capital output ratio on account of the influence of capital on the productivity of labour. These factors reinforcing each other accelerate the pace of development until such time that the economy's capital stock grows large enough to eliminate profits, not of risk. At this stage the stationary state sets in.

The stationary state in Smith's system is distinctly different from under development economies having reached the stationary state is characterised by unchanged population, constant total income, subsistence wage, elimination of profit in excess of the minimum consistent with risk and absence of Net Investment. Adam Smith did not suggest any measures to remedy this 'dull' state of affairs. In his opinion, an economy in the stationary state finds itself at the highest level of prosperity consistent with its natural resources and environment. An under- developed country in contrast, reaches stagnation before it has reached the highest degree of opulence attainable with its resources. Smith has mentioned China by way of an example of an under -developed country.

A Critical Appraisal

(1) Neglect of Middle Class : Smith's theory is based on the socio-economic environment prevailing in Great Britatin and certain parts of Europe. It assumes the existence of a rigid division of society (-) capitalists and labourers. But the middle class occupies and important place in Modern Society. Thus, his theory neglects the role of the middle class which provides necessary conditions to economic development.

(2) One-sided Saving Base : According to Smith, capitalist, land lords and money lenders save.

This is, however, a one-sided base of savings because it did not occur to him that the major source of savings in an advance society was the income-receivers and not the capitalists and land lords.

(3) Unrealistic assumption of perfect competition : Smith's whole model is based upon unreaslistic assumption of perfect competition. The laissez-faire policy of perfect competition is not to be found in any economy, rather a number of restrictions are imposed on the private sector and on internal and international trade in every part of the world.

(4) Neglect of Entrepreneur : Smith neglects the role of the entrepreneur in development. This is a serious defect in his theory. The entrepreneur is the focal point of development, as pointed out by Shumpeter. It is the entrepreneur who organises and brings about innovations, thereby leading to capital formation.

(5) Unrealistic assumption of stationary state : Smith is of the view that the end result of capitalist economy is the stationary state. It implies that there is change in such an economy but around a point of equilibrium. There is progress but it is steady, uniform and regular. But this explanation of the process of development is not satisfactory because development takes place by 'fits and starts' and is not uniform and steady. Thus the assumption of the stationary state is unrealistic.

SMITH'S THEORY OF ECONOMIC DEVELOPMENT

Adam Smith was the first to define the Wealth of Nations. It was not the stock of gold or silver but it consisted of the vendible commodities and services which are of real use to the consumers. Wealth, another very important idea of Adam Smith, could not be increased through a deliberately planned favourable balance of trade as the mercantilists thought or by following physiocratic notion of applying all energies on land; instead wealth of a nation can be increased only by increasing the productive powers of labour, for in the ultimate analysis labour is the cause of all wealth.

This brings us to two of his important factors which determine the rate of economic growth: (i) division of labour and the consequent improvement in "the skill, dexterity and judegment" of workers, and (ii) the proportion of productive to unproductive labour and accumulation of capital. Smith has ascribed a crucial significance to the phenomenon of division of labour as a determinant of economic growth. Division of labour, whether occupational or territorial, creates internal and external economies, including an improvement in technology. Technological improvement not only lowers cost of production but also increases the future productive capacity of an economy. Hence division of labour is looked upon as a major gear in the machine of economic development.

From the Theory of Division of Labour, Smith locally moves to his famous law of market. The increased productive capacity of an economy can be sustained in the long run, only if thee is an adequate effective demand for products. This effective demand itself is constituted of two parts : (i) domestic demand, and (ii) foreign demand. Smith powerfully advocates free trade as a means of intensifying foreign demand. In fact free trade leads to a 'horizontal extension of market' which encourages territorial division of labour. Thus the possibilities are opened upon "reap the advantages of increasing physical returns brought about by overcoming technical indivisibilities of production". (*Myint*)

Smith also makes a strong case for a large population and for paying high real wages to labour. High real wages, associated with an increasing population, would surely stimulate domestic effective demand and encourage occupational division of labour within the domestic economy. Thus, the process of economic growth becomes cumulative division of labour continually leads to fresh internal and external economies. Indeed Adam Smith was an essentially optimistic thinker.

Apart from division of labour, the critical proportion between productive and unproductive labour is another significant determinant of rate of economic development. *Hla Myint* has pointed out the extreme significance of Smithian distinction between productive and unproductive labour. In any case, Smith argues that the proportion of productive to unproductive labour is governed by the rate of capital accumulation. "As the accumulation of stock must, in the nature of things, be previous to the division of labour, so labour can be more and more subdivided in proportion only as stock is previously more and more accumulated." (*Adam Smith*) Smith argued that the annual produce of the land and labour of any nation can be increased in its value by no other means, but by increasing either the number of its productive labourers or the productive power of labour who had been employed. The number of productive labourers cannot be much increased but in consequence of an increase of capital, or of the funds destined for maintaining them. The productive powers of the same number of labourers cannot be increased but in consequence either of some addition and improvement to those machines which facilitate and abridge labour or of a more proper distribution of employment. in either case additional capital is almost always required. Thus, to increase the produce of a nation an increase of capital is necessary.

Smith has examined in considerable detail the difficult problem of capital formation. "Capital is increased by parsimony, and diminished by prodigality and misconduct." In effect, Smith has emphasised the importance of real savings as a factor in capital accumulation. Like other exponents of the Classical School, Smith implicitly assumed that all savings we invested. Thus, he was led to argue that capital formation and economic development would be impossible without real savings on the part of a community. Smith's economics is nearer to the economics of under-developed countries in which savings are less. A developed country suffers from excess savings and under-investment. Thus, he was thinking of an economy where there were unlimited sources of investment.

Adam smith correctly stated that conditioning factor in the growth of an economy ultimately is food. In the chapter 'Of the Rent of Land' he gives a unique position to food. Surplus food production supports the rest of the population. How much ideal labour can be employed depends upon the surplus of food. He thought of food as the limiting factor for demand for labour. When a country tries to develop economically, a shortage of food is bound to occur. Smith said that demand for food is limited by the capacity of stomach. But in underdeveloped countries people are already under-fed. Therefore, demand for food rises when development takes place, for marginal increases in income would first be spent on food. Smith did not develop this aspect fully, though he very well realised the importance of food in under-developed countries.

It has been well established now that Smith's main concern was to increase the physical productivity. He, no doubt, elaborated a theory of distribution also in Book I of the Wealth of Nations, but that was an after-thought—the inevitable effect of Smith's contact with the physiocrats. In the main, Smithian economics drives its 'central unifying principle' from its explicit emphasis on the physical problem of production, i.e., the problem of economic development.

Smith wanted economic development through liberty and free enterprise. State's role is to break monopoly, wherever it exists and perform only routine functions. This will be a correct approach for a country where a class of entrepreneurs is available. But in a country where such a class is conspicuous by its absence, Smith's economics will not prove to be of any practical help—particularly his philosophy of free enterprise and liberty. Their economic development will take a very long time to materialise and the country will be subjugated to foreign rule. Underdeveloped countries suffer, apart from capital scarcity, from a chronic lack of industrial environment, overhead capital, banking, insurance, transport, external economies etc. Such a country cannot stand on its own legs in the face of competition. Thus, while most of Smith's theoretical analysis is applicable to underdeveloped countries, his policies are not.

Laissez Faire or Economic Liberty

Like physiocrats, Adam Smith was a great champion of the principle of economic liberty. He ardently advocated the policy of laissez faire. Toynbee has remarked that Smith's entire economic thought is a plea for liberty. Every page of his writing is illumined by the passion for freedom. He did not have a great faith in the role of Government or in the efficiency of its officials.

Smith preferred economic liberty as it would increase national properity. Really speaking he favoured free trade. He was against state interference in economic activities. For that he gave many reasons. He argued that the Government could not secure economy in expenditure. It could not make correct assessment of the needs of the economy. Further, he believed that the agents of the state are negligent and thriftless. There are malpractices, favouritism and red tapism. He went to the extent of suggesting that payment to the Government servants should be made in proportion to the work done by them.

Functions of State

As a part of his liberalism, Smith advocated the following minimum functions of the Government: (a) Protection against foreign countries (b) administration of law and justice and (c) establishment and maintenance of public works like roads, canals,harbours and schools. However, the state might interfere, if necessary, in matters like foreign trade, banking, education, rate of interest and labour relations.

Public Finance

The Vth book of Wealth of Nations deals with the revenue of the Government. His treatment of this subject has gained universal recognition and his treatment of canons of taxation is classical.

According to Smith public finance is needed to meet the responsibilities of the State. The revenue of the Government is derived from two sources: (1) Funds, land and capital of the state (2) Taxes. In order to guide the revenue authorities, he laid down the following canons of taxation. The later economists followed these in their theories without any change.

Canon of ability

"The subject of every State ought to contribute towards the support of the Government and as nearly as possible, in proportion to their respective abilities". This principle is also known as Ability to Pay or Equality Principle. It implies that people of a country should be taxed in proportion to their respective abilities. Progressive taxation is based upon this principle.

Canon of certainity

This implies that the tax which each individual is bound to pay should be certain and not arbitrary. The time of payment, the manner of payment, the amount to be paid etc., should be clear to the tax payer.

Canon of convenience

"Every tax ought to be levied at the time, or in the manner in which it is most likely to be convenient for the contributor to pay it".

Canon of economy

It implies that taxes should be collected at minimum cost to the Government.

International Trade

The IV Book of Wealth of Nations mainly criticises the mercantilist and Physiocratic doctrines. It is here that Adam Smith has given his ideas in favour of free trade and against protection. He criticised mercantilist idea of control and protection. He is not in favour of accumulating more gold and silver by means of favourable trade. Gold and silver, he says, are just like any other commodity and so their export or import does not affect the prosperity of a nation. Hence he disagrees with mercantilist idea that trade is advantageous because it acquires gold and silver.

According to Smith, the only advantage from foreign trade is that, it carries surplus goods to other countries and brings in commodities which are in demand. Foreign trade is like domestic trade. Foreign trade like domestic trade is equally responsible for extending division of labour, increasing specialisation and for multiplying exchanges. Smith's entire analysis can be summed up into the dictum. "Look after trade, and the gold will look after itself".

The arguments given by him in favour of free trade are summarised below:

a) Free trade brings about a proper distribution of capital within the country. Protection diverts it from one channel to the other.
b) Free trade tends to bring territorial division of labour. It extends markets and increases economic activities which in turn increase national prosperity.
c) Protection is injurious to the development of industry and commerce because, a few industries are protected.
d) Free trade serves the interests of the consumers. Due to the development of commerce, people get commodities produced in a distant country at competitive rates.

Although Adam Smith favoured free trade, he pointed out certain limitations also. He considered the defence of the country as more important than opulence. Hence he thought that the Navigation Act of England was the wisest step taken by the Government. He also suggested the imposition of import duties as a retaliatory measure.

Critical Estimate

Adam Smith has a strong claim as the Father of Political Economy. The Wealth of Nations has become the corner-stone of economic science. J.B. Say rightly remarked, "When we read this work, we feel that previous to Smith there was no such thing as political economy". Though Smith borrowed certain ideas from the mercantilists and physiocrats, he arranged those ideas, gave it a harmonious blending and presented it in an effective manner. He was superior to Quesnay and perhaps to every writer since the time of Aristotle, in the extent and accuracy of his knowledge. As Alexander Gray observes, "Adam Smith's name is incomparably the greatest in the History of Economic Thought",

Merits

1) He was the first economist who defined economics and explained the scope of the subject.
2) Smith developed the price system or value economics which became the central point of modern economic theory.
3) His main contribution to the science of economics is the treatment of taxation. Without any alteration, the later economists incorporated his canons of taxation in their theories.
4) He made a lasting contribution to economic thought through his ideas of division of labour, free trade, laissez faire etc.
5) Smith shifted the emphasis from producer to the consumer.
6) Smith viewed the society on its economic side, working spontaneously under the influence of competition and self interest.

Although the Wealth of Nations has been much praised as the store house of costly gems, from which later economists have freely benefited, yet it could not escape the eyes of the critics. The following are the main defects found in Adam Smith's ideas.

Demerits

1) Smith was essentially a materialistic thinker. That shows an absence of idealism.
2) While dealing with economic theories, Smith did not keep in view the moral end. He had developed excessive individualism, restricting the activities of the State. He has created an imaginary "Economic Man" with great enthusiasm and zeal.
3) His view of wealth was too narrow.
4) His theory of value is ambiguous, confused and inconsistent. It is a two-sided theory.
5) His theory of distribution was pessimistic and incomplete.

His treatment of distribution is inferior to production.

Inspite of the above shortcomings, the Wealth of Nation possesses a literary charm. It provides a starting point for all economists. It is a ground work for modern economics. We may conclude with the words of Alexander Gray, that "It is again a tribute to the greatness of Smith that all schools of thought may trace to him their origins or inspiration".

QUESTIONS

1. What is classicism ?
2. Briefly indicate the philosophy of Adam Smith.
3. State the concepts of Adam Smith relating to Labour and Division of Labour.
4. What were the economic ideas of Adam Smith regarding 'Money', 'Value' and 'Price'?
5. Enunciate Adam Smith's Canons of Taxation.
6. What are the criticisms levelled against 'Wealth of Nations'?
7. Bring out the ideas of Adam Smith about Labour Theory of Value.
8. Elaborate the doctrine of 'Invisible Hand' and 'Natural Order' of Adam Smith.
9. Comment on Smith's Doctrine of 'Free Trade'.

10. Write short notes on :
    (a) Adam Smith's spontaneous orgin of Economic Institutions.
    (b) Value-in-use & Value-in-Exchange.
    (c) Smith's concept of 'Natural Price'.
    (d) Laissez-faire doctrine.

Chapter 9

THOMAS ROBERT MALTHUS (1766-1834)

INTRODUCTION

Thomas Robert Malthus was the second of the trinity, who laid the foundations of English classical political economy. Though he had many contributions in the field of economics, Malthus was best known for his theory of population in the History of Economic Thought. He was also called as a pessimist along with David Ricardo.

LIFE SKETCH

T.R. Malthus was born in Rockery, county Surrey in England in 1766. Young Malthus studied Philosophy. Theology at Cambridge and graduated with honours in 1788. He was soon made Fellow of Jesus College. In 1799, he left for a trip to the continent. He travelled through Sweden, Norway, Finland and Russia. In 1805 he was made Professor of History and Political Economy in the College of the East India Company at Haileybury near London and remained on this post until his death in 1834.

Circumstances and Environment

No thinker can ever remain uninfluenced by the conditions in which he lives and works. So was the case with Thomas Robert Malthus. The prevailing economic conditions and historical environment of England shaped most of his ideas.

The more important perhaps than any one factor in shaping Malthus thought was the condition of England just prior to and during the time at which he wrote. England enjoyed agricultural prosperity during the first half of the eighteenth century. But towards the end of that century agricultural production had declined and prices of commodities rose very high. In the neighbouring country Ireland, there was a recurrence of bad crops and famine condition. The noted Historian T.H. Green says that the miseries of the poeple had increased due to misgovernment and the famine had turned the country into hell.

The evil effects of the Industrial Revolution which had hardly come into view in Adam Smith's days had manifested themselves, unemployment, poverty, disease and riot were among them. They made the agricultural situation still more worse.

To add to the whole dark picture, the English Poor Law was defective both in substance and administration. The rates of grains were enormously high. The freedom of the workers was drastically curtailed leading to pauperism and incompetence everywhere. The miseries of the people prompted Malthus to investigate their causes. Thus a practical interest was created in him, which led to the formulation of his economic theories.

Malthus', famous book "Essay on Population" (seven editions) was published in 1798, 1803, 1806, 1807, 1817. 1826 and 1872. This title was modified as "An Essay on the Principle of Population". Further he published "The Principles of Political Economy Considered With a View to Their Practical Application" in 1820, High Prices of Provisions in 1800, Observations on the Effects of the Corn Laws in 1814, Nature and Progress of Rent in 1815, Grounds of an Opinion of Policy of Restricting the Importation of Foreign Corn in 1815, The Poor Law in 1817, Measure of Value in 1823 and Definition of Political Economy in 1827.

MAIN ECONOMIC IDEAS

1. Theory of Population

Malthus started his Principle of Population with the following two postulates or assumptions:

1) Food is necessary for the existence of man.
2) The passion between the sexes is necessary and will remain nearly in its present state.

From the above two postulates Malthus reached the third conclusion that, "the power of population is indefinitely greater than the power of the earth to produce subsistence for men. Population, when unchecked, increased in a geometrical ratio. Food production increases in an arithmetical ratio."

An analysis of the above assumptions brings out the following important elements in Malthusian theory:

1) Production of food (the means of subsistence) is subject to the law of diminishing returns. Nature is niggardly. It doesn't readily respond to man's efforts to produce more. So as more and more doses of labour and capital are applied to land, no doubt, the total food production increases but at a diminishing rate. Malthus pointed out that food production increases in a slow arithmetical progression (1,2,3,4.......).
2) On the other hand population left to itself tends to grow faster than food production. According to Malthus, population has a tendency to grow in a geometrical progression (2,4,6,8....). Thus

population increases at a much faster rate than food production and has a tendency to double itself every twenty-five years.

3) Food production and population growth are affected by independent factors. Food production is influenced by the law of diminishing returns, whereas the human beings have greater power of reproduction. The force of sex instinct works continuously and universally. "It is a constant tendency in all animated life, hence it surpasses the nourishment produced for it". So in the race between food production and population growth, food production is left behind. Therefore there arises disequilibrium between population growth and food production.

4) Due to this disequilibrium, the increasing population cannot be maintained at the existing level. The cultivation of new lands and emigration are not sufficient to counteract the superior powers of population. So there arises starvation and undernourishment on a mass scale. Famines, floods, earthquakes, epidemics, wars and other natural calamities take the lives of the people. Malthus referred these natural calamities as positive checks. These positive checks are also called natural checks, since they are applied by nature.
However, it should be remembered that these checks are applied by nature only when man fails to check the excessive growth of population through his own efforts.

5) Man could avoid the positive checks by restoring to what Malthus called Preventive checks. Preventive checks are applied by people consciously to limit the number. They include vice, misery and moral restraint. If man applies these preventive checks there will be no need for nature to apply its own checks.

The above main points of the Malthusian theory can be summarised in the form of a chart.

Theory of Population

Population increases in quick geometrical ratio (2,4,6,8,10....)	Food Production increases in slow arithmetical ratio (1,2,3,4,5....)

Results in disequilibrium between population and food supply

↓

Correction of disequilibrium

Positive or natural checks	Preventive checks

Thus Malthus was the first to devote a treatise to the principles of population. He deserves great consideration for calling attention to the economic significance of an important subject which had been neglected. He gave the problem a definiteness and distinctness which made its significance tangible. Malthus must be regarded as the founder of the science of demography.

The Malthusian theory is also important from the fact that it was instrumental in leading Darwin to his doctrine of Natural Selection. Darwin himself has said that his theory of the struggle for existence was only, "the doctrine of Malthus applied with mainfold force to the whole animal kingdom".

Further Malthus collected a number of valuable facts in order to illustrate his doctrine. His principle of population is not based on assumptions. Thus Malthus introduced a dynamic factor into economics. Malthusian theory is essential to an understanding of the problems of social reform.

Criticisms

Inspite of the above merits, the Malthusian doctrine has been criticised on many points.

1. The mathematical character of the theory is opened to objection. Critics have strongly criticised Malthus on this point and pointed out that the increase in population and food production cannot be expressed in terms of geometrical and arithmetical progressions. There are no examples in the history of countries where the population and food production have increased in geometrical and arithmtical progressions. Nor is there any example of a country where the population has doubled by itself in twenty five years.

2) The theory neglects the influence of education and standard of living. On account of the expansion of female education, the young women become family planning conscious and they are reluctant to accept the burden of a large family. Besides, when the standard of living of the people increases, they prefer to have a small family in order to maintain a high standard of living. Thus the spread of female education and the rise in the standard of living have the effect of reducing the birth rate in the country. So population will not increase in quick geometrical ratio, as Malthus expected.

3) Malthus ignored scientific discoveries and inventions. The modern age is full of scientific inventions and discoveries. So there is a possibility to check the operation of the law of diminishing returns in agriculture. As a result the food production can also increase quickly. This was not visualised by Malthus.

4) Too much importance to population and food supply. Malthus has over-emphasised the relationship between population and food supply. "The problem of population as a whole is then, not one of mere size, but of efficient production and equitable distribution. That is, it is a problem not of numbers alone but of wealth," (Seligman)

5) Neglects the effects of over population. Malthus has not explained the full effects of over population. No doubt over population brings poverty, misery and famine but at the same time it increases the labour supply.

As Cannon rightly said, "A baby comes to the world not only with a mouth but also with a pair of hands". Since man is the source of labour, large numbers, sometimes may mean greater wealth, strength and power. But it is unfortunate that Malthus considered only the evils and not the benefits of growing population.

6) Excludes International Trade. This is an age of international trade and commerce. If a country does not grow enough food grains, it can import from other countries.

7) Pessimistic Theory. Malthusian theory is a pessimistic theory because it threatens the poeple with misery, famine, epidemics etc, and thereby shows the future gloomy. Hence William Godwin described this theory, "as a black and terrible demon that is always ready to stifle the hopes of humanity".

8) Incomplete Theory. It is an incomplete theory as it has not explained the declining death rate, the another cause of over population and has not touched the problem of under population.

9) Importance of preventive checks undermined. Malthus has also been criticised on the ground that, he laid too much importance on the positive checks in his theory of population. He could not visualise the growing importance of preventive checks.

10) Malthus failed to provide a satisfactory economic theory of population. An economic theory of population growth must throw light on the determinants of population growth while taking full account of the influence of demand and supply forces producing a child. The demand for producing a child is reflected in the demand for labour and the cost of producing a child includes the cost of rearing that child. Malthusian theory of population growth is a demand-regulated theory and does not take into consideration the cost of production aspect.

But the more realistic view is that the supply curve of producing children is a rising curve implying that more children can be produced only at increased costs. As far as the demand for labour is concerned, it tends to fall as industrialisation progresses. As a result of economic development, a country experiences a falling birth rate. For the sake of criticism, it is true that human beings are not produced under the strict economic discipline of cost-benefit analysis; other non economic determinants also affect the birth rate. But when we become more and more civilised, we prefer to live in rationally chosen and economically better numbers.

Other Economic Views of Malthus

Although Malthus is chiefly known for his theory of population, his other economic views are not less important. They could be gathered from his, "Principles of Political Economy Considered With a View to Their Practical Application" which was published in 1820.

Malthus maintained that man, not wealth was the proper subject of study in political economy. The science of political economy resembled the science of morals.

2. Wealth

Those writers who did not accept the definition of wealth given by Adam Smith, considered wealth as those objects which had value-in-exchange. Sometimes hired labour was also regarded as wealth.

But Malthus considered that mere labour should not be regarded as wealth because nobody would give anything for it if he was sure that it would not give any satisfaction. Therefore Malthus defined wealth as, "the material objects necessary, useful or agreeable to man which are voluntarily appropriated by individuals or nations,". This definition of Malthus includes almost all objects. He also pointed out that a country would be rich or poor in accordance with the abundance or scarcity of those material objects in relation to its territory and population.

Further Malthus believed that even though an increasing population was a powerful element for increasing demand, it would not provide a stimulus to the growth of wealth. In this connection he gave the examples of the countries of Asia, Africa, Spain, Portugal, Poland, Hungary, Turkey etc.

In addition, he listed the following factors which contributed to an increase or decrease in wealth.

1) Heat or climate which makes people indolent and creates obstacles in the way of increasing wealth.
2) Lack of demand reduces wealth.
3) Wealth would increase only when land is cultivated by the skilled and industrious people.

4) Wealth would increase when a newly invented machine brings to the market cheaper goods with the result that the demand for that commodity increases and more hands are required in production – thus unemployment is not created by the introduction of that machine.
5) Wealth also increases quickly when production and distribution are combined in their due proportion.

3. Rent

Malthus did not contribute a separate theory for rent. However his views on rent are found in "An Enquiry into the Nature and Progress of Rent" (1815). To a great extent, Malthus anticipated the Ricardian theory of rent.

The early writers like Adam Smith, J.B. Say and Sismondi regarded rent as a monoply return. For instance, Adam Smith described landlords as monopolists who loved to reap where they had not sown.

But Malthus regarded rent as a surplus due to the bounty of nature. He supported the corn laws and stated that the cause of high prices of food was the population growth and progress. The growth of population leads to the scarcity of food for the production of which good land becomes scarce, consequently prices of the produce raised from the already cultivated land. Since rent arises due to the difference between the price and the cost of production, the rise in price was the sole cause for the origin of rent. Thus Malthus more or less anticipated the Ricardian theory of rent.

Further, Malthus made a distinction between rent and monopoly return. Even though at the outset he had agreed that because the extent of the earth was limited, and there was relatively scarcity of better lands, landownership might be regarded as a "partial monopoly", he considered rent different from high prices for three reasons:

i) The fertility of the soil enables it to yield more than is necessary to maintain agricultural labour. This is peculiar to land and not connected with monoply.
ii) The agricultural produce creates its own demand and hence abundance leads to cheapness and scarcity leads to dearness.
iii) Finally, the fertile land is very scarce. In "common monopolies" there is an "excess price" over cost due to external demand. But in the case of land the excess of price or rent depends entirely upon the degree of fertility–natural or acuquired.

Rent, according to Malthus, would be lowered on account of diminished capital, diminished population, falling price of raw produce and a tedious system of cultivation. These are undoubtedly the indications of poverty and deterioration of the land of superior quality. He admitted that the fertility of land was the only source of a high return to capital.

4. Value

The contribution of Malthus to the theory of value is negligible. He was somewhat confused about it. At one point, he criticised Adam Smith's theory of value and at another point he used Smith's definition of value. He described value as the power of purchasing commodities.

Malthus divided value into three kinds – value in use, nominal value in exchange and intrinsic value in exchange. The nominal value of a commodity is generrally expressed in terms of some metal. Money helped to determine the nominal and relative values of goods.

Malthus also studied the conditions of the supply of a commodity.

i) The labour used in the production of a commodity should be paid so as to encourage its production. Without adequate wages, the supply of the commodity could not be increased.
ii) The assistance given to the worker in the form of implements, food and other materials should continue so that production may not be affected.
iii) The price of commodities should be such as to ensure a continued supply of food and raw materials used by the workers and capitalists.

5. Value of Money

Malthus regarded money as the convenient measure of value. When the value of money falls, the prices increase.

6. Wages

Malthus defined wages as the remuneration paid to the workers for their exertions. He made a difference between nominal and real wages. The amount of money paid to the workers depends upon the demand for and supply of commodities in relation to the number of workers.

Malthus defined the natural price of labour as the "price -------- sufficient to meet the effectual demand". While describing the circumstances that contribute to the character of labourers, he enumerated the following three things–civil liberty, political liberty and education.

7. Theory of Over Production

The name of Malthus has become a by-word so far as the theory of population in concerned. The very prominence of the theory of population has thrown into obscurity other valuable contributions made by Malthus. There is no reason to believe that Malthus is splendid only with his theory of population and he had nothing else of significance to contribute to the theory of economic crisis. In fact Malthus provided the basic foundation for the Keynesian analysis of the working of a capitalist economy which always suffers from a chronic deficiency of demand and periodical ups and downs because of the business cycles. Thus, Malthus was the first theorist of economic crisis. He is considered to be the forerunner of the under consumption theory.

Newman observes that considereing his time and environment, a theory of market glut put forward by Malthus reveals a considerable insight into his past. Malthus was opposed to the capitalism of the classical school regarding the working of the laissez-faire economy. The Great Depression which followed the Napoleonic wars created an interest in the discussion of business crisis among economists.

Before Malthus, all the classical economists believed in the operation of Say's law of market which stated that "every supply creates its own demand". Its implication is that there never could be any overproduction resulting in unemployment. The idea, expressed by Say was further developed by David Ricardo and other writers. They felt that supply and demand were tied together as such in the long run adjustment would take place between supply and demand and therefore there was no possibility for overproduction or glut in the market. There might be overproduction or underproduction in the short run, but generally over production in the long run was not possible. In other words in their opinion, if the supply of any commodity was more than its demand, it would be balanced by others demand being in excess of supply, consequently market gluts were impossible.

This analysis further led them to another conclusion that the accumulation of capital at a rate, faster than investment was also impossible. In other words the classical economists not only assumed a state of full employment but also a balance between production and consumption as well as saving and investment (S = I).

But Malthus never agreed with Say's law of market. He denied the equality between saving and investment. A disparity would arise between saving and investment and supply and demand. Again in Malthus's opinion, capitalist production is not so self-adjusting as was assumed by J.B. Say and Ricardo. Thus Malthus was the first economist to admit that a crisis might arise from the conditions inherent in the capitalist process of production. He did not take effective demand for granted.

In the analysis of effective demand, Malthus differed from Ricardo and other classical writers. Malthus was of the opinion that the level of output at anytime depended upon effective demand. He described the effective demand as demand which was high enough to ensure a continual supply of goods. In other words, production depended upon the existence of effective demand.

Malthus pointed out that value of the product produced by the efforts of labour was always more than the amount of money paid as wages to the workers. Since the wages of the workers are so low that they cannot demand many goods. So lack of demand arises for the goods produced by the workers.

On the other hand the capitalists can demand more goods. But they are interested in saving and accumulation of capital. So in order to increase and maintain effective demand Malthus was in favour of unproductive consumption. Unless a large body of unproductive consumers was maintained, there would be periodic over production, glut in the market and stagnation. In the class of unproductive consumers, Malthus included landlords, statesmen, soldiers, judges, lawyers, physicians, clergymen etc.

Malthus used the concept of effective demand to show that the economic system was not self-adjusting. Unless there is a large body of unproductive consumers, there would be over production and glut in the market. Malthus believed that high wages would not solve the problem because it would increase the cost of production, profits would be reduced and there would be further reduction in investment. Further, Malthus believed that if producers pay less wages to the workers, they would ultimately dig their own graves because low wages in the long run will reduce effective demand and lead to business crisis.

The above analysis can be graphically represented in the following manner:

In the figure $O_1 O_2$ measures the total labour supply. Productive labour is measured from the left and unproductive labour from the right. Line Z which starts from O_1 is the net commodity output line, Line X which starts from O_2 is service line which is a function of unproductive labour.

At an equilibrium wage rate, O_1N_1 productive labour is employed and O_2N_1 unproductive labour is employed. O_1N_1 productive labour produces N_1K output, at point K, where the demand line intersects the supply line Z. So at point K supply is equal to demand. Further at this point Say's law of market is also proved.

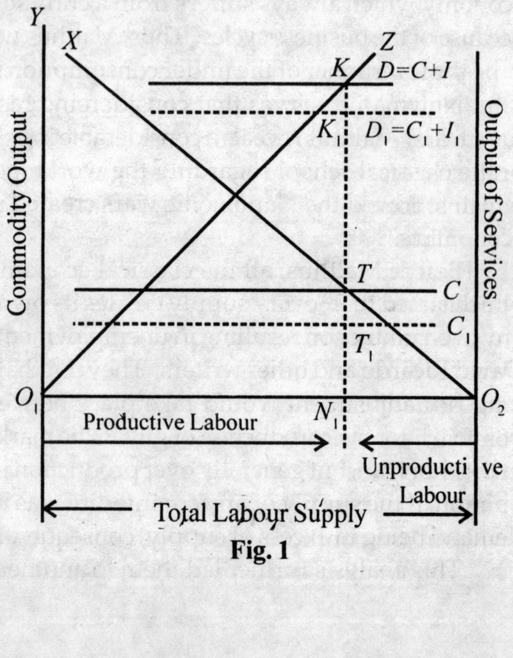

Fig. 1

But as assumed by Malthus, supply will not be equal to demand. The total demand consists of investment demand and consumption demand. ($D = C + I$). Since the demand is made by two different groups of people, there is no co-ordination in the decisions of these two groups.

In the figure, the demand made by unproductive labourers is N_1T_1 and the demand made by productive labourers is K_1T. The total demand is N_1K_1. The glut is measured by the difference between supply and demand. Supply is N_1K. Demand is N_1K_1. So glut or over production is KK_1.

Thus for the first time in the History of economic thought, Malthus has pointed out the possibility of glut or over production.

Malthusian Glut and Keynesian Stagnation

Keynes, in his Essays on Malthus, has quoted one of the letters of Malthus to Ricardo to show how Malthus was concerned with the causes that determined the different levels of output at different times in a country: "....besides I really think that the progress of society consists of irregular movements, and that to omit the consideration of causes of the wealth and poverty of nations—the grand object of all enquiries in political economy..... We see in all countries around us, and in our own particularly, periods of greater and less prosperity and sometimes of adversity, but never the uniform progress which you seem alone to contemplate." Keynes has expressed a feeling that "the almost total obliteration of Malthus's line of approach and the complete domination of Ricardo's for a period of a hundred years has been a disaster to the progress of economics."

Malthus As A Pessimist

In the History of Economic Thought, while Adam Smith was an optimist, Malthus and Ricardo were considered as pessimists.

A given theorist can be considered as an optimist or a pessimist only on the basis of the conclusions which flow out of the theory and which has certain relevance to the course of events likely to happen in future.

Viewed from this point, the conclusion of the Malthusian theory of population spells danger to humanity. Malthus searched pessimistic conclusions on the basis of two lines of reasoning – the one on the race between population and food supply and the other on the basis of the law of diminishing returns, scarcity of fertile soil and a pattern of distribution which has an inherent tendency to go against the interest of the working class.

Truely speaking Malthusian pessimism is based on the law of diminishing returns as advocated by Ricardo which makes it impossible to achieve food production in proportion to the increase in population.

Malthusian pessimism was a reaction to the hasty optimism of his predecessors. A large population was favoured by the mercantilists for the increase of national wealth. They also believed that science and society progressed unhindered. They drew up a picture of peace and prosperity for all. Adam Smith disapproved of any kind of state interference in social and business activities, for he believed that a perfect harmony always existed between the individual and social interests. For all these reasons, it was believed that economic progress caused maximisation of individual and social welfare without any conflict and contradiction in their interests.

But Malthus was opposed to these reasons. The picture of society which he had drawn up leads to misery and starvation of the workers, clash of interest among the different classes of society and an emergence of a stationary state, a state of inactivity. In view of Malthus, the future of society was dark. According to Malthus the unlimited power of reproduction which man possessed was exercised under the sexual passion. Against this power, the means of subsistence were limited by the availability of fertile lands and the fact that agriculture was subject to the law of diminishing returns. So this would lead to over population and it could be checked by adopting certain birth control methods.

But Malthus condemned all kinds of artificial means to check the growth of population. He described them as immoral and unchristian. This attitude was in accordance with Christian ideology. He felt that humanity was doomed to suffer an inevitable disaster. He said, "there is misery in store for mankind, and the poor are the causes of their own poverty".

Further, Malthus in his theory of gluts also stated that how over production or under consumption will be in the economy in future. He never expected that the economy would reach the full employment level. Again in his opinion capitalistic production is not so self-adjusting as was assumed by Ricardo and J.B. Say. He made it very clear that capitalists would not be able to increase the demand for goods. So he suggested that some unproductive consumption should be created so as to equalise the demand with supply.

The pessimism which is very clear in the writings of Malthus rests on two assumptions, namely, the law of diminishing returns and rapid population. These assumptions were influenced by the social and economic conditions that prevailed during his time. By the time Malthus wrote his theories, the evil effects of industrial revolution, namely unemployment, poverty, disease and misery were obvious. So this new situation demanded a new explanation because the earlier economists had not seen such situations.

Further, the second half of the eighteenth century was also a period of great agricultural misery. Ireland was in periodical grips of famine and agricultural production was upset in England. Further in the same period in England population was multiplying faster and agriculture was expanding to meet the greater food demand which resulted in high rent, high price for food materials.

Thus an analysis of Malthusian theories, the social and economic surroundings all clearly show Malthus as a pessimist.

Critical Estimate

Malthus holds a unique place in the history of economic thought. Keynes called Malthus as the "first of the Cambridge economists". Malthus had his one foot in the classical traditions and the other in the Keynesian "New Economics". He not only revised, refined and elaborated the classical system as drafted by Adam Smith but also presented a critique of classicism.

As an economist, he introduced a dynamic element in economics. He not only brought a new subject of study, but also made others to realise the economic significance of the subject. His name has been immortalised by his Principles of Population. Malthusian theory of population has become a starting point for all modern studies of the problem. He has been rightly described as the founder of modern demography. The importance of his essay is all the more enhanced by the fact that it provided the basis to Darwin's Law of the survival of the fitest.

Greater significance than his essay, were his views on rent and over production. His views on rent justify his claim to be regarded as one of the co-discoverers of the theory of rent. His entire analysis of the causes of over production and the principle of effective demand shows that he possessed a keener insight. Keynes has rightly spoken of him as being "far ahead of his time in his analysis" of the role of demand.

His approach to all economic and social problems was scientific. He can be placed as number 'two' after Smith in the list of the builders of economic science. We can conclude with the words of Keynes, "If only Malthus instead of Ricardo has been the parent stem from which nineteenth century economics proceeded, what a much wiser and richer place world would be today...... I have long claimed Robert Malthus as the first of the Cambridge Economists."

COMPARATIVE STUDY OF SMITH AND MALTHUS

Both Smith and Malthus were the leading representatives of the classical school. In fact, critics rank Malthus next to Smith among the founders of the science of economics. Both followed the classical traditions. Smith provided the scientific basis to economics. Malthus introduced population as another key factor in economic analysis. Thus both Smith and Malthus earned an immortal place in the history of economic thought by providing the most durable foundation to the science of economics.

Smith gave an elegant theory of production based on his concept of division of labour. Malthus became a pioneer in developing the problem of population as a separate branch of economics. In fact, Malthus raised the study of population to the status of a science, viz., the science of demography.

To both Smith and Malthus population problems formed an integral part of economics. Smith had thought that population adapted itself to supply and demand. He treated population problem in terms of a self– adjusting cycle. He relied primarily on the economic factor to inhibit his economic man. He did not seem to be worried about over population. Malthus took a different view. Basing his theory on the concept of diminishing returns from agriculture, he found an "inexorable tendency for population to outstrip its means of subsistence". Unlike the predecessors, Malthus took a dismal view of the future.

Optimism marked the major part of Smith's thought but pessimism coloured the economic thought of Malthus especially, in his views on population. Thus Malthusian essay was a reaction against the optimism of Smith.

Naturalism and optimism in Smith's thought had been commended by the critics. Naturalism implied the spontaneous origin of economic institutions based upon the motive of self-interest. Optimism implied that naturally originated institutions were for public good and of a beneficient character. To Smith, naturalism and optimism were not separable. Modern economists have accepted his concept of naturalism but disagreed with the concept of optimism.

In the case of Malthus, his pessimism implied that there was a constant tendency for imbalance between growth rate of population and of food supply. His contemporaries deplored his pessimism. But majority of the English classical school adopted the Malthusian doctrine and it became a pillar of classical economics. Thus both Smith and Malthus through different ideas of optimism and pessimism contributed to the development of classical economics.

Smith realised that in any market and any given time supply and demand will play an important role but under competition price will tend towards cost of production. In this context, Smith discussed effective demand but did not develop a theory of market gluts. Credit goes to Malthus, the lone classical economist, for developing a theory of market glut. The classical economists generally assumed that every demand created its own supply. But Malthus developed a theory of market gluts or a theory of under-consumption which later became a fore-runner to Keynesian economics. If we judged his theory in the light of Malthus' time and environment, it revealed his great insight and theorising ability. According to him, capitalistic production was not self-adjusting or equalizing. Effective demand could not be taken for granted and some way must be found to increase unproductive consumption if the system was not to grind to a halt.

Smith was not very clear regarding his theory of distribution. His theory of rent was not clear and comprehensive. At some places Smith, under the physiocratic influence, treated rent as a gift of nature. At other places his concept of rent was close to the modern concept. On the whole, he was not clear about the relationship between rent and price. It was not generally recognised that Malthus developed a theory of rent. But his ideas on rent were perhaps considered to be more superior than those of Ricardo. In 1815, he published a pamphlet in which he defended the corn laws and stated that the high price of food was due not to legal restrictions on imports of foodgrains but to population growth and progress.

Smith was essentially a materialistic thinker. His economic philosophy was excessively individualistic. But Malthusian theory of population revealed a dualistic philosophy. As a man, Malthus had strong idealistic leanings. But as an economist he emphasised the importance of materialistic factors. But his writings showed that he was not an extremely materialistic thinker.

QUESTIONS

1. Narrate the circumstances and environment that shaped the philosophy of Malthus.
2. What are the underlying principles of Malthusian Theory of population?
3. Make a critical estimate of Malthusian Theory of Population.
4. Is Malthusian Theory irrelevant today ?
5. Write about the "Theory of Gluts".
6. What are the ideas of Malthus about : (i) Wealth (ii) Value of money ; and (iii) Wages ?
7. Estimate the place of Malthus in the History of Economic Thought.

Chapter 10

DAVID RICARDO (1772 - 1823)

INTRODUCTION

Next to Adam Smith, David Ricardo has been considered as the greatest economist of all times. Ricardo's influence in shaping the future course of economic thought has been so profound that none can rival him in this respect. He was a source of inspiration to both of his disciples and to his own opponents. Gray says, "In his hands Classical English Political Economy reaches its final and complete form, so that for the next generation, the leaders of economic thought can do little more than repeat the perfected blend of Adam Smith, Malthus and Ricardo;...... If Marx and Lenin deserve busts, somewhere in the background there should be room for an effigy of Ricardo". Ricardo is chiefly known for his "Principles of Political Economy" which was published in 1817. It was the first complete statement of classical economic Theory.

DEFINITION OF POLITICAL ECONOMY

Ricardo's chief concern was the distribution of wealth and according to him the scope of political economy was to determine the laws which regulate the distribution of the produce of earth into rent, wages and profits. In one of his letters to Malthus he wrote, "Political Economy, you think is an inquiry into the nature and causes of wealth : I think it should rather be called an inquiry into the laws which determine the division of the produce of an industry amongst the classes who concur in its formation". He analysed the course of this division through history. The shift from investigating the nature and causes of wealth to its distribution was due to Ricardo's love for abstract reasoning. Further, economic conditions of Britain had undergone changes and the immediate concern was not the acceleration of economic growth but the distribution of the fruits of economic growth in a proper manner.

Value

Following Adam Smith, Ricardo distinguished between 'Value in use' and 'Value in exchange' and pointed out that to have exchangeable value a commodity must have utility. The other factors which determine the exchange value were scarcity and quantity of labour required to obtain them. In this connection, he distinguished two kinds of commodities. Firstly, those that cannot be multiplied in which case value is determined by scarcity alone, for example, rare statues, coins, scarce books and so on. Secondly, there are those commodities which can be multiplied to any limit and in such cases value is determined by quantity of labour. Ricardo developed the pure Labour Cost Theory of Value in which labour performs the following functions. (a) It is the foundation, source and substance of value, (b) It is the cause of changes in the absolute and relative values, (c) It is the closest approximation to a measure of value, (d) It serves as an ethical and socio-economic justification of prices and (e) It inter-relates economic value and technology.

Ricardo has made a distinction between natural price and market price. Market price may deviate from the natural price because of temporary fluctuations of supply and demand. If market price rises above the normal price, profit will rise and more capital will be used to produce the commodity. On the other hand, if the market price falls, profits will fall and capital will flow out of the industry. In other words, short run price depends on supply and demand and long run price depends on the cost of production.

The presence of capital is not a difficulty to Ricardo. He divides capital into fixed and circulating capital. Circulating capital is used for financing the employment of labour while fixed capital is used in the form of machinery and equipment.

The labour theory of value has been criticised on the following grounds:

1. There is difficulty in measuring labour or cost of production. All workmen are not of equal efficiency. The less skilled may take longer than the skilled over a particular piece of work and so put more labour into it.
2. Labour may be misdirected. An article which cannot fulfill the purpose for which it was intended cannot have value. Misdirected labour does not count as labour.
3. The main weakness of the labour theory of value is that it ignores the influences of demand.

The labour theory of value became a powerful tool in the hands of Karl Marx to demonstrate that there is exploitation of labour in a capitalist economy. Marx found it very convenient for his argument to agree with Adam Smith and Ricardo that the value of a commodity depended on the amount of labour required for its production. On this basis, Marx asserted that the worker was entitled to the entire fruit of his labour. Marx emphasised that a thing can have value only if it is a product of human labour. But there is no hint of exploitation in Ricardo's analysis. It was Marx who made use of Ricardo's labour theory of value to speak about exploitation of labour by capitalists. Ricardo said that labour was the source of wealth. On this basis, Marx developed the socialist concept that the worker deserved the whole product. To this, he added the doctrine of class struggle.

Theory of Distribution

The distribution of wealth is the focus of Ricardian economics. Ricardo opened out a new field of economic enquiry in a comprehensive scientific attempt to determine the shares of land, labour, capital and enterprise in the National Product. "To determine the law which regulates this distribution is the principal problem in political economy", declared Ricardo and thus extended pricing system to the field of distribution.

THEORY OF RENT

According to Ricardo, "Rent is that portion of the produce of the earth, which is paid to the landlord for the use of original and indestructible powers of the soil". Rent was a differential surplus which accrued to superior lands over inferior lands. Differences in the fertility of land was the main factor giving rise to rent.

A group of people settle in a newly discovered island. There are four types of land in the island, classified on the basis of fertility – A, B, C and D. A is the most fertile land and D is the least fertile land. The first batch of people occupy the 'A' quality land for agricultural production. With one dose of labour and capital 'A' quality land yields 100 tons of wheat per hectare. When the second batch of people comes, it has two alternatives: either to occupy the 'B' quality land, which is free or to take the 'A' quality land on rent from the first batch. The rent payable on 'A' quality land would be equal to the difference in the fertilities of the 'A' and 'B' quality lands. If one dose of labour and capital applied to 'B' quality land yields 80 tons of wheat per hectare, then rent on 'A' would be equal to 20 (100-80) tons of wheat per hectare. When the third batch comes it will have three alternatives. It can occupy the 'C' quality land or it can take 'B' or 'A' quality land on rent. If the 'C' quality land yields 60 tons of wheat with the application of a dose of labour and capital, then the rent of 'A' quality land would be 40 tons per hectare and that of the 'B' quality land 20 tons per hectare. When the fourth batch comes to the island, it will have four alternatives before it. It can occupy the 'D' quality land or it can take 'C' or 'B' or 'A' quality land on rent. The rent would be determined by the difference in the fertilities of 'D' quality land on the one side and those of 'C', 'B' and 'A' qulaity lands on the other. 'D' quality land is the no rent land because it earns no rent. The rent is a differential surplus enjoyed by the superior land over the inferior land. This has been illustrated in the diagram.

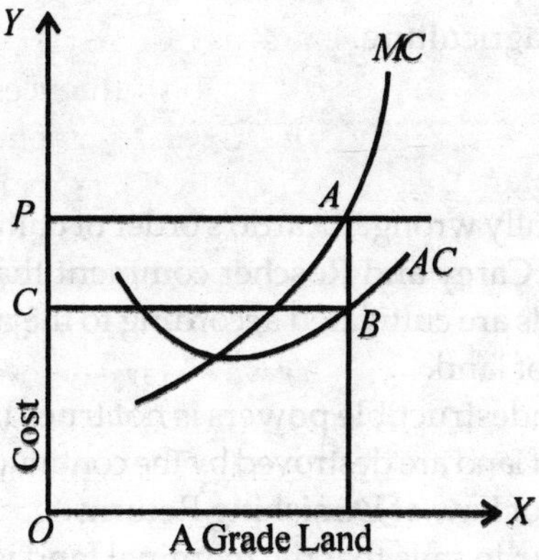

Fig. 1.

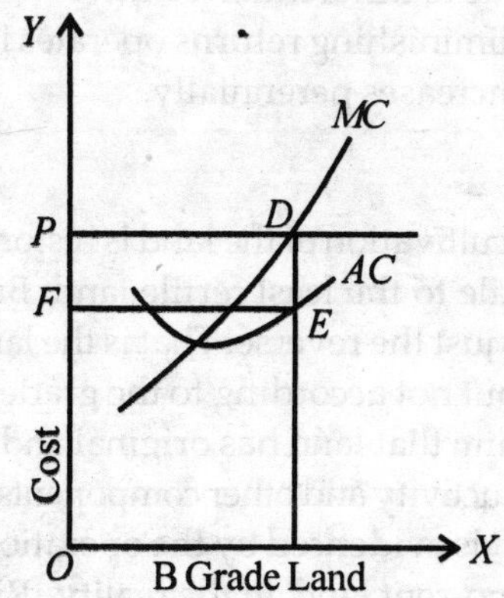

Fig. 2.

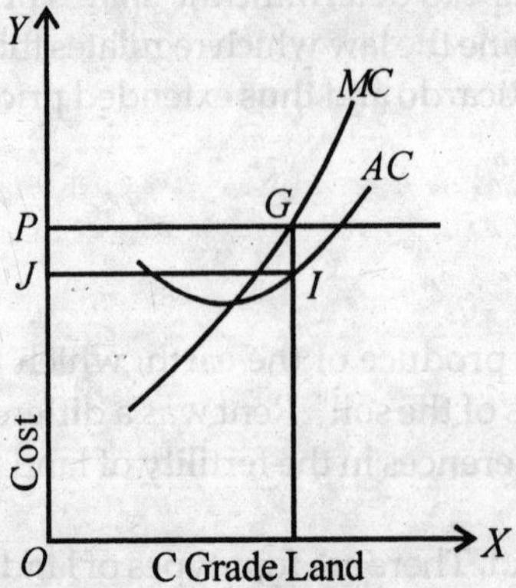

Fig. 3.

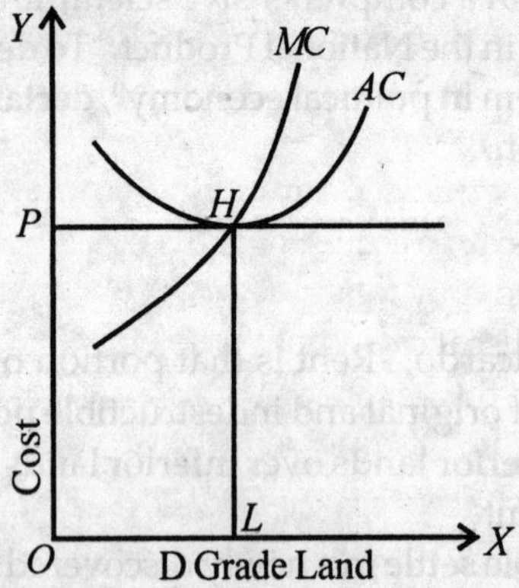

Fig. 4.

Fig 1 shows 'A' grade land which is the most superior land. Fig 2 indicates the 'B' grade land which is the next best. Fig 3 shows 'C' grade land and Fig 4 shows 'D' grade land which is the least productive land or inferior. AC is the average cost and MC is the marginal cost curve. Minimum average cost of production is LH on 'D' grade land. If it is to be cultivated price must be OP. In this case, there is no surplus and hence there is no rent. In case of 'C' grade land, there is surplus equal to PGIJ which is the rent on 'C' grade land. The rent on 'B' grade land is shown by the area PDEF and on 'A' grade land it is PABC.

This theory is based on a number of assumptions:

1) It explains the determination of rent in the long run.
2) It assumes the existence of no rent land.
3) The theory assumes that land is limited both quantitatively and qualitatively.
4) It assumes that land has some "Original and indestructible powers".
5) Rent arises only on land which is a free gift of nature.
6) Land is cultivated in a descending order.
7) Rent arises due to differential fertility.
8) The Law of diminishing returns operates in agriculture.
9) Population increases perennially.

Criticisms

1) The order of cultivation of the land is historically wrong. Ricardo's order of cultivation is from the most fertile to the least fertile land. But Carey and Roscher comment that the order of cultivation is just the reverse. That is the lands are cultivated according to the nearness of the inhabitants but not according to the grades of land.
2) Ricardo's claim that land has original and indestructible powers is not true. In practice, the fertility, productivity and other components of land are destroyed by the continuous cultivation of the land. It is evidenced by the operation of Law of Dimishing Returns.
3) There is no 'no-rent land' in the reality. Ricardo says that the marginal land is no rent land. But this is not true because every land in practice yields rent.
4) Ricardo's statement that rent does not enter into price is not valid. Rent enters into price in

two ways–through cost of production and supply.

5) Ricardian rent does not correspond to the actual rent. The actual rent paid by the tenant to the landlord may be a customary rent or legal rent or competitive rent. But these rents have nothing to do with Ricardian rent which is a differential surplus.
6) Ricardo is criticised for having ignored the other uses of the land. In the statement of his theory, Ricardo contends that rent is paid for the cultivation of land. This implies that land can be used only for cultivation. But land can also be used for construction, playgrounds, and for every use it can command rent.
7) Rent is not the payment for land only. Ricardo associated rent only with land as if land alone is eligible for getting rent. But Marshall contends that rent is payable to other factors of production also.
8) Ricardian theory does not explain the cause of rent. This theory only explains why one area commands a higher rent than a less fertile land; it does not explain the phenomenon of rent. This theory does not point out why the rent arises.
9) Ricardian theory explains differential rent but not scarcity rent or situation rent.

Despite these criticisms the theory is important. It brings out clearly certain points which are of great importance from stand point of policy.

THEORY OF WAGES

Ricardian theory of wages is merely a combination of two concepts - the Smithian concept of wages and the Malthusian theory of population. Ricardo distinguished between natural and market price of labour. According to him, the natural price of labour is "that price which is necessary to enable the labourers, one with another, to subsist and to perpetuate their race, without either increase or diminution". The market price of labour is determined by the forces of demand and supply while the natural price is determined by the level of subsistence of the labour; and the market price tends to conform to the natural price. Ricardo thus treats labour like other commodities. To Ricardo, natural wage consists not of the quantity of money but the quantity of food, conveniences, necessaries that are essential to him which that money purchases.

Ricardo believed that in the long run, both the natural price of labour and money wage would tend to rise because of the increase in the cost of producing food for increasing population. Improvements in agriculture and imports of food grains would lower the cost of living only temporarily. But ultimately, money wages will rise in order to meet the increasing cost of food grains.

Ricardo's idea that in the long run, the wages of workers will enable them to live only a 'subsistence level" is sometimes referred to as the "Iron Law of wages". When the market price of labour rises above the natural price, there will be expansion in the families of workers. As population increases, wages will come down to their natural price. When the market price of labour is below the natural price, poverty and misery will reduce the working population and wage rates will rise. Thus, in the long run, workers will receive wages at minimum subsistence level.

Ricardo also brings in the competitive labour market wherein the wages are determined by relative strength of demand and supply. He advocates non-interference by the government, ignores the existence of non-competing groups and other imperfections which may distort wage rates or which cause wage differentials between workers.

Ricardo's treatment of wages suffers from certain other limitations as well. To quote from Haney, "So abstract and absolute a wage theory as Ricardo's proved thoroughly unsatisfactory. Nowhere does the viciousness of the great economists's abstract method appear more clearly. Overlooking differences in work and workers, non-competitive groups, etc., he assumes an average labourer doing average work under conditions of perfect competition, and receiving a "natural" wage. The effect of laws and customs is virtually ignored....".

Profits and Interest

Ricardo's treatment of profit and interest is least satisfactory and may be styled as, "some remarks on the relation of profits to wages". Ricardo does not clearly distinguish between profit and interest, or the proper relationship between the two. Capital, of course, is divided into circulating and durable capital. Interest is paid on borrowed capital and profit is earned on one's own capital. Profit is a combination of interest, wages of managerial labour supplied by the owner and the return for entrepreneurship. Ricardo does not split the profit income into its components. He does not analyse the origin of this income. Ricardo considers profit as a residual after the claims of rent and wages have been met. In the case of marginal or no-rent lands, the total produce is divided into wages and profit only and profit would vary inversely with wages. Ricardo maintains that with the progress of the society, profit rate would fall. Eventually, a stage would come when it would be no longer paying to save and invest and the economy would get stuck at a stationary state.

Money

Ricardo explains the causes for rise in the price of gold and suggests ways of controlling it. He maintains that printing of bank notes is the main cause of rising prices of gold and other commodities. He believes in the quantity theory of money which tells that the level of prices in the economy is proportional to the quantity of money in the economy. Value of money is its purchasing power and is therefore, determined in the market, like the value of any other commodity, by its labour cost of production. Ricardo also gives us the idea that purchasing power of money depends upon the supply of money, velocity of circulation, confidence and the bank credit policies. But his idea is not the conventional quantity theory in which value of money depends on its supply only. Any excess supply of paper money would be absorbed by the commerce and the only effect will be an increase in prices.

Ricardo advocates restoration of gold standard. Gold standard by acting as a check on the over issue of currency would curb inflation. To eliminate the cost of coinage and to economise gold, gold bullion standard has been suggested by Ricardo.

Foreign Trade

The theory of comparative cost is the major contribution of Ricardo to the theory of foreign trade. It states that every country will produce those goods in the production of which it is favourably placed on account of its climate, the qualities of its other natural resources, the characteristics of its people etc. By concentrating on those goods in which it has special advantages a country produces more than it requires for its own needs and exchanges the surplus with other countries against goods which it cannot produce at all. In other words, every country produces and exports goods in the production of which it has cost advantages and imports those goods in the production of which it has cost disadvantages.

Assumptions

The comparative cost theory is developed on certain assumptions:

1) Labour is the only productive factor.
2) Production is subject to the law of constant returns.
3) Factors of production are assumed to be mobile within a country but immobile between countries.
4) Transport cost is absent.
5) Only two countries and two commodities are considered.
6) There is no barrier for international trade.
7) The two countries have common monetary standard.

When the cost ratio of production is the same in two countries, trade cannot take place.

Equal cost ratios of production

Countries	Quantity of Factor	Production of Cotton	Production of Wheat
India	10 days of Labour	100 Units	80 Units
Pakistan	10 days of Labour	80 Units	64 Units

In both the countries the ratio of exchange between cotton and wheat is: 1unit of cotton = 0.8 unit of wheat.

Hence there is no scope for trade between two countries.

Absolute cost differences

Countries	Quantity of Factor	Production of Cotton	Production of Wheat
India	10 days of Labour	100 Units	50 Units
Pakistan	10 days of Labour	50 Units	100 Units

In this, India has absolute advantage in the production of cotton, while Pakistan can produce wheat cheaply as compared to India. The cost ratio of production is:

India = 1 Unit of Cotton = 0.5 Unit of Wheat
Pakistan = 1 Unit of Cotton = 2 Units of Wheat

Since the cost ratios are different in the two countries, there is scope for trade between them. However, absolute cost differences may not be common and therefore comparative cost differences would be sufficient for trade to take place between two countries.

Comparative Cost Differences

Countries	Production of Cotton	Production of Wheat
India	100 Units	100 Units
Pakistan	50 Units	80 Units

India can produce both the goods cheaply as compared to Pakistan but it has greater advantage in the case of cotton. At the same time, Pakistan is at a disadvantage in both goods but its disadvantage is less in the case of wheat. Trade between two countries depends on the cost ratios of production.

India = 1 Unit of Cotton = 1 Unit of Wheat
Pakistan = 1 Unit of Cotton = 1.6 Unit of Wheat.

Since cost ratios differ in both the countries, there is scope for trade to take place. India's capacity to produce cotton is two times as compared to Pakistan, but it is only 1.25 times in the case of wheat. If there is no trade India will produce both the goods. But if there is trade between India and Pakistan, India will specialise in cotton in which it has comparatively greater advantage. Pakistan is relatively better placed in the case of wheat and if trade takes place between the two countries, Pakistan will specialise in wheat. Terms of trade between India and Pakistan are determined by the cost ratios of production. India wants more than 1 unit of wheat for one unit of cotton and Pakistan wants to offer less than 1.6 units of wheat for a unit of cotton. Actual rate of exchange will be:

1 Unit of cotton = 1 to 1.6 Units of wheat.

India will specialise in cotton and Pakistan will specialise in wheat.

Criticisms

1) A very important criticism against the theory is that it ignores other factors of production.
2) It assumes constant cost of production.
3) Another limitation of the theory is the neglect of transport costs. In some cases, cost of transportation is higher than even production cost. A commodity cannot be exported or imported unless the difference in its cost of production between the two countries exceeds the cost of transporting it from one country to the other.
4) The comparative cost theory is also criticised on the ground that even if its assumptions are accepted, it will not lead to complete specialisation on the part of the two countries which enter into international trade. If two countries – one big and another small - specialise and enter into trade with each other, the small country will be in a position to specialise fully because, whatever surplus it produces, it will be able to dispose it of in the big country. On the other hand, the bigger country will not be able to specialise for, it will not be able to get all its requirments from the smaller country.
5) Comparative cost theory assumes that internally factors of production are perfectly mobile and internationally perfectly immobile. It is unreal and does not accord with facts.
6) For military and strategic reasons, a country may decide to produce certain goods even though they can be cheaply imported from foreign countries. This is to avoid undue dependence on foreign countries which may become dangerous in periods of war.
7) The comparative cost theory is criticised as a clumsy and dangerous tool of analysis. It does not examine as to what extent the cheapness of production in one country is due to low wage, low interest, low transportation and other expenses. It is dangerous since it analyses only two countries and two commodities.

Machinery

Ricardo believes that the use of machinery in any branch of production is good as it provides a labour saving device. The only inconvenience is that of removal of labour and capital. He also admits that when a new machine is invented or applied successfully, the inventor would make additional profits for some time. But when it would come in general use profits would tend to disappear and on account of competition the price of the commodity produced would gradually come down to its cost of production. However, he is aware of the fact that employment of machinery is detrimental to the interest of workers. Though he believes that machinery and labour would always remain in competition yet he suggests that the new savings and accumulation should be invested in the employment of machinery otherwise these would be carried to other countries. In that case, it would become more injurious to the interest of workers. If capital is invested in the country, they get employment; if it is invested in other countries, they become unemployed.

Taxation

Ricardo defines taxes as "a portion of the produce of the land and labour of a country placed at the disposal of the government." According to him when additional taxes are paid to the government out of an increased production, or by a diminished consumption on the part of consumers, the burden will fall upon revenue. But if production does not increase or unproductive consumption does not diminish, the burden of taxes will fall on capital.

Tax on Raw Produce

Any tax which is imposed on the cultivator in the shape of land tax or tithe or a tax on the produce would increase cost of production and price. It would neither be paid by the landlord nor by the farmer but by the consumers in the form of an increased price. Consequently it would increase the wages of workers. Ricardo criticised this tax by saying that when the wages of labourers are increased, profits decline; there is a time lag between the rise in the price of raw produce and rise in wages. During this period wage earners experience great hardships. The delcine in profits discourages capital accumulation. The increase in the price of raw produce causes an increase in the price of all those commodities into which the raw produce enters, as a result of which home-made goods cannot compete favourably with foreign commodities.

Tax on Rent. Tax on rent, according to Ricardo, would affect rent only. It can be shifted by the landlord to any category of consumers. This would discourage cultivation as a portion of this tax would fall on the profits of the landlord.

Land Tax. It is levied in proportion to the rent of land. It is not applicable to that land which does not yield any rent. But the imposition of such a tax would increase price. If equal tax is levied on all land irrespective of quality, price would rise.

Tax on Gold. If gold mines are in the same country, gold tax will not raise the value in relation to other commodities till its quantity was reduced. As the least productive mines cannot pay the tax, they will not be worked. As a result, the quantity of gold produced and quantity of money will be reduced gradually. After sometime, the price of gold will be raised in proportion to the amount of the tax. The proprietors of mines will suffer in the interval. Ricardo mentions two types of taxes on gold: (1) Tax on the actual quantity of gold in circulation and (2) tax on the annual production of gold.

Tax on Houses. House tax falls on the occupier. It is an additional rent on the tenant. Hence the demand for houses will fall. The rates of rent will fall and a portion of the tax equal to the fall in rent will be paid by the owner of the house.

Tax on Wages. Ricardo is against any tax on wages as it will raise wages leading to a fall in profit. He examines the two factors – demand for labour and average price of provisions. The latter determines the amount of money that should be paid to the workers to purchase the commodities of subsistence.

Tax on Profits. While considering the effect of tax on profits, Ricardo took into consideration the profits of the farmer, the landlord and the manufacturer. He held the view that taxation on profits would raise the prices of commodities. The price of raw produce of farmer would rise if his profits are taxed. He will also have to pay an additional price for all commodities he consumed. The tax on the profits of the landlord would not be a burden on him for he would be benefited by the tax on the farmer's profits. He would be compensated for the additional price he would have to pay for purchasing the manufactured goods if their prices were raised.

Ricardo believed that the prices of maunfactured goods would certainly rise if the profits of the manufacturers were taxed. These prices would, however, not rise if money was imported from other countries.

Ricardo's Theory of Economic Growth

Ricardo was much less interested in economic development than in the theory of value and distribution. His views on economic development even if lacking in analytical rigour, deserve some attention precisely due to the position he holds in the classical school.

The Production Function

Ricardo's production function assumes the existence of three factors, viz. land, labour and capital, and in this respect it is similar to that of Adam Smith's production function, However, unlike Adam Smith's production function, Ricardo's production function is subject to restriction of diminishing marginal productivity due to perfectly inelastic supply of land and its variable quality. Ricardo having considered cases of both expensive and intensive margins observed that the marginal productivity of all the factors invariably declines unless it is regulated by technological progress. In agricultural introduction of innovations merely moderates the decline in the marginal productivity of land, while in industry the tendency towards diminishing returns is outweighted by the innovations and as a result, a tendency of increasing returns, sets in. For the overall growth of the economy it is necessary to examine as to which of these patterns prevails with respect to the output of industry and agriculture together. Thus Ricardo's views differ from those of Adam Smith with respect to the pace of economic development. Unlike the economy in Smith's system which develops at an accelerated rate, the economy in the Ricardian system grows at a continuously declining pace.

Ricardo's production function is :

$$Y = f(K, N, L, S)$$

In this production function K, N and L are the same as in Smith's production function. 'S' a new variable denotes technical knowhow. For identifying the determinants of the rate of economy's growth by differentiating the production function we get

$$\frac{dy}{dt} = \frac{\partial f}{\partial k} \cdot \frac{dK}{dt} + \frac{\partial f}{\partial N} \cdot \frac{dN}{dt} + \frac{\partial f}{\partial L} \cdot \frac{dL}{df} + \frac{\partial f}{\partial S} \cdot \frac{dS}{dt}$$

Land and Human Resources

Ricardo's position with respect to land is well defined. In his opinion the factor land included only the original and indestructible powers of the soil. Thus he viewed the supply of land as fixed.

Ricardo's theory of population growth is broadly similar to Smith's. Like Smith he distinguished the market wage rate from the 'natural' wage rate, which is exactly the same as subsistence wage in Smith's system. In Ricardo's opinion, market wage rate could be higher than the natural wage rate; it could also be lower than the latter or even equal to it. Market wage rate above the natural wage rate induces population growth. Conversely, if it is lower than the latter, population shows a tendency to decline. Only in the event of the two wage rates being equal population of a country will show no tendency to change. This similarity apart, Ricardo's views pertaining to population growth differ from those of Smith in a number of respects. In the first place, Ricardo does not endorse Smith's views that growth of labour is strictly proportional to the difference between the market and the natural (subsistence) wage rates. In Ricardo's opinion the growth of labour force is undoubtedly functionally related to the difference between the two wage rates, yet he did not think that the relationship between the two is of equi-proportionality. Secondly, Ricardo's population function is subject to the restriction that there is always an explicit upper limit to the rate of population growth. Such a restriction does not exist in Smith's system. Finally, as against Smith's physiologically determined subsistence wage, Ricardo's natural wage is a historically determined socio-cultural phenomenon.

Generally, market wage rate tends to conform to the natural rate. But the probability of the two differing from each other is not to be ruled out. If the demand for labour exceeds its supply, the market wage rate shows a tendency to rise, which in turn provides an impetus to population growth. The growth of population then first arrests the increase in the market wage, and finally pushes it downward to the subsistence level. Low market wages on the contrary do not permit any increase in population, in fact, over the time population may show a tendency to fall. When such a trend sets in, market wage rate shows a tendency to rise and finally conforms to the natural rate. *Ricardo* asserts that in the long run equilibrium the expansion rate of the labour supply remains in balance with the expansion rate of labour demand. He further states that in the long run the labour force changes are directly responsive to changes in the supply of capital and there are no reasons why changes in the former should not be proportionate to the latter. In the short run, however, the rate of population growth may be slower than that of capital. This will naturally rise the market wage rate, which in turn will provide impetus to population growth. In the long run, equilibrium between the demand and supply of labour will again be restored.

Capital Accumulation

In Ricardo's Theory of Growth, capital accumulation is a strategic factor. In his system the concept of capital includes fixed capital as well as circulating capital. The circulating capital generally grows in a constant proportion to fixed capital, and constitutes the "wages fund." Hence, it is the increase in this variety of capital which determines the increase in the demand for labour. Like Adam Smith, Ricardo ruled out any possibility of leakages between the processes of saving and investment. He asserted, "For no one accumulates but with a view to make his accumulation productive." The rate of capital accumulation in any economy depends on the ability to save and the will to save. While the former is determined by the 'net income' of the economy, the latter depends on the rate of profit. The 'net income' in Ricardian treatment refers to the surplus over the total product required for maintaining labour's subsistence level. Ricardo disagreeing with Smith stated that people's willingness to save and invest "will diminish with every diminution of profit, and will cease altogether when profits are so low as not to afford them an adequate compensation for their trouble, and the risk which they must necessarily encounter in employing their capital productively".

According to Ricardo, capital accumulation is an increasing function of excess profits, not of risk. It will be entirely given up under two situations. First, if surplus above subsistence level falls to zero, and second, if the rate of profit falls to such a low level that it is good only for compensating the risk. Both these conditions are interdependent and related to the productivity of land at the margin of cultivation.

According to Ricardo, profits are determined as a residual over and above the subsistence wages paid to labour on no rent land. Therefore, the rate of profit would inversely change in response to any change in the subsistence wage. The subsistence wage in the Ricardian system has a tendency to rise through time due to the operation of the tendency of diminishing returns. Therefore, the natural tendency of profits is to fall. However, periodically the introduction of innovation might check the tendency toward diminishing returns and thus the share of subsistence wages in total output at the margin of cultivation might also fall. During these periods, profits would rise. Ricardo, however, believed that this tendency could not perpetuate itself for long. Ultimately diminishing returns would set in and the long-run trend of profits will inevitably be downward. In the earlier periods the rate at which profits fall is quite low, and as a result, their share in total output tends to increase. In this period capital accumulation takes place at an impressive rate. Lateron, when share of profits also begins to decline, it reinforces the downward pressure on capital accumulation exerted by the falling rate of profits. At this stage the rate of capital accumulation slows down. But this is not the end of dynamic process. Ricardo asserts that ultimately the pressure of growing population requires the cultivation of the so much inferior land that at margin there is virtually no surplus over an above the minimal rate of profits. If some economy reaches this stage, the accumulation of capital completely stops and further increase in population becomes impossible. In the Ricardian system this is the stationary state.

The Ricardian Dynamic Process

Like Smithian economy, Ricardian economy does not advance towards the stationary state in a sustained manner. Its progress is often interrupted for short intervals by temporary equilibrium during which wages stabilise at the subsistence level, and as a result, population (labour force) does not fall to zero level and the rate of rent on investment in more than what is required as a minimal compensation for risk. These factors naturally induce new investment, raising the demand for labour. Excess of demand over supply raises wage rate above the subsistence level and provides impetus for population growth. In this temporary phase the rise in wages causes a decline in profit rate, leading to a slower rate of capital accumulation. Ultimately when the supply of labour as a result of rapid population growth again catches up with demand, the economy reaches a new equilibrium position. However, the economy's successive equilibrium position differ from each other in atleast two respects. In the first place, the size of population grows with every successive equilibrium position attained. Secondly, the economy's capital stock also grows larger and larger with economy's movement from one equilibrium position to another.

STATIONARY STATE

Ricardo's views on stationary state may be described as follows : To begin with, population is small. When the population is small, only the best lands are used for producing food. This, in turn, means rents are small and there will be a good deal of income to be shared between profits and wages. Everybody, except the landlord, is happy.

In the next stage of society, since profits are high, capitalists will begin accumulating more capital. Then there will be more demand for labourers. The increased demand for labour will raise wages above the subsistence level. When wages are above the subsistene level, population will expand. When population expands, the society is forced to cultivate lands of inferior quality to produce the necessary increase in food supply. This, in turn, means diminishing returns and increased rents. The relative shares of wages and profits fall.

In the third stage, rents rise further and wages and profits fall. The process goes on until population is so large, the pressure on land is so great and rents are so high that wages are at the subsistence level and profits are so low that capitalists do not wish to accumulate more capital. The society is said to have reached the stationary state at this point. Since wages are at the subsistence level, population will not grow. Since profits are very low, there will be no further capital accumulation and no further force to raise wages. The system has come to a halt. Only if there is some external change, such as improvement in agricultural methods, the movement will begin again.

According to Ricardo, there is a natural tendency for the profit rate to fall in the economy so that the country ultimately reaches the stationary state. When capital accumulation rises with increase in profits, total output increases which raises the wage fund. With the increase in the wages fund, population increases which raises the demand for corn and its price. As population increases inferior grade lands are cultivated. This is explained in the following figure:

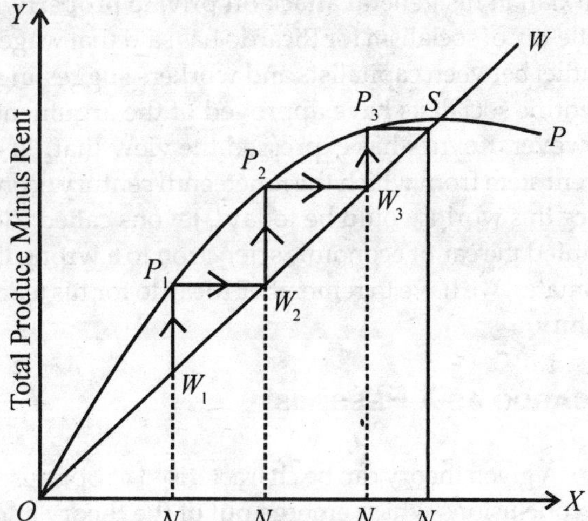

Fig. 5.

As population increases, the *OP* curves flattens out, due to the operation of the law of diminishing returns. The ray through the origin *OW* measures the constant real wage rate. The vertical distance between the horizontal axis and the wage rate line *OW* measures the total wage bill at different levels of population. Thus W_1N_1, W_2N_2 and W_3N_3 are the levels of population, when the wage bill is W_1N_1 the profits are P_1W_1 [Total product – Rent = Wage bill] ($P_1N_1 - W_1N_1 = P_1W_1$). When profits are P_1W_1 investment is encouraged. The demand for labour increased to ON_2, which pushes up the wage bill to W_2N_2 but profits decline to P_2W_2. This will encourage further investment and technical progress and raises the demand for labour to ON_3 and the wage bill will also increase to W_3N_3. But the profit will decline to P_3W_3. This process of capital accumulation increases the population and the wage bill will continue till profits disappear altogether at points from where the stationary state sets in.

The Ricardian theory of stationary state is a brilliant analysis because Ricardo brings together under one head the problems of production, growth and distribution of income which, in fact, remain the major economic problems even today. While Adam Smith looked at the stationary state as a dim and distant prospect Ricardo considered it as a real possibility. The Ricardian system is a major milestone in the development of economic theory. In spite of all his abstract logic, to this day, Ricardo remains an economists' economist.

Conclusion

Opinions differ regarding the contribution of Ricardo to economic thought. According to Gide and Rist, "Next to Smith, Ricardo is the greatest name in economics. Ricardo is the supreme example of abstract reasoning. He will be remembered as the master of deduction in economics". According to Eric Roll, "The main achievement of Ricardo is to be found in the theory of value and distribution". In the opinion of Haney, "One of his (Ricardo's) great services lay in the fact that, more than any predecessor, he separated economics from other branches of knowledge, and from ethics and from government in particular. With Ricardo Political Economy became Economics".

Above all, Ricardo provided the foundation stones of socialism. The Ricardian theory of value is the starting point of modern socialism. Marx developed his theory of surplus value only on the basis of the labour theory of value. The Ricardian theory of rent has become a powerful tool for every Marxian in his general attack on private property. The Ricardian theory of wages has become the battle-cry of socialism for Ricardo has said that wages can increase at the expense of profits. It implied conflict between capitalists and workers suggesting them the idea of a class war. Thus, the so called scientific socialists have approved of the arguments of Ricardo on value, rent, wages and profits. However, Keynes has expressed the view that, "If only Malthus, instead of Ricardo, had been the parent stem from which the nineteenth century economics proceeded, what a much wiser and richer place this world would be today". Jevons called Ricardo, "that able but wrong headed man "who" shunted the car of economic science on to a wrong line". In spite of the above criticisms and varying estimates, we have to remember Ricardo for his teachings dominated political economy for nearly a century.

Ricardo as a Pessimist

A given theory can be characterised as optimistic or pessimistic only on the basis of the nature of the conclusions which emerge out of the theory and which pertain to the course of events likely to happen in future. While going through Ricardo's system of distribution and economic growth, one experiences a note of predominant pessimism throughout the system. Ricardo's theory of distribution predict in clear and unambiguous terms the inevitable misery which lies in store for the mass of people. He painted a new picture of society in which every step forward leads to misery and starvation of the workers, a persistent clash of interest among the different classes of society and emergence of a stationary state–a state of economic inactivity – a stage of stagnation. The future of the society was dark – this darkness overpowered the mind of Ricardo so much that he is generally called a pessimist.

The laws of rent, population and diminishing returns were at the root of Ricardo's pessimistic attitude. All these laws overthrow the harmonious beneficial natural order and exhibit some of its gloomier aspects. The law of rent depicts the antagonism existing between the interests of the landlords and those of all other social classes. For example, the landlord's interest lies in the rising corn prices as they tend to increase rent. But the rising prices tend to reduce real wages of the workers and profits of the capitalists. Moreover, the theory of rent also shows that the landlord's income is anti-social because it is earned without making any effort.

Ricardo accepted the contention of Malthus that population increases much faster than food supply and proceeded to show how this affects the distribution of national income in a society. In his vision of an economy, there are three claimants to national wealth – the capitalists, the labourers and the landlords. The capitalists who direct the production of goods and services play the key role in the economic development of the country. They undertake production, rent the land from the landlords, provide labourers with tools and implements and advance them wages for their maintenance. In brief, it is the capitalists who initiate and maintain the process of economic development.

Whenever the capitalist undertakes new projects, he adds to the Wage Fund meant to be spent on the employment of workers. This increased amount of Wage Fund leads to higher wages. In course of time, the labour would multiply and the real wages would fall back to the old level. The food requirements of the increased population would require the cultivation of new and inferior grade land. The same amount of labour and capital employed upon the inferior land would bring diminishing returns in terms of agricultural output. This would mean an increase in the money wage of labour on the other hand as the same amount of food now costs more. Profits being the residue which is left with the capitalists after paying wages and rent, would decline as a portion of the national income. The progress of the society with its greater demand for food and increasing rents would lead to a reduction of profits, while the wages would remain constant. Finally, when the rate of profit falls so low that it does not appear to be adequate compensation for the trouble and risk involved in further investments, the economy becomes stationary. In such a situation, there will be no capital accumulation, all economic activity would stop and the population would cease to grow. A state of inactivity and stagnation would be the final outcome of all social progress.

The points of pessimism which arise out of the Ricardian analysis of economic development may be summed up as follows:

There is no scope of any improvement in the conditions of labourers. Their lot is predetermined. The wages would always be equal to the subsistence level. So all the efforts on the part of labour to attain higher wages are futile. The only thing which they should do is to reproduce less and voluntarily maintain a labour shortage, which is obviously a difficult and painful process.

There is no harmony of interests in the society as seen by Smith. Instead there is a constant struggle among the different classes. On the one hand, the capitalists clash with landlords because higher rents mean lower profits, and on the other, they clash with the workers because higher wages mean relative decline in the level of profits.

The outcome of all economic development would be a Stationary State in which the rents would be highest and the profits would be reduced to zero whereas the wages remain constant. This will be the end of the process of economic growth.

Ricardo's pessimism was not merely a theoretical impression but a practical reality. Ricardo's theoretical system and his pessimistic tone reflected the current actual situation. General prosperity of the people of France and England, brighter prospect for progress and stable condition of the economy were responsible for optimistic attitude of the Physiocrats and Adam Smith. Ricardo saw no prosperity but problems, no stability but uncertainty, in the country. The businessmen, though they were earning a lot due to industrial revolution, were anticipating uncertain and depressing conditions in future. Scarce land, rapidly increasing population and limited investment opportunities, all made future prospects bleak and convinced the businessmen of declining profits and slowing down of the process of economic growth in the long run. In the days of Ricardo, social classes were not living harmoniously; a tussle for supremacy was going on between the capitalists and the landlords. Under such conditions, it was but natural for Ricardo to paint a dull-shaded picture of the society and its progress.

Smith and Ricardo

Both Smith and Ricardo constituted the foremost exponents of classical economics. But their economic ideas showed certain basic similarities as well as certain differences. Ricardo had a genius for business and he was a successful stock broker of London. In fact his academic interest was aroused by his readings of Adam Smith's book, "Wealth of Nations." Thus Smith was a dominating influence on Ricardo.

But economic conditions that influenced Smith were different from those that shaped the economic thought of Ricardo. Smith lived during the time when Industrial Revolution was taking place. He could not foresee the socio-economic problems created by the Industrial Revolution. Therefore, he concentrated on production and exchange. The entire problem of distribution was of secondary importance to him.

But Ricardo was living at a time when the socio-economic problems and evils of Industrial Revolution had become more pronounced. There was a clash of interest between the landlords and the manufacturers. The landlords received high rents due to growth of population and rise in food prices. But manufacturers had to pay high wages to workers due to high price of food and their profits declined. Under this environment, Ricardo placed the problem of distribution of income in the forefront of his theory. At the same time he accepted Smith's theory of production.

Smith's theory of distribution was confused and scrappy. Ricardian theory of distribution was concerned with the manner in which the proportions of total national income were divided among the three classes–rent receivers, profit receivers and wage earners. In his pamphlet, he discussed the result of certain changes of this proportionate distribution. His ideas were influenced by the battle of the corn law carried out in the Parliament. He assumed that real wages were constant and that profits and wages were the variables. On these assumptions, he made certain conclusions about longrun changes in rent and profits because of the expansion of the economy. According to him, growth of population and capital accumulation will result in an extension of land under cultivation. Instead of using monetary terms, he analysed distribution and exchange on a commodity basis–in quarters of wheat. Under these circumstances, the rent to landlord increased at the expense of profits. Ricardo held that the interest of the landlord was opposed to that of all other classes of the community.

In his 'Principles of Political Economy and Taxation' Ricardo treated a more narrow range of subjects than did Smith. But in many cases Ricardo's treatment of the subjects selected was more intensive. His book never gave illustrative examples of a concrete nature so common in Smith's book. The book is rigorous and abstract throughout, even the examples selected were usually imaginary rather than historical or concrete. From our point of view and compared to a modern treatise, Ricardo's book lacked integration. But it provided the most superior treatment of economic theory compared to that of his predecessors. It was a "tribute to his greatness that both systematic classical economists and economists of socialism look to him for source and inspiration". The most unfortunate aspect of Ricardo's thought was that his theory was not based on solid factual presentation and observation of facts. It reflected the shrewed reasoning of an intelligent and observant man, based on the premises common to the upper class intellectuals of England during his time.

Smith's 'Wealth of Nations' was arranged systematically into 5 books. But Ricardo did not tie various points of his theory together. His treatment of value was apart from his treatment of distribution. In distribution his explanation of rent had no bearing on his explanation of profit. His theory of comparative cost as the basis of internationl trade was not tied to his analysis of cost of production. Ricardo analysed the three different determinants of value without tying them together.

Ricardo took much from his predecessors. He borrowed the labour theory of value from Petty and Smith. But his theory of value went beyond that of Smith in making labour the measure of value even in advanced societies. Ricardian theory of value was confused and towards the end of his life, he admitted his failure to explain the concept of value in a letter to McCulloch. But in his Principles, he developed a theory of value even more dogmatic than that of Smith. Except for very rare objects like great paintings, the exchange value of a commodity was measured by the amount of labour necessary for its production. While Smith held that this theory applied only in primitive societies, Ricardo went further and applied the theory generally. Smith and Cantillon had distinguished between short-term market value determined chiefly by supply and demand and long-run value determined by cost of production. Ricardo ignored the short run completely, and economics was a study of long range tendencies. In this respect Ricardian theory was inferior to Smith's theory.

It was a strange irony that these leading economists, through their labour theory of value, unconsciously provided the basis of Marxian economis.

Ricardian theory of rent was fundamentally different from that of Smith and the Physiocrats. The latter treated rent as a surplus arising out of the bounty of nature. But to Ricardo rent was not due to the generosity of nature. To him rent arose because of the growth of population and diminishing returns in agriculture. Rent thus was the creation of value and not of wealth. The Ricardian theory of rent provided the fatal blow to the beneficient naturalism of Smith.

Both Smith and Ricardo believed in the policy of free trade and competition and opposed the corn laws. Ricardo was a more dynamic advocate of free trade than Adam Smith. He greatly influenced the Manchester school, which organised the anticorn law league.

Ricardo followed Smith broadly in his theory of wages. He distinguished between the short run market price of labour which tended to equal the subsistence wage. Thus Ricardo, like Smith, was pessimistic about the prospects for wage improvements in the long run. Critics point out that Ricardo should not be blamed for these conclusions and these were the product of the socioeconomic conditions of England during his time.

They had different ways of contemplating economics. Smith stressed production, harmony of interest and optimism in his writings. But Ricardian economics stressed distribution and revealed the clash of economic interests in society. It was dominated by pessimism. Smith aimed at a study of economics related to politics and ethics. But Ricardo aimed at developing economics as a pure science.

Smith did not care to find the explanation for the socioeconomic conditions of his time. Ricardo aimed at discovering certain fundamental economic laws of the existing economic environment. Though Ricardo was a disciple of Smith, critics give him the credit for putting the English classical economics on solid foundations. Modern economists, therefore greatly admire Ricardo as a pioneering economist and a founder of pure science.

Smith and Ricardo differed in their philosophical approaches to their economic doctrines. Smith's economic thought was based on nature philosophy which he borrowed from the physiocrats. But Ricardo's economic philosophy was hedonistic and it represented the economic thinking of the manufacturing middle class of England. His economic philosophy was closely related to the industrial revolution which led to the change from domestic system of production to factory system of production. Smith's economic philosophy did not put him at the centre of any controversy. But Ricardo's philosophy put him at the centre of the bitter and fierce controversy during his life time. No economist faced such a great opposition as Ricardo.

To conclude we can say that Ricardo is ranked next to Smith. But even the opponents of Ricardo admired the man and his work. Ricardo completed the work of building the science of economics which was started by Smith.

MALTHUS AND RICARDO

Ricardian thought was influenced by the Malthusian theory of population. Ricardo took his differential rent theory from Malthus. He also borrowed his ideas on population and diminishing returns in agriculture from Malthus. But there was much he forgot to take from Malthus, viz., Malthusian theory of market gluts. Ricardo was a great analytical thinker and he often modified the ideas he borrowed from his predecessors.

Ricardian theory of rent was based upon the Malthusian theory of population and diminishing returns in agriculture. But Malthusian theory of rent was recognised by critics as superior to that of Ricardo. Malthus outlined his ideas on rent in his pamphlet on the corn laws. According to him, high price of food was due not to legal restrictions on imports of grains but to population growth and progress. An increase in population added to the scarcity of good land, would raise the prices of produce on land already in cultivation. As the difference between the price and production cost of food widened, rent would appear on the land in cultivation. It was only at this point that poorer land would come under cultivation. Thus rent preceded movement to poorer lands. But Malthusian theory of rent was not comprehensive when compared to Ricardian theory of rent. Ricardo regarded the landlords as a rather useless functionary. Rent was considered as an economic surplus for the landlord's private pocket rather than any financial advance necessary for the process of production.

Ricardian theory of wages was pessimistic and it showed that wages in the long run would tend to equal the level of subsistence. His theory of wages was influenced by Malthus. Like Malthus, he believed that any increase in wages would be swallowed by the larger population which the better incomes of workers would bring forth.

Malthus differed from Ricardo in his theory of value and theory of market gluts. But Malthus could not rival Ricardo in consistency and elegance of theory. Many observations of Malthus on value were criticisms of Smith and Ricardo. In many ways these observations were more acute and more akin to modern thinking than were theirs. His later reflections on the theory of value led him to a theory of demand which was a great improvement over that of his predecessors.

J.B. Say developed the famous classical law of market that supply created its own demand. The classical economists like Ricardo held that in the long run supply and demand were tied together and therefore over-production was impossible. There might be specific over-production or over production in the short run but there could not be general over production in the long run. But Malthus did not agree with this classical theory of market which ruled out general over-production.

Malthus regarded labour as the best measurement of value. Profits were lumped together with labour in the Malthusian definition of value. For the economic system to function continuously, demand must be high enough to ensure a continued supply. Effective demand was defined by him as demand at a level sufficient to cover costs plus profit for the businessman. It determined production. Therefore, labour was both an element in cost of production and also an extremely important factor in demand. According to Malthusian theory of market glut, the capitalistic production was not self-adjusting or equalising. Therefore, effective demand could not be taken for granted and some way must be found to increase unproductive consumption if the system was not to grind to a halt. Thus Malthus departed from Ricardo and worked out a theory of under-consumption which later influenced Keynesian economics.

Ricardo and Malthus differed considerably in their intellectual approach to almost everything. Malthus wrote to Ricardo asking his opinions on some currency questions. An exchange of letters resulted. They often visited each other and a life-long friendship was remarkable in spite of their basic differences in their approach to economic problems. Malthus had an empirical approach to all problems. He wanted history and statistics before he made generalisations. But Ricardo believed in deductive reasoning and where the facts did not fit in with his generalisations, in rationalisation. Thus Ricardo's method of abstraction was criticised by modern critics.

Both Malthus and Ricardo evinced great interest in the problems of distribution, unlike Smith who concentrated on the theory of production. During their time there was a public controversy among politicians and economists on the corn laws. They published illuminating pamphlets in order to influence the committee of the British Parliament which enquired into the grain trade. Malthus defended the corn laws and stated that high price of food was due not to legal restrictions on imports of grains but to population, growth and economic progress. Ricardo in his pamphlet pointed out that interest of the landlord was opposed to that of all other classes of the community. He showed that rent of land increased at the expense of profits. He did not come out explicitly with any suggestion for import of food. But he assumed that rational and intelligent people would conclude the merchants and manufacturers were in the right in the corn law struggle. But there seemed to be a dearth of intelligent people in England at that time because his pamphlet was poorly received and there were many complaints that Ricardo was unintelligible.

Malthus and Ricardo differed in their philosophical approaches to their economic doctrines. Malthusian thought revealed a dualistic philosophy. As a man he was an idealist. As an economist he was materialist. Ricardo, on the other hand, departed from Smith and Malthus. He was the champion of the manufacturing class of England. His philosophy was hedonistic and it reflected the economic philosophy of the manufacturing class of England during his time.

In spite of his differences with Ricardo, Malthus treated Ricardo with greatest respect and admiration.

QUESTIONS

1. Narrate and explain Ricardo's theory of Distribution.
2. Define 'Rent' according to Ricardo and illustrate that rent is the outcome due to marginal land.
3. What are the criticisms levelled against Ricardian theory of Rent ?
4. Illustrate Ricardian theory of wages and criticise it.
5. What do you men by the 'Theory of Comparative Cost"? Illustrate the doctrine.
6. What are the defects of the theory of Comparative Cost ?
7. Explain the concept of 'Stationary State' as expounded by Ricardo.
8. Discuss about the contribution of Ricardo to Monetary Economics.
9. "If Marx and Lenin deserve busts somewhere in the background, there should be room for an effigy of Ricardo"—Discuss and make a critical appreciation of Ricardo.
10. Write short notes on :
    (a) Rent is paid because the price of corn is high.
    (b) Assumptions of Ricardian theory of rent.
    (c) Ricardian theory of Rent and the Law of Diminishing Returns.
    (d) Theory of Profit and Interest.

Chapter 11

Classical Traditionists

INTRODUCTION

Classical economics did not end with Ricardo. There were many followers of classical school, who contributed to the development of economics. They were known as Classical Traditionists. In this chapter, the contributions of few economists have been dealt with.

JEAN BAPTISTE SAY (1767-1832)

Jean Baptiste Say was a follower of the classical tradition built by Smith, Malthus and Ricardo. J.B.Say made his own contributions to economic thought. He was the founder of the French classical school.

Say came across Adam Smith's "Wealth of Nations" by chance and the book had a profound influence on him. He says that, "When we read this work, we feel that previous to Smith there was no such thing as political economy". Say interpreted the work of Adam Smith. It would be unfair to regard Say as a mere populariser of Smith's ideas. Of course, he was a true disciple of Smith. Say carefully reconsidered and reviewed the ideas of his master with discrimination. He developed some of them and emphasised others. According to Say, "The work of Smith is only a confused assemblage of the soundest principles of Political Economy.... his book is a vast chaos of just ideas, jumbled with positive knowledge". J.B. Say tried to popularise the ideas of Smith by presenting them in a lucid and orderly manner.

Nature and Scope of Political Economy

Since Smith presented a confused idea about political economy, it became Say's mission to put an end to the vast chaos, to bring order and method into the statement of economic principles and also to make the doctrine popular. He had a clear idea about the nature and scope of political economy. According to him, political economy is a study of the laws which govern wealth. He divided the subject of economics into three main divisions–production, distribution and consumption. In the field of distribution, Say said that national income would be distributed in the form of rent, wages and profits. Say believed that the functions of an undertaker were different from those of a capitalist. He described the undertaker as an enterpreneur. This term has found a permanent place in the science of economics. By defining the political economy in such a lucid and simple language, he was equally successful in rendering the subject more popular and even to this day he is read with pleasure.

Say was in favour of inductive method. He argued that methods similar to those used in natural science might be followed in Political Economy. He regarded political economy as a purely theoretical and descriptive science. The role of economists, according to him, was to observe, to analyse and to describe and not to give advice. He emphasised that this subject was not a practical art and that its principles depended upon nature. Thus he regarded political economy as a positive science.

Say rejected the tradition of considering economics as a political art. In this connection, he differed from Smith, his master. Smith was a scientist cum reformer. But Say was a pure scientist. He treated economics as social physics. He thought that economics like Physics was an exact science based upon universal laws, and believed that the laws of economics were of universal application.

Doctrine of Immaterial Products

Smith recognised land to be a productive factor while he regarded doctors, judges, advocates, artists as unproductive. Say protested against this concept and said that nature co-operated with man not only in agriculture but everywhere. According to Say, services of a doctor cannot be called unproductive. Its production consisted in saying it and its consumption in hearing it. It has been consumed simultaneously with its production. Similarly the consumption of a song by an artist will coincide with its production. No doubt, these may linger on in memory, but these will have no exchangeable value once the moment of production is passed. Since they are incapable of accumulation they cannot increase the national wealth. On this point, Say comes quite close to Smith.

In the system as envisaged by Say, the entrepreneur is the most productive of all the factors of production, since he organises all the factors of production so that they may serve the consumers. The entrepreneur gets added bonus in the form of profits. There is no element of exploitation and the economic system works automatically. According to Say, the production of material objects does not imply their creation. Production only means the mere transformation of matter - creation of utilities – "a furthering of that capacity of responding to our needs and of satisfying our wants which is possessed by commodities; and all work is productive which achieves this result, whether it be industry, commerce or agriculture".

Value

Say's theory of value was an improvement over the classical theory of value. He was not convinced about the labour theory of vlaue. Say gave importance to utility. He defined utility as the inherent quality of commodities to satisfy human wants and therefore, it is utility that determines value. Thus he developed a psychological theory of value based on utility.

LAW OF MARKETS

Say's 'Law of Markets' has found a permanent place for him among the galaxy of economists. The Law of Markets is considered to be the greatest contribution of Say to economic thought. J.B. Say enunciated the proposition that "supply creates its own demand".Through this law, Say wanted to disprove the belief that general over-production and unemployment were common occurrences. In Say's words, "It is production which creates markets for goods. A product is no sooner created than it, from that instant, affords a market for other products to the full extent of its own value". The law is applicable to a barter economy where goods are ultimately sold for goods. Every good brought to the market is a demand for some other goods. Work is unpleasant and no one will work to make a product unless he wants to exchange it for some other product. Therefore, the very act of supplying goods implies a demand for them. In such a situation there cannot be general overproduction because supply of goods will not exceed demand as a whole. But a particular good may be overproduced because the producer incorrectly estimates the quantity of the product which others want. But this is a temporary phenomenon for the excess production of particular product can be corrected in time by reducing its production. James Mill supported Say's Law in these words "Consumption coexists with production and production is the cause, and the sole cause of demand. It never furnished supply without furnishing demand, both to an equal extent ..... whatever the amount of annual demand". Thus supply creates its own demand and there cannot be general overproduction and hence general unemployment.

Assumptions

1. The size of the market is not incapable of expansion. It is as wide as the magnitude of products offered in exchange.
2. Say's Law is based on the assumption of laissez faire policy as government interference will come in conflict with the automatic and self-adjusting machanism of the economy.
3. Income is spent partly on consumption and partly on investment.
4. All savings are automatically invested and the equality between savings and investment is brought about by interest rate flexibility.

Criticisms

Say's Law has been criticised severely.

1. Keynes does not agree with Say that since supply creates its own demand, there cannot be overproduction. Keynes points out that in the capitalist society wealth is unequally distributed between the rich and the poor. Marginal propensity to consume of the rich is low and that of poor is high, but the poor have little wealth. This results in deficiency in aggregate demand leading to overproduction and unemployment.
2. Say assumes that whatever is earned is automatically spent. But a part of the income may be saved resulting in a leakage from income-expenditure flows. This renders the law inoperative.
3. Say believed that rate of interest was the equilibrating force between saving and investment, but for Keynes changes in the level of income bring about equilibrium between saving and investment.

4. It has rightly been said that, "Say's Law does not hold in reality, every depression is a proof to the contrary". If this law was correct, then the periods of rising incomes, employment and output will not be followed by periods of falling incomes, employment and output.
5. The fundamental fallacy in Say's Law is that partial equilibrium has been extended to the economy as a whole.
6. Say believed in the automatic working of the economy. But the Great Depression reduced Say's glass house to pieces. Therefore, to keep the vehicle of the economy on set lines, government intervention is a must.
7. Say presumed the existence of perfect competition, but in real world of ours what we have, is imperfect competition both in the factor market and commodity market. Perfect competition is only a myth.
8. Sometimes Say's Law is defended in the excuse of long run equilibrium stating that in the long run total demand tends to be equal to total supply. But as Keynes remarks, "in the long run we are all dead, why worry?"
9. Say's Law considers money only as a device for overcoming the difficulties of barter. But Keynes gave a major role to money in determining output and employment in the economy.

Implications of Say's Law of Markets

1. 'Supply creates its own demand' implies that there can be no general unemployment and no general over-production.
2. According to this law, it will be profitable to have wide markets for, they will increase the demand for goods and raise their prices.
3. Say's Law became the basis for laissez faire policy. It implies automatic adjustment of the economy and hence there is no need for state interference. On this basis Say asserted that, "the very best of all plans of finance is to spend little and the best of all taxes is that which is least in amount".
4. Every one is interested in the prosperity of everyone else. It is foolish to divide the nation into producers and consumers, everyone is both. Further, in a nation, all occupations should flourish together.
5. Say's Law is an essence of free trade doctrine. He asserts that import is not detrimental to home production or industry because what is bought from abroad is purchased only with home products. Thus a market is created.
6. Say was interested in the development of industry. By ruling out the possibility of crisis of over-production, he wanted to avoid everything that might prove unfavourable to the extension of industry.

Conclusion

J.B. Say holds an important place in the history of economic thought. In the words of Haney, "He was not Smith or Ricardo; but he was no mere populariser...The history of political economy would have been different without J.B. Say". He was sincere in his efforts for transmitting the ideas of his master Adam Smith to the French people. He has left an indelible impression upon the French Political Economy.

JAMES MILL (1773-1836)

James Mill was born in 1773. He was the father of the famous economist John Stuart Mill. James Mill earned reputation as a philosopher, economist, utilitarian and historian. He was educated at the University of Edinburgh. He came to London in 1802 and became an editor of the Literary Journal and the Saint James Chronicle. He was a follower of Bentham, the leader of the philosophical radicals.

Economic Views

According to James Mill, the study of political economy raises four inquiries : (a) the laws regulating production; (b) the laws relating distribution (c) the laws governing the exchange of commodities and (d) the laws which regulate consumption.

Wages and Population

He believed that wages depend upon the ratio between population and capital. In his words, "Other things remaining the same, if the ratio which the capital and population bear to one another remains the same, wages will remain the same; if the ratio which capital bears to population increases, wages will rise; if the ratio which population bears to capital increases, wages will fall". Accepting wage fund theory, Malthusian theory of population and the Ricardian theory of distribution, he concluded that, "the grand practical problem was to find the means of limiting the number of births".

Value

Agreeing with the classical economists, Mill tried to revise Labour Theory of Value by emphasizing that capital was only accumulated labour, and profit was a reward for hoarded labour.

He admitted that capital was one of the factors which determine the exchange value of a commodity. He examined the old example of wine the value of which increased when it was left in the cellar. The people who had taken this example wanted to weaken the Ricardian Theory of value; but Mill wrote "Time does nothing. How, then can it create values?"

He believed that when people said that time had increased the value of a commodity, a certain portion of capital had been spent over it. He, therefore, concluded that if the value of the wine increased by one-tenth, it clearly meant that one-tenth more of labour had been expended upon it. This was a great absurdity.

LORD LAUDERDALE

He was born in Scotland and entered Parliament in 1780. He succeeded to Scottish peerage in 1789 and was elected a representative Scot's peer in 1790. On the economic side, he opposed Smith's economic system in a fundamental way. While accepting his individualistic point of view he took the 'Wealth of Nations' to task on the ground that it confused public and private wealth. His contribution to economic literature is to be found in his book whose title is "An Inquiry into the Nature and Origin of Public Wealth, and into the Means and Causes of its Increase". It was published in 1804.

(i) **Distinction between Wealth and Riches.** At the very outset, he emphasizes the importance of defining both the terms 'wealth' and 'riches' and stresses the distinction between the two. Thus he consistently uses the word 'wealth' when the appropriate adjective is 'public', whereas in speaking of the individual, he uses the word 'riches'. He further states that all previous writers confused the individual and national wealth and thereby were led to a mistaken idea that whatever increases the 'riches' of an individual will increase public 'wealth'. He particularly criticizes the views of Adam Smith contained in the passage dealing with the accumulation of capital wherein he says that, "As the capital of an individual can be increased only by what he saves from his annual revenue or his annual gains, so the capital of a society who compose it, can be increased only in the same manner. As against this, Lauderdale thinks that far from being possible to identify the capital (or wealth) of society with the sum total of the capital (or riches) of all the individuals, they are indeed fundamentally opposed. Coming to the sources of wealth and the means of augmenting it, Lauderdale concludes that wealth can be increased only by the means which produce it, namely, production by land, labour and capital.

(ii) **Theory of Value.** Value, according to Lauderdale, may be conferred on any commodity if two conditions are satisfied, firstly, the commodity, as being useful or delightful to man, should be an object of his desire; and secondly, the commodity should exist in a degree of scarcity. Thus, if the demand remains the same the value will increase with scarcity and diminish with abundance. But if the individual's 'riches' are increased by scarcity there must be an opposition between the public wealth and private riches and, as noted above, the increase of the two will depend on different causes. Thus, while the community is interested in abundance of commodities to increase its 'wealth', the individual, who possesses them, is interested in their scarcity to get an increase in the evaluation of his 'riches'. While discussing the four causes which lead to variations in value, viz., diminution and increase of quantity and dimuntion and increase of demand, Lauderdale anticipates what is now called the principle of elasticity of demand.

(iii) **Functions of Capital.** Lauderdale is also notable for his analysis of the function of capital in the production of wealth. He says that land, labour and capital are three original sources of wealth though they will contribute in different proportions depending upon the different stages of development. Regarding the function of capital he criticizes the views of Adam Smith to the effect that the profit of stock is paid out of the value added by the workmen to the raw material. On this view capital would not be an original source of revenue since profit would be "only a transfer from the pocket of the labourer into that of the proprietor of stock. Lauderdale, however, argues that the profit which capital receives is not a simple transfer of this nature, but it arises from its own independent services, i.e., "from its supplanting a portion of labour which would otherwise be performed by the hand of man; or from its performing a portion of labour which is beyond the reach of the personal exertion of man to accomplish". For example, if a man with a spade can do the work of 50 persons using their nails this portion of capital invested in the spade supplants the necessity of 49 people, who are thereby rendered superfluous and the return or profit on this capital arises from this displacement of labour.

JOHN RAE

John Rae (1786-1873) is an American writer though originally Scotch immigrant first to Canada and later to U.S.A. His book was published in 1834 under the title of 'Statement of Some New Principles on the Subject of Political Economy, Exposing the Fallacies of the System of Free Trade, and of Some Other Doctrines Maintained in the Wealth of Nations'. In large measure he also is critical of the foundations on which Adam Smith builds, and in particular of two assumptions; firstly, that the national wealth can be increased by the accumulation of private wealth, and, secondly, that there is a natural harmony between private and national interests. He argues that individuals in general increase their capital by acquiring a larger portion of the common funds. One grows rich while another grows poor; but while one man may add house to house and farm to farm the national capital itself may remain but little changed. In a significant passage, Rae says that "As the individuals seem generally to grow rich by grasping a larger and larger portion of the wealth already in existence, nations do so by the production of wealth that did not previously exist. The two processes differ in this, that the one is an acquisition, the other a creation. "From this, he is led to give greater importance to invention in his scheme of things. Invention can alone be said to create and therefore it is an essential element in the process of an increase of national wealth. He agrees with the views of Lauderdale in general regarding the difference between the public and individual interests which are not always identical. He, however, differs from Lauderdale in that he does not consider this difference in the wealth itself but one in the causes giving rise to individual and national wealth.

Rae also criticizes Smith's statement of division of labour who thought that the encouragement of invention was one of the consequences of the division of labour. Rae, however, holds that division of labour springs from invention (rather than the reverse) and is, therefore, the effect rather than the cause of increased productivity. Knowledge and discoveries mean the multiplication of instruments and tools which it will be wasteful for all men to possess since a bulk of them may lie idle. Thus, division of labour is dependent on the progress of invention and is not a cause but the result of progress.

In harmony with the above ideas Rae is led to a reasoned refutation of the doctrine of laissez-faire, to a plea for enlightened government interference. Since individual and national interests are not always in harmony and men are united in large societies it is the function of the legislature to achieve the public good. The legislature should act but act cautiously and Rae thinks that it should use the weapons of premiums, bounties and duties to achieve the national interest of the country. He much favours the 'infant industry argument' in so far as protection is concerned. According to him, it would be better if the necessary cost of the scheme is borne by the whole community rather than by a single individual since the prosperity of the industry will be in the national interest. Legislation should also promote intelligence and invention and prevent dissipation of the community's funds abroad.

KARL HEINRICH RAU

Karl Heinrich Rau (1792 – 1870), Professor of Political Economy at the University of Heidelberg for about fifty years, was the author of 'Handbook of Political Economy' (1826 – 1837); a standard text book. Rau believed that economics was one thing and the art of administering economic policy was quite a different matter and there need not be a connection between the two. Economic policy will depend upon national needs and local variations. Hence in his theory he followed Adam smith and J.B. Say, but on practical issues he stood for the extension of the functions of the State. Political Policy and expediency is more important than economic theory, so if the two clash, the latter must be subordinated to the former. In Rau's work, the mixture of Classicism and Kameralism is very evident

JOHN RAMSAY MCCULLOCH (1789-1864)

McCulloch was born at Whithorn in 1789 and he was educated at the University of Edinburgh. He was a great follower of Adam Smith and Ricardo and restated their ideas in more lucid and unqualified terms. In 1825, he published his own "Principles of Political Economy" and in 1828 he joined the University of London as Professor of Political Economy.

McCulloch was a great economist and statistician. He collected statistical dictionaries, wrote numerous essays and monographs, and a biography of David Ricardo. He was completely dominated by English classicism.

Wage Fund Theory

McCulloch was an ardent supporter of the wage-fund theory. Though he accepted most of the principles of Smith, he differed from Smith in the classification of labour into productive and unproductive groups. On this he was more a follower of Say than Smith. To him, manufacturers could produce utility and not matter. He gave an example in this connection – "Place us on the banks of river or in an orchard; and we shall infallibly perish either of thirst or hunger, if we do not, by an effort of industry, raise the matter to our lips or pluck the fruit of parent tree". He held that, if the agriculturists labour in growing corn was productive he could not understand why the work of household servant who turned the corn into eatable product was not productive. Even if no new matter was produced these works also were productive. He defined wages as "a compensation paid to the labour in return for the exertion of his physical powers, or of his skill or ingenuity". He, therefore, concluded that wages would necessarilly vary in accordance with the severety of the type of labour to be performed, and the degree of skill required for its actual performance.

Labour Theory

He distinguished between real value and exchange value and held that they ought to be equal to one another. The value should be determined by the value of labour expended in the commodity but this should be greater than the real value and the difference was exacted by the capitalist as profit. Even in this attempt McCulloch could not explain the surplus in any other way than as a mere profit. Although McCulloch helped to clarify certain established doctrines, yet it 'resulted in an indiscriminate mixture of ideas which shows a complete misunderstanding of Ricardo's real problem ..... . His statements on value are eclectic".

HENRY CHARLES CAREY (1793-1879)

Henry Charles Carey was an American and son of a publisher. Carey did not possess much analytical faculty and his observation of facts was also weak. He wrote 13 volumes and 57 pamphlets. His Chief works are: Principles of Political Economy (1837-40) The Past, the Present and the Future (1848); The Harmony of Interests, Agricultural, Manufacturing and Commercial (1851), and Principles of Social Science (1857-60)

Philosophy

Carey was an optimist. He witnessed an era of rapid expansion and vast opportunities. His optimism provided him with a belief in the absurdity of diminishing returns from agriculture and dangers of over population. He believed that the future of man was bright and there was no danger of over population. God would guide man to limit the procreation within desired limits. Increasing population was accompanied by economic progress and with passage of time man's control over nature increases and therefore, there is no reason to be pessimistic. When additional lands are brought under cultivation, labour's productivity increases and economy progresses. Carey believed in "Universal Law of Nature" and it eliminated the conflict of class interest. He also maintained that nature and human intellect would see to it that population does not increase beyond the desired limit.

Method

Carey praised and condemned the deductive and mathematical methods. While giving regard to use and accuracy of facts, he relies on intuition. He also thought that the laws of social sciences and physical sciences are the same. Laws of social sciences are based upon mind and intelligence which are manifestations of matter governed by natural laws.

Value and Distribution

Carey considered value as the centre of a system of Harmony. According to him, value is determined by the amount of labour required for the production or reproduction of a commodity. He regards value as a measure of nature's power over man and believed that value is caused by the obstacles to production. In his system, control of man over nature increases and so there is an ever decreasing resistance of nature to man's efforts in creating values. As labour productivity increases cost of production falls. This is present both in agriculture and industry. Carey believed that labour alone is the cause of value and it depended upon the quantity and quality of labour.

Rent

Carey's views on rent are interesting. He first agreed with Ricardo that best lands are cultivated first. But later on, he rejected Ricardian theory of Rent and pointed out that man cultivated poor soils as they were clear and ready for cultivation. With the increase in population, man started cultivating better and best lands. Carey identified land with capital. Farmer is like a capitalist. He did not agree with Ricardo that rent is paid for the original and indestructible powers of the soil. Carey's criticism of Ricardian theory made the later economists explore the entire field and make the necessary correction in the Ricardian theory. Carey's doctrine spelt an inherent harmony between different classes. In Ricardian theory, rent increased at the cost of profit while wages remained stable. To Carey, the share of both increases though the relative share changes in favour of labour. Thus a new distribution is effected—the proportion to labour goes up and that of capital is relatively reduced.

Profits

Carey considered profit as the return for the capitalist for the use of capital. He defined capital as the compensation for the use of capital–the accumulated labour of the past, while wages were obtained by present labour. It was the reward for time, attention, talent and sacrifice of convenience, comfort and health. Profit was paid for the use of things and wage was paid for the services of men.

Capital

Carey defined capital as "all articles possessing exchange value". He pointed out that capital was scarce and labour was unproductive. When investment increases, the share of labour diminishes. If the machine is perfect, the share of capitalist will be small. He believed that the condition of labour will be improving and the reward of the capitalist will increase in a diminishing ratio in the future progress of the society.

Quality of Labour

Carey admitted that the quality of labour differed from country to country. He observed that the main cause of low wages in India was that workers did a small quantity of useful work. Capital should grow along with the growth of population. The efficiency of labourers will increase with an increase in the reward for labour.

Population

Carey was not worried about increasing population because every addition to population brings both a consumer and a producer. When population increases, capital would increase, business and employment opportunities would be created. Carey criticised the two ratios, given by Malthus. He challenged the contention of Malthus that while man increases in geometrical progression, food supplies increase in an arithmetical progression. He said that if the descendants of Adam and Eve had doubled in every 25 years, they would not have found a room for standing on earth. He believed that if population remained stagnant, misery and vice prevailed, while abundance and prosperity were accompanied by a rapid increase in population. Further, owing to the cultivation of land, animals are destroyed and the carbonic acid which is important for the growth of vegetables would be deficient. Therefore, to furnish the necessry amount of carbonic acid, population should increase. Carey also puts forth that with the growth of civilisation, the rate of growth of population goes on declining. He has also argued that the increase in population means increase of wealth because greater the number of inhabitants, the greater the division of labour. Carey has also objected the conclusions of Malthus that, when people wage war against one another, they waste their time, destroy capital and do not produce foodgrains; when population increases rapidly, food supply also increases rapidly. People are miserable and poor not on account of large population but on account of their own misconduct and idleness.

Thus Carey was oscillating between two extremes, sometimes discarding Malthusian doctrine and sometimes supporting it.

Taxes

Carey divided taxes into four types: Specific tax imposed on each individual; tax on capital, tax on commodities and income tax. He considered the specific tax to be unjust and unequal because a person with large wealth and another with small income were to pay the same amount. He considered income tax justifiable as tax is paid according to their income. He opposed the maintenance of large armies and colonies.

Protection

Carey advocated protective tariff but believes generally in laissez-faire. A peculiar feature of Carey's system was his combination of a doctrine of domestic laissez-faire with protectionism. Carey was a strong protectionist. He began as a free trader but turned into a vigorous advocate of protection. Protection brings consumer and producer together. It leads to harmony of interests and the establishment of peace in society. His theory of protection was based on two considerations; first, the benefit of association, and second, returning to the soil whatever has been taken from it.

Carey was undoubtedly a great economist. He believed in associationism and man's control over nature. His method of study was a mixture of deductive, inductive and statistical methods. He had criticised the law of diminishing returns and the principle of population, the two pillars of classicism. His optimism was of the extreme type and did not find much support. His analysis lacked coherence and system and his ideas were full of inconsistencies. In the field of economic ideas, he has demonstrated a "restrictive emphasis upon theory" and it is this technical deficiency that has affected his reputation. Inspite of these defects, no doubt, he is an important figure in the development of economic doctrine.

HERMANN

Friedrich Bendikt Wilhelm von Hermann (1795-1868), commonly called the German Ricardo, was professor at the University of Munich and later served the Government in various capacities. He published numerous pamphlets on politics, economics and statistics. He did valuable work as a statistician. As an economist his chief title to fame is 'Investigations in Political Economy' (1832).

Hermann declared himself a follower of Adam Smith and quoted him liberally. But on certain issues he showed his disagreement with Smith and the Classicists. He did not believe in the identity of individual interest with general interest. Nor did he believe that the rent of land is different in nature from the return on other factors of production. Like Rau and Say, he recognized the entrepreneur as a distinct factor in production and made a neat distinction between interest and profit. He rejected the Classical Wages Fund theory. For him the real demand for labour did not arise in the employer's enterprise, but in the consumer's demand.

FREDERIC BASTIAT (1801 – 1850).

Frederic Bastiat, French economist and publicist, was attracted by the writings of J.B. Say and the Free Trade Movement of the Manchester School in his early years. He became an ardent liberal himself and spent his life and fortune in popularising his ideas. Possessed of a brilliant journalistic style, his writings had popular appeal and he became the leader of the French anti-socialist group of economists. His main books are 'Sophisms of Protection' (1846) and Economic Harmony (1850).

Economic Ideas

Bastiat was an optimist like Carey. According to him, pessimism was the great source of evil. The sombre prophecies of pessimisms have destroyed all belief in 'natural' laws and in the spontaneous organisation of society, and men had been driven to seek for better fortune in artificial organisation.

The main stress of Bastiat was on the natural harmony of economic interest. He was of the opinion that the principles of liberty and property endanger social harmony, and the free working of these two assures constant improvement of everything. He was a stanuch advocate of free trade. To him the policy of protection was immoral as it allowed more profits to one manufacturer at the cost of others. He attacked both protection and socialism as they represented an unnatural organisation of human society.

Theory of value

According to Bastiat, value is represented not by labour spent, but by labour saved (saved to the purchaser). It represented the labour saved into a valuable service. His was thus a labour theory of value, but put in a juxtaposed manner. To Bastiat "Service becomes the essence of value". He considered the law of value as something basic and central to economic theory and was therefore much elated over his own discovery of this new conception of value. He believed that he had discovered the final truth here and that all other theories of value were nothing but special cases of his theory. For example, a buyer would have to spend more labour if he wanted to get diamonds than water. The seller of diamonds, therefore, provides a greater service and diamonds fetch more value. According to Bastiat, others were groping for the explanation of value in terms of utility, scarcity, cost of production, etc. Bastiat claimed that his "decision is favourable to every one of them, for they have all seen some aspect of the truth; error being on the other side of shield."

Further, according to Bastiat, there are two kinds of utility; or rather he divides the total utility of the product into two layers: (i) The first layer is that of gratuitous utility provided by nature, free of cost. No payment need be made for it in the market, and therefore, it does not carry any value; (ii) The second layer is the 'onerous' utility resulting from toil and effort. This must be paid for in the market and it is this which constitutes the market value of a good. It should be realized that Bastiat's concept of value almost comes near 'labour cost' theory of value; but, his concept of 'service' in the value is not at all clear. The concept of service implies a benefit which need not be there. Moreover, there are many values which are in the nature of 'exactions' and exploitation rather than in the nature of service. It would be difficult to account for capital appreciation in Bastiat's framework of value. It will be equally difficult to see how land rent could be covered by his framework, if we look at the situation from the society's point of view. The real difficulty in Bastiat's theory of value is that the concept of 'service' is a fluid one.

Theory of Distrbution

Being an optimist, Bastiat criticised Ricardian Theory of distribution. Regarding rent, Bastiat held the view that it is only a payment made for the past services of the landlord such as reclaiming the land, constructing fences, drainage and fertilising the soil, etc., and it is not a payment for the orginial and indestructible powers of the soil. According to him, the rent of land would register a fall, as it was only a return for past services rendered, and with the passage of time, the services lost its value. Regarding wages, Bastiat was very optimistic. According to him, the wages increased continually because production became easier and easier and greater in amount. Hence labour's share was naturally greater. He believed that with the progress of industry, the gap between the workers and capitalists would become smaller and the workers would have a fair chance of becoming capitalists themselves.

Regarding interest, Bastiat held the view that it is a payment for postponement of consumption by capitalist. He believed that the rate of interest declined with a larger investment of capital. He contended that though the share of the capitalist declined relatively, he received a greater one absolutely, on account of the growth of capital.

His theory of distribution advocated complete absence of clash between the worker and the capitalist. The teachings of Ricardo and Malthus, according to him, implied antagonism of interests. Under the concept of laissez – faire and the region of liberty, there would be complete harmony of all legitimate interests.

Population

Bastiat did not entirely agree with the opinion of Malthus on the problem of population. He criticised that Malthus had kept his attention largely on the dark side. Distinguishing between the physiological capacity of human being for reproduction and actual reproduction, he contended that man was endowed with foresight; hence, would halt the increasing trend of population. Stating that population could not increase beyond limit, he observed, "If we put a thousand mice in a cage with only enough food to keep them alive from day to day, their number, despite their well known fertility, could never exceed a thousand, or if it did, there would be privation and suffering both of which tend to decrease the number". Using the phrase "means of existence" for "means of subsistence", Bastiat said that population tended to keep at the level of means of existence. Except for the differences in the terminologies used by Bastiat tinged with optimism, his idea on population is more or less similar to that of Malthus.

Free Trade and Lassiez-faire

Bastiat stood for 'Free Trade' and 'Lassiez-faire' doctrine. He believed that there was all-round harmony in nature's scheme of things, in social laws and in the class interests of different members of the society. Moreover, he believed in the subordination of producer to consumer. According to him "Political Economy should be studied from the consumer's standpoint". He preferred free trade to protection; though protection may be good from producer's point of view, it should be discarded from the consumer's point of view. His famous "The petition of the candle makers" is a satire against those producers who seek protection for their industries at the cost of consumers. The producers of these goods face an 'unfair competition' from sun's light which is admitted free to houses through doors and windows. If its importation is checked the producers of candles and other products wound benefit. The manufacturers of candles and other such articles petition to the Legislative Body as follows: "What we pray for is, that it may please you to pass a law ordering the shutting up of all windows, skylights, dormer-windows, outside and inside shutters, curtains, blinds, bull's eyes – in a word, of all openings, holes, chinks, clefts, and fissures, by or through which the light of the sun is allowed to enter houses, to the prejudice of the meritorious of manufacturers with which we flatter ourselves we have accommodated our country...." Though this is humourous, it contains an element of truth. In production, make your choice, but be logical, "for as long as you exclude, as you do, coal, iron, corn, foreign fabrics, in proporation as their price approximates to zero, what inconsistency would it be to admit the light of the sun, the price of which is already at zero during the entire day".

Bastiat's support for laissez – faire within the economy is also based upon his belief in harmony and need to give full freedom to exchange mechanism for the benefit of the customer. Government functions should be limited to the maintenance of order, security and justice and not interfere with the working of the economy.

Evaluation

Bastiat may be criticised on grounds of unrealistic nature of his analysis. He was fond of presenting his findings in the form of dogmatic truths. He has ignored the tactics to which producers and traders resort in their efforts to exploit the consumer. Market mechanism is not a perfect one. To say that value is determined by the "service" rendered by the seller to the purchaser is stating only a half-truth. To assert that cost of production continuously falls even in agricultural production may at the most hold true when new lands are being colonised. There are several inconsistencies and gaps in his theories. He failed to make any serious influence on the French economy. His ideas were mostly shallow and showed complete disregard for the facts of contemporary industrial life.

The ideas propounded by Bastiat were similar to that of Carey and as such he was accused of plagiarism. No doubt, he was an excellent economic journalist; but he was no theorist. Several of his views and analysis started with a big bang; but ended with a whimper. In the words of Schumpeter, Bastiat's case "is simply the case of the bather who enjoys himself in the shallows and then goes beyond his depth and drowns". His attack on protection and socialism presented his negative and destructive side. However, he was the first to give the law of solidarity a position of great honour in political economy which aims at the strengthening of social justice.

QUESTIONS

1. Explain Says 'Definition' of Political Economy.
2. Explain the concept of 'Value and 'Utility' according to J.B. Say.
3. Explain and illustrate Say's Law of Markets.
4. 'Supply creates its own demand'--Elucidate.

Chapter 12

THE EARLY SOCIALIST CRITICS

Robert Owen, Charles Fourier, Louis Blanc and Joseph Proudhon were the early socialist critics of the classical school.

ROBERT OWEN (1771-1858)

Robert Owen was born at Newton in North Wales. He had to leave his schooling at an early age but continued to read books on history, biography, travel etc. At the age of nineteen he set up as a master spinner and was able to expand his business rapidly. At the age of thirty he became a co-proprietor and director of the New Lanark Mills.

As a model employer, he enforced 12 hours of work in place of 17 hours and abolished child labour of 10 years of age and all fines which was a common feature then of all workshops.

In 1832 he established two remarkable things the Grand National Consolidated Trade Union and the National Equitable Labour Exchange, the object of which was to eliminate the use of money in ordinary business. His essays are collected in A New View of Society (1806) and Report to the Country of Lanark (1821). The two famous books written by him are - Catechism of New Moral World (1834) and What is Socialism (1840).

OWEN'S ECONOMIC IDEAS

The following are the economic ideas of Robert Owen.

IMPORTANCE OF ENVIRONMENT

Owen believed that by nature man is neither good nor bad. He is just what his environment has made him. His slogan was "Change the environment and recreate the society." The social environment was the outcome of legislation, education, deliberate individual action and other factors. Owen was the first social philosopher to emphasise environmental influences as factors influencing society.

Abolition of Private Property

According to Owen both labourer and capitalist are good but due to the institution of private property there is concentration of property in the hands of few. Owen wanted to eliminate the profit seeker the parasite, so to achieve this objective he wanted to establish some sort of combination. For instance, in cooperative marketing where the producer and consumer are brought in direct contract without the intervening middleman, whole sale and retail profits will be eliminated.

A cooperative central depot with a few branches, was established with 840 members in September, 1832. All workers were to bring their product to it for sale and price was to be declared in terms of hours of work undergone in making it. They were to be paid in 'labour notes' to that extent and these 'notes' could purchase any other product of a corresponding value in exchange. Commodities would exchange for the real cost of production and thus profits would be abolished. But in actual practice there are lot of problems in the working of the exchange. The value of the product was done according to the money value of the labour involved and prices were exaggerated by the workers. Superior goods were immediately sold and inferior goods were unsold. Some traders of London played a fraud on the exchange. They purchased the labour notes from workers, because they were not registered in their personal names and hence purchased all good commodities from the exchange. This resulted in the collapse of Labour Exchange.

Community Living

He suggested the idea of 'Return to Spade', which meant that workers should go back to their land because agriculture provided them with food. He even suggested the establishment of agricultural manufacturing villages. The number of inhabitants of each such village would range between 300 and 2000, but the optimum number was between 800 and 1200. The people were expected to live in large buildings in the villages arranged in parallelograms.

Owen purchased the community village of New Harmony in 1825 from the Rappites–a religious sect, who had immigrated from Germany in 1804. But the settlement of this colony did not function satisfactorily because the inhabitants who belonged to different groups, did not possess the necessary aptitudes.

Importance of Owen

Owen is sometimes considered as a dreamer of dreams for his ideas like the communist settlements and replacement of money by labour notes. According to Eric Roll his influence on economic thought has not been very great. But according to Schumpeter his ideas within the sphere of thought and action showed even crude common sense. He just did not know how to protect his case against the most obvious.

As a practical reformer, Owen was responsible for inspiring the movement for factory reforms. The first Factory Act of 1819, placing the minimum age limit at 9 years for children employed in

Industry was due to his personal influence. Owen's main title to fame is that he inspired the movements for industrial legislation, cooperative marketing and garden cities.

Owen in England, like Sismondi in France, was the first thinker to condemn the inequality, ugliness and waste of the capitalist social order.

In Labour Exchange Organisation, Owen had assumed the Ricardian theory, that labour determine value. His follower William Thompson in his 'Principles of Distribution of Wealth (1824) refined it — the concept of surplus value–as the source and measure of exploitation of the worker. Thompson in turn influenced Marx for whom the doctrine of surplus value became the chief weapon against capitalism. Owen has been called "The Father of British Socialism", because he gave British socialism a mild conciliatory and compromising tone, but insistent on reform.

FRANCOIS MARIE CHARLES FOURIER (1772-1837)

Charles Fourier was born in 1772 at Besancon. At the time of his father's death he was quite young. At the age of forty he inherited a large fortune from his mother, which helped him to devote his life to writing and experiments. His chief publications are Theory of the Four Movements (1808), Treatise on Domestic and Agricultural Association (1822) and The New Industrial World (1829)

His Social Philosophy. The Law of Attraction was the kernel of his social philosophy which he believed was operative throughout the universe. To him, the existing social evils have resulted from the artificial obstacles that have been placed in a way of operation of this law. It has made men anti social. His aim was, therefore, to remove these obstacles and establish harmony and peace.

Phalanstere or Phalanx or Phalangs. The Phalanstere was a communal organisation of about 1500 persons (400 families). To him, there was no free play of the twelve major passions of mankind, namely, seeing, hearing, smelling, feeling, tasting, enimity, love, fraternity, ambition, desire for intrigue, love of change, and desire for union. When these 12 passions are combined together, the result is brotherly love. He calculated that these passions could be combined in different individuals in 820 ways. It was, therefore, necessary that in an ideal society all these combinations should be possible and there should be a sufficient number of persons to ensure the result. He, therefore, suggested that people should form themselves into such voluntary associations, he called Phalanx.

In a Phalanx, dining rooms, concert halls, schools, kitchens, everything was common, except their living quarters. Services like cooking and cleaning are done together by all residents. The cost of living in such an establishment will be low because of economies of common cooling, heating and lighting and service.

The Phalanstere will be standing in its own grounds, an area of 400 acres, situated in charming natural surroundings on a river side. The land will be devoted to the cultivation of apples, fruits and vegetables, bee keeping and poultry farming. He did not encourage the cultivation of cereals because it is uninteresting. Each member could join any occupation he liked. So, it was a combination of producers and consumers – a self-sufficient world in miniature. The residents of the Phalanx are the co-operative owners of the entire property. They held their share on the joint stock principle, only with this difference that the net product is not distributed among the proprietors in proportion to the value of their shares, but in the following fixed ratio: Labour 5/12, Capital 4/12 and Ability 3/12. Everyone contributes his capital, labour and ability, hence everyone is entitled to draw his share in all the three capacities.

The management of a Phalangs was to be run by able persons elected from amongst the inmates. The inmates were co-partners in that industrial and commercial venture. The Phanlangs was an unique organisation in which the same person was worker, organiser and capitalist, but he had several responsibilities also.

There are seven essential conditions for the successful functioning of a Phalanstere:

(1) Charming surrounding, (2) all inmates as co-partners— no question of wages, all to receive dividends (3) short session of work – for two hours at the most at a stretch (4) work in companies of men spontaneously organised (5) excessive division of labour, (6) Guarantee of minimum of subsistence to free every one from anxiety and (7) development of the spirit of emulation and rivalry. Children are divided into three categories. (1) Nourrissons—upto 15 months, (2) Poupons—from 16 to 33 months and (3) Bambins—from 34 to 54 months. Those children who did scavenging work were called Little Hordes. They had to go to work at 3 O'clock in the morning. Until the age of 6 or 7 years no education was to be given to them. Two-thirds girls and one-thirds of boys, whose work was to design costumes for ceremonies were known as Little Bands.

He distinguished between an ordinary hotel and phalanstere. In a hotel any body can enter whereas in a phalanstere only members are allowed. Phalanstere is regarded as a cooperative hotel—a combination of consumer's cooperative and producers cooperative. Every Phalangs was to be established as a joint stock company. Only members are allowed to work and outside labour was not allowed. Dividends were distributed in the following way: capital—one-third, labour–five-twelfths, and management—three-twelfths. In a phalangs, production of cereals and establishment of large scale industry were prohibited as they would be a nuisance and create ugliness.

Attractive Labour

He wanted that everyone living in a phalanstere should be interested in work in the same way as young men were interested in a gala, to make their life happy.

Back to Land

The idea of back to land aimed at making a phalanstere a well-planned medium village where agriculture and industry prospered side by side. For this purpose a phalanstere should be established near a beautiful river, surrounded by forests and standing near the slopes of a mountain. By 'Back to the land' we generally understand that more emphasis was laid on agriculture, but in the system of Fourier cereals production and old tillage was not to be encouraged. The main emphasis was laid on horticulture and poultry keeping.

Assessment

So far as the influence of his thought is concerned, he must be credited with originating the ideas of the integral co-operative, the garden city movement, attractive labour and education and the greatest of all the co-partnership ideal. Co-partnership has been the ideal of many non-Marxian French socialists, who reject class struggle and expropriation. They maintain and foster the right of property and seek the abolition of wage earning status of labour by making him part-owner of industry. Fourier has just claim to be called the originator of indigenous French socialism with its ideal of co-operation, a trait which continues even to this day.

LOUIS BLANC (1813-1882)

Louis Blanc, a social reformer and an historian, is the founder of state socialism. His important economic writing is "Organisation of Work". It contained a complete attack on competition and a short and simple statement of Blanc's socialist ideal and also a scheme to implement it. His ideal was to create a new society and to prepare for the future without clashing violently with the past.

Economic Ideas

Criticism of competition: Blanc criticised the competitive system of economy. He considered competition as the root cause of all economic and social evils. Competition results in lower wages which brings poverty. Poverty generates crimes. Poverty is also responsible for other social evils such as dissolution of family, infanticide, child labour, prostitution etc. In short competition results in extermination of the poor, impoverishment of the rich, moral degradation, economic crises and crimes. Competition is an evil for both the workers and the society. It has destructive effects on producers. Competition makes commodities cheaper and profits decline. Competition also causes industrial crisis and international wars. Blanc advocated association as the only remedy for saving the society from the effects of competition and as the foundation on which the ideal society would be created in future.

The Social Workshop

Blanc advocated voluntary associations. He advocated the establishment of one social workshop for a trade or industry. In these workshops, state and labour would provide the instruments of production. Capital would be supplied by the Government. Managers will be selected on the basis of their ability. The revenue of the workshop would be used for payment of wages to labourers, to create a fund for repaying the advances made by the Government and for distributing profits among labourers. Wages and profits were to be distributed according to the capacity and needs of the labourers.

The salient features of the workshop are:

a) The social workshop is democratic and an egalitarian organisation. All profits belong to the workers.
b) The state would pay the necessary capital and would initiate the scheme.
c) Wages would be equal for all individuals. However, due to anti-social character of education, equalisation of wages was not possible. Hence there was a need for a new system of education.
d) As the social workshop is democratic, it would be controlled and supervised by the elected representatives of the society.
e) Cost of production in the social workshop comprises of interest and wages.
f) The social workshop is not the ultimate end. It is merely the first step towards establishing the new society.

Criticism of Savings

Louis Blanc criticised the scheme of savings banks. He thought that small deposits were part of an honest labour but increased deposits implied embezzlement and prostitution. He considered saving as unwise and a symptom of selfishness. Saving meant lack of faith in the goodness of the fellow workers. To quote Blank "In itself, thrift is an excellent thing–but when combined with individualism, thrift engenders egoism, it imperceptibly dries up in the best natures, the sources of charity–to save only for one's self is to manifest an act of distrust with regard to one's fellows and with regard to future,"

Role of State. To Blanc social and political reforms are interlinked. The former is the aim and the latter is the means. A strong state is essential to determine and enforce the rules for the society. The power of the state is also needed to materialise the scheme of social workshop. Private initiative cannot be relied upon to undertake such a huge task. The state will act as the founder of the social workshop and the intervention of the state will be temporary. The state is required to give a start to the scheme. "The state will just give it a push; gravity and the laws of mechanics will suffice for the rest."

Blanc occupies an unique position in the history of French socialist movement. He was neither an illustrious author nor an original thinker. He was the first to put an utopian plan into operation with Government help. He was on the border line of state socialism and associationism. He must be credited with having started an idea which acquired great currency in the years that followed – that of Government enterprises.

PIERRE JOSEPH PROUDHON (1809-1865)

Proudhon is the last thinker in the first phase of socialist thought. Coming from a middle class family, he had an early brilliant career and devoted himself to the study of social science and he wrote a number of books expounding his views on the current economic problems. His work on "What is Property" (1840) is important because it contains three important aspects of Proudhon's thought: (i) his scathing criticism of private property (ii) his labour theory of value and (iii) the philosophical background of his Anarchism (system of no government). "The Philosophy of Misery" (1846) was his denunciation of all previous socialists which earned for him a bitter reply from Marx under the caption, "The Misery of Philosophy " (1847). Proudhon did not participate in the revolution of 1848 because he believed that all governments were bad. Proudhon established the people's bank in 1849 which soon failed. His later life was devoted to revolutionary Journalism for which he was prosecuted by the Government.

Proudhon's Economic Ideas

Condemnation of Private Property: Like all socialists he begins with a criticism of the rights of private property. In the very first page of his book "What is Private Property" he says that property is theft and all property holders are thieves. He believed that it is the basis of all social injustice. But Proudhon did not consider all property as theft. Private property in the sense of free disposal of fruits of labour and saving, in his opinion, is an essential condition of liberty. Property is attacked because it gives to the proprietor a right to an income for which he has not worked.

Proudhon considered that labour alone was productive because without labour, land and capital were useless. So the demand of the proprietor for a share is radically false. The capitalist receives payment for doing nothing.

At one point, Proudhon undertakes to explain how it is that capitalist takes a profit from the labourer's product. The capitalist pays each labourer of a group a mere day's wage. But in the combined labour of the group there is an advantage for which he does not pay. There is a union through which the product exceeds the sum of the individual products of the separate labourers. As a remedy he concludes that labour should receive an additional proportion of the product. In accordance with these ideas, Proudhon propounds a labour theory of value.

Labour Theory of Value

He begins by mocking the economists for attempting a science while professing that there is no absolute measure of value. To him, the matter is simple. The absolute value of a thing. then, is its cost in time and expense. A diamond in the rough is worth nothing, cut and mounted it is worth the time and expense involved. But it sells for more than this because men are not free. So, society must regulate exchange and distribution of rarest things, as it does that of most common ones, in such a way that each may share in the enjoyment of them. Value based upon opinion is delusion and robbery.

Implicit in Proudhon's condemnation of property , is the labour theory of value. Proudhon advanced 'Surplus Value' theory thereby providing a hint to Marx. But his explanation for this is absurd. His idea was that many labourers working together will produce more than the total of what they would produce independently but the individual labour is paid according to the individual amount of work he would independently do. Thus the total wage of labour will be lesser than the value of their co-operative production and this difference amounts to the surplus value appropriated by the owner.

Proudhon's Ideal

Proudhon's ideal was the creation of a society based on liberty, equality and fraternity in which justice will be secured for all gradually. The gradual movement was to be in two directions. (i) The Suppression of all property which resulted in unearned income, because the criterian of justice, 'the mutuality of service', was absent in property relationship (ii) the extension of the right of possession of the property, the right of work and the right of exchange assured for every individual. In effect, he wanted that the fundamental attribute of property, i.e., its ability to exploit labour, should be removed. Thus he rejected the previous ideas of associations, as well as socialistic and communalistic schemes which curtailed the individual liberty of the worker. Proudhon wanted to harmonize property and community by limiting the property rights to those things that are clearly produced by labour but abolishing all the rights to interest, rent and profits. His insistence on the principles of liberty and free asociation led him to condemn any form of government. So much so, that he is often classed as an ardent Anarchist. He held "No government" as his ultimate ideal.

The Exchange Bank

Proudhon felt that the chief source of exploitation was capital. Hence the first practical step toward his ideal society was the provision of free credit which was to be done through the establishment of Exchange Banks. It will have the monopoly of credit issue, the workers will be able to obtain the instruments of labour without price. The Bank would issue " Paper money" in lieu of commodities deposited with it or a promissory note issued by the borrower of the capital equipment, because it was to be legally honoured. After the completion of production, the worker was to return his promissory note or commodities and the paper money issued to him was to be cancelled. Thus the worker would be able to get capital without paying any interest. This will ultimately ruin the capitalist who would cease to exist in his scheme of things. This was rejected by the French Assembly as being impracticable. Even the people's Bank established by Proudhon in 1849 was not an exchange bank but was like any other bank except that it had lower rate of interest.

The Bank was to issue notes against commercial goods only. It fixed interest at 2 per cent expecting to reduce it gradually to 1/4 per cent. After three months it was found that the subscribed capital had amounted to 18000 francs only–the number of subscribers being as high as 12000. On April 1,1849 he announced the abandonment of the experiment.

It is difficult to place Proudhon in the history of economic thought. Proudhon is neither a socialist nor can he be classed as an associationist, or an utopian or a communist. He was the great exponent of the ideals of absolute liberty, equality and fraternity which became the slogan of the French Revolution. So he was acceptable to all French Socialists who rejected Marxism.

QUESTIONS

1. What is meany by Utopian Socialism ?
2. What are the characteristic features of Associationism ?
3. Discuss about the experiments and concepts of Robert Owen.
4. 'Robert Owen is the Father of British Socialism'--Elaborate.
5. Discuss the economic ideas of Charles Fourier.
6. Write about the concepts of Joseph Proudhon.

Chapter 13

THE SOCIALIST CRITICS

The socialist critics attacked the old classical economic theory and suggested improvements over them. Among such economic thinkers, the most important were Sismondi and St. Simon.

SISMONDI (1773-1842)

Sismondi occupies a unique position in the development of economic doctrines. He represents the first major revolt against classical economics. He is also described as a socialist. Sismondi was able to highlight the basic conflict in capitalist system of production and distribution. He was able to identify the ailments from which the capitalist system suffered and thus provided a starting point for the socialist economic thought.

Aim and Method of Political Economy

Sismondi accepted the theoretical principles of Adam Smith but strongly criticised the aim, method and end of economics as put by classical economists.The classical economists believed that political economy was the science of wealth or chrematistics. Sismondi felt that economics was not the science of wealth but its main object was man or the physical well being of man. To classical economists, it is the increment of wealth which spells the well being of the society and its members.But Sismondi points out that the object really is to increase happiness of the members of the society. He advocated the way of increasing human happiness. He gave importance to distribution more than the theory of production. Ethical considerations played a large part in his thought and he aimed to put economics upon a new basis and laid down that it should teach how to increase national happiness. Sismondi says that "Political Economy at its widest is a theory of charity". Happiness can be promoted by increase in consumption and it is the sole end of accumulation, and in it lies the true wealth of the nation. Credit goes to Sismondi for regarding economics as a study of man in relation to wealth and not of wealth as such.

With regard to the method of economic analysis, Sismondi was in favour of studying economics by historical method of seeing every fact in relation to its social environment. He disapproved the abstract generalisation of Ricardo and Say but he considered Adam Smith and Malthus sufficiently historical and realistic in their methods. For him the study of economics was to be based on experience, history and observation of the social setting, because it was "a moral science where all facts are interwoven and where a false step is taken whenever a single fact is isolated and attention concentrated upon it alone". In advocating the historical method of study and rejecting the classical method of abstraction, Sismondi was the forerunner of the Historical School. Sismondi can be considered as the first economist to have started the battle of methods.

Over -production

The classical economic theory had established an automatic equilibrium between production and demand. Over-production was considered by classical economists as indicative of general prosperity. But Sismondi believed it to be a great evil caused by maladjustment. He could not assume automatic equilibrium as it was unrealistic. Sismondi did not believe in Say's law of markets or the deductive method of Ricardo in which there was no possibility of over-production. According to Sismondi, over-production resulted when annual production was in excess of annual revenue. He said that even if prices fell, production would continue. He condemned over-production as it created unemployment, reduced the purchasing power of people, and caused an acute distress.

Sismondi believed that over-production was mainly due to (1) the competitive character of the economy. (2) Production is determined by the supply of capital and not by demand and the separation of labour and ownership of means of production.

Competitive character of the economy brings in two types of maladjustment. On the one hand, it brings about uncertainty regarding the demand and on the other entails lack of mobility of factors of production. As the businessmen are unable to judge correctly the market demand, production is based on the availability of capital. This accentuates the problem of over-production. Workers have weak bargaining power and therefore, they are forced to accept low wages. This is the result of the divorce between labour and the ownership of means of production. Sismondi thus describes the increasing concentration of wealth in fewer hands along with increasing numbers of poor workers.

Class Conflict

Through his theory of over-prodcution and crisis, Sismondi was able to lay his finger on the basic conflict of interest between different classes. Sismondi did not believe in harmony of social interests. He was one of the early economists to speak the existence of two social classes, the rich and the poor, the capitalists and the workers. He thought the interests of these two classes were opposed to each other and they were in constant conflict with one another. The workers are not able to share the fruits of increased productivity. The profits go to the businessmen in the form of profits. Thus the gulf between the rich and the poor keeps on widening. It may be pointed out that, "Marx's idea that labour alone created value, and that consequently profit and interest constituted a theft, is entirely foreign to Sismondi." He believed that exploitation of labour meant that labour was getting less than its due. The concentration of capital in the hands of a few persons ruined the small scale producers. The society has been divided into two classes – the owners and the proletariate Property and labour are separated.

Population

Sismondi wanted population to be in such proportion to wealth as would ensure the maximum human welfare. He never suggested a large population. He believed that affection which created an urge for marriage, and egoism and calculation that place a check on the growth of numbers were the two forces that determined the size of the population by their interplay. He also pointed out that the labourers did not marry unless they were employed with an assured earning. Since the poor were exploited and their wages could not be fixed permanently, they do not wait, get married and multiply beyond the natural limit. Sismondi disapproved the Malthusian theory of Population. He criticised the arithmatical and geometrical ratios of Malthus saying that the latter contrasted with reality. According to him, it was the inability to get work and not the means of subsistence that limited the rise of population.

Machinery

The classical writers considered the introduction of machinery beneficial becaue it increases production and as a result, prices fall, demand for goods increases, which in turn means an increased demand for labour and expansion of employment. Thus workers thrown out of the work at the time of the introduction of machinery will now find work. Sismondi was against inventions and machines because they lead to evil consequences. His view was that the introduction of machinery reduces consumption and slackens demand. Machinery produces benefitial results only when those who are unemployed as a result of its introduction are ensured employment elsewhere. He also held the view that all inventions and machines were not bad. The use of invention and machines was justified only when the demand for consumption had surpassed production, so that increased production might benefit the poor people. These inventions and machines would benefit certain nations at the cost of others. In order to save people from the exploitation of inventor countries he suggested that inventions should be made known to all countries at the same time.

Distribution

Sismondi strongly criticised the distribution theory of Ricardo. He said that the end as postulated by the then economists, the largest possible production, did not necessarily coincide with the end to which all activities should be desired. The end was the achievement of greatest possible happiness of the people which could be attained even with a small production which was well distributed. Thus, Sismondi emphasised the need for proper distribution.

Sismondi recognised the existence of three classes of society – landed proprietors, capitalists and day labourers. They could receive for their services rent, profits and wages respectively. Sismondi made an illogical distinction between the annual revenue and annual production and explained that the revenue of the preceding year was spent on the purchase of the annual production. He wanted an equilibrium between production and consumption and effective laws for the regulation of distribution in the interests of the community.

Capital

Sismondi considered that a capitalist industry was necessary for the material happiness of the people. But he opposed concentration of wealth in the hands of a few. Everybody should be enabled to enjoy capital. He admitted that the nation's capital was amassed by the capitalists and their hirelings and the proletariate was left to suffer. He gave a comprehensive exposition of the law of capital concentration which led to pauperism; and the separation of property from toil created evil consequences.

Competition

Sismondi criticised the classical view that competition, in general, was beneficial to the people. Competition is useful only when it provokes the producers to increase production in response to an increase in demand. With stationary consumption, competition means race among the producers for increasing sales by lowering prices. Prices can be lowered by reducing costs and in their bid to reduce costs, the producers are inclined to cut wages and to employ children and women workers and to lengthen the working hours.

Peasant Farming

Sismondi was of the view that the benefits accruing from farming should go to the peasants alone. He praised the efforts of the French peasants to improve the standard of cultivation after their lands had been freed from the feudal lords. Sismondi favoured a small scale cultivator who could cultivate his land according to his choices and skill and enjoy the full benefits of his labour and industry.

Sismondi Reform Projects

Sismondi's aim was to lay down the abuses of the capitalist system in actual life and to demonstrate the necessity of state intervention. He thus became the first of the interventionists. He advocated state intervention to correct the immediate evils of the wage system and worker's misery. Workers should be guaranteed the right of forming trade unions, there should be legal limitation on working hours and guarantee of holidays and restrictions on the employment of children. The employers should be made legally responsible for "Professional Guarantee", a system of insurance for workers, including unemployment, accident, sickness and old age benefits. The financial burden was to fall wholly on the employers and not on the public exchequer. The rapid multiplication of invention was opposed by Sismondi because he feared that it created unemployment and economic crisis. He also opposed mechanised production and the large scale production.

Was Sismondi a Socialist?

Sismondi himself was not a socialist, though his influence on socialists has been profound. He rejected the theoretical principles of the classical school, but not to the extent of identifying himself with socialism. He was in favour of a more equitable distribution of wealth, but he would like it to be brought about without revolutionary means. On the crucial issue of the individual ownership of private property, he is explicit. He considered it both just and necessary. The revenues of proprietors, rent and interest were as legitimate as the wages of workers.

But Sismondi's economic thought reveals a distinct socialist tendency in the criticism of free competition, capitalist system of production, division of society into the rich and the poor, his suggestion for state interventionism for the provision of social security and the achievement of equilibrium between production and consumption.

Gray is right in saying that, "Sismondi as a writer of economics is extremely difficult to place". While having kinship with many schools, he is consequently at home with none. He was at best a social reformer, who stood for social security. A marked characteristic of Sismondi was his concrete and historical method. In brief, he was a historian turned social reformer.

SAINT SIMON (1760-1825)

Saint-Simon was a noble man who led a somewhat dissolute, adventurous life. At the early age of sixteen he took part in American War of Independence. During the French Revolution he gave up his claim to nobility. Towards the end of the Revolution by successful speculation in national property he was enabled to retrieve his fortune to some extent. From 1784 up to his death in 1825 he partly relinquished his interest in philosophy and devoted himself almost exclusively to the exposition of his social and political ideas. As he had seen new developments in the USA and always thought of new things and big experiments, he became a prolific writer. Among his writings on economic problems were included 'Industry (1817)'. 'The Organiser (1819)': 'The Industrial System (1821)' and 'Questions on Industries (1823)'.

Economic ideas

Saint-Simon's economic ideas might be summed up as an apothesis of Industry, using the latter word in the widest sense, much as Smith had employed the term as synonymous with labour of all kinds. He laid great emphasis on increasing the Industrial activity of the country. He stood for equality of opportunity for all people and he wanted that industrials should be given a high place in society. The lists of industrials consisted of farmers, wheel wrights, shoe makers, manufacturers of hats and cloth, sailors on merchant ships, blacksmiths, merchants etc. These industrials were broadly divided into three classes – agriculturists, manufacturers and merchants.

St. Simon's Parable

St. Simon's leading ideas, contained within the compass of a few striking pages, have since become known as "Saint-Simon's Parable".

"Let us Suppose", says he, that France suddenly loses fifty of her first-class doctors, fifty first class chemists, fifty first-class physiologists, fifty first-class bankers, two hundred of her best merchants, six hundred of her foremost agriculturists, five hundred of her most capable ironmasters, etc. (enumerating the Principal of industries). Seeing that these men are its most indispensable producers, makers of its most important products, the minute that it loses these the nation will degenerate into a mere souless body and fall into a state of despicable weakness in the eyes of rival nations and will remain in the subordinate position so long as the loss remains and their places are vacant[1].

From the above parable it is clear that the official Government is a mere facade. Its action is wholly superficial. Society might exist without it and life would be none the less happy. But the disappearance of the servants, industrial leaders, bankers and merchants would leave the community crippled. The very sources of wealth would dry up, for their activities are really fruitful and necessary. They are the true governors who wield real power. Such was the parable. St. Simon wanted to reform the social organisation, he wanted to create an industrial society.

Industrial Order

To provide equality and opportunity the society was to be organised. The main feature of industrialism was that the material resources of the country would be fully utilised. The main citizens of the country would be Industrials – manufacturers, scientists, engineers, workers, agriculturists, artists, bankers, etc. The noblemen had no room in the industrial society as they did not produce; but who dependent upon others. Every one was to earn according to his productive capacity. He held the view that industrial equality consisted in each drawing from society benefits which is proportional to his share in the state.

St. Simon stressed the point in new social order that private property should be abolished but there should not be any class distinctions. He divided the society in to two classes – national party comprising industrials and anti-national party comprising idlers. He wanted the latter to disappear.

Industrial Government

To Saint Simon , the function of the government would be limited to "defending workers from the unproductive sluggard and maintaining security and freedom for the producer. Therefore, to maintain peace in a factory, he thought , that it could even be undertaken by men of secondary level. "France was to be turned into a factory and the nation organised on the model of a vast workshop", which would not require any government . The main task assigned to the government was to organise forces rather than to govern men. He wanted politics to be transformed into a positive science of productive organisation. To Simon, Under the old system, the tendency was to increase the power of government by establishing the ascendancy of the higher classes over the lower. Under the new system the aim must be to combine all the forces of society in such a fashion as to secure the successful execution of all these works which tend to improve the lot of its members either morally or physically. The factory would be run by the government, the executive power would be in the hands of a chamber of deputies recruited from the representatives of commerce, industry,manufacture and agriculture.

This novel concept of government distinguished St. Simon's industrialism from economic liberalism. To him, the main function of the government was not the provision of justice and defence as is done by the modern governments, but the preparation of public works, provision for the defence of industrials, and that of employment so that it might carry out the enterprises of Industrial development and national prosperity.

---

1. Gide and Rist, "A History of Economic Doctorines". Page No.216.

St. Simon was not a socialist but a collectivist. He never proposed the abolition of private property. He wanted knowledge and industry to govern social order, based on universal association. On the one hand , he wanted collectivism and on the other, he defended private property.His industrialism and collectivism greatly influneced French writers like G. Sorrel , Louis Blanc and Anton Menger.His industrial society was intended to secure the greatest advantage for the greatest number.

The deciples of Saint-Simon or the Saint Simonians as they were called , evolved a collectivist doctrine from the philosophy of their great teacher. They made everything subordinate to the end of maximum social utility and hence would not allow any right of inheritance, opposed private property and advocated state ownership of everything.

Economic Ideas of St. Simonians

The St. Simonians have two important contributions to economic thought: (a) their all round criticism of private property from the point of view of justice, utility and history and (b) their advocacy of the suppression of private property and its replacement by collective ownership.

The St. Simonians, Bazard and Enfantin considered private property untenable from the point of view of justice in the distribution of wealth. The capitalist income arises from the ownership of capital,which is not earned, but is the result of exploiting labour. Here private property was bad from the point of the view of equity and common justice in the distribution of wealth.

The St. Simonians opposed the social utility argument for private property–first popularised by the physiocrats and supported by the classical school. Even though private property may lead to inequitable distribution, it was justifiable because without guarantee of the safety of property, the capitalist would not lend it for useful productive purposes. Hence the preservation of private property was essential to enable the socially useful production to continue. Such was the social utility argument. The St. Simonians on the contrary, actually acted as a hinderance to its development. Inheritance was a matter of blind chance and there was no guarantee that private property would pass on to the hands of the persons who were not best equipped or inclined to use it according to the needs of the society.

The historical argument of the St. Simonians against private property was that it was an institution which evolved in the process of the economic development of society. "Prosperity is a social fact which along with other social facts must submit to the laws of progress. Accordingly it may be extended, curtailed or regulated in various ways at different times". Far from being a sacred institution , private property had passed through such historical stages as slavery. The next stage of development of history, the St.Simonians industrialism, demanded that the inheritance of property, should pass on not to the family, but to the state which would secure equal opportunity to everyone of its citizens to enjoy it.

St. Simonian Collectivism

For the St. Simonians, the remedy for the ills of private property was the suppression of inheritance and making the state the sole inheritor of all private property.The administration of the state property and its allocation would be in the hands of competent officials called "Industrial Generals".

St. Simonian collectivism was a new type of social organisation in which economic activity was controlled and directed by the state. Individual initiative and capitalist enterprise were replaced by a system of production in which there was equality of opportunity for every person who earn to work, with ultimate elimination of the parasites who lived on the toil of others.

The St. Simonian scheme was thought out plan. Their collectivism was based on a social criticism of private property and as such is different from the communist schemes of earlier French Socialists.

Conclusion

The doctrine of Saint. Simonians is a mixture of realism and utopianism. Saint Simon's enthusiasm for large scale industry provided the inspiration for big banks, railways, the suez canal and huge industrial undertakings.The St. Simonians realised the importance of the institution of credit in an industrial society. The theory of profit seeking, for the first time, in the history of economic thought, was developed by Saint-Simons and they anticipated most of the doctrines of subsequent socialists.

QUESTIONS

1. Explain Sismondi's ideas of 'Competition' and 'Over Production'.
2. Discuss about Sismondi's proposal for reaching equilibrium in the Economy.
3. Was Sismondi a Socialist ?
4. Elaborate the economic ideas of St. Simon.
5. Discuss about 'Industrial Order' and 'Industrial Government' of St. Simon.
6. Explain the concepts of Simonians. How do they differ from St. Simon's ideas ?

Chapter 14

THE HISTORICAL SCHOOL

A. THE GERMAN HISTORICAL SCHOOL

The birth of the Historical school was a violent reaction of classical philosophy and methodology. The Historical school is the name given to a group of German economists who revolted against the two abstract tendencies of the classical economics in 1843. These economists emphasised the relativity of economic laws and institutions, upheld the inductive and historical methods of economic research rather than abstraction and deductions, and emphasised relationship of economics with allied social sciences like politics, jurisprudence and sociology. The school is divided into two groups of economists – one the old Historical School, which primarily devoted itself to the criticism of classical economics on the issue of the deductive method without substantially building any technique of their own. Roscher, Hildebrand and Knies were the main economists of this group. The other group was called the younger Historical School, which carried on the critical work of the first group, but also made contributions towards a practical application of the Historical Method. Schmoller was the leader of this group.

The thinkers of this historical movement saw that economic life was not isolated from political and social life but had close connections with all civilisation. They revolted against the one-sided and nationalistic doctrines of their predecessors and proceeded to formulate a historical method for political economy. While the Older Group originated that movement, the Younger Group carried the tendency further. The Older Group was negative in its thought in so far as the method was concerned. They did not deny the existence of laws in economics but they attacked the faulty abstract deductive method and consequently its absolutism and abstract deduction from ideal postulates. The Younger Group sought to develop and apply the historical method further and in so doing, they took a positive stand that the Older Group would not have sanctioned. They differed from the older group in that they denied the existence of non-empirical laws in Economics.

OLDER HISTORICAL SCHOOL

WILHELM ROSCHER: (1817-1896)

Roscher was the founder of the Older Historical School. Roscher did not repudiate classical theory completely. He asserted that economic theory should be supplemented with history; and studied in close touch with other sciences like Jurisprudence, political science and history of civilisation. He attempted to introduce the relative character of economics, tying the theory to place and time. "It was exactly because he combined with his new thought a useful exposition of classical economics that his work had a much wider appeal than did that of Hildebrand and Knies, which was differently designed".

Roscher denied absolute truth as to general economic laws. He held that the economist should confine himself to the statement of the laws of government which are applicable to his particular economy. He was not sure about the methodological issues. He regarded history as most important, because it alone can provide the historical sense which enabled the statesmen to solve political problems wisely. At other times, he advocated the collection of historical materials for purposes of illustrations.

Roscher tried to prove four propositions. The first proposition states that political economy is a relative science and cannot be termed absolute. It has to be viewed as one part of the social science along with law, political structure etc. The second proposition is that the current economic relations between individuals reflect both the specific character of the state and the cultural evolution through which it has passed. The state is not just a sum total of its individual members. Thirdly, in order to derive laws of economics, the information should cover as many people as possible, including comparative information of the old and new civilisations. Fourthly, different economic institutions have most probably been partly good and partly bad for all people. Thereore, it is a slow process to arrive at definite conclusions about them through historical method.

His depth of ideas and his contribution have been recognised by world renowned economists. Schmoller has rightly pointed out that, " Roscher is the most universally trained cultural historian among the economists".

BRUNO HILDEBRAND (1812-1878)

Hildebrand was the second member of the trio constituting the older historical school. He has given a much more elaborate and consistent opposition to classicism. He rejected the claim of classical school to have found natural economic laws which would be valid for all times and for all countries. He separated practical problems of economic policy from theoretical analysis and concentrated attention on the latter. According to him, economics had to examine carefully the development of individual people and of mankind as a whole. It had to produce an economic history of culture. It had to work in close collaboration with other branches of history and with statistics. He stated that Adam Smith, like Mercantilists and Physiocrats before him, erred in attempting to build a theory which would apply to all times and all places. The classicists forgot that man, as a social being, is always a child of civilisation and a product of history, his wants, his character, his relations to goods and men being ever-changing. Moreover, they are atomistic, making the individual the head of society and holding that society itself is based upon an exchange contract and private advantage being regarded as the source and bond of community.

Hildebrand cirticised classical economists for their materialistic tendencies saying that the scheme must aim at the welfare of the state. He distinguished three phases of economic development – natural economy, money economy and credit economy. This was a far progressive view as compared with that of Roscher which contained a cyclical theory of historical change involving youth, manhood and decay of the economy. Hildebrand looked at the credit stage as the goal for the economy. He did not suggest any modification in the theories of production and distribution.

Karl Knies (1821-1898)

Karl Knies was the last of the trio of the Older Historical school. But he was the most thorough and logical expositor of the historical method. He was more precise in his formulation of the methodological issues than were his predecessors. Knies not only rejected the view of the classical political economists that there exists natural laws, but even questioned the existence of historical laws of economic development of nations as believed by his predecessors. He distinguished the laws of social science from those of the natural science. The laws of natural science represent exactly similar cause and effect relationship. The laws of social science, on the other hand, are the laws of analogy which make the historical sequence of one nation correspond, in particular conditions, with those of other nations, but never identical to them. He criticised Roscher for having admitted the universal applicability of some economic laws and Hildebrand for making concession in case of pure economic theory.

Knies rejected the absolutism of economic theories. He said that economic theory should cast off its absolute character and instead be a product of historical circumstances. Economic theory is relative and not absolute, applicable to specific historical circumstances and not everywhere and at all times.

The three economists differ in the details and character of their contribution. They all criticised the classical school and their common stand here was that the classical laws could not be universal and perpetual because they had been derived on an abstract basis. Instead they favoured inductive logic. They wanted that the basis of analysis be shifted from the individual as such to the whole society and that the motives of actions be not economic rationality but the totality of the society. They wanted to widen the scope of economics and brought in a fresh approach. But they differed regarding the very existence and nature of economic laws. Roscher supplemented the classical theory with that of inductive analysis; Hildebrand claimed that there were historical laws of development and Knies denied the very existence of even these laws. None of these men, however, was in search of the type of laws which the classical school had put forth. The classical school considered economic phenomena and behaviour independent of the other dimensions of soical existence while the historical school took a much broader view.

The Younger Historical School

While the older historical school stressed a shift from deductive to inductive analysis, it was handicapped by the lack of statistical data and it goes to the credit of the younger historical school that its members could provide as much of insight into historical facts as they did.

The younger school was less handicapped that way. While the older school was more or less content to supplement the classical theories, the younger school wanted to have nothing with deduction and proposed to reconstruct the entire science of political economy by the historical method alone; and this group is characterised to undertake upon itself the task of collecting the necessary vast bulk of systematised data through an endless stream of monographs.

GUSTAV SCHMOLLER (1839-1917)

The younger historical school was led by Gustav Schmoller, the most influential historical economist of Germany. As compared with Roscher, Schmoller was more revolutionary in his methodological views and more interventionist in his social views.

In his outline of General Economic Theory, Schmoller attempted to make a comprehensive and dispassionate historical survey of ethnological, psychological and environmental conditions which influence the economic behaviour of the people and determine the historical laws of economic development. Schmoller treated each economic problem not simply as a logical issue but in its widest possible context. He considered first the genesis of economic institutions related to the problem; second, he demonstrated, with the help of empirical data, the present nature of the problem; third; analysed the problem; and finally, provided solution of the problem.

With the publication of Schmoller's book, the battle of methods, i.e., induction versus deduction ended. He was convinced that the use of both inductive and deductive methods was necessary for economic investigation. This is clear from his oft-quoted statement: "Induction and deduction are both necessary for the science, just as the right and left foot are needed for walking".

Schmoller rejected not only the absolutism of the classical economic theory, but the theory itself. According to him, economic theory, which is based on the unrealistic assumptions and which neglected the historical facts of economic life, should be discarded altogether. In its place, economics should include what the abstract theorists took for granted, i.e., the origin of economic institutions, their present behaviour and the psychology of social classes. Thus Schmoller identified economics with economic history which meant the study of historical laws of economic development.

Schmoller and his followers continued the practical programme outlined by the older historical school. The programme aimed at improving the working conditions of the labouring class through social policy. He also considered the influence of psychology, environment and ethnology. His aim was to develop economic science through historical, descriptive and factual material in order to relate it fully to other social sciences. His man was not fictitious economic man but the actual man revealed by observation and historical analysis.

His work "represented in a real sense an epitome of German historical scholarship". He has been criticised for having failed to develop all aspects of the topics dealt with by him, and for adopting admonition and moralsuation while discussing issues. Judged by all standards of evaluation, the work done by Schmoller was better than that of Roscher.

Friedrich List

List was born in 1789 in Reutlingen. After receiving formal education, he entered into Government service at an early age of 17 as a clerk. In 1817 he was appointed as professor of Administration and Politics in the University of Tubingen. As a professor, he attacked the bureaucratic administration of the civil service and advocated constitutional monarchy. This resulted in his dismissal in 1819. He was elected to State Legislature in 1820. As a member of the State Legislature, he advocated administrative and fiscal reforms like the abolition of tolls on roads, state ownership of industries, taxes on feudal property, excise duties, a reduction in the number of civil service officers and a single direct income tax. He was the founder of the tariff movement. List was a protectionist and the leader of the protectionist group. His great work was "The National System of Political Economy" published in 1840.

The National System of Political Economy

There was economic disunity in Germany. There were 38 inter-state tariffs in German confederation and 67 in Prussia. Germany was an agrarian economy and it was divided into a number of states. These states were weak and economically and politically divided. Hence List wanted to achieve economic unification and nationalism through protection. He believed that political unification was essential for the economic development of Germany. There were many internal tariffs and taxes but there was complete absence of import duties. The unrestricted imports were deterimental to the growth of German industries. Hence German merchants and manufacturers pleaded for uniform tariff and protection.

Theory of Nationality

List rejected the cosmopolitanism of Adam Smith and his followers. All individuals did not belong to one nation and as they belonged to different nations, they have divergent views on economic and political matters. Prosperity of an individual depended on the wealth of nations. If nations had unequal strength, the weak nations would be exploited. Therefore, he believed that classical universalism was a myth and he taught economic nationalism. List defined national economy "as the science which emanating from the idea and nature of the nation teaches how a given nation, in the present state of the world and its own special national relations can maintain and improve its economical conditions". He emphasised that Political Economy was a relative one and not a general one.

Degrees of Culture or Economic Stages

List gave five stages of economic development. (1) The savage stage (2) the pastoral stage (3) the agricultural stage (4) the agricultural and manufacturing stage (5) the agricultural-manufacturing-commercial stage. He considered the fifth stage as the normal one and every nation should try to achieve this. Only when a nation achieved this stage, it could support vast population, retain its independence, maintain a powerful navy, extend its area of influence, establish colonies for the development of foreign trade, and develop its arts and sciences.

The process of development from the first to the last stage depends on the natural resources possessed by the nation. In the first stage the country should develop agriculture, in the second stage the growth of manufactures, in the third foreign trade, in the fourth protective measures and in the last stage temparate climate, vast region and abundant national resources are needed.

Adam Smith had enumerated three stages of economic development, viz., agricultural, agricultural-manufacturing and agricultural-manufacturing-commercial. For him, the third stage was the most important one. These three were borrowed by List from Adam Smith. Thus the theory of economic evolution was not the original idea of List. But there is one big difference between Adam

Smith and List in the approach to the concept of economic evolution. Adam Smith had said that the realisation of the last stage depended upon the natural course. List contempted that it would be brought about by the adoption of protective measure.

Theory of Productive Power

List advocated the generation of future productive power. A nation should give importance to increase in production for the future, than the present production. He distinguished between wealth and causes of wealth. The latter was more important for the progress of nation. A man may be poor but if he could produce more than he consume, then he might become rich. Thus the power of creating wealth was more significant than wealth itself.

List distinguished between the Theory of Value and the Theory of Productive Power with an interesting example of two fathers. Both have five sons each and a surplus income of 1000 dollars a year. One of them invested his savings to earn interest, and got his son employed in some hard work; and the other spent his money on the education of his sons. Two of them became skillful and intelligent land owners and the other three learnt some useful trade. The father who had invested his surplus money on interest, undoubtedly became rich; he acted on the theory of value. But the father who had invested his surplus money in the education of his sons, acted on the theory of productive power. List commended the action of the latter. List considered the theory of value as nothing more than a shop-keeper's theory.

List also pointed out that the present state of nations was the result of the accumulation of the discoveries, inventions, improvements and exertions of the past generation. Present gains should be sacrificed temporarilyfor the future economic development of the country. He pointed out two types of forces which determined the future productivity of the nation: 1) The preservation of moral and social institutions namely control of administration, democratic Government, liberty of the press, freedom of thought and expression, invention of money etc.

2) His preference for manufacture and industry rather than agriculture. According to List in an agricultural economy several factors hinder the economic development of the country like dullness of mind, lack of liberty, prosperity and culture, conservative methods of production and outlook. In a country devoted for manufacture, there was the existence of a strong sense of liberty, increase in skill and moral values leading to increased production. As a result the economic resources of the country were fully utilised. He also criticised Adam Smith for his concept of division of labour, as it was confined only to foreign trade. Smith did not take into account the benefits of division of labour for the whole nation. If division of labour was applied to the entire nation, it was expected to develop the whole nation. Thus List introduced the idea of nationality in contrast to cosmopolitanism and the idea of productive power as contrasted with that of exchange values.

Protection

List advocated the development of industry through protection. Smith and Ricardo believed in the natural development of the economic institutions. But List was of the opinion that industrial development was possible in a planned manner only with the use of protective measures. List pointed out four important features of the policy of protection:

(1) Protection should not be given to agriculture because it will lead to increase in food prices, high cost of living and high wages, which would affect the growth of industries.

(2) Protection was necessary only to provide industrial education.

(3) Protection should be granted only when the domestic industries have failed to compete with established industries of other nations, and protection should be withdrawn after their maturity.

(4) Protection is desiarable only for countries which have their necessary resources and the people who have the necessary ability and aptitude for industrial activity. Protection should be given first to industries that belonged to necessaries of life and List never suggested protection as permanent economic policy.

List suggested that protective duties should be imposed on imported goods. He criticised Adam Smith and J.B. Say for having misunderstood the policies of mercantalists, because they themselves advised nations to purchase from the cheapest market and sell it in the dearest market. He divided the mercantalists into two categories : (i) those who emphasised the importance of industrial potentiality based on the acquirement of industrial and technical training and (ii) those who emphasised the conception of balance of trade. Out of these two, List approved of the first category and outrightly rejected the second one.

The essential difference between the protectionism of mercantalist and List was that the former applied protection as a permanent economic policy to all industries, including agriculture. List's protection was a mere transitory system.

Critical Estimate

List has been rightly called the Father of American protectionism and the messenger of economic nationalism. List gave the new ideas of economic nationalism and future productive power to the science of economics. He emphasised nationality and his ideas provided a great stimulus to the historical school of economics. The classical political economy provided a static concept of economic development. But List introduced dynamism which leads to the achievement of great national power. List has been accepted as the first German hero who sacrificed for the unification and industrial development of the nation.

Critical Ideas of Historical School

The historical school attacked the classical economics on three grounds: (a) Universality of economic laws, (b) Crude psychological assumptions and (c) Use of deductive method.

The belief of the classical writers in the Universality of their doctrines is not justified. The historians pointed out that economic laws are relative and not absolute and therefore cannot be applied everywhere and at all times. Economic laws are subject to change both in theory and in practice. In practice, economic laws cannot be indiscriminately applied to all countries, and in all stages of economic development. In order to make them practically useful, they are to be adapted according to the varying conditions of time and place. For example, the doctrine of free trade is useful in the industrialy advanced countries while that of protection is desirable for the poor developing nations. Theoretically, too, the laws of economics are not as universal and inevitable as the laws of physics and chemistry are. Economic laws are at once provisional and conditional. They are provisional because the progress of history brings to light new facts and economic laws have to be modified accordingly if they are to account for these new facts. They are conditional in the sense that economic laws are only true so long as the assumptions on which they are founded are true and other circumstances do not disturb their operation.

The historians were right so far as they pointed out the relative character of economic laws. But this is not a sufficient reason to separate the economic laws from the laws of other sciences. In fact, all laws, whether economic or physical, are provisional and conditional. The only difference is that while the physical laws are more stable and certain because of the greater uniformity in the conditions that give rise to them and the greater accuracy with which their action is measured, the economic laws are comparatively less stable because of the constantly changing conditions they account for. Under the influence of the historical critics, the modern economists ceased to regard economic laws as absolutely valid. Marshall, for example, considered an economic law as essentially a statement of economic tendencies and not a universal truth.

The second charge which the historians levelled against the classical economists is that their psychological assumptions on which it was based were crude and inadequate. The classical writers assumed that man is solely guided by the consideration of self-interest and is fully absorbed in the gainful activities. The historians, on the other hand, pointed out that self-interest is not the only motivation in the economic world. Man's actions are directed by a variety of motives, such as, vanity, love, pity, glory, pleasure, duty, benevolence, custom, etc. By over emphasising self-interest and neglecting other motives altogether, the calssicists had simply attempted, as Hildebrand remarked to "transform political economy into a mere natural history of egoism".

The classical economists were concerned not with an individual's action but with the action of the crowd. If we leave aside individual differences in special cases and study the various motives influencing economic activities in general, we will find that self-interest is the common and constant motive in almost all the cases.

However, under the impact of the historical economists, the concept of 'economic man' – an imaginary human being, devoid of all motives except self-interest – is abandoned by the modern economists. Now economics is concerned not with an abstract or economic man, but with a man of flesh and blood.

The third criticism is regarding the indiscriminate use of the deductive or abstract method. The classical economists started with a certain prior assumptions and deduced from them all economic laws through the simple process of reasoning. The historical economists considered such laws insufficient as they do not take into account the numerous motives actually operative in the economic world. True theory is that which explains the multiplicity of economic phenomena and such a theory can be constructed only by induction from observed facts about the complex economic life.

But here the historical economists confused two things; the particular use of the deductive method and the deductive method itself. So far as the historians attacked the indiscriminate and wrong use of deductive method by the classical writers and consequently rejected their unsatisfactory analysis and hasty conclusions, they are fully justified in their attack. But to conclude from this that the deductive method itself is illegitimate is not correct. In a science like economics, which deals with complex economic phenomena and where experiments are not possible, abstraction and analysis provide the only means of scientific investigation. It is through this method that we can examine the effect of a particular motive on economic action and escape from all other complex influences. Today, the controversy regarding the relative merit of the two methods is over. The economists are of the view that both the methods are necessary for the proper development of the economic science.

Positive Ideas of the Historical School

The positive contributions made by the historical school are more important, than its criticisms of the classical school. In their positive contribution to economic thought, the historical economists presented an entirely different view of the aim and scope of economics. The fundamental difference between the classicists and historians was that while the classical thinkers approached the economic phenomena from the mechanic point of view, the historians approached it from the organic point of view. The classical economists concentrated their attention only on those economic problems that could be explained by the simple mechanical principles. For example, the problems of price fluctuations, interest rate, wages and rent are all explained by the mechanical interplay of free individuals guided by their self-interests and competing with each other for individual gains. But such mechanical principles tell us nothing about the extremely varied and constantly changing aspects of economic life. In nut-shell, the mechanical conception leaves the actual periods of history unexplained and it is here that the organic approach claims superiority.

The organic approach of the historical economists analysed man's economic activity in relation to his environment. The nature of man's actions and their effects differ according to the physical, social, religious and political conditions in which he lives. Geographical conditions, natural resources, efficiency of labour, entreprenurial skill, level of technology, all these factors which influence the economic institutions and determine the stage of economic development vary from nation to nation and from time to time. Thus, to have a true picture of the complex economic life, man's actions should be studied not in isolation but in relation to his surroundings. The defect of the mechanical approach is that it considers man's activity but ignores his environment. Social environment is constantly changing. It is in the process of transformation and of evolution. Thus to have a proper understanding of present economic life, knowledge of the successive stages of economic development in the past is essential. As Hildebrand has remarked, "Man as a social being is essentially a child of civilisation and a product of history".

The historical school became instrumental in driving home the importance of the truth that there has to be a proper balance between facts and logic. The two must supplement each other. Theory has no meaning unless it can be substantiated by facts and a collection of facts is useless without our being able to derive certain conclusions from them. According to Eric Roll, "Their one positive achievement was to stimulate research in economic history". The historical school had great influence on some leading theoretical economists like Alfred Marshall. However, one main criticism against the historical school is that there is over-emphasis on historical element in their studies. History tells us of sequences and coincidences; but reason alone can interpret and draw lessons from them. The historical inductive method has become complementary to the abstract deductive approach. Marx made great use of historical method. The economists of the historical school are to be thanked for their valuable studies in economic history. These studies have provided us data for verifying and correcting the theory of the classical economists.

B. THE BRITISH HISTORICAL SCHOOL

The deductive method of classical school gave rise to a group of critics known as the 'Historical Critics'. Their objective was not to propound a theory. They were not satisfied with the narrow outlook of the classical economists and desired to broaden the scope of economics. They emphasised that economic problems should be studied with reference to the past as well as to the present. The classical economists used the deductive method because at that time the canons of induction were not so developed as they developed later. They did not make frequent use of historical facts. Ricardo's methodology was the supreme example of abstract reasoning. Thus a host of writers called British Historical School attacked Smith and Ricardo for making abstract generalisation and for narrowing the scope of economics. Chief among these writers were Richard Jones, Water Bagehot, Cliffe leslie, Ingram, Arnold Toynbee, Thorold and Ashley.

Richard Jones (1790-1855)

Richard Jones is generally regarded as an isolated representative of the historical methods in England in the nineteenth century. His major works are "An Essay on the Distribution of Wealth and on the Sources of Taxation," 'An Introductory Lecture on Political Economy', and "Text Book of Lectures on the Political Economy of Nations." Most of his views on economic subjects are found in these important works. Jones blamed Physiocrates for treating agriculture the only source of surplus. He had also made vigorous attack on the Ricardian theory of rent. According to Jones rent was of two types: 'peasant rent' and 'farmer's rent'. From the practical point of view, 'peasant rents' are more important. Jones criticised the abstract suppositions made by Ricardo. Ricardo assumed that (1) lands were first appropriated by those who were prepared to take pains involved in cultivating it and (2) there was free access to uncultivated lands. Jones regarded these assumptions not correct, since these are not supported by historical facts. Credit goès to Jones for inviting attention to the fact that the term rent in common usage means contract rent and not economic rent. Jones also criticised the wages fund theory. The economic ideas of Jones were brought to the outside world by Dr. Whewell who only published his writings.

Water Bagehot (1826-1877)

Bagehot's chief contribution lies in his reconciliation between facts and theories supported by history. He was a banker and writer and edited the "Economist". His greatest positive contribution to economic thought lay in the field of money and banking and the functions of an entrepreneur or capitalist. Entrepreneur was considered a productive agent and his expenses will amount to the cost of production of any commodity.

He wrcte articles on 'International coinage', 'Lambard Street', 'Depreciation of Silver, and Economic Studies'. He wanted the use of both deductive and inductive methods. According to him, the historical and deductive methods were not contrary to each other. Physical Sciences require more verification. However statistics were "Scrap of Scraps". He was the first of the English economist to appreciate the idea of evolution in connection with the social science. His three objections to the English political economy were: (1) the propositions suited to a society of grown up competitive commerce only, (2) their principles did not apply universally as they were abstract and (3) it lacked verification. His criticism was constructive.

John Kells Ingram

Ingram's famous works are "the Present Position and Prospects of Political Economy" and

"History of Political Economy." His views are contained in these works. He was a reputed scholar of philosophy, political science and several literatures. He served for many years as Professor of Greek and Professor of Oratory and English Literature. He treated economics as a branch of sociology. He criticised classical political economy on the following grounds : (1) improper use of deduction (2) too absolute character of theoretical conclusions (3) too much emphasis on wealth and (4) the abstract way of presenting conceptions. The results of these abstractions was that they arrived at wrong conclusions which are useless for practical purposes. Thus the classical writers were too individualistic according to Ingram. He wanted the economic studies to be based on physics and biology. To him economic laws should reflect changing developments. His History of Political Doctrines were essentially relative and has proved that the classical ideas were the product of their environment. He was an optimist, hence he did not accept the Ricardian view that the worker's condition could not be improved under competition and private property. However Toynbee said that free trade, factory legislation, trade unions and cooperative societies have definitely improved the wages of the labourers. He also favoured the extension of public enterprise and public housing. He was not an opponent of deductive method but he criticised the classical writers for making excessive use of the deductive method. He was a vigorous opponent of confiscation and violence.

Thomas Edward Cliffe Leslie (1825-1882)

Leslie an Irish economist was a professor of Political Economy at the Queens College, England, and was the first economist who adopted the historical method of study. His economic ideas are found mostly in his major works like Land Systems and Industrial Economy of Ireland and continental countries. Ingram wanted the economic studies to be based on modern physics and biology.

Arnold Toynbee (1853-1883)

Arnold Toynbee was more a social reformer than an economist. He concentrated his attention on the study of poverty and labour problems. His Lectures were published under the title, "Lectures on the Industrial Revolution of the 18th century in England." Credit goes to Arnold Toynbee for coining the term 'Industrial Revolution'.

Toynbee disproved Ricardian ideas and pointed out that one of the weaknesses of political economy was that it had not been associated with historical facts. He stated that economic theories should be supplemented by historical facts and statistical data. To him historical methods compare the stages of economic development in different countries and thereby enabled the discovery of laws of universal application.

Thorold Rogers (1823-1890)

Rogers emphasised the need for careful historical and statistical investigation. His ideas were similar to those of Jones and Bagehot. His best known books are: History of Agriculture and Prices in England, Manual of Political Economy, Six Centuries of Work and Wages, The First Nine years of the Bank of England and The Economic Interpretation of History. Rogers main opposition was to the Ricardian theory of rent. The movement from more to less fertile lands was not supported by history.

According to him, economics suffered from two things namely, too many definitions and disregard for historical facts. Through historical study he found that much which popular economist believed to be natural, was highly artificial, what they called laws were inaccurate inductions, hasty and inconsiderate.

Conclusion

Thus all the writers have criticised the wages-fund theory and the Ricardian theory. Jones was more concerned with criticism of rent theory, Bagehot with the cost of production and Leslie Essays in Moral and Political Philosophy. His ideas were greatly influenced by Henry Main, Comte, Roscher and Knies. His main contributions were related to prices, wages, distribution of precious metals and agrarian problems.

Leslie objected the classical political economy especially the Ricardian Economics. He believed that Adam Smith had used the inductive method in his generalisation, but Ricardian approach was abstract and a priori which had not given any explanation of the laws of the distribution of wealth. He also criticised the wages fund theory and the Ricardian theory of value. Leslie thought that happiness was not the only and final test and the best aim of the world has been "the progressive improvement of the living creatures". Like Begehot, he prefered the use of both deductive and inductive methods. He said that, "by combining the closest observation of phenomenon with the boldest use of speculation and scientific hypothesis", other sciences had developed.

Nassau William Senior

The Individualistic and Nationalistic Critics created lot of confusion in the economic horizon due to their reaction against classicalists. Hence there was need for revision of classical economics and this was done by a number of writers appeared in various countries. Senior was chief among them. He is one of the best representative of the classical shcool. He exposed both the dark and bright sides of classicism. He was a pioneer to make economics an exact science and thus he richly deserves to be treated as one of the founders of pure economics.

Economic Ideas

Senior was born in 1790 in England, studied at Oxford and got his M.A. degree in 1815. When political economy was founded at the Oxford Universty in 1825, he was appointed as the first professor. His two publications, "Industrial Efficiency and Social Economy", and "An Outline of Science or Political Economy", are worth mentioning.

Scope of Political Economy

According to Senior the subject matter of Political Economy was limited to wealth and not with human happiness. He adopted the deductive method of study. He treated economics as an abstract and deductive science. He stated that "the science of economics depends more on reasoning than on observation". He lays down four postulates from which the deductions are to be made: (1) Man's desire to obtain additional wealth with as little sacrifice as possible (2) Malthusian theory of population, (3) Powers of the factors of production should be indefinitely increased and (4) the law of diminishing returns from land. These days the first postulate is used as the assumption of economic rationality, which means that every economic unit acts with self-interest. For instance a consumer tries to maximise his consumer's surplus, an entrepreneur tries to maximise his profits, a factor of production, its income etc. The second postulate is concerned with the theory of population, the third one laid the foundation for Bohm-Bawerk's theory of production, and the fourth in the familiar law of diminishing returns in agriculture.

Value

Senior defined value as "that quality in anything which fits it to be given and received in exchange." Transferability or marketability, relative scarcity and utility are the three things that contribute value. Scarcity of a good is determined in relation to its demand. Thus he brings in both demand and supply to determine value. Demand rests on utility.

Abstinence and Capital Formation

Senior introduced a cost of production theory. The two productive factors, namely, labour and capital contribute production. As these factors were inadequate a secondary agent, abstinence was needed. Senior emphasised that capital formation could take place due to abstinence. Abstinence he says, "is a term, by which we express the conduct of a person who either abstains from the unproductive use of what he can command....."

Theory of Monopoly

Senior's treatment of monoply revenue was remarkable. He recognised that in practice free competition is not always present. There is often an element of monopoly present in the market, and this could be guaranteed only when everyone had equal access to factors of production. He, therefore, held that in the case of land the element of monopoly is always found to exist. Commodities produced with the help of natural agents are monopoly commodities. He divided monopoly into four kinds– comparative advantage monopoly, absolute monopoly, copy-right monopoly and land monopoly. The most common feature of these monopolies is that income is always more than the cost of production. He regarded land rent as monopoly revenue.

Rent

Due to the scarcity of fertile land labour was applied to inferior lands which results in diminishing returns to labour and capital. Hence the owner of superior land demanded rent. The value of land was determined by the scarcity of superior land and cultivation of inferior lands. If only a part of the most fertile land was cultivated, land had no value. Thus rent would arise so long as a scarce factor of production was used.

Money

Senior suggested the qualities of money as durability, stability, portability and divisibility. Coins should be made only from gold and silver. Paper money should be well regulated. He criticised the Quantity Theory of Money as presented by David Ricardo and James Mill. Hence the value of money neither depends upon its quantity nor upon the velocity of circulation but upon its cost of production.

Wages

Senior propounded the Wages-Fund theory. According to him wages depend on "the extent of the fund for the maintenance of the labourers, compared with the number of labourers to be maintained." Wages were determined according to the size of the wage fund and the number of the labourers. Further he believed that the productive powers of the workers would increase with the introduction of division of labour and mechinery.

He stated that real wages obtained by workers during a year must be the ratio between the quantity of commodities set aside for the maintenance of the working population and the size of that population.

He supported the Malthusian Theory of Population and Adam Smith's division of labour. The advantages of division of labour are mainly depended upon the use of capital or abstinence. Senior did not advocate the laissez faire policy. He also suggested that the state should advance money to facilitate emigration. He welcomed state intervention to solve social problems and for the constitution of public work programmes.

He lacked constructive powers. His greatest contribution to political economy was his Abstinence Theory of Interest. His writings are full of logic and analytical detail but he could not make proper use of these faculties. To conclude, in the words of Haney, "He gave prominence to the unduly abstract character of the classical political economy; his classification of the factors of production lacked coordination, and his definition of monopoly has proved to be inexpedient".

QUESTIONS

1. Trace the origin and development of Historical School.
2. Who were the founders of the old Historical School ?
3. What are the characteristic feature of the Younger Historical School ?
4. Make a critical review of the ideas of the Historical School.
5. Write a brief note on Gustav Schmoller and his work.
6. What were the positive ideas of the Historical School ?

Chapter 15

RESTATEMENT OF CLASSICAL ECONOMICS

INTRODUCTION

Classical Political Economy remained in vogue for many generations. But in their zeal to build up a comprehensive economic theory, the classical economists indulged in certain contradictions and at one stage they were severely criticised. There was lack of unanimity among the builders of classical political economy themselves. The assumptions of the classical shcool regarding the relationship between the individual and the State, the pessimistic outlook, laissez-faire doctrine, etc., were all subject to formidable attacks. The classical economists were criticised on almost all fronts—their philosophy, methods and scope of political economy, logic of their doctrines etc.

John Stuart Mill appeared at a time when the position of classical political economy was dwindling. New changes had started taking place in the economic conditions of England and other countries of the world. People had started realising that the classical doctrines were not suited to the changing conditions and were devoid of practicableness. The principles enunciated by Smith, Ricardo and Malthus, therefore required revision and modification in the context of new problems. Mill's "Principles of Political Economy" fulfilled this task to a great extent. Mill was seen standing on the threshold of a new epoch which was to give due emphasis to the human factor in economic development. Mill represents a two faceted personality—classicist and socialist—merged into one.

JOHN STUART MILL (1806-1873)

John Stuart Mill was one of the builders of classical school. He appeared at a time when political economy required a re-statement. The principles given by A. Smith, D. Ricardo, T.R. Malthus, required revision and modification in the context of new problems. Mill's work heralded the end of one and the beginning of another epoch in economic development.

J.S. Mill, the son of James Mill, was born on May 5th, 1806 in London. He was an extremely brilliant boy and studied Greek, Latin, Logic, History, Literature, Political Economy, Roman and English Law at the age of 15. He served in the office of the East India Company and worked for the economic betterment of the working classes and women suffrage from 1823 to 1868. He died in France in 1873.

He wrote a number of books in various fields, viz., philosophy, political science and economics. His principal works are "The Principles of Political Economy", seventh edition in 1871. It was divided into five books–production, distribution, exchange, influence of the progress of society in production and distribution, and the influence of the Government. He did not add anything to the classical economic theory but he recast the theories of his predecessors. His other works include "Essays on Unsettled Questions in Political Economy" (1844); "System of Logic" (1842) "Liberty of Thoughts on Parliamentary Reform" (1859); "Representative Government". 1861; 'Utilitarianism' (1863); "Comte and Positivism" (1864); "Subjection of Women" (1869); etc.

Sources of Influences on Mill's Writings

Mill as an economist was largely influenced by the fundamental ideas of Adam Smith and Ricardo. He believed in Bentham's principles of utility. He supported individual freedom, liberty and laissez-faire ideas of Physiocrats and Adam Smith. Mill agreed with the Ricardian theory of rent and the Multhusian theory of population. He was treated as a Reformist or as a Philosophical Radicalist, because he advocated the reform of the existing institutions and stood for Government interference in child education and employment. Mill was influenced by John Rae's idea on capital accumulation; on division of labour he relied upon Babbage; in the treatment of value he depended upon Quincey's Logic of the Political Economy, and from Bailey and Senior he derived the Abstinence Theory of Profits. Other writers, for whom Mill had a great regard, were Coleridge, Carlyle, Maurice, Saint Simonian, John Locke, David Hume and Mrs. Taylor.

Mill's Restatement of Classical Ideas

Hedonistic Principle: Hedonistic Principle or law of self-interest means that every individual desires wellbeing and each man knows what is good for himself. It has led to individualism. According to classical writers, self-interest was the main motive behind human activity. Every individual tried to gain the maximum pleasure. This law based on human psychology, was the most rational form of self-preservation. Mill said that individualism never implied egoism and a normal individual was always prepared to give pleasure to others. Once individualism and liberty are realised then there is no clash of interest. But it needed education.

Nature and Scope of Economics

Mill defined economics as the science dealing with "the nature of wealth and the laws of the production and distribution, including, directly or remotely, the operation of all the causes by which the condition of mankind, or of any society of human beings, in respect of this universal object of human desire, is made prosperous or the reverse. He studied not only the laws governing the production and distribution but also the causes by the opeartion of which society is made prosperous or reverse. Mill restated that the laws governing the production and distribution are closely related as well as different from each other. Therefore the study of both these types of laws is essential for economics. The classical writers did not believe in offering advice but Mill wanted economics to be more practical. That is why he distinguished between the laws of production and the laws of distribution.

Scope of Economics

According to classical economists, economics was both a science and an art, that is, the science of economics and art of policy. He made it an art because he aimed at bettering the economic lot of human beings. He was a social reformer. He widened the scope of political economy, so as to include both the positive and negative aspects. It should be supplemented with other social sciences.

Method of Study

He adopted the deductive method of study as had been done by the classical economist. But later on he understood that this method was dangerous for a social science. He, therefore, adopted the concrete deductive method that is a combination of deductive and inductive methods.

Nature of Laws

The classical economists believed that the nature of economic laws were universal. But Mill differed from them. He distinguished between the nature of the laws of production and distribution. The laws of production were based on physical truths and were natural. The laws of distribution resided within the realm of human institutions. This was man made and could be changed. The problem of distribution is the most difficult question in economics. He based the possibility of his socialistic programme on this belief.

Production

According to Mill, labour and natural objects are the two agents of production. He defined Labour as the mental, bodily, muscular or nervous application; and natural object is those which grew up spontaneously. These two are the primary factors in all types of production. He says that, "labour is always and solely employed in putting objects in motion, the properties of matter, the laws of nature do the rest". Some of the natural powers were limited and others unlimited in quantity. For example, water on the banks of rivers or lakes is unlimited; but in cities where people want it for consumption, it is limited. Mill stated that the part played by nature in any work done by a man was indefinite and incommensurate. When nature and labour were required to produce a commodity, it was meaningless to say how much was produced by each one of them. "It is like attempting to decide which half of a pair of scissors has most to do in the act of cutting". He considered J.B. Say's views that the function of labour is that of creating utilities. There are three types of utilities; those which are fixed and embodied in outward objects; those which are fixed and embodied in human beings; those which are fixed or embodied in any object. Mill held that in many cases labour may be of indirect application. There are five ways in which labour operates indirectly in production; (1) labour employed in extractive industries (2) labour employed in the making of tools and implements (3) labour employed for the protection of industry (4) labour employed in the transport and distribution of the produce; (5) labour of the inventors of industrial processes.

Productive and Unproductive Labour

Mill defined productive labour as that, "which is employed in creating permanent utilities, whether embodied in human beings or in any other animate or inanimate objects". These objects he meant only material objects. He included more occupations under productive labour than Smith. It effected an increase of material products ultimately and directly. Cotton spinner, plough man were productive by the direct result of labour. Mill defined unproductive labour as that "which ends in immediate enjoyment, without any increase of the accumulated stock of permanent means of enjoyment". Unproductive labourer might receive for his labour from those who derived pleasure or benefit from it.

Division of Labour

Mill supported Adam Smith's idea on division of labour and its merits and demerits. To him, the extent of division of labour was limited by the extent of market. He gave different causes like high population, poverty, deficiency of roads and waterways, lack of combination of labour, for unemployment. He quoted M. Say who had written that the manufacture of playing cards was divided into 70 operations in which 30 workers were employed. Again he supported Babbage who had pointed out that the work of watch making was divided into 102 distinct operations. Every individual was given only that part of the work for which he/she was best suited. In this connection he wrote that production was most efficient when the precise quantity of skill and strength which was required for each part of the process was employed in it or no more.

Future of Labouring Classes

Mill propounded two conflicting theories—Theory of Dependence and Protection and Theory of Self-Dependence. The first theory stated that the lot of poor labourers should be regulated for them; and it is the duty of high classes to think for them. The second theory explained that in a new country, they find work as hired labourers, after a few years they begin to work on their own account, employing others. Mill predicted that in near future workers, with their increasing powers, would organise themselves into associations which were not meant for the benefit of the individuals but for the promotion of the interest of the cooperative cause. He supported the role of labour associations and their participation in the profits of industries.

Population

Mill appreciated the Malthusian law of population and said that no betterment in the economic condition of workers was possible unless they placed a check on their multiplication. The peasant proprietor class was in a better position as a result of less rapid growth. It was in vain to say that all mouths which were called into existence brought with them hands also, because the new mouths required as much food as the old ones, but the hands did not produce as much. He thought that women were not responsible for too big families, so he suggested that women should have full liberty to decide whether to have more children. Mill supported a legislative measure to prohibit the marriage of the poor. He wrote that the laws forbidding marriage unless the parties could show that they had the necessary means of supporting the family were within the powers of the state, without violating the liberty. This law was followed by many countries of the European Continent.

Capital

Mill assigned a secondary place to capital. He defined capital as the accumulated stock, resulting from industry, which is devoted to reproductive employment. He gave four fundamental propositions for capital:

(1) Industry is limited by capital; but does not reach this limit and that every increase in capital provides additional employment to labour.

(2) It is the result of saving;

(3) It is used for further production;

(4) Capital supports labour and employs it.

According to Mill, capital does not possess any productive powers as possessed by labour and natural agents. The only function of capital is to feed and maintain the labourers during the process of production. He distinguished between two types of capital–fixed and circulating capital. Fixed capital is that portion of capital which consisted in the instruments of production. It is more or less permanent in nature. The effectiveness was not exhausted by a single use viz., buildings, machinery and implements. But it required periodical renewals.

Circulating capital was that capital which after being used once, existed no longer as capital of rendering any service to production viz., alkali used in the preparation of soap, wages to workers etc. Mill analysed that all capital was the product of saving i.e., of abstinence from present consumption. It depends on two things : (a) the amount of net product from which saving could be effected: and (b) the strength of depositions. The greater the net product, the greater the savings. The profit motive provides stimulus to accumulation. But the desire to save is different from individual to individual. Accumulation depended upon the desire for expenditure also.

Cost of Production

Mill believed that unless the value of a commodity was sufficient to repay the cost of production, it would not be produced permanently because the producer would not bear the loss. According to him, there are three components of cost of production: labour, capital and differential tax. For example cloth manufacturing, he said that, its cost of production included the wages of weavers, spinners, yarn makers, brick makers and builder, who erected the factory building, machine makers and carrier who transported the appliances and product. Capital is another element which must be paid its due share i.e., profit. He said that the more largely would profits enter into the cost of production because the greater the proportion of the whole capital which consisted of mahcinery or building or material or anything else which must be produced before the immediate labour could commence.

Causes of Productive Efficiency

The degree of productive efficiency of a community depended upon several factors like abundance of natural resources, energy of labour, skill and knowledge, moral trust worthiness, division of labour. Among the natural resources, Mill included soil, climate, minerals, natural water, power, navigable rivers and good harbours. As far as energy of labour, he considered when workers worked, they should work with all their might and mind. Further he added that the knowledge of natural powers and properties of objects, intelligence and manual dexterity were highly conducive for inventions, division of labour promoted the cooperative spirit, and moral trust worthiness improved the efficiency of organisation. There are two causes for productive efficiency. Firstly, the better educated workmen were entirely sober, discreet, on their enjoyments, had taste for a better society, organised excursions, were economical, honest and trust worthy. The second causes were two (1) Security or protection to be given to the members of community and (2) the enactment of laws.

Scale of Production

Regarding scale of production, he discussed the advantages and disadvantages which accrue from the scale of production. The advantages of large scale production are: (1) Cooperation among the workmen (2) Division of labour (3) Sale of goods at lower rate than small scale production. (4) Economise the cost of superintendence. According to Mill, the production of a large scale system, was again limited by the extent of the market—either the community should be populous and prosperous or there should be the possibility of exports. He said that small scale peasant farming suffered from inferiority in skill and knowledge, which did not exist as a general rule.

Private Property

Mill described that the distribution of wealth depended upon the laws and customs of the society. He examined the institution of private property, under which no injustice would be done to anybody who could follow his line of production independently. It would guarantee to the individuals the fruits of the labour.

Slavery

According to Mill, the landlord owned labour, under this system, the entire produce belonged to him. Nothing should be possessed by the slaves. They were provided only food and other necessaries. The ancient Romans played with the lives of slaves; but the condition of slaves was much less bad in ancient times than that in modern colonies. During long period, slaves obtained full rights of citizenship: both legal rights and property rights. But as far as serfdom is concerned, it was the mildest form of slavery. England was the first country which abolished slavery followed by Denmark, France and the United States. But Mill supported complete personal freedom.

Wages

Mill recognised classical law of wages depended upon the demand for and supply of labour and the natural or subsistence wages. In the short run, these wages are determined by the number of labourers and in the long run wages were determind by the cost of rearing. Workers wages were paid not according to their economic needs and to him, trade unions were helpless in increasing their wages. Mill wrote that, "wages depend, then, on the proportion between the number of the labouring population and the capital or other funds devoted to the purchase of labour, and cannot under the rule of competition be affected by anything else". There are two ways for increasing the wages, either by increasing the wage fund or by limiting the population of workers. The first alternative is beyond the control of workers. Whereas the second is within their power, they should not multiply too fast. Mill suggested that workers must be learnt that the demand for labour grew faster than its aggregate supply, for increasing wages.

Again he had suggested measures for the improvement of the wages of workers. Mill did not support the fixation of minimum wages unless work was found for all the workers who wanted to work. It was the duty of the state or the rich people to see that all poor people found work. Mill offered the following measures to improve the conditions of the workers:

(1) Restrictions should be placed on marriages or those people who cannot support their children should be punished severely.

(2) Small plots of land may be given to workers on fair rent so that they may not wholly depend upon work for hire.

(3) Workers should restrict their numbers.

(4) An effective national system of education should be devised for the children of the labouring classes.

(5) A rational policy of colonization should be adopted so that a considerable fraction of agricultural population might emigrate.

Profits

Mill explained that profits are the "remuneration of abstinence". He analysed gross profit and differences in the rates of profits in different industries and at different places. There are three elements of gross profits, i.e., the remuneration for abstinence, indemnity for risks and remuneration for the labour and skill required for superintendence. According to Mill, rates of profits in different industries and at different places are different owing to the circumstances which render one employment more attractive or more repulsive than another and also under monopoly. Mill said that remuneration for superintendence does not vary much from employment to employment but it varies frequently from individual to individual. Mill did not separate profits from interest, but maintained that the rate of profits generally exceeded to rate of interest. The conditions under which profits differed were risk, nature of employment and time. The two main elements upon which profits depended were–the productive power of labour and the amount of productivity invested for supporting the workers. But the real cause of profit was the fact that labour produced more than was required for its maintenance. He supported David Ricardo's views the "the rate of profit depended upon wages; rising as wages fall and falling as wages rise". But he did not accept Adam Smith's version that the tendency of the profit was to fall as a result of competitive capital; and said that, that theory was unsound and incorrect.

Rent

Mill accepted Ricardo's law of rent and believed that rent arose because of differences in fertility of land. He further said that rent as a differential surplus. Like Adam Smith, he considered rent as the effect of monoply because the landlord had "exclusive power" over his land. Mill has gone a step further in stating that rent also accrues as a result of personal abilities or superior business talent.

Rate of Interest

Mill followed the footsteps of Smith and Ricardo regarding rate of interest. Mill said that the rate of interest is determined at a point where demand for loans is equal to their supply. The market rate of interest fluctuates widely and oscillates round the natural rate. The natural rate of interest depends upon: (a) the accumulation of capital and (b) comparative taste of the people for active participation in industry, leisure, ease etc. The average rate of interest is determined by the total demand for loans and the general loan fund in the country. He does not accept the view that the rate of interest and the quantity of money in circulation are related to each other. The rate of interest may fluctuate with changes in the demand for and supply of loan. Mill said that the rate of interest may be affected permanently by alterations in the proportion of interest receiving and profit receiving capitalists.

Determination of Value

Mill introduced the concept of margin, that is, the value of a commodity was fixed at the margin or at the point of equilibrium at which demand and supply were equal. He said that demand and supply theory of value was simply a vicious circle. He gave two types of value, viz., normal value and market value. Under perfect competition, normal value tended towards the cost of production; but the market value fluctuated towards this fixed point or normal value, in the same way as the sea tends to a level but it never is at one exact level. He extended the classical theory of value.

Value of Money

Mill realised the inconvenience of barter economy and explained the advantages of the introduction of money. He enumerated the qualities which a money-material, gold or silver, should possess in order to serve as money. He defined money as "the medium through which the incomes of the different members of the community are distributed to them and the measure by which they estimate their possessions". According to Mill, money was a commodity and its value depended upon its purchasing power. There is an inverse relationship between value of money and price level. He also recognised the velocity of money. He pointed out that money which was hoarded, cash balance in the hands of people, money in the banks or reserve by private bankers, could not influence prices. The value of money conformed permanently and in a state of freedom, to the value of the metal of which it was made.

Law of Free Competition

The classical writers considered free competition as a supreme natural law. According to Mill, "every restriction of competition is an evil" and "every extension of it is always an ultimate good". Mill said that those people who acted upon the principle of laissez faire were nearer the truth 19 times out 20 times than those who opposed it. It was to be adoped as a practical rule where a better one had not been found. It people found fault with the working of free trade, it was due to imperfect competition. Even though, he had socialistic thinking, yet as socialism suppressed liberty and free trade, he vehemently oppose it.

Criticism of Protection

Like David Ricardo, Mill was a staunch free trader. He believed that to prohibit the importation of foreign goods or to impose protective duties on them was to render the labour and capital of the country less efficient in production than they would otherwise be. At the same time , the difference between labour and capital in the production of two commodities in the two countries would go to waste. He argued that a country which had adopted protection, was destroying the general gain which was to accrue to the world. He defended protective duties only when they were imposed temporarily, particularly in a new country.

Theory of International Trade

Mill developed Ricardian Theory of international trade. Like Ricardo he concluded that it was differences in comparative cost and not differences in absolute cost that gave rise to international trade. He introduced the law of supply and demand into the field of international values. Mill believed that in the case of foreign commodities, the law of permanent value determined by cost of prodution will not hold good. Mill said that trade equilibrium between two countries found each one exporting just enough to cover its imports. This was the "Equation of International Demand or The Law of International values. He never supported protection, but he suggested that the taxes on imports and exports might be so adjusted so that the former could bear the burden of taxes to a certain extent.

Taxation

Mill examined the system of taxation, contributed by Adam Smith and David Ricardo. First of all he reproduced the canons of taxation propounded by the Father of the science. He considered taxation as the means with the help of which greater inequalities of wealth could be reduced. He suggested the imposition of taxes was not for earned fortunes but on unearned incomes. He further suggested that the amount which an individual could acquire by gift, inheritance, shall be fixed by law. He objected to the graduated tax system and permanent incomes were taxed several times. Tax should be levied only once to meet some national emergency. The state should appopriate the whole or part of the income earned without exertion for sacrifice. The incidence of taxes should fall on incomes, not on capital. He added that all savings which had been invested should not be taxed.

Stationary State

Mill wrote a separate chapter on 'Stationary State' in his book. According to him, sometimes the increase in wealth would come to an end; as a result of improvement in the technique and accumulation of capital and competition, profits would decline to zero. Naturally, economic activity and population must come to a standstill position. Under such circumstances rents would rise and wages would remain constant. The stationary state would witness a real moral advancement. If the working population were restrained, an improvement in the economic conditions of workers might be visible. There would be more even distribution of wealth as the result of individual skilfulness and of legislative measures. This would automatically solve many economic problems.

DIFFERENCES IN IDEAS

The ideas on which Mill differed from classical economists are as follows:

Theory of Economic Development

The calssical economists had dealt with the equilibrium state of a static society, whereas Mill believed in a dynamic society. He said that in an advancing society, there were progress in wealth, advancement of material prosperity, increase in production and population, growth of man's power over nature, knowledge of the property and laws of physical objects, increase in security of person and property against the arbitrary power of the government, improvement in business capacity, great capacity of united action, cooperation and association of workers. He accepted the concept that when a society advanced in wealth, population increased faster than the agricultural skill, making food price high.

Functions of Government

Mill opposed the classical economists view of laissez faire policy and extended the Government intervention in those activities which aimed at maximising the human welfare, regulation of working hours, control of public works, scientific experiments, education, administration of charity and preservation of the interests of consumers etc. He classified the functions of Government as authoritative (necessary) and non authoritative (cooperative). He considered that the Government agencies were essential for their performance, and their duties, among others, were to repress violence, to preserve the evidence of facts, to afford protection against force and to provide for the dependants.

Mill and Socialism

Mill was not merely a political economist but also a social reformer. He supported the working class movement. He developed his economic ideas relating to socialism from social thinkers like Saint Simonians, Sismondi and others. He divided human race into two–employers and employed. He said that there should be cooperation among them. There might be association of labourers among themselves. His socialist programme has been described as "individualist socialist programme'.

Mill considered wage-system the enemy of progress, for it deprives man of all interest in the product of his labour. Mill borrowed the ideal of cooperative community from the French socialists. Mill stated that rent is a differential surplus and suggested a tax on land would gradually absorb rent. He advocated peasant proprietorship. He considered the right of inheritance, one of the basic obstacles to individual liberty and a source of danger to free competition. He argued that nobody should be allowed to inherit above a certain sum.

The following are the programmes for social uplift:

(1) to remove all legal and fiscal impediments to the transfer of land,
(2) to restrict within the narrowest limits, the power of tying up land,
(3) to secure the abolition of the law of inheritance,
(4) to claim for the state, the interception by taxation of the future unearned increase of the rent of land,
(5) to promote a policy of encouragement to cooperative agriculture,
(6) to promote the acquisition of land in a similar manner to be let to small cultivators,
(7) to make available land belonging to the crown or public bodies or charitable and other endowments, for the same purpose......as well as for the improvement of the dwellings of working class,
(8) to retain all waste lands for national uses,
(9) to retain less fertile lands for natural beauty,
(10) to obtain for the state the power to take possession of all natural objects.

By all these suggestions Mill aimed at increasing the general happiness of society. He wanted to see that all legal and fiscal hurdles which stood in the way of transfer of land were removed, land was acquired and let out to small cultivators. The dwellings of workers were improved. All waste lands were to be retained for national uses and less fertile lands for beautification and general enjoyment of the community. The prominent three proposals are abolition of the law of inheritance, interception by the State, of the future unearned increment of rent i.e., socialization of rent and organisation of cooperative agriculture, producers' cooperatives and workers associations, i.e., gradual abolition of the wage system.

Critical Estimate

Mill was a great utilitarian philosopher, a staunch free trader and an unparalled exponent of liberalism. Mill supported the fundamental laws of self-interest, free competition, rent and international trade, recast them. He introduced the concept of margin in the theory of value. He showed a little divergence as far as the nautre of economic laws, scope and functions of the Government concerned. He widened the scope of the subject by discussing both the positive and negative aspects. He distinguished between the laws of production and law of distribution. He accepted state intervention in the activities which serve the greatest good of the greatest number. He was the first English economist to use the phrase Laissez Faire and the term unearned advantage.

But he failed to develop the marginal analysis in consumption and production. He did not fully appreciate utility and failed to relate the laws of production and distribution. He did not complete the theory of value. His search for a compromise between the classical economists and the socialists ideal life had many logical inconsistencies. Despite his weakness and failures, Mill can be regarded as a great expositor of classical economic doctrines. Haney said that, "His claim to greatness in economics, however not in his doctrinal contribution, but in his thought concerning the postulates and assumptions of economics and its relation to the social policy. To conclude, in the words of Newman, "Mill did for Ricardo what J.B. Say did for Adam Smith—a job of systematization and popularisation".

QUESTIONS

1. Analyse J.S. Mill's principles relating to 'Nature and Scope of Economics'; 'Production' and 'Distribution'.
2. Discuss about Mill's approach of 'Dynamics of Economics'.
3. Analyse those areas where J.S. Mill disagreed with Classicals.
4. Was J.S. Mill a Socialist ?
5. Explain the concept of 'Stationary State' of J.S. Mill.
6. Indicate the areas in which Mill was in agreement with classicism.
7. Assess the place of J.S Mill in Economic Thought.

Chapter 16

THE MARGINAL REVOLUTION

INTRODUCTION

In the later half of the 19th century the reputation of classical economics had started waning due to its dogmatism and lack of adjustability to time and places. The classicals were given the brand name "materialists" because they over emphasised the objective side of value and excluded the subjective factors. The material and objective considerations of the classical school were questioned by many economists. Thus a marginal revolution took place simultaneously in many countries. Stanley Jevons in England, Carl Menger in Austria and Leon Walras in Switzerland were regarded as the founders of the marginalist school. These economists offered a new approach to economic theory and it was known as subjective approach.

Subjectivism was a reaction against objectivism of the classical economists. According to the subjective economists, human want is the motivating force in economic life and utility is "the manifestation of the relation between goods and the wants which they gratify". In their opinion, the objective phenomenon depends on subjective ones. Ultimately subjectivism is nothing but individualism. It finds in the individual, the seat of pleasure and the faculty of deciding among alternative utilities. For them, the individual is the focal point in all concepts of utility. Subjectivism, thus leads to marginalism since the attention is concentrated on 'points' or 'degrees.' The subjective economists studied the behaviour of man in relation to his environment.

Eventhough subjectivism was raised against classicism, there was not much difference between the two as far as the nature, content and object were concerned. Like the classical economists, the subjective economists also used the deductive method of analysis. Like their classical predecessors, they opposed the use of averages and made use of "marginal utilities". Their object of study was also an "economic man". Just as the classicals believed that man is motivated by "self interest", the subjectivists held that an individual acts in anticipation of pleasure. Thus they substituted the word 'self interest' with 'pleasure'. Not only that, they measured disutility or dissatisfaction or pain. Further like classicals, the subjective economists believed in perfect competion. At the same time, they found fault with the three classical laws, namely, cost of production, doctrine of demand and supply and the principle of distribution.

The classical economists emphasised supply, production and cost, whereas the marginalists gave importance to consumption, demand and utility. They used widely the concept of marginal utility in their analysis. Thus the marginal analysis was regarded as an innovation in the method of analysis. They made use of mathematical expressions and diagrammatic illustrations, to explain the economic problems. Thus economics became an exact science in their hands.

The following are the main ideas of the marginalist school:

(1) The marginalist school used the concept of 'margin' to explain the economic phenomena. They used the marginal principle for the explanation of all theories.
(2) The marginalists followed a micro approach. They did not deal with the aggregate economy. They mainly dealt with problems of an individual buyer, seller, price of a single commodity, output of a single firm and so on. In short they adopted a partial equilibrium analysis.
(3) The marginal school followed an abstract and deductive method.
(4) They believed in the existence of perfect competition.
(5) While the classical school considered cost of production or supply as the determination of value, the marginal school emphasised the importance of demand in the determination of value.
(6) The marginalist analysis is subjective and psychological.
(7) They assumed that man would behave rationally in balancing their pleasure and pain.
(8) They believed in the automatic tendency of the economy towards equilibrium.
(9) Lastly they supported the laissez-faire policy of the classical school.

The subjective school consists of two schools of thought:

(1) Mathematical School and (2) Non-mathematical or Psychological School or Austrian School. While the mathematical school used extensively mathematics for explaining economic theories and problems, the psychological school used mathematics only for illustrations. Among the mathematical writers Cournot. Gossen. Jevons and Walras were prominent. The Austrian school, on the other hand, was represented by three great Austrian economists, i.e.,Carl Menger, Von Wieser and Bohm-Bawerk.

AUGUSTINE COURNOT (1801-1877)

Cournot was the principal founder of the mathematical school. He was a famous French economist who was the first to use Mathematics in this subject. In the opinion of Dr. Marshall, "Cournot's genius must give a new mental activity to every one who passes through his hands. His main contribution, "Researches into the Mathematical Principles of the Theory of Wealth" was first published in 1838. The same book was republished, after omitting the algebraic part, in 1863 as Principles of the Theory of Wealth and in 1876 as Review Summary of Economic Doctrines. His book was recognised only after the publication of William Stanley Jevons' The Theory of Political Economy (1872) and Leon Walras' Elements of Political Economy (1874), who pointed out the virtues of his method in their books. Then he came to occupy a remarkable position in the history of economic thought.

Main Economic Ideas

Cournot extensively examined the changes in value, and dealt with foreign exchange and theory of prices. This theory of prices is the main portion of his book. He assumed that demand for an article varied with its price. It was he who introduced demand curve in economics. He defined market, which is often quoted by modern economists, as "Economists understand by the term market, not any particular market place in which things are brought and sold, but the whole of any region in which buyers and sellers are in such free intercourse with one another that the prices of the same goods tend to equality easily and quickly". He showed that under unlimited competition price equated the marginal cost of production.

In the last chapter of his book he wrote that under special circumstances protective duties increased the national income. He differed from the classical theory of value as he held that the three elements—demand, supply and price were interdependent. Chapters on social income in his book have been considered unsatisfactory.

Cournot's Model of Duopoly

Cournot takes the case of two identical mineral springs operated by two owners who are selling the mineral water in the same market. The waters are identical.

Assumptions

(1) His model relates to the duopoly with homogeneous products.
(2) The owners operate mineral springs and sell water without any cost of production.
(3) Cost of production is taken as Zero.
(4) Only the demand side of the market is analysed.
(5) The market demand for the product is assumed to be linear (straight line demand curve)

Cournot begins his analysis with the fundamental assumption that the duopolist will decide about the amount of output which is most profitable for him to produce in the light of his rival's present output and assume it not to change. Suppose the demand curve confronting the two producers of the mineral water is the straight line *DB* as shown in the following figure (Fig. 1.)

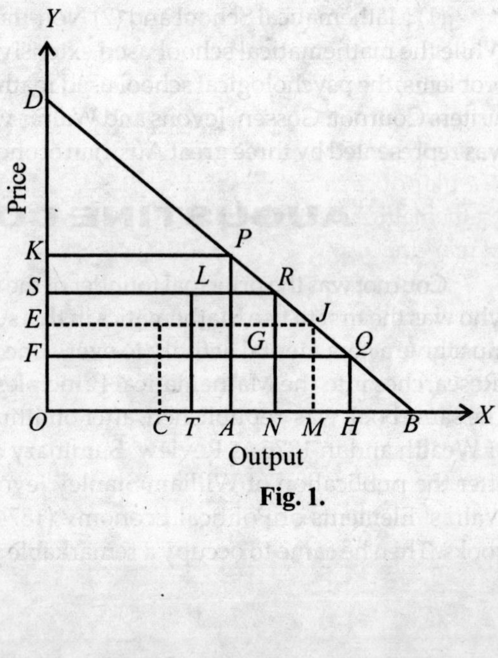

Fig. 1.

Further suppose that $OA = AB$ is the maximum daily output of each spring, total output is $OA + AB = OB$, which is offered for sale in market, the price will be zero. Assume that one producer of the mineral water is monopolist — he starts the business first. He will then produce daily OA output which is his maximum daily output, for his profits will be maximum at output *OA*, and will be equal to *OAPK*. The price which that producer will

charge will be *AP*. Suppose now that the owner of the other spring enters into the business and starts operating his spring. He sees that the former producer is producing *OA* amount of output. According to Cournot's basic assumption, the new producer believes that the former producer will continue to produce *OA* (=1/2 *OB*) amount of output and *PB* as the demand curve confronting him (new producer). With his demand curve *PB*, the producer will produce *AH* (=1/2 *AB*) amount of output. The total output will now be *OA* + *AH* = *OH*, and the price will fall to *HQ* per unit. The total profits made by the two producers will be OHQF which are lese than *OAPK*.

Out of total profits *OHQF*, profits of producer I will be *OAGF* and profits of producer II will be *AHQG*. Now that the profits of producer I are reduced from *OAPK* to *OAGF* by producer II producing output *AH*, the producer I will reconsider the situation. But he will assume that producer II will continue to produce output AH. With producer II producing output *AH*, the best that producer I can do is to produce 1/2 (*OB-AH*) = *OT*. He, therefore, reduces his output from *OA* to *OT*. With output *OT* of producer I and output *AH* of producer II, the total output will be *OT* +*AH* = *ON* and the price of the product will be *NR* and the total profits of the two producers will be *ONRS*. Out of the total profits *ONRS*, the profits to producer I will be *OTLS* which are greater than his previous profits *OAGF* and profits to producer II will be *TNRL* which are greater than his previous profits *AHQG*.

This process of adjustment and readjustment by each producer will continue, until the total output *OM* is produced,(*OM* = 2/3 *OB*) and each is producing the same amount of output. In this final position, producer I produces *OC* amount of output and producer II produces CM amount of output, and *OC* = *CM*. Throughout the process of adjustment and readjustment, each producer assumes that the other will keep his output constant at the present level. So finally the total profits *OMJE* are made by them in Cournot's duopoly equilibrium. It is thus clear that the prices and the profits are lower and output is greater than if they had combined together and formed a monopoly.

To conclude in the words of Fisher, "he exerts a powerful influence on economic thought. It is with him therefore that any survey of modern mathematical economics should begin".

GOSSEN (1810-1858)

Herman Heinrich Gossen is one of the most tragic figures in the history of economics. Gossen was an anticipator of the marginal utility theory. He published his book "Development of the Laws of Exchange Among Men" in 1854. He hoped that his book revolutionised the science of economics. He claimed that he was doing to economics what Copernicus did for astronomy. But his ideas were never popular during his life time. One main reason for that was his treatment of the subject was highly mathematical. But Jevons and Menger praised the poineering efforts made by Gossen in the development of marginal utility theory.

Gossen's analysis of economic system is based on Hedonism and Utilitarianism. According to him everyman tries to maximise his pleasure and minimise his pain. In other words Gossen believed that the aim of all human conduct is to maximise enjoyment.

Gossen believed that the confusion which existed in economic theories before his book was published was due to the absence of mathematical representation. So, he held that a comparison of the quantities of satisfaction might be made with the help of mathematical formulae. Based on the above assumption he wrote in the first para of his book. "Man wants to enjoy life and makes it his chief aim to maximise happiness". In this connection he gave 3 laws of human conduct. These three laws exhibit 3 main features. (1) utilitarianism (2) consumption approach (3) Mathematical method.

Gossen has given certain laws of human enjoyment. Of them, the first two laws are very important.

Gossen's First Law

It states that "The amount of one and the same enjoyment diminishes continously as we proceed with that enjoyment without interruption, until satisfaction is reached". In modern times, this law is known as the Law of Diminishing Marginal Utility'. In other words, the law tells that the marginal utility of a good for a person diminishes with every increase in the stock that he already has.

Gossen's Second Law

The second law tells that each man will spend his money on different commodities in such a way that the amounts of all enjoymets are equal. Thus Gossen explained that maximum enjoyment will result from a uniform level of satisfaction. In modern terms, Gossen's second law is known as the Law of Equi-marginal Utility.

Gossen's views on value are based on the above two laws. According to him value was a relative term. It depended upon the relation between the object and the subject. With an increase in quantity, the value of each added unit decreases until it becomes zero. On this basis he classified goods possessing value into 3 classes. (1) Those which have all the properties for yielding satisfaction, i.e., consumer goods.

(2) Goods of the second class comprise those in which the properties for complete enjoyment is lacking. e.g., pipes. In other words they are required in the production of other goods. (3) Finally comes the production goods. These goods are required in the production.

With regard to cost, Gossen stated that different goods required different amount of exertion for their production. So the value or the cost of the commodity is determined by the degree of exertion spent for the production of the commodity. This was made clear with a diagramatic illustration. (Fig. 2.).

The value reaches a maximum when the quantity 'ab' is produced, i.e.,

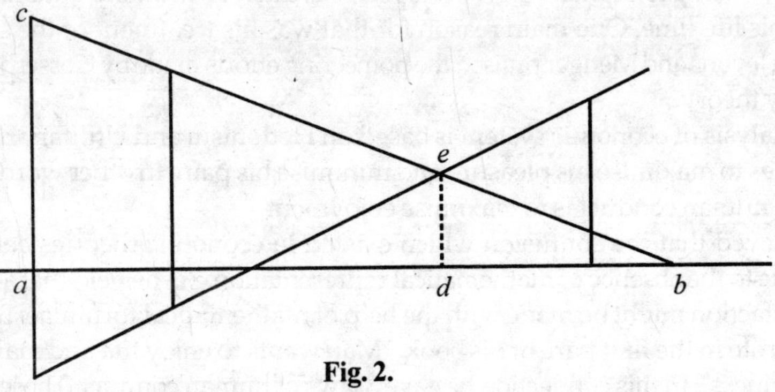

Fig. 2.

when the production is carried on so long that difficulty and value are equal. It follows that in order to obtain maximum satisfaction men have to divide their time and energy spent on procuring different satisfactions, so that the last unit of satisfaction is equal to the amount of difficulty caused on getting that commodity.

Conclusion

The foregoing analysis tells that Gossen's book contains the essential elements of the marginal utility school. Gossen was a great original thinker who believed that mathematical methods were absolutely essential to explain economic phenomena. Unfortunately this German economist anticipated much of recent development in economic theory. He emphasised the subjective side of value. His classification of goods influenced later on Menger. But the main criticisms against his work were his lack of presentation and his failure to deal with market price.

F.Y. EDGEWORTH (1845 – 1926)

Edgeworth took his M.A. degree from the Oxford University in 1877 and was appointed the Drumond Professor of Political Economy in the same university in 1891. He became an emeritus professor after his retirement in 1922. He remained a bachelor throughout. He had profound knowledge of several languages including German, French, Italian and Spanish. For 35 years, he edited the Economic Journal. He taught Economics through Mathematics and Ethics. His chief works are: New and Old Methods of Ethics (1877); An Essay on the Application of Mathematics to the Moral Science (1881) and the Method of Measuring Probability and Utility (1887). His papers appeared in several philosophical magazines on also statistical journals. His papers relating to Political Economy containing 34 papers and economics and 75 reviews was published in 1925. In the same year, the Royal Economic Society published in three volumes, Collected Economic Papers which contained his entire contribution to the subject of economics.

Mathematical Economic Analysis: Edgeworth never attempted a complete treatise on economics, as he was not keenly interested in this subject as Wicksteed, Sidgewick and Marshall. He opitimistically started with the mathematical economic theory and always worked with caution. He criticised the old doctrines and felt that economists regarding their doctrines had avoided some fundamental aspects. He asked them to cultivate open mindedness, candour and sympathy, the absence of which had aggravated the most serious mistakes in this subject in the past. J.S. Mill stated: Even after practical, judgements had been given, there would always remain the room for a modest doubt regarding practical conclusions". Edgeworth also believed that "an academic teacher could not be expected to examine closely all the branches of the subject. This was the reason for his mathematical interpretation of economic theories.

Static and Dynamic Analysis: Edgeworth discriminated between static and dynamic analysis. He charged against contemporary equilibrium theories and found them dangerously vague for want of this distinction. Edgeworth also criticised the obscure dynamics of Walras for suggesting the way by which economic equilibrium is reached. He said that there was no such general dynamic theory which might mark the exact position of equilibrium. "We know only the statical properties of the position".

Indifference and Contract Curves: Edgeworth has given two different ideas – Indifference curve and Contract curves. The indifference curves, perhaps the name was taken from Jevon's Law of

Indifference. Contract curves, he developed just to explain the exchange between two individuals under the barter system. His improvement in the theory of consumer's behaviour, that the utility is not a function of only one commodity, but it is of both or all the commodities, is remarkable and occupies an important place in the history of economic thought.

Three Dimensional Utility: In the economic analysis, utility has been measured only by two dimensions – time and intensity. Edgeworth suggested that economists should apply three-dimensional utility; Ethics being the third dimension, as mentioned in Benthemian Utilitarianism.

Evaluation: Edgeworth gave mathematical treatment to the theories of monopoly and international trade. He wrote on railway rates and taxation also. He did much more in statistics. He developed the Law of Error: the Law of Great Numbers and the Law of Co-relation. At one place he observed, "If the Greeks had been acquainted with the Law of Error, they would have erected an altar to it". His pure theory of monopoly also includes the discussion on duopoly. Due to the influence of Marshallian notions, and his mathematical treatment with the economic theories, Edgeworth, despite his remarkable contribution could never be regarded as a Leader of his branch of investigations.

AN ESTIMATE OF MARGINAL UTILITY SCHOOL

It is generally agreed that the marginal utility school really made a revolutionary advance in economic analysis. Of course, the school has its own critics. One of the major points of criticism against the marginalist school is that it rationalized human behaviour too much. Critics say that it is rather difficult to find their economic man--"the rational maximizer of utility". Second, their theories of market prices are based on the assumption of perfect competition, which we do not have in the real world. They have not dealt with the problems of monopoly price in detailed manner. Third, they have not taken note of the influence of trade unions on wages. In other words, their theories do not deal with the problems of 'big business', big labour, big Government'. Fourth, they have not dealt with the problems affecting the process of economic growth. Fifth, they have not developed any theories of trade cycle. They have said little or nothing on some of the central problems of modern economics, namely, the problems of unemployment and depression. Lastly, they believed that marginal utility was quantitatively measurable. This assumption came in for a lot of criticism. That is why modern economists make use of the 'indifference curve approach' to study consumer's equilibrium where they deal with the problems of different levels of satisfaction and not with different amounts of satisfaction. Modern economists like Pareto and J.R. Hicks have shown that general equilibrium theory can be constructed without assuming a quantitatively measurable utility. Modern economics makes use of a theory of consumers' preference in which the consumer is asked if he prefers one set of goods to another, not by now much he prefers them.

The economists of marginalist school also realized the interdependence of economic life. Instead of having a theory of value, and another theory of production and yet another theory of distribution, the economists of the marginal school demonstrated how all these aspcts of economic activity are related to each other. In the opinion of Prof. T. Gill, "probably the most important technical contribution lay in the development of the tools of what we can call marginal analysis. The particular concept of marginal utility may have gone by the board, but in its place there are marginal rates of substitutions, marginal products, marginal costs, marginal revenues, marginal rates of transformation and a list of other such terms which are at the very core of economic theory of today".

QUESTIONS

1. What is meant by subjectivism in economic thinking ?
2. Explain the concept of marginalism in value analysis.
3. Briefly state "Gossen's contribution" to economics.
4. Write a critical note on Stanley Jevon's utility analysis.
5. Enumerate and expalin Karl Menger's contribution to Economic analysis.
6. Analyse the concept of 'Interest' as envisaged by Bohm-Bawerk.
7. What were the criticisms levelled against the concepts of Austrian School?
8. Write short notes on :
   (a) Friedrich Von Wiser
   (b) Agio theory of interest
   (c) The Theory of Imputation
   (d) Gossen's classification of goods.
9. Critically examine Walrasian general equilibrium analysis.

Chapter 17

AUSTRIAN SCHOOL

KARL MENGER (1840-1921)

Karl Menger has been regarded as a founder of the Austrian school. He was born in Galicia. He had his education in the Universities of Vienna and Prague. Menger was in civil service for a brief period and later became Professor of Economics at the University of Vienna in 1873. He relinquished the post in 1903. Then he devoted his fuli time for economic research. Menger earned a good reputation both as a teacher and a scholar. His important works are: Principles of Economics (1871), Investigations into the Methods of Social Sciences, particularly Political Economy (1883), The Errors of Historismus in German Political Economy (1884) and On the Theory of Capital (1888). Menger's "Principles of Economics" established his fame as the author of the 'Marginal Revolution" of the Austrian School.

According to Eric Roll, "Menger's contributions to economics fall into three main classes : method, money and pure theory".

Method

There was a great debate between Karl Menger and Schmoller, the leader of the younger Historical School over the method of study. While Schmoller advocated inductive method, Menger supported deductive method. The debate was called, "Battle of Methods".

Menger was of the view that economic method must rest on individual foundation. He held that economic phenomena are the result of the behaviour of individuals. So in order to understand the economy, it becomes necessary to study the behaviour of the individuals. Thus like Gossen and Jevons, Menger made the individual the centre of analysis.

Menger held that there were several sciences which study economic phenomena, namely historical, theoretical and practical. In the first group he included economic history and statistics; in the second, economic theory and in the third, politics, public finance and private economics.

Menger believed that the historical method was suitable only for the study of sciences falling in the first group. The historical method or inductive method do not supply all the materials required for the study of the sciences of other two groups. Therefore he suggested deductive method for their study.

However this battle of method came to an end when Schmoller said, "Induction and deduction are both necessary for the science just as the right and left foot are needed for walking".

Needs

In his book "Foundations of Economic Theory" Menger had dealt with some of the important concepts and doctrines of economics. According to him, human needs, goods, and the law of cause and effect are the basic elements in economic science. Satisfaction of human needs is the ultimate goal of the economy and the welfare of the society depends mainly upon an increase and maintenance of the satisfaction of human needs.

Needs represent the conscious effort on the part of a man to live a harmonious life. Needs also imply thought and reasoning. These needs may be the result of the human nature itself or of the social environment. In addition to the individual needs, there are social needs. The satisfaction of social needs is the goal of social economics which is totally different from individual economics.

Theory of Goods

Menger has established a relation between a commodity and satisfaction on the basis of law of cause and effect. A thing if it were to be called as a good should have the following qualities:

1) There should be a human want.
2) It must possess the power to satisfy the human want.
3) Man must recognise the quality possessed by the commodity, namely, the want satisfying power.
4) Man must have command over the thing.

On technical grounds, Menger classified goods into first order, second, third and fourth order goods. Goods of the first order are those which can be used for the immediate satisfaction of human wants., (e.g., bread). Goods of the second order (e.g., Wheat flour) are used for the production of the first order goods. Goods of the third order (e.g., Wheat) are used for the production of second order goods and fourth order goods for the production of third order goods (e.g., land, instruments necessary for cultivation and services of farmers). Thus to quote Alexander Gray, "beyond the bread, is the flour; beyond the flour, the grain; beyond the grain, the field and the plough; beyond the plough, the iron".

In this connection Menger emphasised the importance of consumer goods on which the demand for other goods depended. For example the demand for bread creates the demand for flour, wheat, land, machinery etc. Thus producers' goods derive their value from consumers' goods.

Further Menger classified goods into economic and non-economic goods. Economic goods are those which are relatively less in supply in relation to wants. In the case of non-economic goods the supply of goods exceed their needs and there is no need to economise them.

But Menger pointed out that the classification of goods into economic and non-economic is not a permanent one. It is only relative. Economic goods may become non-economic goods and vice versa, due to changes in wants, supply, technique of production etc.

Wealth

Menger defined wealth as the sum total of "economic goods at the command of an economising individual". He differentiated between individual wealth and public wealth. Just as an individual possess wealth to satisfy his wants, the State, provinces, communities, and associations also have large quantities of economic goods to satisfy their needs which is called public wealth. Today it is called in different names—Government wealth, provincial wealth, municipal wealth, corporate wealth etc.

Theory of Value

According to Menger, supply determines the value of a commodity, Changes in supply, alter the value of a commodity. Menger wanted to show mainly that as the quantity of a good increases, the additional unit has less want satisfying power. Thus Menger's theory of value is subjective in character. "Value is a judgement of the mind; not a property of the thing or an independent entity".

Menger considered the measure of value also as a subjective one. He believed that it was the magnitude of importance attached to a good which determined its value. Value has nothing to do with cost of production or labour. A commodity may have great value to one individual, little or no value to another. Its value depends on the requirements of different individuals and the amounts available to each of them.

Further Menger differentiated use value from exchange value. He defined use value or utility as the power possessed by the commodity to satisfy the human wants directly. Exchange value on the other hand satisfies the human want indirectly. At the same time, Menger held that the utility of the good changes, in different stages of life. For example, toys of a child loose their utility to an adult, the study materials of a student looses their value to a mature man. But when a good looses its use value, its exchange value becomes prominent. All such goods are sold out. Thus the economising individual sells commodities which are not useful for his immediate consumption. This approach is also a subjective one.

Theory of Money

Menger wrote a number of articles in connection with the Austrian currency reform. Menger considered money as a medium of exchange. He recognised the role of money as a standard of measure. As a standard of value, it has two types of value—external and internal. The value of goods can be expressed through money. Thus Menger has given one of the best explanations of the functions of money.

Theory of Exchange

Menger's idea of exchange resembles that of barter system of exchange. He believed that through an act of exchange, the needs of both economising individuals could be satisfied. Both parties gained in the mutual transfer. He pointed out that this theory of exchange holds good for the nations also. For example a country mainly engaged in agriculture and the other in industry would satisfy their needs by exchanging certain portion of their produce.

Menger took great pains to show that in isolated exchange, price would be within limits set by the buyer and seller. He held that under monopoly, price would be set by the offer of the strongest. The monopolist may discriminate between one buyer and another. In competition, discrimination is impossible.

Theory of Imputation

Menger while analysing different categories of goods, developed the theory of imputation. Imputation theory tells us that the value of a good of a high order is derived from the value of a lower order good to which it contributes. For example, the value of flour depends on the value of bread. In this way, rent of land is the value which is imputed to the service of land in the production of agricultural goods.

Distribution

Menger explained the distribution of income among the factors of production. He analysed the problem of factor pricing on the basis of marginal productivity.

Theory of Capital

To Menger, capital consisted only those quantities of economic goods, that were available to be used in future. The difference between capital and wealth was that, the later was concrete durable goods, whereas capital represented economic goods of high order.

Menger believed that free goods might also be regarded as capital, if they are scarce in supply, when used in production.

Critical Estimate

Menger's Principles of Economics was a remarkable publication. It formed the basis for scientific economics. He mostly followed deductive method of study. His treatment of the subject was systematic and comprehensive. His theory of subjective value with its emphasis on demand and utility "might be likened to a pendulum which has moved to the opposite extreme from the classical supply and cost analysis".

If we compare Menger with Adam Smith, we can say that Menger's achievements are narrower than Adam Smith. Smith gave expression to the practical needs of his time, whereas Menger's achievement is purely scientific and analytical. He will always be remembered for the discovery of truths and use of tools in economics.

FRIEDRICH VON WIESER (1851-1926)

Von Wieser was the second member of the Austrian trio who contributed the Austrian School. He was the son-in-law of Karl Menger. He studied for two years in Germany under Knies, Roscher and Hildebrand. From 1903-1922 he served in the University of Vienna as Professor of Political Economy. Wieser also served as Minister of Commerce in the last two cabinets of the Austro—Hungarian Empire. His main works are: The Origin and Principal Laws of Economic Value (1884) ; Natural Value (1889) ; and The Theory of Social Economics (1914).

Wieser was the disciple of Menger and was much influenced by his ideas. The main contributions of Wieser have been in the field of exchange and distribution. Eventhough he elaborated many theories of Menger, he was independent in drawing conclusions. The following are the main economic ideas of Wieser.

Method of Study

Wieser adopted the same method of abstraction followed by Menger. But he questioned the methodological controversy between Menger and Schmoller. He came to the conclusion that Menger had wasted his time and energy over this problem. He suggested that a scientific investigation is the fittest method of study.

Natural Value

Wieser criticised the classical labour cost theory of value. Instead, he developed Marginal Utility Theory of Value. According to him value came from utility. It was derived from the want satisfying power of goods. He defined natural value as one which was found in a community at a high stage of development. He developed the concepts of subjective use value and subjective exchange value.

Law of Imputation of Value

Wieser discussed the law of imputation of value in his book "Natural Value". According to this law, value was imputed to the different factors of production under different conditions of demand, supply and quality. He emphasised the fact that, in the case of production goods, the imputation of value followed the marginal law, i.e., the smallest contribution was imputed to every single quantity.

The theory of Imputation was really a theory of distribution because it explained how the different factors of production were paid. According to this theory, the value of factors of production reflected the value of consumption goods produced by them.

Rent and Wages

Wieser's presentation of the theory of rent was not praise worthy. Because of his confused understanding of the Ricardian theory of rent, he pointed out certain basic errors in the theory. However he was one of the great writers to explain how the rent theory could be used to explain the returns from other factors of production, other than land. Thus Wieser raised the Ricardian theory of rent to a "universal law of differential imputation".

As for as wages are concerned, Wieser criticised the Labour Theory of Value and Subsistence Theory of Wages. He treated the services of labour in the same way as he had treated the services of other factors of production.

Interest

Wieser's theory of capital and interest has three main postulates. He assumed that (a) capital consisted of perishable goods and was used in the process of production (b) capital reproduced a gross product, the value of which exceeded that of capital used in the process of production and (c) supply of capital was fixed.

Wieser maintained that the total return was large enough to replace the capital employed in production and to pay a net return to capital also. The net return paid to capital was known as interest. The payment of interest to capital was justified because capital co-operated in the process of production.

Doctrine of Cost

Wieser made a difference between cost goods and monopoly goods here. Cost goods like coal, wood, unskilled labour, metals etc. were abundant and their production could be increased very easily, whereas monopoly goods were comparatively very rare in supply. Besides, the cost goods were the common, cosmopolitan and indispensable powers of production, and monopoly goods were the specific elements of individual industries. It was with the help of cost goods, the other goods were produced. So the cost goods should be used economically. In short cost goods were production goods.

Wieser made it clear that cost prinicple of valuation should be applied only to these goods where cost goods are used mainly. Cost goods are distributed in such a way as to yield the maximum utility.

Social Economy

In his book "Theory of Social Economics". Wieser gave some new ideas. He tried to integrate pure economics with a theory of society. He pointed out that in the society there were often social conflicts. As a result there was domination of one class over other class. In social economy, there were three types of goods—those used by everyone, luxury goods and intermediate goods. The first type of good was determined by the marginal utility of the poor, the second by the marginal utility of the rich and the third by the middle class.

He referred to growing urbanisation, increasing oppressiveness and harmful effects of inequalities in wealth as causes for social degeneration. He believed that trade unions could take efforts to improve the economic conditions of the workers. For this, Wieser suggested that the trade unions should avoid industrial conflicts and should deal with matters of collective bargaining and determination of wages.

Wieser was in favour of centralised control. To him, the aim of the State shoud be the protection and development of social production. He rejected the idea of progressive taxation and supported economic nationalism and protection.

Critical Estimate

Wieser was an original thinker. His position in the history of economic thought is important. His "Theory of Social Economics" was a magnum opus. Through this book, he made a bold attempt to integrate pure economics with a theory of society. In economic literature this book has the same place as Mill's Political Economy'. While J.S Mill simply re-stated the classical ideas, Wieser contributed his original ideas.

Eventhough Wieser reproduced the theories of Menger, he gave completely different conclusions. He was the first Austrian Economist, who discussed the problem of resource allocation. He adopted the method of abstraction and felt that much time was wasted over the battle of methods.

EUGEN VON BOHM--BAWERK (1851-1914)

Bohm Bawerk was the third pillar of the Austrian school. He was educated at the Universities of Vienna, Heidelberg, Leipzig and Jena. After serving the Austrian Government three times as Minister of Finance, he became a Professor of Economics in the University of Vienna. His important works were: History and Criticism of Interest Theory (1884) ; Outlines of the Theory of Commodity Value (1886) ; and The Positive Theory of Capital (1889). The following are the main economic ideas of Bohm Bawerk.

Methodology

Bohm Bawerk paid little attention to methodological controversy because he was much interested in theoretical analysis. According to him, the main work of economists was not togather more facts, but to study, digest and analyse the facts already known. This could be done by abstraction.

Explanation of Capital

Bohm Bawerk discussed the nature, origin and functions of capital. According to him capital or capital goods were the result of round-about methods of production. Capital goods were used for the production of consumer goods. For him there existed a close connection between saving and capital formation. As for as satisfaction of wants were concerned, capital goods were future goods.

Agio Theory of Interest

Bohm Bawerk's main contribution to economics is in the field of interest. Before developing his own theory of interest, he criticised the existing theories of interest. The problem of interest, according to him, is to find out how and why the owner of capital draws from it, "a permanent net income". He grouped the past theories of interest into various groups like: "The Productivity Theories", "The Abstinence Theories", "The Labour Theories", "The Exploitation Theory" and "Minor Systems".

After rejecting all the old theories, Bohm Bawerk constructed his own theory which is known as Agio Theory of Interest.

According to Bohm Bawerk human beings prefer the present satisfaction to future satisfaction. People generally prefer the present as more important. They discount the future. As the popular saying goes, "A bird in the hand is worth two in the bush". This tendency on the part of the human beings to prefer the present satisfaction, according to Bohm Bawerk is due to three reasons: (1) There is perspective underestimate of the future. Future is not clearly visualised due to lack of imagination. (b) Present wants are felt more strongly than future wants. This is due to the fact that the demand for the present goods is relatively greater than that of the future. (c) There is the technical superiority of the present goods over future goods. Production in modern world is round about. It is a time consuming process, we do not know the nature of the commodity to be produced in future. Hence present goods possess technical superiority over future goods.

Owing to the complexity of the modern capitalist system, the capitalist has to wait for a return on the money that he has invested in production. Meanwhile the other factors of production demand immediate payment for their services. After paying the remuneration to other factors, since the capitalist waits for his return, he is eligible for some reward and that reward is interest. Agio means premium for waiting.

Rate of Interest

According to Bohm Bawerk the rate of interest could be fixed at the macro level for the whole market. Three factors were involved in the equilibrium rate of interest. They were: (1) size of the subsistence fund (2) number of available workers (3) degree of productivity achieved or technological conditions. It must be noted that larger the subsistence fund, lower would be rate of interest and larger the other two factors, higher would be the rate of interest.

Marginal Pairs Theory of Value

Bohm Bawerk presented a novel theory of value. He explained exchange transactions with the help of (a) isolated exchange (b) one-sided competition (c) two-sided competition. Suppose there is a buyer and seller (an example of an isolated exchange). The buyer would not pay a higher price than he considers the commodity is worth to him. The seller would not be willing to accept less than what he considered the object is worth to him. The price would be determined somewhere between these two limits. The exact point depended on their bargaining capacities.

The second case is where there is one sided competition among buyers. The buyer who is willing to pay the highest price (above that of his nearest competitor) will purchase it. Thirdly, combining the two ideas, a market can be considered where a two-sided competition between the buyers and sellers emerges. This is a case of perfect competition. Under this, price would be determined between the limits to be set by two marginal pairs—one marginal pair of potential buyers and sellers who failed to do business and another pair which succeeded in its last transaction. The actual price to be paid would depend upon subjective considerations.

Critical Estimate

Bohm-Bawerk's reputation was firmly established when he published his "Capital and Interest". This book gave a detailed explanation of capital and interest theories. Bohm-Bawerk did not care for the battle of methods that existed during his period and also practical applications. His Agio Theory of Interest was the first systematic theory of interest. It was one of the remarkable achievements in economic theory. His theory of imputation was a great contribution to the Austrian price theory. He was the only Austrian economist who gave importance to the three factors of production—land, labour and capital.

Bohm-Bawerk applied subjective analysis in his theories of capital and interest. His contribution to economics was greater than that of the other two Austrians. He acquired immortality, "On account of his fruitful original ideas, far reaching constructive power, brilliant way of presentation, outstanding gift of leadership, ever-ready preparedness for aggressive and defensive polemics and all the qualities of character and intellect which are the mark of a teacher in the most exalted sense of this word". (Schumpeter)

JOHN GUSTAV KNUT WICKSELL (1851-1926)

Wicksell was the founder of the Swedish School of Economics. He studied the economic theories of Mill, Karl Menger and Bohm-Bawerk for five years. After obtaining his Ph.D. degree in 1895, he became the professor of Economics in 1901 of the University of Lund. Wicksell's main writings are: Interest and Prices (1898), Value, Capital and Rent (1893), Studies in Finance Theory (1896), Lectures on Political Economy Vol. I & Vol. II (1906). "Value, Capital and Interest" contains Wicksell's theories of value and distribution. "Studies in Finance Theory" shows his views on public finance and "Interest and Prices" deals with his views regarding the relationship between rate of interest and price level. "Lectures on Political Economy" is a systematic restatement of the theories of value and distribution and price level.

MAIN IDEAS

Economic Science

Wicksell used the term 'Political Economy" in a wider sense. It has been considered both as a theoretical and practical science. As a theoretical science, it is a statement of economic laws, based on simple assumptions. As a practical science, it examines the question of application of these laws to solve practical problems of real life. It deals with economic policy.

Competition

Wicksell considered perfect competition as good as far as it leads to an optimum allocation of resources and reduces the prices of commodities to its marginal cost. Further the rewards of the productive factors should be determined according to their marginal productivity. At the same time, Wisksell felt that the welfare of the soceity depends on an equal distribution of income and wealth. So in this regard he welcomed state-intervention.

Economic Policy

Eventhough most of Wicksell's writings contained theoretical analysis, he had a definite attitude towards economic policy. He was a strong socialist. He was of the opinion that the welfare oriented economic policy must aim for (a) an optimum allocation and full utilisation of resources and (b) equality of income, wealth and economic opportunities. For achieving these, he suggested that a 'revolutionary programme' must be adopted. This programme includes (a) expansion of public sector (b) development of trade union movement and extension of free education facilities and (c) introduction of progressive tax system and reduction of excise and tariff duties.

Production

Wicksell in his theory of production analysed only three factors of production—land, labour and capital. He left the fourth factor of production namely, organisation due to difficulties of quantitative measurement. Like Bohm-Bawerk, Wicksell also regarded capital as a product of co-operation of the two original factors—labour and land.

All the factors of production are subject to the law of diminishing returns. But Wicksell defined wrongly the law of diminishing returns. It was considered to be a matter of diminishing average rather than marginal returns.

Distribution

Wicksell presented a general marginal productivity theory of distribution. According to this theory, the reward of each factor of production is determined according to the marginal productivity of that factor.

Theory of Capital

Wicksell defined capital as the intermediate good used in production. Capital was not a separate factor of production. But it received remuneration for its services, in the form of interest. Thus interest was the difference between the value of annual product and profit plus payment for land and labour. Wicksell distinguished between natural rate of interest and bank rate of interest. The natural rate was that rate at which the demand for capital and supply of savings are equal. In other words, at the natural rate of interest, savings and investment would be equal.

The Wicksell Effect

The Wicksell effect demonstrates that Von Thunon's marginal productivity principle, which is applicable to labour and land, is applicable to real capital only at the micro level, and not at the macro level. At the macro level, when capital increases, the marginal productivity of capital declines and real savings is absorbed in rising real wages and rent. Thus, the social marginal productivity of capital is smaller than the rate of interest. However at the micro level, the marginal productivity of capital is equal to the rate of interest.

Cumulative Process

Wicksell criticised the traditional quantity theory of money and attempted to explain its method of operation through the cumulative process. Cumulative process is a state of disequilibrium in which a discrepancy arises between the natural rate of interest and market rate of interest.If the natural rate of interest is more than the market rate, investment will be more than savings and there will be a cumulative rise in prices. On the otherhand, if natural rate is less than the market rate, investment will be less than savings and there will be a cumulative fall in prices.

Monetary Policy

Monetary authorities can play an important role in price stability by changing the bank rate. In order to equate the market rate and natural rate of interest, bank rate can be manipulated.

Trade Cycle

Wicksell regarded trade cyle as a real phenomenon and not a monetary one. According to him the main cause for trade cycle is the changes in investment and not in prices. In trade cycle theory, the important contribution of Wicksell is the idea that, "technical progress does not increase in perfect simulaneity with the increase in population".

Appraisal

J.F. Bell remarks, "Wicksell's craftsmanship is at its best in the clarity of expression showing the interdependence of economic factors". His marginal productivity theory of distribution is one of his important contribution to economic theory. His theory of interest shows his originality.

IRVING FISHER (1867-1947)

Schumpeter called Irving Fisher the greatest economist of America in his "Ten Great Economists". Irving Fisher was a mathematician, statistician, reformer and a teacher. He was a man of diverse interests. He took active part in several activities like campaign for prohibition, public health, healthy living etc. He was a great mathematician and used extensively mathematics in economics. His doctoral dissertation was "Mathematical Investigation in the Theory of Value and Price", published in 1892.

Fisher was born in Saugerties (New York). He was educated at Yale, Berlin and Paris. In 1893 he left for Europe for his higher studies in Mathematics. After his return, he taught mathematics for sometime at the Yale University. From 1895 onwards he was appointed as Professor of Economics.

Fisher's other writings include: The Nature of Capital and Income (1906) The Rate of Interest (1907), The Purchasing Power of Money (1911), Elementary Principles of Economics (1910), The Making of Index Numbers (1922), The Money Illusion (1928), The Theory of Interest (1930), Booms and Depressions (1932), Stable Money (1934) and 100 percent Money (1935).

Fisher's main contributions are in the fields of money, interest and capital. He was the first economist who said that income should not be confused with capital. The following are the main economic ideas of Fisher.

Theory of Demand

In his theory of demand, Irving Fisher adopted a cardinal utility analysis. Like Edgeworth, he also developed the concept of indifference curves. He drew price and income lines. He also mentioned about superior and inferior goods and the substitutability and complementarity between goods. For example, when the goods are perfect substitutes, he found that the indifference curves would become straight lines parallel to each other.

Capital

In his book "The Nature of Capital and Income" Irving Fisher discussed about capital. He maintained that capital and income could not be treated as abstract and unrealistic concepts.They were derived from the realities of economic life. Capital was a fund while income from it was a flow. Accordingly the current value of capital was nothing but the discounted value of future income from the capital. This way of looking of the current value of capital has been proved to be useful in both theoretical and empirical studies. Keynesian marginal efficiency of capital is based upon this approach.

Interest

Fisher thought that the main problem in Economics was the determination of rate of interest. For his analysis of interest, Fisher considered three factors namely, impatience or preference for present goods, productivity and uncertainity and risk. Of these, impatience and productivity determined the rate of interest. Here it should be noted that Fisher's concept of productivity is similar to Keynes' marginal efficiency of capital. Fisher emphasised that interest would not arise, if an individual was indifferent towards the present. Interest arose on account of time preference.

Thus Fisher integrated the time preference and productivity theories of interest. Therefore his theory of interest was a non-monetary theory. He did not distinguish between real and monetary rate of interest.

QUANTITY THEORY OF MONEY

Transactions Approach

Fisher stated the theory as, "Quantity Theory asserts that (provided the velocity of circulation and the volume of trade are unchanged) if we increase the number of dollars whether by renaming coins or by debasing coins or by increasing coinage, price will be increased in the same proportion".

In order to explain the direct and proportionate relation between quantity of money and price level, Fisher gave an equation of exchange. The original equation of exchange was

$$PT = MV \text{ (or) } P = MV/T$$

in which 'P' stands for the price level, 'M' quantity of money and 'T' for transactions.

But the later cirtics, criticised this original equation, for not including credit money. So Fisher presented a modified equation of exchange by including credit money.

$$PT = MV + M^1V^1 \text{ (or) } P = \frac{MV + M^1V^1}{T}$$

in which M and V stand for metallic money and its velocity of circulation. M^1 and V^1 for credit money and its velocity of circulation.

Fisher based his quantity theory of money on certain assumptions. He assumed that the velocity of circulation of money and volume of trade to remain unchanged. Further he mentioned certain factors that determined the velocity of circulation of money. They were (1) system of payment (2) development of credit and finance (3) the speed with which money is transported (4) community's consumption and saving habits (5) expectation regarding future incomes and prices of goods and services.

Fisher pointed out that in economically backward countries, the velocity of circulation of money was low. So in order to increase the velocity, Fisher suggested that the people should not hoard their savings but invest them in productive channels.

Fisher's quantity theory of money has been criticised. Some of the criticisms are: (1) It did not explain the changes in the value of money (2) The price level depends on certain non-monetary factors also. (3) The theory did not treat the problem dynamically. (4) The equation did not differentiate between cash deposits and saving deposits, (5) The theory failed to explain the price movements in war times.

Compensated Standard

In order to compensate the changes in the purchasing power of money, Fisher suggested a compensated dollar. Compensated dollar means, the metallic content of the dollar should change in proportion to the changes in the price level. For example, if the price level rose by 10 percent, it meant that the purchasing power of a dollar had fallen by 10 percent. So to compensate this, the metallic content of the dollar should be increased by the same percentage.

Currency Principle

In his book "100 Percent Money", Fisher suggested this currency principle for the banks. He said the banks could follow this principle, in accordance with, the banks were required to maintain 100 percent resources againt deposits. They could not expand the currency unless fully backed by cash. But there were certain practical difficulties in the implementation of the plan.

Theory of Business Cycles

According to Fisher, the main cause for business fluctuations was the changes in credit. He said business depressions were merely the "dances of the dollar". Fisher suggested that in order to lift the economy from depression, prompt action in the form of reflation should be taken by the central bank.

Critical Appraisal

Irving Fisher was a pioneer in the field of econometrics. He opposed laissez faire and pleaded for an equitable distribution of income. Schumpeter says his Theory of Interest is a peak achievement of the literature of interest. Unfortunately he had large number of pupils but no disciples. He did not found a school. So there have been many Ricardians, Marshallians, and Keynesians but no Fisherians.

P.H. WICKSTEED (1844-1928)

Wicksteed stands in the history of economic thought in his own way, not for his originality but for his exposition. Wicksteed was a great contributor to marginalism and was instrumental in popularising the new methodology. He was well known for his marginal productivity theory of distribution. Among his publications were : "Our Prayers and our Politics (1885), The Alphabet of Economic Science (1888), Essay on the Co-ordination of the Laws of Distribution (1894), and The Commonsense of Political Economy (1933).

Appreciation of Fabianism

He was impressed mostly by the social ideas of the Fabians. He believed that the social hardships were mainly due to the collective actions of the present civilisation. At the same time he criticised their industrial and economic organisational ideas as vague. So he suggested that the Fabians and the orthodox economists would work together and offer solutions to the current problems of industrial civilisation. He appreciated the self-interest doctrine and the spontaneity of social order which the socialists failed to understand.

Labour Theory of Value

By applying Jevon's analysis, Wicksteed critised the Marxian Theory of value. He considered the labour theory of value was wrong.

Principle of Marginal Utility

In his book "The Alphabet of Economic Science" Wicksteed introduced the term 'marginal utility'. He insisted that this principle should be used in the allocation of all kinds of resources. Wicksteed believed that the utility of a commodity depended not only upon the quantity of that commodity but also of other goods. In his "Commonsense of Political Economy" he introduced another term 'Significance'. In his market analysis, he emphasised the importance of expectations and the speculative element in all economic activities. Even though he admitted that it was very difficult to establish an equilibrium price due to miscalculations, he claimed that there always existed such a price at any given moment.

Supply Curve

In his paper "The Scope and Method of Political Economy in the Light of the Marginal Principle", Wicksteed spoke about this supply curve. The supply curve was indeed the demand curve. He pointed out that under changing conditions, the same person might be a supplier at one moment and buyer at another moment.

Co-ordination of the Laws of Distribution

This is the most important contribution of Wicksteed to economic analysis. Before Wicksteed, some economists notably Wicksell, J.B. Clark, Marshall, Walras and Edgeworth discussed about marginal productivity Theory. They discussed the rewards of each factor of production separately. So the laws of distribution could not be co-ordinated. He suggested that these laws could be discussed commonly.

Wicksteed believed that the law of exchange value was itself the law of distribution. The exchange value of each good was determined by the marginal unit of that good.

Critical Appraisal

Just like Jevons and Menger, Wicksteed also has an unique place in the history of economic thought. He was an original thinker. Among his contributions, the notable are his theory of distribution, market supply curve, analysis of economic equilibrium and the subjective theory of value. "The Common sense of Political Economy" is the most exhaustive non-mathematical explanation of marginal theory of pure economics.

QUESTIONS

1. What is meant by subjectivism in economic thinking ?
2. Explain the concept of marginalism in value analysis.
3. Briefly state "Gossen's contribution" to economics.
4. Write a critical note on Stanley Jevon's utility analysis.

Chapter 18

KARL MARX (1818-1883)

INTRODUCTION

As Eric Roll observes, "It is a sound tradition which assigns Marx a place in every history of economic thought, but puts him in a separate chapter." He was a revolutionary who used the study of political economy as an instrument of political struggle.

Karl Heinrich Marx was born in Trier in Germany in 1818 in a middle class Jewish family. During his childhood, his family converted to protestantism. Karl Marx studied Law, History and Philosophy in different German Universities (Bonn, Berlin and Jena) and received his Ph. D. degree at the age of 23. After taking doctorate degree, he was influenced by Hegelian philosophy and took up revolutionary journalism. So he was expelled from Germany, Belgium and France. Finally, he came to London where he spent the last 30 years of his life.

In London, Marx spent most of his time in British Museum, the great library. His life was full of poverty and sufferings. His friend and disciple Engels helped him financially. Engels was also a collaborator in the development of Marxian thought. Both of them produced an impressive series of books. They had contact with radical groups everywhere.

His main works are: Introduction to a Critique of Hegelian Philosophy of Rights (1843); The Poverty of Philosophy – A Criticism of Proudhon (1847); Discourse upon the Question of Free Exchange (1848); A Contribution to the Critique of the Political Economy (1859); and the famous book "Das Kapital." The first volume of this book was published in 1867, while the other two volumes were published by Engels after his death in 1885 and 1894.

INFLUENCES SHAPING MARX'S IDEAS

Marx was influenced by his environment. The economic and political conditions of Germany mainly shaped his ideas. During his life time he had seen the economic development of three countries–

Germany, France and England. He drew inspiration from British industrialism and Trade unionism and also French Revolution. He was also inspired by utilitarianism, socialism and German radicalism. Though he was much impressed with Hegelian philosophical ideas, at one stage he felt that it was too conservative to effect changes in the society. Marx was also influenced by the writings of Ricardo, Quesnay and other writers. Thus Karl Marx was the product of different influences, viz, classicism, materialism, Hegelianism etc.

Marxism or Scientific Socialism

Before Karl Marx, there were different types of socialism, advocated by different socialist writers. But they were not able to put forth economic and scientific arguments to substantiate their concept of socialism. It was only with the coming of Karl Marx that socialism entered the main current of economic doctrines. Marixan socialism is called scientific socialism or Marxism.

Marxism is not merely a body of economic ideas; much more than that, it is a comprehensive system of thought embracing almost all the social sciences, such as philosophy, economics, history and politics. The chief merit of Marxism as a system lies in its organic unity. Its different aspects are so closely knit and so logically connected that the act of separating one from the other cannot be accomplished without doing injustice to the later. This explains why a great difficulty is faced when one is engaged in the task of distinguishing Marxian economics from Marxism.

Marxism has provided a new trend to the history of economic thought. It believes that theory and practice go hand in hand. Marxism has originality and initiative. It has a great degree of logical consistency. In short, the following are the main characteristics of Marxism;

(a) Marxism is international in character. It is different from state socialism which is national in character. To quote Haney, "With Marx, socialism took on a purely materialistic garb, and became international or cosmopolitan in its scope as contrasted with the National Industrialism or state socialism of his various predecessors."

(b) Marxism scientifically demonstrates how capitalism will gradually give place to socialism.

(c) There is complete uniformity and full co-operation among all Marxians. If any conflict arises between labour and capital in one country, it is considered as part of international struggle.

(d) Marxism is purely a working class socialism. Marxians generally believe in violence to be used in the final struggle, if necessary. In this respect, Marxian communism is Fascism in technique and Totalitarianism in ideology.

CHIEF TENETS OF MARXIAN THOUGHT

The following are the chief tenets of Marxian thought.

Section I

This section discusses Marxian philosophy, method of approach, money, and division of labour.

Marx's Materialistic Interpretation of History

Marx was perturbed about the various ill effects of capitalism which had progressed throughout Europe. At the same time he was a philosopher deeply trained in Hegelian philosophy. The Hagelian philosophy was one which was generally admitted to be true. Marx, however, found himself dissatisfied with that philosophy and accordingly took to the study of a criticism of it and an improvement upon it. In terms of Hegelian philosophy, history moves on the basic of ideas. It is based upon what is called the dialecticism. Everything has its opposite side. If there is something which we think is true then there must be something which is false to us. Similarly, if there is something good then there must be something bad also. People act on the basis of their ideas and accordingly whatever be the current flow of ideas that would determine the course of action of the people and hence the movement of history. However, the process of dialecticism does not let anything stand still. As has ben stated, according to this approach of dialecticism, thing has its opposite—this also referred to as every thesis having its antithesis. There is always conflict between the thesis and the antithesis and in due course of time the two get merged into one new idea called synthesis. But the moment this synthesis takes place, it becomes a thesis and therefore we get a new antithesis of this new thesis. People then start acting on the basis of the conflict between these new thesis and antithesis. Further, according to Hegel, this mixture of thesis and antithesis into synthesis can be in terms of various proportions of the two elements and accordingly history can take many possible courses. What exact course history will take will depend upon the exact combination of synthesis and antithesis in each case. This combination is in the hands of God, since it is, He who will let the people think along some lines and not the others. Thus history is nothing but the march of God on earth—the unfolding of His will in this world.

Marx maintained that Hegelian interpretation of history was upside down. Ideas did not move on their own, or according to the predetermined will of God; they were also mould on the basis of some deeper elements in the economy. All our ideas, philosophy, actions, political and religious institutions were founded upon the materialistic forces which were at the root of all these things. The dialecticism that moved the history was materialistic dialecticism. Ideas followed the materialistic advantages and conflicts and not the vice versa. Hence his approach is called that of the materialistic dialecticism.

Marx, in order to be thorough in his analysis, starts with what he calls the mode of production in the economy. In an economy, there is always the need to produce and for this the society organises itself into various institutions, methods of work, systems of distribution and exchange etc. All these things put together are called by him the mode of production and this mode of production includes for him all kinds of productive relationships. Within this productive relationship, there may be a system of slavery, here may be a system of workers and capitalists, feudal lords and serfs and so on.

Next plank in Marxian interpretation of history is the concept of surplus value. It is assumed by Marx that whenever labour works it impacts that labour to the raw materials it works upon and in this manner the produced good acquire value. This acquired value, however, is more than the value required for the maintenance of labour itself. When labour works, it spends its labour power the replacement of which needs the use of a certain quantity of goods and services. The labour required to produce these necessary goods and services is the labour cost of producing the labour power. This necessary labour, or the labour cost of labour, is less than then the actual amount of labour power which the consumption of these goods and services can replace. Thus, there is a surplus value over and above the replacement cost.

Throughout history, according to Marx, here has been a fight for the appropriation of this surplus value which the labour is capable of producing. In an economy we might come across various kinds of institutions, rules and regulations, political and religious institutions, theories and philosophies etc., but all these are hovering around one thing only, the surplus value. To Marx, the State plays a decisive role in this sphere. The State is always a class-State—it is always controlled by a particular class in whose economic interest it is to keep on ruling so that the appropriation of surplus value goes on. In other words, that class which rules and that class which appropriates are always the same. The ruling class sees to it that it does appropriate the surplus value. Otherwise what is the use in having the power in the society? All other classes are subject to its exploitation and in this manner the appropriation of the surplus value goes on till this class is ousted and replaced by another class which in its own turn starts exploiting the workers and appropriating the surplus values.

In the beginning, the ruling class is not very cohesive. Nor are, for that matter, the exploited classes of the society either. But as the time passes, the ruling class starts realising more fully the value of keeping its forces joined against the slowly but steadily increasing notes of dissatisfaction from the exploited classes. It must be noted that in the beginning the ruling class, while coming to power had given the exploited classes various concessions, especially in the form of increased productive powers of the economy. Out of these increased productivity, the new ruling class was able to give a larger share to the newly subjected classes and still appropriate a larger share than the ruling class which it replaced. The newly subjected classes, for the sake of these gains had sided with the new ruling class. Thus, when slavery was replaced by the system of feudalism, the slaves were given the chance of improving their lot by becoming serfs instead of slaves. On the other hand, the new system was economically more productive than the old system of slavery. Thus the new nobility classes appeared to be the saviours of the society and were welcomed as such. In due course, however, as Marx says, the ruling class started getting clearer ideas of the fact that their interests were opposed to those of the serfs and similarly the serfs got the ideas that the landlords were exploiting them. In this way, Marx says that to begin with the class idea is hazy but in due course, various classes become more clear about their respective interests and the conflict of their interests with those of the others.

At this stage, the ruling classes start putting forth various philosophies which suit their interest. They try to perpetuate the *status quo* so that the exploitation in their favour can continue unabated. They might believe in the good of those theories themselves so much so that vehemence with which they are presented to the exploited classes is able to convince the exploited classes also for some time. But in due course of time, the class interests prevail upon those philosophies and the exploited classes start realising that there is something wrong about those ideas and philosophies as far as they are concerned. In other words, they come to form the antithesis of the thesis which was being putforth by the ruling classes. Further, even though the ruling classes may be in conflict with one another, and the exploited classes may be in conflict with one another, and the exploited classes may be opposed to each other, but when it comes to facing the other category of class, they become united. In due course, the society is divided into the camps of two clearly divided classes, which are poised for a conflict and an actual conflict ensures. In this conflict a group of people comes up offering better facilities to the exploited classes and organising them against the ruling classes. When the existing society is thrown over and a new one comes into being the leader class becomes the ruling class and starts exploiting the remaining classes, even though compared with the older society the exploited classes are better off.

Marx was able to explain the transition of the society from one type to another with clarity but there were two gaps in his explanation. One was the gap concerning the transformation of what Marx called the Asiatic solicitor communistic societies into slavery and the second one was the course of history which would be taken after the overthrow of capitalism.

The first gap was filled by Engels in his book, "The Origin of Family, Private Property and State". He explains that in an Asiatic society, the production is distributed on the basis of needs. But very soon, the physically strong ones become the rulers of such tribes and they by virtue of their physical strength start appropriating a share of the produce of others. In their wake follow those two may not be physically as strong, but who are able to bring forth some other kinds of force such as the religious fear. Thus a ruling class develops. Then as *Stratchy* explains in his "The Great Awakening", (Lectures) these societies get converted into those of slave societies. This is because earlier it was the custom to kill the members of the vanquished tribe but now it was realised that it was better to keep them alive and make them slaves. They were able to produce more than what was necessary to maintain them. On the other hand, this proposition was a concession to the slaves also. Instead of getting killed now they had a chance to live with a possible escape. Similarly, when slavery gives place to serfdom, the slaves now get more freedom since the owners will not be able to kill them if they so desired. Also the serfs could have some private property which earlier they were not allowed to. Further this system was better from production point of view. The serfs would work more happily as compared with the situation when they were slaves. In the same manner when serfdom gives place to capitalism, the reading classes which are emerging in the last days of feudalism hold out a promise to the serfs of full personal freedom of profession and place of work. With the help of the serfs they are able to throw out the feudal lords and establish their own rule. At this stage, the division of the society is between the workers, the capitalists and the middle class. The middle class gradually gets evaporated while the ranks of the working classes keep on swelling. In due course capitalism also gives way to socialism.

Marx does not explain what would happen once the system of capitalism is ousted. However, according to Marxian materialistic dialecticism, history must move on and therefore to Marx, class conflict will emerge in some form even after the overthrow of capitalism, though Marx admits that he does not know what form it will take. Lenin adds one amplification to this analysis by pointing out that capitalism will make one final bid for survival by resorting to imperialism. However, imperialism will only spread the system of capitalism to hitherto feudal economies and this will not stop the process of history. At the most it can only postpone the downfall of capitalism. That is why Lenin calls imperialism the highest stage of capitalism.

Class Struggle

"The Communist Manifesto" written by Marx and Engels throws light on class struggle. In this Marx wrote that, "The history of all existing society is the history of class struggle." Marx made the class conflict the dominant feature of social life.

In ancient times, there was conflict between the master and the slaves. Under feudalism, there was the struggle between the Lord and the serf. Now under modern capitalism, the struggle is between the capitalists (bourgeoisie) and the workers (proletariat).

Capitalist production created a system under which workers are enslaved to capitalists, to the machines, to the supervisor and to the master. Exploitation of labourers is inherent in the capitalist system. As exploitation increases, there will be two divisions in the society the capitalists and the workers.

Communist Manifesto gave a call to the workers to unite and organise and liberate themselves from the capitalists. It believed that a revolution was inevitable and ultimately socialism would be established. In fact, capitalism itself creates conditions for its destruction.

Being influenced by the Communist Manifesto, a revolution broke in France in 1848, but was not successful. It was only "the small scale dress rehearsal of a gigantic production," which was scheduled for the future.

Method of Approach

Karl Marx first analysed the four broad divisions of economic activity, namely production, consumption, exchange and distribution. He believed that these four divisions are inter-related. Production brought those goods which were needed for the satisfaction of human wants; distribution shared them in accordance with the social laws; exchange distributed and in consumption, the product directly became the servant of individual want.

Further, Marx said that production was subjected to natural laws and distribution to social laws. In order to explain the connection between production and consumption he gave the example of productive consumption and consumptive production–the former shows the use of the product in a new process of production and the later the reproduction of human life. In addition, he emphasised that production, supplied the material for consumption and consumption supplied wants. Thus production and consumption are complementary.

Money

Marx in his theory of money mentioned three important functions of money, namely, measure of value, standard of price and means of payment. When money functioned as a measure of value, it was considered as an ideal money. If two commodities–gold and silver served as measure of value, then all goods had two prices – a gold price and a silver price. If the ratio of exchange between these two remained the same, there would be no disturbance.

Marx believed that the total quantity of money during a given period was determined by two factors – (a) The sum of prices of commodities in circulation and (b) The rapidity with which goods changed their forms.

Marx considered gold and silver as universal money. He said that just as a reserve money was needed for home circulation, a reserve money of gold and silver were required for external circulation in the international markets.

Division of Labour

Marx explained in detail the concept of division of labour in manufacture and pointed out that how in manufacture, a commodity from being a product of an independent workman became a social product, which was the result of the co-operation of so many workers.

Then Marx distinguished between division of labour in manufacture and the division of labour in society or social division of labour. The division of labour in society was created by the sale and purchase of products of different kinds of industry. In the case of division of labour in manufacture, several workers sold their purchasing power to a single capitalist. So the means of production were concentrated in one individual whereas in the case of social division of labour, the means of production were dispersed among many producers. Further in social division of labour, there was a systematic division of labour. Both the organisation and mode of production were simple. Social divison of labour was regulated by the law of nature. But in the case of division of labour in manufacture, the production was complex and was carried on according to the capitalist mode.

SECTION II

This section discusses the Marxian Economic Theories.

Law of Fetishism of Commodities

Fetishism means the mystical character and contradictory nature possessed by the commodities. Every commodity has two values–use value for the consumer and exchange value for the owner.

According to Marx, a commodity was a mysterious one because the social character of labour presented in the commodity appeared to the producer as an objective one. To quote Marx, "This fertishism of commodities has its origin in the peculiar social character of the labour that produces them". To Marx, this social character of labour demanded that the product must be not only useful to him, but useful to others. It should have a common quality i.e., Value.

Labour Theory of Value

Marx considered the labour theory of value a necessary step to arrive at the theory of surplus value which explains the exploitative nature of the capitalist society.

In a capitalist society, a commodity is defined as a carrier of use value and exchange value. As a carrier of use value, it satisfies the human wants. As a carrier of exchange value, it possesses a quantitative relation with other commodities.

Along with this double character of a commodity, there is a corresponding two-fold nature of labour. The one is useful labour, and the other is 'abstract' human labour. Useful labour produces commodities that satisfy human wants. Variety of human wants requires variety of use values. But labour alone cannot produce use value. Matter provides a material on which labour is to be exercised. Besides, a thing may possess use value, but may not require labour to produce it. Air, water, soil are some examples.

If a thing is to be called as commodity, it must have exchange value and to have exchange value, it should have "something common". In Marxian economics, this something common is "The abstract human labour". The value of every commodity is simply the amount of crystallised human labour which it contains, and commodities differ in value according to the different quantities of labour which are socially necessary to produce them". By "Socially necessary labour", Marx meant "labour-time necessary to produce any use-value with the given normal conditions of social production and the social average degree of skill and intensity of labour".

Further Marx emphasised that the value of a commodity would remain constant, if the labour-time required for its production also remained constant.

Criticisms

This theory has been criticised on the following grounds:

1) The argument that, value is the product of human labour is rather wrong because labour is not the only factor which determines value. All factors are necessary to prduce a commodity.
2) According to Marx, the exchange value of a commodity depends upon the amount of labour put in its production. He ignored the dominant role played by demand.

3) It has been pointed out that Marx did not take into consideration the difference in the qualities of labour
4) Marx argued that any commodity which does not involve human labour will not have exchange value. But we find that in practical world, due to scarcity, good lands derive more exchange value.
5) Critics argue that identical commodities may represent different amounts of labour. For example if old methods of production are employed, the amount of labour involved would be greater. Hence value would not be the same.
6) It is purely an objective theory. It explains total value only.
7) This theory is considered half-hearted. For if a chair made after 16 hours of hard labour cannot be used, it will have no value. Hence if labour is misdirected, the commodity will have no value.

Theory of Surplus Value

The theory of surplus value is the corner stone of Marxian economic theory. It provides the framework on the basis of which Marx has built up his theory of capital accumulation.

To Marx, in capitalism, production was not simply production of commodities, but was production of surplus value. The worker produces not for himself but for the capitalist. From capitalist point of view, that labourer alone is productive who produces a surplus.

Under capitalism, labour power itself becomes a commodity and is bought and sold in the market. The main aim of the capitalist is to maximise profit. It is possible for him because labour power has the peculiar character of being able to create more value than is needed for its own production. In other words, the worker can produce more in a day's labour than is needed for his own subsistence. The capitalist pays only those wages with which the latter can purchase the means of subsistence. Thus Marx divided the labour into two kinds–necessary labour and surplus labour.

For example, let us assume that if a labourer works for eight hours a day to produce a commodity, it is sufficient to maintain himself. Then the exchange value of the product should be equal to 8 hours labour. But if the wages paid to the labourer are equal to four hours labour–this labour is the necessary labour and the remaining four hours is known as surplus labour. It creates surplus value which goes to the capitalist.

Thus surplus value is the difference between the selling price of the commodity and the actual wages paid to the labourer. In a capitalist society the workers are thus exploited by the capitalists.

Marx classified capital as constant capital and variable capital. Capital invested in stocks or raw materials or equipments which directly assist the productivity of labour was called by Marx as constant capital. Capital spent for the purchase of labour power in the form of wages was called variable capital. According to Marx, it was only the variable capital which was capable of creating surplus value.

There are three components of the value of commodity: (a) constant capital (b) variable capital and (c) surplus value. Suppose 'C' stands for constant capital, 'V' for variable capital and 'S' for surplus value, then the total value=C+V+S. The rate of surplus value will be S=S/v.

$$S = \frac{\text{Surplus value}}{\text{Variable Capital}} = \frac{\text{Surplus value}}{\text{Value of labour power}} = \frac{\text{Surplus labour}}{\text{Necessary labour}}$$

The annual rate of surplus value can be measured by multiplying the surplus value by the number of turnovers of the variable capital in a year 'n'. Thus the annual rate of surplus value (as') will be

$$as' = Sn/V$$

The rate of profit is equal to the ratio of surplus value to total capital. It is S/C+V.

Marx showed the relation of profit to the rate of surplus value as:

$P_1 + S_1V/C+V$ in which P_1 stands for the rate of profit, S_1 for the rate of surplus value, C for constant capital and V for variable capital.

Marx also distinguished between absolute surplus value and relative surplus value. Absolute surplus value results from an increase in the number of working hours and the relative surplus value from reducing the real wages.

The extent of surplus value can be increased by raising the rate of exploitation. The capitalists can raise the rate of exploitation by the following ways: i) By increasing the working days of labourers, ii) By increasing the productivity of labour and, iii) By reducing real wages.

Criticism

The Marxian theory of surplus value has been criticsed on the following grounds:

1. Marxian theory of surplus value is derived from the labour theory of value. But there is no proof that labour alone creates surplus value.
2. In the real world, we are not concerned with values, but real tangible prices
3. Marxian theory ignores the demand side.
4. Marx exaggerated the scope of exploitation
5. Critics have pointed out that the rate of profit is not only related to variable capital, but also depends on the demand and supply of commodities.

Theory of Capitalist Exploitation

According to Marx, in a capitalist society, there are two classes of people–capitalists and workers. In a capitalist society all the means of production are owned by the capitalists. The workers, on the other hand sell their labour power to the capitalists. The capitalists produce the commodity with the application of labour to machinery and raw materials. Large scale production creates more employment opportunities to the workers. The act of production creates surplus. When the wages are paid less than the market value, exploitation arises.

But over production is another characteristic feature of capitalism in which goods are produced for the market. So when the market contracts, unemployment of workers emerges. Again when market expands, labour power is required again. So such labourers who are temporarily employed form an industrial reserve army. In the industrial reserve army, the farmers who are expelled from land also join.

It should be noted that in Marxian economics, capital means money used for exploitation. In a pre-capitalist society the producer sells his commodities for money. With that money, he buys the commodities of other producers for consumption purposes. So the cycle is C-M-C. Here money simply performed the medium of exchange function. It was not used for the exploitation of any one.

But under capitalism, production is done for profit. So the equation of exchange is M-C-M_1 in which M stands for money or capital, C for commodity and M_1 for money. The difference between M and M_1 constitutes profit or the degree of exploitation.

Thus the capitalist system grows. According to Marx, the capitalist is a vampire which thrives upon the blood of others and becomes stouter and broader the more blood it gets. But very soon in the very root of its expansion are the seeds of destruction.

Law of Capitalist Accumulation

According to Marx, it is the surplus value that creates capital accumulation. Capitalists choose the method of increasing the productivity of labour to maximise their profit. In order to make improvements in the productivity of labour, the capitalists save the surplus value. They reinvest it to acquire a large stock of capital and thus accumulate capital. In this Marx commented," Accumulate, accumulate it, That is Moses and the Prophets."

Evil Effects

The accumulation of capital gives rise to the following evil effects:

1) Large scale production is controlled by a few persons.
2) There is concentration of rural population in towns which leads to an increase in the number of proletariat.
3) As a result of capital accumulation,there is a declining trend in profits.
4) Since in a capitalist system,there is no balance between production and consumption, an industrial crisis occurs. In order to compensate the falling profits, the capitalist try to increase the production, but consumption does not increase at the same rate. So there is over production and under consumption.
5) There is growth of unemployment and pauperism.With the accumulation of capital,technological improvements take up which reduces the demand for labour. So the labour class forms an industrial reserve army. Thus there exist a large mass of casual labourers and paupers.
6) The developments of joint stock companies and banking and credit facilities fasten the growth of concentration of capital.

Thus the General law of Capital Accumulation shows a cumulative process the higher the degree of acumulation,the greater the wealth of society,the greater the industrial reserve army, the greater the concentration of power in a few hands, and the greater the accumulation of misery.

MARX'S THEORY OF CAPITALIST CRISIS

Marxian analysis of the law of motion of a capitalist society brings out the conclusion that capitalism must dig its own grave because of certain inherent tendencies in the order which makes the occurrence of a crisis inevitable. Among the strands of thought which bring Marx to this conclusion, the one that underlines the perennial want of co-ordination between the forces of production and those of consumption occupies a place of great importance. The first proposition of Marx is the division of capitalist society into two classes—the capitalists and the workers. The second proposition is the labour theory of value which underlines the concept of exploitation of the workers. The conclusion which emerges out of these two propositions is the ever-widening gap between the capitalists and the workers. The capitalists go on accumulating capital and undertake further investment in the hope of growing richer and richer. The workers get just enough to support themselves and their families. The subsistence level of wages makes it impossible for the workers to demand anything beyond the barest of their needs. Insufficiency of purchasing power with the workers leads to the phenomenon of under-consumption. Overproduction and under-consumption are, in fact, the obverse and reverse of the same coin. Attracted by their initial success in the acquisition of profits, the entrepreneurs goon investing their savings. Little do they realise that poverty of the masses imposes a great restriction on their capacity to consume. Such of the rich as do not have the incentive to invest, have a great propensity to hoard their savings, which, in effect, have a great propensity to hoard their savings, which, in effect, amounts to withdrawal of so much of money from circulation and a cut in demand of more than the same order. A chronic deficiency of demand is the result. Falling rate of profit is the direct outcome of the falling purchasing power of the masses. A crisis is inherent in such a situation.

Karl Marx conceived capitalist crises as those catastrophic events which are organic in the process of capitalist development. The capitalist society moves in cyclical manner with upswings and downswings and periodic crises. The three volumes of Capital and three volumes of Theories of Surplus Values have references regarding the problem of repeated crises, but "there is nowhere to be found anything approaching a complete or systematic treatment of the subject in Marx' writing". There are scattered notes on the crisis, which have been extended by fellow Maxists and those notes have been systematised into complete theories of crises. To Marx the following three theories of crises are attributed :

1. Law of Falling Tendency of Rate of Profit.
2. Crises arising from Disproportionality,
3. Crises arising from Under-consumption.

Law of Falling Tendency of Rate of Profit

The rate of profit has a tendency to fall, as the accumulation of capital goes on.

$$\text{Total Value} = C + V + S.$$

Where, C means constant capital which "does not in the process of production undergo any quantitative alterations of value". Constant capital remains constant as machine transfers its value to the product but does not increase in value. V stands for 'variable capital' meaning thereby that the value of such capital increase in the process of production. Value of labour power "reproduces the equivalent of its own value, and also produces an excess, a surplus value which may itself vary, may be more or less, according to circumstances". Therefore, V is the value paid to labour, S is the surplus value—excess of the value produced over value paid to labour. Value paid to labour stands for subsistence wage. S is the value appropriated by capitalists and is called profit. The rate of profit

would be equal to $P\dfrac{S}{C+V}$,

where P is the rate of profit, C+V stands for the value invested by the capitalists.

$$P = \frac{S}{C+V}$$

$$= \frac{SV}{V(C+V)}$$

$$= \frac{S}{V} + \frac{V}{C+V}$$

$$= \frac{S}{V}\left\{1-\frac{C}{C-V}\right\} \text{ as } \frac{V}{C+V} = \left\{1\frac{C}{C+V}\right\}$$

Now $\frac{S}{V}$ is the rate of exploitation or rate of surplus value appropriated. This may be denoted by P. $\frac{C}{C+V}$ is the organic composition of capital, i.e., the ratio of constant capital to total capital. It may be represented by q.

$$\therefore \quad P = P(1-e).$$

As the accumulation of capital takes place, constant capital increases in relation to capital or q increases. With e remaining the same as q increases, p must fall. This follows from our equation. Hence, in the process of capitalist development, the rate of profit must decline. This is the falling tendency of the rate of profit. With a decline in the rate of profit, the capitalists struggle to regain their old rates of profit, and hence class conflict emerges. Therefore, crises follow in the presence of this tendency of profit rate to fall. Marx has described that crises arising out of this tendency in Capital Volume III, in the chapter entitled "Unravelling the Internal Contradictions of the Law," in the following words: "It (a fall in the rate of profit) protnotes overproduction, speculation, crises, surplus capital alongwith surplus population". Again he writes, "The barrier of the capitalist mode of production becomes apparent.....in the fact that the development of the productive power of labour creates in the falling rate of profit a law which turns into an antagonism of this mode of production at a certain point and requires for its defeat of periodical crises.

Maurice Dobb in his book 'Political Economy and Capitalism' regards this law to be the sole cause of crises to the complete exclusion of other theories. But before we lay the blame on this law we must note the following :

(a) *First*, there is a contradiction in this law. Marx assumes that the rate of surplus value (p') remains constants or, in other words, the extra productivity due to capital accumulation is proportionately divided between labourers and capitalists. There is an increase in the wages (or value) paid to workers, according to this assumption, which contradicts with his other theory of subsistence wage to labour. If subsistence wage is to be paid to the labour, the whole extra output will go to capitalists and change the ratio to $\frac{S}{V}$. The rate of surplus value would increase, if subsistence wage is paid, and the rate of profit may not decline as the organic composition of capital rises. This can be seen in the equation

$$P = P'(1-q).$$

If q increases, p will decline provided p' remains constant.

If q increases, p' increases, p may or may not decline.

There is an inconsistency in Marxian law of falling rate of profits. Therefore, we cannot rely upon this law as a cause of crises.

(b) *Secondly*, with a fall in the rate of profits, the investment does not decline, as in Marxian system, the inducement to invest is the maintenance of capitalist position by each capitalist. If a capitalist diminishes his investment, he is driven out of the class of capitalists by sheer competitive forces. The higher or lower rate of profit has no impact on the rate of investment. Therefore, the law of falling rate of profit cannot cause crises. The true significance of this law lies in aggravating the class conflict present in capitalist society. The Capitalists on finding that the rate of profit is declining attempt to increase exploitation and thus impinge severe measures on the workers. This law is just another contradiction in a capitalist society, which works for the doom of capitalism.

(c) *Thirdly*, rise in organic composition of capital is slow and hence the tendency of falling rate of profits is perceptible though inherent, only in the long run. The rate of profit falls over a very long period and this periodicity may not coincide with periodic crises (trade cycle) with which we are familar today. But Marx had given the theory of capitalist development embedded with the periodic crises. He believed that the capitalist development takes place in cyclical waves. Those cycles were caused due to exhaustion of reserve army of labour and re-creation of reserve army by technological changes. This type of cyclical revolutions resembles the trade cycles of today. As soon as the unemployed labour force is exhausted and they tend to get higher wages, the capitalists shift to more capital intensive methods, thus creating unemployment once more.

Therefore, the Law of Falling Rate of Profit cannot be the cause of crises.

The above law assumed that all commodities sell at equilibrium values, but the decline in profit may be due to the fact that commodities do not sell at their values. The essential difficulty is that of realising the value, which is already in a physical sense embodied in finished commodities. The crises can arise for lack of realisation of values.

The under-consumption and disproportionality theories are theories of "realisation crises". Paul M. Sweezy states the difference between realisation crises and crises arising out of the tendency of falling rate of profit, in the following words: "The practical capitalist is unlikely to see any difference; for him the trouble is always insufficient profitability from whatever source it may arise. But from the point of view of causal analysis, the two types of crises present divergent problems. In the one case, we have to do with movements in the rate of surplus value and composition of capital, with the value system remaining intact. In the other case, we have to do with as yet unspecified forces tending to create a general shortage in effective demand for commodities, not indeed in the sense that it is insufficient to buy all the commodities offered, but that it is insufficient to buy them all at a satisfactory rate of profit. The starting point of the crisis is in both cases a decline in the rate of profit, but what lies behind the decline in the rate of profit, in one case requires a very different analysis from what lies behind the decline in the rate of profit in the other". We have discussed the crises arising out of falling rate of profit. Now let us pass on to the second group of causes.

The Theory of Disproportionality

There can arise disproportionality between various branches of production, as each capitalist starts production and investment on rough estimates of the market. The capitalist system works on the basis of anticipated demand and hence it becomes difficult to maintain corrector proportions between different branches of production and, therefore, output of one or other industry is sold at prices less or more than its value and this tends to spread to other branches. Hence a general crisis in the economy emerges. The process of adjustment imposed by the forces of competition would not be smooth, but cause an all-pervasive disequilibrium.

Michael Tugan-Baranowsky (a Russian economist) and Hilferding (a German economist) accepted Disproportionality Theory as the only theory of crises advocated by Marx and popularised it. But Marx devoted little space to the discussion of this theory.

Under-consumption Theory

Consumption is the basis of production, but the social relations in a capitalist society are such as impede the expansion of consumption. This is the "Fundamental contradiction" of a capitalist society. The subsistence wage and the increasing proletariatisation of society keep the base for production narrow and restricted. Tugan and Hilferding were not correct in laying the blame for crises only on production, and thus wrongly interpreted that the lack of consumption is the cause of crises in a capitalist society. Karl Marx in Capital (Vol. III) writes, "But to the extent that the productive power develops, it finds itself at variance with the narrow basis on which condition of consumption rests". The laws of distribution are antagonistic to the laws of production.

In the first place, the labour is paid subsistence age and under capitalism, the masses constitute labour. By flooding the market periodically with the reserve army, the capitalist system not only prevents the masses from participating in the benefits that increasing productivity offers but also prevents consumption from rising in proportion to aggregate output, thus threatening the system with under-consumption. The capitalist class shrinks and the proletariat class expands in numbers in the process of development. Therefore, increasing production creates a problem within itself of selling all the production at given values. The prices come down and a general crisis ensues.

Marx states in Capital (Vol. III) : "The last cause of all real crises always remains the poverty and restricted consumption of the masses as compared to the tendency of capital production to develop the productive forces in such a way that only the absolute power of consumption of the entire society would be their limit".

Again he says, "This last named power (i.e., consuming power of society) is not determined either by absolute production power or by the absolute consuming power, but by consuming power based on antagonistic conditions of distribution which reduces the consumption of the great mass of the population to a minimum variable within more or less narrow limits. The consuming power is further restricted by the tendency to accumulate, the greed for an expansion of capital and production of surplus value on an enlarged scale". Self-preservation forces the capitalists to expand the scale of output. "The market must, therefore, be continually extended".

Disproportionality thesis considers lack of proportion in different individual branches (or industries) of production, but under-consumption theory takes disproportionality between production and consumption in consideration.

Karal Marx had devoted a few notes and scattered passages to under-consumption theory, but these can be grouped together to form a theory of crises. Lenin and Bukharin treated under-consumption as one aspect of disproportionality in a capitalist society, but they did not develop a complete theory of under- consumption. Marx laid greater stress on under-consumption as the course of crises.

MARXISM AND CLASSICISM

It has often been remarked that Marxism is essentially a product of classical influence, especially that of Ricardo. Even Marx himself acknowledged his debt to classicism. In "The Critique of Political Economy", Marx clearly mentioned that he studied the classical political economy, while he was collecting material for his Das Kapital from the British Museum Library. It is a better proof to say that his economic theories are based on classical theories, "Marxism" remark Gide and Rist, "is simply a branch grafted on the classical trunk."

According to Prof. Gide, "Marxian theories are derived directly from the theories of leading economists of the early 19th century, especially from Ricardo's. Marxian theory of Value, analysis of conflict between profit and wages, theory of surplus value are derived from Ricardian theories. Again Marxian concept of natural laws shows close connection with classicism.

Marx's abstract, deductive method is essentially Ricardian in nature. Marx made use of the same theoretical tools used by Ricardo. Marxian theory of value is essentially Ricardian in nature. Both Ricardo and Marx accepted that the value of a commodity is determined by the quantity of labour used for its production. For both, value is measured by the hours of work put in by a worker.

Similarly, the theory of industrial reserve army is based on the Ricardian concept of technological unemployment. Another similarity is the universal applicability of Marxian theories. So it is reasonable to conclude that Marxism is a new interpretation of classical theories. The French Marxist Labriola says, "Das capital, instead of being the prologue to the communal critique, is simply the epilogue of the bourgeoise economics." Sorel also meant the same thing when he observed, "Marxism is really much more akin to the Manchester Doctrine than to the utopian."

Inspite of all these similarities, there are certain differnences between Marxism and classicism. There is ample difference in the language used, method of deduction and sociological implication. To a certain extent, Marxian analysis appeared to be an improvement over Ricardian analysis.

While the classical economists sudied economic problems on the assumption that capitalism was fixed and permanent system, Marx regarded capitalism itself as a variable, subject to change. Marx considered it as a transitional stage. Again while the dominant note of classical writings is based on class harmony. Marx regarded class conflict and class struggle as a historical fact.

CHARACTERISTICS OF MARXISM

We are now in a position to enumerate the main characteristic features of Marxism.

1. Marxian socialism is international revolutionary socialism. It is different from state socialism which is national in character.
2. Marxism is a working class gospel. Marxists believe in the organisation of workers and class struggle to do away with capitalism. Prior to Marx, the struggle was for an equitable distribution and for the improvement in the working conditions of the workers. But in the Marxian doctrine, the struggle was given a new name "class war"–workers against the capitalists, the poor versus the rich. The phrase "Class war"contributed much to the success of Marxism.
3. Marxism is purely revolutionary in character. The revolution will be peaceful.
4. Marxism is purely materialistic and not idealistic. It attaches more importance to economic facts.

5. Marxism is scientific socialism which demonstrates how capitalism will gradually give place to socialism.
6. There is complete uniformity and full co-operation among Marxians. If a struggle starts in one country, it is considered a part of international struggle.

Critical Estimate

As remarked by Lenin, "The Marxist doctrine is important because it is true. It is comprehensive and harmonious and provides man with an integral world outlook irreconcilable with any form of reaction or defence of bourgeosis suppression," G.D.H. Cole himself admitted that he was greatly influenced by Marx.

Marx was a revolutionist in whose hands political economy became an instrument of political struggle. As a philosopher, he was an optimist. In the opinion of Seligman," perhaps with the exception of Ricardo, there has been no more original, no more powerful, and no more acute intellect in the entire history of economic science."

Marxian theories of value, surplus value, accumulation, crisis, capitalistic development etc. contain a high degree of internal logical consistency than those of many other post-classical theories.

As Eric Roll put it, "Marx has built for himself an independent sociological frame work". His economic doctrines have a tremendous influence on the future socialist movements. Marxian economics influenced even the non-socialist thinkers. It contains immortal arguments against the evils of exploitation and crisis in a capitalist society.

Marx was a prophet. Marxism became something like a religion. It provided the ways and means for the salvation of human beings. It contained a message for the millions of people. Even today, Marxian economics is a popular gospel for the working class and young men and radical thinkers.

Weaknesses

The following are the weaknesses of Marxian economic thought :

1. Marx's materialistic interpretation of history is inadequate and one-sided. History of man is moulded by many factors. Economic factors are only one of them.
2. The whole Marxian analysis is built on the theory of surplus value. However in the real world, we are concerned with tangible prices and not with value.
3. Marx has proved to be a false prophet. There is no increasing misery of labour in advanced capitalist societies as assumed by Marx. On the contrary, the real wages of workers have continued to rise.
4. Marx pointed out that the technological progress leads to unemployment and thereby rises the strength of industrial reserve army. This is an exaggerated view.
5. Marx failed to visualise that technological innovations may lead to capital saving.
6. Marx failed to understand the flexibility in capitalism.

Conclusion

Inspite of the above critisms, we should remember that Marx developed many insights into the problem of modern industrialisation. The gifted and ingenious writer who called his system as scientific, must be regarded as a religious figure to rank with Christ or Mohammed. His monumental work–Das capital is, in fact, the Dooms day Book of Capitalism. To Loria, this book, "is a masterpiece where in all is great, all alike incomparable and wonderful."

QUESTIONS

1. Analyse the influences that shaped Marx's ideas.
2. What are the chief tenets of Marxism ?
3. Discuss the concept of 'Materialistic Interpreatation of History' as envisaged by Karl Marx.
4. Analyse the concept of 'Labour Theory of Value' as propounded by Karl Marx.
5. What is meant by 'Surplus value' according to Karl Marx ?
6. Make a brief note about class war.
7. Assess the place of Karl Marx in the 'History of Economic Thought'.
8. What are the capitalist's method of creating 'Surplus Value' as envisaged by Karl Marx ? Do you agree with those ideas of Karl Marx ?
9. "Marxism is simply a branch grafted on the classical Trunk"—Discuss.
10. Write short notes on :
    (a) Scientific Socialism
    (b) Dialectical Materialism
    (c) Marxian concept of capital
    (d) Law of concentration of capital

Chapter 19

STATE SOCIALISM

INTRODUCTION

Today, Socialism is followed in some countries. The socio-economic problems of the 18th century shook the belief of the people in capitalistic ideas. Socialism became a popular movement among the workers. Socialism has been defined "as that organisation of society in which the means of production are controlled, and the decisions on how and what to produce and on who is to get what, are made by public authority, instead of by privately-owned and privately-managed firms" (J.A. Schumpeter). According to Sidney and Beatrice Webb, the essential feature of socialism is that industries and services along with the instruments of production should not be owned by individuals; and the industrial and social administration should not be organised for private profit.

TYPES OF SOCIALISM

Socialism is one of the two main movements that have grown out of Marxism. These two movements are commonly known as Collectivism, the right wing of which is socialism and the left wing is Communism. The other forms of socialism are Ricardian socialism, State socialism, Reformism, Fabian socialism, Democratic socialism, Guild socialism, Syndicalism and Christian socialism.

WHAT IS STATE SOCIALISM ?

The year 1848 is very significant in the history of Socialist thought. It was the period when one phase of socialism had ended and the latter was to be started. By this time, all utopian socialists, viz., Robert Owen, Fourier, Blanc, St. Simonians and Proudhon proved to be utter failures, in the trial of their schemes. When the Revolution of 1848 was over, a class of Socialism appeared, known as State

Socialists who recognised STATE as an instrument for the execution of their socialists schemes. In this way, socialism developed mainly in France and England till 1848, was to a great extent utopion and idealistic and moreover, it was dominated by the middle-class spirit. State Socialism developed in Germany during the second half of the 19th century which was based on scientific realism. State Socialism was not merely an economic doctrine; but it was also a moral and social movement. It was based upon "a certain ideal of justice and particular conception of function of society and of the State." Since reforms, both social and economic were to be executed through a nation state, State socialism had a nationalistic character. The socialists, namely Rodbertus and Lassalle presented this idealistic doctrine; they wanted to bring a radical change in the social order with the help of the government. State socialism has also been known as socialism of the chain in Germany because a large number of intellectuals—Professors and writers of contemporary Germany were associated with it; and as Internationalism in France.

The main tenet of State Socialism was that the State should improve and consolidate its position by bringing about legislation for the uplift of the downtrodden. Strictly speaking, it is wrong to call this socialist movement, for it did not advocate abolition of private property and unearned income. It was content with some reforms which were not very socialistic in nature.

The movement developed in two stages. In the first stage, the Laissez-faire was criticised. In the second stage Socialism proper emerged and a manifesto containing objectives of State Socialism was issued. Wagner was the leader of this new movement.

First Phase of State Socialism

In the formative stage, the state socialism began in Germany in the early 19th Century as an economic movement. It was not an organised one, and in fact it was a loose mingling of economic thoughts which generally criticised the free competition. There were several classical economists who criticised the ideal of free competition or Laissez-faire. They were also against individualism. Besides, Sismondi and Cournot in France, Herman and List in Germany, and John Stuart Mill in England felt that the ideal of liberty (which classicists upheld) was likely to create a conflict between individual and social interests. The struggle could only be resolved by seeking state intervention in these matters. Thus, these thinkers and writers were not the forerunners of State Socialism; but their criticism of Laissez-faire and their advocacy of state intervention were unconscious contributions to the tendencies which led to the growth of State Socialism.

Second Phase of State Socialism

A clear-cut formulation of the doctrine of State Socialism took place in 1872 when a historical conference of economists, jurists, administrators, politicians and professors was held at Eisenach. The leaders of this conference were Schmoller Schaffle, Buvhart and Wagner. The Eisenach conference formulated the doctrine of State Socialism, as follows:

"The State was a great moral institution for the education of humanity, which could enable an increasing number of people to participate in highest benefits of civilisation." The citizens of the nation were not merely in economic association with each other but were bound together by the ties of common languages, culture and political constitution. The State was the organ of the moral solidarity of the nation and hence was responsible towards the poorer sections of the society.

The following arguments were put forward by the state socialists in support of their case for state and against individualism and laissez-faire.

(i) Based on the theory of conjectures propounded by Lassalle, they argued that the weakness of individual judgement often led to economic crisis. (ii) As Sismondi, St. Simon and Louis Blanc had stressed, the State Socialists argued that the troubles and uncertainties caused by competition among individual producers should be checked and curbed in the social interest. (iv) The functions of the State were historically evolving. In the early stages of development, individual actions and private charity were adequate. In modern life greater 'Social character' in economic matters is expected out of necessity.

It can be seen that State Socialism was a sharp reaction against the extreme Laissez-faire of classical economists. Schmoller gave the name "MANCHESTERISM" for the extremely optimistic and liberal aspects of classicism which was fully elaborated by Cobden and Bright in England, and Bastiat in France. Thus, State Socialism was opposed to 'Manchesterism', but it qualified its stand. Individual initiative as such, was to be fostered. State interference was to be prevailed upon in such spheres, where individual interest came to clash with the general social interest. In pursuance of this stand, the Socialists did not condemn private property and its fruits, viz., rent and interest. What they wanted was a more equitable social system to give the worker due profit of his labour. In the sphere of distribution, they advocated a step of progressive taxation system which would bring about a levelling of social classes. In the sphere of production, they stood for state control of such industries which are in the nature of public utilities and are likely to become monopolies, if left in the hands of individuals. Thus, they advocated the State administration of transport system, nationalisation of railways, canals, roads, municipalisation of water, gas and electricity and State operation of the banking system.

It would be wrong to presume that this programme of socialists was scarcely socialist in character, because, it upheld private property, rent and interest. It was, in reality a well-meaning programme of reform for national prosperity through state agency. The programme had a moral and ethical, rather than an economic basis. It was a far cry from the militant Marxists Socialist Programme. In fact, it was the nature of compromise.

Assessment

Though State Socialism remained an intellectual rather than a working class movement, its programme was tried and experimented extensively in almost all democratic countries of the world. The German Chancellor, Bismark applied this programme when he provided sickness and old-age insurance measures for the working class. All the state socialist programmes were adopted and implemented in England and France with the beginning of the 20th century. It was not implemented as an application of the theory, but to meet the demand put forth by the progressive democratic opinion. Public control and operation of utility services and progressive taxation and control of employer-employee relations were steps in recognition of more "social" character of modern life in which state interference was essential to preserve the individual's interest. The modern Welfare State when it resorts to a "Controlled" economy, only implements the programme of State Socialism.

JOHANN KARL RODBERTUS (1805-1875)

Rodbertus exerted direct influence upon economic thought than any other social writer. His important books were "To a knowledge of Economic Condition (1842) The Normal Labour Day (1871) and Light upon the Social Question (1875).

Rodbertus's economic thought may be analysed as proceeding from two main ideas: (a) labour theory of productivity and (b) belief in a decreasing wage share. The social idea is connected with the so-called iron law of wages, that is, a subsistence theory. On the basis of these two ideas, he emphasises the problem of distributive justice and evolves a notable theory of justice.

Exploitation of Labour

Rodbertus believed that labour produces all economic goods either directly, or indirectly through tools and machinery. Only those goods are economic which are produced by labour, others being "natural". The law of decreasing wage share was formulated by Rodbertus as early as 1837. The total amount paid in wages may increase, but rent and interest take an increasing percentage of the aggregate income. To Rodbertus, national income is divided into two shares as wages and rent. Rent in its turn falls into 2 parts, i.e., land rent and capital rent. The existence of rent is said to be due to 2 facts : (1) the economic fact that there is a surplus produced by labourer over their subsistence and (2) the juristic fact that private property in land and capital enables the owners to exploit labour and retain that surplus. In this idea, Rodbertus is following the thought of Sismondi, Proudhon and St. Simon. Rodbertus theory of crises is also derived from his theory of a decreasing wage rate. He also stated that poverty and crisis are to be done away with and distributive justice to be attained by an ultimate socialisation of property.

To Rodbertus there are two aspects of distribution : first, distribution between those engaged in the production of wealth and land owners and capitalists, and secondly, between these persons and other members of the society.

Commercial Crisis

His idea on commercial crisis explains that with the diminishing purchasing power of the working classes, the total consumption fail to keep pace with the total production leading to unemployment, further diminution of purchasing power and ultimately to an intensification of the crises. This is because the land lords and the capitalists instead of consuming, invest a considerable portion of their income in productive enterprises. This leads to an increase in the volume of production of those commodities which the labourers are unable to purchase. As a result price falls, the size of production is reduced, factories are closed and unemployment is created leading to further crisis. In this respect also, his ideas have much similarity with the Sismondian theory of over production.

Distributive Justice

Giving suggestion for the removal of the evils of improper distributive justice, he considered state intervention as a necessary one and ultimate socialisation of property. He regarded the latter aspect of distribution as the "secondary distribution". He remarks, "The judge who manipulates justice for society, the physician who heals the sick, the teacher who instructs the youth, receive incomes to the production of which they have contributed no work, incomes which are certainly the production of the labour of others.

He regarded rent, interest and profits as unearned incomes or exploited incomes and the existence of these as the chief characteristics of the present stage will soon be replaced by another which will all the more be close to the ideals of justice and in which the level of human welfare will be much higher. The stage which he visualised, would bring greater prosperity to the working classes. He was of the opinion that the desire of the working class will enable to attain to enjoy the fruits of growing civilisation, culture and progress. He stressed that nobody can stop people from achieving this object, because the working class constitutes a vast majority of mankind. He did not agree with those who said that the realisation of this object will be the end of progress.

Law of Decreasing Wage-Share

To Rodbertus, poverty and crisis were the two main evils of the modern economic system. "A man's poverty", he said, "does not depend so much upon what he has absolutely, as upon the relation in which his possessions stand to those of others about him and upon the extent to which they allow him to share in the progress of the age". Under the present situation, workers are paid only that much which is enough to maintain their living standard which does not keep pace with the increase in their productivity and consequently they are being left behind. Here he has enunciated the law of decreasing wage share. According to this law, the share of labourers in the national income goes on continually decreasing. The total amount of wages paid to the workers may increase but the percentage of rent, and interest in the national income goes on increasing at a faster rate. He concluded that the great mass of mankind is deprived of the income which it creates. In his respect, his ideas appear to be more akin to those of Sismondi, Proudhon and Saint Simonians. This essay on "The Normal Labour Day", he proposed that "in each industry, there should be established a normal day's work and that statistics should be collected indicating the number of such day's work required in the production of each commodity and that exchange between these should be allowed in accordance with the ratio indicated by these figures. He also suggested that after paying adequate remuneration to the capitalists and landlords, the remainder of the income should be distributed among the working classes according to the number of normal days of work of fraction thereof put in by them. He also suggested that the wages should be readjusted according to their productivity so that proportional share in the increase of the national product was guaranteed to them.

Suggestions for Improvement

He suggested that the entire community should be the owner of the means of production. Property should be socialised by an evolutionary process. He further suggested that every individual should contribute something to the national income. He mentioned three stages for nationalisation of property as (1) antiquity in which human beings were enslaved; and their labour was appropriated by their masters (2) Christian Germanic stage in which there was private ownership of property and capital, this was during his own days. (3) Christian social stage which would develop within next five or six centuries and in which land and capital would be fully nationalised.

He suggested the fixation of prices according to the amount of labour involved in the production of commodities; adoption of legal measures for fixing the hours of work; increase in labour's share of the national dividend, protection of workers against the bad effects of trade cycles and reduction in taxes. Under such a system of state regulation of production and consumption there would be as much personal freedom as in any other form in society. Rodbertus had full confidence in the authority of the state in its efficiency and power to bend the individual will to the general will.

FERDINAND LASSALLE (1825-1864)

In the development of German Socialism Lassalle occupies a pride of place. Lassalle was educated at Breslan and Berlin and was a brilliant person and a promising scholar. He was well acquinted with the writings of Marx and he again and again referred to Marx as his master. Like Marx, Lassalle believed that the capitalist exploit the labour by paying him subsistence wages and pocketing the surplus. But to win the masses, he invoked not the doctrine of exploitation of the worker by the proprietors but the brazen law of wages which is the title by which he chose to call the Ricardian law of wages. His chief title to fame is the establishment of the General Association of German workers in 1863. It later developed into Social Democratic Party.

Both Rodbertus and Lassalle are responsible for unconsciously laying the social and moral foundations of the State Socialism.

Producers Association

He felt that capitalism must be abolished and producer's association must be established in its place with a grant of credit by the state. To this end he also wanted universal suffrage so that the workers could control state power. In such a state of affair workers could get their fruits of their productivity. Lassalle's contribution is quite insubstantial in theory, but significant in action.

Lassalle and Marx

Both Marx and Lassalle advanced a theory that wages of labour under capitalism tended always everywhere towards subsistence level. But Lassalle differed from Marx on several points. Lassalle was sceptical about the efficacy of trade unions in improving the workers position under capitalism. Whereas Marx strongly believed in the value of trade unions.

Secondly, Lassalle explained the theory of wages in terms of Malthusian law of population. But Marx did not explain the theory of wages mainly in terms of the Malthusian theory of population.

The effect of these differences was that "whereas Lassalle argued that nothing could be done to help the workers without the capture of the State machine, Marx looked forward rather to a revolution based on the development of the workers movement as an economic force than to a predominantly political agitation for universal suffrage".

To Gray, "Lassalle's position may be said to be based theoretically on a Marxian foundation. He differs from Marx with regard to the programme of action for the immediate future. He also differs from Marx in his conception of what State is and of what can be done by and through the State".

QUESTIONS

1. Explain Rodbertus's Law of diminishing wage share ?
2. Compare Rodbertus's economic ideas with Karl Marx's economic ideas ?
3. Critically evaluate Rodbertus economic ideas ?
4. How Lassalle criticised the concept of division of labour ?
5. What were the suggestions made by Lassalle for the development of co-operative work shops ?
6. Summarise the main economic ideas of Lassalle.

Chapter 20

Neo-Classical Economics : Alfred Marshall

INTRODUCTION

Several changes had taken place in the field of industry due to advancement in technology and physical sciences. The use of machinery and inventions had led to large-scale production. Credit came to occupy a permanent place. The occurence of trade cycles created upheavels in production and consumption. These necessitated the intervention of the state in economic activities. All these factors revealed the inadequacy of classical theories. Hence a re-statement of economic ideas was urgently needed and this work was taken up by Alfred Marshall. Marshall's re-appraisal and restatement of economic ideas resulted in the establishment of neo-classical school. This made Marshall the greatest economist of his generation.

ALFRED MARSHALL

Alfred Marshall was the founder of the Neo-classical school. He was the first economist to re-name political economy as Economics. He was the first one who gave greater importance to the study of human wants and consumption. His Principles of Economics is a masterly exposition and a modern version of the old ideas.

Marshall was born at Clapham in 1842. His book "Principles of Economics" was published in 1890. The eighth edition came out in 1920 and it had been reprinted eleven times. It is divided into six books–Book I deals with preliminary survey; Book II examines some fundamental notions; Book III discusses wants and their satisfaction; Book IV describes the factors of production; Book V deals with demand, supply and value and Book VI presents an analysis of national income and its distribution.

Definition and Laws

Marshall defined Economics as, "Political Economy or Economics is a study of mankind in the ordinary business of life; it examines that part of individual and social action which is most closely connected with the attainment and with the use of material requisites of well-being. Thus it is on the one side a study of wealth and on the other and more important side, a part of the study of man." According to Marshall, Economics is a study of human beings and not of beasts or animals or plants. It deals with the economic aspect of man and not social or political or religious aspect of his life. It explains their ordinary business of life, which consists of earning and spending money, for the satisfaction of their necessities of life like food, clothing and shelter. Marshall classified human activities into activities that contribute to material welfare and activities that do not contribute to material welfare. Marshall shifted the emphasis from wealth to man. Wealth is only a means to welfare. Hence he has given primary importance to man and secondary importance to wealth.

Economic laws are the statements of economic tendencies and are hypothetical. Since economic laws deal with man's actions which are numerous and uncertain, they are to be compared with the laws of tides rather than with the simple and exact law of gravitation.

Marshall' Method

As far as the method of study is concerned, Marshall considered both induction and deduction as useful for economics. Both are complementary to each other. He says, "Induction and deduction are both needed for scientific thought as the left and right foot are both needed for walking".

Marshall was the great interpreter of the method of partial equilibrium. The forces influencing an economic phenomenon are too numerous and it is very difficult to analyse all of them to arrive at a complete explanation of the phenomenon. Therefore, the best method is to keep other forces constant, and study the forces influencing the phenomenon. Thus all the other forces are reduced to inaction by the phrase "other things being equal".

Wants and their Satisfaction

Marshall fully analysed the characteristics of wants and distinguished between necessaries, comforts and luxuries. He believed that consumption was the beginning and end of all economic activities and so he discussed consumption first and production afterwards.

Marshallian Utility and Demand

Price of a commodity is determined not by supply alone as the classical economists believed and not by demand alone as the utility theorists believed but by both demand and supply curves. Marshall takes up the theory of demand to analyse consumer behaviour. A rational consumer aims at maximising satisfaction from his consumption. The amount of satisfaction is closely related to the quantity of that commodity consumed by the consumer. Thus demand is based on the law of diminishing mariginal utility. Marshall stated the law thus, "the additional benefit which a person derives from a given increase of the stock of a thing, diminishes with every increase in the stock that he already has".

Demand refers to the quantity of a commodity demanded at a certain price, other things remaining the same. The individual demand curve can be directly derived from the law of diminishing marginal utility. Assuming the marginal utility of money to be constant as the satisfaction from the additional units of a commodity diminishes, the price offered to additional units will fall. Hence the demand curve slopes downwards. These individual demand curves can be added together to get market demand curve. The market demand curve represents the total demand of all the consumers for a commodity at various prices. On the basis of diminishing utility , Marshall has developed the law of substitution. So far consumer behaviour has been analysed with reference to only one commodity. In practical life, the consumer has to choose between more than one commodity. A rational consumer will spend his money in such a way that his total satisfaction is maximum. He will go on substituting one commodity for another till he gets maximum satisfaction.

Consumer's Surplus

Marshall added the term consumer's surplus to economic literature. According to him, "The excess of price which he would be willing to pay rather than go without the thing, over that which he actually does pay, is the economic measure of this surplus satisfaction. It may be called consumer's surplus". The consumers are generally prepared to pay a higher price for a commodity rather than go without it. But they actually pay less for it. As a result the consumer enjoys a surplus satisfaction and it is known as consumer's surplus. The concept of consumer's surplus has become the basis of welfare economics. In the words of Eric Roll, "The whole field of welfare economics of which Marshall's disciple and successor, Prof. Pigou, is the founder, really rests on considerations of which the consumers surplus doctrine is the intellectual ancestor".

Elasticity of Demand

It is another important concept which Marshall gave to economics. In Marshall's own words". 'The' elasticity of demand in a market is great or small according as the amount demanded increases much or little for a given fall in price and diminish much or little for a given rise in price." He distinguished between five degrees of elasticity—absolutely elastic, highly elastic, elastic, less elastic and inelastic. He laid down that the demand for luxuries was highly elastic, for comforts elastic and for necessaries inelastic.

Elasticity of demand can be measured by the percentage change in the amount demanded/ percentage change in price. Generally, elasticity of demand refers to price elasticity. Marshall was the first to define price elasticity of demand. Marshall gave three kinds of price elasticity—unity, greater than unity and less than unit elasticity. He also enumerated the factors governing elasticity of demand, viz., price level, nature of commodities, variety of uses, substitutes, time element, taste and habit.

Supply and Cost

Marshall developed his theory of supply on the lines similar to his analysis of demand. Just as the consumers obtain utilities or satisfaction from the consumption of commodities, it also involves,costs. Just as the marginal utility diminishes as a consumer increased his consumption of a commodity, the marginal cost rises as the production of a commodity expands. A rational producer aims at minimising costs. The same equi-marginal principle guides the producer in the matters of resource allocation. Like the consumer, the producer too "has to distribute his resources that they have the same marginal utility in each use; he has to weigh the loss that would result from taking away a little expenditure here, with the gain that would result from adding a little there".

Marshall distinguished between real and money cost of production. Real cost of production refers to the efforts and sacrifices involved in making a commodity. Real costs include the exertion of labour and waiting for saving. Money cost of production indicates the sum of money that have to be paid for these efforts and sacrifices.

Marshall divided costs into prime and supplementary costs. Prime cost are variable costs and include wages and raw materials. Supplementary costs are fixed costs and include depreciation, interest on loans, rent and salaries of executives. In the short run, a firm has to cover its prime costs. But in the long run, a firm must cover both prime and supplementary costs.

Factors of Production

According to Marshall, land and labour are the two chief factors of production. Capital is the secondary agent of production. Organisation is just a sort of labour. As a result, land and labour are the primary factors of production. Man being active, is the central force behind all activities relating to production and consumption, but nature plays a significant role as he is moulded by his surroundings and environment.

Population

Marshall agreed with Malthus on the subject of population. Out of the three propositions, he held the first to be valid and second and third as invalid due to the changes that has taken place after the death of Malthus. According to Marshall, population of a country increases either by natural cause or by immigration. Marriages were affected by climatic conditions and lack of means to support a family. He said that large families of healthy and physically fit children are an asset to the country and therefore, it is not true to say that an increase in population is detrimental to the economic prosperity of a nation. He believed that the state gained much from large families of healthy children. He wrote, "The members of a large family educated one another, they are usually more genial and bright, often more vigorous in every way than the members of a small family".

Division of Labour

Marshall held that increased demand for commodities and expansion of the market led to division of labour. Division of labour and improvement of machinery went together. Machinery provides several advantages viz., prevents monotony and relieves the strain of muscles. In order to achieve maximum economy in production, each person should be constantly employed so that the skill and ability may be used in a best possible way. In short, Marshall recognised the importance and the advantages of division of labour.

Laws of Returns

Marshall defined the Law of Diminishing Returns as follows: An increase in the capital and labour applied in the cultivation of land causes in general a less than proportionate increase in the amount of produce raised, unless it happens to coincide with an improvement in the arts of agriculture". In an advanced country twice the amount of labour and capital applied to land would double the yield. Marshall believed that agriculture was subject to the law of diminishing returns in the long run and the manufacturing industry was subject to the law of increasing returns. To quote Marshall, "the part which nature plays in production shows a tendency to diminishing returns, the part which man plays shows a tendency to increasing return".

Marshall stated the Law of Increasing Returns thus. "An increase of labour and capital leads generally to improved organisation which increases the efficiency of the work of labour and capital." In industries, an increase in units of labour and capital would result in more than proportionate increase in production.

Marshall defined the Law of Constant Returns in the following way. "If the actions of the laws of increasing and diminishing returns are balanced, we have the law of constant return and an increased produce is obtained by labour and sacrifice increased just in proportion".

From his Laws of Returns, Marshall arrived at certain policy conclusions. He pointed out that an increasing returns industry would produce more cheaply. But he felt that the difficulty was that it would become a tool of power politics and it might not be put to proper use.

Internal and External Economies

Economies of scale are of two types—internal and external. Internal economies are those which are 'dependent on the resources of the individual houses of business engaged in it, on their organisation and the efficiency of their management. Internal economies arise within a firm when its production increases. External economies are external to a firm and accrue to it when the size of the industry expands. These economies are important to understand the nature of long-run supply curve of an industry.

Book IV, Chapter 11 of the Principles presents the following list of internal economies:

(a) Economy of materials or the utilisation of by-products.

(b) Economy of machinery:

  (i) In a large establishment, there are often many expensive machines which a small manufacturer cannot afford to use.

  (ii) Larger machines are more efficient.

  (iii) Small manufacturers are sometimes ignorant of the best types of machinery to use in their business.

  (iv) Small manufactures cannot undertake expensive experiments.

(c) Economy in bulk buying and selling:

  (i) Larger firms secure discounts for purchasing in huge quantity.

  (ii) Larger firm pays low freights and saves on carriage in many ways.

  (iii) It is cheaper to sell in large quantities.

(d) Economy of skill:

  (i) Each man can be assigned to the task for which he is best fitted and thereby can acquire additional proficiency by repetition.

(e) Economy of finances. Larger firms secure credit on easier terms. Owing to these internal economies, the long-run average costs fail as output rises. But, after a certain level of output, average costs must rise due to growing managerial inefficiencies and marketing difficulties. Thus, internal economies and diseconomies explain why the long-run average cost curve is U-shaped.

As regards the external economies, Marshall discussed two general types: (a) Economies of localisation, such as, cross fertilisation of ideas, the development of auxiliary and subsidiary industries, the availability of skilled labour, (b) The growth of knowledge and progress of arts. External economies appropriate to Marshall's partial equilibrium analysis are those which are external to the firm but internal to the industry. The downward sloping industry's supply curve, which is the result of these economies, is drawn up on the assumption of constant technology because technological change causes a shift in the curve. This is a static analysis. But when we go through Marshall's discussion of external economies, it is surprising to note that in no case they are confined to single industry. All the examples involve, in some way or the other, technological change, which requires a dynamic analysis.

In fact, Marshall failed to distinguish between reversible and irreversible external economies. Reversible economies—a static phenomenon—are destroyed when the output of the industry falls, while irreversible or technological economies—dynamic phenomenon—are retained even when output of the industry falls. Ordinarily, the economies in the industry are due to technological advances and thus are irreversible; reversible economies are very rare.

External economies or decreasing costs are also not compa-tible with Marshall's assumption of perfect competition. This difficulty led to the development of the theory of imperfect competition in the 20th century. When the firms of an industry are producing under decreasing cost conditions as a result of external economies, any single firm will have a strong desire to monopolise all the firms of the industry. In that case, external economies will be internalised by the single monopolistic unit of production that has taken over all the competitive firms of the industry.

Marshallian Theory of Value and Time Element

For a long time, there was a controversy regarding what determined the value of a commodity. The classical economists said that the cost of production (supply) determined value. But the economists of the early marginalist school said that demand based on marginal utility, determined the value of a commodity. But Marshall said that both supply and demand determined value. Marshallian theory of value combines marginal utility with subjective real cost. According to Marshall, the forces behind both supply and demand determine value. Behind demand is marginal utility. Behind supply is real cost. According to Roll "the novelty of this view, compared with the Austrian version, is that cost of production comes into its own once more as a determinant of value".

Marshall likened supply and demand to two blades of a pair of scissors. It is useless to ask which does cutting. In his own words, "we might as reasonably dispute, whether it is the upper or under blade of a pair of scissors that cuts a piece of paper, as whether value is governed by utility or cost of production. It is true that when one blade is held still, and the cutting is effected by moving the other, we may say with careless brevity that cutting is done by the second; but the statement is not strictly accurate, and is to be excused only so long as it claims to be merely a popular and not a strictly scientific account of what happens".

Marshallian theory of value, owing to its emphasis both on supply and demand as forces governing value, is known as the Dual theory of value. It is important to note that the theory emphasises the role of margin. Value is determined by the forces of supply and demand at the margin. It is marginal utility and marginal cost of production that govern value.

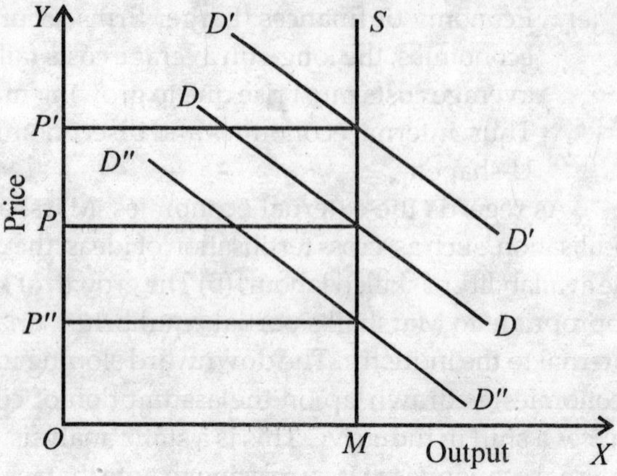

Fig. 1.

On the basis of time element Marshall classified value into four kinds. i. Market value, ii. Short period value. iii. Long period value and iv. secular value.

The market price of a commodity may be defined as the price ruling at a particular period. In the case of market price, the supply is fixed and price depends mainly on demand.

MS is the supply curve. *DD* is the market demand curve. *P* is the equilibrium price level. If the demand increases to $D^1 D^1$ the price level will also increase to P^1 as the supply is fixed. If the demand decreases, price also falls to P''.

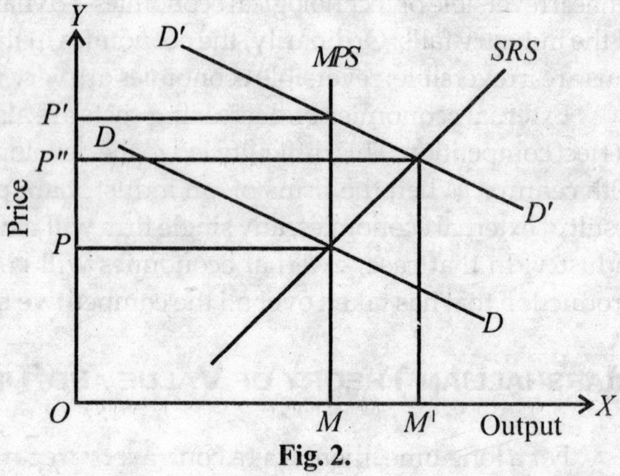

Fig. 2.

In the case of short period, it can be defined as "that period during which the variable inputs can be increased or decreased but the fixed plant can't be changed". So in the case of short period price, both demand and supply determine the price.

DD is the demand curve and MPS is the market period supply curve and SRS is the short run supply curve. When there is an increase in demand, DD will shift to D'D' and the short run price will be *OP*'' at which new demand curve D'D' intersects the *SRS*. The quantity supplied has also increased from *OM* to OM^1. Thus in the short run a greater amount of the quantity is sold and price is not quite as high as in the market period.

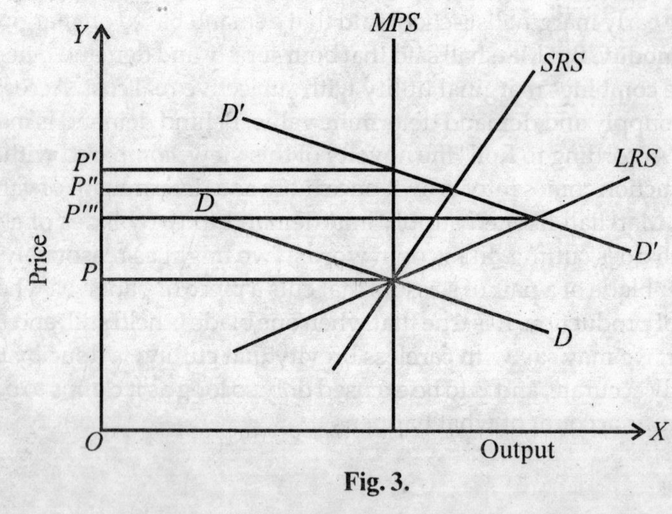

Fig. 3.

In the case of long period, supply means "what can be produced by plant which itself can be remuneratively produced and supplied within the given time". In the long run, cost of production is the most important determinant of price.

LRS is the longrun supply curve. MPS is the market supply curve and SRS is the short run supply curve. *DD* is the market demand curve and *OP* is the price. If the demand increases to *D'D'*, market price will increase to *OP'*. Short period price will be *OP''* at which SPS interesects the *D'D'* curve. But in the longrun the price will be *OP'''* at which LRS intersects the *D'D'* curve.

Marshall's introduction of time element in economic analysis was one of his many significant contributions to economic thinking. In conceiving of market broadly into short and long period, his object was to "trace a continuous thread running through and connecting the applications of the general theory of equilibrium of demand and supply of different periods of time."

Representative Firm

Marshall has defined a representative firm as one "which has had a fairly long life and fair success, which is managed with normal ability and which has normal access to the economies, external and internal, which belong to that aggregate volume of production the conditions of marketing them and the economic environment generally".

Marshall's representative firm is in a sense an average firm. It is neither old nor new, neither very efficient nor inefficient. It is neither earning super normal profits nor incurring losses. It is neither developing fast nor decaying. This type of firm can not be chosen easily. We will have to look the conditions of all the firms. Then only we can find out such an average firm. Marshall says, "the firms rise and fall but the representative firm remains always of the same size as does the representative tree of virgin forest".

Marshall has taken the example of trees in a jungle. There are several types of trees, some are very old and are on the verge of dying. Some are very new and up coming, some trees are there that do not allow the small trees to grow. Only a few will survive. They will gradually grow up. But we can find one such tree that is neither growing nor decaying. It is neither old nor new, that type of tree can be taken as representative tree.

Similarly we can find out our representative firm. The firm will have the following characteristics:

(i) Representative firm will be an average firm. It has a fair amount of internal and external economies.
(ii) It is neither declining nor increasing.
(iii) It's management is neither very efficient nor inefficient.
(iv) It is neither old nor new.
(v) It is neither earning super normal profits nor incurring losses.
(vi) There can be more than one such firm.

Criticisms

Marshall's representative firm is severely criticised by the later economists. The whole concept was regarded as unreal. The following were the main criticisms against the concept of representative firm:

(i) If the law of increasing returns operates in a firm then the firm will be enjoying profits. On the other hand if the firm is subject to the operation of decreasing returns, it will be incurring losses.

(ii) Robbins has said that even the clearest statement given by Marshall for his so called representative firm does not make it clear whether it is a representative plant or a technical production unit or a representative business unit.

(iii) Representative firm is also criticised as an illusory and unnecessary one.

(iv) Robertson has pointed out that in practice it is not so easy to locate a representative firm. A firm which may be representative now may not be in future.

(v) It is assumed that representative firm is neither increasing nor decaying. In practice we can not find firms which will be happy in that position.

(vi) Kaldor regards the representative firm as a state of mind rather than a concrete analysis.

Conclusion

Inspite of the above criticisms, some economists have tried to locate a representative firm. Chapman and Taussig have tried to locate a representative firm in 1914 in England. Prof. J.K. Mehta had also tried to prove that the concept in not altogether incorrect.

Distribution

According to Marshall, the theory of distribution is essentially a theory of factor pricing. The price of factors is determined by market forces, viz., demand and supply. The demand for a factor of production is a derived demand and depends on its marginal productivity. A producer employs more and more of factors of production till its reward is equal to its marginal productivity. Marshalls theory of distribution was essentially marginal productivity theory of distribution. Marshall also accepted Wicksteed's argument about the exhaustion of product. Marshall also admitted that the marginal productivity theory was not a complete theory of factor pricing as it considers only demand, neglecting the supply side. The effective supply of a factor of production at any time, according to Marshall, depends "firstly on the stock of it in existence, and secondly on the willingness of those in whose charge it is, to apply it in production". The equilibrium price of a factor is determined by the interaction of demand and supply.

Quasi-Rent

Marshall introduced the concept of Quasi-rent in economic literature. "Quasi-rent is the income earned from machines and other appliances for production made by man".

The quasi-rent is the surplus earned by the instruments of production other than land. According to Ricardo, the term rent is applied to income from land and other free gifts of nature, whereas quasi-rent is the income derived from man-made appliances and machines. The supply of these man-made producer goods cannot be increased in the short period even-though the demand for them may increase. Marshall therefore coined the term quasi-rent for the earnings of such capital goods in the short period.

Durable factors like machines, ships, house and even human skills are similar to land whose supply is fixed in the short-run. When the demand for them increases suddenly, their supply cannot be increased and they earn a surplus which is not rent but is similar to rent. Marshall preferred to call these earnings in the short period as quasi-rent. This is only a temporary surplus which goes to the owner of capital equipment in the short-run due to the possibility of increase in supply of capital equipment in response to increase in demand.

Due to increase in urban population the demand for houses increases. But the supply cannot be increased because of the scarcity of building materials. Their supply is as much limited as that of land. This abnormal increase in their earnings is quasi-rent. It is not rent proper or pure rent because the supply of houses can be increased in the long-run.

DETERMINATION OF QUASI RENT

A firm under perfect competition must cover variable cost in the short-run. Marshall argues that in the short-run period, the fixed cost need not be covered because even if the firm closed down in the short period, it will continue to incur this cost. The firm will be interested in covering the variable cost of production only. In case the short period price happens to be higher than the variable cost, the firm will get an income which is quasi rent. It does not constitute profit to the firm. This is illustrated in Fig. 4.

AVC is the average prime cost, *PL*, P_1L_1 and P_2L_2 are the price line where AR and *MR* coincide. At *OP* price the firm covers its average prime or variable cost, *AM* by producing *OM* output and quasi rent is zero. If price rises above *OP* to OP_1 or OP_2 Quasi rent emerges. At OP_1 price quasi rent is *JK* per unit and at OP_2 price it is *DE* per unit. In the long-run if price rises above OP_2 entry of new firms will eliminate quasi rent. Similarly at price below OP_2 also quasi rent will disappear due to the exit of firm and thus quasi rent is only short-run phenomenon.

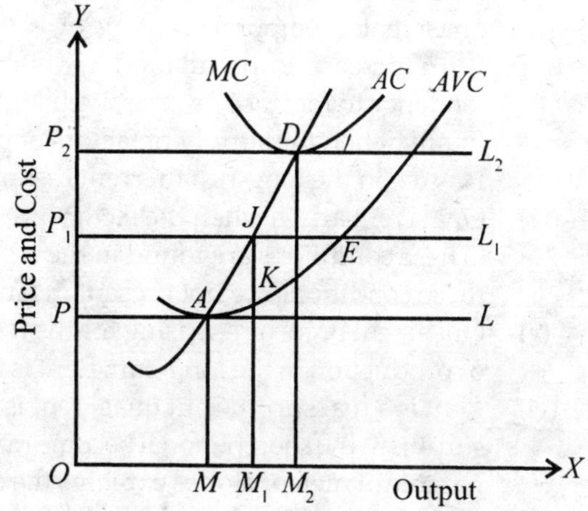

Fig. 4.

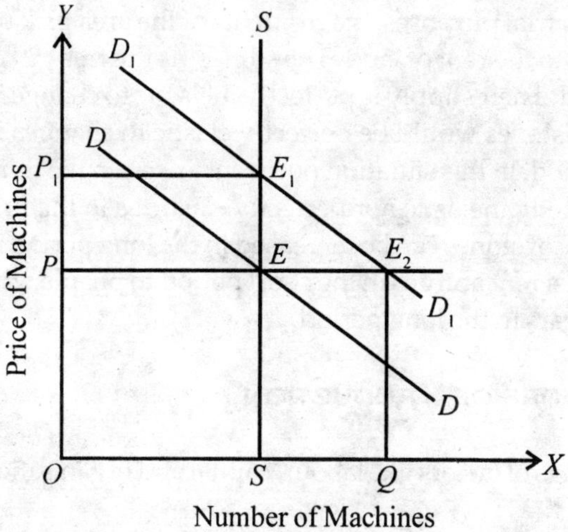

Fig. 5.

The supply of machine or any other capital equipment is fixed in the short period. The surplus earnings will continue. But in the long-run the supply can be increased and the surplus earnings will disappear. This can be illustrated with Fig 5.

In the Fig. 5. *SS* shows the absolutely inelastic supply curve of machines. The demand curve *DD* determines *OP* price at the point of intersection with the supply curve at *E*. When demand in the short-run increases to D_1D_1, the price goes up to OP_1 but the supply of machines remains at OS.

The entire increase in price EE_1 or PP_1 constitutes quasi rent. This is because the number of machines are fixed in the short-run and the transfer earnings are zero. In the long-run the supply becomes perfectly elastic and any number of machines will be supplied at OP price and quasi rent disappears. E_2Q covers just the transfer earning which is quasi rent. It does not constitute profit to the firm.

Difference Between Pure Rent and Quasi Rent

Though quasi rent is similar to rent as a differential surplus it differs from rent in several respects:

(i) Rent is a payment to the land while quasi rent is paid to factors like labour, capital and organisation.

(ii) The supply of land is fixed permanently. Rent is therefore permanent whereas other instruments of production like machinery and buildings etc. are temporarly limited. Therefore quasi rent is temporary.

(iii) With increase in population and subsequent increased demand for land, the rent has a tendency to increase progressively. But quasi rent diminishes progressively and disappears finally when the supply of factors of production becomes elastic. According to Stonier and Hague "in the long-run this rent disappears for it is not true rent but an ephemerol reward".

(iv) Quasi rent arises when the factors are heterogeneous and their supply is perfectly inelastic. "These conditions are found in the labour and capital and therefore quasi rent emerges. But these conditions are not present in land.

(v) Quasi rent or income arising for the fixed factors in the short period becomes part of the cost of production in the long-run. Rent is the reward for the use of land.

(vi) Rent is a real surplus but quasi rent is one "of the nature of a surplus" because though it is a surplus in the short period it becomes a part of the cost of production in the long-run. Marshall's parable of meteor stones explains the difference between pure rent and quasi rent. Marshall assumes three situations. In the first situation a meteoric shower of stones falls at one particular place. As these stones could be used for industrial purposes, the residents of the area pick up the stones. They will enjoy a pure rent equal to the rent of land. The stones, as the free gift of nature have the same property as that of land. Their supply is perfectly inelastic to change in price. In the second situation the supply of stones would be perfectly elastic to changes in demand both in the short and in the long period. In this situation pure rent arises. In the third situation the supply of stones is neither perfetly inelastic nor perfectly elastic as in the first two situations. The short period fixed supply of stones can be increased in the long period in response to an increase in demand. Thus quasi rent accrues in the short period to people who found the stones. However this rent disappears in the long period.

Quasi-Rent in Earnings of other Factors of Production

It is instructive to analyse quasi rent in the earnings of factors like labour, capital and organisation i.e. in wages, interest and profit.

Quasi Rent and Interest

The term interest is applied to a return on floating capital while quasi rent is the return from specialised or sunk capital. Interest on capital is a cost of production in all period, while quasi rent is a cost only in the long-run. In the short-run however quasi rent is a surplus. Usually interest acts as an incentive to save. The higher rate of interest may induce only the marginal investors. But there are other investors who will save even at a lower rate of interest, such as super marginal investors and that surplus is the rent element in interest. Thus quasi rent is price determined while interest is price determining.

Quasi Rent in Wages

Labour is heterogeneous. Labourers generally differ in their efficiency particularly in the case of personal efficiency. The more efficient workers enjoy a surplus or extra wage over the marginal workers. This surplus constitutes the quasi rent.

Quasi Rent in Profit

Entrepreneurs also differ in their ability like labourers. An entrepreneur with his superior organising ability is able to produce more at a lower cost compared to a marginal entrepreneur. Accordingly he is able to enjoy more profit. This is considered as rent element in profit.

Quasi Rent in Personal Incomes

Skilled persons like engineers, surgeons, lawyers and professors due to their abilities earn more than others. Their differential income is the quasi rent. Thus rent element is present in the personal income also.

Wages

Wages are the reward for labour. Wages are determined by demand and supply. The demand for labour arises because labour is productive. "Wages tend to equal the net product of labour; its marginal productivity rules the demand-price for it; and on the other side, wages tend to retain a close though indirect and intricate relation with the cost of rearing, training and sustaining the energy of efficient labour". Marshall attempted to combine the marginal productivity theory of relative wages with the Malthusian subsistence theory of the level of average aggregate wages. The forces governing the supply of labour vary in different market periods. The supply of labour is determined at the level where the marginal disutility of labour equals the marginal utility of labour. The chief force governing the long run supply of labour is the cost of producing labour. Wages must be high enough to cover the worker's expenditures for bare necessaries, for conventional necessaries and for habitual comfort. Thus Marshall did not discard the marginal productivity theory of wages but he regarded it as a part of a complete theory of distribution.

Interest

Marshallian theory of interest is an extension of Abstinence theory of interest of Senior. But he used the term waiting instead of abstinence. He said, "the sacrifice of present pleasures for the sake of future has been called abstinence by economists. But this term has been misunderstood for the greatest accumulators of wealth are very rich persons, some of whom live in luxury, and certainly do not practice abstinence. .... since the term is liable to be misunderstood, we may with advantage avoid its use, and say that accumulation of wealth is generally the result of postponement of enjoyment, or of waiting for it". The rate of interest is determined, on the supply side, by prospectiveness or time preference and , on the demand side, on the productiveness. The demand for capital arises generally from its productiveness, from the services it renders. It is subject to dminishing returns. The supply of capital depends upon the fact that in order to accumulate capital, we must save, wait and sacrifice the present to the future. In the short run, given the stock of capital, the rate of interest is mainly governed by the marginal productivity theory but in the long run, the cost of producing capital determines its return. Marshall ignored some other problems closely related to the theory of interest like the cumulative nature of interest and the effect of saving on invention.

Profit

Marshall gave to organisation the status of fourth factor of production and made profits the reward for organisation or the earnings of management. Organisation involves risk-bearing, business connection, and exceptional abilities of the entrepreneurs. In the long run, the profits are determined by the cost of production of entrepreneurial ability. However, his treatment of profit is vague.

Marshall's Contribution to Monetary Economics

Marshall's book entitled Money, Credit and Commerce appeared in 1923 and his orginality appeared to be more modern in the field of monetary problems. He believed that the value of money was a function of demand and supply. Marshall has also thrown light on the problem of rising price. He made a distinction between real and money rate of interest. For the first time, Marshall explained the causal process by which an increased money supply influences prices and also the part played by the rate of discount was explained by him. Though the purchasing power parity theory was associated with the names of Ricardo and Cassel, it was Marshall who explained the rate of exchange between countries with mutually inconvertible currencies. Marshall also introduced the 'chain' method of compiling index numbers. Marshall also introduced a proposal of paper currency for the circulation based on gold and silver symmetallism as the standard. Symmetallism refers to a method in which a bar of 2000 grams of silver is equal to a bar of 100 grams of gold. Under this system, the government must always be ready to buy or sell a wedded pair of bars for a fixed amount of currency. Marshall thought that this plan could be started by any nation without waiting for the concurrence of others.

EVALUATION

Marshall's Principles cannot be considered a complete and satisfactory work on economics. One finds a number of inadequacies and inconsistencies in Marshall's analysis. (a) He relegated diagrams and mathematical analysis to the appendices or footnotes. (b) He concentrated his attention on the static micro theory and avoided the dynamic macroeconomic problems. (c) His analysis was partial, and not general equilibrium analysis. (e) His concepts of representative firm and consumer's surplus were vague and imaginary. (f) His assumption of perfect competition was unrealistic.

In spite of these weaknesses, Marshall is ranked with the most influential economists and his authority in the subject remains unchallenged. In fact, Marshall's greatness as an economist lay not in his specific analytical contributions to economics, but in his efforts to solve the old problems and to create the new ones for coming generations. He, on the one hand, grasped and synthesised the seemingly conflicting ideas of the earlier writers and solved the age-old dispute between the classical and neoclassical economists regarding the determination of value. On the other hand, he suggested many new directions for the future development of economic science. Schumpeter pointed out a number of such directions while appraising Marshall's work.

(a) Marshall's Principles has guided the work of the generation he taught. Many of Marshall's disciples, such as, Pigou, Robertson, Lavingston, Shove, Joan Robinson and Edgeworth developed, restated and worked up corollaries to Marshallian propositions and pieces of technique.

(b) Marshall was the first economist to show that perfect competition does not always maximise output. Output may be increased beyond the competitive maximum level by restricting decreasing return industries and expanding increasing return industries.

(c) The concept of elasticity has set a fashion of reasoning in terms of elasticities. Now there are about a dozen elasticity concepts in use.

(d) Marshall's distinction between long-run and short-run has opened a new branch of economics, i.e., Short Time Analysis.

(e) Marshall is also the father of the theory of imperfect competition. His comments on the special markets of the individual firms led the economists like Sraffa, Harrod and Joan Robinson to develop the economics of imperfect competition.

(f) Marshall had fully grasped the idea of general equilibrium but he intentionally concentrated his attention on the handier partial equilibrium analysis.

(g) Marshall had a definite theory of economic evolution which as an instrument of research, greatly influenced the writings of H.L. Moore and W.M. Persons.

(h) Marshall also contributed to the development of modern econometrics. He firmly led the way towards, and prepared the ground for an economic science that would be not only quantitative but numerical.

Marshall wielded a great influence on the later economists both in England and abroad. His Principles is still considered a leading text book on economics not only in the country of its origin but wherever economics is studied seriously. Perhaps it is the only 19th century work on economics that still sells in large numbers. In England, Marshall's Principles is ranked with Adam Smith's Wealth of Nations and Ricardo's Principles and commands similar respect. A whole generation of brilliant students (promeinent among them, are, Pigou, Robertson, J.M. Keynes, Joan Robinson, Mauric Dobb, R.F. Harrod) has been brought up on Marshall's work and under his guidance. These students were destined to become leading economists. Marshall's influence was not limited to his home country. His ideas also had their impact on F.W. Taussig and T.N Carver in America, on Pantaleoni and Pareto in Italy and on Cassel in Sweden.

QUESTIONS

1. What is Neo-Classicism ?
2. Analyse the views of Marshall with reference to the definition and methods of Economics.

3. Bring out the idea of Marshall regarding Economic laws.
4. Explain the concept of consumer's surplus introduced by Marshall.
5. Analyse Marshall's concept of 'Representative Firm'.
6. Bring out the art of explaining the concept of value, demand and supply by Marshall.
7. Discuss the role of 'Time' in the theory of value as explained by Marshall.
8. Explain the concept of Quasi-rent of Marshall.
9. State how Marshall has explained the concept of 'Distribution'.
10. Make a critical estimate of Marshall.
11. Write short notes on :
    (a) Marshall's Elasticity of Demand
    (b) Marshall's Law of Diminishing Returns
    (c) Internal Economies & External Economies
    (d) Marshall as a synthesiser.

Chapter 21

INSTITUTIONAL SCHOOL

INTRODUCTION

Institutional economics is a phenomenon of the twentieth century. It is an American product. The institutional approach to economic theory is not new. But as a system of thought it was developed in the hands of the American economists. The seed for a new crop of "institutional" ideas was planted about 1899 with the publication of Veblen's book, "The Theory of the Leisure class". The sapling gained further strength and began to mature by the publication of Veblen's another book, "Instinct of Workmanship". The development and growth of sociological studies, especially the ideas of C.H. Cooley and John Dewey added further strength to it.

The Depression of 1930s provided an extremely favourable atmosphere for the development of institutionalism as a movement in academic thought and as a tool of public policy. The "New Deal" of President Roosevelt was chiefly the result of Institutional Economics. It may be classed as one of the outstanding cases in which a school of economic thought has been closely associated in a direct and practical way with government.

CHARACTERISTIC FEATURES OF INSTITUTIONALISM

The following are the main features of institutionalism:

1) The Institutional school emphasises the role of institutions in economic life. The term "institution" includes customs, social habits, laws, way of living, and mode of thinking. According to the Institutional school, economic life is regulated by economic institutions and not by economic laws. Naturally the institutionalists are interested in analysing and reforming the institutions of credit, monopoly, distribution of national income and so on.

2) They believe that group behaviour, not price should be the central theme of economics.
3) They recognise that human behaviour is constantly changing and economic generalisations should be relative to time and place.
4) They emphasise custom, habit and law as modes of organising economic life.
5) They hold that important motives which influence individuals cannot be measured.
6) They believe that the economy must be studied as a whole. It is in contrast to the "atomistic" approach of the marginal school.
7) They advocate the evolutionary approach in economic analysis. The study of the evolution and functioning of economic institutions should be the central theme in economics.
8) They reject the idea of "normal equilibrium". According to them, mal-adjustments in economic life are not departures from normal equilibrium but are themselves normal.
9) Economic laws are not of universal application. They are relative to time and place. In other words, they believe in the doctrine of relativity.
10) They reject the classical assumption of harmony of interests. They recognise class conflict.
11) They advocate inductive method.
12) They rejected the pleasure-pain psychology of the marginalists.

Institutionalism and Classicism

Institutionalism is a movement against the classical and neo-classical approaches.

According to the classical and neo-classical writers, economic activities are governed by economic laws. But to the institutionalists, economic activities are governed by institutions, instincts and habits.

The classical economists believed that human actions are always guided by self-interest and therefore economic activities are automatically self-adjusted. Nature was considered superior to man and man-made institutions were under-valued.

Institutionalism aims at social reform. In contrast to the static equilibrium of the classical writers, the institutionalists believe in a planned evolutionary rearrangement of economic life. The institutionalists recognise the existence of maladjustments and advocate their correction.

Institutionalists unlike the classicists are not mere theorists. They are reformers. They do not believe in the destruction of capitalism but in eradicating its evils.

Institutionalism and German Historical School

Even though there exist many differences between institutionalism and classicism, the twentieth century institutionalism, to a very great degree resembles with the German Historicism of the nineteenth century.

Both have emerged out of troubled times. Both emphasise the role of institutions in economic life. Both lay stress on evolutionary changes. Both are opposed to the deductive method. Perhaps the only difference between the two, if there is any, is regarding the emphasis given to evolution. The Historicists had no idea of evolution. Their chief concern was with the use of logical method.

Two Groups of Institutionalists

There are two general groups of institutionalists. Veblen, Commons and Mitchell formed the older or negative group. On the other hand the younger or positive group includes W.H. Hamilton, R.G. Tugwell, and W.E. Atkins.

The older school is chiefly concerned with the description of economic life, institutions and maladjustments in the economy. Their approach is essentially critical and negative.

The chief objective of the younger school is to direct social evolution in such a way that social institutions and human activities may move simultaneously. Their approach is positive. They also seek to replace old economics with new economics. Despite their extreme optimism they could not succeed.

In short the main concern of the older school was to analyse and describe economic life as it is, while the younger school was essentially concerned with correcting the maladjustments in the economic system with the help of man-made institutions.

THORSTEIN BUNDE VEBLEN (1857-1929)

Introduction

Veblen was the founder of Institutionalism and the spiritual leader of renaissance in the American Economic thought. He was born of Norwegian parents on a Wisconsin Farm on July 30, 1857. At the age of 23, he graduated from the Carleton college, where he studied political economy under Prof. J.B. Clark. He took a Doctorate Degree in 1884 from the Yale University on "Ethical Grounds of a Doctrine of Retribution".

Veblen remained unemployed for a period of 7 years. When Prof. Laughlin joined the newly founded Chicago University as Head of the Economics Department, in 1892, he took Veblen with him. He was promoted as Assistant Professor at the age of 43. But Veblen never succeeded as a Professor due to his high eccentricities.

Veblen edited the Journal of Political Economy for about 10 years. He served the University of Stanford from 1906 to 1909, the University of Missourio from 1911 to 1918 and the New School of Social Research from 1919 to 1922. He died in California on August 3, 1929.

Veblen was a prolific writer. Among his works are: "The Theory of the Leisure class" (1899); "The Theory of Business Enterprise" (1904); "The Instinct of Workmanship and the state of Industrial Arts" (1919); "The Place of Science in Modern Civilisation" (1919); "The Engineers and the Price System" (1921); "Absentee Ownership and Business Enterprise in Recent Times: (1923); and "Essays in Our Changing Order" (1934).

Main Economic Ideas

The following are the main economic ideas of Veblen:

Criticism of Earlier Schools of Thought

Veblen was an inspired critic. Veblen was not satisfied with the methods, doctrines, and theories of the classical school and marginalist school. His economic views are contained in his articles, published in the Quarterly Journal of Economics and Journal of Political Economy in which he has been critical of the marginal utility economics, the Historical School and socialism. It is only through his criticisms of the existing economic theories, he has contributed to the development of economic thought.

He criticized the existing economics as it was not an evolutionary science. Similarly he holds that the laws of classical economics are based on a wrong conception that there is a natural order in which maladjustments are automatically corrected. The classical economics was therefore unreal and unsound and the conclusions drawn were not universal. He attacked the classical economic theories based on hedonism and rejected the concept of economic man, as always balancing pleasure and pain.

He also criticized the Austrian economists on the ground that they could not make any advance in the direction of reconstructing economic science. Truely speaking he was greatly influenced by the development that took place in the field of social psychology. Social psychology recognised the importance of instincts. Veblen wanted to make economics an evolutionary science based on human instincts and institutions. Calling his own method the evolutionary method of economic analysis, he believed that economists—both past and present had completely failed to grasp the significance of the evolutionary approach. They evaluated the industrial process in terms of money. His main ideas in this regard are contained in his book "The Instinct of workmanship".

Significance of Institutions

Veblen considered the entire civilisation as "a scheme of institutions". He believed that the human behaviour ultimately developed into an institution. Hence he tried to prove that the present institutions were the product of a continuous process of cultural development which had been in operation for many centuries. The growth of institutions was conditioned by two factors—material environment and propensities of human nature. The changing industrial technology considerably affected the changes in the economic institutions.

According to Veblen, industry and business were the two important institutions of capitalism. Around these two institutions, several small institutions like competition, private property, banks, money etc., have developed. He further believed that these institutions have developed because of the process of evolution. These institutions would go on changing in accordance with the changes in the social habits of the people. The development of social institutions is also influenced by such factors as population, physical environment, climatic changes etc. In fact his theory of institutions is not based on any rigid principles.

He has divided the society into two classes—productive and leisure. The former comprise those who work and produce, while the latter depend on acquisition. Veblen believed that the existing institutions have helped in creating class struggle.

Thus Veblen's institutionalism rests on two stones, namely economic conflict and change. Further, even though Veblen has traced the evolution of institutions, he was not sure about their future. Life for him was an endless process which would continue for all times and in which old changes will give place to new changes.

The Theory of Business Enterprise

Veblen's book, "The Theory of Business Enterprise" presents a theoretical analysis of the working of the large scale business enterprises and other institutions of American capitalism.

According to Veblen, it is the machine that provides the scope and method to modern industry. Machine had standardised the human life, goods, processes and consumer taste. It had improved the efficiency of work and decreased the unit cost. But these advantages of machinery are not fully obtained. The industrialists in their desire to get more profit, try to control a large part of the industrial machine and adopt speculative activities. Since every businessman is not alike so far as efficiency, finance, organisational ability etc., often they merge with each other, leading to greater profit at the cost of industrial efficiency.

Veblen, therefore, concludes that it is through the establishment of monopolies and monopolistic activities that the captains of industry meddle with the economic and industrial machanism and the results are wastes, depression and unemployment. In short, the community is deprived of the goods and services to which it is entitled. According to Veblen, large business enterprises are mere parasites on the community, and their activities only add to the instability of the capitalistic system.

Corporations

According to Veblen, technological basis of industry has given rise to a new form of business enterprise, namely corporation. Corporations depend mainly on corporate credit system. They have greater earning capacity and use it only for their benefits and not for the benefits of consumers in the form of lowering prices. Further, these corporations have changed the nature and functions of private property. They have introduced collective action and given stimulus to class conflict.

Further, Veblen feels that the era of corporate enterprise is totally different from full competition. In corporate enterprise era, "there is a division not between those who have something and those who have nothing, but between those who own wealth enough and those who do not".

The Theory of the Leisure Class

In this book, Veblen pointed out that leisure class was an ancient institution. In almost every society upper class men are exempted from industrial occupations which expressed their "superior rank". This class, based on the ownership of property was aggressive. It never helped in providing the necessaries of life. It was always interested in getting money. Veblen regards the activities of this class as waste because they do not serve human well-being. The culture of this class was somewhat savage like because of its dress, ways of living, expenditure etc. This class spent much time, money and energy on unproductive things.

On the other hand in the society, there has developed a class which does not have enough money, but which is faithful to the rich and is always subservient to it. This class much larger in size, supports the leisure class and is unable to fulfil its own basic needs for subsistence. Veblen's analysis of the leisure class appears to be more or less similar to that of Marx.

Trade Cycles

Veblen's analysis of the causes of financial crisis and unemployment is quite interesting. Veblen noticed that in the society there are two classes of people—one was busy in supplying the requirements of human society and the other was engaged in speculation and profit making. He regarded the cyclical occurrences as the result of the finance capitalism.

During the days of prosperity or high profits and rising prices, the captains of industry borrowed large amounts of money to expand their business and earn high profits. During prosperity the banks increase their rate of interest and hence the capitalised value of prospective income declines.

At the later stages of boom, profits decrease and a limit is reached when prices do not increase any further due to increased cost of labour and materials. Bank loans become costlier. Due to the pressure by the creditors for the return of loans, the businessmen get nervous. This leads to the failure of best established firms in the market. Ultimately a crisis occurs.

Veblen thought that the market glut was created by producers themselves because they produced without anticipating demand. They put restraint on the productive efficiency of engineers and technicians. It may be mentioned that Veblen considered "the captains of industry" as mere parasites knowing nothing about the industrial processes. They were interested only in making money and interfered with the industrial techniques.

Had this not been so, the modern industrial techniques could have increased the industrial production and raised the welfare of the society. The efforts made by the entrepreneurs towards the adjustment of supply and demand have been termed by Veblen as "Capitalistic sabotage". He also remarked that whereas in the olden days, producers thoroughly understood the technique of production, in his day, they entirely depended upon engineers and technicians.

According to Veblen, competition is at the root of all cyclical depressions. He therefore suggested that Government expenditure in efficient and low cost public works or preparations for war can ease the pressure of competition and reduce the power of monopolists. In any case, he was not in favour of overthrowing private capitalism. He was only opposed to those producers who were money makers, that is who under-valued productivity, efficiency and gave importance to profit making.

Class Conflict

According to Veblen, under the existing system of production, the society was divided into two classes—productive class and leisure class. While dealing with the concept of class organisation he introduced another concept, that of cultural lag. To Veblen, the technological change was the most important factor that changed the economic institutions and through them, the human behaviour. He emphasised the fact that class conflict arose out of cultural lag.

Value

Veblen differentiated between economic value and pecuniary value. The end products produced by the industrial system possessed economic value. In the Veblenian sense, a commodity has economic value, which statisfies both the individual and social needs.

As against economic value, pecuniary value, or exchange value is the final product of an industry. It is psychological and rests on uncertain foundations of vendibility—that is the capacity of an article to bring the pecuniary gain to its owner.

Critical Estimate

Veblen was the founder of institutional economics. He gave a new look to the subject economics. Veblen's works show that he had varied interests and the topics that he wrote covered a wide range of knowledge. It is difficult to put him in any class. In fact, he was a sharp critic and he looked upon things with a critical eye.

Veblen who was against the captains of industry, financial promotors etc., regarded Marxism as an offshoot of classicism. Though he disagreed with many theories of Karl Marx, he looked upon him as a great teacher and original thinker. P.C. New Man says, "Both Marx and Veblen were institutionalists to the extent that they were interested in studying private property and other economic phenomena in their changing forms".

Veblen criticised the additive method of the classical economists. But he could not satisfactorily discuss his own method of study, namely, evolutionary method. Veblen described the evolution of economic institutions, but was not definite about their future trend. The evolutionary theory checked him from making a forecast.

Though Veblen's influence has waned, his economic thought inspired several writers. To conclude in the words of Eric Roll, "His evolutionary economics presents a body of economic theories which are more relevant to the problem of issues of twentieth century than are the economic theories of the equilibrium economists. This greater relevance of Veblen's institutional economics is derived from its central theories of economic conflict and change. Besides, closing the gap between theory and practice, Veblen's evolutionary economics gives a futuristic slant to economic thought".

JOHN ROGERS COMMONS (1862-1945)

John Rogers Commons was a leading member of the Iinstitutional School. He was born in rural Ohio in 1862 in an impoverished family. Owing to the financially weak position of his father, he acquired first hand knowledge of social and economic problems and realised the necessity of solving them. He graduated at the age of twenty six. He never took his doctorate degree. Since 1904 and until his retirement, he served the University of Wisconsin. He led a very busy life. Besides his major occupation of teaching and writing, he also served on several commissions on state and federal levels.

Though Commons covered a variety of topics like value, monopoly, labour legislation, public utilities, economic thought, housing, trade unionism, social insurance etc., he is generally regarded as a labour economist. While Veblen concentrated on the sociological aspects of the society, Commons contributed to the study of the legal aspects of institutionalism.

The main publications of Commons are:

The Distribution of Wealth (1896), Trade Unionism and Labour Problems (1905), Races and Immigrants in America (1907), A Documentary History of American Industrial Society (1910), Labour and Administration (1913), Principles of Labour Legislation (1916), History of Labour in United States (1918), Industrial Goodwill (1919), Industrial Government (1921), Legal Foundations of Capitalism (1924) and Institutional Economics – Its place in Political Economy (1934).

Main Economic Ideas

The main economic ideas of Commons are the following :

Economic Institutions

In his book "Institutional Economics", Commons defined institution as a "collective action in control of individual action". It may be noted that this definition is different from the one given by Veblen. Veblen defined an institution as a widely prevalent habit of thought. Commons emphasised the mutual dependence of men and the need for co-operation. He emphasised the need for collective action to reconcile the clash of interests which the institution of private property created.

Further Commons believed that all economic institutions were subject to evolution. They evolved gradually. He took the case of capitalism and private property and explained that how these institutions developed gradually.

Institutional Economics

This type of economics started with the conflict of interests. To him, institutional economics took its place as the proprietory economics of rights, duties, liberties and gave to collective actions. He strongly criticised the classical and hedonistic theories because the former emphasised the bargaining between two parties and the latter on pain and pleasure as the sole determinants of economic behaviour. In his opinion, both had failed to recognise the importance of collective action.

Pragmatic Approach

His work was characterised by two qualities, namely historicity and relativity. He shifted from pure theory to pragmatic theory which stressed the importance of inductive analysis. The pragmatic economists were those who had "an eye on the worthfulness of their reasoning for understanding, experimentation, taking chances, and guiding themselves and others in the future".

Economic Transactions

According to Commons, human behaviour was a social phenomenon as it affected the entire society. Men have to depend on one another and the existence of private property created conflict in them. The dependence of man upon man, and the conflicts between human beings should always be kept in order which was possible only by a study of economic transactions.

He classified these economic transactions into bargaining transactions, managerial transactions and rationing transactions. The main defect of the orthodox economics was that it was concerned only with exchange transactions. Bargaining transactions implied an exchange of goods and services between equals. In managerial transactions, a legal superior directs an inferior with the help of the state authority. On the other hand in rationing transactions, three parties are involved, namely, a superior authority, an inferior authority, and a court of law for the enforcement of rules. By superior body he means a trade union or a government.

Bargaining transactions lead to the change in the ownership of wealth, managerial transactions create wealth and rationing transactions ration the burden and benefits of the wealth so created. All these transactions are symbolised in a "going concern".

Theory of Going Concerns

Commons defined a going concern as an institution which promised the expectation of beneficial bargaining, managerial and rationing transactions which were bound together by the working rules. It is these going concerns with the working rules that keep them going all the way from the family, the corporation, the state itself.

This theory of going concern was different from the Duty theory and the Liberty theory of the state. Further Commons differentiated between two other terms—going plant and going business. A going plant is the technological organisation, the main aim of which is to attain the highest degree of efficiency and output. On the other hand, a going business is concerned with the production of money values. In Commons' opinion, the best going business is that in which sales and purchases, technology and business are rightly proportioned.

Public Utility Theory of Labour

According to Commons, labour constituted an important part of the national economy, because they created public utilities. He was fully aware of the psychology of labour and the working of corporate managements. So he was instrumental in bringing about improvements in labour legislation, social insurance, public utility regulation, workmen's compensation etc.

Commons believed that there was a cultural lag between the technological progress and the psychological attitude of employers and workers. He predicted that the future of industry was psychological. So he suggested that the worker should be taught the importance of his job and its significance in the productive process. In short, he was part of the going concern.

Capitalism

Capitalism evolved very slowly during the course of centuries. The present form of capitalism is not what it was in the initial stages. It has lost much of its significance and has now become more congenial.

Commons divided capitalism into 3 kinds, namely, merchant capitalism or mercantilism, employer capitalism, and banker capitalism. In employer capitalism, there was factory-method of production and legal control of commodities was seperated from its physical control. In banker capitalism, the banker entered into economic activities and the stage of abundance caused by an industrial revolution was merged into an era of stabilisation.

Further, in banker capitalism an economic atmosphere was created in which the corporation played a dominant role. It was a flexible institution. It has influenced legislatures and established strong public relations. Commons believed that a regenerated legislature could enforce effective checks on the operation of this kind of capitalism and the state government by protecting the rights of the individual could save the entire system.

Explanatory Principles

Commons introduced 5 explanatory principles namely efficiency, scarcity, working rules, sovereignty and futurity. He discussed the notions of scarcity and efficiency in a detailed manner. Veblen thought that under capitalism a balance could be attained between the two. Whereas the classical economists used scarcity as the basis for value, the Austrian economists adopted hedonistic approach.

Futurity was the most important factor in the collective economics of Commons. Old economists whom Commons called the commodity economists, had ignored the time element. It was the introduction of mathematical statistics which accorded a place to the element of time in economic theory.

Collective Action

Commons discussed elaborately the several stages of the development of the economy of collective action. The impetus for the first stage was provided by the development of the market. Technology and credit led to other stages—the retail shop stage to the wholesale stage. Further according to Commons, three major institutions—corporations, unions and political parties played a dominant role in the repetition and changes of human actions and transactions.

Economic Systems

Comparing the various economic systems, commons felt that under the existing conditions, it was difficult to decide the best system. Under communism and fascism which had evolved in Russia and Italy, liberty was suppressed.

Commons wanted labour to increase its bargaining power and favoured the organisation of trade unions. He never wanted revolutions and strikes, but "collective bargaining on something like an organised equilibrium of equality..... It seems to be the only way to save us from communism, Fascism or Nazism".

Critical Estimate

In the History of economic thought, Commons was regarded as a great labour economist. He was the father of a labour struggle theory. He always emphasised a compromise between the employers and employees as a solution for conflicting problems.

His treatment was a five dimensional interpretation of modern economy. He tried to avoid the errors committed by the formalistic economics of the classical and neo-classical schools and the descriptive economics of the Historical School. In fact he tried to combine these two analyses in order to avoid the over emphasis of logicality and historicity.

While Karl Marx spoke about a class conflict between labour and capital, Commons saw several group conflicts—between labour and capital, between debtor and creditor, between small business and large business, between conservative and radical labour, between farmers and whole salers and between buyers and sellers. Further when Marx had set up dualism, Commons developed pluralism and admitted that the class conflict would continue for ever.

Though Commons admitted that there were certain shortcomings in capitalism, he was optimistic about the progressive improvement of the workers. At the same time he also noted that capitalism itself had changed considerably since the days of Adam Smith.

Today most of his ideas on social reforms are generally accepted. In short Commons made the institutional economics a tool for social reform.

At the same time it must be noted that Commons was not an economic theorist. He simply gave a different point of view to the matters already discussed by his predecessors. He applied the past thinking to the problems of his age, supplemented the work of Veblen and aimed at giving collective action its due place throughout economic theory. His emphasis on legal institutions helped considerably in the development of economic institutions in America.

WESLEY CLAIR MITCHELL (1874-1948)

Wesely Clair Mitchell was one of the three great figures of the Institutional School, the other two being Veblen and Commons. He was a student and admirer of Veblen. He gave an empirical basis for institutional economics. He is well known for his pain taking studies of "green backs" and "business cycles". He did pioneering work in the statistical field and he thought that his statistical studies would provide a firm foundation for the institutionalist ideas of Veblen.

Mitchell was born in Illinois. Though he came from a poor family, he managed to receive university education. He took his doctorate from Chicago University. After serving the Columbia University for a few years, he occupied many important positions. For some time he was Director of the National Bureau of Economic Research. He took an active part in the Social Science Research Council, and the Bureau of Educational Experiments. He served on the Immigration Commission, the Bureau of Labour statistics, The Industries Board, President Hoover's Committee on Social Trends, the National Planning Board, the National Resources Board etc.

He was a visiting Professor also at the Universities of Oxford, California and Cornell. For his outstanding contributions to the science of economics, he received honorary degrees from the Harvard, Columbia, Paris, Princeton, California and Pennsylvania Universities.

Mitchell's outstanding publications are:

History of the Green Backs (1903), Gold Prices and Wages (1908), Busines Cycles (1913), Business Cycle and Unemployment (1923), Business Cycles—The Problem and its Setting (1927), Recent Economic Changes (1929), The Backward Art of Spending Money (1937), and Measuring Business Cycle (1946)

Main Economic Ideas

The main economic ideas of Mitchell are discussed below:

Method of study

Mitchell emphasised the quantitative analysis in economic investigations. Through this quantitative method, he was able to give a systematic account of cyclical fluctuations. He was not interested in the old methodological debate that existed between Historical and classical schools. It is to be noted that he expanded the scope of economics beyond the boundaries of equilibrium.

Institutional Approach

According to Mitchell each individual has lot of instincts which are different from individual to individual. The behaviour of an individual that resulted from inborn capacities is an unreasoning form of behaviour. According to Mitchell, three institutions—arts, writing, speech and religion provided a standard behaviour, habits of feeling, acting and thinking that are approved by the community and finally embedded in a social institution.

Social institutions are powerful agents to direct human behaviour. They are the embodiments of past achievements of human intelligence. They form the basis for the rational behaviour of the individual. Mitchell advised us not to look inside the individual and assess the pleasant and unpleasant characters. Instead he asked us to look outside the individual, to the habits of behaviour which had been gradually evolved by the society.

Mitchell analysed the origin and development of institutions and customs and supplemented them with money, banking and labour problems. In his later researches, he emphasised the physical aspect of economic activities. To him, the traditional economic theory was defective because it lacked an institutional approach. Mitchell was confident that the institutional approach would develop economics into a science of human behaviour and in turn economics would be instrumental in bringing about social change. He felt that the role of money would broaden the scope of economic theory.

Theory of Economic Guidance

The nineteenth century economists provided a rather simple theory. They explained that entrepreneurs occupied a key position in the economic system. They brought together the agents of production in the most efficient manner with the result that economic waste was avoided. The economic needs of the community were satisfied.

But Mitchell in his theory of economic guidance put forward the idea that the introduction of corporate enterprise separated ownership and management. As a result, powers were concentrated in the hands of a few directors and executives. Those who control the affairs of a corporation do it in their own interests. In 1913 when he wrote about this theory, he found that the role of the Government in this regard was less.

Economic Welfare and Planning

Mitchell thought that when economics became a science of human behaviour, it would emphasise more human welfare and less wealth. So he suggested that in economics two things namely, determinants of welfare and the means to be employed to increase it, should be analysed.

To Mitchell, welfare did not simply mean an abundant supply of goods, but also a satisfactory working life, full of interesting activities. The criterion of welfare was to be developed in such a way as it would be appreciable to many lines of efforts, by quantitative methods (Mitchell).

The Depression and the New Deal called for economic planning. Mitchell considered economic planning the most important and difficult task. He believed that planning by business alone would not succeed. Through lectures and talks, he made it clear that planning was essential for an orderly economy but piece meal planning was defective because it ignored the fact that the economic and social processes were interrelated. He was of the view that the work of the national planners was that of an agency for the fulfilment of what the majority desired.

Business Cycle

Mitchell's greatest contribution was the study of business fluctuations. His book entitled "The Rhythm of Business Activity" was the pinnacle of his ideas and findings on the working of trade cycles. He collected huge statistical data and with the help of that he could carry on a deep study of the individual cycles, group of cycles, and parts of the cycle. He has made use of the frequency curves. Further he has made a comparative study of the different trends of changes in the prices during the period of the cycle. The study begins with a review of the existing theories, followed by a survey of general economic organisation and a detailed statistical analysis of various economic factors like prices, interest rate etc., and in the last comes the analysis of the working of cycles.

Mitchell did not consider the study of trade cycles as a branch of economic theory. According to him, the study of trade cycles was more important and fruitful for gaining knowledge about the working of modern economic system.

He attributed business cycles to the imbalance between production and distribution. When imbalances occur, it results in glut in the market. Men and machines are unemployed. Business cycles recur because there is no proper business planning. Business fluctuations are aggravated by factors such as widening of markets, monopolies, migration of people etc.

According to the self generation theory given by Mitchell, each phase of a trade cycle would automatically generate the other. He held the view that business crises were but one feature of a recurrent cycle. A crisis was expected to be followed by depression, depression by recovery, recovery by prosperity and prosperity by crisis and so on. Certain factors like internal political conditions, changes in the monetary and banking systems, war, peace, new industrial methods, international relations etc. were responsible for the slackening or quickening the phases of trade cycle. He pointed out that different industries were affected by the trade cycle in different ways.

Further, Mitchell stated that during the revival period, there would be an increase in the price level, high business expectations, more production, increased demand for goods, and the level of employment would increase. Business optimism, increased investment, heavy orders for machinery would lead to a further increase in the price level.

Later on due to the operation of two factors namely, (1) gradual increase in the operative cost and (2) tension in the money and investment markets, a crisis or recession occurs.

To him, the present economic order which is characterised by high capital investment, middlemen, flexibility of credit and lack of adjustment, was responsible for trade cycles.

Mitchell's treatment of trade cycles is more elaborate, realistic, and authentic, since it is based on statistical and historical proofs. Although studies in different aspects of the problem had been made by Malthus, Sismondi, Karl Marx, Jevons etc., it was only Mitchell who provided an analysis of all the phases of trade cycles on the basis of statistical data. To quote Burns, "No other work between Marshall's "Principles" and Keynes "General Theory" has had as big an influence on economic thought of the western world".

Inspite of several merits, the theory is not without its criticism. It has been criticised by modern writers on several counts. Firstly, it simply takes other factors behind. Secondly, it treats cyclical movements as the movements of a machine. In the opinion of Homan, it is a static theory in which economic institutions are a relatively constant factor not highly variable.

Critical Estimate

Mitchell who made a deep study of business cycles, was undoubtedly the leading exponent of institutionalism. His business cycle is considered a masterpiece in economic literature. Mitchell's use of the statistical method and quantitative analysis has made economists to be more realistic in their studies. He wanted that inductive method should be used in the study of economic problems. Since collection of facts is more painstaking, tiring and time consuming, he had earned all praise from American economists. He had realised that the modern economic life was quite complicated and its problems could not be handled successfully with the help of traditional analysis. He therefore pleaded for an integrated study of all related disciplines such as history, statistics, sociology etc.

Institutionalism—An Evaluation

With the exception of Veblen, no one has added anything material to the body of economic science. They have made valuable descriptive studies and criticisms but they have neither said anything new nor they have provided any scientific basis for the reconstruction of the science.

As critics, the institutionalists have exposed the weaknesses of classical economics, unreal assumptions and the abstract method. But they have emphasised the usefulness of the role played by institutions. Their emphasis on evolutionary process had been fruitful.

Its Weaknesses

Prof. Haney has pointed out the following weaknesses in the institutional thought:

(1) In certain respects, institutionalism is abstract and is based on unreal assumptions which render it unsatisfactory to the scientist.

(2) Like the classical economists, the "economic man" of the institutionalists does seem to be real. They have treated man as a mere creature of habits.

(3) While making use of the words such as "effective", "serviceable", "workmanlike", "futile", they have not prescribed any criteria for the measurement of these. Their thought is full of abstractions and unrealistic.

(4) Their thought leads to the adoption of the test of "survival" which is not only a strong materialistic concept but is vague.

(5) Their thought contains important deductions which cannot be verified. For example, their statement that present conditions are bad and they can be improved by changing "institutions" appears to be a mere assumption, because it is difficult to know what institutions are good and what are bad.

(6) Their thought suggests a sort of "Kinematics" to the extent that they conceive of economics as dealing with ever moving bodies governed by no casual forces and tending towards no equilibrium.

(7) The relation between "Instincts" and "reason" and the part played by "institutions" are not all clear. Their plan lacks uniformity and a specific goal.

QUESTIONS

1. What is meant by Institutionalism ?
2. What are the features of Institutionalism ?
3. Emumerate the views of Veblen.
4. Can you equate Veblen with Marx ?
5. Make a critical appraisal of Institutionalism.
6. Write short notes on :
   (a) Capitalistic Sabotage.
   (b) Veblen's view of 'Trade Cycle'
   (c) The Theory of Leisure class
   (d) Works of Veblen
   (e) Economic ideas of Mitchell.

Chapter 22

WELFARE ECONOMICS

INTRODUCTION AND DEFINITION

Welfare Economics is that branch of economic science which aims at evaluating the social desirability of alternative social states. It is a normative study for it lays down criteria on the basis of which policies can be adopted to maximise social welfare. It is futile to try to define welfare economics. Curiously enough a lot of energy of the economists has gone into identifying the concept of welfare and even then the term has not been given, unambiguous meaning. Right from the day welfare economics has come to be recognised as a separate branch of economics, writers have attempted to define welfare. It is no easy task for welfare depends on many factors.

A genuinely historical treatment of welfare economics should begin with the classical period. Briefly it can be said that classical writers regard political economy as a science which has to do with external valuable things on economic goods – ie with wealth. While defining economics as a science of wealth, they proceed to assert that wealth promotes the economic welfare of many and that economics should be essentially concerned with welfare on atleast material well-being. This peculiar idea of welfare is of course challengeable. One can also conclude that welfare economics in its modern sense is conspicuous by its absence in the classical scheme. None the less, the classical writings seem to emphasise that instead of studying the effects of various measures on the wealth of a nation, economic analysis should go to step further and study the welfare of the nation as affected by these measures. However the trouble is that classical economic theory is usually so written that the purely scientific model and the welfare arguments based on it are often intertwined; because of this one fails to have a clear grasp of the classical welfare ideas.

The broadening of the economics of wealth into the economics of welfare was actually effected by the marginal utility school which rejected the classical wealth oriented definition of economics, welfare, utility, ophelimity. These were the terms around which expositions of economic doctrines began to revolve.

Only in the 1920s a fully self-conscious welfare theory began to be written. This self-consciousness about its distinct character and even the name welfare economics are due to Prof. A.C. Pigou. Prof. Pigou is considered as the father of welfare economics. His great book, 'The Economics of Welfare', may fairly be taken as marking the beginnings of fully self-conscious welfare analysis.

ARTHUR CECIL PIGOU

Arthur Cecil Pigou succeeded Prof. Marshall as the Professor of Economics at the University of Cambridge. After Marshall, he became the leading neo classical economist. He is the founder of "Welfare Economics" His leading ideas on welfare economics are found in his "Economics of Welfare" (1920). Prof. Pigou popularised the word welfare and gave a concrete meaning to it. In his book, Pigou dealt with three things: (1) a definition of economic welfare (2) spelling out the condition under which welfare is maximised and (3) pronouncement of policy recommendations for increasing welfare.

Prof. Pigou gave a clear meaning to the concept of welfare. He defined individual welfare as the sum of satisfactions obtained from the use of goods and services. Social welfare is the summation of all individual welfare in a society. Since general welfare is very wide and complicated, he limited his study to economic welfare. He defined economic welfare as that part of social welfare "that can be brought directly or indirectly into relation with the measuring rod of money."

Pigou regards economic welfare and national income as coordinate. He lays down two conditions for maximisations of welfare: (i) Given the taste and income distribution, an increase in national income represents an increase in welfare. (ii) For welfare maximisation, the distribution of national income is equally important. If national income remains constant, transfer of income from rich to the poor would improve welfare. With income subject to diminishing marginal utility, transfers of income from the rich to the poor will increase social welfare by satisfying the more intense wants of the poor. Thus it is economic equality that maximises welfare.

Prof. Pigou had a dual criterion for detecting the increase in social welfare. First, he measured the economic welfare of the society in money value and thus, given the supply of resources, an increase in national dividend meant an increase in social welfare. Second, Pigou favoured an income equalisation policy and therefore, reorganisation of the economy which increases the share of the poor without offseting adversely "productive effort enterprise and development of capital equipment was to be taken as a gain in social welfare."

Pigou has made a distinction between private and social costs. The private marginal cost of a commodity is the cost of producing an additional unit. The social marginal cost is the expense or damage to society as a consequence of producing that commodity. Private marginal benefit can be measured by the selling price of the commodity. Social marginal benefit refers to the total benefit that society gets from the production of an additional unit. By making a distinction between social and private valuations of economic activity, he paved the way for the analysis of external effects or externalities in social welfare economics.

The presence of external effects in production was seen by Prof. Pigou in the divergence between social net product and private net product. He defined social net product "as the aggregate contribution made to the national dividend" and the private net product as the contribution which is capable of being sold and the proceeds added to the earnings of the person responsible for investment. The divergence between the two products shows itself in the form of external effects of production associated with marginal increments of output. In some cases social net product is more than the private product while in others private product is greater than the social product. As an example of the former, Pigou pointed out to the greater social benefit from technical training of workers by a private firm. As an illustration of the latter he cited the fact that the smoke rising from the chimneys of private factory spoils the atmosphere of the locality and increases the laundry bills of the people of the neighbourhood. But people are not compensated in any way by the factory owner. He was of the opinion that the state should equalise the private net product with social net product, if in an industry where private net product is more, it should be taxed, and if another industry shows a lesser private net product, it ought to be subsidized. Of course, Prof. Pigou recognised that the divergence between private net product and social net product cannot always be quantified and measured in terms of money.

Prof. Pigou made the first attempt to lay down the conditions of social optimum which he termed "the ideal output" of the economic system as a whole. In his view, the social optimum prevails when marginal social products are equal in all industries and thus production of real wealth is maximised. Assuming that all the productive resources are being employed and that there is no cost of movement between different occupations and places, it can be concluded that the national dividend is the largest when the values of the marginal social net products are equal in all industries. If this arrangement prevails, the society is having its" ideal output".

Pigovian welfare conditions presuppose the existence of the following assumptions:

1. It was assumed that every body as consumer acts rationally to maximise his satisfaction.

2. Pigou believed that utility is not measurable cardinally. But inter personal and intra personal comparisons of utilities are also possible so that it is possible to find out quantitatively whether welfare has increased or decreased.

3. Pigou put forward a basic postulate that a man possesses equal capacity for satisfaction when placed in similar circumstances. Pigou held that different people derive the same satisfaction out of the same real income.

4. Pigou also believed that the marginal utility of money income falls as money income increases. As a result, the marginal utility of an addition to the income of a poor man is greater as compared to the loss of utility from the loss of the same amount of income to a rich man.

EVALUATION

Pigou provided the first systematic theoretical base of welfare economics and intergrated the normative problems with the positive ones. He provided a rationale for state intervention at places where private and social net product diverged. But his policy recommendations were all value based. As such his study was more normative than theoretical.

Though Pigou's Economics of Welfare was the first clear analysis of welfare economics, yet the Pigovian conditions of welfare have been criticised on the following grounds. Pigou lays emphasis on the maximisation of welfare, but he does not clarify the notion of maximisation.

Pigovian assumption of equal capacity for satisfaction is scientifically untenable. This represents a broad value judgement in favour of equal distribution of wealth. The capacity for satisfaction of any individual is a subjective thing incapable of objective quantification.

Another trouble with Pigovian welfare economics, is the lack of rigour and operational content in the distinction between private and social products. Pigou seems to have assumed that the divergence between the two is not inherent in the working of the free enterprise system. It is traceable to and can be corrected through governmental intervention. In the real world, structural failures resulting from immobility, indivisibility and imperfect knowledge are so numerous as to defy correction through social action.

The classification of general welfare into 'economic' and 'non-economic' welfare has also benn criticised as too superficial to be made the basis of all welfare analysis.

The most destructive criticism of the Pigovian welfare economics was the unrealistic nature of the assumptions of cardinal additivity of the individual utility functions to get the social welfare functions. Economists do not agree with this view because quantitative measurement of utility is not possible.

Pigou's welfare conditions are related to national income. But it is not easy to calculate national income. Again, social welfare does not increase by a mere increase in national income. It is possible that national income may increase due to inflationary rise in prices and poor may become worse off than before.

Welfare economics is closely related to ethics but Pigou does not clarify it. Welfare economics is essentially a normative study in which value judgements and inter personal comparisons are made. By not relating these concepts with his notion of welfare, Pigou's economics of welfare is not considered as an objective study of the causes of welfare.

Marshall made the concept of consumers surplus as the central tool of his welfare analysis. Marshall considered the community's welfare to be maximum when its satisfaction is maximum. There were two basic assumptions of this maximum welfare analysis of Dr. Marshall 1. Equal sums of money measure equal utilities to all 2. A fall in the price of the product results in a fall in output and hence loss of satisfaction.

Marshall advocated that an industry which is working under increasing returns must produce beyond its equilibrium point and an industry working with diminishing returns should stop producing before their equilibrium output. For this he suggested the policy of giving a bounty to increasing returns industry and levying a tax on the industries subject to diminishing returns. The proceeds of the tax could be used for giving bounties.

PARETIAN WELFARE ECONOMICS

Pareto's "Manual of Political Economy" (1906) represents a decisive watershed in the history of subjective welfare economics. Pareto broke away from the traditional utilitarian economics. He rejected the hypothesis based on cardinal utility and also the additive utility function and arrived at his welfare conclusions which do not require any inter-personal comparison what so ever. Some have therefore called Paretian welfare economics as "New Welfare Economics".

Pareto had three objectives in mind in giving his concept of the social optimum.

1. To clarify and quantify the concept of economic welfare.
2. To develop welfare propositions which are "scienctifically" free of value – judgements.
3. To clearly state what it is that economists have to say on matters of public policy.

Social Optimum

Pareto defined social optimum as a position from which no reorganisation of production and exchange can be effected to make anyone better off without making somebody else worse off.

Pareto's welfare criterion

From the Paretian concept of social optimum follows his criterion for judging an increase or decrease in welfare. The criterion may be stated thus: given some form of distribution, a reorganisation of production and exchange would increase social welfare, if it makes atleast one person better off without harming anyone else. Since the criterion requires that there should be unanimity among individuals about the maintenance of the condition in which welfare has increased, it is also called "Pareto's Unanimity Rule".

Conditions

The concept of the social optimum given by Pareto was introduced into the English language by A.P. Lerner and J.R. Hicks. Lerner detailed the conditions of production and exchange which are necessary for the attainment of social optimum in the form of marginal equalities and hence are called "Marginal conditions". Prof. Hicks pointed out that besides these marginal on first order conditions, there are other conditions which must be satisfied to ensure that these marginal conditions define a maximum. These are referred to as total or second order conditions.

Assumptions

The assumptions underlying the Pareto social optimum are:

1. Individual ordinal utility functions remain invariant when economic changes are effected.
2. Each individual owns definite quantities of each product and factor.
3. The individual attempts to maximise his satisfaction.
4. Each producer strives to earn maximum profit and is in equilibrium only when producing at the lowest average cost.
5. Each firm has a given transformation function determined by the given technology.

The conditions can be stated geometrically.

I. Optimum allocation of products:

The allocation of products between individuals can be optimal only when the Marginal Rate of Substitution (MRS) between any two goods is the same for any pair of individuals owning the two goods. If MRS between any two goods is not the same for any two individuals, they can enter into exchange which would increase the satisfaction of both or one without diminishing that of the other.

II. Optimum allocation of factors:

The marginal rate of technical substitution between any pair of factors must be the same for any two firms using both to produce a given product. If this condition is satisfied, it is not possible to produce any more of a good without producing less of some other goods. If the condition is not satisfied, there remains a possibility of increasing total production by shifting resources from one firm to the other.

III. Optimum degree of specialization:

This condition determines the optimum output of each product to be produced by each firm. This will prevail when the marginal rate of transformation between any two goods is the same for any two firms which produce both the products. Marginal Rate of Transformation between two goods is the rate at which one good must be sacrificed to obtain more of the other good without varying the input used. Thus if MRT between two goods is not the same for the two firms, it would always be possible to increase the combined output of both the goods on atleast one of them.

IV. Optimum factor utilisation:

This condition states that the marginal rate of transformation between any factor and any product must be the same for any pair of firms using the factor and producing the product". It means that the marginal productivity of any factor in producing a particular product must be the same for all the firms. If the marginal productivity of factor to produce a given product is low, the total product would increase by transferring some units of the factor to the high productivity firm.

V. Optimum direction of Production:

This condition relates to the substitution of products to conform to the structure of consumer's preferences. The general optimum will be attained only when exchange optimum in the consuming sector and production optimum in the producing sector are simultaneously reached. It requires that the subjective rate of substitution between two products for any pair of individuals must be equal to the objective rate of transformation for all pairs of goods in the economy.

VI. Optimum allocation of a factor – unit's time:

The condition relates to the substitution of leisure for work on product on intensity of use of factors. It states that the marginal rate of substitution between leisure and work must be the same as the marginal rate of transformation between work and its product for the community as a whole. The private rate of substitution between leisure and work for every factor must equal the social rate.

VII. Optimum inter – temporal allocation of assets:

This condition requires that "The marginal temporal rate of transformation between every pair of factors and products as well as the marginal temporal rate of substitution between every pair of factors and between every pair of products must be equal to the rate of interest on riskless securities". It therefore relates to borrowing and lending between producers in the absence of risk or uncertainty. This condition implies that the rate of interest at which an individual producer is willing to lend a given amount of capital must equal its marginal productivity to the borrowing producer.

THE SECOND ORDER AND TOTAL CONDITIONS

To ensure that the marginal conditions define a maximum, it should be supplemented with some second order conditions. These second order conditions require that in the neighbourhood of the optimum all indifference curves must be convex to the origin and all transformation curves must be concave to it.

KALDOR – HICKS COMPENSATION PRINCIPLE

There are two main lines along which efforts have been made to rehabilitate Welfare Economics. The first line of improvement was suggested by Kaldor, Hicks and Scitovsky by introducing the concept of a compensating payment on value free foundation given by Pareto. They believed that the concept of compensating payment helps us to test the desirability of economic changes which benefit some and harm others and all this without bringing in value judgement. The second line of effort to rehabilitate welfare economics is that of Bergson, Samuelson and Tinther. In their view, it is neither possible nor advisable to do without ethical norms. These economists admit that inter-personal comparisons involve value judgements but assert that the welfare economists cannot evaluate any kind of policy change without some kind of value judgements.

Compensation Principle

Kaldor, Hicks and Scitovsky have given their tests for judging an increasing in welfare. Like Pareto, they isolate the problem of production from that of distribution. They deal with policy change with ambiguous welfare effects saying that if the people benefiting from it can gainfully compensate the losers, then the policy change is desirable otherwise not. This extension is popularly called the compensation principle.

This compensation tests are based on several restrictive assumptions. 1. It is assumed that individual tastes do not change and there are no external effects. 2. It is assumed that inter-personal comparisons of welfare are inadmissible. 3. It is assumed that individuals are the best judges of their own welfare. 4. It is implied that although social welfare depends on the level of distribution and the level of production, it is possible to study only the changes in the level of production.

The compensation principle that underlies all the welfare criteria was proposed by Kaldor. His formulation is: Let there be a policy measure which takes the society from state A to state B, then state B of the society is preferable to state A, if the gainers from the policy measures can compensate the losers and still be in a better position.

Prof. Hicks proposed a test which is the reverse of Kaldor test. He pointed out that in any policy proposal there are two parties, one gainers and the other loses. In the event of a decision of the proposal the losers may try all the means to forestall this. to keep this eventually out and this criterion Hicks proposed the reverse test: state B of society is socially preferable to A if the losers from the policy change from A to B can't profitably bribe the gainers into not making the change from A to B.

SCITOVSKY'S PARADOX

Scitovsky has pointed out that the Kaldor – Hicks compensation test has a contradiction. He pointed out that it is possible according to Kaldor-Hicks criteria that state B is better than state A, but once the society moves to the state B, the same criteria may reveal that the return move from B to A is also desirable on welfare grounds. This contradiction has been called the 'Scitovsky Paradox'. Scitovsky pointed out that to get at the correct criterion of welfare we must remove this contradiction. He has therefore offered his own criterion called the "Scitovsky Double criterion".

Scitovsky wanted an economic change to satisfy double test-the fulfillment of Kaldor-Hicks test plus the non-fulfilment of the reversal test. This means, that a movement from state A to state B must be desirable in terms of the Kaldor-Hicks criteria but a return from B to A should not be an improvement on these criteria.

The essence of Kaldor, Hicks and Scitovsky criteria can be expressed thus: The Kaldor-Hicks criteria are met if in an economic change, "gainers can over-compensate the losers, "The reversal test is satisfied" if losers are able to bribe the gainers to stay in the old position". The Schtovsky double test is satisfied "By the fulfilment of the Kaldor-Hicks test plus the non-fulfilment of the reversal test".

DR. LITTLE'S CRITERION

Dr. Little has developed a reaction against the compensation criteria proposed by Kaldor, Hicks and Scitovsky. In form, it is also a compensation criterion, but in spirit, it differs markedly from the earlier Kaldor-type criteria. Dr. Little asserts that neither the Kaldor-Hicks test nor the Scitovsky double test, either alone or together, can possibly be taken as a criterion of welfare.

Since Little believes that value judgements are essential in welfare economics, he bases his criterion on two value premises. 1. The well being of an individual is supposed to be greater in a chosen position that it is in any other position. 2. Any social alternation that makes everybody better off is a good thing.

Based on these value judgements, the criterion can be stated in this way: An economic change constitutes social improvement (a) if the resulting redistribution is no worse than the old and (b) if it is impossible to make the community as well off in the initial position as it would be after the change.

There are 3 main features of Littles criterion, as pointed out of Prof. A.K. Sen (1) Little bases the overall economic welfare on the welfare of the individual members of the society. (2) Like Pareto, Little assumes that if atleast one person is better off and none worse off than in an alternative state. Then this state is better. (3) Little says nothing about the exact nature of welfare judgements.

SOCIAL WELFARE FUNCTION

Bergson and Samuelson make use of social welfare function which describes the factors on which the welfare of all individuals in a society depends. It makes welfare of the society depend upon economic as well as non-economic factors-the amount of each and every kind of goods consumed and services performed, the amount of capital investment undertaken and so on.

The Social Welfare Function possesses some special properties which give it an edge of superiority over the earlier ones.

1. It introduces value judgements into the welfare analysis and does not in any way feel shy of them. Thus the function involves inter-personal comparisons and hence value judgements.
2. It is a general welfare function. Any set of assumptions of compounding individual utility functions into the social welfare function can be fed into the Bergson Social Welfare Function.

3. The ethical norms on which the Social Welfare Function is built are assumed to be ordinal in nature. So the assumption of additivity of individual utilities is not there.
4. The Social Welfare Function does not have any element of indeterminacy in it. It deals with distribution of welfare as much as production and exchange condition of welfare.

Assumptions:

1. It assumes that social welfare depends on wealth and income.
2. It assumes the presence of external economics and diseconomics.
3. It is based on ordinal utility.
4. Inter-personal comparisons are possible.

A social welfare function is simply a set of social indifferences curves where an increases in one individual's welfare, all other individual's welfares remaining the same increases social welfare. Hence the social welfare function is an ordinal index of society's welfare and is also a function of the level of satisfaction of all individuals.

ARROW'S THEORY OF SOCIAL CHOICE

Prof. Arrow, in his monumental work, Social Choice and Individual Values, published in 1951, shows that the task of constructing a social welfare function to reflect the aims and aspirations of a free democratic society is an impossible one. Arrow has proved a general theorem about the impossibility of constructing an ordering for society as a whole which will in some way reflect all the individual orderings of the members who make up the society.

Arrow's main concern is to consider if a social choice can be satisfactorily derived from individual decisions. The problem is easily solved by dictatorship under which social decisions are made by single individual in small group. In a democratic society, each and every individual will have their idea of social welfare function. It is therefore difficult to construct a social welfare function which reflects the individual orderings. Therefore Arrow lays down five reasonable conditions which social choices must meet in order to reflect individual's preferences.

The first condition may be called universality condition. It states that a definite social ordering is derivable from a reasonably wide range of individual orderings. This social ordering must have the properties of connexity and transitivity. By the axiom of connexity, any two alternatives must be related either by preference or indifference. Thus for any two alternatives X and Y, either X is preferred to Y, on Y is preferred to X or the two are indifferent. By the axiom of transitivity if X is preferred on indifferent to Y and Y is preferred on indifferent to Z, then X must be either preferred on indifferent to Z. These two axioms constitute the foundation of modern choice theory.

The second condition is called Responsiveness condition. It states that social ordering is positively related with the individual orderings. On simply social choices must move in the same direction as individual choices.

The third condition is called by Arrow the Independence of Irrelevant Alternatives. It simply, states that the choice made by a society depends on the orderings of individuals in that environment and not on the orderings of alternatives outside that environment.

Fourth is the non-imposition condition also called the conditions of citizens' soverignty. It required that there should be no external control over a society's choice. The social welfare function is not to be imposed.

Condition number 5, called, the condition of Non-dictatorship is a part of the condition 4. It permits the construction of social choices by collective methods and not by dictatorial ones. Hence the condition is the social welfare function is not to be dictatorial.

Condition I specifies the scope of social welfare function and other four are value judgements. Arrow next considers whether a social ordering can be derived from any set of individual orderings. He demonstrates that impossibility of doing this without violating atleast one of the value judgements as expressed in five conditions. This is his "General Possibility Theorem".

GENERAL POSSIBILITY THEOREM

Arrow first considers a simple case where there are only two alternatives and shows that in this case the method of majority decision yields a social welfare function satisfying all the five conditions.

But when there are three or more alternatives difficulty emerges and no valied social welfare function can be derived therefore a social welfare function may be eiher imposed on dictatorial.

Arrows offers three important deductions-consequences 1,2 and 3. The three alternatives are X,Y,Z and there are two individuals. Consequence I states that whenever both individuals prefer X to Y, society will prefer X to Y. Consequence 2 states that, if in four given choice the will of individual 1 prevails against the opposition of 2, then individual 1 prevails against the opposition of 2, then individual 1's view will prevail if 2 is indifferent on if he agrees with 1. Consequence III states that, if two individuals have opposing interests, then the society will be indifferent between the two alternatives.

Based on these consequences, the General Possibility Theorem is stated in its simplest form. Let there be two individuals and three alternatives X,Y,A. If individual 1 prefers X to Y and individual 2, Y to X, the society is indifferent between the two.

If individual 1 has X,Y,Z and individual 2 has the ordering Z,X,Y. Since individual one prefers Y to Z and individual 2 prefers Z to Y, the society should be indifferent between the two. For both X is preferred to Y and society also prefers X to Y. By the axiom of transitivity society prefers X to Z.

By since individual 1 prefers X to Z and 2 prefers Z to X we are to concluded that the society is indifferent as between X and Z. But this contradicts the earlier conclusion that X is preferred to Z. it can't be that for society X is both preferred and also indifferent to Z.

QUESTIONS

1. Give an account of Pigovian welfare economics.
2. State the conditions of Paretian social optimum.
3. State and explain Kaldor-Hicks compensation principle.
4. Briefly explain Arrow's Theorem

Chapter 23

JOHN MAYNARD KEYNES (1883-1946)

INTRODUCTION

One of the greatest and the most controversial economists of the twentieth century was John Maynard Keynes. Many major developments in modern economics are associated with his name. The term "Keynesian Revolution" is often applied to describe the economic ideas of Keynes and it is also called as "New Economics". He was born in 1883, son of a noted British economist John Neville Keynes. He graduated from the Cambridge University and served in the India Office. He was the leader of the British delegation to the Bretton Woods Conference in 1944 and served as a Governor of the I.B.R.D. and I.M.F. He served his country in various capacities and in appreciation of his services to the nation, his Government made him the first Baron of Tilton in 1942. He died on April 21, 1946.

His publications include: Indian Currency and Finance (1913), The End of Laissez Faire (1926), A Treatise on Money (1930), The Means to Prosperity (1933), The General Theory of Employment, Interest and Money (1936), and How to Pay for the War (1940),

Besides ten books and five booklets, he wrote about 300 articles and about 50 reviews on official and non-official reports.

INFLUENCES

Keynes' writings reveal the impact of the influences of the mercantilists, the physiocrats, Marshall and his own colleagues at Cambridge. His thought was also influenced by the writings of Lauderdale, Sismondi and Malthus. Keynes adopted the notion of Hobson–of under employment caused by undue exercise of the habit of saving; and by giving a lengthy quotation from "The Physiology of Industry" by

A.F. Mummery and J.A. Hobson. He tried to show that their criticism of classical theories and institutions were very significant and well-founded. Keynes' thought was influenced by Proudhon and Karl Marx also. The German economic thinkers like Lederer and A. Hahn and Fisher, Hawtrey, Macleod had been emphatic in explaining that there was lack of co-relation between saving and investment and this fact was later elaborated by Keynes. The writings and ideas of his teacher Dr. Alfred Marshall and other contemporaries considerably influenced his thought. Marshall suggested gap between income and spending, laid emphasis on the rate of interest and equality between saving and investment. His treatment of time element and money was of considerable help to Keynes. His thought was also influenced by the ideas of D.H. Robertson, R.F. Harrod, Mrs. Joan Robinson, R.F. Kahn and R.G. Hawtrey.

Keynesian economics or Macro economics is based on broad national aggregates like national income, consumption, saving, investment, full employment etc., which have a strong bearing on the economic prosperity of a country. Rejecting the classical approach Keynes held that mal-adjustment in the economic system of a country was a normal feature which might lead the national economy to the ravages of trade cycles. His approach was fundamentally different from that of the classicists. For the smooth and uninterrupted functioning of the national economy he suggested the policy of state intervention.

KEYNES VERSUS CLASSICALS

Keynes differs from the classical school in almost all ideas and has severely criticised each and every concept.

1. The classicals believed in laissez faire policy. But according to Keynes free enterprise system leads to fluctuations in trade cycles, so government intervention is a must.

2. The classicals assumed full employment and there is no deviation from full employment. Even if there are temporary deviations, the economy has the tendency to reach full employment. Whereas Keynes stated that under employment equilibrium is in the reality and full employment is a distant goal. Achievement of full employment is very difficult and maintenance of it on a permanent basis is still more difficult.

3. The classicals said that there exists in the economy a state of perfect competition which allocates resources ideally and ensures maximisation of output and welfare. But Keynes argued that perfect competition is a myth. Today's market structure is characterised by imperfect market which restricts output leads to wastage of resources, and exploitation of consumers. Ideal allocation of resources is not ensured.

4. The classicals believed in invisible hand or flexible price mechanism which ensures maximisation in all market and also in allocation of resources and distribution of resources and national income. Keynes said that private motives do not coincide with public welfare. Indiscriminate attachment to profit leads to depression, unemployment and other evil consequences. So there are no invisible hands, or automatic price mechanism which ensures the welfare of one and all in society. Artificial hinderances in the price mechanism has led to exploitation, misallocation and improper distribution of income.

5. According to the classical economists there is automatic self adjusting character of the economy. There is no such automatic or self adjusting system in Keynesian economics. If such a force is there, depressions and booms can be easily avoided and fluctuations averted.

6. The classical contributions constitute the core of 'Micro Economics'. The classicals assumed a fixed quantity of resources and concentrated on ideal allocation among firms, industries and individual units in the economy. They studied 'micro elements' and implicitly believed that what principles and rules govern the micro problems are completely valid for macro problems also. Therefore no separate theory is required for macro problems. Keynesian contribution relates to macro problems and according to him, micro problems require one set of policies and for macro problems, another set of policies is required. The same policy tools or instruments cannot be applied for both. Macro is not a mere addition of micro elements. The nature, magnitude and intensity of macro problems vary from that of micro problems.

7. Wage-price flexibility is advocated by classicals for solving unemployment problem. If at anytime the economy slips down from the level of full employment it can be restored by cutting down real wages. Since wages are determined by marginal physical product of labour and MPC is subject to the operation of the Law of diminishing returns, more labour can be employed only if wages are reduced. As long as wages are flexible downwards, full employment can be easily achieved. The classical school assumed that workers will accept a lower wage. Thus wages are flexible both ways for them. According to Keynes, wage flexibility is not found in the modern economy, especially downward flexibility of wages. Modern trade unions never accept wage cut for solving disequilibrium. Keynes has explained the following consequences if real wages are reduced:

(a) In modern economy where there are strong trade unions, workers will not accept a reduction in real wage. The union may resort to strike in which case production will be completely affected.

(b) When wages are reduced, it may affect the consumption level of workers. A distribution of income takes place from wage earners, whose MPC is high, to propertied class (low MPC) which means overall reduction in consumption. Since consumption is an important element of aggregate demand, effective demand will fall short of aggregate supply and employment, instead of increasing, will decline further.

(c) Even accepting that wage reductions can solve unemployment, this reduction in real wage can be accomplished in a different and painless manner than what the classical school thinks of. By keeping the money wage constant, a gradual and unnoticeable increase in price level will bring down the level of real wage and such a reduction in real wage will promote employment. The workers will be happy that they continue to get the same money income and feel that they are not aware of the fact that because of the gradually increasing price levels, their real income has come down. When people have such a false satisfaction, they are said to be subject to 'money' illusion. Taking advantage of this illusion the economy can reach full employment.

(d) Keynes raises one more objection to wage cut policy of the classicals. When wages are cut, more employment is offered, output increases and prices fall. If the fall in prices is in proportion to the fall in money wage, then real wages of workers will remain the same. When there is no fall in real wage how can the economy reach a state of full employment. So for Keynes wage cut is not an advisable policy for removal of unemployment or for reaching full employment.

8. The classical school believed in the flexibility of interest rate in bringing about an equilibrium between savings and investment. Saving is a function of interest rate and higher the rate of interest higher will be the level of savings and vice versa. Investment is also a function of interest rate, lower the interest, higher the level of investment and vice versa. Interest rate because of its flexibility restored

equilibrium between S and I at full employment equillibrium. Too much importance was given by classical for interest rate machanism. Keynes explained that neither savings nor investment are functions of interest rate. Savings depend on the capacity of the people to save and this capacity is determined by income. So S= f (y) and not interest rate. Just because the rate of interest is high, people will not starve and save money when their incomes are low. Investment is also not a function of interest rate. It is the rate of return or profit which determines the level of investment. Investment is a function of MEC and not interest. So mere interest rate flexibility cannot bring about an equality between savings and investment.

9. Money plays a passive role for classicals. It has only one function, viz., medium of exchange. The 'store of value function' of money was not given due attention. Moreover money being a precious commodity can never be kept idle as liquid cash. Either it should be spent for consumption or invested immediately. Money is demanded for three motives for Keynes—transaction motive, precautionary motive and for speculative motive. No asset is as liquid as cash. So if interest rates are very low people may prefer to hold their savings in the form of idle cash than in the form of interest earning assets like bonds and shares. Their expectations about future changes in the rate of interest, influence this volume of liquid cash which in turn exercise tremendous influence on the level of investment, employment and output in the economy.

10. The classical economists did not integrate the theory of value with the theory of prices or money. By inventing the concept of speculative demand for money, Keynes successfully integrated the theory of value with the theory of prices. Both money and real markets are interdependent and not independent. Money causes many confusions in the economy. Liquidity preference has a major impact on the level of investment and other variables in the system. So money plays a very active role and not a passive role.

11. The classicals considered only real variables like MPP, real profit, real wage and real sacrifice. Keynes considered monetary variables and at the same time connected them with real variables.

Consumption Function

Keynes psychological law of consumption is of basic importance in the analysis of income, output and employment. Keynes based his law on the general psychology of the people that when they find an increase in aggregate real income there is a tendency to increase aggregate consumption too. In his own words "Men are disposed, as a rule and on the average, to increase their consumption as their income increases, but not by as much as the increase in their income".

This psychological law is a statement of common experience based up on three propositions:

1. When aggregate income increases consumption expenditure also increases. This is because as a person's income increases, more and more wants are satisfied.

2. The second proposition is that when income increases the additional income is spent between consumption and saving. This is also a common experience that when income increases, people spend only a portion of their additional income and save the remainder.

3. When income increases, both consumption and saving increase but consumption increases less than proportionately.

The three propositions form Keynes' psychological law of consumption and it is based on the following assumptions: (i) It is assumed that the habits of the people regarding spending do not change. The propensity to consume is assumed to be stable. This means that we assume that only income changes, whereas the other variables like price movements, income distribution, growth of population etc., remain more or less constant. (ii) The second assumption is that the conditions remain normal and there are no abnormal conditions like hyper inflation or war. (iii) The third assumption is that of a capitalistic laissez-faire economy. The law will not hold good in an economy where the state interferes with consumption or productive enterprise.

Keynes explained the concepts of propensity to consume namely average propensity to consume (APC) and marginal propensity to consume (MPC).The average propensity to consume is the ratio of absolute consumption to absolute income, i.e., C/Y. On the other hand the marginal propensity to consume refers to the ratio of a small change in consumption due to a small change in income i.e., DC/DY.

Factors Determining Consumption Function

According to Keynes two principal factors, the subjective factors and objective factors influence consumption function. The subjective factors are endogenous or internal and the objective factors are exogenous or external to the economic system.

The subjective factors are the psychological nature of human race. They are the outcome of individual and business motives. There are eight psychological individual motives, which determine individual's spending. They are: (i). the desire to keep reserves for emergency (ii). the desire to provide for old age and sickness (iii) the desire to enjoy an enlarged future income through interest and appreciation (iv). the desire to improve standard of living (v). the desire to have financial independence (vi). the desire to do forward trading and speculation (vii). the desire to bequeath a fortune (viii). the desire to satisfy a purely miserly instinct.

There are four business motives:

1. Enterprise, the desire to do big things,
2. Liquidity, the desire to meet emergency successfully.
3. Income raise, the desire to secure larger income and to show successful management.
4. Financial prudence, the desire to provide adequate financial resources against depreciation, obsolescences and to discharge debt.

These subjective factors remain constant during the short run and keep the consumption function stable.

The objective factors are given by Keynes and his followers.

1. Change in the Wage Level. Increase in wages will increase consumption. Therefore the consumption function curve will shift upward. If however, the rise in the wage rate is accompained by a more than proportionate rise in the price level, the real wage rate will fall and consumption will decrease. This will tend to shift the consumption function curve downward. A cut in wage rate will reduce consumption and shift the curve downward.

2. Windfall Gains or Losses. Unexpected gain will increase consumption and shift consumption function curve e.g., the windfall gain in American stock market in 1925 led to a rise in consumption. Unexpected losses lead to the downward shifting of the consumption curve.

3. Change in the Fiscal Policy. The fiscal policy of the government relating to taxation, expenditure and public debt affect consumption. A reduction in taxation will leave more post-tax incomes with people which would tend to increase their expenditure on consumption. In contrast, an increase in taxation will reduce consumption. Progressive taxation and public expenditure on welfare programmes will shift consumption function upwards by altering the distribution of income.

4. Changes in Expectations. If the consumers expect a shortage or rise in prices of certain goods, they may rush to purchase such goods far in excess of their current needs. This would raise the consumption function. Such things happen during war. On the other hand, if the people expect a plenty, or a decline in prices of certain durable goods, they would tend to postpone purchase of such goods, which would lower the consumption function.

5. Changes in the Rate of Interest. If the interest rate is high the cost of holding money as liquid asset increases, people will find it less profitable to keep idle cash. They may begin to invest. This will reduce total consumption and increase saving. If on the other hand the interest rate is low people may find that keeping liquid cash would be more profitable. This will reduce savings and increase consumption.

6. Financial Policies of Corporations. If corporations and companies retain more reserves and give lesser profits in the form of dividends, the disposable income of the shareholders will be smaller. On the other hand if more profits are distributed as dividends, more will be spent on consumption.

7. Holding of Liquid Assets. Liquid assets in the form of cash balances, savings and government bonds in the hands of the consumers also influence the consumption function. If people hold larger liquid assets they will have a tendency to spend more out of their current income and the propensity to consume will move upward and vice versa.

8. The Distribution of Income. If the income distribution is more even, then the propensity to consume will be high. If there is wide spread disparity of income, the income will go into the hands of a handful capitalists who have greater propensity to save than to spend. Hence the over all propensity to consume will be less.

9. Attitude toward Saving. If the consumers value future consumption more than present consumption, they will tend to save more and consume less and the consumption function curve will shift downward. Such a tendency is reinforced by the state through compulsory provident fund, life insurance and other social insurance schemes to keep the consumption function low. In a high saving economy, consumption function is low.

10. Duesenberry Hypothesis. According to James Duesenberry the expectation of an individual depends not on his current income but also on his past income and standard of living. Even if the current income is reduced, the individual might continue to spend the same amount on current consumption, out of past saving, because he has been accustomed to a particular standard of living. He also talks about 'demonstration effect'. He says that the consumption standards of low income groups are largely influenced by the consumption standards of the high income groups. Such habits will weaken the propensity to save and increase consumption.

11. Selling Effort. Selling cost and advertisement may increase the consumption of one good at the expense of other. Nevertheless, given the level of income, an increase in selling effort may increase the total volume of consumer expenditure. But this factor has not been given much importance due to three reasons. In the first place there is no independent measure of the volume of effective selling effort. Secondly, this volume probably does not fluctuate much in the short period. Thirdly, it has not been considered, at least, in the past, subject to social control.

12. Changes in Relative Prices. Like selling efforts, changes in relative prices increase demand for some products at the expense of other products. Much attention has not been paid to this factor because there is no specific hypothesis as to which this influence is important and in which direction it operates.

13. Volume of Wealth. The larger the wealth possessed by an individual the higher will be the propensity to consume. This is because when wealth is more the marginal utility would be lower and as such the weaker would be the desire to add to future wealth by reducing current consumption.

14. Demographic Factors. Factors like size of the family, stage in the family life cycle, place of residence, occupation etc. affect consumption function. Other things remaining the same a large size family will spend more than a small size family. Families with children of college age would spend more than those with children of primary age. Normally the urban families will have a tendency to spend more than the rural families. Farmers and small businessmen tend to spend less than service people. But changes in demographic factors, occur only in the long period and therefore be ignored in the short-run analysis.

15. Terms of Consumer Credit. Easy availability of credit will increase the propensity to consume of consumer durables. In recent years, there has been a considerable increase in the volume of purchases of consumer durables financed by consumer credit and as such its cost and availability have assumed great importance.

16. Permanent Income. It is also known as normal income. A family's expenditure on consumption is determined not by its current income but by its permanent income. If the latter is more, consumption function will be more, or else it will be less.

17. Consumer Durables. The short-run instability of consumption expenditure in relation to income is concentrated much in the area of consumer durables. The factors affecting the timing of purchase of durable goods can significantly affect aggregate demand causing irregularities between current consumption and income. The timing of purchase of consumer durables depends on nature and obsolescence of the existing stock.

18. Pigou Effect. The changes in the real value of liquid assets also affect consumption function. This is known as 'Pigou Effect' or 'Real Value of Money Assets Effect' or 'Wealth Effect.' It was given by A.C. Pigou in 1943. He argued that when money wages are cut, prices fall and the value of money rises. This will result in the real value of assets such as stocks, shares, bank deposits, government securities, bonds etc. for example, if prices fall by 50 percent the real value of each rupee will be doubled because it will buy twice as much as it did before. The increase in the real value of fixed assets will make their owners feel richer than before. They will therefore save less out of their current income and spend more on consumption. This will increase aggregate demand and output and will generate automatic full employment in the economy. As a result of Pigou effect the consumption function will shift upward. Pigou effect is based on the assumption of flexible wage, flexible absolute price and a constant stock of money.

Implications of Consumption Function

Most of the economists agree with Prof. Hansen's view that the Keynesian formulation of consumption function is an epoch making contribution to the tools of economic analysis. This is clear from the implications of Keynes psychological law mentioned below:

1. Vital Importance of Investment. One of the most important implications of Keynes' psychological law of consumption is that it brings about the crucial importance of investment if we want to attain higher level of income and employment. The law says when income increases the gap between income and consumption increases. The gap is to be filled by bringing more and more investment failing which there will be shortage of effective demand and the economy would slip down. Thus the law highlights the vital importance of investment.

2. General Over Prodution. Since the marginal propensity to consume is less than unity, with every increase in income, consumption would tend to lag behind income which would result in overproduction and unemployment. Thus the law tells us that there can occur a general overproduction and unemployment.

3. Repudiation of Say's Law. Keynes with the help of his law of consumption repudiates Say's law which states supply creates its own demand. Since the marginal propensity to consume is less than unity all that is supplied is not automatically demanded. The supply fails to create its own demand resulting in glut of products in the market.

4. Need for State Intervention. As there is no automatic and self adjusting mechanism between supply and demand the government should interfere actively to ensure that aggregate effective demand does not fall below aggregate supply.

5. Over Saving Gap. Since the increase in consumption expenditure does not keep pace with the increase in income, there arises the danger of oversaving gap. This danger is more for rich countries than for poor countries.

6. Decline in MEC. As a result of the propensity to consume remaining stable with an increase in income the expected rate of profitability or the marginal efficiency of capital may tend to decline. This can be prevented only by increasing consumption with an increase in income because ultimately the decisions to undertake investments are guided by the volume of consumption.

7. Income Propagation. Keynesian theory explains the slow nature of income propagation. Since the marginal propensity to consume is less than unity, injection of increasing purchasing power into the income stream leads to smaller and smaller successive increments to income.

8. Under Employment Equilibrium. Equilibrium would be attained at full employment only if investment demand happens to be equal to the gap between aggregate income corresponding to full employment and aggregate consumption expenditure out of that income. But Keynes believed that the typical investment demand would not be adequate to fill the gap between the amount of income corresponding to full employment and the consumption demand out of that income. As such the aggregate demand and supply schedules would intersect at a point less than full employment.

9. Secular Stagnation. With the increase in income, since consumption cannot be easily increased and investment demand becomes weaker and weaker the economy may sooner or later reach a stage where it may not be able to provide outlets for its growing savings which is necessary for maintaining full employment. This stage is known as secular stagnation. Such a situation could be avoided if the consumption function were not stable.

10. Turning Points of Trade Cycle. Keynes' psychological law of consumption is very helpful in explaining the turning points of the trade cycle. When the business cycle reaches the highest point of prosperity, income has increased, but the marginal propensity to consume being less than unity, consumption does not increase correspondingly and the result is the downward start of the cycle. Similarly when the business cycle reaches the lowest point, income has declined very low but since people do not reduce their consumption to the full extent of decline in income, the upward phase of the cycle starts.

Thus consumption function occupies a very important place in the theory of employment.

Investment

To Keynes investment refers to real investment which adds to capital equipment. It leads to increase in the level of income and production by increasing the production and purchase of capital goods. Real investment is to be increased to maintain stable national income growth. According to Keynes investment depends on marginal efficiency of capital and rate of interest.

The Marginal Efficiency of Capital (MEC)

MEC refers to the expected profitability of a capital asset. It may be defined as the highest rate of return over cost expected from the marginal or additional unit of a capital asset. First we must go to the marginal unit of the capital asset and secondly its cost has to be deducted from its return. Now the MEC in its turn, depends on two factors: the prospective yield of the capital asset and the supply price of the capital asset. The MEC is the ratio of these two factors.

The prospective yield of a capital asset is the total net return from the asset over its life time. The supply price of an asset is the cost of producing a brand new asset of that kind and not the supply price of an existing asset. It is referred to as the replacement cost. If the supply price of a capital asset is Rs. 20,000 and its annual yield is Rs. 2000, then the marginal efficiency of this asset is 2000/20000 x 100 = 10 percent. Thus the marginal efficiency of capital is the percentage of profit expected from a given investment on a capital asset.

Keynes relates the prospective yield of a capital asset to its supply price and defines MEC "as being equal to that rate of discount which would make the present value of the series of annuities given by the returns expected from the capital asset during its life equal to its supply price". This may be put in the form of an equation.

$$Sp = \frac{R_1}{(1+i)} = \frac{R_2}{(1+i)^2} + ... + \frac{R_n}{(1+i)^n} - \quad ...(1)$$

Where Sp is the supply price or the cost of capital asset, R_1,R_2...... Rn are the prospective yields or the series of expected annual returns from the capital asset in the years 1,2....... n, and i is the rate of discount. This makes the capital asset exactly equal to the present value of the expected yield from it. This can be explained with a numerical example. Let us assume that: 1. The life time of a capital asset (n) is 2 years. 2. The supply price of the capital asset (Sp) is Rs. 3000. 3. The expected yield from the asset at the end of one year (R_1) is Rs. 1100. 4. The expected yield from the asset at the end of 2 years (R_2) is Rs. 2420.

The MEC or the rate of discount which will equate the future yields of the asset with its supply price is 10% as shown below:

$$\text{Since Sp} = \frac{R_1}{(1+i)} + \frac{R_2}{(1+i)^2}$$

$$\text{Rs. } 3000 = \frac{1100}{1.10} + \frac{2320}{(1.10)^2}$$

Rs. 3000 = Rs. 1000 + Rs. 2000

In this way, discounted prospective yields of capital asset can be brought into equality with the curent supply price. Thus investment will take place only if the net prospective yield of an asset is greater than its supply price and given the income flow the higher the supply price of the capital asset, the lower will be the rate of discount.

The various factors that bring about shifts in MEC are short run or endogenous factors and long run or exogenous factors.

The short run factors are:

1. Expected demand. If the demand for the product is expected to be high in future, the MEC will be high and the investment will increase. On the other hand if the demand for the product is expected to decline in future the MEC will be low and investment will fall.

2. Costs and prices. If the costs are expected to decline and if the prices are expected to increase, the expectation of the producer will go up. On the other hand if the costs are expected to go up and prices are to decline the MEC will receive a set back and the investment will be less.

3. Propensity to consume. If the propensity to consume is more then the volume of investment will be more and vice versa.

4. Changes in income. An increase in the level of income will stimulate investment while a decrease in the level of income will discourage investment.

5. Current state of expectation. Businessmen while making expectations take into account the current state of affairs regarding costs, prices, returns etc. If they are high the MEC is bound to be high for new projects of investment.

6. Level of confidence. During period of optimism the businessmen over estimate and boost the MEC of capital assets. During period of pessimism they under estimate and reduce the MEC of capital assets.

The long run factors which influence the MEC are as follows:

1. Population growth. A rapidly growing population means a rapid increase in the demand for all types of goods and hence investment rises and conversely, a decline in population will decrease the demand investment.

2. Development of new areas. When a new area is developed heavy investments in all fields such as agriculture, industries, electricity, housing etc., are to be undertaken.

3. Technological factors. New invention or new discovery may necessitate the installation of new machineries in the industrial enterprise and encourage investment.

4. Productive capacity of the Industry. If the existing capacity is fully utilised then any further increase in demand will be met with by making fresh investment on new capital equipment.

5. Level of current investment. If the existing level of investment is already high there will be little scope for further investment and vice versa.

Criticism of The Marginal Efficiency of Capital

Keynes used the term marginal efficiency of capital in a vague manner. Secondly, Keynes failed to recognize that interest rates are also governed by expectations like the marginal efficiency of capital. He considered marginal efficiency of capital in the field of dynamic economics and rate of interest in the field of static economics.

MARGINAL EFFICIENCY OF INVESTMENT

The rate of discount or yield i.e., r is conventionally called the Marginal Efficiency of Investment (MEI). Keynes originally called it the 'Marginal Efficiency of Capital'. Brooman says that it is preferable to use a term which refers explicitly to investment (i.e MEI). The MEI (or MEC) ought to be distinguished from the 'Marginal product of capital' which refers to the increase in current output resulting from the addition of one more unit of capital. It is clear that the marginal product of capital is a physical quantity similar to the marginal product of any other factor. The MEI is a percentage rate, and not the physical quantity. Again the marginal product of capital does not involve expectations about the yield from the unit of capital during the remainder of its life. But the MEI is very much concerned with such expectations about the yield.

Strictly speaking, however, there is a difference between the MEC and the MEI. The MEC is derived as the relationship between i (rate of interest) and the optimum level of capital stock. The MEI is derived as the relationship between i (rate of interest) and the optimum change in capital stock. It can be said by way of corollary that the MEC and the MEI are interrelated. The MEI really indicates the decision to invest whereby there is change in the capital stock. This relationship between investment as the change in capital stock and the actual capital stock presents a difficulty in determining the MEI. If investment is change in capital stock, it can be assumed that the capital stock is fixed once investment is underway. Keynes recognized this difficulty and sought to overcome it by stating that he was interested in short period changes in investment. In the short period change in investment would be insignificant relative to the entire capital stock; therefore, the impact of investment on capital stock could be ignored.

The relationship between MEC and MEI is illustrated in the figure 7.

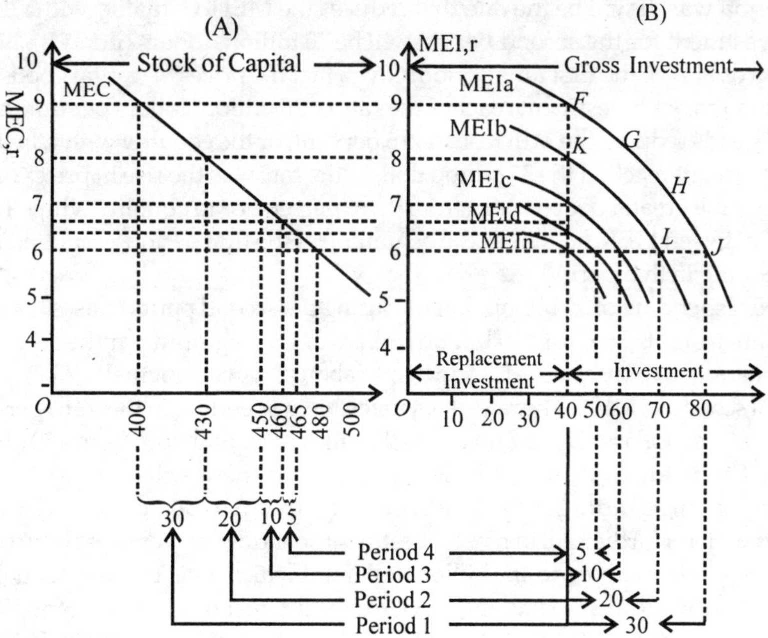

Fig. 1.

MEI schedule indicates the rate of investment spending per time period at each possible market rate of interest for different levels of the stock of capital. Part A shows the MEC schedule. When the rate of interest is 9% and capital stock is 400 billion dollars, the net investment is zero. MEI schedule labelled MEIa shows that at point F, when the rate of interest is 9%, the net investment is zero. If rate of interest falls to 6%, net investment will be 30 billion dollars. At G, the MEI is 8%, because the rise in net investment spending from zero to 15 billion dollars has raised the prices of capital goods which has reduced the rate of interest to 8%. As this is higher than MEI (6%) higher rate of net investment is needed. At point H, MEI has fallen to 7 per cent because higher rate of net investment spending has pushed the prices of capital goods to a higher level. The MEI is still above 6 percent, so a still higher rate of net investment spending is wanted. At point J, MEI is 6 percent. It is no higher or lower than the initial rate of interest.

From the beginning to the end of this first time period, with net investment of 30 billion dollars during the period, the capital stock will have risen to 430 billion dollars from its beginning level of 400 billion dollars. As shown in Part A, this increase of 30 billion dollars reduces the MEC about 8 per cent (actually 7.87) from its previous level of 9. Because r is still 6 per cent, further growth in the capital stock is called for. The amount by which it grows in the second period, or the rate of net investment spending in the second peiod, depends on the MEI schedule. With MEC now at 8 per cent, the new MEI schedule, relating investment expenditures to the interest rate, must show zero net investment at an interest rate of 8 per cent (point K). Therefore, MEI_b, the new schedule, lies below MEI_a because of the increase in the stock of capital in the first time period; the whole MEI schedule must fall to a lower level with each movement to a lower point on the given MEC schedule, MEI_b slopes down ward for the same reason that MEI_a sloped downward—the rising supply price of capital goods as the rate of output of these goods is expanded in response to invesment spending.

The rate of net investment spending in the second period is determined in the same way as the rate in the first period was. It will be the rate that reduces the MEI to equality with r. Schedule MEI_b shows that net investment for the second period will be 20 billion dollars (point L). Note that this is below the 30 billion dollars of the first time period. Given that the prices of capital goods rise with their rate of output as soon as net investment reaches the rate of 20 billion dollars per time period, the rise in prices of capital goods reduces the MEI from 8 to 6 per cent, or the equality with r. In the first period, only when net investment reached the 30 billion dollars the rate was the rise in prices of capital goods sufficient to produce the greater drop in MEI from 9 to 6 percent, or to equality with r. In other words, the greater spread between MEI and the r at the beginning of the first period permitted the higher rate of investment spending in that period.

Net Investment spending of 20 billion dollars during the second period raises the stock of captial to 450 billion dollars from its level of 430 billion dollars at the beginning of the second period. The increase in the capital stock reduces the MEC further to about 7 percent (actually 7.12) which produces the new, lower MEI schedule, MEIc. The rate of net investment spending in the third period as given by this schedule is 10 billion dollars. This again raises the stock of capital now from 450 billion dollars to 460 billion dollars. This in turn reduces the MEC and creates the new, still lower MEI schedule, MEI_d. The rate of net investment spending in the fourth period is then 5 billion dollars. With no shift in the MEC schedule and with no further fall in r, net investment spending, lower in each succeeding period, eventually raises the stock of capital to 480 billion dollars, at which level the MEC equals r. The actual stock of capital is now the profit-maximizing stock for the interest rate of 6 per cent. With the capital stock at 480 billion dollars, the relevant MEI schedule is MEIn, which shows net investment to be zero and gross investment equal to replacement investment per time period. We have reached a new equilibrium, which will be upset only by a shift in the MEC schedule or by a change in the market rate of interest.

ECONOMIC IDEAD

The General Theory of Employment, Interest and Money of the late Lord Keynes appeared in the year 1933. The purpose of the book was in the words of the author himself "primarily a study of the forces which determine changes in the scale of output and employment as a whole". The book is called the General Theory in order to distinguish the approach from the earlier partial equilibrium theories which examined the economies of particular commodities and industries on the assumption that all other things remain equal. They also dealt with mainly the problems of pricing in the short run excepting perhaps Adam Smith who had attempted a systematic study of the working of the economy as a whole. It was taken for granted that the economy would automatically work at the level of full employment and produce the full employment level of output under the guidance of the "invisible hand" which was no more than the demand conditions in the market. Spontaneous market forces constituted a sort of unplanned plan to guide production and allocation of resources as between different industries. Everything would be in its own right place. Those goods would be produced that were in the highest demand. Resources would shift in favour of the highest of earnings. There would be nothing like involuntary unemployment. Everything would be in its own right demand. Every man would get his due. There would be a virtual paradise on earth if only the government allowed the principle of laissez faire to work uninterrupted. Disturbances that come periodically by way of business cycles were either completely ignored as of little importance or were assumed to be corrected automatically very much like a healthy man coming back to his health after a temporary period of illness. No remedies were thought to be necessary. "Normally everything goes well on its own" was the assumption of the pre-Keynesian school of thought.

What Lord Keynes did was to blow up the complacency. He exploded the blissful assumptions of spontaneous full employment and full employment levels of production. He sharply pointed out the fallacies in the reasoning and the premises of the classical school of thought. The depression of the thirties was too much to be bypassed Laisse faire had let loose terrific disturbances in the economy. The total national income had sunk considerably because of the depression. A large number of workers were out of job. The Keynesian revolution conceived of the working of the economy as a whole even the secular period as distinguished from the study of fluctuations in connection with the business cycles. That is the reason why the general theory deals with investment, employment and output and studies in particular the role of monetary institutions in dermining employment and output. The study of the aggregate output of an economy, is nothing but the sudy of economic growth especially, when attention is paid to the problems of long term growth. That is how Keynesian revolution is taken as the precursor to the recent models of growth.

In the backward countries of the world a close attention is being paid to the study of the problem of extremely low level of output perhead which makes it possible for the bulk of the people to gain access to even the barest necessities of life. These so called under developed economies languish in the most apalling conditions of poverty because of their current inability to raise the aggregate output as fast as is desirable to provide the fundamental means of life to the community. The growth models study the causes for the low aggregate output in the backward economies and present certain hypotheses as to how these economies would fare on certain assumptions about the rate of growth of population, the rate of savings, investment, the capital, output ratio etc., and try to explain how best to achieve these goals. The growth models endeavour to find out what the net national output would be at certain future date, if the economy works on certain assumed lines. The growth models very much like the Keynesian model are concerned with the long term growth of an economy as measured by the changes in the other important variables. In order to illustrate what a growth model tries to do we might take an equation given by Prof. Mahalanobis which gives a formula to study the growth of income over time. The equation is as follows :

$$n_t = n_o (1+ab-p)t$$

in which 'n' stands for income after a period of time t, n_o the initial income, 'a' the rate of investment, b the capital-output ratio and p the rate of growth of population. The growth model of Mahalanobis holds that the income after a certain period of time depends on three variables namely, the initial income, the proportion of that income which is saved and invested and thirdly, the rate of growth of population which acts as a denominator in determining the net income per head. This is very much similar to Harrods model of gowth which hinges on two crucial variables namely the rate of investment and the capital out put ratio. Whatever the growth model that we wish to study the purpose is to study the long term rate of the economy in terms of saving, investment and the fruitfulness of investment in terms of the capital output ratio. In the economic circumstances of backwardness, with the existing low levels of income, low levels of savings and therefore, of the low levels of investment, how to raise the aggregate output as fast as possible is the problem dealt with by the growth models.

QUESTIONS

1. Analyse the fundamental mistakes committed by classical economists in their theories, according to Keynes.
2. Why do we call Keynesian theory as "New Economics"?
3. Give a brief outline of Keynesian theory of employment.
4. What are the solutions offered by Keynes to remove unemployment in the economy ?
5. Explain the concept of 'Multiplier' and how this tool has been used in Keynesian analysis.
6. Analyse the theoretical importance of Keynesian theory.
7. Enumerate the influence of Keynes in 'Practical Policies'.
8. Briefly analyse the critisms levelled against Keynes' theory.
9. Bring out the relevance and limitations of Keynesian economics in backward and developing countries.
10. J.M. Keynes was a 'toolmaker' like Marshall-Elucidate.
11. Explain the concept of under-employment equilibrium.
12. Explain the concept of equality between savings and investment.
13. Write short notes on :
    (a) Y = C + I
    (b) Liquidity preference theory of interest
    (c) Autonomous investment
    (d) Marginal efficiency of capital
    (e) Theory of prices

Chapter 24

DEVELOPMENT OF ECONOMIC THEORIES

In this chapter it is proposed to analyse the development of the theories of rent, wages, interest, profit and trade cycle.

(a) THEORIES OF RENT

In ordinary language, the term "rent" denotes a periodical payment made for the hiring of, say, a plot of land, a house, a machine, etc., a payment made for use of a fixed factor of production. In the past, rent was a payment for the use of land only. *In ordinary language*, rent is a periodical payment for the use of land, buildings, machinery, etc., i.e., for the use of a fixed factor. *In Ricardian sense*, rent is a payment by a tenant-farmer to the landlord for the use of land (which is fixed). *In modern sense*, payment for any factor of production over and above the minimum transfer cost is called rent.

RICARDIAN THEORY OF RENT

Ricardo defines rent as "that portion of the produce of the earth which is paid to the landlord for the use of the original and indestructible powers of the soil". The essential features of Ricardo's definition are as follows:

a) Rent of land is a payment made by the tenant to the landlord, not for any services of the latter but for the services of land.
b) Land possesses certain original and indestructible powers; these powers are fertility and location.

c) Rent is the difference between the price of corn and the cost of cultivation, and as such rent is determined by price.
d) The amount of rent for any plot of land depends upon the fertility of that plot of land as compared to the fertility of the marginal land.
e) Marginal land is a no-rent land, since the price of the product and the cost of cultivation of the marginal land will be equal.

How Rent arises in the Ricardian Sense

Let us take the case of a new country which is relatively vast and the settlers are few. Land is free and people can have any amount of land. Obviously, people will settle down on the best land, start cultivating it. The cost of cultivation will consist of three items, viz., wage of labour, interest on capital invested and a margin of profit for the trouble of cultivating and producing food for others. If the cost of cultivation of corn is Rs. 100 per quintal, the price of corn in the market must be equal to the cost of cultivation; otherwise the farmers will produce just the quantity needed for themselves and will not produce anything for the market.

Suppose that, in course of time, more people come to the new country to settle down and that population increases. The demand for corn increases accordingly and cultivation is extended to the second best land (as the best lands are already cultivated). The cost of cultivation of the second best land is higher since the latter is of inferior quality say, Rs.120 per quintal. The price of corn will have to rise so as to cover the cost of cultivation of the second best land (viz., the marginal land). If the price of corn goes up to Rs. 120, then obviously, the first land where cost of cultivation is only Rs.100 will be getting a surplus income of Rs.20. This extra amount is due to the superior productivity of the first grade land.

Suppose that the demand for corn rises still further because of increased population. The margin of cultivation is extended to the third best lands. Again the cost of cultivation on this land will be higher say Rs. 140 and accordingly, the price of corn will have to rise. If the market price is not equal to the cost of cultivation of the marginal land (in this case, the third best land), then the latter will be brought under cultivation. If the corn produced by this land is required, the consumers should be prepared to pay the price which is at least equal to the cost of cultivation of this land. If the market price of corn is Rs. 140 per quintal, the best land gets a surplus of Rs.40, the second best land gets a surplus of Rs.20 and the third land gets nothing. In the third case, the price of corn (Rs.140) and the actual cost of cultivation (RS.140) are the same, hence no surplus arises.

In this way, with every increase in production and in demand for corn, increasingly inferior lands are brought under cultivation. The cost of cultivation obviously goes up and consequently the price of corn also rises. The marginal land does not yield any surplus because the price of corn and the cost of production on the marginal land are equal. But the superior lands will yield surpluses.

Assumptions of Ricardian Theory

Ricardo develops his theory on the basis of certain assumptions. First, he assumes that nature is niggardly and the volume of land available is limited. Secondly, Ricardo assumes that land has certain "original and indestructible powers" for the use of which rent is paid. Thirdly, Ricardo assumes that land having different grades of fertility will be cultivated strictly in the descending order of fertility in such a way that the best lands will be cultivated first and the inferior lands later. Fourthly, Ricardo assumes the existence of the marginal or no-rent land. Finally, Ricardo assumes two tendencies – the tendency to diminishing returns in agriculture and the tendency towards increase in population.

Given all these assumptions, the growth of population will leap to increased demand for agricultural goods and extension of cultivation to inferior lands; as a result, the superior lands will get surpluses which the landlords can appropriate by way of rent of land from the tenants. The increase in population may mean suffering to different sections of people, except the landlords, for the greater the population pressure on land, the higher will be the price of agricultural goods and higher will be the rent of land.

Critical Evaluation of the Ricardian Theory

The Ricardian theory of rent has been the subject of many serious criticisms.

(i) *Ricardo's concept of land is wrong*. According to Ricardo, land possesses original and indestructible powers for which rent is paid. Critics, however, argue that land does not possess any original powers nor are its powers indestructible. For one thing, whatever fertility which land possesses now is mainly due to man's effort-irrigation, manuring, drainage, etc. By using wrong agricultural practices, it is possible to destroy the properties of land.

(ii) *Ricardo's order of cultivation is faulty*. Critics have found fault with Ricardo's order of cultivation. According to Ricardo, the most fertile and most favourably situated land will be cultivated first. However, this may not always be the case. Even in a new country (about which Ricardo talks) the new settlers need not necessarily choose the best lands. They may not know which are the best lands.

(iii) *The differential surplus concept of rent is defective*. Ricardo assumes differential natural advantages of superior lands over inferior lands and bases his concept of rent on this difference. In the Ricardian analysis, if all lands possessed equal fertility, there would be no rent. Further in the Ricardian theory, the marginal land is a no-rent land. The supply of land is limited as compared to the demand for it and accordingly rent will exist because of the scarcity of land. All lands including the marginal land will secure rent.

(iv) *The relation between rent and price is wrong*. An important criticism leveled against Ricardian theory of rent concerns the relation between rent and price. According to Ricardo, price determines rent. The higher the price of corn, the higher will be the rent. The price of corn is determined by the cost of producing corn on the marginal land which is rent-free. Critics, however, disagree with Ricardo on this question. They argue that rent of land is a cost, and as such enters into the price of the product.

(v) *Rent is not peculiar to land*. Modern economists argue that rent is not peculiar to land because differential surpluses similar to that of rent of land are widespread both in labour and capital payments. So long as a factor of production is inelastic (in relation to the demand for it) during a given period of time, a surplus income i.e., rent arises. There is no reason to argue that land alone can be fixed or inelastic in supply. Modern economists, therefore, have extended the concept of rent to refer to an income which any factor of production may secure over and above its minimum transfer cost.

MODERN THEORY

Whenever a factor unit gets a payment over and above what is really necessary to induce it to work, the extra payment is economic rent. The payment which is necessary to make a factor unit work is called transfer earnings of the factor unit i.e., the payment it can get from the next best alternative occupation. If this minimum payment is not made by an industry, the factor unit will transfer itself to the next best occupation. The minimum payment made to a factor unit may also be called its opportunity cost or alternative cost. If, however, any payment is made to the factor unit above its transfer earnings, the extra payment is surplus (over transfer earnings) or an unnecessary payment (to get the services of the factor unit). This surplus is known as economic rent.

It is necessary to distinguish between rent of land which is the payment for the use of land (similar to the wage of labour or the interest for capital) and economic rent which is surplus over transfer earnings and which may arise for any factor of production. Thus, whenever a factor of production – whether labour, capital enterprise or land – receives a payment over and above its minimum transfer earnings it is said to receive economic rent. In other words, economic rent may be part of wages received, or part of interest paid for the use of capital or part of profit received by the organizer or part of rent of land which is made for the use of land. Economic rent may, therefore, be calculated as follows:

Economic rent =Actual Remuneration for a factor unit minus its Transfer earnings.

(a) The surplus income above transfer earnings is known as economic rent. When the supply of a factor is perfectly elastic, the factor will be earning only transfer income;

(b) When the supply of a factor is less than perfectly elastic (i.e., relatively fixed), the income of the factor will contain transfer earnings and also an element of rent; and

(c) When the supply of a factor is perfectly inelastic (i.e., the supply is absolutely fixed), the income of the factor is completely rent.

(b) THEORIES OF WAGES

INTRODUCTION

Wage may be defined as the price paid for the use of labour. The term may refer to piece wage, money wage, money wage, real wage, etc. But normally in all economic discussion, the term is used to mean the money wage, ie., rate per hour or per day or per week or per month, for the services of a person. It represents to the firm the labour cost of production. From time to time various attempts have been made to explain the determination of wages.

THE SUBSISTENCE THEORY OF WAGES

The theory was formulated by physiocrats. According to them wages would be equal to the amount just sufficient for subsistence. Lassale, a German economist developed this theory. According to this theory, wages are determined by the cost of production of labour or subsistence level. The wages so determined will remain fixed. It actual wages are higher than the subsistence level, then population will increase leading to an increase in labour supply and lower wages. If on the other hand, the actual wages fall below the subsistence level, population will decrease resulting in a decline in labour supply and rise in wages. Since there is a tendency for the wages to remain fixed at the subsistence level, it is called as Iron Law of Wages or Brazen Law of Wages.

This theory is based on two assumptions. 1. Food production is subject to the law of diminishing returns, i.e., there is a limit to expansion of food production 2. Population increases at an increasing rate.

Criticisms

1. The subsistence theory of wages explains wages from the supply side and ignores the demand side.
2. If all labourers must get the bare necessaries of life, all must get equal wages. But there are many differences in wages. Thus this theory ignores wage differences.
3. This theory asserts that wages are fixed at the subsistence level. Therefore, it assumes that the trade unions are powerless in increasing the wages. This is a wrong notion.
4. This theory is based on the Malthusian theory of population according to which a rise in wages above the subsistence level will lead to rapid increase in population. But experience shows that a rise in wages leads to higher standard of living and not increase in population.
5. This theory is pessimistic because it excludes all possibility of improvement in the conditions of labour either through increased efficiency or due to general economic progress.

Standard of Living Theory

This theory is an improved and refined version of subsistence theory. According to this theory, wage is determined by the standard of living of the workers. Standard of living refers to the bare necessaries of life and also education, and recreation to which the worker is habituated.

Merits

This theory has two merits:

1. This theory gives importance to the efficiency and productivity of the worker.
2. When workers are paid a high wage rate for a considerable period of time, they become accustomed to a high standard of living and they will try to maintain the same high standard of living.

Criticisms

In spite of its merits, the theory has been subjected to many criticisms:

1. Individuals do not have any fixed standard of living. Critics point out that there is no such thing as a standard of living to which a worker is accustomed.
2. When wages depend on standard of living, the latter should not change. But workers' standard of living remains fixed for sometime but wages change frequently.
3. No doubt, wages are determined by standard of living. It is also true that standard of living is determined by wages.

WAGE FUND THEORY

This theory was developed by J.S.Mill. According to him, the employers set apart a certain amount of capital to pay wages for labourers. This is fixed and constant. This is called as wages fund. Wage is determined by the amount of wages fund and the total number of labourers. According to J.S.Mill, "wages depend upon the demand and supply of labour or as it is often expressed as proportion between population and capital. By population is here meant the number only of the laboring classes or rather of those who work for hire and by capital, only circulating capital.....".

$$\text{Wage rate} = \frac{\text{Wage fund}}{\text{Number of labourers}}$$

An increase in wage rate is possible only by an increase in wage fund or by a reduction in the number of labourers. Thus there exists a direct relation between wage rate and wages fund and inverse relation between wage rate and number of labourers. This theory also states that trade unions are powerless in rising the general wage rate.

Criticisms

1. Wage fund theory states that the wage rate is found by dividing the wage fund by the number of workers. But it does not tell us about the sources of wages fund and the method of estimating it.
2. Wage fund theory is unscientific and illogical because it first decides the wages fund and then determines wages. But in reality, wages should be found first and from that wage fund should be calculated. This theory neglects the quality and efficiency of the workers in determining the wage rate. This is considered to be a basic weakness of the theory.
3. This theory neglects the quality and efficiency of the workers in determining the wage rate. This is considered to be a basic weakness of the theory.
4. This theory assumes that wages can increase only at the expense of profit. This is not correct. The operation of the law of increasing returns will lead to a great increase in total output which may be sufficient to raise both wages and profits.
5. The wages fund theory has been criticised by the trade unions for its assumption that wages cannot be increased through bargaining.
6. Wages fund theory has failed to explain the differences in wage rate.
7. This theory believes that wages are paid out of circulating capital. But when the process of production is short, wages are paid out of current production. When the process of production is long, wages are paid out of capital.

RESIDUAL CLAIMANT THEORY

This theory was propounded by Walker. According to this theory, rent and interest are contractual payments. After deducting rent and interest from total product, the employer will deduct his profits. What remains after deducting rent, interest and profits is wages. It is possible to increase wages by increasing the total product by improving the efficiency of the workers.

Criticisms

This theory has several defects:

1. This theory assumes that the share of landlords, capitalists and entrepreneurs are fixed and it is absolutely wrong.
2. It is not the worker who is the residual claimant but the entrepreneur.
3. It does not explain the influence of trade union in wage determination.
4. The supply side of labour has been totally ignored by the theory.

MARGINAL PRODUCTIVITY THEORY OF WAGES

Marginal productivity theory of wages is an extension of marginal productivity theory of distribution. According to this theory, wage for labour should be equal to the value of the marginal product under conditions of perfect competition. Marginal product is the addition made to total product by the employment of one unit of labour. The value of the marginal product of labour is equal to the price at which the marginal product can be sold.

Under conditions of perfect competition, an employer will continue to employ more and more of labourers till the value of the marginal product is equal to marginal factor cost(MFC). Marginal factor cost is the cost of employing an additional worker. In order to find out the marginal productivity of labour we have to keep the quantity of other factors constant while employing one more unit of labour. The difference in total production is the marginal productivity. The employment of an additional unit of labour will result in increase in output and cost. As long as MPP is greater than MFC, the employer will employ additional units of labour. But he will stop employing additional units of labour when MPP=MC.

Assumptions

This theory is based upon the following assumptions:

1. There is perfect competition in factor market and in product market.
2. Labour is homogeneous.
3. The law of diminishing returns operates in production.
4. There is free entry and exit of the firms.
5. There is perfect knowledge about the market conditions.
6. All factors of production can be substituted for each other.
7. There is free mobility of factors of production.
8. Factors of production are divisible.

Criticism

The theory is found to be unsatisfactory and various criticisms have been leveled against this theory.

1. The theory deals with the demand side only. The supply side is totally ignored.
2. This theory is unjust because wages are determined by the marginal productivity. But justice demand that workers should be paid on the basis of average productivity.
3. Further, marginal productivity of the worker cannot be calculated as factors are not divisible into small units.

4. Factors of production are neither mobile nor perfect substitutes. Their knowledge is also imperfect.
5. This theory assumes perfect competition in the product market. But the market for goods is characterised by imperfect competition.
6. Marginal product of labour depends not only on its support but also on the supply of other factors. If other factors are plentiful and labour is scarce, marginal product of labour will be high and vice versa.
7. This theory fails to explain the differences in wages.

Rejecting the marginal productivity theory Marshall states, "This doctrine has been put forward as a theory of wages. But there is no valid ground for any such pretension... Demand and supply exert equally important influences on wages; neither has a claim to predominance; any more than has either blade of scissors, or either pier of an arch... The doctrine throws into clear light, one of the causes that governs wages".

DISCOUNTED MARGINAL PRODUCTIVITY THEORY OF WAGES

Taussig has given a modified version of the Marginal Productivity theory of wages. According to this theory, the wage for labour is determined not by its marginal product but by the discounted marginal product.

Labourers cannot get the entire amount of the marginal product because production is a long drawn out process. In the same way, sales also take time. As the labourers are poor and cannot wait till the product is sold, they have to be supported by the employers. The employer does not pay the full amount of the marginal product of labour. In order to compensate the risk involved in giving advance to the workers, the employer deducts a certain percentage from the final output. This deduction is made at the current rate of interest. It is the discounted marginal product that determines the wage of the labourers.

Criticisms

1. This theory is abstract. It is "a dim and abstract one remote from the problem of real life".
2. It is very difficult to determine the discounted marginal product of labour.
3. This theory fails to take into account other factors which determine the wage rate.
4. This theory has failed to explain differences in wage rate.

Taussing's theory is another version of the Residual Claimant Theory of wages. Therefore, it is subject to all criticisms put forward against the Residual Claimant Theory.

(c) THEORIES OF INTEREST

Theories of interest seeks to explain two important issues namely how interest arises and how the rate of interest is determined. Some classical theories like Productivity Theory and Abstinence Theory explains only the first aspect while the classical, Loanable and Keynerian Liquidity Preference Theory explains both the aspects.

Classical Theories of Interest

1. Productivity Theory of Interest

This theory was propounded by Physiocrats and developed by German economists. According to this theory, interest is paid for the productivity of capital. According to Wicksell, "interest is the payment by the borrower of capital by virtue of its productivity". Capital is productive in the sense that labour, assisted by capital produces more than labour without capital. for example, a fisherman with a net can catch more fish than without it. An agricultural labour with tractor can produce more than without a tractor. Thus capital is as productive as other factors of production.

Criticisms

1. Economists criticise this theory for having ignored the scarcity, efficiency and supply of capital that determine the rate of interest.
2. If interest depends merely on productivity, interest rates should vary in proportion to the productiveness of capital. Actually pure rate of interest tends to be the same in the market.
3. Even if loans are taken for consumption purposes, interest has to be paid on them. But loans for consumption purposes are not productive.
4. Productivity theory explains interest from the side of demand only and ignores the supply side altogether.
5. Mere physical productivity of capital does not explain interest. If people are willing to lend unlimited amounts of loans (money) without interest, business would expand. Interest would not be a cost. But interest is a cost which every entrepreneur must bear with. Hence price in the long-run, must cover all costs including interest.

Abstinence or Waiting Theory

Senior, the classical economist is the exponent of the abstinence theory of interest. According to J.S.Mill, interest is the remuneration for mere abstinence. Abstinence theory explains interest from the side of supply whereas the productivity theory explains from the demand side. According to Senior saving involved a sacrifice which he calls it 'abstinence'. Senior explains that capital is the result of savings, which in turn are the result of abstinence. People usually may consume their entire income. They save a part of their income only by abstaining from the present consumption. Thus saving was an act of abstaining from consumption. It was necessary to reward people to abstain from consumption since abstinence is regarded as painful. Interest is thus the reward paid for those who saved rather than consumed their incomes.

Criticism

1. This theory has failed to explain the demand for capital, hence it is one-sided theory.
2. This theory emphasises that all capital is the result of abstinence, but it is not true.
3. This theory is also criticised on the ground that rich people save without least inconvenience and they do not undergo discomfort on account of saving.
4. Marshall substituted the term waiting for 'abstinence'. Saving means waiting. When a person

saves, he does not abstain from consumption for ever. He just postpones present consumption to a future date. Generally people do not like to wait; an incentive is necessary to encourage this postponement of consumption. Interest is thus an incentive.

Agio or Austrian Theory of Interest

This theory was first advanced by John Rae and later developed by Bohm Bawerk of the Austrain School of Economics. According to this theory interest arises because people prefer present goods to future goods. If people prefer the present goods, there cannot be savings and capital. To induce people to save and accumulate capital an agio or premium or price must be given. Thus agio is nothing but interest. People generally prefer the present goods to the future goods for three reasons. According to Bohm Bawerk the first reason is an under valuation of the future purchasing power as compared with the present purchasing power, moreover future is uncertain. In the second place present wants are felt more keenly than the future good. Yet another reason is that a person expects improvement in economic position in future as a result of which the marginal utility of his income will decline. He therefore prefers to use his income at the present when the marginal utility of his income is high. A premium or agio must be given to the lender if he has a part with his income at the present. This premium is the so-called interest.

Criticism

1. This theory failed to explain the forces of demand and supply for capital that determine the rate of interest.
2. The reasons given by Bohm Bawerk do not apply always.
3. The technical superiority of present goods of Bohm Bawerk has been criticised by Irving fisher.

Fisher's Time Preference Theory

This theory is associated with Irving Fisher who emphasises time preference as the central point in the theory. This theory is based on the subjective valuation of income and people's time preference. According to this theory "interest is the price of time". In the words of Fisher "interest is an index of community's preference for a dollar of present over a dollar of future income".

People in general prefer the present to the future. This is what he calls the time preference. By time preference Fisher means individual's preference for the present to the future or people's discounting or under estimating the future.

There is a tendency on the part of the people to vary the income meant for consumption from time to time by saving and borrowing. Interest is the price paid to the people for present income rather than for future income. According to Fisher the rate of interest varies according to the time preference.

The time preference depends upon the size of income, the distribution of income over the period of time, the composition of income, the certainty of enjoying income in the future, the temperament and the character of the individuals and expectation of the life of the people. If the income size is large, individual will satisfy present wants more and discount the future at a lower rate. The distribution of income may take place in three different ways. It may be uniform throughout the life or increase with age or decrease with age. If it is uniform individuals will have their time preference according to the size of their income and temperament. But if the income increases with age, individuals will tend to discount the future at a higher rate because their future is well provided. If the income decreases with age, the future will be discounted at a lower rate.

Regarding the degree of enjoying the income in the future, greater the certainty of enjoying income in the future smaller is the degree of time preference. But if the enjoyment of income is not certain the degree of time preference will be greater. The character of individuals also influences time preference. A person of forethought discounts the future at a low rate compared to a spend thrift. Similarly a person who expects to live long has less time preference than one who expects to live short. These factors determine individual's rate of time preference. When the rate of time preference is higher than the market rate of interest, the individuals will borrow; if it is lower he will lend to the market.

Criticism

1. Fisher's theory fails to show the influence of the banking system on rate of interest.
2. This theory gives too much importance to willingness or preference; moreover this theory lays much emphasis on consumption expenditure out of income.
3. Fisher did not give importance to the impact of expectations on interest rate. The concept of productivity is free from the element of uncertainty. Both the factors namely expectation and uncertainty are crucial factors to Keyesian concept of marginal efficiency of capital.
4. The theory is based on the assumption of fixed purchasing power of money between the present and the future. In the real world, fluctuations in the value of money are the most common.

The time preference theory is superior to the other theories since it explains the rate of interest by reference to demand for and supply of capital. The demand for capital depends upon the marginal productivity of capital to investors while the supply of capital depends upon the time preference of individuals. The rate of interest will be determined at the point of equilibrium between demand for and supply of capital. The time preference theory is a complete theory and is the basis of the modern loanable funds theory of interest rate.

The Classical Theory of Interest

The classical theory of interest was propounded by the old classical economists. Later it was developed by Marshall, Pigou, Walras, Taussig and Knight. According to this theory rate of interest is determined by the demand for and supply of capital. The rate of interest settles at the point where the demand for capital is equal to supply of capital. The demand for capital arises from investment and supply of capital from savings. This means that the rate of interest is determined by the volume of savings and volume of investment. This theory explains the rate of interest in terms of saving and investment; this theory is called the saving investment theory of interest.

Classical theory is also known as real or non-monetary theory of interest. This theory refers to saving as real savings and investment as real investment. Real saving refers to those goods which are employed for investment purposes instead of consumption. Real investment refers to the production of capital goods like machinery, buildings, etc., rather than monetary investment, such as stocks and shares. Thus money does not play an important role in the determination of rate of interest. According to classical economist the rate of interest is determined by the demand for savings to invest in capital goods and the supply of savings. The two sides of the interest determination, namely, the demand for capital and the supply of capital can be analysed.

Demand for Capital

Demand for capital arises on account of its productivity. Firms desire to make new capital goods which are demanded to produce consumer goods. For any type of capital good it is possible to draw a marginal revenue productivity curve showing the addition made to the total revenue by an additional unit of a capital at various levels of the stock of that capital. The more the capital assets an entrepreneur has, the less revenue or income he will earn by purchasing one more unit of capital. Under perfect competition, it is profitable for a firm to purchase any capital up to the point at which the price of that capital equals its marginal revenue productivity. The entrepreneur will demand capital goods up to the point at which the expected rate of return on the capital goods equals the rate of interest. At a higher rate of interest the demand for capital is low and it is high at a lower rate of interest. Thus the demand for capital is inversely related to rate of interest and the demand schedule for capital slopes downward from left to right. However there are certain other factors which govern the demand for capital such as the growth of population, technical progress, the standard of living of the community, etc.

Supply of Capital

The supply of capital depends upon savings and hence the will to save and the power to save of the community. Some people save irrespective of the rate of interest. They would save even if the rate of interest is zero. Others save because the current rate of interest is just enough to induce them to save. There are potential savers who will save if the rate of interest increases. In an economy, there may be three types of savers, viz., individual savers, institutional savers like banks, insurance companies, etc., and the government. Saving involves certain inconvenience like sacrifice, or waiting as they have to forgo present consumption which has to be compensated. The higher the rate of interest, the larger will be the community savings and the more will be the supply of funds. The supply curve of capital thus slopes upward indicating that more funds will be saved and supplied at a higher rate of interest.

Determination of the Rate of Interest

The rate of interest is determined by the intersection of the demand for capital (or investment demand) and supply of savings. This is shown in the Fig.

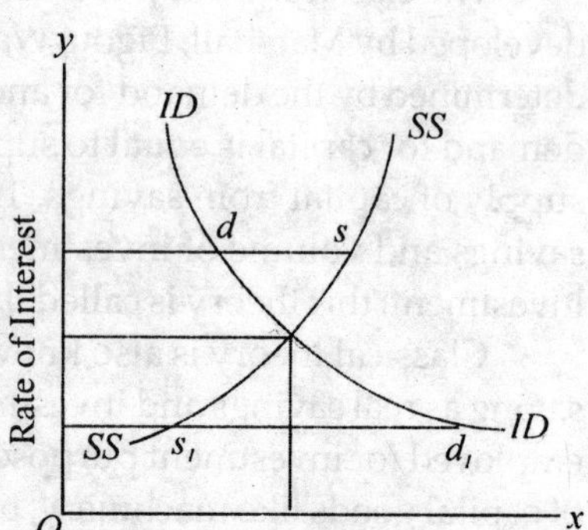

The point of equilibrium is E at which investment demand is equal to saving. 'r' is the natural rate of interest. OQ quantity of capital is demanded and supplied, at 'Or' rate of interest. Rate of interest cannot be higher or lower than 'r' since charges in saving and investment will force the rate back to 'r'. For example, if the rate of interest rises above to Or_1 the demand for investment funds will fall and the supply of funds will increase. Since the supply of capital is more than the demand by 'ds' the rate of interest will come down to the equilibrium level 'Or'. If the rate of interest falls to Or_2 the demand for capital will be greater than the supply by S_1d_1 and the rate of interest will rise to 'Or'. At the lower rate of interest, people will save less but the demand for investible funds will increase which will raise the rate of interest to the equilibrium level.

Criticism

The real theory of the classical economists as propounded by Marshall and Pigou has been criticised by Keynes.

1. Keynes has condemned the classical theory as a useless and unrealistic theory. Keyness does not agree with the classical idea that saving is interest elastic. In fact the level of income has more important influence upon the amount saved than the rate of interest. For instance, the rich persons in a community will save automatically, even if the rate of interest is zero. Middle income group also save, because they would like to provide security for their families for the future, so they will save even if the rate of interest is zero. If the rate of interest is high, the low income groups may not be in a position to save.
2. Keynes did not agree with the classical relationship between investment and rate of interest. The classical theory assumes that investment demand will be larger at lower interest rate. Keynes shows that investment does not depend upon rate of interest alone but also upon marginal efficiency of capital.
3. Keynes does not agree with the classical theory that the rate of interest equates saving and investment. According to him, any difference between saving and investment will be removed by changes in the levels of income and expenditure rather than by changes in the rate of interest.
4. The classical theory believes that saving and investment are interest elastic, i.e., both are influenced by interest rates. But it is not true; investment, for instance is influenced by marginal efficiency of capital.
5. Another important defect of the theory is that it has not taken into account monetary factors and credit money that determine the rate of interest.
6. Keynes criticizes the basic assumption of the classical theory, namely that the resources in a society are fully employed. He believed, in less than full employment situation, where resources are unemployed interest is not essentially an inducement of saving.
7. The classical theory includes savings out of current income for supply of savings which makes it inadequate. Bank credit and past savings are other sources of supply of capital. The classical theory remains incomplete by neglecting these factors in the supply schedule of capital.
8. Classical theory is criticised as indeterminate. Since savings depend upon the level of income it is not possible to know the rate of interest unless the income level is known before hand. The income level itself cannot be known without knowing the rate of interest. For each income level a separate saving curve will have to be drawn. These are circular reasons which offer no solution to the problem of interest.
9. This theory also neglects the influence of the demand for idle money balances on the determination of the rate of interest on the demand side.
10. This theory ignores consumption loans and takes into account only capital used for productive purposes.

LOANABLE FUNDS THEORY OF INTEREST

Introduction

The loanable funds theory known as the neo-classical theory explains the determination of interest in terms of demand and supply of loanable funds. This theory was developed by Swedish economists and first formulated by Knut Wicksell but contributions were made by other Swedish economists such as Bertil Ohlin, Gunnar Myrdal, Eric Lindahl and English economists like Pigou and Roberston. The term loanable funds means the total amount of money which is supplied and demanded in the market. According to loanable funds theory interest is the price paid for the use of loanable funds. There are several sources of both supply and demand of loanable funds.

Supply of Loanable Funds

The supply of loanable funds comes from four basic sources namely, savings disboarding, bank credit and disinvestment.

(a) Savings

Private savings, individual and corporate savings are the main source of saving. In the loanable funds theory savings are classified as planned (exante) and unplanned (expost) savings of individuals and households. Exante savings are planned by individuals at the beginning of a period in the hope of expected incomes and anticipated expenditure on consumption. In the Robertsonian expost sense savings is the difference between the income of the preceding period and the consumption of the present period. In both the cases the amount saved varies at different rates of interest. More savings will be coming at higher rates of interest. Just like individual, business sector will also save. A part of the earnings of the business is declared as dividend and the undistributed part constitutes business or corporate savings. Corporate savings also depends upon current rate of interest. A higher rate of interest encourages business savings.

(b) Dishoarding

Dishoarding also brings forth the supply of loanable funds. When people dishoard the previous hoardings, the supply of loanable funds increases. Cash balances remaining idle in the previous period, becomes active balances in the present period, are available as loanable funds. At higher rate of interest more will be dishoarded.

(c) Bank Credit

Money created by banks adds to the supply of loanable funds. By creating credit money banks advance loans to the businessmen. The supply of loanable funds varies with rate of interest. Generally the banks will lend more money at higher rates of interest.

(d) Disinvestment

Sometimes, due to disinvestment funds, flow into capital market adding to the supply of loanable funds. Due to structural changes, the existing stock of machines and other equipments are not replaced.

They are allowed to wear out. Hence a part of the revenue from the sale of the commodities will not be needed to keep the machines in proper condition or to replace them. Instead this will increase the supply of loanable funds. Disinvestment increases when the rate of interest is high. These components of loanable funds are denoted by savings(s), dishoarding (DH), disinvestment (DI) and bank credit (BM).

Demand for Loanable Fund

The demand for loanable funds mainly comes from three sectors namely government, businessmen and consumers who need them for purposes of investment, hoarding and consumption. The government borrows funds for the provision of public goods, for development purposes or for war preparations. Major part of demand for loanable funds comes from business firms which borrow money for purchasing or producing new capital goods and for starting investment projects. This is the most important constituent of demand for loanable funds. Rate of interest is the price of the loanable funds required to purchase the capital goods. Businessmen will find it profitable to purchase large amount of capital goods, when the rate of interest is low. Thus the demand curve for loanable funds for investment purposes is interest elastic and slopes downwards to the right. The demand for loanable funds on the part of the consumers is for the purchase of durable consumer goods like scooter, houses, refrigerators, television sets, etc., Lower rates of interest will induce them to borrow more. Hence demand curve for loanable funds for consumption purposes is also downward sloping. Funds are also demanded for the purpose of hoarding them in liquid form as idle cash balances. This is to satisfy their desire for liquidity preference. It is important to note that a person who supplies the loanable funds is the same person who demands loanable funds for hoarding purposes. A saver for instance who hoards his savings supplies loanable funds and also demands them to satisfy his liquidity preference. Hoarding is also interest elastic. The rate of interest is determined by the equilibrium between the total demand for loanable funds and the total supply of loanable funds.

The loanable funds theory is more realistic than the classical theory in several respects. The classical theory neglects monetary influences on interest. The loanable funds theory takes into account bank credit on the supply side. The theory recognises the role of hoarding as a factor influencing the demand for funds.

Criticism

1. This theory is unrealistic for combining monetary factors with real factors. It is not proper to combine non-monetary factors like saving and investment with monetary factors like bank credit and dishoarding without bringing changes in the level of income.
2. The theory exaggerates the effect of rate of interest on savings. In fact, the rate of interest does not influence the volume of savings as suggested by the theory. Generally speaking people save not to earn interest. People save more even without any increase in the rate of interest; they save even if the rate of interest falls to zero. Thus for some people savings are interest inelastic.
3. Loanable funds theory like the classical theory is criticised on the ground that it is indeterminante. The supply of loanable funds consists of savigs, bank credit and dishoarding. Since savings varies with the level of income, the total supply of loanable funds will also vary with income. Thus loanable funds theory is indeterminate unless the income level is already known.

4. Another criticism against the loanable funds theory is that it is based upon the assumptions of full employment of resources, which does not exist in the real world. Loanable fund theory implies that it is not applicable to the situation of less than full employment. However the theory takes into account the increase in the level of income due to investment and its influence on savings. If full employment is assumed, income would not increase at all.
5. The theory states that the supply of loanable funds can be increased by releasing cash balances from savings and decreased by absorbing cash balances into savings. This means that the cash balances are elastic. This is not true because the total cash balances available are in fixed proportion to the supply of money at any time. Even if there are variations in the cash balances they are in fact, in the velocity of circulation of money rather than in the amount of cash balances in the community.

Liquidity Preference Theory

Keynes introduced a monetary theory of interest in his famous book, "The General Theory of Employment, Interest and Money". According to him "interest is a reward for parting with liquidity. His theory is known as liquidity preference theory of interest. Liquidity preference means the demand for money to hold or the desire of the public to hold cash. According to Meyer, "liquidity preference is the preference to have an equal amount of cash rather than a claim against others". To Keynes interest is purely a monetary phenomenon because the rate of interest is determined in terms of money. Money is the most liquid asset and people would like to keep their assets in cash. To make them surrender the liquidity, they must be paid a reward. This reward is paid in the form of liquidity. The more the desire for liquidity, higher shall be the rate of interest demanded to part with liquidity. This theory is characterised as the monetary theory of interest, as different from the real theory of classical economists.

Factors Determining Liquidity Preference

Liquidity preference depends upon many factors. According to Keynes the desire for liquidity or the desire of the people to hold liquid cash arises because of three motives, namely, (i) the transaction motives (ii) the precautionary motive and (iii) speculation motive.

Transaction Motive

The transaction motive refers to the demand for money or the 'need for cash for the current transactions of personal and business exchanges'. It is divided into income and business motives. The income motive is meant to bridge the interval between the receipt of income and its disbursement. The business motive refers to the interval between the time of incurring business costs and that of the receipt of the sale proceeds. If the time between expenditure to be incurred and the receipt of income is small, less cash will be held by the people for current transactions and vice versa. Most of the people receive their income weekly or monthly, while the expenditure is to be incurred everyday. Therefore it becomes necessary to keep certain amount of ready money in hand to make current payments. Similarly the businessmen and the entrepreneurs also require ready cash to meet their current expenses, especially, for payment for raw materials and transport, to pay wages and salaries and to meet other expenses. Money held for this business motive depends to a large extent on the volume of trade of the firm. Changes in the transaction demand for money depends upon the level of income.

The Precautionary Motive

Precautionary motive for holding money refers to the desire of the people to hold cash balances for unforeseen contingencies. Both individuals and businessmen keep cash in reserve to meet expected needs like sickness, accidents, travel, unemployment and other contingencies. Money held under the precautionary motive is rather like water kept in reserve in a water tank. The precautionary demand for money depends upon the level of income, business activity, the nature of the individual, availability of cash, the cost of holding liquid assets, financial soundness and accessibility to the credit market.

Speculative Demand for Money

Money held under speculative motive is for "securing profit from knowing better than the market what the future will bring forth". In other words it reflects the desire to hold one's resources in liquid form in order to take advantage of market movements regarding the future changes in the rate of interest. Individuals and businessmen who have funds after keeping enough for transactions and precautionary purposes like to gain by investing in bonds.

Supply of Money

Among the two determinants of the rate of interest the supply of money refers to the total quantity of money in circulation for all transactions at any time. It is exogenously determined by monetary authorities. Thus the quantity of money is fixed by the monetary authorities and hence the supply curve of money is assumed to be perfectly inelastic. Supply of money consists of coins, notes and bank deposits.

Determination of the Rate of Interest

According to Keynes the demand for money namely the liquidity preference and supply of money determine the rate of interest. The rate of interest like the price of a commodity is determined at a level where the demand for money equals the supply of money.

Criticism

The Keynesian theory of interest has been severely criticised by Hansen, Robertson, Knight and others.

1. This theory explains the working of everything through the bond market and regards bonds as the only alternative to money. Thus the theory lacks realism.
2. This theory points out the rate of interest as purely a monetary phenomenon; real forces like productivity of capital and thriftness or saving by the people also play an important role in the determination of the rate of interest.
3. Keynes' concept of demand for money is not comprehensive. To him the demand for money means liquidity preference. But money is demanded also for consumption and investment purposes.
4. Keynes states that liquidity is essential for interest rate. But as Hazlitt says, even "if a man is holding his funds in the form of time deposits or short-term treasury bills, he is being paid interest on them.

5. Robertson dubbed this theory as 'at best an inadequate and at worst a misleading account'. This theory is an incomplete theory because it has not taken into account the factors like credit money and loanable funds for the determination of rate of interest.
6. This theory assumes the supply of money to be constant. Hence the rate of interest is influenced by the demand for money. This theory is thus one-sided.
7. Keynes' theory explains interest as a short-term phenomenon. So it cannot be applied to long period.
8. The greatest fallacy in Keynes' analysis is that it ignores the influence of real factors in determining the rate of interest. Knut Wicksell was the first economist to present a real-cum-monetary theory of interest which was further refined by Irving Fisher.
9. The concept of 'liquidity trap' is also wrong. In reality the liquidity preference schedule may not be perfectly elastic at low rate of interest. Especially during depression, general pessimism prevails in the economy. It is therefore not correct to argue that the rate of interest will go up in future.
10. The Keynesian theory is also indeterminate like the classical theory. The supply and demand for money schedules cannot give the rate of interest if the income level is not known. In the classical theory also the demand and supply schedules for savings offer no solution unless the income is known. Thus according to Prof. Hansen "Keynes' criticism of the classical theory applies equally to his own theory".
11. Hicks, Lerner, Hansen and others opine that the rate of interest, along with the level of income is determined by factors like investment demand function, the supply of savings function, the liquidity preference function and the quantity of money function. Keynes does not bring all these factors into his theory. Thus Keynes fails to provide an integrated and determinate theory of interest.

(d) THEORIES OF PROFIT

There are several theories of profit propounded by economists. No theory deals with all aspects of the problem. Each one explains a particular aspect of profit. The central problem in the phenomenon of profit is to explain why the profit is paid.

Rent Theory of Profit

This theory was first propounded by the American Economist Walker. It is based on the ideas of Senior and J.S.Mill. According to Mill, "the extra gains which any producer obtains through superior talents for business or superior business arrangements are very much of a kind similar to rent. Walker says that "Profits are of the same genus as rent". His theory of profits states that profit is the rent of superior entrepreneur over marginal of less efficient entrepreneur. According to these economists, there was a good deal of similarity between rent and profit. Rent was the reward for the use of land while profits was the reward for the ability of the entrepreneur. Just as land differs from one another in fertility, entrepreneurs differ from one another in ability. Rent of superior land is determined by the difference in productivity of the marginal and super marginal land; similarly the profits of the marginal and super marginal entrepreneurs. In short it is the intra-marginal lands that earn a surplus over margial lands. So also intra marginal entrepreneurs earn a surplus over marginal entrepreneur. Just as there is the marginal land, there is the marginal entrepreneur. The marginal land yields no rent; so also marginal entrepreneur is a no profit entrepreneur.

The marginal entrepreneur sells his produce at cost price and gets no profit. He secures only the wages of management not profit. Thus profit does not enter into cost of production. Like rent, profit also does not enter into price. Profit is thus a surplus.

Criticism

1. According to critics there cannot be perfect similarity between rent and profit. Rent is generally positive and in rare cases it may be zero. But rent can never be negative. When entrepreneur suffers losses profit can be negative.
2. The theory explains profit as the differential surplus rather than a reward for an entrepreneur.
3. Profit is not always the reward for business ability. Profit can be due to monopoly or it can arise due to favourable chance to the entrepreneur.
4. This thecry maintains that there is no profit entrepreneur just as no rent land. But in practical life there is no such entrepreneur because whether the entrepreneur has ability or not be gets profit as his reward.
5. The system of joint stock enterprise has become more important in the modern economy. The manner in which dividends are distributed among the shareholders is not at all related to latter's ability. Both dull and intelligent shareholders enjoy the same dividends. In fact, the less able may secure more dividends if they possess more shares.
6. This theory assumes that profit does not enter into price. But this is unrealistic because profit as a part of the cost of production does enter into price.
7. Rent is a known and expected surplus. It is also a contractual payment. Profit is unknown.
8. Walker has analysed only surplus profit. But profit can be several other types.'
9. Walker failed to understand the true nature of profit. According to Walker, profit arose on account of the ability of the entrepreneur to undertake risk. Critics point out that profit is not the reward for undertaking risk but it is the reward for the avoidance of risk.

Wage Theory of Profit

This theory was propounded by Taussig, the American economist. According to this theory, profit is also a type of wage which is given to the entrepreneur for the services rendered by him. In the words of Taussig, "profit is the wage of the entrepreneur which accures to him on account of his ability". Just as a labourer receives wages for his services, the entrepreneur works hard gets profit for the part played by him in the production. The only difference is that while labourer renders physical services, entrepreneur puts in mental work. Thus an entrepreneur is not different from a doctor, lawyer, teacher, etc., who do mental work. Profit is thus a form of wage.

Criticism

1. The main defect of this theory is that it does not make a distinction between wage and profit. Wages are fixed and certain, but profits are uncertain income.
2. The entrepreneurs undergo risk in production; but the labourer undertakes no such risk.
3. Entrepreneur bears the entire responsibility to organize the business, but labourer need not do so.

4. Profits tend to vary with price but wages do not vary so.
5. The labourer get his wages if he has put in the required amount of labour, but the entrepreneur may not get profit even if he works hard.
6. Profit may include chance gain while wages do not include such an element.

Risk Theory of Profit

This theory is associated with American economist Hawley. According to him profit is the reward for risk-taking in business. Risk-taking is supposed to be the most important function of an entrepreneur. Every production, that is undertaken in anticipation of demand involves risk. According to Drucker there are four kinds of risk. They are replacement, obsolescence, risk proper and uncertainty. The first two are calculated and therefore they are insured. But the other two are unknown and unforeseen risks. It is for bearing such risk profit is paid to entrepreneur. No entrepreneur will be willing to undertake risks if he gets only the normal return. Therefore the reward for risk-taking must be higher than the actual value of the risk. If the entrepreneur does not receive the reward, he will not be prepared to undertake the risk. Thus higher the risk greater is the possibility of profit.

According to Hawley the entrepreneur can avoid certain risks for a fixed payment to the insurance company. But he cannot get rid of all risks by means of insurance. If he does so he is not an entrepreneur and would earn only wages of management and not profit.

Criticism

1. Risk-taking is not the only entrepreneurial function which leads to emergence of profits. Profits are also due to the organizational and coordinating ability of the entrepreneur. It is also reward for innovation.
2. According to Carver profit is paid to an entrepreneur not for bearning the risk but for minimizing and avoiding risk.
3. This theory assumes that profit is proportional to risk undertaken by entrepreneurs. But this is not true in practical life because even entrepreneurs who do not take any risk are paid profit.
4. Knight says that it is not every risk that gives profit. It is unforeseen and non-insured risks that account for profit. According to Knight risks are of two types viz., foreseeable risk and unforeseeable risk. The risk of fire in a factory is a foreseeable risk and can be covered through insurance. The premium paid for the fire insurance can be included in the cost of production. The entrepreneur can foresee such a risk and insures it. An insurable risk in reality is no risk and profit cannot arise due to insurable risk.
5. There is little empirical evidence to prove that entrepreneurs earn more in risky enterprises. In a way all enterprises are risky, for an element of uncertainty is present in them and every entrepreneur aims at making large profits.

The Dynamic Theory of Profit

Prof. J.B.Clark propounded the dynamic theory of profit in the year 1900. To him profit is the difference between the price and the cost of production of the commodity. Profit is the result of progressive change in an organized society. The progressive change is possible only in a dynamic state. According to Clark the whole economic society is divided into organized and unorganized society. The organized society is further divided into static and dynamic state. Only in dynamic state profit arises.

In a static state, the five generic changes such as the size of the population, technical knowledge, the amount of capital, method of production of the firms and the size of the industry and the wants of the people do not take place; everything is stagnant and there is no change at all. The element of time is non-existent and there is no uncertainty. The same economic features are repeated year after year. Therefore there is not risk of any kind to the entrepreneur. The price of the good will be equal to the cost of production. Hence profit does not arise at all. The entrepreneur would get wages for his labour and interest on his capital. If the price of the commodity is higher than the cost of production, competition would reduce the price again to the level of the cost of production so that profit is eliminated. The presence of perfect competition makes the price equal to the cost of production which eliminates the super normal profit. Thus Knight observes, "Since costs and selling prices are always equal, there can be no profit beyond wages for the routine work of supervision".

It is well known that the society has always been dynamic. Several changes are taking place in a dynamic society. According to Clark five major changes are constantly taking place in a society. They are (1) Changes in the size of the population, (2) Changes in the supply of capital, (3) Changes in production techniques, (4) Changes in the forms of industrial organisation, and (5) Changes in human wants. These dynamic changes affect the demand and supply of commodities which leads to emergence of profit. Sometimes individual firms may introduce dynamic changes. For example, a firm may improve its production technique, reduce its cost and thereby increase its profit. The typical dynamic change is an invention. This enables the entrepreneur to produce more and reduce costs, leading to emergence of profit.

Criticism

1. It is wrong to say that there is no profit in static state because every entrepreneur is paid profit irrespective of the state of an economy.
2. This theory does not fully appreciate the nature of the entrepreneurial function. If there are no profits in a static state, it means there is no entrepreneur. But without an entrepreneur it is not possible to imagine how different factors of production would be employed.
3. Mere change in an economy would not give rise to profits if those changes are predictable. It is only the unpredictable, provision can be made for such changes and the expenditure can be included in the cost of production.
4. This theory assumes the existence of perfect competition and static state. But they are far from reality.
5. This theory states that profit arises because of dynamic changes. But Knight says that it is only unforeseen changes that give rise to profit.
6. This theory associates profit for imitating progressive changes in the economy. But in reality profit is paid to entrepreneur for other important functions like risk taking and uncertainty bearing.
7. According to Taussig, "dynamic theory has created unnecessary and artificial distinction between "profits" and wage of management".

Schumpeter's Innovation Theory

This theory was propounded by Schumpeter. This theory is more or less similar to that of Clark's theory. Instead of five changes mentioned by Clark, Schumpeter explains the change caused by innovations in the production process. According to this theory profit is the reward for innovations. He uses the term innovation in a sense wider than that of the changes mentioned by Clark. Innovation refers to all those changes, in the production process with an objective of reducing the cost of commodity so as to create gap between the existing price of the commodity and its new cost. Innovation may take any shape like introduction of a new technique or a new plant, a change in the internal structure or organizational set up of the firm or change in the quality of raw material, a new form of energy, better method of salesmanship, etc.

Schumpter makes a distinction between invention and innovation. Innovation is brought about mainly for reducing the cost of production and it is cost reducing agent. Profit is the reward for this stratagic role, Innovations are not possible by all entrepreneurs. Only exceptional entrepreneurs can innovate. They are capable of tapping new resources, technical knowledge and reduce the cost of production. Thus the main motive for introducing innovation is the desire to earn profit. Profit is therefore the cause of innovation.

Profits are of temporary nature. The pioneer who innovates earns abnormal profit for a short period. Soon other entrepreneurs, "swarm in clusters", compete for profit in the same manner. The pioneer will make another innovation. In a dynamic world innovation in one field may induce other innovations in related fields. The emergence of motor car industry may in turn stimulate new investments in the construction of highways, rubber, tyresm and petroleum products. Profits are thus causes and effects of innovation. The interest of profit leads entrepreneur to innovate and innovation leads to profit. Thus profit has a tendency to appear, disappear and reappear. Profits are caused by innovation and disappear by imitation. Innovational profit is thus, never permanent, in the opinion of Schumpeter. Therefore it is different from other incomes, such as rent, wages and interest. These are regular and permanent incomes arising under all circumstances. Profit on the other hand is a temporary surplus resulting from innovation.

Prof. Schumpeter also explained his views on the functions of the entrepreneur. The entrepreneur organizes the business and combines the various factors of production. But this is not his real function and this will not yield him profit. The real function of the entrepreneur is to introduce innovations in business. It is innovations which yield him profit.

Criticisms

1. This theory concentrates only on innovation, which is only one of the many functions of the entrepreneur and not the only factor.
2. This theory does not consider profit as the reward for risk-taking. According to Schumpeter it is the capitalist not the entrepreneur who undertakes risk.
3. This theory has ignored the importance of uncertainty bearing which is one of the factors that determines profit.
4. This theory attributes profit only to innovation ignoring other functions of entrepreneur.
5. Monoploy profits are permanent in nature while Schumpeter says that innovate profits occur temporarily.

6. This theory has presented a very narrow view of the function of the entrepreneur. He not only introduces innovation but he is equally responsible for proper organisation of the business. As such profit is not merely due to innovation. It is also due to organizational work performed by the entrepreneur. As it is well known, every entrepreneur does not innovate and yet he must earn profit if he is to stay in business.
7. It is an incomplete theory because it has failed to explain all the factors that influence profit.

UNCERTAINTY BEARING THEORY OF PROFIT

This theory was propounded by an American economist Prof. Frank H. Knight. This theory, starts on the foundation of Hawley's risk bearing theory. Knight agrees with Hawley that profit is a reward for risk-taking. There are two types of risks viz. foreseeable risk and unforeseeable risk. According to Knight unforeseeable risk is called uncertainty bearning. Knight, regards profit as the reward for bearing non-insurable risks and uncertainties. He distinguishes between insurable and non-insurable risks. Certain risks are measurable, the probability of their occurrence can be statistically calculated. The risks of fire, theft, flood and death by accident are insurable. These risks are borne by the insurance company. The premium paid for insurance is included in the cost of production. According to Knight these foreseen risks are not genuine economic risks eligible for any remuneration of profit. In other words insurable risk does not give rise to profit.

According to Knight profit is due to non-insurable risk or unforeseeable risk. Some of the non-insurable risks which arise in modern business are as follows:

(a) **Competitive risk:** Some new firms enter into the market unexpectedly. The existing firms may have to face serious competition from them. This will inevitably lower down the profit of the firms.

(b) **Technical risk:** This risk arises from the possibility of machinery becoming obsolete due to the discovery of new processes. The existing firm may not be in a position to adopt these changes into its organization, and hence suffer losses.

(c) **Risk of government intervention:** The government, in course of time, interferes into the affairs of the industry such as price control, tax policy, import and export restrictions, etc., which might reduce the profits of the firm.

(d) **Cyclical risk:** This risk emerges from business cycles. Due to business recession or depression, consumer's purchasing power is reduced, consequently demand for the product of the firm also falls.

(e) **Risk of demand:** This is generated by a shift or change of demand in the market.

Prof. Knight calls these risks as 'uncertainties' and 'it is uncertainties in this sense which explains profit in the proper use of the term'. These risks cannot be foreseen and measured, they become non-insurable and the uncertainties have to be borne by the entrepreneur. According to this theory there is a direct relationship between profit and uncertainty bearing. Greater the uncertainty bearing the higher the level of profit. Uncertainty bearning has become so important in business enterprise in modern days, it has come to be considered as a separate factor of production. Like other factors it has a supply price and entrepreneurs undertake uncertainty bearing in the expectation of earning certain level of profit. Profit is thus the reward for assuming uncertainty.

In the modern days production has to take place in advance of consumption. The producers have to face their rival producers and the future is uncertain and unknown. These are uncertainties. Some entrepreneurs are able to see it more clearly than others and therefore able to earn profit.

Criticism

1. According to this theory, profit is the reward for uncertainty bearing. But critics point out that sometimes an entrepreneur earns no profit in spite of uncertainty bearing.
2. Uncertainty bearing is one of the determinants of profit and it is not the only determinant. Profit is also a reward for many other activities performed by entrepreneur like initiating, coordinating and bargaining, etc.
3. It is not possible to measure uncertainty in quantitative terms as depicted in this theory.
4. In modern business corporations ownership is separate from control. Decision-making is done by the salaried managers who control and organise the corporation. Ownership rests with the shareholders who ultimately bear uncertainties of business. Knight does not separate ownership and control and this theory becomes unrealistic.
5. Uncertainty bearing cannot be looked upon as a separate factor of production like land, labour or capital. It is a psychological concept which forms part of the real cost of production.
6. Monopoly firms earn much larger profits than competitive firms and they are not due to the presence of uncertainty. This theory throws no light on monopoly profit.

Knight's theory of profit is more elaborate than other theories, because it combines the conception of risk, of economic change and of the role of business ability.

Marginal Productivity Theory of Profit

The general theory of distribution is also applied to the factor, entrepreneur. According to Prof. Chapman, profits are equal to the marginal worth of the entrepreneur and are determined by the marginal productivity of the entrepreneur. When the marginal productivity is high, profits will be high.

Just as marginal revenue productivity of any factor represents the demand curve of a factor the marginal revenue productivity curve of entrepreneur is the demand curve of an entrepreneur. As more and more firms enter into the industry, the marginal revenue productivity (MRP) of entrepreneurship decreases. The slope of the MRP curve will be negative. The supply curve of entrepreneur will be perfectly elastic under perfect competition.

Criticism

1. This theory is not a satisfactory theory of profit because it is very difficult to calculate the marginal productivity of entrepreneurship.
2. Like land, labour, or capital the marginal revenue productivity of entrepreneurship is a meaningless concept in the case of a firm because unlike other factors, there can be only one entrepreneur in a firm.
3. This theory is based on the homogeneity of entrepreneur, in an industry. Entrepreneurs differ in efficiency. It is therefore, not possible to have one marginal revenue productivity curve for all entrepreneurs. This theory thus fails to determine profit accurately.
4. This theory fails to explain why entrepreneurs sometimes earn windfall or chance gains and even monopoly profits.
5. It is one-sided theory which takes into account only the demand for entrepreneurs and neglects supply of entrepreneurs.

6. It is a static theory according to which all entrepreneurs earn only normal profits in the long-run. In the real world entrepreneurs earn more than normal profit due to its dynamic nature.

In conclusion it can be stated that there are essentially three kinds of profit theories which have been developed during last two centuries. The functional theory of profit regards profit as a reward for a factor of production. Secondly the rent theory of profit regards profit as a residual income or as excess of price over costs. The institutional theory emphasises unearned nature of profit as monopoly profit.

None of the theories is satisfactory. Each theory explains profit in terms of one function rather than in terms of all the functions. Economists are of the opinion that it is very difficult to state an adequate theory of profit.

(e) THEORIES OF TRADE CYCLE

A trade cycle refers to fluctuations in economic activities specially in employment, output and income, prices, profits etc. It has been defined differently by different economists. According to Mitchell, "Business cycles are of fluctuations in the economic activities of organized communities. The adjective 'business' restricts the concept of fluctuations in activities which are systematically conducted on commercial basis. The noun 'cycle' bars out fluctuations which do not occur with a measure of regularity". According to Keynes, "A trade cycle is composed of periods of good trade characterised by rising prices and low unemployment percentages altering with periods of bad trade characterised by falling prices and high unemployment percentages".

FEATURES OF A TRADE CYCLE

1. A business cycle is synchronic. When cyclical fluctuations start in one sector it spreads to other sectors.
2. In a trade cycle, a period of prosperity is followed by a period of depression. Hence trade cycle is a wave like movement.
3. Business cycle is recurrent and rhythmic; prosperity is followed by depression and vice versa.
4. A trade cycle is cumulative and self reinforcing. Each phase feeds on itself and creates further movement in the same direction.
5. A trade cycle is asymmetrical. The prosperity phase is slow and gradual and the phase of depression is rapid.
6. The business cycle is not periodical. Some trade cycles last for three or four years, while others last for six or eight or even more years.
7. The impact of a trade cycle is differential. It affects different industries in different ways.
8. A trade cycle is international in character. Through international trade, booms and depressions in one country are passed to other countries.

PHASES OF A TRADE CYCLE

Generally, a trade cycle is composed of four phases - depression, recovery, prosperity and recession.

Depression: During depression, the level of economic activity is extremely low. Real income, production, employment, prices, profit etc. are falling. There are idle resources. Price is low leading to a fall in profit, interest and wages. All the sections of the people suffer. During this phase, there will be pessimism leading to closing down of business firms.

Recovery: Recovery denotes the turning point of business cycle form depression to prosperity. In this phase, there is a slow rise in output, employment, income and price. Demand for commodities go up. There is increase in investment, bank loans and advances. Pessimism gives way to optimism. The process of revival and recovery becomes cumulative and leads to prosperity.

Prosperity: It is a state of affairs in which real income and employment are high. There are no idle resources. There is no wastage of materials. There is rise in wages, prices, profits and interest. Demand for bank loans increases. There is optimism everywhere. There is a general uptrend in business community. However, these boom conditions cannot last long because the forces of expansion are very weak. There are bottlenecks and shortages. There may be scarcity of labour, raw material and othere factors of production. Banks may stop their loans. These conditions lead to recession.

Recession: When the entrepreneurs realize their mistakes, they reduce investment, employment and production. Then fall in employment leads to fall in income, expenditure, prices and profits. Optimism gives way to pessimism. Banks reduce their loans and advances. Business expansion stops. This state of recession ends in depression.

THEORIES OF TRADE CYCLE

Many theories have been put forward from time to time to explain the phenomenon of trade cycles. These theories can be classified into non-monetary and monetary theories.

Non-Monetary Theories of Trade Cycle

1. **Sunspot Theory or Climatic Theory:** It is the oldest theory of trade cycle. It is associated with W.S.Jevons and later on developed by H.C.Moore. According to this theory, the spot that appears on the sun influences the climatic conditions. When the spot appears, it will affect rainfall and hence agricultural crops. When there is crop failure, that will result in depression. On the other hand, if the spot did not appear on the sun, rainfall is good leading to prosperity. Thus, the variations in climate are so regular that depression is followed by prosperity.

However, this theory is not accepted today. Trade cycle is a complex phenomenon and it cannot be associated with climatic conditions. If this theory is correct, then industrialised countries should be free from cyclical fluctuations. But it is the advanced, industrialised countries which are affected by trade cycles.

2. **Psychological Theory:** This theory was developed by A.C. Pigou. He emphasized the role of psychological factor in the generation of trade cycles. According to Pigou, the main cause for trade cycle is optimism and pessimism among business people and bankers. During the period of good trade, entrerpreneurs become optimistic which would lead to increase in production. The feeling of optimism is spread to other. Hence investments are increased beyond limits and there is over production, which results in losses. Entrepreneurs become pessimistic and reduce their investment and production. Thus, fluctuations are due to optimism leading to prosperity and pessimism resulting depression.

Though there is an element of truth in this theory, this theory is unable to explain the occurrence of boom and starting of revival. Further this theory fails to explain the periodicity of trade cycle.

3. Overinvestment Theory: Arthur Spiethoff and D.H. Robertson have developed the over investment theory. It is based on Say's law of markets. It believes that over production in one sector leads to over production in other sectors. Suppose, there is over production and excess supply in one sector, that will result in fall in price and income of the people employed in that sector. Fall in income will lead to a decline in demand for goods and services produced by other sectors. This will create over production in other sectors.

Spiethoff has pointed out that over investment is the cause for trade cycle. Over investment is due to indivisibility of investment and excess supply of bank credit. He gives the example of a railway company which lays down one more track to avoid traffic congestion. But this may result in excess capacity because the additional traffic may not be sufficient to utilise the second track fully.

Over investment and overproduction are encouraged by monetary factors. If the banking system places more money in the hands of entrepreneurs, prices will increase. The rise in prices may induce the entrepreneurs to increase their investments leading to over-investment. Thus Prof. Robertson has successfully combined real and monetary factors to explain business cycle.

This theory is realistic in the sense that it considers over investment as the cause of trade cycle. But it has failed to explain revival.

4. Over-Saving or Under Consumption Theory: This theory is the oldest explanation of the cyclical fluctuations. This theory has been formulated by Malthus, Marx and Hobson. According to this theory, depression is due to over-saving. In the modern society, there is great inequalities of income. Rich people have large income but their marginal propensity to consume is less. Hence they save and invest which results in an increase in the volume of goods. This causes a general glut in the market. At the same time, as majority of the people are poor, they have low propensity to consume. Therefore, consumption will not increase. Increase in the supply of goods and decline in the demand create under consumption and hence over production.

This theory is not free from criticism. This theory explains only the turning point from prosperity to depression. It does not say anything about recovery. This theory assumes that the amount saved would be automatically invested. But this is not true. It pays too much attention on saving and too little on others.

5. Keynes' Theory of Trade Cycles: Keynes doesn't develop a complete and pure theory of trade cycles. According to Keynes, effective demand is composed of consumption and investment expenditure. It is effective demand which determines the level of income and employment. Therefore, changes in total expenditure i.e., consumption and investment expenditures, affect effective demand and this will bring about fluctuation in economic activity. Keynes believes that consumption expenditure is stable and it is the fluctuation in investment expenditure which is responsible for changes in output, income and employment.

Investment depends on rate of interest and marginal efficiency of capital. Since rate of interest is more or less stable, marginal efficiency of capital determines investment. Marginal efficiency of capital depends on two factors – prospective yield and supply price of the capital asset. An increase in MEC will create more employment, output and income leading to prosperity. On the other hand, a decline in MEC leads to unemployment and fall in income and output. It results in depression.

During the period of expansion businessmen are optimistic. MEC is rapidly increasing and rate of interest is sticky. So entrepreneurs undertake new investment. The process of expansion goes on till the boom is reached. As the process of expansion continues, cost of production increases, due to scarcity of factors of production. This will lead to a fall in MEC. Further, price of the product falls due to abundant supply leading to a decline in profits. This leads to depression. As time passes, existing machinery becomes worn out and has to be replaced. Surplus stocks of goods are exhausted. As there is a fall in price of raw-materials and equipment, costs fall. Wages also go down. MEC increases leading to recovery. Keynes states that, "Trade cycle can be described and analyzed in terms of the fluctuations of the marginal efficiency of capital relatively to the rate of interest".

The merit of Keynes' theory lies in explaining the turning points-the lower and upper turning points of a trade cycle. The earlier economists considered the changes in the amount of credit given by banking system to be responsible for cyclical fluctuations. But for Keynes, the change in consumption function with its effect on MEC is responsible for trade cycle. Keynes, thus, has given a satisfactory explanation of the turning points of the trade cycle, "Keynes consumption function filled a serious gap and corrected a serious error in the previous theory of the business cycle". (Metzler).

Critics have pointed out the weakness of Keynes' theory. Firstly, according to Keynes the main cause for trade cycle is the fluctuations in MEC. But the term marginal efficiency of capital is vague. MEC depends on the expectations of the entrepreneur about future. In this sense, it is similar to that of Pigou's psychological theory. He has ignored real factors.

Secondly, Keynes assumes that rate of interest is stable. But rate of interest does play an important role in decision making process of entrepreneurs.

Thirdly, Keynes does not explain periodicity of trade cycle. In a period of recession and depression, according to Keynes, rate of interest should be high due to strong liquidity preference. But, during this period, rate of interest is very low. Similarly during boom, rate of interest should be low because of weak liquidity preference; but actually the rate of interest is high.

6. Schumpeter's Innovation Theory: Joseph A. Schumpeter has developed innovation theory of trade cycles. An innovation includes the discovery of a new product, opening of a new market, reorganization of an industry and development of a new method of production. These innovations may reduce the cost of production and may shift the demand curve. Thus innovations may bring about changes in economic conditions.

Suppose, at the full employment level, an innovation in the form of a new product has been introduced. Innovation is financed by bank loans. As there is full employment already, factors of production have to be withdrawn from others to manufacture the new product. Hence, due to competition for factors of production costs may go up, leading to an increase in price. When the new product becomes successful, other entrepreneurs will also produce similar products. This will result in cumulative expansion and prosperity. When the innovation is adopted by many, supernormal profits will be competed away. Firms incurring losses will go out of business. Employment, output and income fall resulting in depression.

Schumpeter's theory has been criticised on the following grounds. Firstly, Schumpter's theory is based on two assumptions viz., full employment and that innovation is being financed by banks. But full employment is an unrealistic assumption, as no country in the world has achieved full employment. Further innovation is usually financed by the promoters and not by banks. Secondly, innovation is not the only cause of business cycle. There are many other causes which have not been analysed by Schumpter.

Monetory Theories of Trade Cycles

1. Over-Investment Theory: Prof. Von Hayek in his books on **"Monetary Theory and Trade**

Cycle" and **"Prices and Production"** has developed a theory of trade cycle. He has distinguished between equilibrium or natural rate of interest and market rate of interest. Market rate of interest is one at which demand for and supply of money are equal. Equilibrium rate of interest is one at which savings are equal to investment. If both equilibrium rate of interest and market rate of interest are equal, there will be stability in the economy. If equilibrium rate of interest is higher than market rate of interest there will be prosperity and vice versa.

For instance, if the market rate of interest is lower than equilibrium rate of interest due to increase in money supply, investment will go up. The demand for capital goods will increase leading to a rise in price of these goods. As a result, there will be a diversion of resources from consumption goods industries to capital goods industries. Employment and income of the factors of production in capital goods industries will increase. This will increase the demand for consumption goods. There will be competition for factors of production between capital goods and consumption good industries. Factor prices go up. Cost of production increases. At this time, banks will decide to reduce credit expansion. This will lead to rise in market rate of interest above the equilibrium rate of interest. Investment will fall; production declines leading to depression.

Hayek's theory has certain weaknesses.

1. It is not easy to transfer resources from capital goods industries to consumer goods industries and vice versa.
2. This theory does not explain all the phases of trade cycle.
3. It gives too much importance to rate of interest in determining investment. It has neglected other factors determining investment.
4. Hayek has suggested that the volume of money supply should be kept neutral to solve the problem of cyclical fluctuations. But this concept of neutrality of money is based on old quantity theory of money which has lost its validity.

2. Hawtrey's Monetary Theory: Prof. Hawtrey considers trade cycle to be a purely monetary phenomenon. According to him non-monetary factors like wars, strike, floods, drought may cause only temporary depression. Hawtrey believes that expansion and contraction of money are the basic causes of trade cycle. Money supply changes due to changes in rates of interest. When rate of interest is reduced by banks, entrepreneurs will borrow more and invest. This causes an increase in money supply and rise in price leading to expansion. On the other hand, an increase in the rate of interest will lead to reduction in borrowing, investment, prices and business activity and hence depression.

Hawtrey believes that trade cycle is nothing but small scale replica of inflation and deflation. An increase in money supply will lead to boom and vice versa, a decrease in money supply will result in depression.

Banks will give more loans to traders and merchants by lowering the rate of interest. Merchants place more orders which induce the entrepreneurs to increase production by employing more labourers. This results in increase in employment and income leading to an increase in demand for goods. Thus the phase of expansion starts. Business expands; factors of production are fully employed; price increases further, resulting in boom conditions. At this time, the banks call off loans from the borrowers. In order to repay the loans, the borrowers sell their stocks. This sudden disposal of goods leads to fall in prices and liquidation of marginal firms. Banks will further contract credit. Thus the period of contraction starts making the producers reduce their output. The process of contraction becomes cumulative leading to depression. When the economy is at the level of depression, banks have excess reserves. Therefore, banks will lend at a low rate of interest which makes the entrepreneurs to borrow more. Thus revival starts, becomes cumulative and leads to boom.

Hawtrey's theory has been criticised on many grounds.

1. Hawtrey's theory is considered to be an incomplete theory as it does not take into account the non-monetary factors which cause trade cycles.
2. It is wrong to say that banks alone cause business cycle. Credit expansion and contraction do not lead to boom and depression. But they are accentuated by bank credit.
3. The theory exaggerates the importance of bank credit as a means of financing development. In recent years, all firms resort to plough back of profits for expansion.
4. Mere contraction of bank credit will not lead to depression if marginal efficiency of capital is high. Businessmen will undertake investment inspite of high rate of interest if they feel that the future prospects are bright.
5. Rate of interest does not determine the level of borrowing and investment. A high rate of interest will not prevent the people to borrow. Therefore, it may be stated that banking system cannot originate a trade cycle. Expansion and contraction of credit may be a supplementary cause but not the main and sole cause of trade cycle.

QUESTIONS

1. State and explain Ricardian Theory of Rent.
2. Give an account of the Theories of Wages.
3. 'Interest is a reward for parting with liquidity' – Explain.
4. Review the various Theories of Profits.
5. Trade Cycle is a monetary phenomenon – Elucidate.
6. Describe the non-monetary Theories of Trade Cycle.

Chapter 25

JOSEPH ALOIS SCHUMPETER

INTRODUCTION

Schumpeter was born in 1883 in the Austrian province of Moravia. He studied in University of Vienna and received the degree of Doctor of Law in 1906. He practiced law for few years and then he decided to specialise in Economics. He studied Economics under Professors Weiser. Philippovich and Bohm-Bawerk. In the seminars he attended, he came into contact with Mises Bauer, Semary and Hilferding. His teaching career began in 1909. He taught at the Universities of Czernowitz, Graz (Austria), Bonn (Germany), Columbia and Harvard. Schumpeter was famous for his scholarly achievements. He was the president of Econometric Society from 1937 to 1941 and of the American Economic Association in 1949. His best known works are: The Theory of Economic Development (1912), Business Cycles - Two Volumes (1939), Capitalism, Socialism and Democracy (1942), Ten Great Economists (1951), Essays (1951), Imperialism and Social Classes (1951), History of Economic Analysis (1954), and Economic Doctrine and Method (1957). He died on January 8, 1950.

INFLUENCES

Schumpeter was influenced by Walras, Fisher, J.B. Clark, Weiser and Bohm-Bawerk. He thought that without studying Walrasian general equilibrium analysis, one cannot be a good theorist. He was influenced by Fisher and Clark in his analysis of capitalist process. Wieser and Bohm-Bawerk influenced him in his ideas relating to marginal productivity, order of goods, opportunity costs etc.

METHODS OF STUDY

Schumpeter believed that both inductive and deductive methods are necessary for the study of economic science. Deductive method was effective in price theory and inductive method was suitable for the study and analysis of economic organisation. He followed statistical method in his study of business cycles and later he realised that it was not useful. Historical method was the most important one for him. At the same time, he accepted mathematics as an important tool in the science of economics.

Theory of Economic Development

Role of Entrepreneur

According to Schumpeter in economic development, entrepreneur played a key role. The credit for innovations and outburst of economic activity belonged to the entrepreneur. Innovation consisted in the introduction of a new good, new method of production, opening of a new market, the discovery of a new source of supply of raw materials or semi-manufactured goods and introduction of a new organisation in an industry. In a world full of risk and uncertainty, only exceptional entrepreneurs succeed by introducing innovations. The main motivating factor behind an innovating entrepreneur was profit expectations. Thus entrepreneur played an important role in determining the rate of economic growth. In his absence, the growth rate is bound to be slow.

Innovations

Schumpeter developed his own system in which he analysed the effects of various changes occurring with the introduction of a new technique of production. In his initial model, Schumpeter eliminated profits and interest from general equilibrium theory. He assumed that all values were created by demand and that all costs were opportunity costs and as there was no surplus, there was no profit. Interest would not arise as the entrepreneur had perfect knowledge of future. He then studied the effects of innovations on the working of economic system. He defined innovation as "an introduction into economic use of an invention". After the introduction of innovation, cost falls below the competitive level and profit appears. He concluded that profit arises only in a dynamic society. Then Schumpeter proceeded to analyse long-run processes of business cycles. In the long run, prosperity and inflation led to the introduction of innovations since capital was in abundance. These innovations depended upon the expectation of profit and financed by credit creation. According to Schumpeter, the innovator borrowed money from the bank and moved into the market to outbid others. Other entrepreneurs followed until a new equilibrium is reached. Schumpeter's model is limited to the economic changes introduced by innovations. However, Schumpeter did not analyse the inter-relationship of various causes leading to economic changes. Schempeter's theory is not comprehensive as he did not analyse the relationship between public policy and economic change. Further, he did not take into account the degree of competition and its effects as he assumed a state of perfect competition. He also did not study the economic changes introduced by innovations from the point of view of an individual firm.

Schumpeter's Innovation Theory

Joseph A. Schumpeter has developed innovation theory of trade cycles. An innovation includes the discovery of a new product, opening of a new market, reorganisation of an industry and development of a new method of production. These innovations may reduce the cost of production and may shift the demand curve. Thus innovations may bring about changes in economic conditions.

Suppose, at the full employment level, an innovation in the form of a new product has been introduced. Innovation is financed by bank loans. As there is full employment already, factors of production have to be withdrawn from others to manufacture the new product. Hence, due to competition for factors of production costs may go up, leading to an increase in price. When the new product becomes successful, other entrepreneurs will also produce similar products. This will result in cumulative expansion and prosperity. When the innovation is adopted by many, supernormal profits will be competed away. Firms incurring losses will go out of business. Employment, output and income fall resulting in depression.

Schumpeter's theory has been criticised on the following grounds. Firstly, Schumpeter's theory is based on two assumptions, viz., full employment and that innovation is being financed by banks. But full employment is an unrealistic assumption, as no country in the world has achieved full employment. Further innovation is usually financed by the promoters and not by banks. Secondly, innovation is not the only cause of business cycle. There are many other causes which have not been analysed by Schumpeter.

Capital

Schumpeter did not identify capital with concrete goods; but regarded it as a separate agent or factor representing a fund of purchasing power. In this respect he departed from the economic ideas developed by Bohm-Bawerk and F.A. Von Hayek. Capital became significant only when economic development took place. It explained the emergence of interest during the process of economic development. Interest did not arise in a static state and therefore it was an aspect of dynamic analysis. Capital was a price paid for the new productive forces accrued under innovation. It arose in the money market which was a creation of economic development.

Capitalism and Socialism

Schumpeter agreed with Marx that capitalism was sowing the seeds of its own destruction, due to inner contradictions. Capitalism was killed by its own achievement. Schumpeter had infinite faith in the potentiality of capitalism but he believed in a Marxian fashion. The very success of capitalism would breed the germs of its ultimate decay. It was not economic barriers but social factors which undermine capitalism. According to Schumpeter, the economic and social foundations of capitalism crumbled on account of the destruction of the industrial framework the decay of the entrepreneurial function and the disintegration of the protecting political framework. Innovation thus degenerated into a dispersonalised routine activity. The concentration of business and the growth of monopolies destroyed the institutions of private property and freedom of contract. The social class that used to protect capitalism also lost its political power and unwilling to support the established trade and industry. The educated unemployed was another group of 'have-nots' against the capitalist class of 'haves'. Labour also organised itself to fight against capital and the intellectuals supplied the leadership. All these new forces led to the gradual decay of capitalism and strengthen the movement towards socialism. Capitalism could not function in this new atmosphere.

To conclude in the words of Seligman that Schumpeter was not a reformer. He was not interested in public policy. He was neither a marxist nor a socialist. Instead he was an objective scientific investigator, with no particular axe to grind. He was no man's pupil, and he founded no school. In her review of Schumpeter's capitalism, socialism and democracy, Joan Robinson wrote, "Professor

Schumpeter, as many fast phrases reveal, has little love for socialism, and none at all for socialists. His natural sympathy is all with the heroic age of expanding capitalism. But yet he regards capitalism as doomed and socialism as inevitable".

As an economist, Schumpeter occupies a unique position. He founded no school and hardly had any follower. He was a class by himself. He possessed mastery over all branches of economics. He was independent in his ideas and style. Despite the originality of ideas and expression, his writings suffer from ambiguity and lack of coherence. "The result of complexity, diversity and universality of his mind was that he could not fully integrate his ideas", and that is why he could not gain that position which was held by his contemporaries, especially Keynes.

QUESTIONS

1. Explain Schumpeter's theory of economic development.
2. Write short notes on :
   (a) Schumpeter's theory of economic development
   (b) Schumpeter's innovation theory.

Chapter 26

CONTRIBUTIONS OF NOBEL ECONOMISTS

This chapter deals with the contributions of Nobel Laureates in the field of Economics.

(a) PAUL A. SAMUELSON (1970)

INTRODUCTION

Paul A. Samuelson has been awarded the second Nobel prize for economics in 1970 for his brilliant contributions. He has been given Nobel prize for his work, "Development of New Economic Theories" and for finding new applications for old theories. The Swedish Academy, while declaring this award, has rightly said that Samuelson has done more than any other economist to raise the level of scientific analysis in the field of economic theory". He has tried his best to shape the U.S. economic and fiscal policies all through. Samuelson was the first to receive the Nobel prize in Economics from America.

Samuelson has always advocated the use of mathematics as a means to explain and explore the economic problem. In 1949, he published the book, "Economics, an Introductory Analysis" which has become world famous. Samuelson remarked that "Economics never was a dismal science. It should be a realistic science".

HIS CONTRIBUTIONS

Samuelson's contributions are mainly in the fields of economic analysis, public expenditure, consumer welfare, etc. He introduced the notion of revealed preference. Rather than harping on tastes and utilities which cannot be observed, he developed an approach based on the actual choice made by the consumer. The theory of revealed preference has been a practical instrument.

1. Theory of Revealed Preference

In revealed preference theory, the consumer is supposed to reveal his preferences. When a consumer selects a combination out of various alternative combinations open to him, he reveals his preference over all other alternative combinations. Thus 'Choice reveals preference'.

Revealed preference hypothesis can be shown graphically in the following figure 1.

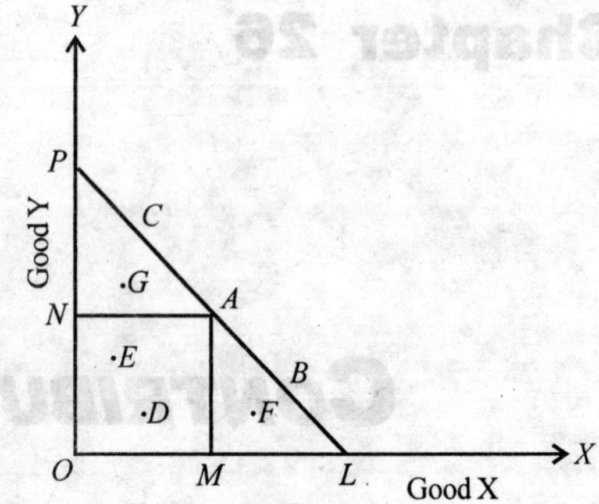

Fig. 1

Give the price of two commodities and income of the consumer, the price line *PL* is drawn. Given the price income line *PL* the consumer can choose any combination within or on the triangle *OPL*. The combinations *A,B,C* lying on the line PL and *D,E,F,G* lying below the *PL* line are alternative combinations available to the consumer. If the consumer selects the combination *A*, it means he reveals his preference for A over all other combinations. At *A*, the consumer is buying *OM* of commodity *X* and *ON* Quantity of commodity *Y*.

Assumptions

The revealed preference hypothesis is based on the following assumptions:

(1) The consumer is rational aiming at maximum satisfaction.

(2) It assumes consistency of consumer behaviour. If A is preferred to B in one situation, B cannot be preferred to A in other situation.

(3) The theory is based on the assumption of transitivity. If A is preferred to B and B to C, then the consumer must prefer A to C.

(4) The consumer prefers a combination of more goods to less in any situation.

(5) The tastes of the consumer do not change.

(6) Revealed preference theory assumes that the income elasticity of demand is positive, i.e., as income increases, demand for the commodity must also increase.

(7) Revealed preference theory is based on strong ordering. By choosing one combination and rejecting others, the consumer reveals his definite preference.

Merits

Revealed preference theory is an improvement over the Marshallian utility analysis and Hicks – Allen indifference curve technique.

(1) Revealed preference theory is more realistic and scientific. It studies the actual behaviour of a consumer and not an imaginary consumer.

(2) Samuelson's revealed preference theory does not assume continuity.

(3) Samuelson uses the consistency principle to derive the demand theorem and drops the utility maximisation principle.

Demerits

Revealed preference theory is not free from defects.

(1) The Revealed theory preference is based on strong ordering and neglects indifference. Sometimes, the consumer is faced with alternatives which are equally desirable and therefore he is hesitant to choose among them.

(2) The Revealed preference theory is based on the positive income elasticity of demand. It cannot explain Giffen's paradox in which the income effect is negative.

(3) The assumption of choice reveals preference has also been criticised. Choice always does not reveal preference. Choice requires rational consumer behaviour. Since a consumer does not act rationally at all times, his choice may not reveal his preference.

(4) The revealed preference approach is applicable only to an individual consumer. Individual demand curve can be drawn for each consumer. But market demand schedule cannot be drawn with the help of this approach.

(5) Since the revealed preference theory is based upon the actual behaviour of the consumer it is not possible to distinguish between income effect and substituion effect.

Therefore Samuelson's theory gives only a partial explanation of a change in demand as a result of a change in price. Revealed preference theory is superior to other demand-theories as it is scientific and behaviouristic.

BUSINESS CYCLES

Prof. Samuelson has developed a model of multiplier-accelerator interaction to explain the process of income propagation and also the different types of cyclical fluctuations.

Samuelson shows five types of cyclical fluctuation in the following figure 2:

Types of Fluctuations

Case	Values		Behaviour of the cycle
1	a = .5	b = 0	Cycleless path
2	a = .5	b = 1	Damped fluctuations
3	a = .5	b = 2	Fluctuations of constant amplitude.
4	a = .6	b = 2	Explosive cycles
5	a = .8	b = 4	Cycleless explosive path.

Figure A (case 1) shows cycleless path. Income moves upward or downward at a diminishing rate. As accelerator is zero, there is no cycle. It is based only on multiplier. Figure B shows damped oscillations (case 2), i.e., they will become weaker and weaker and slowly disappear. Figure C depicts (case 4) explosive fluctuations. The cycles will become stronger and stronger. Figure D (case 3) illustrates cycles of constant amplitude. This type of cycle is a regular one. Figure E (case 5) relates to a cycleless explosive path. Income moves in an upward path.

Prof. Samuelson has shown that for different combinations of values of multiplier and accelerator, it is possible to get cycles of various types.

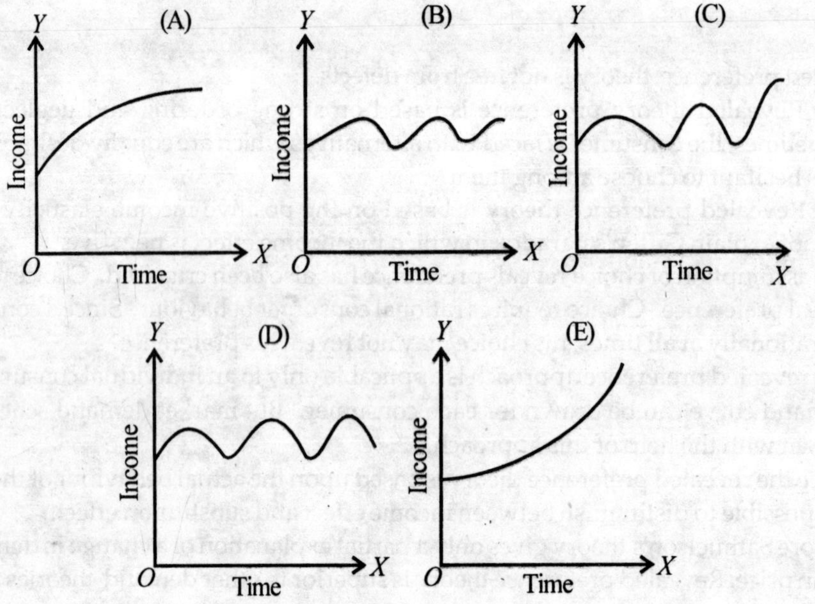

Fig. 2

In the following figure 3. the combinations of multiplier and accelerator which fall in region B will produce damped oscillations. Similarly, those combinations of multiplier and accelerator that fall in regions A, C and D will produce either explosive cycles or cycleless path. Multiplier and accelerator combinations that fall along the line E produce cycles of constant amplitude.

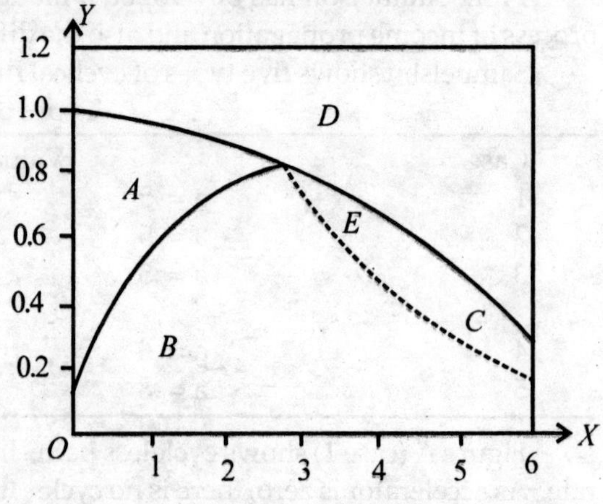

Fig. 3

In case 1 the economic system moves to a new equilibrium without any fluctuation. There is no cycle here. Case 5 produces explosive movement without cycles. Only other three cases are cyclical in nature. Of the three, case 3 illustrates cycles of constant amplitude which has not been experienced. Case 2 shows damped oscillations and this has taken place in the last century. They are the result of exogenous factors such as war, inventions, changes in crops etc. Case 4 represents explosive cycles but this type of fluctuations are absent due to endogenous economic factors.

Limitations

Samuelson's theory has got certain limitations.

(1) Samuelson did not explain the length of each period in different cycles.

(2) He assumes a constant marginal propensity to consume and a constant accelerator. But in

reality, consumption changes change with the level of income.

(3) He assumes a stationary state but this is unrealistic as the economy is always in a process of growth.

Uses

Samuelson's study has paved the way for a more accurate analysis of nature of cyclical fluctuations. It also serves as a useful tool for understanding the process of income generation. It also helps in formulating a stabilisation policy. Prof. Kurihara points out, 'It is in conjuction with the multiplier analysis that the acceleration principle serves as a useful tool of business cycle analysis based on the concept of the marginal propensity to consume and a helpful guide to stabilisation policy."

Social Welfare Function

Samuelson makes use of his social welfare function which describes the factors on which the welfare of all individuals in a society depends. It makes welfare of the society depend upon economic as well as non-economic factors – the amount of each and every kind of goods consumed and services performed, the amount of capital investment undertaken and so on.

The social welfare function possess some special properties which give it an edge of superiority over the earlier ones.

1. It introduces value judgements into the welfare analysis and does not in any way feel shy of them. Thus the function involves inter-personal comparisons and hence value judgements.
2. It is a general welfare function. Any set of assumptions of compounding individual utility functions into the social welfare function can be fed into the Bergson social welfare function.
3. The ethical norms on which the Social Welfare Function is built, are assumed to be ordinal in nature. So the assumption of additivity of individual utilities is not there.
4. The Social Welfare Function does not have any element of indeterminancy in it. It deals with distribution of welfare as much as production and exchange condition of welfare.

Assumptions

1. It assumes that social welfare depends on wealth and income.
2. It assumes the presence of external economies and diseconomies.
3. It is based on ordinal utility.
4. Inter – personal comparisons are possible.

A social welfare function is simply a set of social indifference curves where an increase in one individual's welfare, all other individual's welfare remaining the same, increases social welfare. Hence the social welfare function is an ordinal index of society's welfare and is also a function of the level of satisfaction of all individuals. Economists have developed two equivalent ways of finding the point of maximum welfare.

Samuelson's Utility Possibility Approach

It was given by Samuelson. It consists of representing the social welfare function by a family of social indifference curves. A family of curves is shown in the figure by, W_1, W_2, W_3, W_4 VV^1 is the utility possibility frontier. It shows all possible comb-inations of utility to A and B, given the resource base, production functions and individual preference order-ings. The social indifference curves show utility combinations that result in equal levels of social welfare. The higher the curve, the greater is the aggregate social welfare.

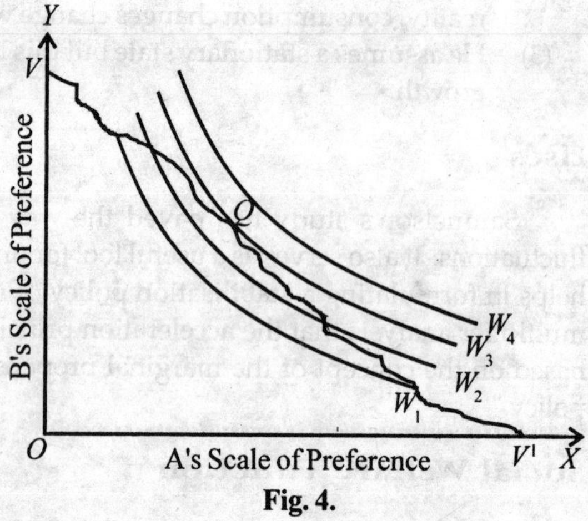

Fig. 4.

Maximum social welfare is attained at Q where a social indifference curve is just tangent to the utility possibility frontier. The unique equilibrium Q is called the point of "Constrain bliss" because it represents the unique organisation of production, exchange and distribution that leads to the maximum attainable social welfare. The society, of course, would be more blissful, on W_4. But a state on this higher curve is not attainable. The resource endowement and technology constraint the society to a point on VV^1. In view of the constraint, society reaches its point of constrained bliss at Q.

Inflotion : Samuelson has emphasized the problem of inflation. Inflation occured whenever the sum of consumption, investment and Government expenditures exceed the full employment capacity of production. Samuelson regards the Phillips Curve as an important concept in the formulation of modern policy. He advocated a system of rationing to fight scarcity of resources. He gave a welfare interpretation of the concept of national income. He has suggested a Leontief– type Input-Output structure. He has writtèn an important theorem in the pure theory of normative growth in his "Linear programming and Economic Analysis". He emphasized that mixed economy idea is coming up in many countries.

Samuelson has a great public image not only in U.S.A. but in the entire world. Through his works and articles, he has impressed the world much more than any other economist of the day.

(b) SIR JOHN HICKS (1972)

INTRODUCTION

Sir John Hicks of Oxford University was awarded the Nobel Prize in Economics in 1972 along with Kenneth J. Arrow of the United States. Hicks was the first British economist to receive the Nobel Prize. They were awarded the prize for their "pioneering contributions to the general economic equilibrium theory and welfare theory", As Bertil Ohlin puts it, "The general equilibrium theory is the basis for most of the direct application of economic theory such as the localisation of industrial plant, resource allocation, financial and employment theory and foreign trade, all this being used to increase the welfare of the people".

Hicks was born in Warwick in 1904. He graduated in 1925 at Oxford. He was a lecturer at the London School of Economics from 1926 to 1935, Cambridge and Oxford Universities. He retired from Oxford University in 1965. He was knighted in 1964.

Prof. Hicks served as a member of the Revenue Allocation Commission for Nigeria in 1960 and on the Royal Commission on the Taxation of Profits and Income. He became a Fellow of All Souls, Fellow of the British Academy and Honorary Fellow of the London School of Economics.

His important works are:

Theory of Wages (1932), Value and Capital (1939), The Social Framework: An Introduction to Economics (1942), The Problem of Budgetary Reform (1948), A Contribution to the Theory of Trade Cycle (1950), A Revision of Demand Theory (1956), Capital and Growth (1965), and Critical Essays in Monetary Theory (1967),

"Value and Capital" is one of the monumental works of Hicks. It became the starting point for the subsequent micro economic theories in Britain and United States. It starts with an elementary problem of consumers preference and leads upto unemployment and the future of capitalism.

The chief characteristic of Hick's work was that he moved away from the partial equilibrium approach of Alfred Marshall back towards the older "general equilibrium" approach of Walras. He also introduced a dynamic dimension with his work on period analysis and his theory of the elasticity of expectations. This book is one of the rarest books in economic science which marked a definite stage in the advance of a science.

More than any other economist, Hicks has rehabilitated and extended the indifference curve apparatus. The book contains in its first 52 pages, the best exposition of the contemporary theory, The Social Framework and A Revision of Demand Theory are his other pioneering works.

The Social Framework is a beautiful introduction to economics. Prof. Pigou said that, "beginner coming to this book will find concepts with which he has long been familiar in a vague way clarified and given a more significant meaning and that he will also acquire a good deal of actual knowledge". While praising this book, Prof. Harrod observed that, "It is an introduction to economics written by an economist of the highest calibre. His style is easy and popular.....the presentation is straight forward and dignified".

Hick's book, 'A Revision of Demand Theory' has been acclaimed as "a superb exercise of exposition" and "probably the last word there is to be said on this aspect of demand theory". He has shown that the law of demand can be extended to study the behaviour of groups from that of individuals. The theory of demand for a single commodity is only the beginning of a demand theory. The general theory of demand is a theory of the relation between the set of prices, at which purchases are made, and the set of quantities which are purchased.

MAIN ECONOMIC IDEAS

The following are the main economic ideas of Lord Hicks:

Definition of Economics

To Hicks, economics is essentially a branch of human science. He has defined economics as "the science which deals with business affairs". He considers it to be superior to other human science in the sense that it has been able to apply scientific methods to the study of human conduct in a better way. His only suggestion is that since economics deals with facts, efforts must be made to arrange these facts rightly, otherwise they will be of no use.

Consumer Equilibrium

Hicks has made notable contribution to the study of consumer equilibrium by making use of indifference curve approach. The ordinalist approach of Hicks is considered superior to the Marshallian utility approach or cardinalist approach. Indifference curve technique assumes what is called "ordinal measurement of utility". Another distinct improvement made by Hicks is unlike Marshall, he explains consumer's behaviour without the assumption of constant marginal utility of money. Further through his indifference curve technique, Hicks distinguished between income and substitution effects.

The distinction between income effect and substitution effect of a price change enables us to gain better understanding of the effect of a price change on the demand for a good.

The amount demanded of a good generally rises as a result of the fall in its price due to two reasons. Firstly, because real income rises as a result of the fall in price (income effect) and secondly, because the good whose price falls becomes relatively cheaper than others and therefore the consumer substitutes it for other (substitution effect).

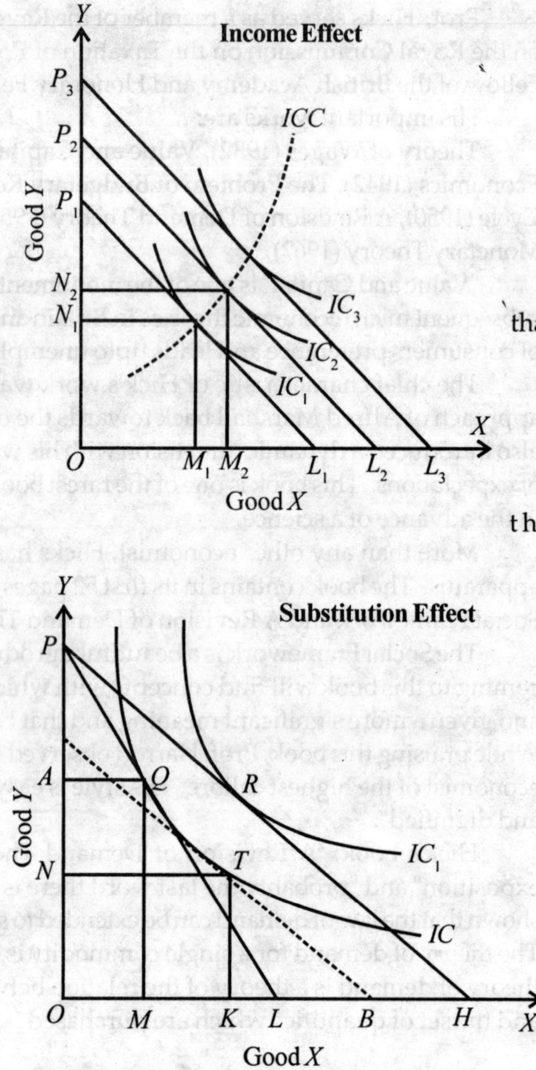

Fig. 5.

Revision of Demand Theory

Hicks in his "Revision of Demand Theory", has taken note of some of the recent developments in demand theory and incorporated them.

He used ordinal utility theory but he rejected indifference curve technique for two reasons:

(1) Indifference curve technique is useful only if we have to select between two goods. If there are more than two goods, then we have to rely on mathematics.

(2) Second disadvantage of indifference curve is that it is based on the assumption of continuity.

He therefore dispenses indifference curve along with this assumption of continuity.

Assumptions

1. It is based on preference hypothesis. It states that the consumer selects the one which he prefers the most from among the alternatives open to him.

2. More of a commodity is always preferred to less of it.
3. It is based on weak ordering that is items cannot be arranged one after another. It can only be grouped. Those groups can be strongly ordered but within the group ordering is not possible.
4. Weak ordering depends on two conditions : (a) two term consistency condition and (b) transitivity condition
5. There are two commodities x and m. Price of x changed and that of m remain constant. M is a composite commodity. The difference between revealed preference theory and revision of demand theory is shown in fig. 6.

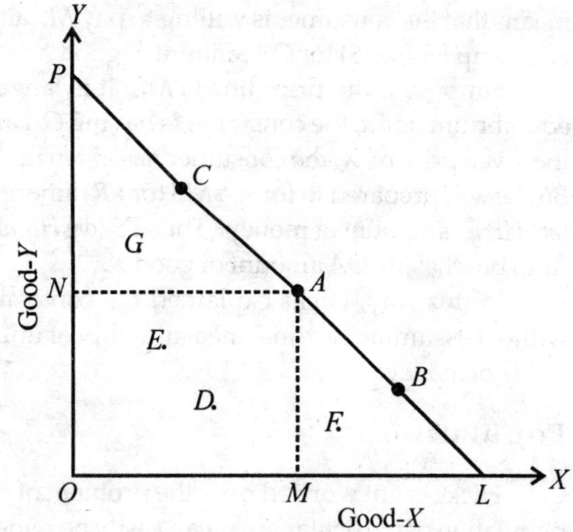

Fig. 6.

According to revealed preference theory, which is based on strong ordering, chosen point is preferred to all points within and on the triangle. Revision of demand theory is based on weak ordering in which chosen point 'A' is preferred to all points with in the triangle but may be indifferent to other points on the boundary line.

CONSUMER'S SURPLUS

Consumer's surplus, as developed by Marshall is based on the assumption that the marginal utility of money is constant. This assumption is considered wrong. If we relax the assumption, the size of the consumer's surplus is smaller than the Marshallian theory. Indifference curve analysis has been used by Hicks to demonstrate this.

Indifference curves technique does not make the assumption of cardinal measurability of utility, nor does it assume that marginal utility of money remains constant. How consumer's surplus is measured with the aid of indifference curves is illustrated in the following figure (Fig. 7).

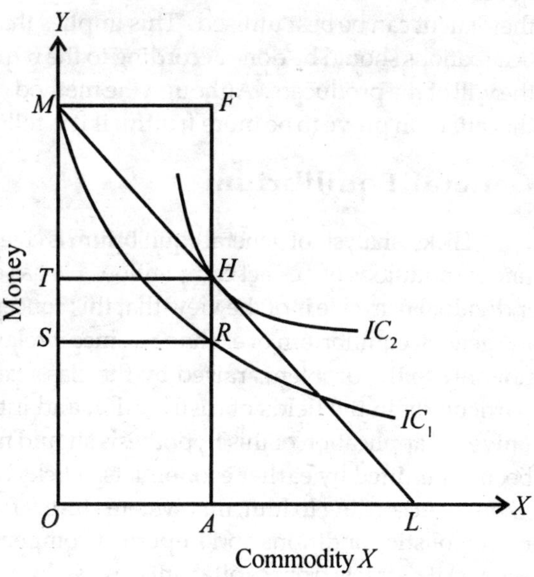

Fig. 7.

Suppose a consumer has *OM* amount of money which he can spend on good *A* and other goods. The indifference curve IC_1 touches this point *M* indicating that all combinations of money and commodity *X* give same satisfaction to the consumer. *For* example at point *R* on IC_1, *OA* amount of commodity and *OS* amount of money will give the same satisfaction. In other words, it means that the consumer is willing to pay *MS* amount of money for *OA* amount of *X*. He is prepared to give up *FR* (=*MS*) for *OA* amount of good *X*.

Suppose if the price line is *ML*, it is tangent to the indifference curve IC_2 at point *H*. In this equilibrium point, the consumer is having *OA* amount of good *X* and *OT* amount of money. Thus at the given price of *X*, the consumer has given up *MT* amount of money for acquiring *OA* amount of *X*. But he was prepared to forego *MS* (or *FR*) amount of money for *OA*. Therefore the consumer pays *TS* (*or*) *HR* less amount of money. Thus *TS* (*or*) *HR* is the consumer's surplus which the consumer derives from purchasing *OA* amount of good *X*.

In this way, Hicks explained the consumer's surplus with his indifference curve technique without assuming cardinal measurability of utility and without assuming constancy of the marginal utility of money.

Population

Hicks is not worried over the problem of over population in a country. He feels that "the over population of particular areas can easily be remedied by industrialisation". In this connection he has cited the example of Great Britain. He is of the view that for meeting the needs of food, clothing etc. of an increasing population, the production should also be simultaneously increased. If agricultural production cannot be increased owing to the shortage of land, industrial production must be increased.

Right Man On The Right Job

According to Hicks, the economic organisation of a community must be done in such a way that the working force is utilised in an efficient manner. He means to say that persons with particular qualifications and talents should be employed on those jobs for which they are best suited or where their talent can be best utilised. This implies that the distribution of labour force among the various occupations should be done according to the requirements of the community and should not be left to the will of the producers. Although the method of incentives is better than the method of compulsion, the latter can prove to be more fruitful if it is followed by an adequate system of selection.

General Equilibrium

Hicks' analysis of general equilibrium is chiefly concerned with the problem of general equilibrium under conditions of perfect competition. He has only studied the problem from the point of view of an individual firm. He is of the view that this concept of equilibrium has a wider application than that of the general equilibrium of exchange, since it relates to production. This analysis can be made to apply not only to the problems raised by the classical economists, but also to other long term problems, particularly in the fields of distribution and international trade. He has however warned that the universal application of this hypothesis should not be tried, since it may lead to the same errors as has been committed by earlier economists. Hicks has been quite frank in stating the weaknesses of his system. According to him, this system suffers from three defects: (a) it does not take into account the monopolistic conditions and imperfect competition (b) It detracts from the economic activity of the state (c) it detracts from capital, interest, saving, investment and speculation.

Economic Dynamics

According to Hicks, Economic statics includes the study of those elements of economic theory, whose dating is not required. On the other hand economic dynamics treats of those parts where every quantity must be dated. Further in economic statics, the economist is concerned with knowing that the producer, after employing certain quantities of factors of production, has been able to produce a certain amount of product and not with such questions as to when those factors were employed and when the commodities were produced.

In economic dynamics these questions are the most significant and the economists after knowing the "when " of the problem try to create a relationship between the variation in time, the quantity of factors and the goods produced and also the way these changes in dates have affected the relationship between factors and products.

Stationary State

According to Hicks the stationary state is a special case of dynamic system. In such a state, tastes, techniques and resources remain stationary over a given period of time. Again in such a state, the problem of distinguishing between actual price and expected price, income and commodities, money and real rate of interest, is not felt.

Hicks feels that, it is the treatment of the stationary state that has hampered the development of a proper theory of interest. In such a state, equilibrium is not only established when demand and supplies are equal, at the current prices, but also when the prices are constant over a period of time. Hence he concludes that equilibrium over a period of time can only be possible in a much longer period and therefore, it cannot be achieved in real life. It may be ideal from the theoretical point of view but from the practical point of view, it is an impossibility. Therefore Hicks says that the economists should be interested in temporary equilibrium.

Theory of Trade Cycle

Hicks contribution to the "Theory of Trade Cycle" has been regarded as one of the major contributions to trade cycle theories. It is apt to quote, "A beautiful theory of the cycle is here built up with an admirable economy of means..... undoubtedly a tour de force".

Hicks has developed the thoery by making use of the accelerator—multiplier interaction principle and autonomous and induced investment. Dussenberry describes it as an, "ingenious piece of work" and "the first coherent theory of the cycle to appear in some years". The multiplier is related to the autonomous investment of the government. The acceleration is based on induced investment. We can show the influence of the two types of investment on the level of income and cyclical fluctuations with the help of a diagram.

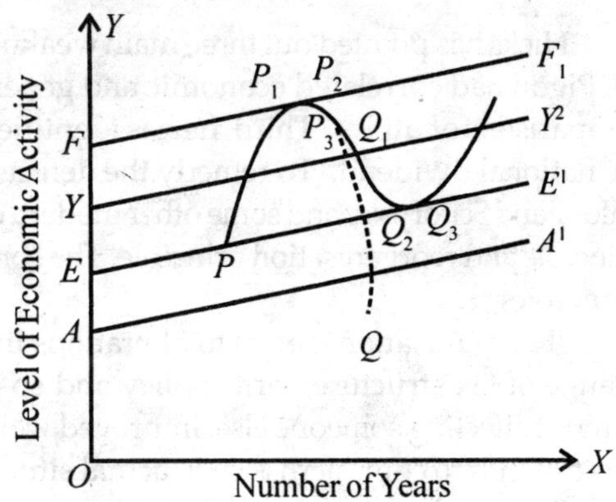

Fig. 8.

In Fig.8, the horizontal axis represents the number of years and the vertical axis, the level of economic activity. Line AA^1 represents the progress over the years. It slants upward at a uniform rate to indicate that autonomous investment grows over time at a constant rate. Line EE_1 represents the income or output corresponding to the autonomous investment line AA^1 but EE^1 is at a higher level because it represents the combined influence of multiplier and acceleration effects as a result of autonomous investment (AA1). In fact the distance between AA^1 and EE^1 will depend upon the combined influence of the multiplier and acceleration effects. Finally, line FF_1 represents the level of full employment income—"full employment ceiling".

Suppose the economy is at point P and a certain invention is introduced. As a result, there is a burst of autonomous investment. But the induced investment will push output, employment etc. upward along the path marked PP^1, away from the EE^1 line. The upward trend touches full employment ceiling at P_1 and it cannot raise further. When the path has touched the ceiling, it must move in a downward direction after some time.

This downward swing, according to Hicks is inevitable. The initial burst of autonomous investment is shortlived and after a stage it will fall to the usual level. But the induced investment which was the result of the initial autonomous investment and the initial increase in output would continue and push ahead on path PP_1. But the induced investment is not sufficient to support a growth of output along the path FF^1 It is sufficient to support an output which expands along the equilibrium path EE^1. Therefore output will return from FF^1 back to EE^1.

The downward swing can be gradual along the path $P_2\ Q_1Q_2$ or more rapid along $P_2\ Q_1Q_2$. At first, the downward swing may appear to be gradual but, in practice it will be rapid. The reason is that once the decline in output is initiated, it gathers momentum, and tends to proceed at a fast rate. Hicks gives a monetary explanation to this. As the downward movement starts, it becomes increasingly difficult to sell goods and consequently the burden of fixed cost becomes oppressive. Firms become bankrupt. Liquidity preference records a sudden and abrupt rise and reacts most adversely on credit situation. At the same time the stringent conditions in the credit market, by forcing business activity to fall to the lowest ebb, tend to aggravate the situation.

Thus Hicks' theory makes use of multiplier and accelerator principles and autonomous and induced investments. It is induced investment which is finally responsible for the upward push and downward swing of output and income, prices and employment.

Welfare Economics

Hicks has pointed out three main weaknesses in Pigou's approach to welfare economics. First of all, Pigou had correlated economic and general welfare. Second, he has made use of interpersonal comparisons of utility. Third, he has identified the sum of consumer supluses with the real value of the national dividend. To remedy the defects in the analysis of Pigou and Pareto, Hicks along with Kaldor and Scitorysky and some other modern economists have introduced the concept of compensation principle and reorganisation principle. The compensation principle is generally known as new welfare economics.

"Reorganisation" refers to alterations in economic circumstances. For instance, there may be change of tax structure, tariff policy and so on. A change in tax structure which helped someone without affecting someone else, improved welfare. Theoretically, it was an ideal reorganisation. But it was difficult to come across such actual situations.

So Hicks has introduced the compensation principle. According to the compensation principle,

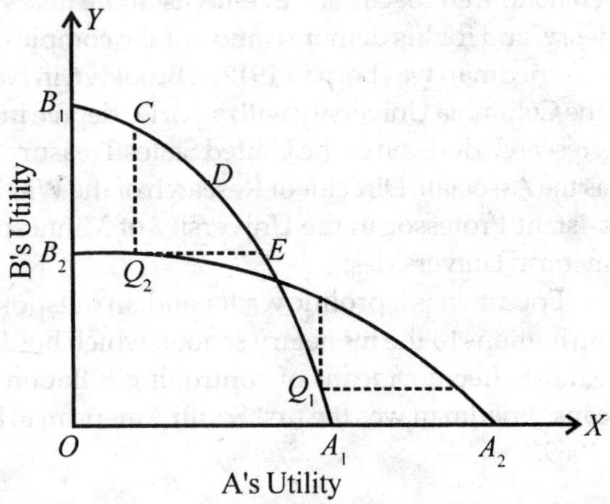

Fig. 9.

a society's economic welfare would increase if it were possible for those gained from a reorganisation to compensate those who lost and still retain some net advantage. Hicks has given the compensation principle as, "If A is made so much better off by change that he could compensate B for his loss and still have something left for, then the reorganisation is unequivocal improvement".

Hicks has proposed a test for the compensation principle. He pointed out that in any policy proposal there are two parties—gainers and loosers. Hicks is of the opinion that State B of the society is socially preferable to A, if the loosers from the policy change cannot bribe the gainer's. This can be illustrated diagrammati- cally (Fig.9).

The initial equilibrium is at Q_2 on the utility possibility curve A_2B_2. Any move from Q_2 to C,D,E is an improvement in terms of Pareto criterion. But a move from Q_2 to Q_1 cannot be evaluated in terms of Paretian criterion, but can be done in terms of Kaldor-Hicks criterion. This can be done by finding out the amount that B is willing to pay to prevent the move (since he is the looser) and finding out how much *A* is willing to pay. If the amount paid by *A* is greater, then A will be gainer and is willing to compensate loser and still be in a better position. To put it simply Q_2 should lie below Q_1.

Conclusion

By his brilliant contribution in the field of economic theory, Hicks has joined the rank of immortals like the earlier economists like Alfred Marshall and Keynes. He has a language of his own and his style and diction are uncommon among other economists. His language is full of profoundity of sense and the real meaning could be available at times at a further distance. He has been outstanding as a clear and tireless thinker, a widely read scholar and a lucid expositor. He is the pioneer who has laid theoretical ground work for the renewal of the equilibrium theory. His books on "Value and Capital" and "The Theory of Wages" are the masterly works in the field of economic science. For the most parts, he was worked with labour and capital only. He correctly perceived that capitalism has shown greater growth of capital than of labour. Even more important is his analysis of how technical invention affects distribution. By virtue of his original contributions, his name will remain immortal for any time to come in the annals of the history of economic thought. He is one of the ablest living economists of the day who richly deserves the award.

(c) MILTON FRIEDMAN (1976)

INTRODUCTION

The Nobel prize for the year 1976 has been awarded to Prof. Milton Friedman of Chicago University. The Royal Swedish Academy while announcing the reward, had said that Friedman had been honoured for his achievements in the fields of Consumption Analysis, Monetary History and Theory, and for his demonstration of the complexity of stabilisation policy.

Friedman was born in 1912 at Brooklyn in New York, studied in Rutgers University, passed out of the Columbia University with a Ph. D. degree in 1946. He had worked as Principal Economist of the tax research division of the United States Treasury Department during 1940-41. From 1941 to 1943, he was the Associate Director of Research of the War Research Division of Columbia. He had worked as Assistant Professor in the University of Minnesota. He was the visiting professor of many of the American Universities.

Friedman is a prolific writer and an outspoken conservative thinker. He is best known for his contributions to the monetary school, which holds that monetary rather than tax and fiscal policy is the most effective means of controlling inflation while keeping unemployment within acceptable means. Friedman was the first South American to be honoured with this award since it was instituted in 1969.

Quantity Theory of Money

Friedman in his essay, "The Quantity Theory of Money—A Restatement" published in 1956 beautifully restated the old quantity theory of money. In his restatement he says that "money does matter".

For a better understanding and appreciation of Friedman's modern quantity theory, it is necessary to state the major assumptions and beliefs of Friedman.

First of all Friedman says that his quantity theory is a theory of demand for money and not a theory of output, income or prices.

Secondly, Friedman distinguishes between two types of demand for money. In the first type, money is demanded for transaction purposes. It serves as a medium of exchange. This view of money is the same as the old quantity theory. But in the second type, money is demanded because it is considered as an asset. Money is more basic than the medium of exchange. It is a temporary abode of purchasing power and hence an asset or a part of wealth. Friedman treats the demand for money as a part of the wealth theory.

Thirdly, Friedman treats the demand for money just like the demand for any durable consumer good. The demand for money depends on 3 factors : (a) The total wealth to be held in various forms (b) the price or return from these various assets and (c) tastes and preferences of the asset holders. Friedman considers five different forms in which wealth can be held, namely, money (M), bonds (B), equities (E), physical non-human goods (G) and human capital (H).

In a broad sense, total wealth consists of all types of "income". By "income" Friedman means "aggregate nominal permanent income" which is the average expected yield from wealth during its life time.

The wealth holders distribute their total wealth among its various forms so as to maximise utility from them. They distribute the assets in such a way that the rate at which they can substitute one form of wealth for another is equal to the rate at which they are willing to do. Accordingly the cost of holding various assets except human capital can be measured by the rate of interest on various assets and the expected change in their prices.

Thus Friedman says there are four factors which determine the demand for money. They are: price level, real income, rate of interest and rate of increase in the price level.

The demand for money is unitarily elastic. The relationship between the demand for money and real income (output of goods and services) is also direct. But it is not proportional as in the case of price. Thus while changes in the price level cause direct and proportional changes in the demand for money, changes in real income create direct but more than proportional changes in the demand for money.

The rate of interest and the rate of increase in the price level constitute the cost of holding cash balances. If money is kept in the form of cash, it does not earn any income. But if the same money is lent out, it could earn some income in the form of interest to the owner. The interest is the cost of holding cash. At higher interest rate the demand for money would be less. On the other hand, a lower rate of interest creates an increase in the demand for money. Thus there is an inverse relationship between the rate of interest and the demand for money.

The rate of increase in the price level also influences the demand for money. There is an inverse relationship between the rate of increase in the price level and the demand for money. When the price level increases at a high rate, the cost of holding money will increase. The people would like to hold smaller cash balances. The demand for money will decline. On the other hand when the price level increases at a low rate, the cost of holding money will decline and the demand for money increases.

Fourthly, Friedman believes that each form of wealth has its own characteristics and a different yeild or return. In a broad sense money includes currency, demand deposits and time deposits which yield interest. Money also yields real return in the form of convenience, security etc., to the holder which is measured in terms of price (P). When the price level falls, the rate of return on money is positive because the value of money increases. When the price level rises, the value of money falls and the rate of return is negative. Thus P is an important variable in the demand function of Friedman.

The rate of return on bonds, equities and physical assets consists of currently paid interest rate and changes in their prices.

As far as human wealth is concerned it is very difficult to measure the conversion of human into non-human wealth due to institutional constraints. But there is some possibility of substituting human wealth for non-human wealth. Freidman calls the ratio of non-human wealth to human wealth or ratio of wealth to income as W. According to Friedman, income elasticity of demand for money is greater than unity.

Besides, there are certain variables like the tastes and preferences of the wealth holders which also affect the demand functions. These variables are represented by m.

FRIEDMAN'S DEMAND FUNCTION

On the basis of the above assumptions and formulations, Friedman has derived a demand function for an individual wealth holder. It may be symbolically expressed as

$$M = f\left[p, r_b - \frac{1}{r_b}\cdot\frac{dr_b}{dt}; r_e + \frac{1}{p}\cdot\frac{dp}{dt} - \frac{1}{r_e}\frac{dr_e}{dt}; \frac{1}{p}\cdot\frac{dp}{dt}; w; y; m\right] \quad ...(1)$$

Where M is the total demand for money, P is the general price level,

r_b is the market interest rate on bonds,

r_e is the market interest rate on equities,

$\frac{1}{p}\cdot\frac{dp}{dt}$ is the nominal return from physical goods,

W is the ratio of non-human to human wealth,

Y is the money income available to the wealth holder,

m is the variables affecting tastes and preferences on the wealth holders.

By assuming rb and re to be stable, Friedman replaces the variables representing the ruturn on

bonds and equities $\left[r_b, \frac{1}{r_b}\cdot\frac{dr_b}{dt}\right] + \left[r_e + \frac{1}{p}\cdot\frac{dp}{dt}\frac{1}{r_b}\cdot\frac{dr_e}{dt}\right]$

in equation I by simply r_b and r_e. As a result of this replacement, the demand function can be written as

$$M = f\left(P, r_b; r_e; \frac{1}{P}\cdot\frac{dp}{dt} w; y; \mu\right) \qquad ...(2)$$

Further Friedman says that when there are changes in price and money income, there will be a proportionate change in the demand for money. This means that equation 2 must be regarded as homogenous of the first degree in P and Y, so that equation 2 becomes as

$$lM = f\left(\lambda P, r_b; r_e; \frac{1}{P}\cdot\frac{dp}{dt} w; \lambda y; \mu\right) \qquad ...(3)$$

putting $\lambda = \frac{1}{P}$

equation 3 can be written as

$$\frac{M}{P} = f\left(r_b; r_e \frac{1}{P}\cdot\frac{dp}{dt}; w\frac{\gamma}{P}; \mu\right) \qquad ...(4)$$

In this form, the equation 4 expresses the demand for real cash balances as a function of "real" variable.

Putting $\lambda = \frac{1}{Y}$ equation 3 can be written as

$$\frac{M}{Y} = f\left(r_b; r_e \frac{1}{P}\cdot\frac{dp}{dt}; w; \frac{P}{y}; \mu\right) \qquad ...(5)$$

or

$$M = f\left(r_b; r_e \frac{1}{P}\cdot\frac{dp}{dt}; w; \frac{P}{y}; \mu\right) Y \qquad ...(6)$$

In Friedman's modern quantity theory of money, the supply of money is independent of demand for money. Due to the actions of the monetary authorities, the supply of money changes, whereas the demand for money remains more or less stable. It means that the amount of money which people want

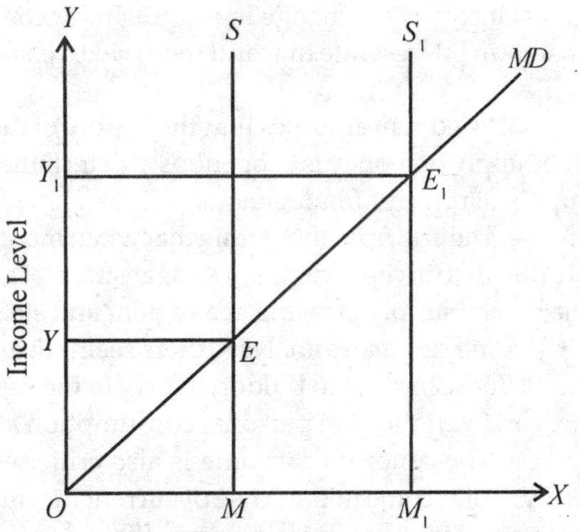

Demand and Supply of Money

Fig. 10.

to have as cash or bank deposits is more or less fixed to their permanent income.

If the central bank purchases securities, people who sell securities to the central bank receive money and this leads to an increase in their cash holdings. The people will spend this excess money partly on consumer goods and partly by purchasing assets. This spending will reduce their cash balances and at the same time there is a rise in the national income.

On the other hand, when the central bank sells securities, the money holding of the people reduces, in relation to their permanent income. Therefore, they will try to increase their cash partly by reducing their consumption and partly by selling their assets. This will reduce national income. Thus in both cases the demand for money remains stable.

If the demand for money is given, it is possible to predict the effects of changes in the supply of money on expenditure and income. If the economy is at less than full employment level, an increase in the supply of money raises the expenditure, output and employment levels. But this is possible only in the short run.

Friedman's quantity theory of money can be explained diagrammatically in the following figure (fig.10).

In the figure while the X-axis shows the demand and supply of money, Y-axis measures the income level. *MD* is the demand curve for money which changes along with income. MS is the supply curve for money. These two curves intersect at point E and the equilibrium income level *OY* is determined. If there is an increase in money supply, the supply curve shifts to M_1S_1. At this level the supply is greater than demand and a new equilibrium is established at E_1. At the new equilibrium level the income increases to OY_1.

Critical Evaluation of Friedman's Quantity Theoy of Money

Even though, Friedman through his modern quantity theory, revived interest in the role of money as a causal factor in economic activity , many economists raised controversial issues against this theory. The main criticisms against this theory are as follows.

1. Friedman has been criticised for his broad definition of money which includes not only currency and demand deposits but also time deposits. This broad definition ignores the effect of interest rate on the demand for money. If the rate of interest on time deposits increases, the demand for them rises. But the demand for currency and demand deposits falls. So the overall effect of the interest rate will be negligible on the demand for money.

2. Critics have questioned about Friedman's explanation of the transmission of monetary change to the real economic change. In Friedman's analysis, a change in M is passed on to a change in P, a fall

in real income and change in output and income. But the ciritics argue that a change in M creates a change in interest rate first and then makes changes in investment, employment, output, income and prices.

3. Friedman assumes that the supply of money is independent of changes in price and income. The supply of money is exogenously determined by the monetary authorities. But the fact is that the supply of money is endogenous.

4. The critics further argue that when money has a dynamic role to play in a modern economy, it is difficult to accept Friedman's suggestions of a steady monetary policy. Further it is difficult to keep the money supply growing at a regular and steady rate.

5. In Friedman's analysis, there seems to exist a positive correlation between money supply and GNP. But according to Kaldor, in Britain the best correlation is to be found between the variations in cash and variations in personal consumption at market prices.

6. The concept of income is also criticised by the critics. Keynes and his followers used the concept of income in the sense of current income. But Friedman uses the term income in the sense of permanent income. But it is very difficult to quantify and measure permanent income.

7. Again Friedman's concept of wealth is too broad and imprecise and concepts like "human capital" are difficult to quantify.

Inspite of the above criticisms, as H.G. Johnson says, "Friedman's application to monetary theory of the basic principle of capital theory—that is, the yield on capital and the present value of income—is probably the most important development in monetary theory since Keynes's General Theory. Its theoretical significance lies in the conceptual integration of wealth and income as influences on behaviour".

Permanent Income Hypothesis

Friedman gave the Permanent Income Hypothesis as an explanation of the short and long period consumption function. According to him, there is no tendency for the proportion of income saved to increase at higher income levels. He rejects the use of "current income" as the determinant of consumption expenditure. He divides consumption and income into "permanent" and "transitory" components, so that

$$Ym = Yp + Yt \text{ and}$$
$$Cm = Cp + Ct$$

where Y stands for income, C stands for consumption and m,p and t stand for their measured , permanent and transitory components.

Permanent income is to be defined as the means of income which is regarded as permanent by the consumer. It depends on time-horizon and farsightedness. It includes non-human wealth like personal attributes of the earners. Y being the measured income or current income, it may be larger or smaller than his permanent income in any period. The differences between measured and permanent income are due to the transitory component of income (Yt). The transitory income may rise or fall depending on cyclical variations. If the transitory income is positive, the measured income will be higher than the permanent income, if it is negative it will be lower than the permanent income. The transitory income can also be zero in which case measured income equals permanent income.

Permanent consumption is the amount planned to consume in a given period. Measured consumption is divided into permanent consumption (Cp) and transitory consumption (Ct). Measured consumption may be more than permanent consumption if the transitory consumption is positive. It will be less than permanent consumption if the transitory consumption is negative and it will be equal to permanent consumption if the transitory consumption is zero.

Permanent consumption is a multiple (K) of permanent income Yp

$$Cp = KYp$$

and $$K = f(r,w,u)$$

Therefore $$Cp = K(r,w,u,) Yp$$

where *K* is the function of the rate of interest (*r*), the ratio of income to wealth (*w*), and the consumer's propensity to consume (*u*) . This equation tells us that in the long period consumption increases in proportion to change in *Yp*. Thus K is the permanent average propensity to consume. Friedman contended that the secular decline in (*r*) since 1920s has tended to raise the value of *K*. But there has been a long run decline in wealth (*w*) which tends to reduce the value of *K*. Three factors have said to influence the propensity to consume. Firstly, there has been a deep decline in farm population increasing consumption with urbanisation and ultimately increasing *K*. Secondly, there has been a sharp decline in the size of the families leading to more saving and less consumption and reducing the value of *K*. Thirdly, the large provision of social security reduced the need for keeping more savings. It has increased the propensity to consume resulting in a higher value of *K*. The cumulative effect of all these factors is to raise consumption in proportion to the change in the permanent income component.

The relationship between the permanent and transitory components of income and consumption are based on the following assumptions:

1. There is no correlation between transitory and permanent income.
2. There is no correlation between permanent and transitory consumption.
3. There is no correlation between transiatory consumption and transistory income.
4. The differences in permanent income alone affect consumption.

The Permanent Income Hypothesis can be diagrammatically depicted Fig.11.

X axis measures income and Y axis consumption. *C1* is the long run consumption function and *Cs* is the short run consumption function. At OY_0 income level *Cs* and *Cl* coincide at *Eo*. At this point changes in permanent income and measured income (i.e., current income) are identical. So are permanent and measured consumption as shown by OCo. If we move to the left of point *Eo* on the *Cs* curve at E_3, the measured income declines to OY_3 due to negative transitory income component. As the permanent income OY_4 is higher than the measured income OY_3, permanent consumption will remain at OC_3 (= Y_4 E_4) and will also equal to measured consumption ($Y_3E_3 = Y_4E_4$). Thus when permanent income is less than one it is possible for measured consumption Y_3E_3 to be higher than measured income OY_3 because of the stability of permanent income. This generally keeps the measured consumption static.

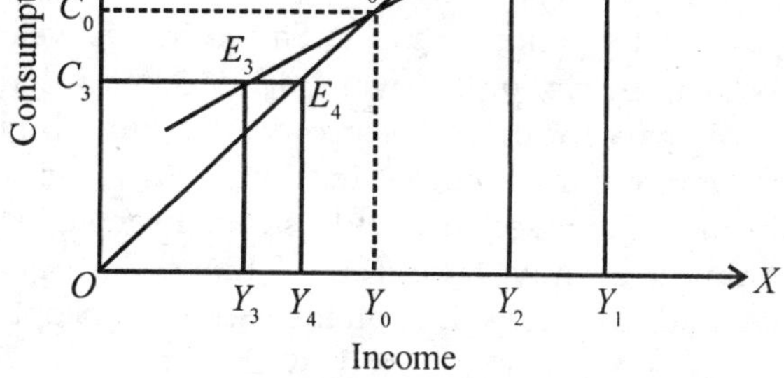

Fig. 11.

On the other hand a movement to the right of point *Eo* on the *Cs* curve at E_1 shows the measured income to be OY_1. Here the measured consumption is OC_2 (=Y_1E_1). But OC_2 (=E_2Y_2) level of consumption can be maintained permanently at the permanent income level OY_2. Thus $Y_1 Y_2$ is the positive transitory income component of measured income OY_1, which is higher than the permanent income OY_2.

The Permanent Income Hypothesis of Friedman is consistent with cross-section budget data. It suggests that current consumption or measured consumption will tend to be high during recession and low during boom period.

Criticism

Friedman's Permanent Income Hypothesis is criticised on the following grounds.

Firstly, Friedman's assumption that there is no connection between transitory components of consumption and income is not real. This assumption says that when measured income increases or decreases it does not affect consumption but it does affect only savings. But this is very much contrary to the natural behaviour of the consumers. A person who have windfall gain does not deposit the entire amount in the bank but enjoys a whole or part of it in current consumption. Similarly a person who has met with a loss would definitely reduce or postpone his consumption than rush to the bank to withdraw the amount to meet his requirements.

Secondly, Friedman's hypothesis states that the APC of all families,whether rich or poor is the same in the long run. But this is not true. The consumption of low income families is higher relative to their incomes and the saving of high income families is higher relative to their incomes. Even among the persons with level of permanent income same saving and consumption differ.

Thirdly, the usage of terms like 'permanent', 'transitory' and 'measured' have tended to affect the clarity of the theory. The concept of measured income creates confusion by mixing with permanent and transitory income on the one hand and permanent and transitory consumption on the other.

Fourthly, the distinction between human and non-human wealth is sadly missing in Friedman's theory.

Inspite of all these weaknesses it can be fairly concluded with the words of Micheal Evans "that the evidence supports this theory", and that Friedman's formulation has reshaped and redirected much of the research on the consumption function.

Milton Freidman and Savage Hypothesis

Milton Freidman and L.J. Savage in their well-known article, put forward a hypothesis that explains why the same group of people buy insurance and also engage in gambling. In buying insurance they seek to avoid risk and in engaging gambling they take risk. This seemingly contradictory behaviour on the part of the people could not be explained with Bernoullian Hypothesis of diminishing marginal utility of

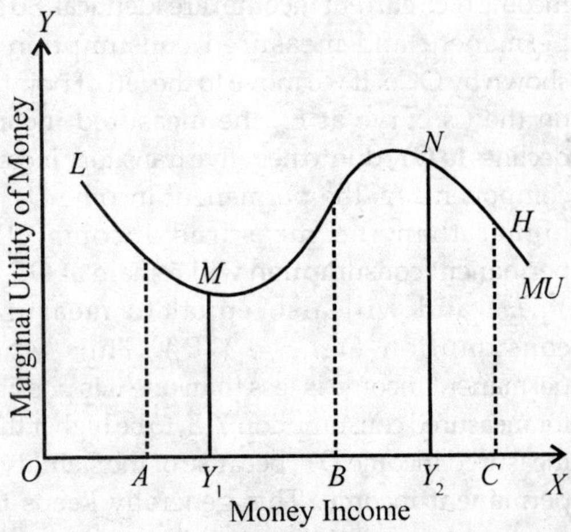

Fig. 12.

money. Freidman and Savage abandoned this hypothesis of diminishing marginal utility of money for all ranges of income and instead adopted another hypothesis. According to Freidman-Savage hypothesis, for most people, marginal utility of money income diminishes upto a certain level of money income, it increases from that level to a certain higher level of money income and then beyond that level it again diminishes. With this hypothesis both types of behaviour of buying insurance to avoid risk and of indulging in gambling and thereby to take risks are explained. Freidman-Savage hypothesis is depicted in the Figure (Fig.12). The curve of marginal utility of money income has three segments over *LM*, (that is, upto income level OY_1), marginal utility of money income diminishes, segment *MN* (that is, between income level Y_1 and Y_2) where marginal utility of money income rises and segment *NH* (that is, income higher than OY_2) where marginal utility of money income again diminishes. Segment LM represents marginal utilities of money income at lower level, range MN represents marginal utilities of money income at middle range and segment NH represents marginal utilities of money income at higher level.

Suppose an individual has an income *OA* which lies in the first segment of diminishing marginal utility of income. Such an individual would be induced to buy insurance and thereby avoid risk, since the payment (insurance premium) is small as compared with the loss of utility he would suffer without insurance. The loss of utility is very large for the marginal utility of money to the left of A is higher. With such an income individual will be unwilling to take risks in a gamble or risky investment, since the gain in utility from any income will be smaller than the loss of utility from it. Now suppose the individual's income is OB which lies in the middle income segment MN where the marginal utility of money income is increasing. With *OB* income, the individual will be willing to buy lottery tickets, indulge in gambling or undertake risky investment since the gain in utility from extra money will be much greater (marginal utility of money income is rising) than the loss of utility from the small payment for a lottery ticket or from equal monetary loss in a gamble.

A person with an income beyond Y_2 in the segment *MH* enjoys quite high income and therefore marginal utility of money to him is declining. As a result of this he would be unwilling to take risk either in a gamble or in undertaking risky investment except at very favourable odds.

Freidman-Savage think that the curve of marginal utility of money indicates the behaviour or attitude of people in different socio-economic groups. They of course admit that there are many differences between the persons within a same socio-economic group; some have great preference for gambling and others are unwilling to take any risk at all. Even then Freidman and Savage think the curve described the propensities of broad classes. The middle group with increasing marginal utility of money are those, they argue, who are eager to take risks to improve themselves. The expectation of more money means much to this group of persons; if their efforts succeed, they will lift themselves up into the next soico-economic class. These persons want not just more consumer goods; they look up in the social scale. They want to rise, to change the pattern of their lives. No wonder that marginal utility of money increases for them.

According to Friedman, the Great Depression of 1930s should be called the 'Great Contraction'. He has analysed the trend between 1928-1933 and explained that the Federal Reserve System bears the main responsibility for the Great Depression. The sharp and unprecedented decline in the stock of money was a consequence of the monetary authority's failure to provide the liquidity that would have enabled the banks which were failing to meet their obligation. Friedman has pointed out that perhaps the most remarkable feature of the record is the adaptability and flexibility that the private economy has so frequently shown under such extreme provocation".

Friedman along with A.J. Schwartz has written a book entitled A Monetary History of the United States, 1867-1960. Here they have analysed the America's economic history. In his another book titled" A Programme for Monetary Stability " he points out that for effective and successful operation of a private market economy, a stable monetary framework is essential.

Friedman is an uncompromising supporter of the free market mechanism. This world renowned economist has 23 books and 40 papers to his credit.

(d) AMARTYA KUMAR SEN (1998)

INTRODUCTION

Amartya Sen has been identified as the single most important thinker in the area of general equilibrium theory and welfare economics after Hicks and Arrow by the Nobel Committee. Sen has been awarded the Nobel Prize in Economics for the year 1998. This is the most significant achievement in eonomics. Sen is the first Asian and the Indian to achieve this distinction of the Nobel award in economics. The Nobel citation refers to (a) Sen's contributions to social choice theory (b) Sen's work in development economics, specially in the analysis of the relation between poverty and famines and (c) Sen's concepts of entitlements and capability development. Sen's work covers a vast domain in the above areas. He is proficient in symbolic logic and in the use of the axiomatic approach. His ideas cannot be labelled as belonging to any particular school of political economy. However he should be credited for having established his own special paradigm in welfare economics, particularly in the analysis of the relation between poverty and human development. He has put forth a number of new measures like poverty index and the capability index, which have been attempted to be empirically estimated.

Sen's social choice theory, his work on Bengal famine, his efforts to relate inequality and the depth of poverty, and his notions of capability and entitlement are the most important contributions to welfare economics. The social choice approach, as generally understood in the tradition of Pareto, Bergson and Arrow, proceeds by treating the community's aggregate welfare as a function of the welfare of each individual taken separately. The impossibility theorem of Arrow, in his constitution, was based on the assumptions which are reasonable in the tradition of Pareto, Bergson, etc. Arrow showed that there is no social choice satisfying all the assumptions. Samuelson has argued that Arrow has departed from the approach to social welfare function in Bergson who did not necessarily rule out cardinality and inter-personal comparisons. Sen's contributions have also shown this possibility by removing the requirement of ordinality in the Arrow procedure and substituting it by cardinality and inter-personal comparisons. In later writings Sen seems to have gone against procedures based on utilities. Sen has argued that the Rawlsian procedure does involve belief in utilities, their diminishing nature and their inter-personal comparisons. This is the way to distinguish between the rich and the poor and among the poor pick out the ultra poor.

Sen must be complimented for the axiomatic approach to widen the range of social welfare function models. He has tried to bring in the form of his extended social choice appproach, issues like poverty, inequality, famine etc. The field of application of social choice theory in the Sen direction can be equated with alternative political economy and social action models concerning development. It is in this direction to which Sen has taken welfare economics that seems to have won the admiration of the Nobel Committee. Social decisions are then taken by individuals, each of whom may have a separate sphere in which they do consider improvement in their own well-being, as the dominant yardstick in ranking social choices. Removal of poverty, unemployment, restriction on population growth, control of inflation, provision of subsidised social sector facilities, etc, can be defended on social utilisation grounds in democracies. Ethical consideration need not be brought in.

Poverty and Famines

Sen's "Poverty and Famines", an essay by Sen on Entitlement and Deprivation (1981) is both theoretical and applied work. In the essay, several famines have been studied in the working of a general theoretical frame work from an original angle. He examined various meanings of poverty and drew attention to the incidence of absolute and relative deprivation. He relates the head-count ratio of poverty to the measure of inequality of deprivation of people below the poverty line. Sen identified various causes that lead to different famines and demonstrated that the decline in aggregate food availability is not the primary cause. Sen gives very interesting data on how with relative rise in rice prices and the collapse of the rural labour's entitlements of purchasing rice, there was a relative fall in the prices of a number of other commodities, like wheat flour, mustard oil, cloth, milk, fish, and hair cuts. Sen's theory led to a controversy on whether food availability decline was not the cause for the Bengal famine. The two factors which he has highlighted are, the adverse effects on the poor of the steep rise in the price due to the inflation of currency by the government and the reduction in market supplies due to speculative hoarding which also helped to boost prices further. Sen disputes the thesis that aggregate food decline was the chief factor causing the famine.

The Nobel Committee has correctly appreciated Sen's analysis of the mechanism of the famine, which is important in itself irrespective of the controversy concerning empirical causes of the famine. The Nobel Committee has done well in identifying 'Amartya Sen' as the leading international economist of modern times who has addressed himself to the studies in famines and hunger in different parts of the world. His plea for regular assured food entitlement and the avoidance of inflation should surely be welcomed in all poor countries.

Poverty and Inequality

Sen has carried out massive work on poverty and inequality in India. Sen's major point has been that the gap simpliciter approach will not do. The distribution of income/consumption among the persons below the poverty line is to be taken into account. One has to be assumed that the initial distribution below poverty line would remain more and less unchanged. The intuitive finding was that the more skewed the distribution below the poverty line, the larger would be the Sen gap. Sen produced a neat formula, termed as the poverty measure, known as the Sen index.

$$P = [\,1 + (1\text{-}1)\,G\,]\,H$$

Where P is the poverty index, 1 is the measure of distribution, G is the Gini coefficient, and H is the head count proportion of the people below the poverty line. The procedures adopted by Sen, seems to treat the inequality measure about the poverty line and that the poverty line as largely independent of each other. Sen measure is sensitive to changes in distribution parameter in the poverty line groups, changes in the price index of wage-goods, changes in the relative prices of wage-goods due to productivity changes in the latter etc.

Sen's view is that the causes of poverty in India are illiteracy, poor health care, unemployment, bureaucratic administration etc. An illiterate person can hardly engage himself in production or in service. He is unaware of modern means of livelihood. Sen has suggested removal of illiteracy, malnutrition, unemployment etc. within a specific time period. He found that unequal distribution of wealth and income or concentration of wealth in fewer hands, illiteracy were the causes of poverty in countries like India. In Indian system, women members of a family are deprived of sufficient food, medical facilities etc. From the records of deaths during the period of famine, he found that among the victims, the number of women surpassed the male counter parts. Old women and female children died in larger numbers.

The Concept of Capability

The concept of capabilities developed by Sen has been cited as a better index of wellbeing than commodities or utilities. Capability, as defined by Sen, is the ability to transform Rawlsian primary goods to the achievement of wellbeing. Capability of human being is his ability of functioning in different capacities in a society such as to enable him to achieve the components or the constitutions of his well-being. Such functioning ability con- cretely implies access to adequate and nutritious food. Some measures are general and probably technical education, medical and health care facilities and a measure of security regarding the availability of the above. Sen has helped to induct indicators regarding the above in the human development index. A separate capability index for different countries has also been developed. Capability includes also an environment of freedom of choice and ability to make use of the various freedoms. Hence capability is prior to the attainment of the desired welfare states of individuals. Sen has argued that poverty is a result of capability failures. Sen has a wide ranging critique of conventional welfare economics on account of neglect of the capability dimension. His ideas in this area are continuously evolving and further break through may be expected. Capability is a normative concept. Capability development involves costs to society though the benefits may exceed the cost. If capability is deemed as a measure of surplus in human beings, classical economic analysis can be applied to it.

Entitlement

The concept of entitlement in the United States refers to the legally enforceable rights against the state like those of old age pensions. Sen has included in the concept of entitlements items like nutritious food, medical and health care, employments, security of food supply in times of famine etc. He considers famine as arising out of the failure of establishing a system of entitlements. He recognises that the market can provide entitlement provided all people can get work and a reasonable wage. The market will not provide entitlements in respect of some capability improving items. There are no identifiable reciprocities of commercial significance..

Sen has vigourously asserted that expansion of market is among the instruments that can help to promote human capabilities and gave the imperative need for rapid elimination of endemic deprivation. It would be irresponsible to ignore that opportunity. There are major gains to be made in globalisation. But if a country has globalisation at the highest possible speed and pays no attention to lack of social opportunity, illiteracy and lack of health care, it was creating problem for itself. In that case, the blame lies not with globalisation but with concomitant policies with which it was being married to. Globalisation need to be put in a broader context of social and economic policies. It could be a major force for prosperity only if it is backed by adequate national policies in a conducive social and economic environment.

Sen has compared the Indian Index of Human Development with a Chinese Index of Human Development in which China is in a much higher scale. But he has compared the human development of China with human development index of Kerala, in which Kerala is better placed without any coercion inspite of low income in comparison to so many states in India. Kerala's data on human development show the regional variation and mismatch between income and human development in Indian States. The data also shows the variations in the public action in different states in India because Kerala's progress on human development front is a result of public action and not the policies of globalisation and liberalisation.

Choice of Technique

Sen's 'Choice of Technique' was a research work where he argued that in a labour surplus economy, generation of employment cannot be increased at the initial stage by the adoption of labour intensive technique. He pleaded for adoption of capital-intensive technique in a developing country like India. His argument was that capital-intensive technique strengthens the economic foundation of the country which help in further expansion of the economy. The expansion of capital - intensive projects has a snow - balling effect on development in general including agriculture and industry. The scope of expansion of employment opportunities is more in capital - based project compared to labour - based projects. This idea of Sen cannot be said to be totally new one, because the Indian planners adopted Mahalanobis capital-intensive four sector model in the second five year plan before the publication of 'Choice of Technique' in 1960.

The Time Series Criterion

A.K. Sen begins with the problem of an investment planner who has to make a choice between various techniques. This person has to start with the estimates of real income flows corresponding to each technique. If (m_1/m_2) is the ratio of the volumes of investment with technique I and technique 2 respectively and if (r_1/r_2) is the ratio of reinvestment that would be possible when the investment planner choose the respective techniques, technique I will lead to a higher or lower rate of growth depending on whether m_1r_1 is greater or less than m_2r_2. But this is not enough to make a choice between the two techniques; it is very much possible that a higher growth rate does not provide a higher level of social welfare. Sen, therefore, argues, "After getting the two time series of income flows we have to apply the relevant rates of time discount. The time discount is necessary because of at least two reasons: (a) the diminishing marginal social utility of income with the rising income level, and (b) the uncertainity of the future. If marginal social utility of income falls quickly and becomes negligible as income rises beyond a certain level, it is possible that higher rate of growth of income may not give us a higher sum of total social satisfaction". Sen admits that beyond a point these rational calculations cannot be applied, because it is very difficult to foresee all that is going to happen in the future. He, therefore, suggests a less satisfactory but more workable method under which a period of time that is to be considered is to be fixed and then one should see whether the loss of immediate output due to the choice of the more capital - intensive technique is more than compensated by the extra output from it later, before the period under consideration is over. He conceives a period of recovery and defines it "as the period of time in which the total output, with the more capital-intensive technique, is just equal to that with the less intensive technique". In figure (Fig.13) which Sen uses, OT represents the period of recovery, as the surplus area for the capital intensive techniques, (BCC_1) is exactly equal to the deficit area (BAA'). H and L curves indicate the time series of consumption flows from the capital intensive and labour intensive techniques respectively.

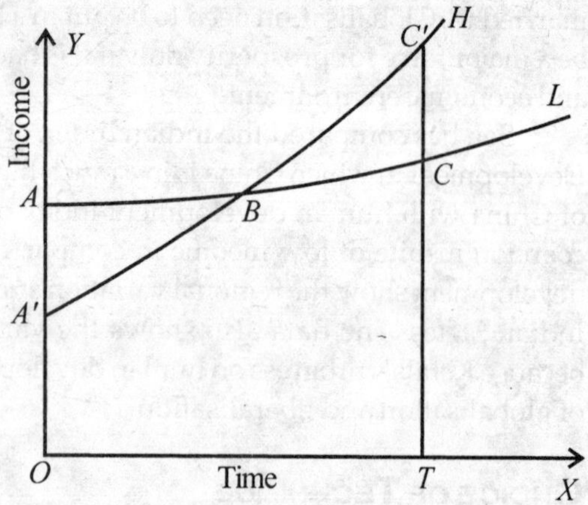

Fig. 13.

But the investment planner wishes to consider period U which lies between O an d T. If U = T, the investment planner would be indifferent between the two techniques. He would choose technique L if U < T, and technique H if U > T.

Limitations

Sen himself is aware of the limitations of this approach. According to him there is an arbitrariness involved, since it is assumed that there is no time preference up to the end of the period U and thus each unit of income has an equal value. But beyond the peroid U income is of no value. Thus the time factor is suddenly introduced. Sen, however, assures that such arbitrariness cannot easily be avoided on account of the very nature of the porblem. He further states that if extreme values of U are not chosen, it will become less arbitrary than the Kahn - Chenery approach of the S.M.P. criterion or the Galenson – Leibenstein approach of reinvestment criterion.

Further there is not much reality in Sen's period of recovery approach. If we assume U = 1, Sen's approach becomes exactly the same as the Polak-Buchanan rate of turnover criterion. It implies that the investment planner's interest is limited to the first period only and therefore, that technique is to be preferred which could provide a higher rate of immediate output. If we assume U = a, Sen's approach becomes similar to the Galenson - Leibenstein rate of reinvestment criterion, according to which, it is the higher rate of growth all that is wanted. A.K. Sen and Maurice Dobb explicitly introduce dynamic elements while stating their criterion, but even they do not take into account the relevant constraints that may become effective at future points of time.

Other Economic Ideas

Sen was in favour of *land reforms.* In 1962, he opined that there was an inverse relationship between farm size and productivity . Sen believed that productivity on a small plot of land owned by a single person is higher because the owner of the land can devote personal energy to cultivation. The farmer considers the land as the only source of his income or livelihood and he whole heartedly tries to increase productivity of that plot of land. Personal care by the farmer helps to increase production. Sen's idea about farm size and productivity is controversial in nature. But his concept of farm size and productivity has not been proved to be correct. Sen himself changed his view of farm size and productivity in 1980.

Sen has opined that an opportunity for a break from the past could have been seized when economic reforms were initiated in 1991, but the focus of attention in that programme has been almost exclusively on the opening up of the Indian economy and no broadening the reach of the markets. Those are certainly worthy goals, and the need for reform had been strong for a long time in the over regulated Indian economy but the lack of any initiatives towards a radical change in social policies, including those in basic education and elementary health care, is a major failure with deeply negative implications on the prospect of improving living conditions and even on the changes of success of the market reforms themselves.

According to Sen, there is a deep seated complimentarity between various economic arrangements including market mechanism and social opportunities. On the other hand, the opportunity offered by a well functioning market may be difficult to use when a person is handicapped by, say, illiteracy or ill health. On the other hand a person with some education and fine health may still be unable to use his or her abilities because of limitation of economic opportunities related to the absence of markets, or over zealous bureaucratic control, or lack of access to finance, or some other restraint that limit economic initiatives. The use of economic opportunities by one person can open up further opportunities for others through backward and forward linkages in supply and demand.

Sen has given greatest strategic importance to the expansion of health and education especially primary health and education in the process of economic development for having the influences that go much beyond the immediate personal effects. If machinery did nothing to raise production, it would be quite eccentric to value its existence, nevertheless, where as being educated or being in good health could be valued even if these would do nothing to increase the production of commodities, because the human resource is not only means of production but ultimate end also.

Sen is especially worried about the fact that agency of women as a force for change is one of the most neglected aspect of the development literature. Inequality between men and women is one of the most crucial disparity and social failures in many societies including India and it would not decline automatically with the process of economic growth. By simply decline in poverty which is of course a matter of deprivation, cannot assure a simultaneous decline in inequality. Recognition of women as agent of social change is essentially needed for which specific focus should be given on women sector in the process of human development efforts.

Conclusively, Amartya Sen, more than just an economist, is an ethical philosopher. He is a lover of freedom and a humanist. He has focussed on the poor, viewing them not as objects of pity requiring charitable hand - outs, but as disempowered fold needing empowerment, education, health, nutrition gender equality, safety net in times of distress, all are needed to empower people. Sen opines that is the role, the state should play rather than taking over the means of production while neglecting social sectors. On these grounds, Sen has influenced the IMF and the World Bank so much that today, they sometimes sound like Sen himself. Truly speaking, Sen's contribution to applied economics is a momentous and relevant to the contemporary world as J.M. Keynes' Theory of Employment during the years of the Great Depression about seven decades ago. Economics to him, is like it was to Marshall - a hand maid of ethics and servant of practice.

(e) ROBERT A MUNDELL (1999)

INTRODUCTION

Professor Robert Mundell of Columbia University, USA, has been awarded the Nobel prize in Economics for the year 1999. The Nobel committee in their citation has rightly mentioned about his fundamental theoretical contribution on the inter dependence of monetary and fiscal policy in an integrated world economy under alternative exchange rate regimes when financial capital are perfectly mobile across countries in response to interest rate differentials. This aspect of his contributions is so fundamental to the theory of economic policy that they are part of any sensible textbook On macro economic theory that have so far been written. But there are quiet a few other theoretical contributions of Prof. Mundell which have influenced many of the contemporary researches on the subject. These areas belong to the theory of international trade and macroeconomics, on which Mundell's pioneering works have stimulated research as a result of which the current status of the subjects have attained significance.

THEORY OF INTERNATIONAL TRADE

One fundamental corollary of the celebrated Heckscher-Ohlin Theorem of international trade has been the Factor Price Equalisation Theorem, which suggests the important theoretical premise that free commodity trade across nations is a substitute for international factor mobility. This theorem is based on a set of crucial assumptions, most of which are common with the Heckscher-Ohiln Theory of international trade. Given the set of assumptions, Mundell's theoretical contribution has been to prove the converse of the Factor Price Equalisation Theorem. The crucial analytical assumptions underlying the Factor Price Equalisation Theorem are:

1. Full intersectoral mobility of the factors of production which are however, internationally immobile.
2. Constant return to scale technology for each industry, with distinct and irreversible ranking of the products of these industries by factor intensities.
3. Profit maximization by the producers under perfectly competitive commodity and factor markets.
4. Difference in factor endowment position between countries and
5. Free trade across nations with zero tariffs and zero transport costs.

The theorem states that equality of commodity prices via the channel of free trade between nations is sufficient for complete equalisation of both relative and absolute factor prices at the past trade equilibrium scenario even though the factor prices are supposed to be different between nations, thanks to the international immobility of factors of production. There exists a one to one correspondence between commodity price ratios and factors price ratios which is crucial for proving this theorem.

THE MUNDELL-FLEMING MODEL OF AN OPEN MACRO ECONOMY

The open economy version-the flexible exchange rate version of the standard IS-LM model with output demand determined and prices taken as given in the Mundell-Fleming model, was developed in the early 1960s in the contributions made by Robert Mundell (1963) and Marcus Fleming (1962).

The simplest comparative static version of the Mundell-Fleming model is a direct extension of the IS-LM model. Mundell introduced foreign trade and capital movements into the so called IS-LM model of a closed economy, initially developed by John Hicks. This model is stated in highly simplified assumptions in terms of fixed domestic prices and static expectations about the exchange rate. Later researchers relax these assumptions and allow price adjustment when the economy deviates from full employment.

Exchange rate expectations also enter prominently in a frame work of rational expectations. In the Mundell - Fleming macro economic model of flexible exchange rates under conditions of perfect capital mobility, the openness of the economy is introduced with given prices at home and abroad, changes in the exchange rate, change in the terms of trade and the allocation of demand, output and employment.

The Optimum Currency Area Argument

The credit of developing the first theory of optimum currency goes to Mundell. Mundell in 1961 developed it as branch or an extension of the fixed versus flexible exchange rate. An optimum currency area is an area within which exchange rates should be fixed. Mundell claimed that the optimum currency area is the 'region' which is defined as an area within which factors of production are mobile and from which they are immobile. Mundell argued that if currency areas are smaller than existing countries then:

* There is considerable inconvenience in converting currencies.
* There is exchange rate risk in local business activity.
* In addition this currency markets can experience monopolistic private speculation.

Mundell therefore limited the optimum currency area to something larger than a nation. This makes the problem one of asking which countries should have fixed exchange rates.

The Monetary Approach to the Balance of Payments

Mundell's new ideas on the monetary approach to the balance of payments are presented in 'International Economics' . The monetary approach explains the balance of payments in terms of difference between the supply of money and the demand for meony, and also to show the effects of change in the supply of money. The monetarist approach is also used by its proponents to explain why some countries have persistent deficits. The monetary approach shows that if too much money is created deficit will occur. It also argues that the balance of payments is essentially a monetary phenomenon and must be viewed in its entirety. It stresses that the money supply and demand are strong forces in determining a country's external position as indicated by the change in the country's foreign currency reserves.

Prof. Robert A. Mundell in his seminal paper on "The Appropriate use of Fiscal and Monetary policy for Internal and External stability", considers the problem of achieving internal stability and balance of payment equilibrium in a situation when alternations in the exchange rate are ruled out and trade controls are considered inadvisable. The external and internal balances can be respectively achieved by various combinaions of fiscal and monetary policies.

In the diagram (Fig.14) the *FF* line represents the 'Foreign Balance Schedule' which traces the locus of pairs of interest rates and budget surpluses (at the level of income compatible with full employment) along which the balance of payments is in equilibrium. The *XX* line or 'Internal Balance Schedule' is the locus of pairs of interest rates and budget surpluses which permits continuing full employment equilibrium in the market for goods and services. Both the internal balance and the foreign balance schedules have negative slopes.

The *FF* schdule has a negative slope because an increase in the interest rate, by reducing capital exports and lowering domestic expenditure and hence imports, improves the balance of payments, while a decrease in the budget surplus, by raising domestic expenditure and hence imports, worsens the balance of payments. Any point of the *FF* schedule represents equilibrium. Points above and to the right of the FF schedule refer to balance of payments surpluses, while points below and to the left of the *FF* schedule reflects balance of payments deficits.

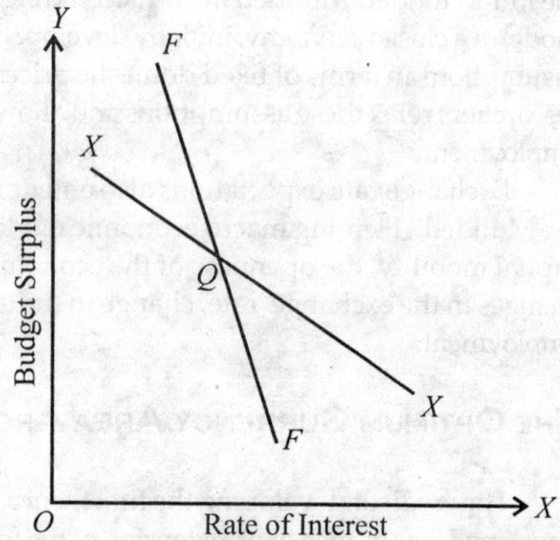

Fig. 14.

The internal balance line XX has a negative slope, since increase in the interest rate are associated with decreases in the budget surplus in order to maintain domestic expenditure constant. The crucial point is that the external balance *FF* is steeper than the internal balance locus *XX*. This is because of the responsiveness of capital inflows to change in interest rate. The more mobile is capital and the lower is the marginal propensity to import the slope of *FF* becomes greater in absolute value than the value of *XX*. In the figure, the situation of overall equilibrium exists at *Q*. If this equilibrium is disturbed by an increase in the rate of interest, there would be deflationary pressure and a balance of payment surplus.

In the figure, the two schedules separate four quardrants, distinguished from one another by the conditions of internal imbalance and external disequilibrium, only at the point where the FF and XX schedules intersect are the policy variables in equilibrium. The conclusion that follows from Mundell's diagrammatic argument is that in countries where employment and balance of payments policies are restricted to monetary and fiscal instruments, monetary policy should be reserved for attaining the desired level of the balance of payments and fiscal policy for preserving internal stability.

The opposite system would lead to a progressively worsening unemployment and balance of payments situation. That is the use of fiscal policy for external balance and monetary policy for internal balance drives the interest rate and budget surplus further away from equilibrium while the alternative system moves the instruments closer to equilibrium.

In the domain of monetary theory and macro economics Robert Mundell's seminal contribution has shaped the subsequent researches. Robert Mundell pointed out that whether the equilibrium rate of interest would be affected by monetary expansion or not, depends not only on the mode of monetary expansion-dificit financing versus open market operations, but also on what the government does with the interest income that accrues to it in the common stock that it purchases through the open market operations of the central bank. If the government decides to neutralise this receipt of interest income. Mundell was perhaps amongst the first to point out the importance of this contraints and much of the discourses on modern macroeconomics since then have tried to point out this constraint as an intergral part of macro-modelling.

Fiscal-Monetary Mixtures and the Assignment Rule

Looking more closely at the basic demand policy dilemma, Robert Mundell and Fleming noticed that monetary and fiscal policy, those two main arms of demand management have different relative impacts on internal and external balance, monetary and fiscal policy can be mixed so as to achieve any combination of aggregate demand and overall payment balance.

The pattern of policy prescriptions reveals a useful guideline for assigning policy tasks to fiscal and monetary policy. This is Robert Mundell's assignment rule, assign to fiscal policy the task of stabilising the domestic economy only and assign to monetary policy the task of stabilising the balance of payments only.

Robert Mundell's work is more than a bench mark. Mundell's contributions on monetary dynamics proved to be a watershed for research in international macro economics. He has reshaped the macro economic theory for open economics. His analysis of stabilisation policy and exchange rate systems constitutes the core of policy research. His theory of optimum currency areas has great importance. His monetary approach to the balance of payments is a foundational work for a number of researches to build on. Mundell's contributions at the University of Chicago serve as basic research in international macro economics. Mundell's analysis of monetary and fiscal policy in open economics stimulated the creative research activities. His work also initiated the necessary reapproachment between Keynesian short run analysis and classical long run analysis. His research findings have been applied in practical economic policy making. His analysis has attracted the attention of policy makers in connection with the common European currency. Recently it has been emphasised that SAARC countries must work towards common currency on the lines of Euro so that the region became a powerful trading block.

Conclusion

Robert Mundell's analytical and practical contributions in the field of economics has been enormous and varied. He is acclaimed mostly for his fundamental contributions in international monetary theory and policy, and also for his insightful and penetrative diagnosis of the working of the international monetary order, which he rightly considered to be biased against the interests of developing nations. But this fundamental theoretical insights in proving the reverse of the factor price equalization theorem, and in emphasizing the importance of government budget constraint in macroeconomic theory are often over-looked, although these have sustantially influenced the subsequent researches in the theory of international trade and macro-economic theory.

(f) JOSEPH E. STIGLITZ, JOSEPH A. AKERLOF AND A. MICHEAL SPENCE (2001)

INTRODUCTION

Three distinguished US economists Dr. Joseph A. Akerlof (61) of the University of California at Berkeley, Dr. A. Micheal Spence (58) of Standford University and Dr. Joseph E.Stiglitz (58) of Columbia University have been awarded the Nobel prize in economic science on October 10, 2001, for their analyses of markets with asymmetric information, referring to the fact that some market players have better information than othe.:s, as cited by the Royal Swedish Academy of Sciences at Stockholm Sweden.

They did their pioneering research in the 1960s and 1970s which incorporated imperfect or asymmetric information into economics in contrast to the mainstream economics. Their basic research has countless applications that extend from traditional agricultural markets in developing countries to modern financial markets in developed countries.

The three distinguished economists pioneered the view that markets, when confronted with imperfections, may not be the best way to allocate resources, that changed "economics", said Dr.Alankarueger of Princeton University. Their fundamental research convinced the view that government must play a strong role in a market system to prevent damage from imperfect information.

According to the Nobel Committee, Dr.Stiglitz's work is the broadest of the three. Joseph Stiglitz's many contributions have transformed the way the economists think about the working of markets, said the citation. Of the three, stiglitz is possibly the most distinguished and prolific economic theorist.

Dr. Akerlof was honoured mainly for an outstanding (1970) essay on the market for Lemons, "which was described by the Nobel Committee as the single most important study in the literature on economics of information".

The Nobel award came to Dr.Spence mainly on the strength of a single path-breaking paper on "Market Signals" published in 1973.

THE ECONOMICS OF SCREENING

Professor Joseph Stiglitz stressed the importance of the availability and transmission of information about alternative opportunities in making the education system as a more effective vehicle for income redistribution. In his paper on "Information and Economic Analysis", Stiglitz surveyed widely all the current works in the area of the economics of information and screening in education, labour and insurance markets.

He laid the foundation for constructing an "economics" of information-production and dissemination of information. He analysed two kinds of information. "One is associated with 'research and development' and the other with 'screening'". These two kinds of information are viewed as "polar cases"; while other kinds of information are thought of a mixture of the two.

J.E. Stiglitz defined screening as simply "the process of discrimination, of distinguishing among "things" which, in the absence of screening, would, for economic purposes, be treated the same, even though it may be known that they differ in perhaps some important ways".

Stiglitz discussed screening device with examples and examined the screening mechanisms by examination and self-selection, motivations for screening in monopoly and competitive market choices associated with differential information, screening costs and imperfect information on both sides of the market. Most of the analysis focused on imperfections of information on one side of the market. But Stiglitz focused on imperfections on both sides, e.g., in education market including examination system, insurance market, labour market and capital market. Screening was examined in a variety of contexts in these markets and the analysis has been extended to welfare economics also.

Spence in his insightful work (1973, 1974) focused on what has been referred to as self-selection mechanism and also on signals. Akerlof's seminal paper on the market for lemons and the literature on the economics of discrimination by Arrow, Phelps and Stiglitz and Spence work are noted as the two important antecedents of the Theory of Screening.

The development of the theory of imperfect information and non-convexity of technology altered the conventional fundamental analysis of markets. The seminal contributions questioned the assumptions of perfect competition, convexity of technology and the concept of equilibrium.

Traditional Vs Behavioural Theories of the Firm

The traditional theory of the firm (the neoclassical theory) assumes a single owner entrepreneur. There is no separation between ownership and management. The owner-entrepreneur takes all the decisions. The entrepreneur is further more assumed to have unlimited information, unlimited time at his disposal and unlimited ability to compare all the possible alternative actions and choose the one that maximizes his profit. There is no time, information or other constraints in pursuing the single goal of profit maximization.

Clearly the neoclassical (marginalist) assumptions are unrealistic, considering the complexity of modern enterprises. In the modern business world the firm is a complex organization, characterized by the divorce of ownership and management. This gives discretion to the managers to pursue goals other than profit maximisation.

Information is not unlimited. It acquisition involves expenses. Further more it is often distorted as it passes through the various hierarchical levels of administration. As recognized by the behavioural theories firms have no perfect knowledge of their costs, revenues and their environment and they operate in a world of uncertainty. Entrepreneurs attitudes towards risk plays an important role in actual decision-making.

Information activity is problematic in the behavioural theories. That is, a search is made whenever a problem is identified. Information flow is not costless, as the conventional theory of the firm assumed. Furthermore a search is not made on marginalistic rules, as the neoclassical theory postulated. Nobel economists have recognized that information is not costless, but they have treated information search as a resource absorbing activity. Information affects expectations and hence demands and goals of management.

Asymmetric Information

A very widespread economic situation is that of the relation between a principal and principal-agent relation. The interactions between the two are almost universal in the economy and are significant almost in all transactions. The problem acquires interest only when there is uncertainty at some point, and in particular, when the information available to the two participants is unequal. In technical language, there is asymmetric information between the two sides.

Asymmetric information is a situation where one party in an economic relationship (e.g an agent) has more information than another (e.g. the principal). The inherent dangers for the principal in these relationships are that the agent knows more about the situation than the principal and also the agent may well not act in the principals best interests and may be able to get away with it because of the principal's imperfect knowledge.

The main problem is where the agent's action is not directly observable by the principal and where in addition the outcome is affected but not completely determined by the agent's action. Technically the outcome is a random variable whose distribution depends on the action taken.

More generally, there may be many agents for a single principal. Each takes an action and the output of the system is a random function of all the actions. The principal cannot observe the actions themselves but may make some observations of the output and possible others (hidden action type). Also the agent makes an observation and bases his action on that observation and the principal does not know whether or not it is the most appropriate (hidden-information type). These are two types of principal-agent problems: hidden action and hidden information, respectively.

The Principal-Agent Problem

The principal-agent theory can be interpreted both normatively and descriptively. It can also be interpreted as an attempt to guide principal-agent problems in the real world and acts as a foundation for social engineering. It can be interpreted as an attempt to explain observed phenomena in the empirical economic world, particularly exchange relations which are observed but not explained by more standard economic theory. For example the case of a physician-patient relation. Here, the patient is the principal and the physician is the agent. The physician has a superior knowledge and the patient cannot check to see if the actions of physician are as diligent as they could be.

How can principals Tackle the Problem?

There are two types of solutions:

1. The principals must have some way of monitoring the performance of their agents and
2. There must be incentives for agents to behave in the principal's interests.

Conclusion

In economics, the issue of the divorce between the ownership and control of a company is known as the principal-agent problem. The principal-agent problem refers to a situation where people (principals), as a result of lack of knowledge cannot ensure that their best interests are served by their agents. One of the features of a complex modern economy is that people (principals) have to employ others (agents) to carry out their wishes. The point is that these agents have specialist knowledge and can save the principal, a great deal of time and effort. It is merely an extension of the benefits of the specialization and division of labour.

(g) DANIEL KAHNEMAN AND VERNON LOMAX SMITH (2002)

INTRODUCTION

American economists Daniel Kahneman (68) and Vernon L.Smith (75) won the 2002 Nobel Memorial Prize in Economics for their pioneering works in psychological and experimental economics. Daniei Kanneman was born in TelAviv and Vernon Lomax Smith was born in Wichita. Their works highlight the nexus between psychology and economics in explaining decision-making and behaviour of financial markets. Their research in contrast to the works of conventional economists has brought together the fields of experimental economics and cognitive psychology. Psychology emerged as the top field with economics, paving the way for scientific fraternity to rely less on observation of actual economics in decision-making and more on controlled laboratory experiments.

These economists have been conducting a number of experiments to determine how markets actually work in the real world. These experiments are part of the new fast – growing field of experimental economics, which has provided some very interesting results. Economists "have to invent new wisdom for a new age" and to "appear unorthodox", said J.M. Keynes. Keynes's characterization suits well to the two towering American economists in their formation of experimental economics.

DECISION MAKING UNDER RISK AND UNCERTAINTY

A behavioural scientist by training and temperament, Daniel Kahneman of Princeton University in New Jersey (U.S) brought to economic research quite a different bag of tools and insights from those of the technical economist. As a social psychologist Kahneman has integrated insights from psychology into economics, "especially concerning human judgement and decision-making under uncertainty" said the Royal Swedish Academy of Sciences in it's citation. He was so impressed by the complete lack of connection between the statistical information and the compelling experience of insight that he coined a term for it: "the illusion of validity". It was the first cognitive illusion he discovered. Kahneman is the great entrepreneur of controlled laboratory experiments, and for this methodological interest alone the economics profession owes him an immense debt.

A simple example of the discussion of the anomalous experimental results of decision-making under uncertainty can be found in D.Kahneman and A.Tversky's work when they argue that there are biases in the perception of probability distributions. Moreover, experimental psychologists like D.Kahneman, P.Slovic and A.Tversky do not accept that events, which are driven by stochastic processes, are stochastic by nature. Kahneman's experiments in probability theory showed a shortsightedness in interpreting data that could explain large fluctuations on financial markets and other phenomena that elude existing models.

His assignment involved two tasks,

(i) There were personality dimension that mattered more in some combat jobs than in others,

(ii) To develop interviewing guidelines that would identify those dimensions.

D.Kahneman made a discussion about predictions and observations. Observation in the experimental psychological literature often reveal that laboratory experiments or clinical studies are more realistic than actual surveys. He invented a statistical technique for the analysis of multi-attribute heteroscedastic data, which used to produce a complex description of the psychological requirements of the various units. By being able to control the environment, clinics avoid the pitfall of actual market observations. Clinics can provide useful information about how the participants, say consumers, in a stipulated store react to change in the commodity price, product packaging, displays, price of competing products and other factors affecting the demand for a firm's product. Participants in the experiment can be selected so as to closely represent the socio-economic characteristics of the market of interest. In contrast to the conventional surveys, the clinical studies undertake the continuous monitoring of the psychological variables such as the attitudes, expectations and intentions of the participants.

The clinical method mimics the essential features of the real world situation. However, the sample of participants must necessarily be small because this procedure is expensive. Also, the results are questionable because participants are aware but they are in an artificial situation. Unlike clinical experiments, which are conducted under strict laboratory conditions, market surveys can be conducted on a large scale to ensure the validity of the results and participants are not aware that they are part of an experiment. Nevertheless, clinical experiments are supplemented with market surveys.

He had devised personality profiles for a criterion measure, and now he needed to propose predictive interview. He developed a structured interview schedule with a set of questions about various aspects of civilian life which the interviewers were to use to generate ratings about different aspect of personality.

Functioning of Markets and Experimental Economics

Vernon L. Smith of George Mason University in Virginia (U.S) laid the foundations for the field of experimental economics, demonstrating the importance of alternative institutions. Smith "established laboratory experiments as a tool in empirical economic analysis, especially in the study of alternative market mechanisms".

The Royal Swedish Academy singled our Mr. Smith's use of "wind tunnel tests", where trials of new, alternative market designs are carried out in the lab before being implemented. That could be useful, for example, in deciding on deregulating electricity markets and the privatization of public monopolies. Vernon Smith shows how the "home made leverage theorem" is vulnerable to default risk.

In game theory, not all games are zero sum. Also negative-sum games are possible in which both parties loose. A two-person, non zero sum game where the payoffs are negative is given by the "prisoner's dilemma". It has been found that the best strategy for playing the prisoner's dilemma is a "tit for tat" behaviour, which can be summed by "do to your opponent what he has just done to you". That is, as long as your opponent cooperates, you cooperate. If he betrays you, the next time you betray him back. If he cooperates again, the next time you cooperate also. As viewed by Vernon Smith, controlled experiments with human participants have shown that such a tit-for-tat behaviour leads people to cooperate and reach a better outcome than with any other form of behaviour.

Experimental economics or the probing of human behaviour through laboratory experiments has recently gained popularity in analysing complex situations (such as game theory), where useful or practical and theoretical conclusions have been hard to obtain.

The experiments are conducted with volunteers, often college students, who are provided money to buy and sell a fictitious commodity with in a simple specified institutional framework. The participants are allowed to keep some of the money that they earn by acting in an economically rational way. For example, in a recent time Vernon Smith handed out several thousand dollars of his own money to a group of students participating in a stimulated stock market study, which provided very interesting results. One is that stock market or speculative "bubbles" occur regularly with in the experimental framework.

Traders seem to be carried away in a raising market and continue to bid stock prices up for past the expected dividend and price/earnings ratio of the stock-inevitably lead to an eventual crash. Smith's experiments showed that imposing limits on price declines only postpones the crash and makes it deeper when it comes. Only the availability of futures trading seemed to reduce the size and duration of speculative bubbles. These experimental results could have important practical implications in devising regulations to make stock market less volatile in the real world. Despite the very simple setting in which these experiments were conducted, their outcome closely mimics the actual stock market crash of 1987.

Conclusion

It must be pointed out that experimental economics is still in, its infancy; and many economists remain skeptical of the real-world usefulness of results obtained in such simplistic institutional settings and of their applicability in devising regulatory policies in the real world. No doubt, the field of experimental economics has boomed in recent years. Most economists seem to be watching hopefully from the sidelines.

(h) ROBERT F. ENGLE AND CLIVE W.J. GRANGER (2003)

The time-series analysts, Robert F. Engle (b. 1942) of the U.S. and Clive W.J. Granger (b.1934) of the U.K., won the 2003 Nobel Economics Prize for their use of statistical methods for economic time-series, the Royal Swedish Academy Sciences said on October 8, 2003 at Stockholm (Sweden). The Academy said in its citation that the research was used to gather data for time-series, such as chronological observations or for estimating relationships and testing hypotheses in economic theory. Such time series show the development of gross domestic product (GDP), prices, interest rates, stock prices, etc.

Men live with change and the focus of interest of economists will be the nature of the long-run changes in aggregate economy and their implications for the functioning and structure of the economy. An observer looking at the statistical record or even glancing about the past century cannot but be impressed by the pervasive nature of long-run economic change, an ever-changing economy places a premium upon understanding the nature of change and the forms in which it is manifested. Understanding change is essential to the appraisal of future economic conditions, as addressed by Nobel economists. The Nobel prize-winning contributions on statistical analysis rely on time-series data.

R.E. Engle (60) obtained his B.A. Degree from Williams College in 1964, M.S. Degree from Cornell University in 1969 and Ph.D. from Cornell University. His academic affiliation shows that he served as Professor of Economics in the University of California at San Diego since 1975 and also in the

Massachusetts from 1969-75. He is currently on the faculty of economics at the New York University. His major field of research reflects time series analysis and econometrics.

C.W.J. Granger (69) received his B.A. Degree in 1955, Ph.D., in 1959 and D.Sc. from the University of Nottingham in 1992. His fields of specialisation include Econometric Modeling and Prices, Business Fluctuations and Cycles. His main area of research belongs to long run equilibrium of economic series. His analytic probes cover: C.W.J. Granger and P. Newbold, Forecasting Economic Time Series ; C.W.J. Granger, Forecasting in Business and Economics. Granger has developed methods that help us model variables that follow trends over time and in particular to estimate relationships between such variables. One example would be exchange rate and relative price levels.

The findings of these laureates' are important because on financial markets, random fluctuations and volatility can affect share prices and value, along with other financial instruments. Their research had helped economists and financial experts "measure and estimate volatility and how volatility varies over time". This had most of its applications in financial markets, for instance how the volatility of stock returns and investment returns in general vary overtime.

Time-series behaviour of Economic-data

For policy analysis, to investigate the relative effectiveness of policies (eg., monetary and fiscal policies), it is important to ascertain that the conceptual model for such empirical exercise is correctly specified. The rationale behind this methodology is based on the assumption that most macroeconomic variables exhibit substantial co-movements. It is therefore important to examine the time-series characteristics of the data to be estimated and also to distinguish between correlations that arise from shared trend and one associated with underlying casual relationships. The estimation of non-stationary time-series may yield spurious regressions and erroneous inferences which may have adverse consequences for macroeconomic stabilisations.

For example, when the dependent and other explanatory variables are non-stationary, conventional estimation methods using observations on the levels or first differences of those variables will likely find statistically significant relationship, even when there is no meaningful economic relationship. To avoid such problems, the data used are to be subjected to a battery of econometric tests in order to establish their uni-variable time-series behaviour.

Statistical Methods in Economics Research

The progress of a science is dependent on the reciprocal influence and simultaneous advancement of both the theoretical and empirical parts. The theoretical part of science is, presumably based on exact ascertainments, and its purpose is to develop the structure, relationships, and results of hypotheses. The appropriateness and applicability of a conceptual model involve the confirmation or reputation by observation of the hypotheses which enter into the model.

In economics research there are three general uses of statistical methods: they may 1. serve as information culminating in hypotheses and theories, 2. be applied to the testing of hypotheses or theories, and 3. Furnish estimates of quantities in economic analysis. Economic theory is of a 'deductive' nature; it deduces conclusions from given assumptions. Statistics, however, is of an 'inferential' nature; it infers something about a totality from a limited body of evidence.

Statistical attempt to quantify the degree of confidence one can place in a theory. The only way to strengthen the confidence in the validity of a theory is to confront it with as much evidence as possible that could conceptually disprove it. A connected role of statistics is to estimate the parameters of economic theory.

'Economic forecasting' refers to the predictions relating to the future course of total economic activity or of the major sector accounts in Gross National Product (GNP). In 'business forecasting' in appraising the potential of a given company, an important element is the outlook for its industry and the market for products it produces. Often prediction of the future course of events of a particular set of prices or the market for an industry or a commodity, cannot be divorced from an assessment of the state of general business. Each may be influenced in a major way by the total level of economic activity and in these circumstances some prediction of the aggregate is essential before an attack can be made on the specific problem. Time-series analysts stress that long-runs of observations require the assumption that the underlying economic structure has been stable for that length of that time. What is more important is that economic world is not homogeneous through 'space' and 'time'.

Today most economics research is attempted by the experimental approach. The experimental approach combines the theoretical considerations (a priori criteria) with the empirical observations available and is designed to extract the maximum of information from the available data. The laureates' pioneering study on statistical laws confine to the empirical work to aggregative time-series samples. Their contributions on statistical analysis rely on time-series data. The two outstanding economic statisticians are rightly recognised by the Nobel committee for their invaluable work in analysing the economic time-series.

(i) FINN E.KYDLAND AND EDWARD C PRESCOTT (2004)

INTRODUCTION

Norweign Finn E.Kydland (60) of Carnegie Mellon University in Puttsburgh, Pennsylvania and the University of California at Santa Barbara and American Edward C.Prescott (63) of Arizona State University, Temple, Arizona, received the 2004 Nobel Memorial Prize in Economic Sciences for shedding light on how government policies and actions affect economics world wide. They examine the key policy issues and their repercussions stemming from the contributions of the Nobel Laureates for the year 2004.

NEW CLASSICAL MODEL

To the "rational expectationists", counter cyclical monetary and fiscal policies will not make the economy more or less stable than it would otherwise be; they believe that such policies will not make the economy more or less stable than it would otherwise be; they believe that such policies simply have no systematic effect on the economy's real variables such as output and unemployment. In opposition to both the monetarists and the rational expectationists, the Keynesians hold the view that has long been their gospel: counter-cyclical policy can make a positive contribution to the stability system.

In the rational expectations framework, the availability of information and the ability of decision makers to acquire new information play central roles. Advocates of the rational expectations framework argue that after repeated attempts by the government to stimulate the economy, people catch on to the policy and come to expect inflationary pressure. But inorder to stop inflation the government must announce its intentions in advance and convince people that it will do what it says.

Models of Optimizing Agents

F.E. Kydland and E.C.Prescott have developed models of optimizing agents. The government, anticipating the reactions of the private sector to its policy can maximize its objective function. This solves the problem of designing an optimal policy for government, which incorporates the private sector's reaction. In order for this solution to be stable, however, the private sector must trust the government. Otherwise, the private sector could put themselves in bad situations and wait for the government to save them. An Adaptive Regression Model designed for its application to time-series data is associated mainly with the names of T.F. Cooley and E.C. Prescott.

Business Cycle Models

Business cycles generally occur as a result of shifts in aggregate demand. Given the wide swings in economic activity, economic forecasting is one of the most important tasks of economists. Kydland and Prescott build their equilibrium business cycle model upon the assumption of utility maximization. The technique combines "equilibrium business cycle modeling "with modern tools of public finance and contrasts sharply with the conventional techniques-such as econometric model simulation.

Some of the most important business-cycle models along with their proponents are given under:

- Monetary theories attribute the business cycle to the expansion and contraction of money and credit
- Innovation theories attribute the cycle to the clustering of important inventions such as surrounding the railroad or the automobile.
- The multiplier-accelerator model proposes thereby generating regular, cyclical fluctuations in output.
- Real-business cycle proponent hold that productivity shocks spread through the economy and cause fluctuations.
- Equilibrium-business-cycle theories claim that misperceptions about price and wage movements lead people to supply too much or too little labour, which leads to cycles of output and employment.

This list just hints at the variety of explanations of movements in output, unemployment and prices. An economics entered the age of statistics and computers, macro economics forecasting has made great progress.

Models of Unemployment

Any attempt to explain unemployment, especially at the macro economic level, must have a suitable theory of the labour market. The move to 'supply-side economics' at the very least turns attention to this neglected aspect. But it is important that both sides be constantly kept in mind. A theory, which deals only with the demand side, cannot be a full explanation; but the same is true of a theory, which considers only the supply side. Unemployment, like inflation, is riddled with confusion and it seems everyone is suffering from these two economic diseases namely unemployment and inflation at the national and global levels.

Classical, Keynesian, Monetarists And New Classical Models Of Unemployment

In the classical model, the only unemployment is the difference between 'full employment' and the working population. J.M. Keynes assumed that money wages were inflexible downwards and explained his concept of 'Involuntary unemployment' through the influence of aggregate demand. In addition, the term 'natural unemployment' was introduced into the literature by Milton Friedman. Search theory is one explanation for the growing level of voluntary unemployment. It is apparent that Search Theories are a sub-group of the new classical economists. The reduction in the uncertainty is a means of increasing the efficiency of labour market.

Search Models Of Unemployment

New classical economists assume that free markets are efficient and equilibrium will always be achieved. In order to reduce the level of unemployment, the labour market must be rid of the distortions-trade unions, social security benefits etc., which impede the free market from working. It, is therefore, quite consistent to hear monetarists argue for a curb on trade union power and a reduction in unemployment benefits. A rise in aggregate demand will simply lead to higher prices.

Another different view has also emerged in the literature, namely the relationship between search time and unemployment wherein a rise in the level of aggregate demand will raise the equilibrium of employment of labour due to price effect, demand and supply forces. The money wage will accordingly rise and those seeking jobs perceive an improvement in job opportunities.

Search theorists argue that the bulk of the natural rate of unemployment can be explained by this uncertainty and the need to search. A reduction in the natural rate of unemployment, therefore, requires improvement in methods of search; namely, improved information about the job market. The uncertainty on the supply side-skill and sustainability alters the level of unemployment, while the uncertainty on the demand side-wage and working condition alters the level of vacancies.

Rational Expectations And Economics Policy

Finn Kydland and Edward C.Prescott investigated the implications of rational expectations for choosing among alternative fiscal policy rules in their paper "A competitive Theory of Fluctuations and the Feasibility and Desirability of Stabilization Policy", Kydland and Prescott consider a model in which the neutrality and non-neutrality hypotheses both obtain and their analysis focuses on the effects of changes in technology and shifts in fiscal policies on aggregate employment. In their model, these effects are persistent, but not permanent. Kydland and Prescott conclude that tax rates should not respond either to fluctuations in economic aggregates or to temporary changes in public expenditures. The tax rates should remain constant or nearby constant over the cycle with the budget being balanced on average. This does not minimize fluctuations but does minimize the deadweight burden of financing government expenditure.

The choice among fiscal and monetary instruments depends on issues on timing and of the mix of demands to be affected. The government's limited ability to forecast the future course of the economy and the effects of different stabilization policies is to be still the main reason for limiting policy activism.

Conclusion

Mr. Kydland and Mr. Prescott were able to show "how such effects of expectations about future economic policy can give rise to a time consistency problem". "If economic policy makers lack the ability to commit in advance to a specific decision rule, they will often not implement the most desirable policy later on".

Mr. Kydland and Mr. Prescott made fundamental contributions to both those areas not only in macro economic analysis, but also for the practice of monetary and fiscal policy in many countries.

(j) THOMAS SCHELLING AND ROBERT J. AUMANN (2005)

Introduction

Thomas Schelling, an American and Robert J. Aumann, an Israeli, won the 2005 Nobel Prize in Economics for their game theory to explain conflict resolution. The Royal Swedish Academy of Sciences awarded on October 10, 2005 the $1.30 million prize to Thomas Schelling and Robert Aumann for work that has found uses in "Security and disarmament policies, price formation on markets, as well as economic and political nagotiations. Their work has helped in the understanding of trade disputes, organized crime, political decisions and wage negotiations, as well as outright shooting wars.

They did not stop at explaining the economic phenomena alone and had extended their analysis to the study of racial and sexual discrimination. Their work has transformed the social sciences for beyond the boundaries of economics using the game theory-interactive decision scenarios-the laureates concentrated on why some persons and countries managed to cooperate while others suffer from conflict.

The laureates have "enhanced the understanding of conflict and cooperation through game theory analysis". They have helped to explain economic conflicts such as price wars and trade wars as well as why some communities are more successful than others in managing common pool resources.

Schelling, teaches at the University of Maryland. He produced his main work during the Cold War, which pitted the United States against the Soviet Union, using game theory methods to explain the era's most vital issues, global security and the arms race.

Robert Aumann, was born in Germany but is an Israeli and U.S. Citizen who teaches at the centre for Rationality at the Hebrew University of Jerusalem. He was cited for his work in looking at how real world situations can affect the theory. In many real world situations cooperation may be easier to sustain in the long-term relationship than in a single encounter.

Proper understanding of any social situation would require game-theoretic analysis. As seen by John. C. Harsanyi, the Nobel laureate, "Game theory is a theory of strategic interaction. That is to say it is a theory of rational behaviour in social situations in which each player has to choose his moves on the basis of what he thinks the other players' counter moves are likely to be".

Game theory as first established as a systematic theory in 1944 by Von Neumann and Morgenstern with the publication of "The Theory of Games and Economic behaviour", and even as it had been further developed up to the late 1960's, was restricted to games with complete information now extended to games with imperfect information. After Schelling and Aumann, seemingly irrational behaviour could suddenly be explained. "The repeated – games approach clarifies the raison d'etre of many institutions, ranging from merchant guilds and organized crime to wage negotiations and international trade agreements". Game-theoretic frameworks have been specifically developed to analyse situations in which 'players' or agents interact strategically. Game theory is concerned with the choice of the optimum strategy in conflict situations.

Psychological evidence indicates that most altruistic behaviour is more complex: people do not seek uniformly to help other people; rather, they do show according to how generous these other people are being. Indeed, the same people who are altruistic people are also motivated to hurt who hurt them. Clearly, these emotions have economic implications in game-theoretic situations.

Thomas Schelling has given a wide variety of social interaction situations where the social outcome was surprisingly different from individual motivations.

"The theory of games gets it name and much of its force from an analogy with social games. The rules of the game are social. More generally, individual behaviour is always motivated by social relations", as remarked by Kenneth J. Arrow, the Nobel Laureate.

Having working on the Marshall plan the U.S. post-war aid programme for battle-ruined Europe and at the White House in the 1950s, Schelling was well placed to examine the rationale behind the superpower's nuclear standoff.

Schelling's seminal work, "The Strategy of Conflict" became a classic and has influenced generations of strategic thinkers. "These insights have proven to be of great relevance for conflict resolution and efforts to avoid war", said the Nobel jury. Building on Schelling's original ideas Aumann applied the tools of mathematical analysis to highlight the alternatives available to one's own country and the opponents in times of conflict. Schelling showed that the ability to retaliate can be more useful than the ability to resist an attack and that it may be good to keep the enemy in the dark over how ones retaliation will look.

Some games are not strictly competitive, for there are aspects that make cooperation both beneficial and feasible. Such games are called cooperative games. Cooperative games are defined explicitly as having the feature that players can make agreements regarding the strategies they will play. Such agreements can drastically affect the outcome of the game. In a cooperative game an agreement is made by a coalition.

CONCLUSION

The game is widely studied by political scientist, because it captures well situations in which nations challenge each other. Each country hopes to "dare" while the other country backs down' but both dread most of all the outcomes in which neither nation backs down. Game theory is a science of strategy, which attempts to determine what actions different "players" be they trading partners, employers and unions or even crime syndicates-should take to secure the best outcome for themselves.

(k) EDMUND S. PHELPS (2006)

Edmund S. Phelps (73) an American Economist, a New Keynesian won the Nobel Economics Prize on October 9, 2006 for his analysis of short-term and long-term trade offs in macro-economic policy. Great men with glittering credentials in the field of economics are honoured for their prodigious intellectual resources and path-breaking contributions by the Swedish Academy of Science at Stockholm from 1969. The Swedish Academy recognized eminent men by considering "not only the extension of knowledge for knowledge's own sake, but also its applied aspects, its potential benefits to manking".

Background

Edmund S.Phelps born in 1933 was educated at Amherst College, obtained his B.A. degree in 1955 and got his Ph.D from Yale University in 1959. He has been the Professor of Economics at New York University during 1978-79 and has also taught economics at University of Paris during 1968-71. He is currently a Professor of Political Economy in the Department of Economics at Columbia University, New York and working since 1971. His research interest includes Political Economy, Unemployment, Monetary and Fiscal Policy and Public Finance. His publications include pioneering theoretical and empirical contributions to economic analysis that have ranged over such varied topics as Micro Foundations of Macro Economics (New Micro Economics), Inflation Theory, Modern Market Theory of Labour Market (Search Theory), Expectation Model and New Keynesian Theory and Golden Rule of Accumulation (Neo Classical Growth Model).

The Nobel Committee honoured Prof. Phelps for explaining how economic policies to deal with inflation and unemployment today, can have big effects on behaviour and welfare in future. Phelps recognised that inflation does not only depend on unemployment but also on the expectations of firms and employees about price and wage increases. His work is characterized by a strong practical content. He has devoted his attention to real problems. As observed by John Kenneth Galbraith: "Economics deals with matters which men consider very close to their lives".

Phelps has emphasized that not only the issue of savings and capital formation but also the balance between inflation and unemployment are fundamental issues about the distribution of welfare over time. Previously economists believed that a fall in unemployment would cause a rise in inflation. As a result, Governments tended to regard inflation as a secondary problems to unemployment. But in the late 1960s Phelps challenged that view.

Main Economic Ideas

Building on the foundations laid in the late 1970s by Stanley Fischer (1977) and Edmund Phelps and John Taylor (1977), a large number of authors, young and middle-aged alike, since the late 1970s have produced an outpouring of research literature on "New Micro Economics" within the Keynesian tradition that attempts to build the microeconomic foundations of wage and price stickiness. The adjective "New-Keynesian" properly juxtaposes the body of research with its arch-opposite, the new classical approach. The label "new-Keynesian" should be attributed to Michael Parkin.

The word, 'new' rather than 'neo' to describe the recent work in the classical tradition distinguishes it from what Paul Samuelson in the early post war period called "neoclassical synthesis" of old-Keynesian Macroeconomics and Classical Microeconomics". Hence, the word 'new' rather than 'neo' is used for the recent work in the tradition, juxtaposed to the new classical approach. Edmund Phelps, New Keynesian incorporated the insights of modern market theory where consumers, producers and labour market participants make decisions with incomplete information.

TRADE-OFF BETWEEN INFLATION AND UNEMPLOYMENT

Phelps pointed out that current inflation depends not only on unemployment but also on inflation expectations. Such dependence is due to the fact that wages and prices are adjusted only infrequently. Consequently, when adjustments are made, they are based on inflation forecasts. Thus, the higher the anticipated rate of inflation, the higher the unemployment required to reach a certain actual inflation rate. Phelps formulated the so-called expectations-augmented Phillips curve. The intertemporal perspective implies that current inflation expectations affect the future trade off between inflation and unemployment. A higher current inflation rate typically leads to higher inflation expectations in the future, so that it has then becomes more difficult to achieve the objectives of stabilization policy.

The argument that a "long-run" relationship between the unemployment rate and the inflation rate is very different from the short-run relationship has been associated mainly with the names of Milton Friedman and Edmund Phelps. They independently developed the same idea.

The existence of a short-run trade-off between inflation and unemployment depends crucially on how expectations are formed. The breakdown of the empirical Phillips relationship between inflation and unemployment in the late 1960s coincided with new theoretical work, notably by M. Friedman (1968) and E.Phelps (1967), which denied the existence of a permanent trade-off between inflation and unemployment of the simple Philips curve of 1960s.

Milton Friedman and Edmund Phelps had criticized the idea of a permanent inflation-unemployment trade-off in the mid-1960s on the ground that the behaviour of inflation expectations, themselves endogenous to the structure of the economy, would render any such trade-off temporary.

The apparent short-run trade-off between output and inflation as predicted in the neoclassical theory needs to be rationalized. This has resulted in a reworking of neoclassical choice theory to include uncertainty and incomplete information. This approach has come to be known as the "New Micro Economics".

The major innovation of the new micro economics is that the assumption of complete information is dropped. The essential feature of the neo classical theory stating that markets clear is retained, though the market clearing equilibrium is only temporary if expectations turn out to be wrong. A crucial feature of this new approach is that when expectations are being falsified by the outcome of the events, only short-run temporary equilibria can exist. Economic agents base their buying and selling plans on their expectations about the future, while trying to maximize their utility over time. Market prices adjust to reconcile the demands and supplies that are conditioned by expectations. When expectations turn out to have been wrong, agents revise their plans. The 'new micro economics' analyses the dynamic changes in the economy by means of market which are always in market clearing equilibrium.

A major weakness of the new search theory is that it does not explain why workers become in employed through either layoffs or redundancy and it offers no explanation of job rationing. A crucial factor is that all unemployed workers while searching for jobs have a reservation wage that is compared with the wage available from current job offers. If they reject current employment opportunities on the grounds that they pay less than their reservation wage, they are choosing to prolong their unemployment.

An alternative explanation of the Philips relation to that given by Search Theory is the bargaining popular approach by L.Kahm (1980). This gives explicit recognition to the role of trade unions while challenging "Philips Curve" (1958)-the idea of a stable inflations-unemployment trade-off, Phelps (1967) added the expected rate of inflation.

Conclusion

The relationship between inflation and unemployment and the trade off between the welfare of current and future generations are key issues in macroeconomic research. They have a strong influence on the choice of macroeconomic policy. Both issues concern trade off between different objectives. In particular, he had the insight that the balance between inflation and unemployment reflects a fundamentally intertemporal problem. No doubt, Phelps is truly a phenomenon with a lasting impact on the economics of modern age.

QUESTIONS

1. Explain Schumpeter's theory of economic development.
2. "Choice reveals preference" examine.
3. Critically examine Hicks' contributions to economic thought.
4. Explain the important contributions of Milton Friedman in the field of monetary economics.
5. What are the main contributions of A.K. Sen towards Indian Economic Development.
6. Review the contributions of Mundell in the fields of international and macro economics.
7. Give an account of the contributions of nobel laureates Since 2000.
8. Describe the ideas of Edmund Phelps.

Chapter-27

INDIAN ECONOMIC THOUGHT

INTRODUCTION

This chapter analyses the main contributions to economic thought by some important Indian thinkers.

(a) KAUTILYA'S ARTHASHASTRA

The main source of information regarding the economic thought in ancient India are the Vedas, the Upanishads, the Epics and treatises like Kautilya's Arthashastra. Thiruvalluvar's Thirukkural throws light on the economic thought in ancient South India. The Vedas depict the life and work in the early Vedic period. Kautilya's Arthashastra gives details of the political, social, economic and military organisation of the Mauryan Empire.

Kautilya's Arthashastra is the chief source of information. He was the Chief Minister of Chandra Guptha Maurya. He was responsible for getting Chandra Guptha the Kingdom of Land. Kautilya has given a vivid description of the administrative procedures, duties of Kings, Ministers and Government officers. Kautilya's Arthashastra is based on earlier treatises and is divided into fifteen chapters covering 430 pages. The treatment in his book is quite comprehensive and systematic. It covers almost every aspect of theory and practice of Economics. It also deals with the Government of towns and villages, law courts, rights of women, maintenance of the old and helpless, marriage and divorce, public finance, maintenance of Army and Navy, diplomacy, agriculture, spinning and weaving and a number of other subjects. His book contains ample ideas on a welfare state.

ECONOMIC IDEAS OF KAUTILYA'S ARTHASHASTRA

1. Wealth

The concept of wealth as held by Kautilya was very wide in its scope. To him, wealth included money, commodity, the acquired wealth, public or private property, precious metals, the accumulated wealth, negotiable and transferability and the power of appropriation. He also included labour and forest produce in wealth. To him, "wealth is to be acquired grain by grain, as learning is to be acquired every moment. Acquisition of wealth is always beneficial if it is acquired for the sake of a good wife, a son or a friend, or for giving away charity". Thus Kautilya justified wealth which was earned through proper means, and also he thought that accumulation of wealth was a safe method for protecting the people against famines.

2. Varta

Ancient thinkers used the word Varta to mean the science of national economy. Kautilya included agriculture, animal husbandry and trade in Varta. According to Mahabharat, Varta was the roof of the world, a thing which was most essential for economic stability. It was necessary for the King to learn about the essentials of national economy from scholars and specialists in order to discharge his functions successfully as a ruler.

3. Agriculture and Animal Husbandry

Agriculture and Animal Husbandry formed the important components of Varta. These were regarded as the basic sources of new wealth. Agriculture was given the pride of place among the occupations adopted by the people. Shukracharya was of the firm belief that by birth nobody was a Brahmin or Kshatria or Shudra. It was on the basis of their occupation that they are distinguished from one another. Agriculture occupies a place of first stage importance in Kautilya's Arthashastra. The art of agriculture reached a high degree of perfection and our ancient scholars well understood the minutest details of agricultural techniques. They have mentioned in their books, rotation of crops, intensive and extensive cultivation, large and small scale farming, use of fertilizers, crop diseases and their eradication, irrigation by rivers and tanks, cattle farming, seed selection, evils of the fragmentation of holdings etc. To them the largest source of State income was land revenue.

In those days the state and the community were responsible for the development of agriculture for which the waste lands were to be cleared. The value of the land was determined on the basis of its fertility. The fair prices of agricultural produce were fixed by the state to save cultivators from the clutches of traders.

4. Labour

The ancient sages appreciated the dignity of labour for 100 years. Manu and Kautilya have dealt with the methods for the regulation of wages and for the settlement of disputes between employers and workers.

Kautilya did not recommend slave labour. But hired labour was there. Kautilya had laid down a code of labour discipline. For instance, he suggested that a wage worker who abandoned his work before the term had expired, was to pay the whole amount of stipulated wages to his employer and a fine to the King. On the other hand, if an employer dismissed a workman whom he had hired before the expiration of the term agreed upon, he must pay the full amount of wages stipulated and a fine to the King, unless the workman was to blame.

5. Trade

Gold and bullion was regarded as a means of producing wealth, and trade was the sum of industrialised capital. Kautilya devoted a good deal of attention to the problems of trade such as regulation and development of trade by the state and the different taxes to be levied on the commodities that entered into trade. He even advocated state trading in certain commodities through departmental agencies. Kautilya advised the state to build rest houses and store houses for the caravans of traders for whom police escorts were recommended. Also trade was approved only when the supplies of commodities were left over after satisfying local needs.

6. Value

Regarding value, the ancient thinkers of India seemed to have some ideas on value which are relevant to modern times. We should take the value of each commodity according to time and place but there can be no value (price) of that which is incapable of being exchanged. Again whatever one pays for obtaining a thing must be taken to be the cost. The value is determined by the easiness, or otherwise of obtaining, and also by the inherent utility of it (Shukracharya).

7. Population

The ancient thinkers had no fear of growing population. The Vedas were for more married couple. Population could not grow beyond a reasonable limit owing to the high death rate due to constant wars between small states and loss of life due to the inadequate medical facilities. Kautilya recommended that the king should establish colonies for facilitating immigration.

8. Slavery

In Ancient India, a slave was treated as a member of family, and was not asked to do a degrading work. A slave was a hereditary domestic servant who could not use his personal earnings and could not own property. But economically he was better than a hired labourer. Slaves could not be employed by Buddhist monks. In ancient India all slaves were as good as others and hence Megasthenes wrote that slavery was unknown in ancient India.

9. Welfare State

The ancient Indian writers had a clear idea of the welfare state. According to Shukracharya, the state is a tree of which the king is the root and the counsellors are the main branches, the commanders are the lesser branches, the armies are blossoms and flowers, the people are the fruits and the land is the seed". The same idea has been echoed by Kautilya, "In the happiness of his (king's) subjects lies his happiness, in their welfare, his welfare".

To Kautilya, the state was to promote the economic welfare of the people and fully regulate its economic life. The state had to give subsidies for the development of trade, agriculture, irrigation, mines, cattle welfare etc.

Economic Functions of State

Kautilya's concept of state is founded on Industrial edifice. According to him, there are guiding principles for the state, first, the state should undertake those industries which help directly in making the nation self-sufficient and self-reliant, e.g., gold, silver, dimonds and iron and other metals should be in the charge of the state. Secondly, the activities related to farming, spinning and weaving, arts and crafts should be left to the individuals and the right of the ownership should be recognised. Finally, the state should see that the activities relating to production, distribution and consumption are carried out efficiently and in accordance with the rules framed by it. The duties of men, women, saints and sages, lords and the kings used to be clearly defined so that their observance may help in achieving the objective. The private people can also undertake the production of goods under the supervision of the State. In addition to the above function, the State regulated the wages and working condition of workers, and helped the farmers in times of calamities.

10. Public Finance

Taxation was one of the most important sources of revenue of the state. It was known as 'rajkar'. The rate of tax was determined in accordance with the dictates of Hindu religion. Land Revenue was an important source of taxation in ancient India. The early writers have described the features of a good tax system. "The tax system should be such as not to prove a great burden to the public. The king should act like the bee which collects honey without inconveniencing the plant". Taxes were the remuneration for the services rendered by the king as a public functionary for providing internal security to his subjects. Kautilya suggested forced loans for meeting deficit budgets.

He divided income from taxes into the following three kinds:

(a) Income from taxes on commodities produced in the country.

(b) Income from taxes on commodities produced in the capital and

(c) Income from taxes imposed on imports and exports

The usual import tax was 20 per cent which varied from time to time in case of precious stones and rare commodities. Heavy taxes were imposed on the importation of luxury goods. The policy of the state was to discourage the import of luxury goods and those which were harmful for the welfare of the State. Kautilya suggested an efficient machinery for audit. Two principles were followed in connection with the realisation of taxes:

(1) A tax should be levied once a year, and should not prove burdensome (ii) Taxes should be levied according to the ability to pay.

Sources of Revenue included taxes on land, forests, monopoly and property, customs and excise duties, fines, profits of state, factories and crown monopolies, from manufacture and sale of saffron, salt, intoxicants, trade in horses, fine wool and elephants and port dues, road tolls, fruit and tree tax etc. Similarly public expenditure included public administration, defence, salaries of ministers, Government departments, maintenance of national store houses and granaries and acquisition of valuable-ornaments, gems and precious stones. Whatever amount was left unused, was deposited either with the treasury or the war chest.

Town Planning and Social Security

Town planning included the re-orientation of main roads and streets and the subdivision of city areas. The villages were grouped together from the point of view of economic necessities and for national defence. The metropolitan city was established after a detailed and careful planning, and due emphasis was laid on the maintenance of sanitation and prevention of fire.

Kautilya believed that it was the prime duty of the state to set up charitable institutions and poor houses. Further, the state should protect the weak and the aged, to provide jobs to the unemployed.

Private Property

Ancient economic thinkers supported the institution of private property, both movable and immovable. The right in land was transferable and saleable. As revealed by ancient law books, the following eight sources of property were recognised in those days—gift, conquest, inheritance, partition, purchase, gain of agriculture and trade, discovery and seizure. The owner of land on which a treasure was discovered, could get the large share of it, not the whole of it.

Justification on Interest

Though interest was justified in ancient India, no interest was allowed on the mortgaged property. The rate of interest was also varied from class to class depending upon the purpose for which money was borrowed, economic resources of the borrower etc. The same were the considerations for charging compound rate of interest. Thus, interest in those days was part of profit. If a loan made in kind or money was to be returned in kind, interest did not exceed half of the money value of the original capital.

Consumption and Production

For consumption purposes, family was regarded as an economic unit. Consumption should have four ideas, namely, Dharma, Artha, Kama, and Moksha. The individual was subordinate to the family or the community. As far as production was concerned, the four agents of production namely, land, labour, capital and organisation were recognised. Land was considered as the main source of wealth. The importance of labour was also duly recognised. "An employer not taking work from his labourer, or an employee not doing his employer's work, should be fined", The ancient writers believed that the accumulated wealth, earned through hard labour was sufficient for a man's life. The high rate of interest prevailed in the economy was due to shortage of private capital. So the state was asked to provide cash and kind to the farmers and cash to the industrialists.

Comparison of Valluvar and Kautilya

Sometimes a comparison is made between the economic ideas of Kautilya and Valluvar. The basic economic ideas of Valluvar are different from that of Kautilya.

1) Arthashastra ia based on the caste system but Valluvar does not speak of the caste system.
2) Thirukkural is based on ethics. For Valluvar good ethics is good economics. But Arthashastra emphasised that economics and politics are different from ethics.
3) Taxation by consent is the main feature of Kural. But taxation by fear is the central teaching in Arthashastra.

4) But both Valluvar and Kautilya accorded the pride of place to agriculture.

So we may conclude by saying that the fundamental economic ideas of Thiruvalluvar are similar to those of Adam Smith rather than of Kautilya. For both, economic ideas are based on moral philosophy. Both advocated individual freedom.

Critical Estimate

The ancient thinkers did not regard economics as a separate discipline. The study of economics was combined with the study of religion, ethics, philosophy, law, politics and public administration. According to Kautilya, the study of four sciences namely, philosophy, ethics, economics and politics was combined together and was essential for the salvation of individual. The economic teaching emphasised a moral life.

Secondly, the concept of welfare state was the kernal of the ancient Indian economic thought. The state was responsible for the economic prosperity of the people.

Finally, economic life as well as thought in ancient India was governed by moral sanctions and religious ideals. The social equilibrium was maintained by the system of 'Varna ashram' a system of mutual checks and balances emphasising the virtues of hard work.

(b) THIRUVALLUVAR

The economic ideas of Thiruvalluvar are found in his immortal work, Thirukkural, a book of ethics. Even though scholars differ widely over the estimation of the period of Thiruvalluvar, it is generally believed that, he belonged to the Sangam Age in TamilNadu, around 3rd century A.D. Thiruvalluvar's work is marked by pragmatic idealism.

Thirukkural contains three important parts, viz., Aram, Porul, and Inbam which literally means Dharma (Ethics), Artha (Polity) and Kama (Bondage or love), which are the aims of life of a Hindu. The fourth aim of life was Moksha or Veedu (Liberation). Thiruvalluvar deliberately excluded this fourth division in his book, as it is the exclusive area of spiritual literature. Thus Thiruvalluvar did not mix spiritualism with earthly things.

A large part of Valluvar's economic ideas are found in the second part of Thirukkural-the Porutpal. It deals with wealth.

Thiruvalluvar was a pragmatic thinker and his porutpal shows three characteristic features of the author. Firstly, Thirukkal has certain elements of classicism. So he can be identified as a classical economist. Secondly, his economic ideas were based under ethics and hence he can be called as normative economist. Finally, his treatise speaks about general welfare and hence he can be identified as a welfare economist. Thus he had in him, classicism, normatism and welfare ideal.

Thiruvalluvar was a fundamental thinker. He believed that rains were the basic support of life. Since rain furnishes food, it forms the basis for stable economic life. Agriculture which is the most fundamental economic activity depends on rain, "It is rain that both ruins and aids the ruined to rise".

Factors of Production

Thiruvalluvar has made many passing references about the factors of production viz., Land, Labour, Capital, Organisation, Time, Technology etc. He says, "Unfailing harvest, competent body of men, group of men whose wealth knows no diminution, are the components of an economy", (Kural 61). Further he says, "Executing the work at the proper time is sure to deliver goods (wealth)", "Nothing is impossible if done with the help of time and technology". Finally, he says, "anyone who executes at the appropriate time with appropriate technology, he can conquer the world." From this we can understand the importance given to factors of production by Thiruvalluvar.

He has also emphasised the importance of capital formation. He has insisted on the need for savings. He says, "Profit cannot be had without capital".

Agriculture

According to Thiruvalluvar, agriculture is the most fundamental economic activity. They are the axle-pin of the world, for on their prosperity revolves the prosperity of the other sectors of the economy, "The ploughmen alone", he says, "live as the freemen of the soil; the rest are mere slaves that follow on their toil."

Valluvar believed that agriculture is superior to all other occupations. "Husbandmen are the lynch –pin of society, for they support all those that take to other work, not having the strength to plough." He goes on to say," who ploughing eat their food, they truly live. The rest to others bend subservient, eating what they give. "Valluvar considered the 'agriculturists", "the intellectuals" and 'the capitalists' are the important ingredients of an economy.

Here we can see certain similarities between Thiruvalluvar's views and Physiocrats of France on agriculture. As the French Physiocrats glorified agriculture as the only productive occupation and other occupations as 'sterile', so also Thiruvalluvar highlighted the importance of agriculture. Like Physiocrats, Thiruvalluvar also had the belief that agriculture was superior to all other occupations.

Public Finance

Thiruvalluvar elaborately explained Public Finance under the headings Public Revenue, Financial Administration and Public expenditure. He has stated these as (1) creation of revenue (2) collection of revenue (3) management of revenue, and (4) public expenditure.

Valluvar was against the method of collecting tax compulsorily. He compared a king who collected taxes by force to a highway robber. The three main sources of revenue are : (1) Wealth that comes by itself; (2) Customs duties; (3) Tributes paid by the defeated kings, i.e., 'reparation'. It should be noted that Valluvar did not mention land revenue which was the main source of revenue in those days.

Public Expenditure

Valluvar recommended a balanced budget. "It is not a great misfortune for a state if its revenues are limited, provided the expenditure is kept within bounds." He gave certain guidelines for a budgetary policy. "Budget for a surplus, if possible, balance the budget at other times, but never budget for a deficit."

Valluvar advocated the following main items of public expenditure : 1) Defence 2) Public Works and 3) Social Services.

External Assistance

Valluvar was against seeking external assistance. According to Kural 739, countries seeking external assistance are not to be considered as countries at all. In other words, he advocated a self-sufficient economy.

Poverty and Begging

Valluvar considered freedom from hunger as one of the fundamental freedoms that should be enjoyed by every citizen. According to him 'poverty' is the root cause of all other evils which would lead to ever-lasting sufferings. Valluvar considered it foolish to redress the ills of poverty by begging. He condemned poverty and begging as the greatest curses of a society. It is wrong to say that some were made to beg by fate. If people were to live by begging, he said, "may the creator of the universe who has decreed so, go abegging and perish."

Wealth

Valluvar regarded wealth as only a means and not an end. He said, "Acquire a great fortune by noble and honourable means." He condemned hoarding and described hoarded wealth as profitless richness. To him industry is real wealth and labour is the greatest resource.

Ethics

The entire teachings of Thiruvalluvar was based on ethics. He was against unlawful and illegal methods of realising the objectives. There should be ethics not only in objectives, but also in realising those objectives. He considered drinking, gambling and prostitution as evils that did harm to the socio-economic life of a society.

Welfare State

Thiruvalluvar was for a welfare state. In a welfare state there will be no poverty, illiteracy, disease and industry. The important beautifying elements of a state are 1) perfect health of the people without disease 2) abundant wealth 3) good crop 4) prosperity and happiness and 5) full security for the people. Finally, one of his kurals shows the main characteristic features of a peaceful state. "It is that country which can be called a good country wherein there are no several parties, where there are no internal dissensions; where there are no internal enemies."

(c) DADABHAI NAOROJI (1825-1917)

Dadabhai Naoroji, "The grand old man of India" was one of the founders of Indian Nationalism. His teacher called him "The Promise of India". Born in a Parsi family of Bombay, Naoroji became the first Indian Professor in Elphinston college, Bombay, the founder of the East India Association (1886), the first Indian to be elected as member of British Parliament (1893), the first Indian member of the Royal Commission, and above all, first Indian economist of the 19th century. He was elected President of the Indian National Congress thrice in 1886, 1893 and 1906.

Naoroji's economic ideas are contained in his book, "Poverty and Un-British Rule in India" (first published in 1901 and reprinted in 1962). Naoroji analysed the effects of the British rule on the Indian economy. He pointed out how the Britishers were responsible for causing drain on the Indian resources and generating poverty in India. He also suggested some remedial measures for the improvement of the Indian economy.

National Income of India

Naoroji was not satisfied with the official estimates regarding the national income of India during the British rule. "The Indian Economist" was the only journal which gave such knowledge in those days. Naoroji regarded this information regarding the country's prosperity as insufficient and misleading. He pointed out that unless complete information about (a) the average annual income per head and (b) "the requirements of labourer to live in working health and not as a starved beast of burden" was supplied every year, it was useless to make unsounded statement that India was progressing.

On the basis of the official data, Naoroji himself calculated the per capita income for the years 1867-70 at Rs. 20 only. On the other hand, the basic requirements of an ordinary labourer, as calculated by him was about Rs. 34. He concluded that even for such food and clothing which was provided to a criminal, a good seasonal production was not enough. The high and middle classes get a larger share, while the poor masses did not get enough for their basic necessaries of life. It was in this context of growing disparities of income that Naoroji spoke of two Indians one the prosperous and the other poor. The prosperous India was the India of the British and the foreigners, while the poor India was the India of the Indians.

But while calculating the percapita income, Naoroji had equally apportioned the value of agricultural produce and manufactures among all the people without taking care of the actual number of persons employed in agriculture, industries and other professions. Though the method adopted by Naoroji was criticised by F.C. Danvers, an employee of India office, Dr. V.K.R.V. Rao had supported the method adopted by Naoroji and paid a great tribute to him as a statistician. While replying Danver's criticism as to how people were able to live with Rs. 20 per annum when their actual expenditure was Rs. 34, Naoroji said, "As the balance of income every year available for the use of people of India did not suffice for the works of the year, the capital – wealth of country is drawn upon, and the country goes on becoming poorer and poorer and more and more weakened in its capacity of production."

Another criticism was that Naoroji did not include in the calculation of total income of the country, items like railway wealth, government stock, house property, trade profit, salaries, non-agricultural income etc. Replying to this criticism, Naoroji maintained that mere movement of goods by the railways did not add to the existing wealth of the country. The railways in no way increased the material wealth of the country. Regarding the Government stock, he believed that it did not increase the material wealth of the country. For example, the interest paid on a government bond was made from the revenue of the country. In the same way house property and internal trade did not create material production. He also said that profits of India's foreign trade were enjoyed by England. Regarding the payment of salaries and pensions, Naoroji argued that these were paid out of the revenue of the country.

Taxation, Military Expenditure and Public Department

A glaring example of exploitation of Indian resources and discrimination of the Indians is the taxation policy adopted by the British Government. While in England, taxes constituted 8 per cent of the income, in India it was about 15 per cent. He criticised the then Indian Government for abolishing the duties on cotton imports from Manchester as it was harmful to the newly established Indian factories.

According to Naoroji, the main cause of India's poverty was the excessive expenditure on European services and interest paid on public debts. In 1870 itself Gladstone admitted that India was "too much burdened." In 1893 he said that the military expenditure of India was alarming. So Naoroji suggested that the military expenditure should be limited and England should pay her share for the maintenance of British army in India and for other military services.

In the case of railways, Naoroji argues that the entire benefit was enjoyed by the Britishers, and the burden of foreign debts was borne by India.

Drain Theory

Naoroji was famous as an economist for his "Drain Theory". He developed this theory to explain the conditions of poverty in India. The drain theory emphasized the fact that the management and institutions of British India were prone to a mechanism of the economic drain.

Naoroji felt that under the British rule, India had the costliest administration in the world. It had a disastrous effect on the Indian economy. Naoroji estimated that the drain which was to the tune of 3 million pounds in the beginning of the 19th century increased to 30 million pounds at the end of the last century.

The drain of wealth took place is several ways. 1. Large remittances were made by European officials of their savings in India. 2. Large remittances were made in the form of salaries and pensions. 3. India had to pay for government expenditure in England also. 4. Non-official Europeans made remittances from their business profits in India. The money which had gone out of India, to England came back as British capital and foreigners had monopolized trade and industry. It had once again resulted in the drain of wealth. Thus the drain became continuous and it had affected capital formation in India.

Naoroji collected a lot of statistical data to prove his drain theory. He examined the imports and exports between 1835 and 1872 and pointed out that the value of exports was greater than that of imports by 500 million pounds. The drain would have been greater, if interest had been calculated on the amount. No country could bear such a drain upon its resources without sustaining very serious injury.

Further, when the railways were built in India, Indians had to spend large sums on salaries and allowances to European staff for all the top posts were manned by the Britishers.

Naoroji felt that the former rulers who plundered India's wealth by their invasions now and then were now better than the British rulers. He said, "The former rulers were like butchers hacking here and there, but the English with their scientific scalpel cut to the very heart ...... there is no wound to be seen, and soon the plaster of the high talk of civilisation, progress and what not covers up the wound."

Thus according the Naoroji, the economic resources of India were drained in two ways: (a) through internal drain, i.e., through the transfer of purchasing power by means of taxation, interest payments and profits from poor classes/regions to the rich classes/ regions. (b) through external drain, i.e., through unrequired exports which produced no equivalent returns in the form of imports. The dynamics of the process of external drain is functionally related to a net transfer of funds, with its adverse effects on India's terms of trade. Thus while internal drain refers to the exploitation of poor regions or individuals by the rich within a country, external drain implies the exploitation of a poor country by the rich.

The effects of external drain on the Indian economy can be explained with the following model.

$$P > Y \qquad ...(1)$$

$$Y - T = E - (X - M) = (C + 1d) - (X - M) \qquad ...(2)$$

As a result of economic drain or unilateral transfer (T), national income (Y) remains below its total production (P). T is a leakage from Y. On the expenditure side, the corresponding leakage is export surplus (X-M), where X stands for the value of exports and M for the value of imports. Export surplus is to be deducted from total expenditure E; C and Id, i.e., consumption and domestic investment, being the constituents of E.

In this model, T has to be interpreted as net transfer because in actual practice its size depended upon the reverse flow of sterling loans as a balancing factor. If X-M is insufficient to be equal to T, or if there is an exceptional rise in T, the gap had to be filled by sterling loans. This inflow of capital in the form of loans produces adverse balance of trade in the borrowing country. As Haberler remarked, " A country making large unilateral payments will tend to import capital in one way or another. In this way, the direct effect of these payments on the balance of trade and services will be suspended or weakened". Haberler's conclusion is fully applicable to India.

J.S.Mill opined that, "it was an extraction of the life-blood from the veins of national industry which no subsequent introduction of nourishment is furnished to rescue." Naoroji quoted F.J.Shore, J.B.Norton, Robert Knought, Sir George Campbell, Colonel Band Smith and many others who had written to the Government that India was getting from bad to worse; and the poverty of the country and its people had gone up to "an extent almost unparalleled".

Naoroji himself wrote – "Even an ocean if it lost some water everyday which never returned to it, would be dried up in time, under similar conditions, wealthy England even would be soon reduced to poverty."

Naoroji suggested the following measures to remove India's poverty and to reduce the drain.

1. Indians and Englishmen should be paid equal salary for the same type of job. Regarding the Britishers employed in India and the Indians employed in England, he suggested that a fair and reasonable apportionment between the two should be made.
2. Britishers were getting high salaries and so they should not be paid any pension.
3. No country could invade India through the sea and so she should not be charged for the maintenance of the India navy.
4. Indians should be given due representation in the government and foreign capital should come but not the foreign capitalist who took everything from India.

Criticism of British Administration

Through the speeches in the House of Commons, Naoroji severely criticized the British administration in India. The main attack was on the unjust, destructive and exploitative attitude of the East India Company. It was, on the one hand destroying the internal trade of the country and on the other hand, employing the imported labour in administration. Thus Indians were denied their due share in the administration of the country. He felt that it was wrong to consider India as Nature's tragedy and the Indian agriculture, a gamble in the hands of the monsoon. He said that, "If India did not progress under the Englishmen there was no justification for their existence here".

Critical Estimate

Naoroji was the first economic thinker who provided the pattern of economic thought for modern India. As he emphasized the material concept of wealth and the circulation of National income, we can say that he had been considerably influenced by the physiocratic school. He was the first Indian to calculate the percapita and national income. He believed that the economic phenomena were linked with the moral, social and political factors. The inductive method predominated his writings. His main contribution was the Drain theory. He gave a picture of the Indian economy in a realistic sense.

(d) MAHADEV GOVIND RANADE (1842-1901)

Mahadev Govind Ranade has been called as the father of Renaissance in western India. He influenced everyone who came in his contact. Ranade was born at Nasik on 18th January, 1842. After taking his M.A. Degree from Bombay University in 1865, he qualified himself for the degree of Law. He taught economics at the University of Bombay for some time. Later on, he entered judicial service and became the judge of the Bombay High Court. Since then, Ranade was popularly known as Justice Ranade. He was in that post till his death in 1901.

In 1878, Ranade started the publication of the 'Quarterly Journal'. In 1884 he helped in founding the 'Deccan Education Society'. The aim of this society was to provide western education to the rising generation without exposing it to the antinational bias of English educators. From this, it is deduced that while recognising the merits of western education, Ranade wanted to adopt it without loosing the spirit of rationalism.

The economic ideas of Ranade are found in his most important works : "Essay on Indian Political Economy" (1898) and "The Rise of Maratha Power" (1900).

Economic Ideas

Method and Scope of Political Economy

After a careful study of the economic systems of various European countries, Ranade believed that inductive or historical method was the best. In his words, "The method to be followed is not the deductive but the historical method which takes into account the past in its forecast of the future; relativity and not absoluteness, characterises the conclusion of the economic science".

Again, while the classical economists believed in the universal application of economic laws, Ranade considered economic laws were only relative. In other words, he believed in the doctrine of relativity. Ranade criticised Adam Smith, David Ricardo, Malthus, James Mill and Meculloch for their absolutism and assumptions. He said that their ideas were applicable only to a static society. He held the view that in India, institutions like family and caste were more powerful than the individual in the determination of his economic position. Wealth was not the only thing to be aimed at.

He said that the traditional assumptions of economic thoery were true only for England. Being influenced by the ideas of Adam Muller and List, Ranade emphasised the many sided development of productive powers. Further he suggested that the study of theory and practice should go side by side. "Theory" says Ranade, "is only relation to proximate causes".

Economic Education

Ranade emphasised the importance of economic education in promoting the wealth of a nation. He said, "the nation's economic education is of far more importance than the present gain of its individual members, as represented by the quantity of wealth measured by its value in exchanges. In a sound and normal condition all the three departments of national activity must be fully developed. Commerce and manufactures are, if possible, more vital in their bearing on education, on the intelligence and skill and enterprise of the nation than agriculture."

Economic Development

Ranade held that economic development was a complex phenomenon and it had many inter-related causes. It was connected with economic institutions. Thus economic development of India depended on economic, social and political institutions. It was the duty of the state, to direct and channelise the activities of individuals and institutions, towards a well determined goal. In India, since the private initiative was shy, the state should undertake measures for the industrial development of the country.

"The State", said Ranade," is now more and more recognised as the national organ for taking care of national needs in all matters in which individual and cooperative efforts are most likely to be so effective and economical as national effort..... To relegate them to the simple duty of maintaining peace and order is really to deprive the community of many of the advantages of the social union".

India's Poverty

Dutt and Naoroji believed that poverty of India was the result of the British rule. Ranade believed that mass poverty had been there in India even before the British rule. Ranade thought that India inherited poverty from the past generations, which had increased on account of foreign rule. According to Ranade the main causes for poverty were the predominance of agriculture, backward state of industries, lack of credit facilities and defective land policy. Predominance of agriculture was due to the economic policy of the government, which encouraged the production of raw materials to be transported to England. Secondly, industries were in a backward state due to their inability to face severe foreign competition. Thirdly, the credit system was highly unorganised and banking facilities were inadequate. Lastly, the land policy was also defective because the assessment of revenue was highly arbitrary.

Remedies

In order to eradicate poverty and to make India economically prosperous, Ranade made certain suggestions. He wanted a balanced and well planned development of agriculture, industry and commerce. He thought that without reducing the number dependent on agriculture, there could not be agricultural development. He advocated state action in order to promote large scale farming. Thus Ranade opposed the laissez-faire policy of the state and believed that the state should play an active role in removing poverty and promoting the welfare of the state.

In order to absorb the surplus agricultural population, Ranade suggested the establishment of agro-based industries by the state. Further he advocated changes in land policy to serve the interests of the cultivators. He suggested a liberal land policy and a permanent Ryotwari system. Fifty percent of the profit from land should go to the cultivators and the farmers might be allowed to pay their tax in kind, if it was convenient for them. Further he advocated re-organisation of credit system and formation of committees of capitalists to finance agriculture.

Ranade opposed the policy of free trade because it was harmful to the local industries. So he advocated a policy of protection to the Indian industries. Not only that, he wanted the government to follow a positive policy for promotion of industrial development of India. The indigenous resources should be utilised to produce commodities in state factories. For the proper utilisation of resources of the various regions, Ranade suggested the redistribution of population. He advocated a balanced redistribution of population by sending people from thickly populated areas to sparsely populated areas.

Conclusion

Ranade occupies a significant place in the history of economic thought. In order to make economic studies more realistic and meaningful Ranade suggested the study of economic problems in the national context. He was really a national economist. He has been characterised by Sir J.C. Coyajee as an economic relativist and by Prof. D.G. Karve as the first economist who suggested planning. Many of Ranade's suggestions were put into practice. His suggestion for re-organisation of credit system led to the establishment of land mortgage banks. His advocacy of many-sided economic development and state action helped to a great extent in the eradication of poverty. Besides being an eminent economist and able historian, he was a leader of thought and great patriot. We may conclude in the words of Prof. Karve, that Ranade was, "a great man, a fervent patriot, a religious reformer, a leader of thought, a guide of men, an able historian, an eminent economist and the prophet of liberal India."

(e) ROMESH CHANDRA DUTT (1848-1909)

R.C. Dutt belonged to an eminent educated Bengal family. He was born in 1848 in Calcutta. He joined the Indian Civil Service in 1869 and served in many capacities. In 1899, he was elected as the President of the Indian National Congress. In his later years, he was appointed as a lecturer in Indian History at the University of London. The economic ideas of Dutt are found in his two important books : (1) The Economic History of India – 2 volumes and (2) Famines in India – 2 volumes. Gadgil described Dutt's Economic History of India as "almost the first history of a colonial empire." Thus while the first book deals with the economics of colonisation, the second one deals with the conditions of agricultural population in India and the causes and remedies of famines on India.

R.C. Dutt's another book "Famines in India" provided such a vivid description of the conditions of agricultural population in India that Prince Kropotkin of Russia wrote to Dutt that, "the conditions of your agricultural population are awfully terribly similar to those of the Russian peasants, and I now will often think that whatever we do in Russia for awakening the consciousness of the agrarian evil—and anywhere in Europe as well will be in an indirect way for hundreds of millions of people whom we cannot approach without feeling love for them."

ECONOMIC IDEAS

R.C. Dutt believed that there was a close relationship between political and economic phenomena. The social and economic equilibrium was dynamic. He did not follow a systematic method of study. Eventhough, he did not favour government interference in the private activities, under special circumstances he suggested that the government might remove obstructions so that the economic force might work satisfactorily.

Problem of Poverty

Dutt was chiefly concerned with the problem of India's poverty. In his book "Famines in India", he analysed the causes for the frequency of famines in India. The chief cause was the British rule and its policies.

Dutt referred to the following as the causes for India's poverty: (a) recurrence of famines (b) low productivity (c) land tax system (d) decay of cottage industries etc. Among the causes responsible for low productivity of land, he pointed out unfavourable climate, old agricultural techniques, poor soil, inadequate equipments etc. In his opinion, the low standard of living of farmers was due to high density of population, low agricultural prices, land tenure system and agrarian structure.

Though it was true that famines occur due to failure of monsoon, they were aggravated by resourcelessness of Indian peasants. He historically discussed all these facts and showed that the agrarian structure of the country was a great hurdle for economic development and welfare.

The Indian tax payer was taxed 40 per cent more than the tax payer of Great Britain and Ireland. The heavy burden of taxes was due to the expensive financial administration. The poverty of India was aggravated by the extravagant, selfish and unsound financial administrative policies of Britain. He felt that nearly half of the revenue received in India was remitted out of the country.

He held that in many ways the sources of Indian national wealth had been narrowed and the Indian Industries declined due to the selfish commercial policy adopted by the British Government. In the words of Dutt, "all our village industries have been killed by a free competition with the steam and machinery of England. Our cultivators and even our village industrial classes therefore virtually depend on the soil as the one remaining source of their subsistence".

Further the village self-government also became a victim of the British rule in India. In "Economic History of India", Dutt remarked' "one of the saddest results of British rule in India is the effacement of that system of village self-government which was developed earliest and preserved longest in India among all the countries of the earth."

Remedies

Dutt suggested many measures to eradicate poverty from Indian soil. He outlined a complete overhauling of the economic structure of the Indian society. The principal suggestions are : (1) revival of cottage industries to remove unemployment and underemployment (2) extension of irrigaton facilities to reduce dependence on monsoon (3) economy in government expenditure and reduction of purchase stores in England (4) the rate of interest on public debt should be lowered.

Dutt suggested a comprehensive scheme of reforms in the land revenue system:

1) Land settlement should not be for more than 30 years.
2) The cess on land tax should not exceed 6 percent
3) In those areas where the permanent settlement had not been introduced, the revenue collected by the land lords on behalf of the state, should not exceed 15 percent of the produce.
4) As per the directions of the state, in those areas where the land revenue was collected, it should not exceed 20 percent and the average revenue for the district should not exceed 10 percent.

Further, Dutt suggested the withdrawal of excise duties on the Indian mill industries, reduction in the rate of interest on public debt, creation of a sinking fund, sharing of the civil and military expenditure incurred in that country by Great Britain, larger employment of Indians in civil services, prohibition of railway construction from the state loans etc.

Conclusion

R.C. Dutt may be regarded as one of the builders of modern India. He has combined history, politics and economics to demonstrate the impact of British rule in India, and the causes of India's poverty. He did not stop with analysing causes, but suggested remedies also. He was the first to produce an economic history of far-reaching importance. His experience as a successful administrator helped him considerably in passing sound judgement on questions of practical economic importance. Dutt has secured an eminent place for his thought in the economic and political history of India.

(f) GOPAL KRISHNA GOKHALE (1866-1915)

Gopal Krishna Gokhale was born at Kolhapur in Ratnagiri district on 9th May, 1866. He had his higher education at Rajaram College, Kolhapur, Deccan College, Poona and Elphinstone College, Bombay. He taught history and economics at the Ferguson College, Poona from 1866 to 1902. He was elected as a member of the legislative council of Bombay in 1899. He became a member of the viceroy's council in 1901. In 1905, he was chosen as the president of the Indian National Congress. He founded the "Servants of India Society" in the same year. He visited England several times to give evidence before the Welby Commission, Decentralisation Commission and for other purposes. He died on 19th November, 1915.

Though short-lived, the life of Gokhale was a brilliant one. He became a graduate at 18, professor at 20, secretary of the provisional conference at 22, editor of the Quarterly of the "Poona Sarvajanik Sabha" at 24, secretary of National Congress at 29, one of the witnesses of the Welby Commission at 30, member of the Provincial Legislative Council at 34, Imperial legislator at 36, president of the Indian National Congress and founder of the "Servants of India Society at 39, and member of a Royal Commission on Public Services at 46.

Gandhi was very much impressed with the personality of Gokhale and wrote, "He seemed to me all I wanted as a political worker – pure as crystal, gentle as a lamb, brave as a lion and chivalrous to a fault."

Economic Ideas

In economic matters, Gokhale was a disciple of Ranade. He was an expert in fiscal economics. He was interested in financial control and fiscal administration in India. He suggested a number of reforms in taxation and budgetary policies.

Indian Finance

With regard to Indian Budget, Gokhale held the view that, it should be passed item by item. In such a case, people having sound knowledge of Indian conditions would get an opportunity to express their opinion on various items of expenditure. Suggestions made by non-official members should be referred to a committee of control.

Gokhale was not in favour of surplus budgets. He held that a policy of surplus budget was unsound. He believed that a surplus budget would demoralise even the most conscientious government for resorting to wasteful expenditure. He thought that a succession of surplus budgets would made the government indulge in extravagant expenditure. He thought it would be, "Specially true of countries like India where public revenues are administered under no sense of responsibility, such as exists in the West, to the governed." Gokhale was against using the budget surpluses for repaying the debt incurred for the construction of Railways. As the railways were a commercial undertaking, it should meet its debt commitments from its own income and not from the proceeds of taxation.

The finances of the local bodies and provinces were poor. So Gokhale suggested an equitable distribution of tax revenue between the centre and provincial governments and local bodies. So he suggested that land revenue, excise and revenue from forests might be given to the provinces. Opium, salt, customs, post and telegraphs might be given to the Imperial government. The quinquennial revenue settlement might be given to the local bodies.

Decentralisation of Power

Gokhale was an advocate of decentralisation of power. He suggested the creation of punchayats at the village level and then local boards and district councils. He suggested the creation of a council of members in the provinces to assist the Governors. He held that the provincial legislation should discuss important matters relating to finance and the budgets.

In 1896, the British Government decided to increase the duty on salt to meet the deficit of 1.5 million pounds which arose as a result of the annexation of Burma. Gokhale opposed this as it would place a heavy burden on the poor. Again in 1879, the government removed the 5 percent import duty on textiles and in 1896 imposed 3 1/2 percent excise duty on Indian cotton goods. Gokhale attacked these two measures.

Land Revenue

Gokhale suggested certain reforms in land revenue system also. He suggested that in the Ryotwari areas, where the cultivators paid revenue directly to the government, the revenue should not be more than 20 percent of the gross produce.

Public Expenditure

Gokhale was highly critical of large increase in public expenditure. He pointed out that India's monetary resources were mis-spent in extending northern and north eastern frontiers and in using troops for imperial purposes. He charged that the British government was looking after the interests of British traders and it did not bother about the Indian tax payer. So he emphasised the need for controlling public expenditure in India.

A Royal Commission was appointed in 1895, "to enquire into the administration and the management of the military and civil expenditure, and the apportionment of charges between the government of the United Kingdom, and of India for the purposes in which both are interested." Gokhale was one of the non-official witness of this commission. He divided his evidence into 3 parts—the first one dealing with the machinery of control, the second with the progress of expenditure and the last portion dealing with the apportionment of charges between England and India.

Gokhale pointed out that in England and other countries, public expenditure was controlled by tax payers. But in India, there was no popular control over the public expenditure. The Indian tax payers had no voice over this matter.

With regard to progress of expenditure, Gokhale expressed the view that ever since the transfer of power from the East India Company to the crown, there was a tremendous growth of public expenditure. The average expenditure increased to Rs. 73 crores from Rs. 3 crores.

As far as the apportionment of charges between the United Kingdom and India was concerned, Gokhale suggested that the India office charges should be shared on 50:50 basis, the army charges should be paid by the crown, the public debt of India should be charged to the crown and the crown should pay a reasonable share of the cost of maintaining the British army stationed in India.

Gokhale suggested the following remedies to check the growth of public expenditure : (1) The expenditure should be incurred with a spirit of economy. It should not be allowed to exceed the normal revenue except under conditions of war, famine etc. (2) Military expenditure should be cut down and the size of the army should be maintained to the extent of Indian requirements. (3) More number of Indians should be employed in public services. Indians should be paid salaries at same rate as were being paid to the Englishmen. (4) The audit should be made independent. The audit report should be laid before the parliament so that effective criticism of the financial administration may be possible.

Education

Gokhale stated that an illiterate nation could not make any progress. So educational facilities should be extended to all in the country. The expenditure on education must be an imperial charge. Education must receive same attention as army and railways.

Trade

Gokhale criticised free trade policy. He pointed out that a number of countries adopted protection for the growth of the economy. Gokhale suggested that for the development of industries, protection was necessary.

Conclusion

Gokhale made a remarkable contribution to the study of fiscal administration. His ideas on budget, fiscal policy, provincial autonomy and military expenditure are great. He realised the importance of well-informed public opinion of governmental policies. The importance of Gokhale lay in emphasising the need for a systematic public expenditure. His criticisms helped in shaping the future financial and economic policies of the country. Above all he was the political guru of Mahatma Gandhi.

(g) GANDHIAN ECONOMICS (1869-1948)

INTRODUCTION

The economic ideas of Gandhi and his followers may collectively be called Gandhian Economics. Gandhi himself was not a professional economist. He was a great political and spiritual leader. But consistent with his philosophy of truth and non-violence, he gave a set of economic ideas which are sharp in contrast against the traditional economics of the west. Gandhi's ideas have considerable influence on Indian thought and policy. Further, some of his followers, normally J.C. Kumarappa have attempted in recent years to refine and restate Gandhian economics as a counter theory to western economics and it is claimed to be more suitable for building up a more peaceful and stable future.

Mahatma Gandhi, The Father of the Nation was born in Porbander on October2, 1869. He came from a well-to-do family and had his early education in London. He settled down as a lawyer in South Africa, where he took part in a political movement against racial discrimination. He had been deeply infuenced by Christianity and the ideas of Tolstoy, Ruskin and Thoreau. So he devised the technique of non-violence as an active method of political agitation. Coming to India in 1906, Gandhi assumed political leadership of the country. At the same time, he developed his economic ideas as well. Gandhi continued to be the virtual guide and the inspiration of the Indian National Congress and the political movement in India upto his death.

INFLUENCES ON GANDHI

In his economic thought, Gandhi was greatly influenced by Ruskin's Unto This Last. From this book he learnt a) that the good of the individual is contained in the good of all; b) that a lawyer's work has the same value as the barber's in as much as all have the same right of earning their livelihood from their work, and that a life of labour, i.e., the life of the tiller of the soil and the handicraftsman is the life worthliving. Further Gandhi was inspired by the idea of Thoreau, Tolstoy and Kropotkin. Tolstoy's prinicples of simplicity, asceticism and equalitarianism became a part of Gandhi's philosophy. Besides Indian scriptures, Gita and Upnishads and Indian saints Kabir, Mira, Nanak also left a deep impression on Gandhi's mind.

Three Phases of Gandhi's Economic Thought

The economic ideas of Gandhiji developed in three phases : a) the negative phase upto 1919 during which he criticised the western pattern of economic development and adopted a non-materialistic attitude which is embodied in his book Hind Swaraj (1909). b) the positive phase (1919-1934) : During this phase, he presented an alternative to the western civilisation in the ideal of Swadeshi. c) the constructive phase (1934-1948): In this phase, Gandhi became more practical. He gave a contructive programme for village regeneration and put forward the ideal of Sarvodaya.

Economic Ideas of Gandhi

Gandhi considered human beings as wealth and not gold and silver. He said, "The final consummation of all wealth is in producing as many as possible, full-breadth, bright-eyed and happy-hearted human beings." He considered a country to be richest if it nourished the greatest number of happy individuals. Thus in Gandhian economic thought, man occupied a prominent position than wealth.

Gandhi did not isolate economics from other sciences, particularly from ethics. Economics should aim at material and moral progress of the society. It must help in producing and increasing wealth and also promote social justice and moral progress, "An economics that inculcates mammon – worship and enables the strong to amass wealth at the expense of the weak is a false and dismal science." Gandhi considered economics as a practical science as it suggested measures for maximizing human welfare. He laid great emphasis on human values and condemned the monetary basis of human relations.

Economic Laws

According to Gandhi, economic laws which aim at material progress as well as social harmony and moral advancement, should be formulated according to the laws of nature. There is no conflict between the laws of nature and laws of economics. The laws of nature are universal. The laws of economics, which deal with practical problems are not universal. The economic laws of a country are determined by the climatic, geological and temperamental conditions of that country. Hence they vary with the conditions of the nations.

Non-violent Economy

Gandhi advocated non-violence and hence his economics may be called economics of non-violence. The principle of non-violence is the principle of Gandhian philosophy. As there was no industry and no activity without certain violence, he wanted to minimize it. He believed that violence in any form breeds greater violence. He defined a non-violent occupation as one "which is fundamentally free from violence and which involves no exploitation or envy of others". The solution to Indian basic problems lies in the practice of non-violence. Gandhiji opposed capitalism as it resulted in exploitation of human labour. He believed that nature produced enough for the satisfaction of the people's wants and there would be no pauperism and starvation if everybody took only that much that was sufficient to him.

DECENTRALISATION: COTTAGE INDUSTRIES

Gandhi was not in favour of large scale industrialisation, as it was responsible for many socio-economic evils. He believed that large scale use of machinery led to drudgery and monotony. He was in favour of decentralised economy. In such an economy, exploitation of labour would be nil. His belief was strong in the context of the Indian economy. India has plenty of human resources but capital supply was poor, therefore labour intensive technology should be followed. Gandhiji advocated a decentralised economy. Production should be organised in a large number of places on a small scale. As Gandhiji was for the development of cottage and rural industries, he suggested delocalisation of industries. Gandhiji believed that decentralisation was essential for the survival of democracy and for the establishment of a non-violent state. Gandhi preferred the decentralisation of small units of production to the concentration of large scale units in few places. He wanted to carry the production units to the homes of the masses, particularly in villages. Cottage and village industries help increasing employment. Commodities can be produced cheaply as there is no need for a separate establishment; very few tools are needed. There is no problem of storage. Transport cost is negligible. There is no overproduction and wastes of competition. All these factors make the production by the small units economical and thus, provide logic to the Gandhian scheme of decentralisation of village and cottage industries, Integration of cottage industries with agriculture provides work to the farmer in their spare time and thus harnesses "all the energies that at present run to waste" In fact, these industries are best suited to the rhythm of rural life. These industries increase the income of the villages and satisfy their basic requirements. They not only remove poverty and unemployment from the villages but also make them self-sufficient economic units.

KHADI INDUSTRY

Every Indian needed at least 13 yards of cloth per year. Gandhiji believed that multiplication of mills could not solve the problem of cloth supply; therefore he stressed the development of Khadi industry. For Gandhiji, khadi was the "symbol of unity of Indian humanity of its economic freedom and equality". Khadi means the decentralisation of production and distribution of the necessaries of human life. Khadi movement began only after Gandhiji's return from South Africa. He believed that Khadi industry would save millions of people from starvation and would supplement the earnings of poor poeple. To him, the music of the spinning wheel was sweeter and more profitable than harmonium. Gandhiji advocated the use of charkha due to its advantages. Charkha requires a small amount of capital; it is simple in operation. It is a source of steady income; it does not depend upon monsoon; it helps in solving the problem of unemployment. Charkha was considered to be the symbol of non-violence. His slogan was "swaraj through spinning".

His khadi scheme included the following:

1. Compulsory spinning in all primary and secondary schools.
2. Cultivation of cotton in areas where it was not grown.

3. Organisation of weaving by the multipurpose co-operative societies.
4. All employees in the department of education, co-operation, municipalities, district boards and panchayats shoud be required to pass a test in spinning, otherwise they may be disqualified.
5. Control of prices of handloom cloth woven of mill yarn.
6. Imposition of a ban on the use of mill cloth in areas where the hand woven cloth was in abundance.
7. Use of hand-spun cloth in all Government and textile and weaving departments.
8. The old cloth mills should not be allowed to expand and new ones should not be opened.
9. Import of foreign yarn or cloth should be banned.

However Gandhiji's belief in charkha as a means to solve the problem of poverty was criticised as stupid, and childish. Some people criticised Khadi as an non-economic proposition because its roughness caused it to soil more quickly than the mill made cloth. It required more frequent washing and its thickness used up more soap and therefore khadi wear was not economic but expensive. Further the wages paid to spinners were low. Khadi arrested the forward march of prosperity.

Use of Machines

Gandhiji described machinery as 'great sin'. He believed that the modern technology was responsible for human frustration, violence and war. It was also responsible for the multiplication of material wants. The use of machines created a class of wealthy people and led to unequal distribution of wealth. Gandhiji was not against machinery. He says "the spinning wheel itself is a machine; a little toothpick is a machine, what I object to is the craze for labour saving machinery. Men go on saving labour, till thousands are without work and thrown on the open streets to die of stravation". But he was against all destructive machinery. He welcomed such instruments and machinery that saved individual labour and lightened the burden of millions of cottage workers. Gandhiji emphasised that he was against large scale production only of those things which villages can produce without difficulty. He believed that machinery was harmful when the same thing could be done easily by millions of hands. He wrote "mechanisation is good when the hands are too few for the work intended to be accomplished. It is an evil when there are more hands than required for the work, as is the case in India". In 1938 in 'Harijan' he wrote, "if I could produce all my country's wants by means of 30,000 people instead of 30 million, I should not mind it, provided that the 30 million are not rendered idle and unemployed." In short, Gandhi was aware of the menace of technological unemployment. He emphasised the need for labour-intensive methods of production in a country with surplus labour. Gandhiji's ideas on machinery are still relevant. In spite of more than six decades of planned, machine using and power driven economic development unemployment is still there and is still growing.

Regeneration of Villages or Village Sarvodaya

Gandhiji evolved the ideal of Village Sarvodaya. Speaking about the old village economy, Gandhiji said, "Production was simultaneous with consumption and distribution and the vicious circle of money economy was absent. Production was for immediate use and not for distant markets. The whole structure of society was founded on non-violence." Gandhiji wanted the revival of ancient village communities with prosperous agriculture, decentralised industry and small scale co-operative organisations. He also wanted that there should be the participation of people at all levels. He declared that the real India was to be found in villages and not in the towns and he accepted the remark that an Indian village was "a collection of insanitary dwellings constructed on a dunghill". His desire was that every Indian village may be converted into a little self-sufficient republic. His ideal of Village Sarvodaya implied that an ideal village must fulfil the following conditions:

(i) There should be orderliness in the structure of the village : (ii) there should be fruit trees ; (iii) it should have a dharamshala and a small dispensary; (iv) it shoud be self-sufficient in matters of food and clothing ; (v) the roads and lanes should be kept clean ; (vi) the places of worship should be beautiful and clean ; (vii) there should be gutters for draining of water in every lane ; (viii) the village shoulld be well protected against robbers and wild animals ; (ix) it should have a public hall, a school and a theatre hall ; (x) it should have an efficient water supply ; (xi) it should have a play-ground, cattle sheds, etc., (xii) if space permits, cash crops excluding tobacco and opium may be grown ; (xiii) adequate education upto the basic standard must be made compulsory ; (xiv) rural activities may be organised on co-operative basis ; (xv) rural administration and government should be in the hands of panchayats, consisting of 5 members duly elected every year by the adult villagers ; (xvi) the village panchayats would enjoy judicial, legislative and executive powers; (xvii) a system of village guards must be made compulsory for every village (xviii) the caste system should be abolished.

He was confident that if all the villages in India are regenerated along these lines, there would not be any worries for her. But Gandhiji knew that it was not easy to establish ideal villages and, therefore, he emphasised the revival of village industries.

THE TRUSTEESHIP DOCTRINE

Gandhiji remarked that the capitalist who had amassed a large sum of money was a thief. If a person had inherited a big fortune or had collected a large amount of money by way of trade and industry, the entire amount did not belong to him. It belonged to the entire society and must be spent on the welfare of all. He wanted to avoid a violent and bloody revolution by gearing a permanent stability of economic equality. He wanted the capitalists to be trustees and he enunciated the doctrine of trusteeship. All social property is meant for all people—rich or poor. Capitalists being trustees would take care of not only themselves but also of others. The workers would treat the capitalists as their benefactors and would keep faith in them. In this way there would be mutual trust and confidence with the help of which the remarkable ideal of economic equality could be achieved. His entire ideology is summed up as follows:

(i) "Trusteeship provides a means of transforming the present capitalist order of society into an egalitarian one. It gives no quarter to capitalism, but gives the present owning class the chance of reforming itself. It is based on the faith that human nature is never beyond redemption.

(ii) "It does not recognise any right of private ownership of property except in as much as it may be permitted by society for its welfare.

(iii) "It does not exclude legislative regulation of the ownership and the use of wealth.

(iv) "Thus, under state-regulated trusteeship, an individual will not be free to hold or use his wealth for selfish satisfaction or in disregard of the interest of society.

(v) "Just as it is proposed to fix a decent minimum living wage, even so, a limit should be fixed for the maximum income that could be allowed to any person in society. The difference between such minimum and maximum incomes should be resonable and equitable and variable from time to time so much so that the tendency would be towards obliteration of the difference.

(vi) "Under the Gandhian economic order the character of production will be determined by social necessity and not by personal whim or greed".

Law of Bread Labour

The Law of Bread Labour was propounded by T.M. Bondaref and popularised by Ruskin and Tolstoy. This law emphasises that man must earn his bread by his own labour. To Gandhiji the law of bread labour related to agriculture alone. But as every body was not a cultivator, he could earn his bread by doing some other work. If all people laboured for their bread, there would be enough food and clothing for all, they would be healthier and happier, and there would be no problem of food shortage, no disease and no misery. He strongly believed that without physical labour no one was entitled to get his food. He advised the rich also to do bodily labour for the bread.

Food Problem

Gandhiji had seen the worst famine of his life during 1943-44, when Bengal suffered heavily owing to the country-wide shortage of food. To start with, Gandhiji thought that this scarcity of food had been artificially created. But after visiting Madras, Bengal and Assam, he arrived at the conclusion that the shortage of food was real and not artificial. He suggested the following measures for solving the problem of food shortage in India : (i) every individual should curtail his or her requirements of food to the minimum and as far as possible the consumption of food grains and pulses should be reduced to the minimum by substituting vegetables, milk, fruits, etc., for them ; (ii) every flower garden should be utilised for cultivation purpose ; (iii) the consumption of food grains and pulses by the army personnel should be economised ; (iv) black-marketing should be stopped ; (v) deep wells should be sunk by the government so as to provide irrigational facilities ; (vi) export of oil seeds, oil cakes, etc., should be stopped. Gandhiji was against food controls, because he thought that it not only created artificial scarcity, but made the people to depend upon others. They become spoon-fed. That is why, in November, 1947 he asked the Government of India to remove food controls.

Population

The most important problem which attracted the attention of Gandhiji was the rapid increase in population. Gandhiji opposed the use of contraceptives as its use in India would make the middle class male population imbecile through abuse of the creative functions. Gandhiji was in favour of birth control through self-control or brahmacharya and not through the use of artifical methods. He considered self-control as the "infallible sovereign remedy". He wanted the propagation of sex passion. He criticised those who angued that birth control was needed for solving the problem of overpopulation. He said, "in my opinion, by a proper land system, better agriculture, and a supplementary industry, this country is capable of supporting twice as many people as there are to-day". Gandhiji was against the sterilisation of women, as it was inhuman. But he was not against vasectomy, especially in the case of those men who suffer from chronic diseases, because he thought that it were men who were the aggressors.

Prohibition

According to Gandhiji, the use of coffee, tea, tobacco, and alcohol was detrimental to the mental, physical, and moral development of an individual. In his opinion, the use of liquor was a disease rather than a vice. He had no objection to the use of liquor if taken under medical advice. He would have preferred India to be reduced to a state of pauperism than have 'thousands of drunkards in our midst'. In one of his articles, he wrote that if he were appointed dictator of India, only for an hour, he would, in the first instance, close all the liquor shops without compensation, and compel the mill-owners to start refreshment rooms to provide harmless drinks to the workmen. He thought that the evil of drinking liquor could not be eradicated by legislative measures alone. Other measures suggested by him are as under:

(a) public opinion should be educated ;

(b) refreshment rooms shoud be opened for selling harmless drinks ;

(c) the income derived from the sale of intoxicants should be used for cultivating public opinion in favour of prohibition. He did not agree with those who contended that by prohibition, the revenue of the government will fall and it would not be able to incur expenditure on nation-building activities like education. He said that if the evil was removed, other resources of revenue could be developed without much difficulty.

Labour Welfare

One of the important fields where Mahatma Gandhi extended his right for economic equality was the factory. He saw that workers were subjected to gross injustice and the treatment meted out to them was below dignity. To him, the employment of children was a national degradation. He always pleaded for shorter hours of work and more leisure so that workers might not be reduced to the condition of beasts. He also demanded safety measures inside factories.

Mahatma Gandhi laid emphasis on the welfare of the worker, his dignity and proper wages. In the Harijan dated June 9, 1946 he wrote that all useful work should bring to the worker the same and equal wages. Until then, he should be paid at least that much which could feed and clothe himself and his family. In order to improve the condition of the worker, first of all he laid claims on a minimum living wage so that a family of 4 to 6 members might live a human life. He wrote as far back as 1920 that the worker should get more wages, and should be given less work to do so that the following four things might be guaranteed to him — clean house, clean body, clean mind and a clean soul.

In so far as the relation between labour and capital is concerned, Mahatma Gandhi always suggested harmony between them. He argued that if the distinction of high and low disappeared, it would have a healthy reacion on all aspects of life. Consequently, the struggle between labour and capital would come to an end; and would give place to co-operation between them. According to him, "capital should be labour's servant, not its master". Moreover, he believed in the formation of labour unions. If the rights of workers were not conceded, they could go on a strike which shoud be based on non-violence and truth.

Simplicity

Mahatma Gandhi was against the multiplication of human wants. In order to lead a simple life

— a life untouched by immorality, untruth and political gain, he did not want many things. He eventually succeeded in complete renunciation. He firmly believed that Western materialism and industrialisation had increased human wants. He always pleaded for a simple life, life of plain living and high thinking, so that the requirements of such a life could be satisfied easily.

To Mahatma Gandhi, happiness lay in the curtailment of wants, and not in their multiplication. As he observed — "The less you possess, the less you want, the better you are, better not for the enjoyment of this life but for the enjoyment of personal service to one's fellow beings, service to which you dedicate yourself, body, soul and mind".

Exchange Economy

Gandhian idea on exchange economy is based on the swadeshi spirit. Every Indian village should be a self supporting and self contained unit exchanging only necessary commodities with other villages where they are not locally producible.

The person who has accepted the discipline of swadeshi would not mind physical discomfort or inconvenience caused by the non-availability of certain things which he has been using. He would gradually learn to do without those things which up to this time he has been regarding as necessary for his life.

Mahatma Gandhi asked people not to worry about the non-availability of such things as pin and needle, because these were not manufactured in India. He was prepared to buy from other countries those commodities (like watches from Switzerland, surgical instruments from England, etc.) which were needed for his growth; but he was not prepared to buy an inch of cotton of the finest variety from England or Japan or any other country of the world because the importation of cloth had caused the ruin of the home industry : it had harmed the interests of the millions of inhabitants of this country. The guiding principle that he laid down in respect of all foreign goods was that those things should not be imported which were likely to prove harmful to the interests of the indigenous industry.

Mahatma Gandhi recognised money as a token of exchange only. In the economy envisaged by him, commodities were to be exchanged with commodities. The part played by money was insignificant. It became instrumental in the exploitation of the weak by the strong. To him, money was as useful as labour. He suggested that in order to make khadi universal, it should be made available in exchange for yarn, i.e., yarn-currency.

Constructive Programme

Mahatma Gandhi's constructive programme was a big undertaking which included 18 items enumerated below: Communal unity, removal of untouchability, prohibition, khadi, other village industries, village sanitation, uplift of women, basic education, adult education, hygiene and health, economic equality, propagation of national language, provincial languages, kisans, labour adivasis, lepers and students.

Untouchability

Gandhi believed that untouchability was a sin against God and man. It was "like poison slowly eating into the very vitals of Hinduism". It degraded both the untouchables and the touchables. He felt that Swaraj had no meaning if about 4 crores of people were kept under prepetual subjection; and were deliberately denied the fruits of their labour and national culture." To him, untouchability was not only part and parcel of Hinduism but a plague which every Hindu should try to combat.

Mahatma Gandhi admitted that untouchability was an old institution; but as it was an evil, it could not be defended on this ground. He held that if some shastras had given sanction to it, it was a sin committed by Hinduism; this sin must be removed. Once he went to the extent of saying: "If this is Hinduism, O lord, my daily prayer is that the soonest it is destroyed, the best." When he came to know that there was untouchability even among the untouchables, he concluded that the evil was all-pervading; and suggested that cultured Hindus should try to get rid of that curse as soon as possible.

Mahatma Gandhi laid the entire blame for the cancer of untouchability on the Hindus. To him, the removal of untouchability meant fighting against the impurity found in man. It meant also love for, and service of , the whole world. It would remove the barrier between man and man.

Assessment of Gandhian Economics

Gandhian economics is very different from traditional economics, as it has no clear cut theory. Gandhi himself never studied any economics. He was unfamiliar with the thought of Keynes or Marshall. He read Marx as late as 1942 during detention and his impression was that if he had to write "The Capital", he would probably do it in a much more simplified manner. It is natural that the traditional economists do not find Gandhian ideas scientific. Moreover, there are numerous contradictions in his thought which were brought about due to the evolution of his ideas as his personality matured. For instance, his extreme apathy to machinery, as evident in "Hind Swaraj", was considerably softened in his later years.

In assessing Gandhian thought, it all depends upon whether one agrees with the Gandhian postulates or not. If the critic agrees with simplicity, non-violence, decentralisation and ethical and moral considerations which form the basis of the Gandhian ideas, he would probably find that entire system of Gandhian thought is very logical. Otherwise, the traditional economist will find that Gandhian thought is extremely lacking in coherence on such modern issues as public finance, the problems of defence and international trade, monetary management and economic planning. In Gandhi's economics, there is a fundamental postulate that all countries would be organised on the non-violent pattern. Whether such a situation is practicable or not, is quite a different matter.

"The relationship between Gandhism and Socialism is interesting. Gandhi himself declared that he was a socialist and his ideal of Sarvodaya was the traditional Indian Socialism. But technically, Gandhi is not a socialist. He would uphold private ownership of property by asking the capitalists to become the trustees of public property. At best, he asked them to be enlightened capitalists and uphold the welfare of the workers at all costs.

From the Marxist point of view, Gandhian economics is reactionary in its outlook. Gandhi refused to recognise class-struggle and the fact that history had developed from one stage to another and, as such, must pass on to the higher stage of Socialism from the persent state of Capitalism. Like Sismondi Gandhi's solution of the problem of capitalist society consists in suspending material progress and technical inventions and to go back to a decentralized and simple system of economic organisation. The Marxist charge is that Gandhi was trying to put the clock back and as such was unconsciously extending capitalist and feudal interest. The most outspoken critiques of Gandhian economics have come from the Indian Marxists.

Many socialist thinkers, specially J. B. Kripalani, Jai Prakash Narain and Ram Manohar Lohia have accepted Gandhian 'Sarvodaya' as the ideal of Indian Socialism. They hold that Praja Socialism is Socialism plus Gandhism and believe that Marxism was suitable to the Western industrial nations and as such is inapplicable to Indian conditions. The Indian variety of socialism suitable to a poor and agricultural country must necessarily follow the non-violent and decentralized pattern of the Gandhian 'Sarvodaya'. A comprehensive theory of Praja Socialism has yet to be worked out, but these have been advanced by some Praja Socialist leaders in recent articles and speeches.

Yet another controversy that has sprung up recently, is due to the ideas of J. C. Kumarappa and Sunderlal, themselves veteran Gandhities. They hold that the points of difference between Marxism and Gandhism are very few. Gandhism is Marxism minus violence. They assert that the Gandhian principles of simplicity, non violence and decentralisation of power are actively pursued in post-Revolution China, which is evidently being built up on the basis of the Marxian philosophy of the Chinese Communist Party.

Influence of Gandhian Economics

The influence of Gandhian economic ideas on Indian thinkers has not been very fundamental. Gandhi was universally accepted as a great political leader and the Father of the Nation. But many of his immediate followers did not see eye to eye with his economic views. Probably, the only organised attempt to put Gandhian ideas into practice is due to the various organisations started by Gandhi himself, the All India Charkha Sangh, the Go-Seva Sangh, the All-India Spinners Association and the All-India Village Industries Association. Recently Vinoba Bhave and many Socialist leaders, like Jai Prakash Narain, have taken active interest in the Bhoodan Yagya Movement, which aims at the redistribution of land on Gandhian lines.

The influence of Gandhi's economic ideas on Government policy has been very little. The Planning Commission has talked about moral values, non-violence and decentralisation as desirable characteristics of a national economic policy of India, but the Five Year Plan in itself is hardly Gandhian in outlook. In fact, staunch Gandhites, like Kumarappa and Sunderlal, were sharply critical of the Government policy of reconstructing villages with foreign aid, as was being done under the Community Development Programmes. Recent attempts by the Government to revitalise handloom and Khadhi industry are not in the nature of the application of Gandhian theory to economic policy. They are obviously directed by the political necessity of fighting unemployment which looms large on the Indian horizon.

So far as traditional economists are concerned, they have accepted two ideas from Gandhian thought: (1) the importance of cottage industries in our rural economy and (2) the necessity of decentralisation of the economic structure. Most economists also agree with the Gandhian contention that the village improvement and rehabilitation of agriculture must be the first step towards any economic improvement in this country.

(h) K.T. SHAH (1888-1953)

INTRODUCTION

K.T. Shah studied in the University of Bombay and the London School of Economics and Political Science. He served as Professor of Economics at the Mysore University (1918) and at the Bombay University (1921). His important works include Sixty Years of Indian Finance (1921), Federal Finance in India (1929), Principles of Planning (1943), India's National Plan (1947), etc.

ECONOMIC IDEAS:

Indian Finance

Shah points out that during 1919 to 1958 land revenue had declined from Rs. 35 crores to Rs. 20 crores. He suggested the abolition of drink traffic and minimisation of military expenditure and home charges. The loss in income should be made good by direct taxes.

Trade, Tariffs and Transport

Shah considered transport facilities and tariff regulations were indispensable for the development of international trade. He was in favour of protection, though he was aware of its limitations also. He gave a scheme for adopting protectionist legislation for India. He pointed out that the scientific protection formulated by List and J.S. Mill was only a temporary fiscal aid given to selected industries.

Municipal Government and Municipal Finance

Shah favoured both nationalism and democracy—nationalism to achieve brotherhood and democracy to save people. He advocated the revival of local self-government. He felt that the municipal government is a necessity as industries had developed in cities and towns. He also suggested that the local character of municipal finances should be maintained and items of revenue and expenditure should be re-classified. The entire revenue system should be modified. He gave the following ways by which the revenue system could be changed: (1) Taxes should be reduced to the minimum. (2) Indirect taxes viz., octroi and town duties should be abolished. (3) To compensate the loss the rate of direct taxes should be raised proportionately. (4) Taxes should be realised only when the municipal trading enterprise falls.

Federal Finance

Shah pointed out that in India, federal principles had been hardly recognised though finances had been decentralised. After examining the financial evolution in India, financial position of the Government of India and financial relation between the Government of India and the Indian states, he gave his own suggestions. In the opinion of Shah, financial resources and obligations should be divided among the various states according to the division of powers and duties. Regarding the evolution of federal finance, he pointed out three things:

1. There was no logical division of resources and obligations.
2. The division already adopted was not in accordance with the well coordinated and scientific principle of federal finance; and
3. Indian states could no longer be left out.

Shah pointed out that a tripartite arrangement between the Government of India, British Provinces and Indian states should be evolved. In order to govern the country more economically, there was room for retrenchment and readjustment in public expenditure. This was necessary for the promotion of economic welfare also. He also suggested a reduction in defence expenditure and an increase in expenditure on health and education. The central government should give grants to provincial governments and the basis of income tax should be changed.

Economic Planning

As Shah had acted as the Honorary General Secretary of the National Planning Committee he was very much interested in the development of planning. He wrote two books on Principles of Planning and India's National Plan. Principles of Planning deals with the objectives of planning, production, forms of production, industries, labour and population, distribution, trade and administrative organisation and public finance. The second book examines more fully the administrative organisation. Planning meant a simultaneous advance on all points and in all sectors—economic, cultural and spiritual values and the human side of life. The aim of planning was the attainment of national self-sufficiency and the doubling of the standard of living of the masses within a period of ten years. Therefore the National Planning Authority should scientifically distribute industries and systematically organise resources in every state. He also suggested that the administration should be decentralised, and agency of that authority should be instituted in every state.

Economics in Ancient India

In his work on 'Ancient Foundations of Economics in India', he showed that the economic ideas of Indian servants thousands of years ago were similar to modern economic ideas. He believed that all allied branches of social science, namely, economics, ethics and politics were interdependent.

Agriculture and animal husbandry were the main occupations of people in those days. Material wealth was not an end in itself. He had discussed the organisation of production, socio-economic institutions, regulation governing the distribution and consumption of wealth, trade, currency, credit, taxation, its basis and justification and the role of state in production and distribution.

Payment for War

In his "How India Pays for the War" Shah discussed the ways by which India paid for the Second World War. India had to pay for the war by direct and indirect taxation, tax on transport and communications and through currency receipts. Indirect taxes included customs duties on imports and exports, central excise, salt duty, and direct taxes included income tax, corporation tax, super tax, cess, profits tax and investment in war loans.

(i) RADHAKAMAL MUKERJEE (1889-1968)

INTRODUCTION

Dr. Mukerjee began his career as a lecturer in 1910 and studied in Calcutta University. He served as Professor in Economics in various Indian Universities, viz., Calcutta University in 1917, University of Lucknow in 1921, and became Vice-Chancellor in 1955-57 in the same University. He served on several committees and commissions as Chairman and participated in many international conferences and lectured on different economic problems. He published number of books like The Foundations of Indian Economics (1916), Principles of Comparative Economics (1923), Land Problems in India (1933), Regional Balance of Man (1938), The Political Economy of Population (1942) and The Economic History of India (1946).

ECONOMIC IDEAS

Balanced Development of Industries

Dr. Mukerjee laid emphasis on Cottage and Village industries which was passing through a great economic revolution in India. There was a great vitality for cottage industries even under the unfavourable conditions. There was a great future for these industries if they formed economic organisation, mechanical processes and business management. He justified cottage industries on the ground that they were the product of environment as well as of social and ethical ideals cherished by the country. They supplement the slender earnings of poor cultivators, at the same time. Western industrialism had created large inequalities, but he was not against large scale production. He supported the development of an industrial system based on the Indian heritage. According to this, for sound economic development both large and small industries have their proper scope and importance.

Regional Economics

Dr. Mukerjee stated that economic regions are determined by regional geography, physiography, internal organic factors and historical traditions. The analysis of economic institutions may be scientific because these factors should be considered dynamically. Praising communalism of East, he said that this communalistic ideal of each for all and all for each is sought to be realised in the constitution of the social unit in India, such as the family, the social group and the community.

Institutional Theory of Economics

According to Dr. Mukerjee, the institutional theory can be studied both by inductive and deductive methods, the outlook throughout being regional, historical, comparative and normative. Economics must base itself on social psychology which reveals unity between the individual's behaviour and social institutions. As he pointed out that the institutional equilibrium was the result not of an automatic adjustment of economic, political and social forces, but of deliberate planning. The institutional approach could only prevent a relativistic analysis of an individual's actions and bridge the existing gulf between economic theory and economic policy. He further added that throughout the course of economic history, social norms and institutions always affected economic values.

Rural Reconstruction and Rural Planning

Ground works of Economics, Rural Economy of India, Hand Problems of India, Changing Face of Bengal and Planning the Country Side, all these five books of Mukerjee, explained the rural problems of India. He suggested co-operative farming, the organisation of caste guilds on district, regional basis, agricultural practices and methods of more efficient regions should be introduced in the underdeveloped regions of the country. Peasant farming should be rehabilitated on the basis of an appropriate land settlement, utilization of human waste, intensive cultivation, consolidation, co-operative irrigation and development of rural transport. Guilds and co-operative societies might be developed into regional associations of producers and consumers to eliminate the middlemen.

Mukerjee stated that the plan included the co-ordination of activities in agriculture, education, marketing, panchayat, sanitation and forestry. He included the problem of drought or famine, human and cattle diesease and this underlined the importance of the development of canal and well irrigation, erosion control, pest control, use of improved seeds, cattle development, stability and security of employment, permanent lights in land, fair rents, protection from usury or exploitative credit. He further added that planned industrialisation was essential to rural development. Rural reconstruction could not be successful unless it was linked with the development of communications and rural industrialisation.

Planning in India

Dr. Mukerjee felt that economic planning had assumed a great significance because of the growth of economic nationalism. After the second world war planning became pervasive and now it covers all aspects of our economic life; and aims at social welfare. The main aim of our five-year plans should be crop and food planning, reconstruction of agriculture, forestry, soil and river management, development of key, light and agricultural industries, maintenance of cost-price equalisation, rationalisation of money and credit, improvement in the standard of living and population control. Co-ordination between regions, between agriculture and industry and between all the sectors of economic life, is the key to economic planning.

Population

In his book "Migrant Asia" he suggested emigration to new countries where the pressure of population was comparatively less. In another book he suggested intensive cultivation, the introduction of dairy farming and an intensive system of mixed farming combined with dairying. He further added industrial planning for providing employment opportunities. To control over population of the country he suggested a ban on child marriage and polygamy, spread of education, birth control, and the creation of a desire among the masses for a better standard of living. To check the overpopulation in backward and less literate classes, he suggested inter-caste marriage, widow remarriage, spread of education and the abolition of hypergamy.

Ecological Theory of Population

Mukerjee emphasised that the study of population should depend upon the linking of economic factors to the ecology of different regions and cultures. According to him, the study of population required a many-sided and synthetic approach as the process of population involved several dissimilar elements—physical and ecological factors of land and resources, biological factors of fertility and expectation of life, economic factors of productivity and standard of living, institutional factors of sex, habits, cultural traditions and personal and social attitudes concerning marriage and children. He suggested certain laws to control these elements viz., the statistical law of probability, the ecological law of conservation of economic resources and regional and occupational balance, the economic laws of equimarginal utilities and returns and the sociological law of the optimum, selection and control of population. Planned population should be harmonised with the world economic policy and world peace could be effectively guaranteed in the future only by an international population policy.

Industrial Labour

Dr. Mukerjee said that the rapid development of industries and increase in the number of landless workers who migrated from villages for the sake of employment to towns and cities, did not allow time for either a smooth adjustment of relations between labour and management. Rapid industrialisation aggravated the situation with the result that human requirements of these workers were not adequately satisfied. Trade unionism. developed as a strong force in industry in other countries, but in India there was disorganisation which led to serious hindrances in the way of industrial development. As he was not satisfied with the plan the Government had formulated for the betterment of the economic conditions of Indian workers, Mukerjee suggested that a more comprehensive plan like the Beveridge plan should be adopted here.

Economic History

In his book The Economic History of India, he described the changes that had taken place in agriculture, industry, trade, commerce, population etc. He maintained that during the 17th century India's trade with other countries and shipping had developed, the economic condition of cultivators was not depressed, and cottage industries were flourishing. Indian exports shrunk due to competition from England and the British monopoly of shipping during eighteenth century. In the middle of the nineteenth century, the export of cotton and silk piece goods entirely ceased, which marked the complete decline of our industries. There was economic and social changes and political upheavals in the two centuries. It represented the golden era of Indian trade and industry and the beginning of her economic downfall which was as sudden as it was complete and unprecedented. At the same time, real wages declined; the burden of agriculturists increased as a result of an increase in prices.

(j) C.N. VAKIL (1895-1979)

Prof. Vakil was born at Hasot (Gurajat) on 22nd August 1895. He has done pioneering work in research training in Economics for over a generation. He is specially known for the large number of distinguished economists that he has trained. A look at the Bibliography will convince any one of the vast amount of solid work that he was instrumental in producing, in almost all branches of Economics, by inspiring a band of devoted workers to a new field of activity. Several of his works were the first research contributions in their respective fields and have stimulated further work on the subject. He died at Bombay on 26th October 1979.

PLANNING

Prof. Vakil (along with Prof. P.R. Brahmananda) put forward an alternative approach to Indian planning, which was opposite to that of the Mahalanobis model, at the time of the formulation of the second five year plan for India. Vakil's plan frame was related to *Marxian concept of variable capital (v)*. This model is based on classical economic philosophy, in particular Ricardo, Marx, Rosenstein Rodan and Ragnar Nurkse. All these models are based on the assumption that, there exist a massive reserve army of labour in rural areas of developing economies. In other words, the disguised unemployed formed the savings potential. This is based on the view of that labour could be transferred from agriculture, without decreasing production and deployed for producing real capital goods. In short, for the development of the Indian economy, with large-scale disguised unemployment, the bottleneck good is not the basic and heavy capital goods (as felt by Mahalanobis) but the wage-goods.

ASSUMPTIONS

The plan frame proposed by Vakil was based on the following assumptions:

1. Wages are paid in advance of production. This assumption is similar to that of Marx, Van-Neumann, Leontif, Nurkse, etc.
2. Variable capital or wage goods constitute exclusively food.
3. Labour could produce capital goods without the assistance of other factors of production.
4. The role of the potential surplus might not be procurable and further that there might be a need to provide for slightly higher consumption levels than in agriculture to workers engaged in Non-agriculture (consumption). The model is developed with a multiplier formula which is based/autonomous increase in the stock of wage foods in the hands of planning authorities.
5. In rural areas there prevails disguised unemployment to a great extent. Therefore, existence of large industrial reserve army.
6. The transfer of disguised unemployed workers from rural sector does not lead to the decrease in the output in the farm sector.
7. There exists a gap in accumulation of wage goods. To the extent of that/gap, forced savings have to be effected by reducing present consumption (by imposing taxes) or by importing wage goods.
8. The wages paid to the newly employed workers will be higher than the consumption of disguised unemployed.

WAGE-GOODS MODEL

According to Vakil, the rate of growth of the economy is influenced by several economic and non-economic factors. Among economic factors, accumulation of capital is the most important, which in turns depends upon technical progress. So as non-economic factors are concerned, institutional changes are important. The living conditions of people are very poor. Higher level of investment will break this vicious circle. Demand for investment depends upon the demand for consumption goods. The demand for consumption depends upon the size of the market. But due to low level of income in developing economies, the size of the market is limited. The lower productivity of labour leads to lower level of income and hence the size of the market end level of investment is low, that is, small investments have to be made in several avenues.

In the context of the large-scale employment that was prevailing at the time of the finalization of the second five year plan frame, vakil suggested a wage-goods strategy as the best alternative to the Mahalanobis model.

The model suggested that disguised unemployed be regarded as potential saving. To transfer these workers from agriculture to industry by itself, did not lead to the existence of a wage-goods gap. By filling the wage-goods gap only could one increase employment in developing economies. Since economic system does not supply wage-goods in the short-run, employment and investment will decrease. The rate of transfer of unemployed workers from the farm sector to the non-farm sector (capital goods sector) depends upon the rate of increase in the supply of wage-goods.

Until this wage-goods gap is removed, it will not be possible to remove workers from the farm sector to the non-farm sector. Thus the provision of wage goods constitutes the most important element of Vakil's planned model. In India, the population is high, but the avenues to provide employment to them are limited. Capital unemployment is less harmful than labour unemployment. Therefore, the problem of unemployment has to be tackled without sacrificing technical progress and rapid accumulation of capital, Vakil felt that, the Mahalanobis model does not solve the problem of unemployment and economic growth in India, because the model has a contradiction between theory and statistical frame. Therefore, provision of unemployment to the tune of 11 million people (of which 8 million people in non-agricultural sector was the target) would not be achieved in the second five year plan period because the employment target was not fixed on the basis of demand and supply of additional wage-goods. Vakil says that, in a country like India it is not only the availability of fixed capital which leads to provision of employment, but also the level of wage goods. Scarcity of both types of capital is the cause of unemployment. In the Vakil Plan frame, there is a complementarity between consumption and investment whereas, in the Mahalanobis model there is a conflict between consumption and investment. This is because, an increase in consumption goods output leads to decrease in investment, which in turn leads to decrease in the growth of the economy. When more resources are allocated to the capital goods sector, allocation of resources to consumption goods sector has to be reduced. But this conflict is not present in Vakil's model, as the consumption goods sector and capital goods sector are complementary to each other. By increasing wage goods production, at a rapid rate, the resources needed for investment in capital goods sector can be mobilized without decrease in the output of wage-goods sector as labour can be reduced in the latter.

Role of Technological Progress

Vakil emphasized that technological progress is a powerful engine of growth in output as it did not cause unemployment in developed economies (at the full employment level) and also that it led to increase in the standard of living of people. However, in a country like India, if the required capital accumulation does not take place technological progress aggravates unemployment.

Vakil was of the opinion that labour intensive techniques are not always relevant in labour-abundant economics. After a certain stage, abundance of labour does not increase factor price. To increase capital accumulation, employment has to be increased. This leads to profitability in the agricultural sector which was for long discouraged. By decreasing luxury goods production, avenues for investment will increase in under-developed countries. Abundance of unskilled labour is available but availability of skilled labour for employment is limited.

In short, Vakil argued that, for the development of the Indian economy, what was needed was an abundant of wage goods, technological progress, reorganisation of institutions, changes in the price policy, and mobilisation of resources for investment through taxation and compulsory savings. To mobilize compulsory savings, taxes, adjustment in monopoly prices, and other receipts are needed. Though deficit finance also forms a part of compulsory savings, the model envisaged keeping it at a low level. To mobilise investible resources, the model reorganised the role of public and private sectors. The classical economists (particularly Ricardo) stated that scarcity of supply of foodgrains is a hurdle to economic growth. Similarly, in Vakil's model, the wage-goods equation determines level of employment and growth of the economy. Increase in the supply of wage-goods by one unit will lead to an increase in employment by certain units. This relation is described by Vakil as the consumption multiplier.

Consumption Multiplier

The consumption multiplier developed by Vakil is based on certain specific assumptions, as under:

1. The marginal propensity to consume of wage-goods producers is zero.
2. The money and real wage rate remain constant.
3. Price level remains constant.
4. Large-scale disguised unemployment exists in the wage-goods farm sector. The average wage goods consumption of the disguised unemployed worker (d) is less than the real wage (W).
5. The supply of credit is perfectly elastic, therefore, rate of interest remains constant.
6. Increase in the activities of the public sector does not lead to disincentives in the private sector.
7. There are not difficulties in the mobilization and transportation of goods.
8. The size of the population remains constant.

Poverty

According to Prof. C.N. Vakil, poverty in a country may be due to defects either in the production of wealth or in its distribution. Both these problems are equally important, but it is obvious that if the production or the national dividend is small, the question of distribution would be of comparatively less importance. Further, he viewed the causes as two separate entities, internal and external.

1. Internal Causes

(a) Not enough work for the vast mass of the agricultural population during the off season: The majority of our people demand upon agriculture directly or indirectly. In spite of the presence of employment opportunities provided by industries and also other secondary occupations in different parts of the country, the majority of the agricultural population did not have enough work during the off season,

which extends to about five months in a year.

(b) Presence of the type of social life where there are few active workers in each family: According to Prof. C.N. Vakil, the number of dependants in an average family in the country is large. Usually, an only earning member supports a large family. This kind of situation exists not only among the agricultural population but also among urban population and the higher classes.

(c)Presence of a large number of able-bodied beggars miscalled sadhus: Prof. C.N. Vakil rightly pointed out that India the number of persons doing religious service is quite high. They are called as Sadhus. He is of the view that the Sadhus are not doing any kind of religious service in the true sense, either for themselves or to the society. They are actually living off society. Their presence in large number, Prof. Vakil feels, adds to the burden of poverty on the productive members f society.

(d) Climatic disadvantages: Presence of different climates in different parts of the country stands in the way of continuous and sustained work, either physical or mental. This again increases the number of unemployed, another index poverty.

(e) Fatalism and consequent want of determination to struggle against odds: The peculiar cause operating in our country against greater production, as stated by Prof. C.N. Vakil was the mental attitude which may be described stated by Prof. C.N. Vakil was the mental attitude which may be described as the lack of economic motivation either due to the philosophic idea of renunciation of all desires, or to the continuous state of helplessness and poverty in which the people have been living, or to the want of education and consciousness about their own potentialities, or a combination of these.

(f) Faculty educational system: Prof. Vakil also mentioned the faulty or one-sided educational system which creates large numbers of educated but in people, suitable for no fit work other than that of the liberal professions or clerical occupations. The great magnitude of unemployment or under employment among the educated young men of the country was due largely to ills of the educational system.

2 External Causes

(a) International trade and Commerce: Prof. Vakil is of the view that the chief external cause of poverty is the great change in the economic life and organization of the people brought about by international trade and commerce, facilitated by modern means by communication. According to him, the nature of our commercial relations with other countries has not been to our best advantage, and the internal adjustment in the internal economy of the people required by the great change is not yet complete.

(b) Commercial and industrial relations with other countries: He has brought out well the main features of India's commercial and industrial relations with other countries. During British rule in India there was a silent and pervasive economic invasion of the country, supported by the highly organised industrial system of England and other countries and patronized by the Indian administration. On the one hand, India produced large quantities of varied manufactured articles, the introduction of which had been systematically encouraged; on the other, a large number of foreign capitalists had been allowed to settle in the country for the purpose of industrial and commercial exploitation. This can definitely affect the internal production, employment, etc. and finally aggravate conditions of poverty.

REMEDIES

Prof. C.N. Vakil has suggested several measures to remove poverty. He stated that stress had to be laid on increased production and equitable distribution. He advocated consolidation of holdings, for agricultural improvement, as in the use of better inputs in terms of seeds, implements, and manure, sinking of large number of wells and creation of other irrigation facilities, concerted efforts to promote the co-operative movement and suitable education to assure enough employment opportunity and reward to the agricultural family.

He further suggested that in order to overcome the problem of indebtedness of farmers, there should be Land Mortgage Banks, to take over the existing debt of the farmers from the sowcars on easier conditions. In addition, finance should be provided through the co-operatives.

He advocated the development of cottage industries to provide more employment opportunities for those who were not willing to migrate from rural to other areas and also for the small farmers during the off season.

Regarding land tax, Prof. Vakil stated that it should be brought in line with the income tax, where an exemption limit below a certain specified income from land could be fixed with reference to agricultural life and conditions. It may be possible at the same time to allow Local Bodies to tax agriculturists to a certain extent, by some ceses on the land the proceeds to be utilized for the benefit of the people of the area concerned.

He is of the view that unless steps are taken to prevent foreigners or non-Indians from enjoying the fruits of the industrial exploitation of the country, the problem of Indian poverty can not be solved.

In order to bring about desired social change, he advocated the prevention of early marriages, lowering of mortality rates and incidence of diseases, provision of sanitation, removal of purdah system and provision of suitable work to them etc. Further, he reminds us that unnecessary ceremonial expenditure should be curtailed since it is not productive.

Prof. Vakil believed that free and compulsory primary education was desirable. He was also of the view that rural universities should be established to create an interest in the better understanding of and efforts to solve, the problems that affect the life of the rural people in their proximity.

DEFICIT FINANCING AND PUBLIC EXPENDITURE

Prof. Vakil strongly objected to deficit financing as a means to finance the plans. He floated the idea that, "...it is the Keynesian concept of pumping money into the economy to offset a depression which is one of the evils of capitalism. This is a short-term remedy for developed countries to remove depression or to bring out equilibrium in the economy. It has created a great havoc, inflation and poverty also. His significant contribution lay in truncating the public expenditure by appointing a Public Expenditure Commission. One Public Expenditure Commission was set up in 1921 by the Britishers, since then we have no such Commission. It had a salutary effect in bringing things to reasonable proportions.

INTERNATIONAL TRADE

On the question of protection, he emphasized that, "Protection should only be for a temporary period and once an industry has been properly established, it should be able to face competition. This is the only way to safeguard the interest of the consumer which one usually ignored in such matters. Thus he was in favour of slow and partial competition rather than opening of the whole economy at once. He welcomed the New Gold Policy of the Government to sell gold at international price and t import gold. He described it as anti-inflationary, employment-oriented and for checking smuggling. He was in favour of joint ventures abroad, consultancy in Gulf countries and trade with OECD countries in primary products. Branch offices in foreign countries like Japan were to be activated to keep pace with the world demand by supplying quality goods at competitive prices with timely deliveries. He also proposed setting up an Import-Export Bank for international trading, commerce and financial matters.

Extension Work

Prof.Vakil laid much emphasis on extension work without which the colossal task of rural development was not possible. He stressed that people with a missionary zeal should be enthused for this task and devoted officers were to be entrusted to implement the plans. A class of young volunteers and trainees should be raised to integrate knowledge of agricultural sciences, agricultural economics, rural sociology, village industries, public administration health and family welfare and so on. Agricultural polytechniques and a centre for rural development were needed to fill the gap between higher education and the needs of the people.

The proposed research centres might select a few villages and appropriate methods. He lamented the bureaucratic methods, due to which "a large percentage of plan expenditure for rural development, about 60 percent was spent for administration. It was not known whether or not remaining 40 percent reached the farmer. Therefore, the machinery for implementing the same, had to be created as the existing bureaucratic machinery has failed to function effectively so far".

Inflation

Vakil was the first Indian economist who drew attention to the price rise spiral. The definition of inflation, as given by Prof. C.N. Vakil is that, when supply of money in a country increases and the supply of goods does not increase to the same extent, the situation is described as one in which more money chases scarce goods. Such a tendency is called inflation. If it continues for a long period, it causes a lot of disturbance to the economy which gets distorted. Excess supply of money may be due to either government expenditure exceeding its receipts from revenue and loans from the public, which is known as deficit financing or larger credit given by banks to the commercial sector not supported by the latter's productive activities. The Reserve Bank regulates the latter by imposing restrictions on credit in order to bring about some equilibrium. The former can be controlled by government imposing greater self-discipline and keeping its expenditure within the limits of its resources.

Prof. Vakil said that, "We inherited inflation on Independence and we have followed an inflationary policy due to incorrect notions or wrong application of western theories to our conditions. This has seriously interfered with our attack on poverty and our efforts at planning". Vakil had suggested that the immediate object of policy should be to roll back prices to a lower level and to reduce significantly the incidence of 'black money'. This necessitates immobilisation of say 30 per cent of money supply through partial remonetisation and issuance of 20 years fixed interest-yielding but illiquid savings certificates and black accounts; there should be a national ceiling of 5 per cent on the annual growth rate of money supply during the Fifth Plan; Government borrowing from the entire banking system should be completely eschewed during the first two years of the Fifth Plan. The step up in government expenditure contemplated in the Fifth Plan should be brought about through rationalization of expenditure and maximum dependence upon non-inflationary sources of receipts. The growth rate of credit to the industrial commercial sector should be pruned with reference to the Macro-ceiling of 5 per cent. The proportion of value of inventories financed by bank credit should be reduced to about 33 per cent; rationalisation of government expenditures can be achieved by economizing severely on non-accumulation expenditure.

All future capital projects must be examined with reference to their fiscal viability before they are sanctioned. Norms of work standards should be laid down for all levels of employees in the government. The services of Defence personnel should be considered for deployment in short gestation projects, and in step-up of emergency production schemes particularly in food articles. Suitable arrangements should be made to examine continuously the desirability and feasibility of granting of, or of the continuance of, subsidies of various types from the public exchequer. All subsidies to certain categories of consumers and government and public servants in the form of supply of goods at subsidized rates, loans at concessional interest, quarters, travel concessions, etc., should be subject to periodical review.

A drastic upward revision is needed in the level of the Bank Rate, the structure of deposit rates and yield rates. The term-structure of rates should be so devised as to favour the medium-term and the long-term savers. The lending rates by banks for prime borrowers should be increased.

The instrument of taxation should be effectively used to reduce luxury consumption by individuals and firms of siphon off excess demand on scarce commodities to encourage exports, to promote savings in specific financial and other assets and generally to realign the pattern of private production along a product-mix enabling the speedy attainment of self-reliance. Discriminatory excise taxes, exemption of increment in savings from income tax, tax credit schemes based on degrees of utilization of capacity, are all in order. Tax loopholes should be closed. The tax revenue from agriculture should be raised to 3 per cent of net output of agriculture.

Exchange reserves should be built up to stand normally at a level of about six months of annual imports. Through appropriate redesigning of construction, encouragement of indigenous methods of transport, greater use of public transport, promotion of organic manures and in input mix, the direct and indirect repercussions of the oil crisis can be partly overcome.

At a time when India is facing the problem of containing the spectra of double, digit inflation, one can't but appreciate the ideas of C.N.Vakil, many of which have currency even today. The quote Alexander Gray, "No point of view, once expressed, ever seems wholly to die; and in periods of transition like the present, our ears are full of the whisperings of dead man". For both academic and practical reasons, Vakil's contribution to inflation will be remembered.

Prof.Vakil can be rightly considered as the originator and propounder of certain standpoints and approaches relevant to modern economics in India.

1. He was among the earliest of economists anywhere to have empirically applied the fulfledged quantity theory to understand price behavior. He took into account the quantity of money, the velocity of money and the supply of real output. He separated the monetary factors from the real factors.
2. Vakil was among the earliest to have pursued the non-autonomy of money supply and its changes in a country which lodges its glod/foreign exchange/foreign security reserves in a

foreign country and makes its own money supply determined by the former.

3. Prof.Vakil noticed the strong relation between deficit financing in the form of sales of ad hoc treasury bill and currency supply.
4. Prof.Vakil emphasized the need for linking money supply changes to aggregate real output changes rather than to volume of trade changes. He thus rejected the link between money supply and the needs of foreign trade. Total trade changes, foreign as well as internal would be a better proxy for real output changes.
5. Prof.Vakil widended the concept of the brain to include more items than the 'English'(Home) charges. The entire financial policy of the British Government had to be scrutinized in order to understand the magnitude of the excess brain-burden imposed on the Indian people.
6. Prof.Vakil also was the earliest in India to have related the incidence of the public expenditure and taxation to the per captia income of the community. The case for a reduction in public expenditure was argued on the score of its adverse effects on the poor people of the country.
7. Prof.Vakil voiced concerns at the growth of defence expenditure in India and urged the case for close economic monitoring of defence expenditures.
8. Prof.Vakil also recognized the need for large scale regional and urban social surveys to understand the economic conditions of the people. He was also instrumental in recognizing the need for scientific surveys of public opinion in matters like group tensions, effects of war and rising prices on the middle class, etc. his achievement in this connection is parallel to that of Prof.Mahalanobis, who pioneered National Sample Surveys, to understand the economic conditions of the people.
9. Prof.Vakil was also among the few public men who thought that the basic causes behind communal tensions and riots was economic insecurity along with economic disparities.

(k) J.K. MEHTA

INTRODUCTION

Professor J.K. Mehta was a philosopher, economist, follower of Mahatma Gandhi, and worked as a Professor of Economics in Allahabad University. His notable publications are: Studies in Advanced Economic Theory (1946), Lectures on Modern Economic Theory (1959), Foundations of Economics (1959), A Philosophical Interpretation of Economics (1962), and Macro Economics (1969). He published Public Finance in 1949 along with S.N. Agarwal.

ECONOMIC IDEAS

Scope and Definition of Economics

Mehta has defined Economics, "as a science which studies human behaviour as a means to the end of wantlessness". Human behaviour is the subject matter of the science of Economics. It is generally the result of a state of disequilibrium of human mind. Disequilibrium is due to more pain than pleasure. Pleasure means the removal of pain. To him, want and pain are concurrent phenomena.

Perfect equilibrium can never be attained, because there is continuously increasing pain. The real relief from pain consists not only in removing present wants but also not creating new wants in future.

State of Wantlessness

Wantlessness consists neither in not eating and drinking, nor in not earning income. All that is required is to do all such things with a selfless motive; to earn not for our own use but for the use of all those whom our conscience would like to be served. Such a wantless attitude to life would secure, therefore not only our own happiness but would enable us to contribute to social welfare.

Nature of Economic Generalisations

Economic theory teaches to arrange facts in proper order of their magnitude or in the order of their place in time. Economic generalisations, again, make us realise that isolated single experiences have no meaning; they have to be related to one another. One relation is mathematical and the other philosophical. They do not give us a vocational training, they give us general education, liberal education.

Static and Dynamic Economics

According to Mehta dynamics is not a positive concept, it is the negation of statics. By introducing time element, as a variable in statics then it is dynamic. Static economics refers to the economic system which is in equilibrium. But dynamic economics is to determine the temporary points of equilibrium within a short period at successive moments of time. It changes from time to time and is not concerned with the end results; its concern is to show the path, an economy takes to arrive at the final result. It shows the position of an economy an intermediate points of time. Dynamics will consider loss in the production during short period. Static economics has nothing to do with trade cycles. He feels that his developmental economics corresponds to Tinbergens economic dynamics involving endogenous processes.

Consumer's Surplus

To Professor Mehta, Marshall's consumer surplus, is merely a buyer's surplus. It is the difference between the utility that he expects to derive from the consumption of the commodity and the cost of buying it. The greater our want for commodities now as compared to future wants, the greater the consumer's surplus. To him, it is due to the possibility of putting one's resources to multiple uses which are not equally beneficial to the consumer.

Theories of Interest

According to Mehta that both from theoretically and practically the theories of interest in economics are most important. He has defined interest as the earning of capital which is determined by it marginal productivity. Interest can be explained by:

(1) Marginal productivity of capital
(2) abstinence of effort
(3) Price of waiting and

(4) interest is the tangible expression of time preference.

It means that the present day enjoyment is preferred to an equal enjoyment in the future. The earning of capital is determined by the productivity of the last unit of capital in use, the amount of capital by the available supply, the available supply by the cost of creating capital or by the cost of waiting and the cost of abstinence by the time preference. In the opinion of Mehta, the two theories, classical and Keynesian, as a matter of fact are one and the same.

Welfare Economics

Mehta stated that a man's welfare at any given time is measured by the amount of satisfaction that he enjoys at that time, Welfare is an ethical concept. Social Welfare is a kind of welfare which is located in the mind of a particular man. It is difficult to measure social welfare because only a super man is competent to measure them. To him, the concept of super man serves a useful purpose; it makes us realise that social welfare is the sum total of satisfactions in the mind of a man. He feels that every study of economics has been a welfare study in some sense. In order to maximise social welfare we must introduce all those changes which make the gainers gain more than the losers lose. Later on, compensations should be allowed as stated by Hicks, Kaldor and Scitovsky.

Economics of Fasting

Fasting means not eating and not drinking, but if a man has to fast, his body and mind both must be fasting. Mind fasting means stop thinking which is impossible for ordinary people and body fasting refers to removing the poisonous matters from the body. It will improve the quality of action and ultimately the future condition of living. It will be instrumental in removing undesirable thoughts. Likewise a firm should undertake two kinds of fast—firstly bodily fast, i.e., it should not add to its building, plant, machinery, stock of goods etc. Secondly, mental fast, i.e., the organiser should think piously; he should not think of capturing the markets of other producers of improving technical efficiency which will increase unemployment. In other words, he should be non-violent. Owing to violence and selfishness some business are diseased. They should be persuaded to undertake a fast.

Growth and Investment

Growth, according to Professor Mehta, means the growth of population, wealth, and per capita income. When income grows, the economy is growing but morally it might be declining. He concluded that there is an inverse relationship between growth and moral progress. In the same way development leads to material prosperity, but it need not lead to moral progress. He feels that quantitative or qualitative improvement of human factors is more important than increase in either capital goods or the production of wealth. He has laid great emphasis on the efficiency of organisation.

Mehta has stressed innovations and increased investment which are needed for economic growth. The first condition is that capital shoud be more productive. The second condition is the period of production. There is a time lag between investment and final production. If the gestation period is small more investment will be needed. Thus lower the rate of time preference, the greater the investment. Time preference is a psychological phenomenon; so there is an element of uncertainty in investment also.

Macro Economic Growth

According to Professor Mehta, the development of a backward economy requires a change of social, cultural and economic infra-structure or structural constants. It needs banking system, a good system of transport and communications, an efficient organisation and capital formation. But the problem in developed country is not insufficient income but insufficient consumption. Professor Mehta believes that profitable investment would increase if the purchasing power in the hands of labourers increases.

(I) D.R. GADGIL (1901 - 1971)

Introduction

Dr. Dhanajay Ramachandra Gadgil, M.A., M.Litt., D. Litt., was a notable economists in the Indian scene for nearly five decades. He was educated at Nagpur and Cambridge Universities. He served the country in various capacities. He was Additional Secretary, Finance Department, Government of Bombay during 1924-25 and served as Principal M.T.B.College, Surat from 1925 to 1930. He occupied the position of Director, Gokhale Institute of Politics and Economics for a long time from 1930 to 1966. He was Deputy Chairman of Planning Commission from 1967 to 1971. He had served on several Committees including the ALL INDIA RURAL CREDIT SURVEY. He died on May, 3, 1971. He had published 24 books and many articles. In him, we can see the rare combination of academic pursuit with practical wisdom.

Economic Ideas

His book 'The Industrial Evolution of India in Recent Times' throws abundant light on Gadgil's industrialisation concepts. According to him the most important event in the economic transition of the country was the decline of handicrafts on account of railway policy, free trade policy and lack of technical education in India. The commercialisation of agriculture and increasing population were responsible for starting industries in India. During the early part of the British rule, cotton textile and jute industries made commendable progress. Regarding future trend he observed, "no big industries requiring complicated machinery of a thorough use of by-products are likely to spring up. The chief direction of progress will be that of the accessory industries and industries chiefly connected with agricultural operations or with the further working up of raw agricultural produce grown in the country". During 1914-28, the notable feature in the industrial scene of India was the establishment of the iron and steel industries. The war made the Government realise the importance of an all-round industrial development. As a consequence, the Industrial Commission was set up in 1916 and the Tariff Board in 1923 on the recommendations of the Fiscal Commission, to afford discriminating protection to industries. According to Professor Gadgil, these events had far-reaching significance which dominated the economic history of India. Further the world-wide trade depression and the emergence of provincial autonomy in 1929-30 had another profound impact on the economic scene of India. The trade depression heavily brought down agricultural prices and the State did nothing to help agriculturists. When popular ministers began to function in 1937-38 under the scheme of Provincial

Autonomy, they did not visualise the problems facing the country in right perspective. They could not solve the agrarian problems. Though factory production had increased under protection, the purchasing power of the farming community was very low. According to Gadgil "while in all countries of the world, old prejudices were rapidly thrown over, and an enormous amount of experimentation in the direction and control of economic life was undertaken, India alone marked time".

Prof. Gadgil's ideas about industrial labour can be understood in his publications of Regulation of Wages and other problems of Industrial Labour in India in which topics related to wages, employment, standard of living of workers, industrial relations effects of rationalisation of industries are covered. Gadgil points out the great evils in the existing wage rate system : (i) low level of wage of industrial workers, and (ii) disparities between the wages paid for similar work. Of course the latter continues even today. In order to remove disparity in payment and improve the lot of workers, Gadgil suggested that wages should be regulated at a higher level. It would decidedly improve their efficiency. Further, Gadgil sympathised with industrial workers and suggested besides higher wages, several welfare programmes, such as industrial housing, unemployment insurance, holidays with pay, sickness insurance etc. While examining the scheme of rationalisation of industries, he felt that though in the long run it would increase national income and employment in other industries, in the short run, it would create the embarrassment of unemployment. It was the State to decide how far rationalisation would help the Indian industries.

Gadgil's book War and Indian Economic Policy throws light on the inflation created during the war period 1939-43 due to expansion of currency. This had created enormous sufferings to the poor wage earners. For checking inflation, Gadgil suggested several fiscal measures such as increasing the direct taxes, public borrowing, full utilisation of productive resources, economy in administrative expenditure, control over profits and investments; price control and rationing, transport regulation with a priority to the movement of essential commodities and co-ordination of all these activities.

Regarding price policy Gadgil maintained that stabilisation of agricultural prices and holding the price line are closely related; and he further suggested regulation of prices of commodities like foodgrains, cloth, sugar, gur, edible oil, soap, tea, tobacco and kerosene oil which are essentially needed for the rural population. Regarding distribution, Gadgil laid emphasis on co-operative consumer societies.

(m) DR.RAMMANOHAR LOHIA (1920-1967)

INTRODUCTION

Dr. Rammanohar Lohia, a great leader of 20th century, saw the first ray of the sun on 23rd March 1920 at Akbarpur in Faizabad District (U.P.) in a Vaishya Family. His ancestors had acquired the surname of 'Lohia' for their dealing in the business of Lohia (Hardware). His father, Hiralal was a nationalist and from his father Lohia inherited the feelings of Nationalism, love and affection for the poor and needy. The environment in which Lohia spent his childhood was free from caste feelings. Even as a child, Lohia took keen interest in helping the poor, the needy and downtrodden and the weaker section when they were exploited.

Lohia completed his primary education at his native place Akbarpur, passed Matriculation in 1925 from Marwari Vidyalaya, Bombay, Intermediate in 1927 from the Kashi Vishwavidyalaya, Banaras and B.A. in 1929 from Vidyasagar College, Calcutta. He did his Ph.D. from Berlin in 1932. Since his very childhood Lohia took active part in public life. In 1920 on the death of Lokmanya Tilak, Lohia at the age of 10 years, took initiative in organizing a strike in school. His major passion was to free India from the foreigners rule. He, therefore, became a freedom fighter at a very early age and played a magnificent role in organizing the Quit India Movement in 1942.

After the achievement of Independence Lohia took active part in organizing many movements which he thought were beneficial for the Country. He struggled throughout his life for human freedom. He went to Goa and fought for the establishment of democracy in Nepal. He not only defeated the western imperialism but also Vehemently opposed the forceful entry of Soviet Union troops into Hungri in 1956 and Chinese troops into Tibbet . Though he was a political opponent of Nehru, he had love for him and had no hestitation to accept that Nehru was a veteran politician and the Congress had great need of his. While Gandhi was a dream for him, Netaji Shubhash was a brave leader in his eyes. He after independence, fought for many years to establish non-Congress governments in the states. His long cherished political desire could be fulfilled in 1967 when there was non-Congress government in eight states of Indian Union. He was an eloquent speaker, a great freedom fighter, a brave soldier of democracy and socialism, a courageous critic and independent ideologist, thinker and above all a great humanist. He left this earthly world for heavenly abode in the year 1967. After his death the socialist movement got divided into many factions.

Dr. Lohia's contributions to economic thoughts and action came out of this single-minded preoccupation with the need to free the individual from the shackles that chained him all-around.

ECONOMIC IDEAS OF DR. RAM MANOHAR LOHIA

INTRODUCTION

Economic ideas of Dr. Ram Manohar Lohia are embedded in his political philosophy and it is very difficult to separate them completely. Sometimes, they overlap each other. Due to this problem, it is very natural that readers may view some of his economic ideas as his political thought and vice-versa. In spite of this, a sincere effort has been made in this paper to put his economic ideas as separately as possible and any criss-cross is simply regretted and may kindly be excused. Unless we touch the border line of his political philosophy, we cannot fully understand and appreciate the economic ideas of Dr. Lohia. In fact, there is not a water-tight compartment between his economic ideas and his political philosophy.

INDIVIDUAL FREEDOM

Like most of the classical economists such as Adam Smith, J.B. Say and J.S. Mill, Dr. Lohia advocates Individual Freedom. He holds that men are by nature equal and free. His mind was tremendously influenced by the German Philosophers and Scholars – namely Kant, Hegel, Karl Marx and others. He agrees to Kantian view point that the individual is rational and has will of his own. Like Kant and Laski, he considers Liberty and equality as the necessary attributes of the individual. Lohia in the preface to his monumental book 'Marx Gandhi and Socialism', has mentioned seven revolutions, through which a better society can be established which will result in the progress of both individual and the society. His seventh revolution aims at protecting privacy against encroachment by the collective. He regrets to see the modern trend in which the individual has been steadily losing his sovereignty to organization. Laski and Russel have also expressed similar views. According to Lohia, the individual welfare and happiness, education and health, also his leisure and much of his life and thought are subject to planning of various kinds. "This planning is rigorous in lands of communism but a growing element of organizational compulsion is present everywhere".

Lohia further argues that there are certain spheres of life which should be free from the control of State, Government, Organisations and Groups. Rights of privacy in the sphere of house keeping, entertainment, marriage should be maintained. An individual should have full freedom for choosing any profession and membership of any political party. State or Government or Political party should not interfere with the private life of individual. Every individual should have right to lead his life according to his choice upto a certain limit. Lohia fears this right may be misused by the individual. But when one's right is recognised and if that is misused then what should be done. In this connection Lohia says let the individual suffer. Lohia surpasses Mill, when the firmly opines that every man or woman should have even the right to commit suicide. No body has right to interfere with this personal matter of individual, his choice of committing suicide. Mill allows interference in purely personal matter when one is about to commit suicide or insists on doing something whose dangerous nature is not known to him. It will never be an attack upon one's liberty if individual is prevented from committing suicide. Mill justifies such intervention on the ground that the individual at the time of committing suicide does not know his own true interest; society knows it better and so can legitimately restrain him. The notion of individual freedom as advocated by Lohia has divided freedom into two parts – the first is connected with non-property matter and second one is connected with property. He advocates full freedom to individuals in non-property matters. He asserts, "Rights of privacy and freedom must be recognised in all those spheres which are not directly connected with property". It shows that Dr. Lohia also accepts certain degree of interference in property matters but even in property matters Lohia never approves of complete State control as is prevalent in the communist system. He wants to restrain state interference only in those spheres which are directly connected with property.

Lohia is a staunch supporter of liberty for backward people which Mill refuses to grant. Lohia wants to give preferential treatment to backward people for a certain period. In this connection, he surpasses Mill who proves to be a bit conservative in his approach to liberty.

Planning

Lohia does not outrightly oppose State planning. He says that State Planning always aims at doing good. But he does not like such a planning which is rooted in compulsion and curtails much of the individual freedom. Lohia fears that State Planning may encroach on the individual privacy.

Lohia points out the defect of the then Congress in matter of planning. The Congress had not planned things well. It is protected the capitalist. It is like a person in whirlpool reaching out its hands in whatever direction it can without success. He observes, "Thus, while classless society is declared as its goal, the Congress in practice aligns itself with Landlords and Capitalists". The pattern of big fish devouring small fries is prevailing under the Congress regime. Poverty, increasing population, unemployment lawlessness, corruption, deceit, arson and loot have become the normal features of the society. As a result, there is frustration everywhere. To quote Lohia, "owing to the planlessness and the initial blunders of the Congress, the country is at a standstill with an everincreasing population;

this means retrogression. Production is declinging, poverty is on the increase, and there is disillusionment and distrust all round".

Gender Difference

In Lohia's view, there is no distinction between men and women. Men and women both should be equally placed in the society. Like Plato, Indian saints and other thinkers, Lohia also advocates equality between men and women. He observes "women will be given equal status with men in all matters – political, social and economic. In the sphere of education women will receive preferential treatment to enable them to overcome existing disparities with men". Through legislation and through propaganda and education, all social customs and practices that go against the principles of equality of women with men will be ended. Lohia holds the view that women have always been neglected in the society. Their status is very low. They are backward in all respects. Therefore, it is necessary to bring them on equal footing with men. He further says that women can be equated with men only by preferential opportunity rather than equal opportunity. Lohia opines that "equal opportunity would not solve the problem of inequality between the sexes. When a group of people is held down by debility, physical or cultural, the only way to bring it up to equality with others is through conferment of preferential opportunity. An Indian woman is a bond maid at the mercy of her parents till her marriage and after marriage a slave to her husband. Lohia wants this to be done away by giving preferential treatment to the fair sex. Like men, participation of women in the socialist movement is equally necessary, as Lohia says – "A socialist movement without the active participation of women is like a wedding without the bride".

Solution to Food Problem–Ghera dalo Andolan (Gherao)

Lohia has suggested Ghera Dalo Andolan for the solution of food problems during the time of famine. The socialist party believes in the method of Ghera Dalo Andolan which makes an appeal to the Government either to – "give bread" to hungry people or "send them to jail". According to Lohia, "under the Ghera Dalo Andolan hungry people should Gherao the Government's offices, Government's godowns, godowns of big traders and hoarders upto the time they get food or they get themselves arrested". Such movements were launched at Deoriya in U.P. and Daltonganj in Bihar and people got success in the year, 1958. This Ghera Dalo Andolan should be strictly peaceful and non-violent in Gandhian way. Lohia has suggested two other movements for solving food problem. First, the socialist two other movements for solving food problem. First, the socialist party should lauch Anna Banto or distribute food movement. Under this movement, hungry masses should peacefully seize godowns, weigh foodgrains, maintain an account of the total food grains and then distribute foodgrains among themselves. Later on, when they become capable of paying, they return the taken food grains plus one-fourth more or pay in cash. But Lohia says this movement is possible only when the people are strong and police weak.

Secondly, without weighing and maintaining account of food grains, hungry masses should distribute foodgrains among themselves but this should be performed peacefully and non-violently. In this connection, Lohia warns people that "godowns or retailers or commission taking goledars should not be seized. Such type of movement was prevalent in Germany".

Ghera Dalo Andolan, Anna Banto and Anna Banto Movement without keeping records of foodgrains – all these three movements suggested by Lohia for solving food problem during famine are sound in theory but impracticable, unmanageable and undesirable in practice. These will create chaos and anarchy in the society, and the problem may be further complicated.

Imperialism and Colonialism

Lohia was against imperialism and colonialism. According to him all forms of colonialism are shame to mankind and serious impediment to growth of equal world. Political rule of an occupation army and of one nation over another must go. All colonial states of the world must be set free. "Socialist internationalism must stand behind all struggles against colonialism and render all possible assistance to freedom fighters".

International Trade and Aid and Assistance toUnder Developed countries

Lohia favours international trade but he warns that such trade should not be a one-way traffic rather it should be a two-way traffic. According to Lohia aid to underdeveloped countries must come through a World Development Authority to which every nation contributes according to its ability from which every nation receives according to its need. He further points out that "until such an authority comes into being, international socialism may attempt to setup model projects through a capital collected from all such organisations and men as would listen to its appeal". Even within a nation, the more fortunate persons are called upon to assist the less fortunate ones, so in the international world, the more favoured ones should assist the less advanced. Backward nations should be helped to acquire the economic apparatus by which they can raise themselves. Our fight should be against hunger, disease and illiteracy. Economic inequality is the main source of discord and war in the world. In order to remove the economic disparities, a World Development Authority should be established. Like Lohia, Radhakrishnan also supports the concept of World Economic Development Programme. Foreign aid in its present form is not only humiliating and dangerous to the receiving countries but can never be adequate to meet their needs and requirements. Such aid definitely, corrupts the backward countries. Such a one sided giving and taking is one-way traffic and is erroneous in conception and harmful in consequences. Technological skills and economic aid should be voluntarily exchanged between rich and the retarded states through World Development Authority. And this mutual exchange should result in approximation not in imposition. This concept of two way traffic in the field of International Trade, Aid and Assistance is sound in theory but difficult in practice so long as distinction between Big and Small exists in the International field.

The Concept of Four-Pillar State and Decentralisation of Economic and Political Powers

Lohia belives in decentralisatin of economic and political powers. For giving a solution to the malady of Indian administration, he gives the concept of Four-Pillar state which is based on the principle of division of powers. According to him Four-Pillar State constitutes four limbs of the State. They are the village, the district, the province and the centre with sovereign powers. All these four limbs of the State will organically function. They will work interdependently. Sovereign powers must not reside alone in the centre and the federating units but also with district and villages which are the primary political institutions where a group of men and women work for the interest of the whole community. Thus Lohia considers that the greatest defect of Indian administration is the concentration of economic and political powers either in the centre or in the federating units. He suggests that there should be decentralization of political and economic powers in the four limbs of the Four-Pillar State. Unless this is done, democratic institutions can not flourish and active participation of people in administration can not be reality. Concentration of economic power give rise to inequality and is a characteristic feature of capitalism where the economic power remains concentrated in the hands of a few.

Democracy and Democratic Institutions

Lohia considers democracy and democratic institutions very important for any nation. He says that democracy and socialism are the two sides of the same coin. "Democracy in all circumstances shall be the sheet-anchor of the ideas and programmes of the socialism. Democracy means the inevitable answerability of elected assembly. It also means the recognition and respect of limited personality of individual, party, Government and the State-four categories which together constitute the agencies of political action".

Thus Lohia is fully convinced that it is only through democracy that freedom of thought can be best maintained. At the same time, he believes if democracy is organised on the principles of socialism, both freedom of mind and economic security to the individual can be attained. The enjoyment of individual liberty can not take a concrete form unless the state assures economic security or equality to the individual. Nobel laureate Prof. Amartya Sen later testified it through practical examples of famines that took place in many countries. Countries with democratic system saved countless lives whereas people in large number died in other system of Governance.

Socialism, Capitalism and Communism

Lohia is an exponent of socialism. He believes in the system of socialism. He is a born critic of capitalism and communism. He criticises capitalism and communism on the ground that both the systems have failed to prepare the soil for the germination of the seeds of liberty and equality evenly. Therefore, Lohia prefers the system of socialism which believes in the equal growth of liberty and equality both.

According to him "if socialism is to be defined in two words then they are equality and prosperity. I do not know if this definition has been given earlier at any time. If so, I could call it the best definition given so far".

Lohia says real freedom is not possible in capitalism and communism because capitalism breeds inequalities on the one hand and communism kills the spirit of individual freedom on the other. Therefore, both the systems are inimical to the true spirit of democracy which signifies liberty and equality both. Lohia, Russel, Laski and Nehru want to establish a democratic socialist society which will constantly move on the axis of liberty and equality. Liberty thus implies equality. Liberty and equality are not in conflict nor even separate, but are different facets of the same ideal. Lohia opines: "Freedom and bread are inseparable, at least in Asia, and neither communism nor capitalism can supply these two articles to us. I would suggest that Asia can be saved from communism only if it is saved from capitalism and feudalism".

Therefore, to Lohia and Laski, equality is the primary condition of attaining freedom or justice. No one can dare to believe that it can be obtained under the capitalist system which practices privileges and distinctions. The real point that they wish to place in their discussion of liberty is that in the present hierarchically organised economic and political order, opportunities for creative self-expression are denied to all but small group of men. Liberty in the sense of free play of the relative impulses of men and a high degree of individual diversity is incompatible with the present system of property, for its result is a concentration of power in a few hands which makes for the political personalizing of the average citizen ineffective. Inequality is an inherent characteristic of capitalist society, while a Socialist Society will necessarily be an equal society. Both Lohia and Laski argue that economic inequality is the root cause of all other inequalities. They also say that freedom is meaningful only to a small minority in capitalist society which owns and controls property. Great inequalities of wealth make impossible the attainment of freedom.

The removal of inequality from the human society is one of the seven revolutions of Lohia. He points out that "the poorer the country, the greater is the inequality within it". Lohia is firm in his thought that the capitalist society breeds inequality which proves antithetical to freedom. Similarly, he dislikes communist system which is based on fear; whereas, the capitalist system works under the temptation of profit. "Such systems which depend on temptation and fear for their dynamism and growth must inevitably breed inequality".

Capital Formation

Lohia holds the view that Industrialisation is not possible without capital formation. As per his prescription, in a poor and diseased country like India, Capital could be formed only through the way of equality. "Capitalism cannot perform its own functions here. Capitalism cannot create capital, prosperity and thereby capital formation can come only through equality".

Other Contributions

Lohia's thought was not confined to the national boundary. He advocated World Civilization, World Parliament, World Government, World Development Authority and World Citizenship. Lohia was opposed to 'United Nations' in its present form and was in favour of replacing it by a world parliament which will be organised on the principles of universality and equality. He was having a broad outlook and so he visualised the concept of World Civilization, World Parliament, World Government, World Development Authority and World Citizenship. He further explains that under the atmosphere of capitalism, imperialism, colonialism and racialism, the above concepts cannot be a reality. Therefore, for the realizations of world citizenship, economic inequality, political slavery and the feeling of racialism must stop without any delay. He gives the example of India which is gripped by poverty and torn by example of India which is gripped by poverty and torn by religions and castes. According to him, it seems ridiculous to make the submerged and hungry landless labourer a world citizen. Lohia shows the boldness to say that our attempt to create a new civilization through World Government must not cease. In this context, he finally concludes, "And yet this movement for World

Government in conjunction with socialism may be that lever which raises the submerged millions to new hope and endeavour".

TECHNOLOGY

"The technology of Modern Europe is an imperialist technology in origin and in current substance is incapable of reproduction all over the word unless an abundance of colonies in other planets were discovered". The industrial revolution of Europe and modern technology are incapable of repetition in Asia and Africa. Too little land and too many men and too few tools are a mark of Asia, so a full application of a mass production is utterly impossible. Lohia further says that existing technology made possible by the imperialist control which European civilization exercises over the rest of the world is no longer valid. In a way, Lohia favoured the use of labour intensive technique for a country like India where there is abundance of labour and death of capital.

Conclusion

Dr. Lohia was an ardent supporter of Individual Freedom, Democratic Institutions and Socialism. He advocated democratic socialism. He was critical of hig powers which were either following capitalism or communism. He was against direct aid of any kind from developed economies to underdeveloped economies like India because of the fact that in such aid there was a feeling of domination in the givers and a feeling of subjugation in the receivers. He recommended such aid through world Development Authority where rich nations may contribute to the poor ones. He favoured international trade but it should not be a one-way traffic rather it should be a two-way traffic. The chief contribution of Lohia lies in analysing and exposing the danger of modern capitalism and communism and putting up a proposal for a socialistic system which can ensure maximum welfare to the people through material comfort and at the same time assure freedom for the full development of individual.

(n) JAWAHARLAL NEHRU (1989-1964)

LIFE-SKETCH OF NEHRU

Jawaharlal Nehru was born on 14th November 1889 at Allahabad. His father, Pandit Moti Lal Nehru, was a famous lawyer and rich man and as such Jawaharlal was brought up like a prince. He received his primary education at home but after passing his Matriculation Examination went to England for higher studies. After taking his degree in Law he came back to India in 1912 and started practice at Allahabad. In 1916 he was married to Kamla. He came under the influence of Mahatma Gandhi and left his practice in 1921 to join the National Movement started by Gandhiji. He was sent to jail several times and was elected president of the Congress four times. He was undoubtedly very hardworking, courageous and bold, scholarly as well as a believer in truth, non-violence and universal brotherhood. During his lifetime he was loved and respected by all and became a great leader. He became the first Prime Minister of the Indian Republic after independence and died on 27th May, 1964.

The auto-biography of Jawaharlal Nehru and the two other important books—'The Discovery of India', the 'Glimpses of World History' as well as many historical speeches and writing give a clear impression of this great man of destiny of history', a man of action and of thought and the master spirit of an epoch in India History.

Nehru and the National Philosophy of India

For Jawaharlal Nehru, every State needed a 'National Philosophy or 'national ideology' to hold it together and give it coherence and sense of direction and purpose. In his view the need for such a philosophy was particularly great in a new country like India whose people were divided on religious, ethnic, linguistic and other grounds, economically undeveloped, socially static and politically inexperienced. As such they desperately needed a shared public philosophy to unit them and provide them with a set of clearly defined 'goals' or 'objectives'. As India's fist Prime Minister he thought it one of his most important task to develop such a national philosophy.

Like most nationalist leaders Nehru was convinced that India had become deeply degenerate and required radical restructuring. Its regeneration consisted in modernising itself along the lines of modern European societies, which too had, for centuries, remained degenerate and turned the corner in the nineteenth century by comprehensively reorganising themselves along the lines required by the modern industrial civilisation. For Nehru 'modernisation' was India's national philosophy and involved seven 'national goals', namely, national unity, parliamentary democracy, industrialisation, socialism, development of the scientific temper, secularism and non-alignment.

National Unity

For Nehru national unity or what he sometimes called national integration was the *sine qua non* of national independence. 'We must give topmost priority to the development of a sense of unity in India because these are critical days'. Over the centuries India had fallen prey to foreign rule because of such factors as the lack of a strong central government underpinned by a nationwide structure of authority, narrow regional loyalties, divisions among its people sometimes so deep that they did not mind inviting outside help to settle old scores, and the absence of pubic spirit and patriotism. Unless India put these right, it was doomed. Nehru thought that the Constitution of India had taken care of some of them and for the first time in its history given it a strong state, reconciling the regional aspirations for autonomy with the need for a central government strong enough to hold them all together and protect them against external threats.

Parliamentary Democracy

Parliamentary democracy was the second 'national goal' for Nehru. He was convinced that India needed a democratic form of government not only because the latter respected the Individual and was inherently desirable, but also because a diverse, vast and divided country could not be held together and governed in any other way. He also thought that it, especially the national and state elections, had the great advantage of drawing the masses into the conduct of public affairs and giving them a stake in the new polity.

Nehru knew that parliamentary democracy depend for its success on a strong and united opposition, and that India not only had none but was unlikely to have one for some time. Since he was convinced that it was the only appropriate form of government for India, he explored ways of compensating for the absence of opposition. He regularly consulted and briefed opposition leaders, and unsuccessfully tried to involve them in supervising the work of government departments. He urged his party to think of itself in national terms, encouraged vigorous internal debates and even welcomed dissent. On many occasions he internalised the opposition and himself acted as the leader of opposition, publicly criticising his colleagues and even himself and acknowledging his mistakes.... He also encouraged the press to play the appositional role and chided chief ministers who tried to penalise over critical journalists. None of these came anywhere near filling the role of a strong opposition party but they did humanise the exercise of power and introduce a moderate degree of check on its abuse.

Industrialisation

Industrialisation was the third component of the national ideology. Though Nehru was persuaded that India needed to encourage cottage and small-scale industries to ease the problems of poverty and unemployment, he saw them as a temporary expedient only necessary until the country became fully industrialised. Unlike Gandhi he was convinced that India could not permanently eliminate poverty and satisfy the legitimate aspirations of its people without large-scale industrialisation. More importantly the modern world was industrialised, and a country that failed to keep pace with it remained weak and vulnerable to foreign domination.

For Nehru industry, not agriculture, was the lever of economic development. He thought that industry-led growth transformed the economy far more quickly and effectively than agriculture-led growth. For Nehru agriculture was a primitive and culturally inferior activity. It was tied to land, parasitic upon the forces of nature, made man a plaything of nature and encouraged 'fatalistic' and 'obscurantism' ways of thought. It also fragmented the country, confined man's vision to the narrow limits of his village, and was a breeding ground of ignorance, traditionalism, passivity, narrow-mindedness and superstition. As such it lacked the power and energy to haul the country out of its 'traditional grooves' and 'propel' it along the path of modern ways of life and thought. As Nehru repeatedly argued, villages had been responsible for India's degeneration and changing their 'antiquated' ideas and habits was the 'very basic problem' of independent India. He did not therefore think much of agriculture as an activity and of the peasantry as a social class.

Socialism

For Nehru socialism was both a 'scientific method of social analysis and a normative doctrine describing a 'desirable' society. Like Marx, by whom he was once deeply influenced, he found it difficult to integrate the two and ran into all kinds of difficulties.

For Nehru the 'socialist method' explained phenomena no other method could. The British had colonised India not in a fit of absent-mindedness, nor to 'civilise' its people, but to procure cheap raw material and a captive market for their goods.

Nehru remained a socialist all his adult life and entertained the same broad view of it. For him socialism was not just an economic doctrine, nor just a form of social organisation, but a 'new civilisation' based on a radically transformed 'humanity'. It was classless, democratic, provided the material and moral conditions necessary for the fullest development of the human potential, and encouraged co-operative and non-acquisitive impulses. Production was planned, organised on co-operative lines, and directed towards the satisfaction of human needs rather than accumulation of profit, and the basic freedoms and rights of citizens were fully guaranteed. It was striking that unlike Marx and other socialists, Nehru did not define man as a producing being, or place much emphasis on popular participation, egalitarianism, gradual withering away of the state class struggle and new forms of communal living. His socialism was basically aesthetic and liberal, concentrating on the individual rather than the community and stressing self-expression, individuality, social justice and human creativity.

Scientific Temper

The fifth national goal consisted in the cultivation of the 'scientific temper', 'culture' or 'approach to life'. By this Nehru meant not so much the development of science and technology, which was but a part and product of it, as fostering rational and empirical ways of thought and life. For nearly a millennium India had remained in 'deep slumber' and come to grief because it had become dogmatic, mystical, speculative, uncritical, inward-looking and addicted to undisciplined fantasy. If it was to turn the corner and become a strong and vibrant society like Europe, it had to learn to think and behave scientifically. Nehru's view of scientific thinking was fairly conventional. It involved checking and relying on facts alone, taking nothing on 'blind trust' or faith, changing beliefs in the light of new evidence, being precise and exact, relying on the method of trial and error, ceaselessly searching for truth, keeping an open mind, and in general developing the 'hard discipline of the mind' characteristic of the 'modern age'. Such an approach applied to beliefs as much as to social practices. Nehru advocated economic planning on the ground that it was the only scientific way of running the economy.

Secularism

Nehru vigorously pleaded for a secular state, but his view of secularism was complex and vague. He distinguished between the spiritual and ideological-cum-institutional dimensions of religion. He was intensely hostile to the latter but deeply sympathetic to the former, especially during the pre-independence days and the last years of his Prime Ministership. Though he frequently talked about spirituality, he never clearly defined the term. Sometimes he equated it with morality. On other occasions he used it to refer to concern with the nature and destiny of man and the meaning and purpose of life; to be spiritual was to be sensitive to these important and 'irrepressible' questions. On yet other occasions Nehru gave the term substantive content and took it to mean a broadly advaita metaphysic, spirituality consisted in recognising the presence of a creative force or vital energy at work in all living beings and appreciating the unity of life.

Non-Alignment

International affairs were Nehru's favourite area of interest. During the independence struggle he constantly drew his countrymen's attention to their vital importance, and was the principal architect of many an important Congress resolutions on international subjects. During his period in office as prime minister he remained his own foreign minister.

Nehru insisted that India should follow an independent foreign policy. He justified this on three grounds. First, it was a necessary expression and an indispensable means of preserving Indian independence. Second, it was the only common ground on which Indians of different ideological persuasions could be united. *Third* India could not mediate between the superpowers, mobilise world opinion on important issues, retain a fresh and pragmatic perspective on world affairs, open up and reconstitute the rigid international system on a broader basis, and speak for the third world if it aligned itself to one of the power blocs.

Thanks to Nehru's foreign policy, India acquired high political visibility and played a creative international role. It mediated and contributed towards a better understanding between the two superpowers and between the metropolitan countries and their ex-colonies. It brought the countries of the third world together, helped forge common bonds between them, and made them a moderately effective world force. India also linked up with the progressive elements in the west and helped create a powerful world opinion in favour of peaceful co-existence and the economic development and territorial integrity of the new nations.

The Nehru Strategy

The principal components of the Nehru Strategy of building modern India were the institution and strengthening of the planning process, establishment of the public sector in Industry, laying the base of modern agriculture by the overthrow of the feudal system, creation of a modern scientific and technological base and attainment of economic independence by systematic development of heavy and basic industries and maximum development of our natural and human resources. Within the framework of mixed economy, the public sector was to be built upto attain the commanding heights of the economy'. The concept of mixed economy itself was, and remains valid for mobilising all productive classes including the national bourgeoisie for promoting sustained and rapid economic growth. In the rural areas, while the concept of private ownership of land was an indispensable element for ushering in modernisation of agriculture, a co-operative sector was promoted along with the community development organisations to assist the process of social transformation. Politically the strategy implied an alliance of all productive classes, including owners of property. Hence the broad anti-imperialist alliance forged by Gandhiji was continued. This continuity imparted a great deal of strength to the process of modernisation in the initial stages.

Industrial Development: Policy and Relation

India must be industrialised as rapidly as possible. And industrialisation includes, of course, all kinds of industry—major, middling, small, village and cottage. However, rapid our industrialisation may be, it cannot possibly absorb more than a small part of the population of this country in the next ten, twenty or even thirty years. Hundreds of millions will remain who have to be employed chiefly in agriculture. These people must, in addition, be given employment in smaller industries like cottage industries and so on. Hence, the importance to agriculture and food and matters pertaining to agriculture. If agricultural foundation is not strong then the industry will not have a strong basis either. Certain basic and key industries have been given due consideration. The essential basis for development of industry is power-electric power. The progress made by a country can be judged by the electric power it has.

INDUSTRIAL POLICY

There is much discussion about the public sector and the private sector. He attached great importance to the public sector. The pattern of society that he look forward to is a socialist pattern of society that he looks forward to is a socialist pattern of society which is classless, casteles. As the socialist pattern grows, there is bound to be more and more nationalised industry, but what is important is not that there should be an attempt to nationalise everything, but higher production and employment. In a country like India, where money, trained personnel and experience are lacking, we have to take advantage of such experience, training and money as we have. We want to make this business of building up India a co-operative enterprise of all the people.

Some people might talk about private enterprise and laissez faire, but practically nobody now believes in laissez faire. There is regulation and control all-over the world in regard to industry and imports and exports. Everywhere, even in the most highly developed countries of the capitalist economy, the State functions in a way which possibly a socialist fifty years ago did not dream of.

INDUSTRIAL RELATIONS

This business of strikes and lock-outs should be faced. Apart from the wastage involved, this conflict is illogical and wrong. The only other way is to find mutual agreement, or if there is no mutual agreement, to bring in some third party in the shape of conciliator, arbitrator or tribunal.

THE POVERTY BARRIER

India is struggling to get out of the morass of poverty, and to reach the stage of what is called "the take-off into sustained economic growth". It wants to cross the barrier of poverty and reach the stage where growth becomes relatively spontaneous. The under-developed country is on this side of the barrier. There are certain cumulative processes at work which in a developed country, tend to encourage its growth further and further and which, in an under-developed country, pull it back all the time. The poor becomes poorer. Poverty becomes is own curse. It repeats itself. Planning is essentially a process whereby we stop those cumulative forces at work which make the poor poorer, and start a new series cumulative forces which make them get over that difficulty.

Defence

Defence does not consist in people going about marching up and down the road with guns and other weapons. Defence consists today in a country being industrially prepared for producing the goods and equipment of defence.

You cannot have a factory producing tanks in the absence of other industrial development in the country. A factory producing aircraft can be created only, if there is large supply of technically trained people. Therefore, the immediate object should be, both from the point of view of economic development and that of defence, to build up industry, heavy industry in particular.

Socialism

All individuals in India should have equal opportunities of growth, from birth upwards, and equal opportunities for work according to their capacity. The process of bringing socialism to India, especially in the democratic way, will inevitably take time.

Public Sector

It is interesting to see other countries where there are public enterprises; there they have arrived at the conclusion that they must give freedom to the man in charge. Of course, if there is a major loss, if the whole thing goes to pieces, then the man in charge will suffer. But the point is that he is given responsibility. Every person who has advised us, whether he is an American like Dr. Appleby or a great Russian leader like Mr. Mikoyan, has told, us : 'Do not interfere with your enterprises give your executive responsibility. Do not interfere".

Population Control

Some kind of limitation of the rapidly growing population becomes an urgent matter. It was for this reason that India was driven to consider this question of family planning as a part of national planning. If educational standards in the country go up, the problem becomes simpler. If the general living and economic conditions improve, it becomes simpler again. This fact should be appreciated because then the movement of family planning becomes a part of the larger movement for raising the standard of living of the people.

Price Control

It goes without saying that it is of utmost importance that prices should be under control. But a price policy is not separated from fiscal or monetary or commercial policy, and it might well involve controls. In certain essential articles, if necessary, it may involve all kinds of approaches including controls.

Deficit Financing

Finance is important but not so important as people think. What is really important is drawing up the physical needs of the people and then working to produce things which will fulfil such needs. If you are producing wealth, it does not matter very much if you have some deficit financing because you are actually putting money back through goods and services. Therefore, it does not matter how you manipulate your currency so long as your production is also keeping pace with it. Of course there is the fear of inflation. We must avoid it.

Importance of Technicians

Scientific and technical personal should be introduced not only in the technical processes but in administration also. The administrator is an able man and does a good deal but his thinking is on different lines from that of a technical man. There should be a greater inclusion of the technical and scientific type of thinking in administration. It is good to mix the pure administrator with the technical man and the scientific man. After all, all problems today are problems of science and technology. An able administrator or an able politician, just as an enable lawyer, can grasp the broad outlines of a problem, but it is another thing to have grown up with all the processes. Therefore, the scientists and technicians should be associated more and more with administration and planning.

Women's Progress

A social revolution includes everyone, but it especially pertains to women. If the women do not change or progress, social life remains more or less static. And one of the most interesting and far-reaching changes which are coming over India today is the change among the women of India. It has occurred to a great extent in regard to women in cities and towns and has begun even in the rural parts of our country. Once it spread adequately in the villages, this social revolution will bring tremendous results.

Rural Development

Over 80 per cent of our people live in villages. India is poor because the villagers of India are poor. India will be rich if the village's of India are rich. Therefore, the basic problem of India is to remove the poverty from the Indian villages. Firstly, each village should have a semi-autonomous panchayat. It should have a co-operative. It should have a school. The co-operatives have in the past been chiefly societies for credit purposes. But the co-operative should perform many other services. While the panchayat will represent the administrative aspect of village life, the co-operative will represent the economic side of village life.

Land Reforms

A proper land policy is essential for the progress of agriculture. We have gone some way towards achieving this by putting an end to the zamindari and jagirdari systems in many states. We must complete this task, eliminate all intermediaries and fix a limit for the size of holdings. We hope that the next step will be co-operative farming which will take advantage of the latest agricultural techniques.

Employment

Every modern economic theory today bases itself, unlike the previous ones, on full employment in the country. We cannot produce employment by legislation. Our economic approach must be such that we can reach the stage of full employment within a measurable period of time. Every one of our steps must be aimed at that.

Education

According to Nehru : "Right education must be all round development of the human being, harmonising of our internal conflicts and a capacity to co-operate with others." Nehru attached great importance to the practical aspect of education. Examination oriented education was never favoured by Nehru. He attached more importance to real education, and by that he do not mean examinations and the like. In his opinion proper intellectual training is essential to do anything efficiently; but far more important is the background of this training—the habits. ideals, ideas, objective the internal harmony, the capacity for co-operation, the strength to be true to what one considers to be right, the absence of fear. Real education, according to Nehru, aims at, "internal freedom and fearlessness. Time and again he reiterated that education divorced from life can never be of any use. "Afterall education is meant to fit you for life, that is to say, not only your narrow spheres but you will have lateron understand the big problems of life".

Of late a lot of fuss has ben made about value oriented education. However, only a vague idea is conveyed through this phrase. It is interesting to note that Nehru was fairly free from doubts as to the value education aimed at. There is not a great difference between his and Gandhi's conception. Both insist the individual virtues to be inculcated, however, the former gives no less importance to the social aspect. He hates an education system that reduces a human being to a bookworm or an island by himself. The greatest value on can expect from academic training is the feeling of co-operation and equality.

Nehru always warned as against inaction and indolence. 'Aram Haram Hai' was his ever-echoing watchword. In his opinion, the greatest feat of education would be to make people shrug their lethargy off and work ceaselessly for the welfare of society. Dignity of labour was considered by him much greater than higher intellectual pursuits.

NATIONALISM

Nehru's nationalism was free from all bigotry and narrow-mindedness. He had evolved so healthy an outlook that it was impossible for him to confine his interests to his own nation. Humanity, love and justice were the values he was all for. However, he was like any other nationalist against the British rule in India. He could never get condescend to the unjust laws and administration of the British. His love for India was deeply romantic and emotional. At the same time he was seriously concerned about the well-being of the Nation. And to this cause he was fully dedicated. All suffereings and troubles he sustained for this very cause. Naturally his ideals of education is closely associated with nationalism. Nationalistic education he thought, must come from the national genius. To Nehru, devotion to learning was meaningless in the absence of devotion to the nation. The immediate and recognisable unit of society is nation and therefore nation and society are synonymous.

Though the first job of a student is to train himself for future, his indifference to politics is undesirable. 'The pressure of political circumstances' and 'the stranglehold of economic conditions' deny the opportunity of education to vast masses of people. A national awareness, as such, was necessary in order to create a favourable atmosphere for proper education. But it does not mean only politicians are the builders of India's destiny. The academic including students and teachers also have an important rather seminal role to play in the reconstruction of the nation. Politicians and states men may strive for political and economic changes but they can't play the part of foundation layers. 'The real basis' of that society must be laid in the teachings of our schools and colleges.

Art and culture, though not so important as science and technology, are very essential for the general refinement of a people's attitude and ways of life. Nehru never undermined the value of art. In his opinion art and culture are necessary to make a complete man or a woman. They give a grace of life and broaden viewspan. However, too much concentration on the artistic side does not let us keep with the fast progressing world. We cannot go on living and relieving our past. Nehru's progressive thoughts, though deeply influenced by the industrial world of the west, were not very different from those of

Gandhiji. The latter believed in small scale technology with a special weight on individual effort, while Nehru insisted on socialistic pattern of industrialism, this is the reason that Nehru put art and culture in the second place.

Nehru's views on women's education are reflected specially in his letters to his daughter. He was directly related to this problem. Though he never imposed his ideas on her, he expressed frankly what he thought and meant by education for women. He disliked the education which prepared a girl to play a part in the drawing room and nowhere else. Women had an equal role to play in the making of the nation. He treats women on par with men in every walk of life.

Non-Violence

Gandhiji's abhorrence for violence was shared by Nehru even if he did not accept nonviolence as a creed. Gandhiji told Fischer, "I am a social revolutionist. Violence is bred by inequality, non-violence by equality". Nehru took a historical view of violence. He told the Lok Sabha in 1954, "Where upheavals occur they are products of history, and violence, defeat and civil war govern the subsequent events. Some Hon. members seem to think that in order to have progress they must destroy. They think that by increasing the conflict and bitterness they can have a clean slate to write upon. No country has ever had a clean slate to write upon, not even after the biggest of revolutions. No one should deliberately destroy something which is worthwhile in order to build something which may be good in certain circumstances". His objection to communism was its emphasis on violence. "Communism charges the capitalist structure of society with violence and class-conflict. I think this is essentially correct. The question is how to get rid of inequality and have a classless society with equal opportunities for all. Can this be achieved through methods of violence, or is it possible to bring about changes through peaceful methods? Communism has definitely allied itself to the approach of violence. Even if it does not indulge normally in violence, its language is of violence, its thought is violent". He repeatedly said, "We want to do away with classes, but by the method of winning over people. I admit class struggle, but I do not want to aggravate it. I do not want to be obsessed with it. I want to get rid of it as far as possible without aggravating it".

Mixed Economy

It was precisely to avoid a violent eruption of class struggle in the country that Jawaharlal Nehru opted for a mixed economy. He repeatedly pointed out that acquisitive society and the "free enterprise system" had outlived their relevance and were controlled and restrained even in the countries in which they first came up. He emphasised that the"strongest urge today is for social justice and equality", and unless the state responded to it "it might well become a police state". But he also saw that fully controlled economies led to authoritarianism and totalitarianism which he regarded as irrational growths. He was faced with another dilemma. From the historical point of view he saw that the 'shell' of the Indian system was capitalistic while its 'essence' remained feudal; in this context the slow pace of growth that would take place without the state taking on certain economic responsibilities would lead to "monopolies and aggregations of economic power". At the same time, he realised, as he told the Lok Sabha once, "the price paid for rapid industrialisation has been terrific in some socialist countries. I am certain no country with any kind of parliamentary democracy can possibly pay it". He wanted India to be a parliamentary democracy for various reasons, but he knew that " if there is economic inequality in the country all the political democracy and all the adult suffrage in the world cannot bring about real democracy". At one stage he was even prepared for adjustments in the political system to meet the demands of the task of building a non-acquisitive and egalitarian society, but he emphasised that "political democracy will only justify itself if ultimately succeeded in producing these results"—by 'these' he meant economic advance in a manner that social tensions (including class war) were reduced and finally defused.

Mixed economy was his answer to the problem of planning economic advance in a democratic set-up. Besides, he believed that "change is essential, but continuity is also essential. The future has to be built on the foundations laid in the past and the present. To deny the past and break with it completely is to uproot ourselves and, sapless, dry up". Mixed economy was to be his instrument of change without a break with continuity. Transition from feudalism had not been accomplished anywhere without a break caused by industrial revolution which had taken place in western countries before they took to democracy and in socialist countries in conditions in which civil liberties were not available to their citizens. It was an uncharted path that he took, and he made it clear that, for India, planning was to be a method of trial and error; he had no ready-made model before him but he was sure that India would learn from the mistakes of others. But mixed economy was not an end in itself. As early as 1948 when he was not even sure of how to describe it ("call it what you like—mixed economy or something else"), he was clear that it was to be a "transitional stage of economy". He also felt that the transition was not to be smooth. "I rather doubt myself whether it is possible without a conflict or repeated conflicts to bring about these changes because people who are used to possessing certain interests or certain ideas do not easily accept new ideas, and nobody likes to give up what he has, at least no groups like it; individuals sometimes do". His doubts were not unjustified; during the years since he spoke, the conflicts which, he thought, would arise did come to the fore resulting in distortion in the path he sought to pursue.

PLANNING

The leadership of Jawaharlal Nehru as the Chairman of the National Planning Committee (NPC) set up in 1938, gave a great impetus to thinking on planning in the country. While articulating the concept of planning Nehru was no doubt impressed by Russian experiment. But he had all the realisation of difficulties associated with such kind of experiment. He had a very deep understading of the world history as can be seen from his Glimpses of World History. But his concept of planning never claimed to have its origin in doctrinaire philosophy of history. What he understood by a planned economy was a regime where things could be made to happen through foresight, goodwill and co-operation. In contrast, in market economy things just happen.

Though Nehru was impressed by the experiment of Russian Revolution, when it came to the selection of suitable option for development of independent India, he preferred "Mixed economy" model. His concept of planning envisaged that people's participation should be ensured at every stage. The things which are going to affect the people, may be decided and moulded by them in perfectly democratic way. That is, his concept of planning was democratic planning. In the articulation of the concept of planning in India, he strongly favoured democratic framework which ensures that things are decided in a co-operative manner, seeking the willingness of all concerned. Nehru tried to keep away the element of 'coercion' in the concept of planning.

Nehru's contribution in the articulation of the concept of planning has been best summarised by Dr. P.C. Mahalnobis as follows :

"Under the leadership of Nehru, India made big advances. He initiated thinking on planning in India. Through his speeches and through planning committees and the Planning Commission, he has exercised a profound educative influence and made India conscious of the need for national planning, Through the Congress Party and the Government, he has made planning an instrument of national policy on the biggest scale outside the communist countries, and has persuaded India to accept socialism as her goal. He has brought to Indian planning a full appreciation of the scientific revolution which is transforming the world, a sensitive awareness of human values and cultural traditions, an inherent sense of democracy and an international outlook".

The Planning Commission of India is the brainchild of Jawaharlal Nehru. Nehru exercised a tremendous political will in the formation of Planning Commission which was to chalk out the course of planned development not only for Central Government but also for State Governments. This was more so in the light of quasi federal structure of Indian Constitution. When Nehru inducted Dr. P.C. Mahalnobis into the Planning Commission, he wanted to ensure that planning process in India should be scientific, based on facts and figures. He had the foresight in realising that adequate and accurate statistics formed the basis of planning. The National Sample Survey started in 1950 is a testimony to this.

Perspective Planning

(1) We are to build up, by democratic means, a rapidly expanding and technologically progressive economy; (2) we are to establish a social order based on social justice and offering equal opportunity to every citizen. These objectives have to be kept in view all the time. Therefore, it is necessary to have not only a Five Year Plan, but a plan with longer perspective.

When it came to the question of 'Planning from below', Nehru envisaged the machinery of Panchayat Raj Institution, i.e. three tier system of democratic decentralisation. These Panchayati Raj Institutions or local-self governments were entrusted with the responsibility of chalking out suitable plans at the block level and initiation of Community Development projects. Nehru's idea of planning was sufficiently flexible to accommodate any change suitable to local needs. When he was convinced that adequate degree of powers must be vested with local institutions, he showed political courage to create that type of machinery. His attempt was to create necessary framework to carry out the experiment of planning in India. He was open to any suggestions since he wanted that planning should not be merely blueprint but a way of life of people. He wanted that institutional framework for carrying out planning which will ensure adequate degree of involvement of people for whose welfare plans are being prepared.

Institutional Reforms

At the time of implementation of the second Five Year Plan, Nehru strongly felt that the objectives of planning will not be fulfilled unless institutional reforms are introduced with political courage. The decision to introduce these institutional reforms was certainly with some political cost which he readily accepted. At this stage in the country's development, he felt concerned at slow progress in carrying out co-operative farming and in implementing the programme for land reforms. On both these issues, there had been considerable discussion at the highest level and Nehru threw his decisive weight on the side of co-operative farming and agrarian reforms. The second plan had envisaged such essential steps being taken as would provide sound foundations for co-operative farming so that over a period of ten years or so, a substantial proportion of agricultural lands could be cultivated on co-operative lines. Similar proposals were made in the plan to adopt common approach for land reforms to be accepted and pursued by each state as a part of National plan. These institutional reforms were accepted by various States only because of Nehru's political will and stature.

It may be noted that the contribution of Nehru lies in the fact that he not only popularised the concept of planning but created appropriate institutional structure within which working relations between the Centre and the States were directed and regulated. He created a machinery like Planning Commission and body like National Development Council which could translate has vision into reality. It was not only he aspect of deep commitment and scientific outlook which made planning a successful experiment, but it was more his political will which could give planning a concrete expression in Indian context. While evaluating Nehru's contribution to Indian planning many a time, we blame Nehru for the failures of planning. In our vein of criticism, we produce the statistics of families below the poverty line. But it may be borne in mind that Nehru provided us scientific methods of planning and necessary tools for achieving our goals. If these tools are not successful, the fault lies with us and not with Jawaharlal Nehru.

Use of Foreign Capital

Nehru believed that for financing our plans foreign capital was essential and could benefit India in its industrial growth as it had benefitted America. After the new Industrial Policy Resolution of 1948, then Prime Minister Nehru announced on 6th April 1949, "Indian capital needs to be supplemented by foreign capital not only because our material savings will not be enough for the rapid development of the country on the scale we wish, but also because in many cases scientific, technical and industrial knowledge and capital equipment can better be secured alongwith foreign capital". The position was also cleared by the Prime Minister as regards the remittance of profits and the repatriation of capital and it was pointed out that in case of nationalisation fair and equitable compensation would be paid. Dr. P.S. Loknathan, former Director General, National Council of Applied Economic Research, while delivering the Jawahar Lal Nehru Memorial Lectures organised by the University of Rajasthan on the "Economic Philosophy of Nehru" in Feb. 1968 said the late Prime Minister Nehru discovered in the wake of the Chinese aggression that 'there is a price to be paid for foreign aid and capital". Dr. Loknathan pointed out that Nehru's attitude to the entry of foreign private Capital into India was essentially 'pragmatic'. Nehru after independence had gained confidence in the ability of independent India to utilise foreign capital without fear of being dominated politically or economically. Whether the confidence was justified or not is debatable but this cannot be disputed that no one besides Nehru could have obtained so much foreign capital without losing the country's independent policies.

Essence of Nehru

The essence of Nehru, in the context of present conditions, was that, while he followed the highest standards of probity and integrity, he kept himself as far away as possible from vested interest.

One thing that distrusted was big business, and all those who claim to follow him can study him usefully from this point of view. He was not doctrinaire, when he was Prime Minister, but his "pragmatism" was based on a clear and firm grasp of the essentials of socialism. He used Marxism, which he studied early, as a tool and a test and understood the spirit of social conflict, which could be ignored but could not be wished away. Every annual address to the Federation of Chambers of Commerce and Industry was a rebuke to the ugliness of capitalism. If he could not advance the cause of socialism as much as he wanted to, it was because of the limitations under which he had to work, especially the limitations of the party. He knew the people well, their genius and their conditions, but he never gave up basic principles. He cannot be reduced to a guide-book of pragmatism, which can degenerate into opportunism, just as Gandhi, who was essentially a social revolutionary, cannot be reduced to a mere guidebook of morals. The new congress emerges from a great struggle as a radical organization and cannot give up its role. We do not mind what happens to this forum or that, but we hope everyone claiming to be a follower of Nehru will work for socialist transformation and that Nehru will not be reduced to a reactionary and a defender of the status quo, as Gandhi has been reduced by a set of Gandhians.

In all fairness, it must be admitted that Jawaharlal Nehru loved Gandhi and his ideas. He was an amalgam of science and philosophy. He broke away from Marxism but its influence still permeated his thought. He hated Hitlerism and Stalinism. Despite all this his ideas were progressive. He was deeply a humanist. He wrote of his ambition and of the people of India as given below :

"I have hardly any ambition left, I have been a very ambitious person in many ways. But there is one ambition left in me and it is this that in the years to come and in the few years left to me, I should throw myself with all the strength and energy left in me into the work of building of India. I want to do it to the uttermost till I am exhausted and thrown away on the scrap heap."

It is enough to me that I have exhausted myself, my strength and energy in India's task I do not care what happens to my reputation after I am gone, But if any people choose to think of me, then, I should like them to say, 'This was a man who with all his mind and heart loved India and the Indian people. And they, in turn, were indulgent to him and gave him their love most abundantly and extravagantly".

The lines quoted above indicate the character and the trend of outlook of the great personality. Great men do not demand gratitude and in the case of a great man like Jawaharlal Nehru neither the quarter-century of the contribution to the freedom struggle of the country nor the seventeen years of the arduous life in office as Prime Minister together with his contribution in thought and action can be erased or easily forgotten.

(o) V.K.R.V. RAO

Dr.V.K.R.V.Rao, a father figure among the 20th century Indian economists, was one of those rare intellectuals who sincerely cared for national interests in general and economists in particular. Dr.Rao has an active work span of about six decades. During this period, he presided over most of the professional conferences and served as an active member in various governmental committees and accepted various assignments, as Vice-Chancellor of Delhi University, as member of the Planning Commission and a Cabinet Minister of the Government of India. He founded and nursed a leading Research Journal, "The Indian Economic Review". Professor V.K.R.V.Rao was an internationally renowned economist. In the economic literatue, his contributions will always be remembered. His pioneering research contributions include development and planning, employment and unemployment, essays in economic development, food, nutrition and poverty, national income, socialism, values and economic development, deficit financing for capital formation and price behavior and freedom and development. Needless to say, his contributions helped in shaping the economic planning in India.

Economic Activity

V.K.R.V. Rao examined the relation of economic activity to the end of all human activity. The methods employed for securing economic goods, or what is called economic activity, can either promote or hinder the development of human personality. There are four elements in economic activity which have a bearing on the development of human personality and, therefore, on the ultimate end of human activity. These are: (1) The art element in work; (2) The dignity and pride element in work; (3) The personality-killing element in work; and (4) The character-forming element in work.

The art element gives an opportunity to the individual to develop his personality though his work has no special value for the economist and is rejected by him in favour of a way of production which will yield a larger output per unit cost in terms of money. The dignity and pride element in work is also not taken into account by the principle of economy. The third factor, viz., the personality-killing element in work performs, by its presence, the negative function of getting economic activity to thwart the end of human activity. The fourth factor, effect on the character and outlook of the worker, can be either positive or negative. It may promote ability and willingness in the worker to develop his personality or it may result in the opposite. That the mechanized industrial system of today based on the principle of economy – tends to do the opposite is an admitted fact.

Features of Underdeveloped Countries

Dr.Rao identified the following, features of an underdeveloped economy: (1) Prevalence of disguised unemployment; (2) Dominance of production under household enterprises; (3) A significant extent of production for self-consumption (4) Predominance of Agriculture; (5) Deficiency of technical knowledge; (6) Deficiency of capital equipment; (7) A marginal propensity to consume equal to, or about unity; (8) A high proportion of incremental demand towards food in any incremental income-generation. Dr.Rao argued that whereas a primary increase in investment would take place, a subsequent, secondary and tertiary affects through the expansion of output in the consumption goods sector would not take place. Consequently, the multiplier process would not be operation. Dr.Raw came to the conclusion even that the money income multiplier would be working but real income multiplier would not be working. He drew attention to the inelasticity in the agricultural output, and more particularly, to the probability of some decline in proportion of such output coming to the market, consequent upon a rise in prices of food and other agricultural commodities.

Industrial Development

Dr.Rao believed that industrialization would provide a solution to the population pressure in agriculture. However, during the years prior to his passing away, Dr.Rao had started voicing strong concern at the hiatus between the raising share of industry and the falling share of agriculture in national output accompanied by a falling share in agriculture of employment.

National Income Methodology

Dr.Rao applied pure scientific exercise in the estimation of National Income. This was his unique achievement at that time and gave credibility to his work over the years he became more and more assertive on the analytical limitations of inter-country comparisons of national and per capita income. He was bothered truly by three issues. First, at great deal of what becomes marketed and exchange-value derived output in developed countries gets unrecorded and underestimated in developing countries. Secondly, a significant portion of national income in developed countries represents compensation or countervailing costs of final goods. This is so both in the material production and teritiary sectors. Thirdly, there is no scientific basis for estimating values of government expenditures not all of which may have a marketable/commercial significance. Dr.Rao's own theoretical and applied contributions to national income analysis can bear out a full-fledged research dissensation of interanational significance.

Institutional Development

Dr.Rao founded the three major institutions of post-graduate work, training and research. These are: Delhi School of Economics, 1948, the Institute of Economic Grwoth in 1957 and the Institute of Social and Economic Change in 1972. The Delhi School of Ecomomics is among the foremost of University Post-graduate Teaching Institutions in the country in the orientation to mainstream modern economic theory; it has wide international contacts. The Institute of Economic Growth is among the leading research institutions in the country with its staff intimately involved in governmental consultation and delegation. It has record of national level research work. The Institute of Social and Economic change is largely devoted to regional research spheres and is closely connected with the State Government. These three institutions reflect Dr.Rao's perception of balance among international, national and regional angles and facets in economics. As a minister of education Dr.Rao initiated in 1965 the Indian Council of Social Science Research which is now founding the number of research institutions in the country. He also innovated Agro-Economic Research Centres and Research Units in demography in different parts of the country.

Poverty

V.K.R.V. Rao examined various issues and dimensions relating to poverty and undernutrition in India and also criticized research studies undertaken by eminent economists like Dandekar, Rath, Bardhan and Sukhatme, etc., on the extent and measurement of poverty in rural and urban India.

According to Rao, a method commonly employed for the measurement of poverty is to take the nutritional norm in terms of daily calorie intake by consumer unit, and the cut-off point by the expenditure class which has an average daily calorie intake per consumer unit nearest to the norm and then treat half the population lying in this expenditure class and the entire population in the lower expenditure classes as the poor. This is the method employed by Dandekar and Rath (1971) in their famous book 'Poverty in India'. And it has been followed by more studies using a more or less similar method... but the methodology... does not appear to be correct. While the proportion of undernutritional poverty undoubtedly declines with increasing income, and the paradoxical result was found that the poor as defined also include the non-poor and that the non-poor include the poor (*Rao*, 1977). Rao seemed to believe that Dandekar and Rath got the 'paradoxical result' because they based the estimates of poverty on the sole criterion of calorie intake. He says: 'The balanced diet approach is ... preferable to the calorie intake approach. And this is what writers like Bardhan (1974). Rudra (1974) and others have done, unlike Dandekar and Rath (1971) who have only used the calorie intake criterion'. Rao preferred the balanced diet approach because he believed that it took into account the nutritional quality of the calorie intake. Though he prefers the balanced diet to calorie intake as a criterion for determining the poverty line, Rao was not entirely satisfied with the balanced diet approach either. He said: 'Poverty has to be identified with deficiency in the total level of living. And total level of living includes not only energy requirements but also balanced diet needed for health, and the other basic needs essential for human existence at a tolerable level.

Deficit Financing

Dr.Rao has pointed out that in case of deficit financing by the government the danger of initial rise in prices is greater due to expansion of currency, absence of direct return or absence of the supplies of goods and services, absence of saleable securities and greater possibility of wastage and failure to promote greater productivity. There can be forced savings for financing economic development. The only question is the extent to which it can be resorted, because it is bound to result in a certain rise in prices due to the following factors:

(a) Attempt on the part of the Government to make up for the fall in the real value of its deficit-financed outlay;
(b) Failure on the part of the Government to mop up for the exchequer any part of the increase in profit that follows deficit financing;
(c) Failure of the Government to prevent the banking system from adopting a liberal credit policy;
(d) Failure on the part of the Government to undertake an effective system f price control and controlled distribution of essential wage goods;
(e) Compensatory rise in money wage rate; and
(f) Use of deficit financing for unproductive expenditure which adds neither to consumption nor to capital formation.

For reducing this rise in prices, Dr.Rao has suggested that it is better to use bank credit rather than credit money for meeting the deficit expenditure. The size of induced outlay should be reduced as much as possible; and the flow of output should be increased simultaneously. A suitable fiscal policy should be adopted under which the increments in income should be mopped up by means of taxes and loans. A rise in the money rates of wages should be prevented. The reserve ratio of banks should be raised and the flow of additional bank credit should be well-regulated under credit policy. In addition, public-understanding and co-operation are needed since taxation, wage, credit and price controls normally create resentment.

Fiscal Policy

According to V.K.R.V. Rao fiscal policy should aim at maximizing the mopping up of deficit-induced increment in incomes by means of both taxes and loans; and the more these can be built-in with the increase in income, the more automatic and effective will be the flow-back into the exchequer. Wage policy should take the form of preventing to the maximum possible extent a rise in the money rate of wages. In order to do this, it would be necessary to control the prices of basic wage goods and also arrange for their controlled distribution wherever expedient. It would also be necessary to get the positive support of labour for the policy of deficit-financed investment by an appropriate choice of projects and by seeking its cooperation and participation not merely in the choice the projects but also in their implementation.

Rao emphasised the role of public understanding and public cooperation as a positive factor intending to diminish the price effect of deficit financing. Taxation, savings, credit controls, wage controls, price controls, and controlled distribution, all these normally cause resentment. It is only when their rationale is fully understood and the purpose for which they are used fully accepted and supported that they get the best chance of successful functioning; hence the imperative need for promoting public understanding and cooperation when undertaking deficit financing for capital formation. As a logical result of the argument, policy conclusions emerge for preventing deficit financing from degenerating into inflationary finance and enabling the mobilization of a given measure of forced saving for the successful achievement of capital formation.

Income Tax

In his work "Taxation of Income in India", which dealt with the history of income tax from 1860 to 1929, he concluded by saying that "the Indian system of income tax reveals an absence of any background of the theory or principle. No attempt has so far been made by the government to examine the fundamental principle underlying its levy or to analyse its incidence. Such improvements as have been made from time to time are of a piecemeal character". Hence, for improving the system he suggested the following measures:

i) Gross and net incomes should be clearly distinguished;
ii) Hindu undivided families should be statutorily recognized;
iii) Agricultural incomes should not be exempted;
iv) The rate of tax should be properly graduated; and
v) The courts of appeal should be established.

Price Policy

V.K.R.V. Rao emphasized that price is an important economic mechanism that has certain functions to perform; and any policy that is formulated has to be in this functional context, viz., it has to help in the more adequate and more efficient performance of these functions. Primarily this function is to bring about the required equilibrium between demand and supply both of goods and of factors of production.

The Human Factor in Economic Growth

V.K.R.V. Rao emphasized that science and technology have succeeded in devising measures for reducing the death rate without the prerequisite of a high standard of life. But they not succeeded in devising measures for bringing about a similar reduction in the birth rate in the context of underdevelopment. What is needed, therefore, is a deliberate effort on the part of science and technology to devise methods that would lead to a sharp fall in the birth rate and are capable of application in the underdeveloped world. There is need to include in the role of the human factor in economic growth an important place for deliberate regulation of the growth of numbers and a drastic reduction in the birth rate. The psychological and sociological factors necessary for this purpose have of course to be studied and acted upon by the governments and peoples of the underdeveloped countries; but a conference that deals with the application of science and technology for promoting economic growth, should also give adequate attention to the application of science and technology for reducing the birth rate in the underdeveloped countries to something like half or less of their current rates and that too within a period of not more than one or two decades at the outset.

There is one more element concerning the role of the human factor in the underdeveloped countries which needs stressing. In all underdeveloped economies, there are large number of people who are not able to take advantage of even the limited facilities that are available for modernization and increase in productivity. These classes are described in India as the weaker sections of the community. They are weak and unable to grow partly because of their sub-human economic status and also because of their social organization, their traditional values and ways of living, and other sociological, cultural and psychological characteristics that are inhibitive of their taking advantage of the facilities that planning and economic development places at their disposal.

Rao depicted that underdeveloped economies have tended to pay far more attention to the role of capital and investment in the promotion of economic growth and in fact have been so obsessed by this factor that, on the one hand, they set their targets low and, on the other, lean unduly on foreign aid.

The result has been that progress in slow and the gap continues to widen between the developing and the developed economies. Especially countries like India, which are rich in human resources, have to adopt a far more positive and studied approach to the productive use of the human factor than they done so far.

Full-Employment and Economic Development

After reviewing the ideas of Keynes, William Fellner, Ohlin, Beveridge, Mrs.Robinson, A.P.Lerner, etc., about full –employment and frictional unemployment Dr. Rao feels that in under developed counties there is another category of unemployment – disguised unemployment which is different from the type of involuntary unemployed which is found in developed countries. It is the most formidable problem for the solution of which the first committee of UN-experts had suggested economic development; and the second committee pointed out that the task of economic development was to create new employment rapidly. In other words, economic development would create employment opportunities thus raising the level of employment. Now emphasis is shifted from reaching a given level of full-employment to creating additional employment. Whereas full-employment is essentially a short period concept, economic development is a long period one involving movement form one level of full employment to a higher level. This process is continuous; and is determined by the rate of development. The disguised unemployed, with nil product, begin to produce output under economic development, and add to the average productivity of all the employment works. When such persons get employment, they add to the volume of employment.

According to Dr.Rao, economic development involves something more. In this connection, he has quoted the UN Sub-commission on Economic Development. "The objective is the promotion of higher standards of living, full employment and condition of economic and social progress and development in the countries concerned, and the manner for achieving it is a sound, efficient and fuller utilization of man-power, natural resources, energy and capital". Dr.Rao concludes that the Keynesian treatment of full employment is not only unsatisfactory as regards the removal of the types of involuntary unemployment in both developed and undeveloped economics, but is also deficient as regards the productivity of employed labour".

On Relevance of Keynesian Multiplier Principle to Under-developed Countries

How far Keynes' theory is relevant to under-developed countries is a question which Dr.Rao had attempted to answer about four decades ago. According to him, Keynes' theory of employment, and more particularly the multiplier principle has little relevance for policy decisions in under-developed countries. He thought that as in under-developed countries, supplies of consumer goods fail to respond to price changes, Keynesian multiplier principle works with reference to money income only. Any attempt to attain significant improvement in real income or employment by increasing investment would fail as the multiplier principle would not work with reference to any of these. Thus the investment or income multiplier (K) and the employment multiplier (K')would normally be smaller than the multiplier linking up increment in money investment to increment in money income. But all these multipliers must have a positive value and should move in the same direction, if the Keynesian multiplier principle is to have any relevance for policy decision in the under-developed counties.

Dr.Rao has underlined the following conditions which must be satisfied in an economy, if the multiplier principle is to be applied in practice:

i) There must not exist unemployment in any form other than Keynesian unemployment.
ii) The economy must be primarily industrial and the supply curves of consumer goods must have a positive slope.
iii) Excess capacity should exist in the consumer goods industries which would enable them to expand their output in response to increasing demand for their products.
iv) There has to be abundance of capital in the country, making the supply of working capital required for increased output fairly elastic.

Dr. Rao asserts that these conditions are rarely satisfied in under-developed economies and, therefore, Keynesian multiplier principle remains inoperative in these countries.

India must follow the ideals suggested by V.K.R.V.Rao which urns as follows: Poverty must go. Disparity must diminish. Injustice must end. These are but essential steps towards our ultimate goal – the goal of an India which is united and strong, an India which lives up to its ancient and enduring ideals, yet is modern in thought and achievement, meeting the future with vision and confidence.

QUESTIONS

1. Write Briefly about the salient contents of 'Arthasashtra'.
2. Enumerate the concept of Kautilya regarding Public Finance.
3. State briefly about the salient features of Economic Thought of Tiruvalluvar.
4. Write about Dadabhai Naoroji and his 'Drain Theory'.
5. What were the economic ideas of Mahadeva Govind Ranade?
6. Discuss about G.K. Gokhale's economic ideas and views.
7. Write about Gandhi's Trusteeship Doctrine.
8. Write about Gandhian Economic Thought.
9. Assess Prof. Gadgil's role as an economist.
10. Discuss Nehru's ideas about Economic Planning.
11. Discuss the economic measures adopted by Nehru to transform the Indian economy.
12. Write short notes on :
    (a) R.C. Dutt
    (b) Sarvodaya
    (c) Prohibition
    (d) K.T. Shah
    (e) R.K. Mukerjee
    (f) C.N. Vakil
    (g) J.K. Mehta

BIBLIOGRAPHY

Adam Smith	Wealth of Nations
Alexander Gray	The Development of Economic Doctrines
Alfred Marshall	Principles of Economics
Bell. J.F.	A History of Economic Thought
Cole. G.D.H.	A History of Socialist Thought
Edmund Whittaker	Schools and Streams of Economic Thought
Eric Roll	History of Economic Thought
Frank Neff	Economic Doctrines
Gide and Rist	A History of Economic Doctrines
Haney. L.H.	A History of Economic Thought
Heimann. E.	History of Economic Doctrines
Ingram. J.K.	A History of Political Economy
Keynes. J.M.	The General Theory of Employment, Interest and Money
Lekachman. R.	A History of Economic ideas
Malthus. T.R.	An Essay on Population
Newman. P.C.	The Development of Economic Thought
Schumpeter. J.A.	Ten Great Economists
Schumpeter. J.A.	A History of Economic Analysis
Scott. W.A.	The Development of Economics
Seligman. B.	Main currents in Economics
Shah. K.T.	Ancient Foundations of Economics in India
Spiegal (ed)	The Development of Economic Thought
Taylor. O.H.	A History of Economic Thought
Scott. A. William	The Development of Economics

INDEX

A

B

C

D

E

F

G

H

I

J